On the Manners and Customs of the Ancient Irish

ON THE

MANNERS AND CUSTOMS

OF

THE ANCIENT IRISH.

A SERIES OF LECTURES

DELIVERED BY THE LATE

EUGENE O'CURRY, M.R.I.A.,

PROFESSOR OF IRISH HISTORY AND ARCHAEOLOGY IN THE CATHOLIC UNIVERSITY OF IRELAND; CORRESPONDING MEMBER OF THE SOCIETY OF ANTIQUARIES OF SCOTLAND, ETC.

EDITED, WITH

AN INTRODUCTION, APPENDIXES, ETC.,

BY

W. K. SULLIVAN, PH.D.,

SECRETARY OF THE ROYAL IRISH ACADEMY, AND PROFESSOR OF CHEMISTRY TO THE CATHOLIC UNIVERSITY OF IRELAND, AND TO THE ROYAL COLLEGE OF SCIENCE.

VOL. II.

LECTURES, VOL. I.

WILLIAMS AND NORGATE,

14 HENRIETTA STREET, COVENT GARDEN, LONDON,

AND 20 SOUTH FREDERICK STREET, EDINBURGH.

W. B. KELLY, 8 GRAFTON STREET, DUBLIN.

SCRIBNER, WELFORD, & CO., NEW YORK.

1873.

DUBLIN:
JOHN F. FOWLER, PRINTER,
3 CROW STREET, DAME STREET.

CONTENTS.

ENCES TO THE PASSAGES QUOTED FROM IRISH MANUSCRIPTS IN THIS VOLUME.

Page	
—	See Vol. ii., p. 241.
—	Vellum MS., T.C.D., H. 2. 16, f. 10, a. b.
3—4	Cormac's Glossary.
—	Vellum MS., R.I.A., Book of Lecan.
—	MS., R.I.A., No. $\frac{23}{D. 5.}$ p. 294.
—	See Vol. ii. Appendix, Poem on the Fair of Carman.
27	MS., T.C.D., H. 4. 22; and MS., R.I.A., $\frac{23}{M. 24.}$
29—30	MS., R.I.A., No. $\frac{23}{D. 5,}$ p. 1.
—	Vellum MS., R.I.A., *Lebor na h-Uidhri* and *fac-simile*, published by the Royal Irish Academy.
—	See Transactions of the Ossianic Society, vol. v., p. 34.
36	Vellum MS., T.C.D., H. 2. 18 (Book of Leinster), f. 12, a. b.; and MS., R.I.A., Book of Lecan, f. 17, a. b.
38—39	Vellum MS., T.C.D., Liber Hymnorum, f. 5, a.
44	Vellum MS., R.I.A., Book of Lecan, f. 11.
45	Vellum MS., T.C.D., H. 2. 16, col. 780.
46	The O'Conor Don's MS., p. 190.
47	Vellum MSS., T.C.D., H. 2. 18, f. 156, b. b.; and H. 2. 16.
48	Vellum MS., T.C.D., H. 2. 16, col. 917.
49	Vellum MS., T.C.D., H. 2. 16, col. 917.
51	The O'Conor Don's MS.
52	Vellum MS., R.I.A., Book of Lecan, f. 189.
53	Vellum MS., T.C.D., H. 2. 18, f. 118, a. a.
54	Ibid., f. 112, a. a.
55	Vellum MSS., R.I.A., *Lebor na h-Uidhri* and *fac-simile*, p. 51, col. 2; and Book of Lecan, f. 190.
56	Vellum MS., R.I.A., Book of Lecan, f. 188.
57	Vellum MS., R.I.A., Book of Ballymote, f. 50, a. a.
58	Vellum MS., T.C.D., H. 2. 18, f. 16, a. b.
60	Ibid., f. 106, b. a.
61	Ibid., f. 106, b. a.; and MS., R.I.A., Book of Lecan, f. 191, a. b.
62	Vellum MS., R.I.A., Book of Ballymote, f. 14, a. a.
63	Ibid., f. 13; and Book of Lecan, f. 274

Page	Note	
109	64	Vellum MSS., R.I.A., Book of Ballymote, f. 1[illegible] Book of Lecan, f. 274.
"	65	Vellum MS., R.I.A., Book of Ballymote, 14, a. a.
"	66	Ibid., f. 16, a. a.
110	67	Vellum MS., R.I.A., Book of Lecan, f. 16; and [illegible] MS., T.C.D., H. 2. 18, f. 3, a. b
111	68	Vellum MS., T.C.D., H. 2. 18, f. 5, b. b.
"	69	Ibid., f. 8, a. b.
"	70	Vellum MS., R.I.A., Book of Lecan, f. 15, b. a.
"	71	Vellum MS., R.I.A., Book of Ballymote, f. 19, b.
112	72	Vellum MS., R.I.A., Book of Lecan, f. 16, a. a.
"	73	Ibid., f. 16, b. a., and 293, b. b.
"	74	Vellum MS., T.C.D., H. 2. 18, f. 11, b. a.
113	75	Vellum MS., R.I.A., Book of Lecan, f. 267.
"	76	Ibid., f. 235, b. b.
117	80	Vellum MS., R.I.A., Book of Ballymote, 105, b. b
"	81	Ibid., f. 106, a. a.
118	82	MS., R.I.A., No. $\frac{23}{F.16}$, p. 79.
"	83	Ibid.
"	84	MS., R.I.A., No. $\frac{23}{F.16}$, p. 70; and MS. 22. 5, p. [illegible]
119	85	Vellum MS., H. 2. 15. f. 181.
120	86	MS., R.I.A., $\frac{23}{P.13}$, p. 99.
121	87	MS., R.I.A., No. $\frac{23}{G.S.}$; and No. 32. 5, p. 70.
"	88	Vellum MS., R.I.A., Book of Ballymote, f. 16, a.
123	90	MS., Brit. Mus., Bibl. Egerton. Plut. cl, xvi., [illegible] lanea Hibernica, fol. 18.
124	91	MS., Brit. Mus., Egerton 90, f. 17, a. b.
125	92	Ibid.
127	94	Vellum MS., T.C.D., H. 2. 15, p. 181.
128	95	Vellum MS., T.C.D., H. 2. 15, f. 181.
129	97	MS., R.I.A., No. $\frac{23}{L.34}$, p. 165; and No. 2. 25, p.
135	102	M.S., Brit. Mus., Harl. 5280.
142	108	Vellum MS., Book of Ballymote, f. 204, a. a.
143	110	Brit. Mus., Bibl. Egerton Plut. cl, xvi, fol. 18.
144	111	M.S., R.I.A., No. $\frac{23}{D.13}$, p. 8.
"	112	Ibid.
145	113	Vellum MS., Book of Ballymote, f. 221, a. a.
148	114	Vellum MS., T.C.D., H. 2. 18, f. 17, a. b.
149	115	Vellum MS., R.I.A., Book of Ballymote, 225, a. a
150	118	Vellum MS., R.I.A., Book of Lecan, f 28, a. a.
"	119	Ibid., f. 24, b. b.

Page	Item	
,,	120	Ibid., f. 25, a. a.
151	122	Vellum MS., T.C.D., H. 2. 18, f. 14, a. b.
,,	123	Vellum MS., R.I.A., Book of Ballymote, f. 225, a. a.
,,	124	Vellum MS., T.C.D., H. 2. 18, 147. b. b.
153	125	Vellum MS., R.I.A., Book of Ballymote, f. 228, a. b.
154	126	Vellum MSS., T.C.D., H. 2. 18; and R.I.A., Books of Ballymote and Lecan.
155	127	Ibid.
,,	128	Vellum MS., T.C.D., H. 2. 18, f. 146, b. a.
156	129	Vellum MS., R.I.A., Book of Lecan, f. 68, b. a.
,,	130	Vellum MS., T.C.D., H. 2. 18, f. 147, a. b.
159	131	Ibid., f. 104, a. b.
,,	132	Ibid., f. 148, a. b.
160	133	Vellum MS., R.I.A., Book of Lecan, f. 44 b., col. 4.
,,	134	Ibid., f. 20, a. a.
,,	135	MS., R.I.A., No. $\frac{23}{Q.\ 1.}$
,,	136	MS., R.I.A., No. $\frac{23}{P.\ 8.}$
,,	137	MS., R.I.A., No. $\frac{23}{P.\ 8,}$ fol. 39. a. b.
162	139	MS., R.I.A., No. $\frac{23}{P.\ 8.}$
163	140	Ibid., f. 47.
164	141	Ibid., f. 40, b. b.
165	142	The O'Conor Don's Vellum MS., p. 160; and M.S., R.I.A. No. $\frac{23}{P.\ 8,}$ fol. 47, a. b.
,,	145	Vellum MS., T.C.D., H. 2. 18.
[illegible]	146	Vellum MS., R.I.A., Book of Lecan, f. 58, b.
172	152	Vellum MS., R.I.A., Book of Ballymote, *Leabar Olloman.*
175	154	Vellum MS., R.I.A., *Lebor Brec* and *fac-simile*, part I., published by the Royal Irish Academy, 77.
176	156	MS., T.C.D., H. 2, 18.
[illegible]	—	See Vol. ii., p. 102.
[illegible]	177	Vellum MSS., T.C.D., and R.I.A.; H. 2. 18, and Books of Ballymote and Lecan.
[illegible]	—	Mason MSS., vol. iii., and Vellum MS., R.I.A., Book of Lecan, f. 231, b. a.
[illegible]	191	Vellum MS., R.I.A., Book of Lecan, f. 231.
,,	192	Battle of *Magh Tuired*, MS., Brit. Mus., Harleian, 5282.
[illegible]	193	Ibid.
[illegible]	199	Vellum MS., R.I.A., Book of Ballymote, f. 191.
[illegible]	200	Keating's MS., Hist. Cath. Univ. of Ireland, p. 65.
[illegible]	—	Vellum MS., T.C.D., H. 2. 18, f. 42, b. b.
[illegible]	212	MS., R.I.A., No. 205. H. and S.

INDEX TO THE

FIGURES OF SPEARS AND OTHER WEAPONS OF WARFARE

GIVEN IN VOL. I. (INTRODUCTION), AND REFERRED TO IN THIS VOLUME.

In writing the Introduction, it was found inconvenient to adhere to the order of subjects originally intended, and consequently the numbers by which the figures are referred to in the notes to the Lectures, do not correspond to those attached to them in Volume I.

VOL. II.			VOL. I. (INTRODUCTION).	
Page	Note	No. of Fig.	No. of Fig.	Page
240	180	1	not given	.
,,	,,	2	15	ccccxxxix
,,	,,	3	not given	
241	182	4	17	,,
242	183	5	not given	,,
,,	,,	6	16	,,
243	184	7	14	ccccxxxviii
,,	185	8	30	cccclv
,,	,,	9	31	,,
,,	,,	10	32	,,
,,	186	11	33	,,
244	187	12	39	cccclxii
,,	188	13	32	ccccxlix
,,	,,	14	33	ccccl
245	,,	15	35	,,
,,	,,	16	35	ccccli
,,	,,	17	36	,,
,,	,,	18	37	,,
,,	,,	19	38	,,
,,	,,	20	39	,,
,,	189	21	41	cccclii
,,	,,	22	40	,,
,,	,,	23	42	,,
263	194	24	18	ccccxl
,,	,,	25	19	,,
,,	,,	26	no figure	
,,	,,	27	21	,,
,,	,,	28	22	,,
,,	,,	29	20	,,
,,	,,	30	23	,,

VOL. II.			VOL. I. (INTRODUCTION).	
Page	Note	No. of Fig.	No. of Fig.	Page
255	294	31	24	ccccxl
,,	,,	32	25	,,
,,	,,	33	26	ccccxli
,,	,,	34	27	,,
255	195	40	28	ccccxlii
259	202	41	29	,,
265	207	42	54	cccclvii
,,	,,	43	55	,,
272	210	44	43	ccccliii
,,	,,	45	44	,,
,,	,,	46	45	,,
,,	211	47	46	,,
,,	,,	48	56	cccclix
,,	,,	49	57	,,
,,	,,	50	47	ccccliii
,,	,,	51	49	,,
,,	212	52	48	,,
,,	,,	53	58	cccclx

The numbers 35, 36, 37, 38, 39, used in note 194, page 194, refer to the same figures as Nos. 30, 31, 32, 33, and 34, namely, figures 23, 24, and 25, page ccccxl, and 26 and 27, page ccccxli.

CORRIGENDA.

The following errors have been noticed in preparing the In

				FOR	READ
Page	11,	line	24,	heads,	descendants.
„	„	note	4,	nam,	inan.
„	15,	line	43,	*Chonnachtact,*	*Chonnachtach.*
„	33	„	11,	*Caelain,*	*Caelan.*
„	35	„	22,	of seven,	twice seven.
„	40	„	3,	*Mes Seda, Misroeda, Mesdeda,*	*Messed, Mesroed, ded.*
„	50	„	13,	*Ugainé Mór,*	*Eogan Mór,* and wh the genitive, *Ugai* curs.
„	51	„	9,	*Lecain,*	*Lecan,* and wherev genitive case, *Lec* curs.
„	„	„	35,	*Bricrinn,*	*Bricriu,* the nomi should be substitu this or the other the genitive, *B* wherever it occur
„	67	„	32,	*Daire Cearba,*	*Dairé Cearb.*
„	81	„	45,	*Finguine,*	*Finghin.*
„	83	„	34,	*Fionntain,*	*Finntan.*
„	91	„	19,	nine "waves",	"nine waves".
„	92	„	6,	fifth,	eleventh.
„	104	„	20,	*Gormliath,*	*Gormlaith.*
„	133	„	35,	*Suimhairé,*	*Snimhairé.*
„	„	„	36,	*Suathad,*	*Snathad.*
„	„	„	40,	*truaircnigh,*	*tuaircnighe.*
„	150	„	17,	who were warmed by fire,	who showed emulati
„	151,	note	122,	ca dé at,	cad eat.
„	153	„	125,	e altaig,	ealtaig.
„	„	„	„	ir gait,	ir gait.
„	161,	line	26,	*Fiacha,*	*Fiachra.*
„	162	„	41,	chiefship,	chieftainship.
„	172	„	15,	*Enan,*	*Eman.*
„	187	„	41,	*Cesarn,*	*Fathach, Cesarn.*
„	207,	line	11,	southward,	westward.
„	„	„	21,	but, said he,	no matter, said she.
„	„	„	22,	I am preparing incantations, said he.	I am putting inca in that wisp whic my shoes.

		FOR	READ
Page 213,	line 33,	*Magh Raith*,	*Magh Rath*.
" 218,	" 20,	*Albain*,	*Alba*, the nominative, and wherever the genitive, *Albain*, occurs.
" [illegible]	" 18,	*Sreng* his two *Sleghs*,	*Sreng* one of his two *Sleghs*.
" 245,	" 13,	Northern Battle of Magh Tuireadh,	Battle of Northern *Magh Tuireadh*.
" 254,	" 183, line 3,	noeрnaѵ,	n-ѵeрnaѵ.
" "	" " "	clorомb,	clorомb.
" 276,	" 214 " 2,	hиргaіle,	h-иргaіle.
" 284,	line 12,	four *Colmans*,	two *Colmans*.
" [illegible]	" 11,	blade,	blades.
" [illegible]	" 24,	Missive Shields,	turned handled missive darts.
" [illegible]	" 24,	sent share,	sent a share.
" [illegible]	" 2,	chastises you as a loving woman would her son,	throws you as a lewd woman would throw her son.
" [illegible]	" 7,	*loga* should perhaps be	*foga*.
" [illegible]	note 37,	H. 2. 16,	H. 2. 18.
" [illegible]	line 26,	shield,	sword.

" [illegible] { " 7, } { note 243, } The stanza given here is made up of two half quatrains, and is consequently incorrect. The following is the correct text and translation:

[illegible] be clar оірсаc,	It was by me an oratory was first built,
Ir срaі сloсe.	And a stone cross.
[illegible] ronbói im Chрim-thann	It was my cloak that was upon *Crimthann*
[illegible] Осе.	In the battle of *Oche*.
[illegible] iaрnn, moрсіаc uma,	My *Lorica* of iron, my shield of bronze,
[illegible] mo caрaс,	My skin [protection], my friend,
[illegible] péin, рор na n-aіреc	He admitted himself the chief of the chiefs,
[illegible] ронanacс.	Thus it was it that saved him.

[illegible] means literally skin, but here and in the *Táin Bó Chuailgne*, and [illegible] places, it is put for skin protection in the sense of a shirt of mail. [illegible] he describes his "*Lorica* of iron", as "My skin, my friend". See [illegible] on the *Manuscript Materials of Irish History*, p. 488.

		FOR	READ
" [illegible]	line 34,	fifteen,	seventeen.
" [illegible]	" 6,	the wisely and arrogant,	arrogant counsellors.
" [illegible]	" 18,	*Ceannfeadhua*,	*Ceannfeadhna*.

LECTURE I.

[Delivered [illegible] May, 1857.]

[illegible] The subject of the former course. Subject of the present [illegible] Social Life, Manners, and Civilisation of the people of ancient [illegible] of a definite system of Civilisation in Erinn at an [illegible] The Milesian monarchy; *Amergin*, son of *Milidh* (or Mile-[illegible] a Poet. Of Professors of Music and Poetry among the [illegible] Of the working of gold mines by *Tighearnmas*, B. C. 915. [illegible] at the same time of ornamental drinking cups, and of [illegible] Of the law of *Eochaidh Edgudhach* as to colours in [illegible] introduced by *Enna Aighneach*; Chains of gold, by [illegible] The first *Ogham* inscriptions by *Cetcsimnigh*, A. M. 3941. Of [illegible] Antiquity of the *Feis* of Tara. Of the three *Fercsirtnes*. [illegible] of the province of *Connacht*. Of the *Feis* of Tara. Of the [illegible] military organization by *Ollamh Fodhla*. Keting's descrip-[illegible] of Tara. Of the Kingdom of *Oirghialla* (or Oriel). Of [illegible] Description of *Cormac MacArt* at the Feast of Tara. [illegible] Traditions of the bringing of the law of Moses from [illegible] Profession of Poet-Judges deprived of their privileges, temp. [illegible] Account of the more remarkable of the early Judges [illegible] the *Senchus Mór*.

[illegible] lectures I entered, as fully and minutely as the [illegible] Introductory Course on the Manuscript Materials [illegible] would allow, into the extent, character, and [illegible] large and valuable mass of that ancient historic [illegible] which the wreck of ages, and an accumulation of [illegible] almost unparalleled in history for duration [illegible], have still left us.

[illegible] in those Lectures to trace the progress and [illegible] Literature, in all its varied forms, from the [illegible] to which existing authority and reasonable [illegible] carry us back, down to our own times. I en-[illegible] on the minds of my hearers, and I wish I [illegible] in impressing it on the minds of all the rising [illegible] Irishmen, the great educational importance of [illegible] ancient Gaedhelic Language, and of working as [illegible] be worked, the mines of philological, ethnological, [illegible] treasures which that language preserves. And I [illegible] expressing the pride I felt in observing that, not-[illegible] great deficiencies of the humble advocate to [illegible] this venerable cause was heard by my audience [illegible] so cordial, as to induce the hope that some of

LECT. I.

them at least, if not many, will soon turn their practical atten-tion to a study now acknowledged by the most distinguis[illegible] scholars in Europe as one not only of an extraordinary lo[illegible] national interest and importance, but even of paramount nece-ssity in the investigation of the philology, the ethnography, a[illegible] the history of the family of European Nations at large.

Subject of the present Course.

The subject of the course of Lectures which it is now [illegible] duty to open is different. I hope I have already proved t[illegible] the materials for a copious history of our ancient nation e[illegible] in abundance, although it is true that as yet nothing deserv[illegible] of the name of a History of Erinn has been written; for it [illegible] now at least be admitted that the various compilations publi[illegible] at different times (though often by men of considerable abi[illegible] under the name of "Irish History", are not only entirely [illegible] serving of that ambitious title, but are full of mistakes so g[illegible] and of omissions so very large as to convey, I will not say m[illegible] an inadequate, but an altogether false view of what that Hi[illegible] really was. The accounts which all the writers upon the s[illegible] ject have ventured to give of Life and Manners in Ancient E[illegible] are, of course, yet more meagre than their statements of hist[illegible] events, and they are, if possible, still more false—perhaps, [illegible] cause those who have treated of this latter subject, (till t[illegible] commencement of the publications of the Irish Archaeologi[illegible] Society), have been still more ignorant of that which th[illegible] have pretended to explain to the world. And as the Hist[illegible] of a nation can be but little understood without some acqu[illegible] ance with the Life, the Habits, and Social Ideas—in a w[illegible] the peculiar *Civilization* of the people whose actions are [illegible] corded in it,—it appears to me that my next duty, in connect[illegible] with the Chair I have the honour to fill, is to give some acco[illegible] of the authentic materials we possess towards the illustration [illegible] the SOCIAL LIFE, MANNERS, AND CIVILIZATION OF THE PEO[illegible] OF ANCIENT ERINN. This shall, then, be the subject for [illegible] consideration during the present session.

Existence of a definite system of civilization in Erinn at an early period.

It is but reasonable to think that such a people as [illegible] Gaedhils of Erinn, whose love of literature and support [illegible] literary institutions are now universally acknowledged by h[illegible] torians to have been so remarkable during the darkness of [illegible] middle ages, must have commenced at a very early period [illegible] construct some kind of social and political system, regula[illegible] by fixed and determinate rules, and suited to foster and prot[illegible] the exercise of their peculiar genius, not only in the walks [illegible] literature, but in the various other arts of civilization with[illegible] the presence of which literature could never have been app[illegible]

[illegible] to maturity among a people, nor even [illegible] to live, had it been imported in full [illegible] other country.

[illegible] system and such rules or laws, were in [illegible] and efficiently sustained, in this country, at a [illegible], and were carried down without material [illegible] peculiar spirit (though with some modifications [illegible] subject to many vicissitudes), even to the close [illegible] century, I shall, I think, be able to demonstrate [illegible] doubt. And without further preface I [illegible] with this design, following the same course I [illegible] take, on the former occasion: that, namely, [illegible] path of our investigation from the authorities [illegible] their chronological order.

Foundation of the Milesian Sovereignty, B.C. 1694.

[illegible] the chronology of the Annals of the Four [illegible] (founded on the Septuagint), the Milesian colony [illegible] the year of the world 3500—that is, about [illegible] according to that computation, before the Incarna[illegible].

[illegible] our most ancient writings and traditions, [illegible] before them here, and conquered, the [illegible] colony,—a people remarkable for their [illegible] domestic if not the higher arts of civilized [illegible] in a higher state of civilization than their [illegible] little, however, is certainly known of the [illegible], that it would be impossible for me, on the [illegible], to treat at large, with any sufficient distinct[illegible] interesting people, who so mysteriously disappear [illegible] our history immediately on their subjugation. [illegible] defer to some future lecture any further refer[illegible] is recorded of their skill in the arts, and shall [illegible] draw from the more tangible history of the [illegible] body of my illustrative facts with reference [illegible] and Manners of our early ancestors.

Amergin (son of Milesius), a Judge and a Poet.

[illegible] on the authority of the "Book of Invasions", [illegible] the Book of Leinster (a collection be it remem[illegible] from more ancient books about the year [illegible] *Amergin*, one of the Milesian brothers who led the [illegible], was a Judge and a Poet; and indeed some [illegible] of legal decisions, and of verses, ascribed to [illegible] in our oldest manuscripts. A short primary [illegible] Gaedhelic is also attributed to him, of which [illegible] preserved in the very old grammatical tract [illegible] the Books of Ballymote and *Lecain*, as well as [illegible] books. So that, even with the very coming of

LECT. I.

the Milesians, they must have brought with them some system of positive Law, and some definite literary Education.

Professors of Music and Poetry among the early Milesians.

There is, also, another record or tradition, belonging to the same remote period, with regard to the original existence and causes of certain marked tastes which characterize the Northern and Southern Inhabitants of Erinn, from which the same conclusion may be drawn. For we find it stated in our very oldest books, that when the two surviving leaders of the first Milesian colony—the brothers *Eber* and *Eremon*—had obtained possession of the island, they divided it into two parts between them, the former taking the southern, and the latter the northern half; that they then divided between the two portions of their kingdom the surviving officers, soldiers, and civilians of the expedition; and that after this division there remained two distinguished personages, who belonged to none of those classes; namely, a learned poet named *Cir*, the son of *Cis;* and a celebrated *Cruitiré*, or harper, named *Ona*. And it is recorded that for these noble followers the two brothers cast lots, by which the poet fell to *Eremon*, and the harper to *Eber*; and that it was from this circumstance that the Eremonians, or northerns, continued to be distinguished for their poetry, and the Eberians, or southerns, for their music.

This statement is supported by the following short ancient poem, found in the "Book of Conquests", which Dr. Keting quotes from the *Saltair* of Cashel, and of which the following is a literal translation:

"The two renowned sons of Milesius,
Who conquered both *Erinn* and *Albain;*
With them hither there came
A comely poet and a gifted harper.

"*Cir*, the son of *Cis*, was the fair-haired poet;
The harper's name was *Ona* the fair-haired;
For the sons of the noble renowned Milesius
Was the harper wont to tune his harp.

"For the chiefs, who by battles many and fierce
Had conquered the sovereignty of Erinn,
Their sweet and well-timed notes they raised,—
For *Eber*, and for *Eremon*.

"They in a friendly way cast lots
For these professors of the sweet arts,
Until to the southern chieftain fell
The accomplished and most dexterous harper.

"Sweetness of string-music, comeliness of race,
Belong to the southern parts of Erinn;
Thus shall it be to the end of time,
With the noble race of valiant *Eber*.

... of the northern chieftain fell
... with all his varied gifts;
... without contest, to the north belongs
... of poetry and the chief of poets[7].

... few lines may appear as mere specimens of ... they bring down to us valuable evidence to ... it here for no other purpose than to show), ... have been the quality of the poetry and ... race in Erinn, they themselves at all ... a very early period, that the cultivation of ... among them was as old even as their own ... of the country.

... steps the new and successful colony took ... perpetuate such literature and civilization as ... brought with them into this country, as well as ... and that of their predecessors, (the Firbolgs, ... etc.), our ancient records preserve no

... to be found in our ancient authorities, throw- ... upon the progress of our early civilization, is ... of the reign of *Tighearnmas Mac Follaigh*, ... Milesian kings of Erinn. *Tighearnmas*, who ... of *Eremon*, became king in the year of the ... according to the Annals of the Four Masters, or ... to the chronology followed by MacGeoghegan: ... 1620 years before Christ, according to the former, ... before Christ, according to the latter authority. ... is everywhere recorded as having been the first ... and to work gold mines, in this country. The ... of these original gold mines is not laid down ... recorded that it was in the forests standing on ... the River Liffey that the ore was smelted for ... and that it was smelted by a worker in metals, of ... who was a native of that district.

Gold mines worked by *Tighearnmas*, King of Erinn, B.C. 1620 [or 915?]

Iuchadan the first worker in Gold.

... therefore, fairly infer that the gold itself was dis- ... Leinster; and this opinion is strengthened by our ... people of *Laighin*, or Leinster, called afterwards ... or the Lagenians of the Gold; because (as ... was in their country that gold was first disco- ...

Gold in Leinster.

... short but significant entries respecting the reign ... are recorded, which are similarly useful as mark- ... of the arts of mere luxury at this early period. ... stated to have been the first that introduced ... drinking cups, or horns, into Erinn; and it is also

Introduction of ornamented drinking cups, and of colours in dress, by *Tighearnmas*.

recorded that he first caused colours and borders to be worn in clothes, as well as ornaments and brooches of gold and silver.

It would appear that, at this time, some system of idolatrous worship was either established, revived, or continued; since we find that this same King *Tighearnmas*, together with a vast number (three-fourths, say the annalists) of the people of Erinn,—men, women, and children,—died in the plain called *Magh Slecht* (that is, the Plain of Adoration), in the present county of Sligo, while engaged in the worship of the great idol *Crum-Croich*, which stood in that plain; the same idol it may be remembered which is said to have continued to receive the homage of the Milesian race, down to the coming of St. Patrick by whom, only, it was at last destroyed for ever.[1]

Death of *Tighearnmas*, in *Magh Slecht*, A.M. 3656.

The death of *Tighearnmas* and his people happened according to the Annals on the ancient festival of *Samhain* (or November eve), in the year of the world 3656, and in the seventy-seventh year of his reign.

Of *Eochaidh Edgudhach's* Law as to Colours in dress.

Tighearnmas was succeeded in the monarchy by *Eochaidh*, surnamed *Edgudhach*, (that is, *Eochaidh* of the Robes),—who was descended of the Ithian race of Munster. He obtained the surname of *Edgudhach* (i. e. of the Robes) because he first introduced a sumptuary law, as effective as it was simple, by which the people were divided into different classes, distinguished by the colours of their clothes. *Eochaidh* ordained one colour for the clothes of servants; two for husbandmen; three for soldiers and warriors; four for gentlemen; five for captains, or military leaders; six for the chief poets, or *ollamhs;* and seven for kings and queens: and it is from this circumstance, says the Book of Leinster, (folio 8), that all those colours have come into the vestments of a Bishop at this day.

Other ancient authorities ascribe the institution of this sumptuary law to *Tighearnmas*, but I have followed the Book of Leinster.

After a reign of four years, *Eochaidh* was slain in the year of the world 3667.

Proceeding with the early Annals, we find the following entries in succession.

Silver Shields first made under *Enna Aighnech*.

In the year of the world 3817 died the monarch *Enna Aighnech*, of the Eremonian race. It was this *Enna* that first made Silver Shields, (at *Airget Ros*), and bestowed them on the men of Erinn, together with horses and chariots. [*Airget Ros* (that is, the Silver Wood) was situated in the present

[1] See as to this Idol, the author's *Lectures on the MS. Materials of Ancient Irish History*,—p. 103,—and App., pp. 538 and 631.

[illegible] ancient fort of *Rath Betha*, (in the [illegible] Rath, in the barony of Galmoy, near [illegible] Brenann died and was buried, stood in it.] LECT. I.

[illegible] world 3872 died the monarch *Muinemon*, [illegible] It was this *Muinemon* that first caused [illegible] be worn on the necks of kings and chiefs [illegible] Chains of Gold first made under Muinemon.

[illegible] lived *Mainmairis*, King of Munster, [illegible] He was the first that purchased gold and [illegible]

[illegible] died the monarch *Fail-dearg-doid* (that is, [illegible] Hands), of the line of *Eber*. He [illegible] Rings of Gold to be worn on the fin-[illegible]

[illegible] flourished *Cetcuimnigh*, King of Mun-[illegible] *Eber*. He was the first that inscribed [illegible] The first Ogham inscriptions by Cetcuimnigh, A. M. 3941.

[illegible] this *Cetcuimnigh*, succeeded his father, and [illegible] Chariots built in Erinn.

[illegible] the world 3991 died the monarch *Fiacha* [illegible] race of *Ir*, after a reign of twenty years. He [illegible] Spring Wells in Erinn.

[illegible] the world 4176 died the monarch *Roitheach-*[illegible] *Eber*, after a reign of seven years. He [illegible] a chariot with four horses in Erinn.

[illegible] the world 4463 died the monarch *Lughaidh* [illegible] *Eber*, after a reign of seven years. He [illegible] "invented" Bronze and Bronze Spears in [illegible]

[illegible] versions of this list of "inventors" ex-[illegible] followed the Book of Leinster and the Annals [illegible] and as criticism upon their entries would [illegible] here for my present purpose, I shall, with your [illegible] what I have to say as to the accuracy of the [illegible] recorded, for a future occasion.[1]

[illegible] interrupt the foregoing list, I have been obliged [illegible] to a later date in the march of the country's [illegible]; and I shall now go back again from the [illegible] world 4463, where I stopped, to the time of the [illegible], who is recorded to have succeeded to the

[1] [illegible] intended to have concluded the whole series of these [illegible] examination of the authorities whose statements he fol-[illegible] of his work. Unfortunately, the whole series was not des-[illegible] before he was taken from amongst us.]

LECT. I.

monarchy in the year of the world 3882, and died in the year 3922, after a reign of forty years.

Of Ollamh Fodhla (Monarch A.M. 3882-3922).

The original name of this prince was *Eochaidh;* but, from his great learning he obtained the distinction of *Ollamh*, or Doctor, before his accession to the throne; and after he became King of Erinn, he was called *Ollamh Fodhla*, or "the Doctor of *Fodhla*", which was one of the ancient names of Erinn.

Ollamh Fodhla erected a new court at *Teamair*, or Tara, which ever after was called *Mur Ollamhan*, or "*Ollamh's* Court". This court has been often represented to have been a college of *Ollamhs*, or learned Doctors; such, however, is not the meaning of the name, but, simply, the Court of King *Ollamh* himself.

That *Ollamh Fodhla* was a man of power and distinction as a legislator and a scholar, may be, I think, very fairly allowed, as we find this character given to him in a very ancient poem of thirty-two lines, preserved in the Book of Leinster, and ascribed to the Ultonian poet *Ferceirtné*, who was attached to the Court of *Conor MacNessa*, the celebrated King of *Uladh*, and flourished so long since as about the time of the Incarnation of our Lord.

Antiquity of the *Feis* of Tara.

This little piece contains evidence of the high antiquity of that Feast of Tara, which we shall presently see was, in fact, the supreme legislative assembly of ancient Erinn; and thus refers to a very remote period indeed the existence of an institution which necessarily implies that high degree of civilization which the annalists always attribute to our early ancestors.

The poem was written to commemorate the name of *Ollamh Fodhla*, his three sons, and his descendants, who succeeded him one after another and occupied the sovereignty 210 years without interruption from any other family. As this poem appears to me to be certainly authentic, and of great historic value, I am tempted to give here a literal translation of the whole of it. It is as follows:—

"*Ollamh Fodhla*, of furious valour,
Who founded the Court of *Ollamh*,
Was the first heroic king
That instituted the Feast of *Teamair*.

"Forty sweet musical years
He held the high sovereignty of Erinn;
And it was from him, with noble pride,
The Ultonians [or Olltonians] took their name.

"Six kings of valiant career
Of *Ollamh's* race reigned over Erinn;
For two hundred and ten full years,
No other person came between them.

[illegible] the gifted;
[illegible] the great sweet voice;
[illegible] the sharp gifted weapons;
[illegible] warrior *Bengal*,
[illegible] (Doctor) by natural right,
[illegible] of *Fiacha Finscothach*;
[illegible] king,—royal his face,—
[illegible] son of *Milidh*.
[illegible] of brilliant fame,
[illegible] of the Royal Branch,
[illegible] deserved renown,
[illegible] descendants of *Ollamh*.
[illegible] with his ample force,
[illegible] in *Dinnrigh*,
[illegible] host from beyond the sea;—
[illegible] Lagenians [lit. lancemen] are named.
[illegible] Greater than any other man,
[illegible] son of *Mofemis*;—
[illegible] of old was named.
[illegible] Ultonia is from *Ollamh*".

[illegible] felt the difficulty of authenticating the [illegible] this short simple poem will afford much [illegible] than may at first appear.

[illegible] of the author, *Ferceirtné*, and of the time [illegible] reasonable doubt can exist.

[illegible] poets and historians of this name found in [illegible] Pagan Erinn, preserved in the Book of [illegible] *Ferceirtné* (as I have shown in a former [illegible] to the person and fortunes of *Labhraidh* [illegible] of Leinster; the second, the present *Ferceirtné*, [illegible] Conor MacNessa's court at Emania; and the [illegible] to the court and person of *Curoi MacDairé*, [illegible] Munster, at *Cathair Conroi* (near Tralee, in [illegible] of the Ultonian race, one of the heroes of [illegible] and contemporary with Conor; and after [illegible] treacherous death at the hands of the [illegible] Ultonian warrior, *Cuchulainn*, *Ferceirtné* com- [illegible] for the fallen hero, in which he celebrates his [illegible] his honour, and his munificence to poets [illegible] describing in a long list his gifts and pre-

Of the three *Ferceirtnés*.

[illegible] copies of this most curious and ancient poem [illegible] a manuscript in the British Museum, (Egar- [illegible] another in Trinity College, Dublin, (H., 3, 18);

Difficulty of the language of poems attributed to *Ferceirtné*.

LECT. I.

but their style and diction are so antiquated as to place th beyond the comprehension of those Irish scholars who h either not been able, or have not undertaken the labour, prepare for themselves glossaries and concordances from su other very ancient pieces of composition as have come do to our time. For, let me observe, that no acquaintance wi the corrupt writings of Irish Bards of the last two hund years, and no lexicon yet published, will be found of a value in dealing with this piece and others of its class, writ as they were in forms of language so ancient and now so v obscure; and yet there are pretended Irish scholars of the p sent day, who never saw these most ancient writings, nor e even heard of them but casually, and who nevertheless affec familiarity with them, nay actually pretend to translate the with a confidence in the public credulity which only ceases surprise us because we know how often it has been succes in imposing on the ignorant.

But to return to the poem on *Ollamh Fodhla:* the points it to which I would particularly desire attention are these the existence and antiquity of the great Feast of *Teamair* the author's time (that is, the time of the Incarnation); th existence of the *Craebh Ruadh*, or House of the "Royal Branch at the same time, at Emania; and, among other things, origin of the names of *Laighin* (Leinster), *Mumhain* (Munste and *Uladh* (Ulster).

Of the name of the province of Connacht.

Why, it may be asked, is not the origin of the name *Connacht* found with the other three provincial names in th poem? This is a curious and I can assure you an impor question in relation to the antiquity of the piece; but it c be answered positively by the fact that the name "*Connac* had not yet existed in the poet's time.

You will have seen that *Ferceirtné* derives the names of th three provinces from the names of distinguished men; but th province of *Connacht*, as it happens, was at this time call *Ollnegmacht*,—and did not receive the name of *Connacht* ("the land of the descendants of *Conn*"), until after the time o *Conn* of the Hundred Battles, who died, Monarch of Erinn, a late as the year of our Lord 157.

It is true that it was attempted in later times to give romantic, or rather mythological, origin to the name *Connac* For in the same Book of Leinster we find recorded an ancie legend, which tells us that there ruled over *Connacht*, at so unknown period, a King whose name was *Conn;* that this Ki was one of the greatest Druids of his time; that not only w he able to resist all the druidical power of the *Tuatha D* [illegible] attempted against him, but became in [illegible] with their own chosen weapons; that, hav[illegible] carried off all their cattle, and pillaged [illegible] dwellings, in order to protect himself and to [illegible] Snow, he enveloped himself and the whole [illegible] several feet deep; that thereupon the *Tuatha* [illegible] themselves to *Dalach*, the King's brother, [illegible] of high renown; that *Dalach* ordered them [illegible] white cows with red ears, to take out their [illegible] spread them upon a certain plain (in the [illegible] Roscommon), where he pronounced druidical [illegible] and that immediately their heat melted the [illegible] plain and the province; that this plain there[illegible] name of *Magh Aoi*, or the "Plain of the [illegible] retained ever after; and that the province re[illegible] *Connsneachta*, or Conn's Snow, which name [illegible] to the more euphonious form of *Connachta*.

[illegible] hardly say, no argument to show the purely [illegible] this derivation of the name *Connacht;* and [illegible] agree with me in preferring the authority of [illegible], the King-Bishop Cormac MacCullinan, [illegible] Glossary, at the word *Icht*, derives the [illegible] as follows:

[illegible] heads or children, ut est, *Connachta*, id est, [illegible], the Children of *Conn*".[3]

[illegible] is found more copiously sustained in the very [illegible] called *Coir Anmann*, or the Explanation of [illegible] copies are preserved in the Books of Ballymote, [illegible] says this tract:[4]

[illegible] is, *Conn-Ichta*, that is, the *Ichta* of *Conn* [illegible] Battles; that is, the Children of Conn; for [illegible] Children, or Race.

[illegible] that is, the *Acht* of *Conn;* that is, the Act [illegible] Conn; because it was *Conn* that made forcible [illegible] and *Acht* is the same as a deed".

[illegible] are two important authorities—(Cormac Mac[illegible] ninth century,—and the Book of *Lecain*),—to [illegible] name *Connachta*, (the People), and *Connacht*, (the [illegible] derived from *Conn* of the Hundred Battles, who [illegible] of our Lord 157; so that this name could not

[3] [illegible] clann, ut est, Connachta edon conn-icht, edon

[4] [illegible] Connachta .i. ichta Chuinn cet cathaich .i. clann [illegible] clann, no cenel. No Connacht .i. acht Chuinn .i. [illegible] do ronai tir claidem di doreicin, ar is inand

LECT. I.

be found in *Ferceirtné's* poem, who must have been d
the same number of years before; and thus the traditi
Feast of *Teamair*, found in *Ferceirtné's* verses, would
back at least to a period anterior to the Incarnation.

Of the *Feis* of Tara.

According to *Ferceirtné*, then, *Ollamh Fodhla* was
monarch that instituted the Feast of *Teamair*, or T
besides the many allusions to this Feast, and to the
of the triennial assembly of the powerful and learned
Erinn, we have the positive statement taken by Keti
ancient books (of which I on a former occasion[5] gave
count as having been still in existence in the time
learned priest, though since lost to us), that the assem
Tara was held at the beginning of November, every thi
and that it was a sort of parliament, at which all the
and principal scholars of Erinn met, to institute ne
or to renew and extend old ones, and to examine, to
pare, and to correct the national annals and history
country.

Military Organization under *Ollamh Fodhla*.

Ollamh Fodhla is stated[6] (by the same authorities)
been the first that ordered a military leader, or captain,
cantred, and a chief, or gentleman-farmer, in every vill
of whom were to do service to the monarch of Erinn.
ordered a particular place, according to rank, for every
that attended the great Feast of *Teamair*, an arrangeme
continued without material alteration down to the abando
of that ancient seat of the monarchy, in the sixth centu
our era.

Of the still existing authorities on the subject of the F
Tara, as it was celebrated by the successors of *Ollamh F*
I shall here refer to some of the most important.

The following extract from a poem of *Eochaidh O'Cl*
(who lived about the year of our Lord 1000) will give yo
idea of the sort of order which was observed during the ho
of the feast:—

"The Feast of *Teamair* every third year,
For the preservation of law and rule,
At that time was proudly held
By the illustrious kings of Erinn.

"*Cathair* [*Mór*] the popular held
The far-famed Feast of Royal *Teamair*;
There assembled unto him, to his delight,
The men of Erinn, to the one place.

(5) See *Lectures on the MS. Materials of Ancient Irish History*, p. 21.
(6) *Annals of the Four Masters*; A.M. 3922.

...*Samhain*, at all times,
...after, by ancient custom,
...of high aspirations
...feast for the whole week.
...theft, no wounding of the person,
...during all this time;
...of weapons, no cutting,
...no threatening boast.
...guilty of any of these
...mortal, venomous foe;
...such crime was from him received,
...the immediate spot".

...is taken from the thirteenth stanza of a poem ... written by *O'Ciarain*, on the origin of the ... history of *Loch Garman* (now Wexford), ... Books of Ballymote and *Lecain*.

... have sufficient authority to show the time at ... by whom, the great Feast of *Teamair* ... we have no detailed account, that I have ... arrangements of the meeting but what ... Keting has left us; and although that ... access to many ancient and important ... lost to us, there is good reason to think that ... Feast of *Teamair* was obtained particularly ... *Leabhar na h-Ua Chongbhala*, or Book of ... preserved at Kildare in his time.[7]

... that the arrangement of which Keting ... detailed account could not have existed so ... of *Ollamh Fodhla*; because the provincial ... fully established, nor down to the reign of ... *Feidhlech*, in the century immediately ...

...of *Teamair* was but of limited extent, down ... monarch *Tuathal* (about the year of our ... the restoration of the legitimate monarchy, ... of the democratic revolution, *Tuathal* esta... of *Midhé*, or Meath, to be the mensal lands ...; and this he did without much injury ... ancient provincial divisions originally made ... for, as the provinces of Ulster, Leinster, ... met in a single point (at a great stone ... the hill of *Uisnech* in Westmeath), so he cut

Of the royal domain of Tara.

... the MS. *Materials*, etc.; p. 13 (etc.).

LECT. I. off from them their converging points, to a certain joined these to the old and limited territory of Bregia, *Teamair* originally stood; and it was after this that the new divisions of the new province took the geographical of East and West Meath. *Tuathal* afterwards built a each of these divisions cut off from the four provinces.

Keting's description of the Feast of Tara, temp. Tuathal Teachtmar. The following is the description of the Feast of in the reign of *Tuathal Teachtmar*, as preserved by

"The fourth of these royal residences was *Teamair*, is situated in the part which was added from Leinster to where the feast of *Teamair* was held every third year, they had made offerings to all their gods at *Tlachtga*, as said above, preparatory to that Royal Convocation which called the Feast of *Teamair*, at which they were accustomed order laws and customs, and to test the Annals of that such parts of them as were attested, were written chief *ollamhs* (or doctors) in the Roll of the Kings, was called the *Saltair* of *Teamair;* and any other history of Erinn which did not agree with this chief book not estimated as of truth. We shall not here recite the laws or the customs which were ordered at the *Teamair*, because the Book of the People's Laws is full I shall, however, set down here the order which was at the Feast of *Teamair* for the distribution in their halls, of the nobles and the warriors, when assembled at

"There was no Territorial *Ollamh* in History and in Erinn who did not write in the Roll of *Teamair* the of the nobles who were lords of Territories, each according his rank, as it was ordered at the Feast of *Teamair;* and chief (or leader) of warriors who was retained to guard protect the land of Erinn had his name enrolled by *ollamh* in like manner; and there was not one of these, Lords of Territories or leaders, who was not attended shield-bearer.

"The form of their banquet halls was long and with tables at both sides of the house, and a rack on side over the seats of the company, having only the a shield between every two hooks of it; and upon those the genealogist suspended the shields of the nobles and before they took their seats, each of them under his own both noble and warrior. The lords of Territories, however had a choice of the two sides; and the leaders (or captains) occupied the other; while the *ollamhs* and chief poets

(8) *Vide* MS. H. 3, 17. T.C.D.

LECT. I.

The Feis of Tara.

judges, musicians, etc.) occupied the
attendants who waited on the guests, the

too, that no one of them sat opposite to
with his back to the wall, both lords of
under their own shields.
custom to have women in their banquet
place for themselves, where they were

custom also, that preparatory to the serving
leave the house but three,—namely, a
of the house; and a trumpeter with his
in. This trumpeter sounded his horn
first blast the shield-bearers of the nobles
door of the banquet hall, and the marshal
the shield of each noble, and under the
genealogist placed each shield in its own proper
then sounded the second blast, when
the warriors came to the door of the ban-
marshal received the shields from them, and
the direction of the genealogist, on the
over the table of the warriors.
afterwards sounded the third blast, at which
assembled in the banquet hall, and each
his own shield, so that there was neither
for places among them".

Keting's description of the same Feast, temp. Laeghaire Mac Neill.

from his ancient authorities, on the ordi-
of the great Feast of *Teamair*, in the
but he quotes another short article
of the feast on a state occasion of special
Laeghaire MacNeill, who was the monarch
of Saint Patrick's arrival:—
was convoked by *Laeghaire* to renew
laws of Erinn, in conformity with the prac-
who preceded him.
and learned men of Erinn came to this
King, or Monarch, with his court, occupied
namely, the *Teach Miodhchuarta*, or great
and each of the provincial kings had a
too. The King of Munster had the *Long*
House; the King of Leinster had the *Long*
House; the King of Connacht had the
or Connacht Banqueting House; and the
the *Eachrais Uladh*, or Assembly House of

LECT. I

THE FEIS OF TARA.

"There were three other buildings at *Teamair* at
The first was *Carcair na n-Giall*, or the Prison of the
where the monarch's hostages were kept. The
Realta na bh-Filiodh, or the Star of the Poets,
judges and poets of Erinn sat to dispense justice to
were charged with breaches of the laws and regulat
country. The third was *Grianan na n-Inghean*, or
House of the Women, where the provincial queens we
each with her own attendants, in separate sections of
blishment.

"When, however, the great assembly sat to enact
the national laws and customs, the *Teach Miodhchuarta*,
Banqueting Hall, was the seat of their deliberations.
lowing was the order in which they sat in that house
King of Erinn sat in the centre of the hall, with his face
west; and the King of Munster on the south side of
it was to the east and to the west that the two ends
house looked; the King of Leinster sat opposite him
King of Connacht behind him; and the *Ollamhs* (or
Doctors) of Erinn behind the King of Connacht; wh
King of Ulster sat on the north side, on the Monarch's
hand; those kings being each attended by a select p
their most distinguished nobles. And this arrange
manifest from the old heraldry which had been estab
in Erinn in the ancient times. The following is an
plification of this fact, as given briefly by an a
poet:—

"The men of Munster on the south side,
Without injustice, without constraint;
And the men of Leinster, full of strength,
Face to face with their High King.

"The Connacht men at the monarch's back,
They who in history preserved all truth;
The chief of *Dal Araidhé*, among the rest,
Sat in a distinguished separate place.

"The right hand of *Teamair's* powerful king,
Without injustice, without reproach,
To the Oriellians doth belong,
Without decision of law, without dispute".

So far Keting. The three verses which he quotes a
second, third, and fourth stanzas of an anonymous po
thirty-two stanzas, which describes the peculiar privile
the Oriellians, or *Clan Colla;* as granted to them by *Dia*
the son of *Fergus Cerrbheoil* (the last monarch that r

[illegible] about the year 536), and confirmed to [illegible] son of Aedh, (who died, 639).[18] LECT. I.
[illegible] great interest, not only in carrying [illegible] the Feast of Temair more than a [illegible] own time, but because also they [illegible] on which it is to be regretted that [illegible] learned Irish scholar did not offer some [illegible] they do not exactly agree with the [illegible] explanation of this discrepancy will be [illegible] connection with my present purpose.

[illegible] observed that while the prose piece places [illegible] the monarch's right hand in the great [illegible] according to the strict precedence of [illegible] designation, the poem gives that place [illegible] or Oriell.

[illegible] that the prose is the more ancient [illegible] it must originally have been written [illegible] Lord 331, for it was only down to that [illegible] kingdom of Ulster remained intact, and [illegible] representative at *Temair*. In that year, [illegible] *Colla*, of the Eremonian race, overthrew [illegible] of the Irian race) at the great battle [illegible], (in *Farney*, in the present county [illegible] the sovereignty of the province from [illegible] the parts comprised in the present coun-[illegible] Down; and into that district they drove the [illegible] the Irians, over the river *Righ*. This [illegible] inhabited by the original race of Ulster, de-[illegible] modern writers (to distinguish it from [illegible] province of Ulster), subsequently obtained the [illegible] permanent, name of *Oirghiall*, (Angli-[illegible] Oriell).

Of the Kingdom of Oirghialla, or Oriall.

[illegible] Uladh, too, or the true Ultonians, received [illegible] of *Dal Araidhé*, (Anglicised or Latinised [illegible] *Fiacha Araidhé*, King of all Ulster about [illegible] Lord 240; whose descendants continued to [illegible] lords of the smaller territory of *Uladh* down [illegible] invasion; and who are represented at the [illegible] Mac Ennises, or Magennises, of Iveagh, in [illegible]

Of the Dal Araidhé.

[illegible] Tara was held A.D. 554, and the last king [illegible] died in 558, the same year in which died

[illegible] of this poem preserved in the Royal Irish Academy, [illegible] —("Ye learned of the poetic

LECT. I.

the monarch *Diarmait*, son of Fergus, in whose time *Teamair* was cursed by Saint *Ruadhan*, and with whose death it ceased to be a royal residence.

It is evident, then, that this poem must have been originally written after the year 332, when *Colla Uais* took the dignity of king of Ulster, and before the year 558, the last year in which the petty king of *Dal Araidh* could have occupied the distinguished separate place at the Feast assigned to him by it.

Cormac Mac Airt at the Feast of Tara.

The following brief sketch of the celebrated monarch, *Cormac Mac Airt*, as he appeared at one of those Feasts of *Teamair*, is preserved in the Book of Ballymote, in the Royal Irish Academy (folio 142), and taken from the more ancient *Leabhar na h-Ua Chongbhala*, or Book of Navan, already mentioned:[10]

"A noble illustrious king took the sovereignty and rule over Erinn at another time: namely, *Cormac*, the grandson of *Conn*.

"The world was replete with all that was good in his time. The fruit and fat of the land, and the gifts of the sea, were in abundance in this king's reign. There were neither woundings nor robberies in his time, but every one enjoyed his own in peace.

"The nobles of the men of Erinn came to drink the Feast of *Teamair* at a certain time. These were the kings who presided at the Feast, namely: *Fergus* the Blacktoothed, and *Eochaidh Gunnat*, the two Kings of Ulster; *Dunlaing*, the son of *Enna Niadh*, King of Leinster; *Cormac Cas* (the ancestor of the Dalcassians), son of [illegible] and *Fiacha Muilleathan*, the son of *Eoghan* [illegible] the two Kings of Munster; *Nia Mor*, son of [illegible] the son of Cormac's own mother; and [illegible] son of *Conall*, the two Kings of [illegible] of the Bloody Spear [illegible] and *Fearadhach*, the son of [illegible] King of [West] Meath.

"[illegible] and assemblies were attended [illegible]: Every king was clad [illegible] helmet on his head for [illegible] crowns but in the field of battle [illegible].

"[illegible] this great assembly; for the [illegible] excepting *Conaire Mor* son of [illegible] *Cathbadh*: or *Aengus* the son of [illegible].

[10] The [illegible] Appendix, No. xxvii. to the [illegible] MS. *Materials of Ancient* [illegible]

LECT. I.

[illegible] was the appearance of *Cormac* in that assembly. [illegible] curling golden hair, upon him. A red buck[illegible] [illegible] animals of gold and fastenings of silver, upon [illegible] cloak in wide descending folds upon him, fas[illegible] by a golden brooch set with precious stones. [illegible] of gold around his neck. A white shirt, with a [illegible] interwoven with red gold thread, upon him. A [illegible] with precious stones around him. Two [illegible] of gold, with runnings of gold, upon him. [illegible] golden sockets, in his hand, and with many [illegible]. And he was, besides, himself symmetrical [illegible], without blemish or reproach".

Dr. Keting's authorities.

[illegible] it will be observed, in the course of this Lec[illegible] Rev. Geoffrey Keting's History of Erinn,—a work [illegible] native Gaedhelic about the year 1630,—as an [illegible] as the authority of that eminent scholar is even [illegible] insufficiently acknowledged at the present day, [illegible] should be led to suppose that he took occasion [illegible] imagination, for want of original authorities, in [illegible] of the valuable work to which I have referred, [illegible] a list, which I gave on a former occasion, of [illegible] books which he had before him:—The Book [illegible] Book of *Dromsnechta*, or extracts from it; the [illegible] the *Leabhar na h-Uidhré* of St. *Ciaran;* the [illegible] Mac Egans; the Book of *Glenn-dá-Locha;* the [illegible] (in Ormond); the Annals of the ancient [illegible] *Eidnech;* the Book of the *Ua Chongbhail* (or [illegible] Book of St. *Fintán*, of *Cluain Eidnech;* the [illegible] St. *Moling;* and the Black Book of St. *Molaga.* [illegible] were more full by far than those which now [illegible] of the credit due to a man of Dr. Keting's [illegible] learning I apprehend no one can suggest a [illegible] perfectly certain that he has told us only what he

[illegible] endeavoured to abstract as authentic, clear, and [illegible] as I could, of the institution and arrange[illegible] great Feast or Convocation of the States of Erinn, [illegible] continued to meet, and to make or renew [illegible] of the country, during the long term of 1800 [illegible] to the chronology of the Four Masters. We [illegible] the personages were who, in right of their rank [illegible], sat as legislators in that famous assembly in [illegible]. They were: the Monarch; the Provin[illegible] the nobles, or Chiefs of Territories; the chief

LECT. I.

Judges; the chief Poets; and the chief general Sch[illegible] nation. In short, the legislative assembly appears [illegible] at this remote period not only a representative [illegible] one as popular as the existing distinction of classes [illegible] any propriety have allowed it to be.

Tradition of the bringing of the law of Moses from Egypt.

It is stated in very old copies of the "Book of Inv[illegible] other ancient documents, that it was the Mosaic la[illegible] Milesians brought into Erinn at their coming; that [illegible] learned and received from Moses, in Egypt, by *Cas* "[illegible] *thach*", [*Cae*, "of the Fair Judgments"], who was [illegible] Israelite, but had been sent into Egypt to learn the [illegible] that country by the great Master *Fenius Farsaidh*, [illegible] "the Antiquarian"], from whom the Milesian broth[illegible] conquered Erinn are recorded to have been the twent[illegible] generation in descent; and it is stated in the prefa[illegible] *Seanchas Mór* that this was the law of Erinn at the [illegible] coming of St. Patrick, in 432.

It is also stated in the preface to the *Seanchas Mór*, [illegible] in a quotation in the Book of Ballymote, in the Roy[illegible] Academy, and in the Yellow Book of *Lecain* (H. 2, 16[illegible] nity College Library), [taken from the more ancient [illegible] *na h-Ua Chongbhala*, (or Book of Navan)], that from [illegible] that *Amergin*, the son of Milesius, gave judgment betw[illegible] brothers *Eber* and *Eremon*, on their arrival in Erinn, [illegible] ing the division of the produce of a certain chase in whic[illegible] respective people took part, the office of Brehon or judg[illegible] conceded to the poetic or philosophic profession; and that [illegible] continued down to the time of *Concobar Mac Nessa*, Ki[illegible] Ulster, who was contemporary with our Saviour.

The Profession of Poet-Judges deprived of their privileges, temp. *Concobar Mac Nessa.*

It would appear that for some time before this period [illegible] learned Poet-Judges were accustomed to deliver their judg[illegible] in language so obscure as to be almost unintelligible to the [illegible] nobles, and chiefs, who attended at the *Airechts*, or courts [illegible] happened that a great contest took place in *Concobar's* [illegible] at Emania, the royal palace of Ulster, between *Aithirn[illegible]* chief poet and satirist of that province, and *Neidhé*, the so[illegible] *Adhna;* as to which of them should wear the *Tuidhen F[illegible]* or poet's gown, and occupy the poet's chair at court, [illegible] which had been just left vacant by the death of *Ne[illegible]* father. This contest or discussion was a public one; and [illegible] was carried on between the learned antagonists in so obscur[illegible] style of language and construction, that the attending mult[illegible] tude must have felt disappointed at not being able to under[illegible] stand it. King *Concobar*, who was present all the time, fel[illegible] so much annoyed at not understanding the discussion himself, [illegible] of his unskilled people, he made an [illegible] the office of judge should no longer [illegible] of the poetic art, but should be [illegible] themselves for it, not however exclud- [illegible] talented tain. This order was adopted [illegible] nation, and produced immediate and [illegible] office of judge became thenceforth an [illegible] [illegible], and numbers of talented men, [illegible] too, were called to it, by the una- [illegible] church, and people.

[illegible] remarkable of these judges a short list [illegible] the preface to the *Seanchas Mór*; but [illegible] of those whose names are preserved in these [illegible] to Ulster, and to the first century.

Account of the more remarkable Judges of Erinn, from the Seanchas Mór.

[illegible] the parties in the above discussion, *Neidhé* [illegible] of course to change their language in [illegible] *Fergus* the poet, son of *Aithirné*;—*Sean* [illegible];—and *Brigh*, his daughter, who criti- [illegible] father's errors;—*Fachtna* the wise, son [illegible] *Mac Durthacht*, King, or Chief of [illegible] in the county Monaghan);—*Eoch-* [illegible] King of North Munster;—*Fergus Fiannaitt*, [illegible] *Fiannait* (near Tralee, in Kerry);—and [illegible] [i.e., "of the mild judgments"] of Con- [illegible] *Connla* that held a celebrated contest with [illegible] asserted that they were the creators of the [illegible] earth; but they were defeated by *Connla*, who [illegible] to prove their great powers by causing the [illegible] appear in the north; this, of course, was not [illegible] were confounded.

[illegible] also flourished *Feradhach "Finn Feacht-* [illegible] and righteous"], who became monarch of [illegible]. He is mentioned in the preface to the *Seanchas* [illegible] all our ancient books, as an eminent judge. [illegible] *Morann*—(of the fabulous collar, which is said [illegible] on his neck when falling into the delivery of [illegible] judgment),—was the official judge and adviser [illegible] *Feradhach*. *Morann's* instructions to his son [illegible] *Neré*, on the qualifications and duties of a judge, [illegible] and will, probably, appear in the forthcoming [illegible] Brehon Law Commission.

[illegible] *Sencha*, the son of *Ailill*, occupying the place [illegible] monarch *Tuathal Techtmar*, whose reign closed [illegible] our Lord 106.

[illegible] *Techtmhar*, the son of *Tuathal*, succeeded to the

LECT. I. monarchy in the year 111, and died in the year 11[illegible] ceived the surname of *Rechtmhar*, (or "the lawgiver"), [illegible] having in his reign introduced into Erinn the Lex [illegible] which ordered payment in kind for all injuries; such as [illegible] for an eye, a tooth for a tooth, an arm for an arm, a [illegible] cow, and so on.

Conn "of the Hundred Battles" succeeded to the [illegible] the year 123. *Conn* had, attached to his court, a [illegible] chief judge, a wealthy member of his own family—who [illegible] strange name of *Caratniad* "of the false judgments" [illegible] title referred only, however, to the unusual literary [illegible] which he delivered them, which appears to have been [illegible] strangest. For we are told that every cause that [illegible] adjudication to the monarch was handed over by [illegible] *Caratniad*, who delivered his decisions in such a way [illegible] they always appeared at first to be false and unjust, but [illegible] decisions upon critical examination were always found [illegible] strictly just and legal.

We may pass over the reign of *Art*, son of *Conn*; and [illegible] immediate successor, *MacCon*, who was his own Judge [illegible] come down to *Cormac*, the son of *Art*, and grandson of [illegible] who came to the monarchy in the year 227, and died in [illegible] year 266.

So much has been said of *Cormac*, in my former lecture [illegible] that I need only repeat here that he was one of the ablest, [illegible] not absolutely the wisest, of all the monarchs of Erinn down [illegible] his time. He was not only a judge and lawyer, but he himself compiled an abstract of all the ancient laws of the country for the special use of his son and successor *Cairbré Liffeachair*. This book was compiled at *Acaill* (now the hill of Screen, near Tara), and has on that account been called the "Book of *Acaill*". There are copies of large fragments of it, if not of the whole book, extant at this day; but as I have described it in a former lecture, it is not necessary to do more than refer to it here.[11]

Cormac, though himself, according to *Cuan O'Lochain's* poem, a most eminent judge, had also an eminent chief judge and adviser in the wise and acute *Fithal*, and after him in his prudent and learned son *Flaithri*.

There is a curious and very ancient little tract preserved in the Book of Leinster, under the name of *Sean-raidhté Fithail* (that is, "the old, or wise, sayings of *Fithal*"), consisting of a series of moral, philosophical, and legal maxims, said to have been spoken by the wise *Fithal* to his great master *Cormac*.

[11] See *Lectures on the MS. Materials of Ancient Irish History*, pp. 47, 48.

King Cormac's order regulating the household of a Monarch.

[illegible] *Cormac*, according to Keting, that made an order [illegible] monarchs of Erinn should be at all times accom[illegible] persons, consisting of a chief, a judge, a druid, a [illegible] an historian, a musician, and three servants. [illegible] to sit at the king's shoulder; the judge, to ex[illegible] and customs of the country in the king's pre[illegible] for sacrifice and prophecy, of good or evil, to [illegible] his pagan knowledge; the doctor, for attending [illegible] the king, queen, and household; the poet, for [illegible] all persons according to their deserts; the [illegible] the genealogical branches, and the history [illegible] the nobles, from time to time; the musician, to [illegible] and sing songs and poems before the king; the [illegible] servants, with a sufficient company of assistants, to [illegible] and his company at table.

[illegible] continued in force from *Cormac's* time to the [illegible] monarch *Brian Boroimhé*, in the year 1014; [illegible] times a bishop took the place of the druid [illegible] attendants.

[illegible] an ancient poem for this arrangement, but [illegible] nothing more than he gives in this prose.

[illegible] account of any change in, or addition to, the [illegible] the country, from the time of *Cormac* to the [illegible] and the compiling of the *Seanchas Mór*.

LECTURE II.

[Delivered [illegible] May, 1857.]

(I.) Legislation; (continued).—Of the existence of a regular System [illegible] in Erinn before the time of St. Patrick. Of the revision of the Laws [illegible] St. Patrick. The Law of *Adamnan*. Of the *Seanchas Mór*: Crimin[illegible] Code; Law of Contracts; Law of Ranks in Society; Military Laws [illegible] as to the Land; various Special Laws. *Law of Eric* (or compos[illegible] murder) introduced with Christianity. Of the mode of Legislation [illegible] passing of new laws. Of the *Meill Bretha*, (temp. *Conn*). Of local [illegible] lation by the several Tribes. Mode of making the *Nos Tuaithe*, or [illegible] Law. Of the Twelve Books of Laws of West Munster (A.D. 690). Of [illegible] Laws not passed in assembly;—e. g. the *Cain Domhnaigh*, or Law of S[illegible] (II.) System of Classes of Society. Of the division of Classes of [illegible] in ancient Erinn. Of the *Flaith*, or noble. Of the *Ceile*, or tenant [illegible] the Four Classes of *Bo-Airech*. Of the Seven Classes of *Flaith*. Of the [illegible] of *Carmán* (Wexford); ancient accounts of the Legislative Assembly of [illegible] Kingdom of Leinster held there.

In my last lecture I opened the subject of the ancient [illegible] zation of Erinn, so far as we can with certainty trace [illegible] evidences of it in the comparatively meagre annals exis[illegible] concerning the very early eras of our national history. [illegible] as the growth of some System of Law, and its gradual prog[illegible] to maturity, affords the best history of the civilization of [illegible] nation,—as it is also the most important of all the results [illegible] that civilization,—I applied myself in the first instance to [illegible] branch of the subject selected for the present course.

System of Laws before St. Patrick's time.

That some system of law—and by this I mean, not mere[illegible] some body of separate enactments, but really a *system*—exi[illegible] among the Milesian race, from a period contemporary wit[illegible] not anterior to, their original landing in the island, is perfec[illegible] plain from all their traditions and records. I have as yet [illegible] touched on the most important proofs of this fact, in pointing [illegible] to you the existence of a national Legislative Assembly, certa[illegible] some centuries, probably many, before the era of the g[illegible] revision and completion of the Irish code in Saint Patrick's t[illegible] As this is the Code of which the greater part still remains to [illegible] now happily destined to see the light under the direction [illegible] the Brehon Law Commission, I cannot pass over so shortly [illegible] history of its construction. Pending, however, the expec[illegible] publication, it is not my intention, because it would not [illegible] proper for me, to enter at all into the details of these ancien[illegible] Laws; full though they are of the most minute and the most [illegible]

[illegible] civilization I have spoken of, in all [illegible] as well as of political life. I proceed, [illegible] where we left off.

[illegible] of the Christian religion in Ireland by [illegible] of *Laeghaire MacNeill*, it was found [illegible] of the ancient Pagan enactments, [illegible] national code, in order to bring them into [illegible] milder spirit of the Christian dispen- [illegible] monarch *Laeghaird* (according to the [illegible]), on his conversion, convoked the [illegible] of *Teamair*; and after sufficient [illegible] that the whole of the ancient code [illegible] explained to Saint Patrick, in order [illegible] such parts of it as it would be desirable [illegible]

Revision of the Laws, temp. St. Patrick.

[illegible] that this statement implies, of course, the [illegible] a complete Code of Laws; and the convo- [illegible] to revise and republish the laws [illegible] the account quoted by Keting of the [illegible] assembly in earlier times.

[illegible] the three most distinguished *ollamhs* (or [illegible], Literature, and Law, then attached to the [illegible] selected, namely, *Dubhthach*, the *ollamh* [illegible] history (the first convert in *Teamar*); *Ros* [illegible] of the *Berla Feiné*, or technical law; and [illegible]. These three having made a general [illegible] laws, and *Dubhthach* having explained [illegible] saint then proceeded to mark out every- [illegible] in them to the teaching of the Gospel. [illegible] assembly proceeded to appoint what may [illegible] language, a Committee of nine, to carry out [illegible]. This committee consisted of three kings, [illegible], and three Christian bishops. The three [illegible], the monarch; *Dairé*, King of Ulster (or [illegible]) King of Munster. The three *ollamhs* were [illegible] learned men—*Dubhthach*, *Ros*, and *Fergus*. [illegible] were—Patrick, *Benen*, and *Cairnech*.[12] [illegible] seem, however, to have only had power to [illegible] recommend the necessary changes.

[illegible] recorded proves that the supreme legislative [illegible] with the whole body of the assembly con- [illegible]. For we find that, after the revision of the [illegible] completed by the personages just mentioned, the [illegible]

[illegible], [R.I.A.] fol. 76, b.

LECT. II.

purified code was next laid before the National Assembly, received its formal assent; and thus it was that the revised Co became the law of the land, preserved under the distin name of the *Seanchas Mór*, or Great Body of Laws; a which it received, I should tell you, not from the magnitu the work, but from the greatness in number and nobility assembly that passed it. And it was under this great laws that this country continued chiefly to be governed, native judges, from the year 439, in which it was revised, to the year 1600, when it practically ceased to exist in my county of Clare; the last, I believe, in Ireland, that retaine It was at this time of Saint Patrick, too, of course, tha ecclesiastical element entered into our native legislation; *Teamar* ceased to be the seat of government in the year and as no one particular locality was ever after chosen fo monarch's residence, the long-revered Feast of *Teamar* thenceforward to be held, as far as I have been able to as tain, excepting in one single instance; and that was w Saint *Adamnan* procured the convocation of the states of nation there, in the reign of the monarch *Loingsech*, betw the years 694 and 701, for the purpose of enacting a spec law to prohibit the presence of women in battle.

The Law of *Adamnan*.

A copy of the curious law-tract containing this law, by Father Michael O'Clery from the ancient Book of *Boith* [Raphoe], in Donegall,—(a church founded by *Adamnan* himself),—has been lately recovered, I think I say through my own perseverance, by the Brehon Law Co mission; and of this I have made a transcript and transla which will appear along with the other parts of the an Institutes of Erinn in the forthcoming publication under direction of the commissioners. I may add, as an intere feature of this curious tract, that it contains the names of the personages, lay and ecclesiastical, who were present at passing of the law, and who gave it their assent.

The *Seanchas Mór*.

Of the detailed contents of the laws passed by *Laeghaire* am not at liberty, as I have already observed, to give any acco at present, even could the limits of these lectures allow of But, as a proof of that civilization of which it appears to me the existence of a matured system of law is the greatest and consequence, I shall only say, that when this *Seanchas Mór* shall be brought out by the Brehon Law Commission, it will found to contain all the details of a general legal system.

Criminal Law.

It includes, in the first place, a System of Criminal Law, which crimes of every sort are defined, and under which has its special punishment; by which judges and officers [illegible] into all crimes and accusa- [illegible] punishments are enforced in every [illegible] the power and authority of the state. [illegible] ancient Criminal Law, as it now [illegible] much older than the time of *Lao-* [illegible] the very criminal code, or the [illegible] held down in the Book of *Acaill*, [illegible] through *Cormac Mac Airt*, one [illegible] years before the compilation of the [illegible]

[illegible] *Seanchas Mór* contains a System of [illegible] in which every species of Contract, [illegible] is defined, and the competency or [illegible] rights and duties, of the contracting [illegible] a penalty is incurred for the non- [illegible] kind of contract; false and frau- [illegible] and fraud punished; and under [illegible] are provided to decide all disputes [illegible] decisions of such judges being in all [illegible] power and authority of the state. It is [illegible] under this ancient system, neither the [illegible] of the latter of whom there were, it [illegible] classes,—was held harmless in cases of [illegible], or faulty or incompetent advocacy.

[illegible] the definition of a very nice and some- [illegible] of Ranks of Society, from the king [illegible] having its own peculiar privileges, on [illegible] other the rights of the inferior classes [illegible] defined and protected.

[illegible] the laws included a Military System, for [illegible] Country, and for the support of the powers [illegible] law and of the rulers throughout the [illegible] peculiar principles of the constitution [illegible] was governed.

[illegible] *Mór* settles the division of the whole [illegible] various tribes or families, and assures the [illegible] and family to the possession of particular [illegible] particular tribes to particular privileges [illegible]

[illegible] remarkable of these laws, both in point [illegible] the minute attention to all the details of [illegible] they display, I may particularly allude to:

[illegible] all the different species of Bargains, Con- [illegible] between man and man.

[illegible] Property entrusted or given in charge

LECT. II.

The Seanchas Mór.

Law of Contracts.

Law of Ranks in Society.

Military Laws.

Law as to the Land.

Various special Laws.

LECT. II. THE SEANCHAS MOR.

by one man to another; and the Liability of the person in case of loss or damage, whether by accident or de

The laws respecting Gifts and presents, and respec and Endowments.

The laws as to Waifs and Strays, Derelictions, and the donment and Resumption of Property.

The law of Loans, Pledges, Accommodations, and Se

The law of Prescription, of Lapse, and of the Reco Possession of Property.

The laws concerning the relation of Father and the legal and illegal contracts of the son as connected

The laws respecting Illegitimate Children; and as to tions, and the Adoption of children.

Laws minutely regulating the Fees of Doctors, Lawyers, and Teachers, and of all other professional p

A series of laws concerning the varied species of Ind such as Weaving, Spinning, Sewing, Building, Brewi concerning Mills and Weirs; concerning Fishing; con Bees, Poultry, etc., and so on; (full of most interesting

Laws with respect to Injuries to Cattle; by neglect, by driving, etc.

Laws concerning Fosterage, and the relative duties of and Children, Foster-fathers and Foster-mothers; incl details of a very curious kind, respecting the training, clothing, etc., of all foster-children, from the king to the

A very complicated, yet clearly defined series of laws Landlord and Tenant, and Master and Servant; explaining different species of lords and of masters, of tenants servants; and the origin and termination of Tenantry Service.

Laws concerning Trespass and Damage to Land, whether man or beast.

A curious series of laws concerning Co-Occupancy of and concerning the dividing, hedging, fencing, paling, dit and walling, and the ploughing and stocking of land.

Laws of Evidence; of Corroborative Testimony; and Compurgation.

The law of Distress and Caption; including most mi details, which appear to embrace almost every possible p that could be made concerning the legality or illegality a Distress or Seizure.

The laws of Tithes and First Fruits; and concerning the lations of the Church with the state or nation (a law, doubtl introduced at the direct suggestion of Saint Patrick).

Laws concerning the regulation of Churches and the tena

THE SEANCHAS MOR.

[illegible] lands, and the servitors of Churches and Ecclesiastical [illegible].

[illegible] Law: complete laws respecting Manslaughter [illegible], distinguishing accurately between principals and [illegible] before and after the fact.

[illegible] concerning Thefts, and the receiving and recovery of [illegible] property; in the greatest possible detail.

[illegible] concerning the infliction of Wounds and the shedding [illegible] and with regard to the commission of violence by [illegible] well as sane persons.

[illegible], laws concerning Accidental Injuries; as from [illegible], flails, hatchets, and other implements con[illegible] peaceful labour.

Law of Eric or composition, (for Murder, etc.), introduced by St. Patrick.

[illegible] to the *Seanchas Mór* we find it stated that [illegible] Patrick's coming over with the Christian faith, there [illegible] or composition in cases of wilful murder, but [illegible] with death, as under the ancient Hebrew law. [illegible], in the spirit of the new Gospel, introduced the [illegible], or *Eric*, in mercy to the criminal; by which [illegible] the homicide was saved, should the aggrieved [illegible] to accept the *Eric*, and that he or his friends [illegible] pay it. If they were not, however, he should [illegible] happened that he was not redeemed, by [illegible] or neighbours; (sometimes by an individual; in [illegible] he became the bondman of him who redeemed [illegible] time as he should be able to redeem himself, or [illegible] voluntary manumission).

[illegible] aggravated manslaughter, when a man could not [illegible] he was put into a boat and set adrift on the sea.

Law of Contracts like that of the Jews. (Service for debt.)

[illegible] of the ancient Milesian to the Hebrew law is [illegible] that of Contracts. For, according to the [illegible], a man who failed to fulfil his lawful contracts, [illegible] of any fraud, if not able to pay the legal fine, [illegible] go into the service of the plaintiff or person [illegible] wronged, until by the profit of his labour he [illegible] the debt and expiate the crime he had com[illegible]

Accounts of the passing of particular laws.

[illegible] scarcely any particular records of the passing of [illegible] at the national convocation or parliament of [illegible] only that, so long as the palace of Tara conti[illegible] of the central government, laws continued [illegible], or the more ancient laws revised and added [illegible] magnates of Erinn. The general revision [illegible] time matured and completed the whole body [illegible] generation: and the same code seems to have

LECT. II. been found sufficient (and reasonably, as its publication will abundantly demonstrate,) for the social and political the people for many centuries afterwards. Some first there are, however, of special laws having been added to the code, such as that of Adamnan, (in the to which I have already alluded.

The codification (if I may call it so) under King was of course the re-arrangement of a vast number of laws that must have been passed from time to time vious generations. Of the passing of one of these itself indeed a system of law with respect to a certain subjects) long before the great revision of which I have a very curious hint is preserved to us in an allusion to the lative meeting of Tara, which is contained in the entry in a MS. in the British Museum [Egerton, 88].

Of the *Meill Bretha* (temp. Conn). "The *Meill Bretha* ("Good Judgments"), written in the time of *Conn* of the Hundred Battles, by *Bodainn* *Modan*.

"The cause of making this book was a quarrel pened in the middle of the plain of Bregia, on November between two parties of the youths who were fostered under the care of *Fuaimnech*, daughter of King Conn she extorted a promise from the kings and nobles of Tara to enter on the solution of the law questions of Erinn reparation was made for her foster-children. And they mitted the case to *Bodainn*, the judge, who gave judgment and drew up this scheme of law for the future government juvenile sports".

Such is the short history of this law; but whether these are the laws provided for such cases, and to be found our present collections, it is now impossible to say.

So much for the laws of *Tara*,—the laws regulating the people of ancient Erinn.

Of local legislation by the several Tribes. But, though the general system of law (law of contract criminal law, etc., etc.) had need to be the same throughout the whole island, yet many local rules and laws must been required to meet the exigencies of particular tribes, cumstanced with reference to property or otherwise in peculiar manner. And so we find that, according to the ancient constitution, every tribe or territory under the government of *Righ*, or king, could make local laws for itself, binding only course, within the territory. Such laws were necessarily plemental only to the general law of the whole nation; they were, in fact, framed solely with a view to the spec [illegible] and peculiar wants of the tribe. With respect to [illegible] laws, we find an interesting entry explaining exactly [illegible] in which they could be passed. And in an extract [illegible] I shall also presently refer to, it will be seen that in [illegible] to the labours of a Committee (such as that by which [illegible] *Mór* was revised), a public general assembly of [illegible] seems to have been necessary to give the required [illegible] to these local laws also.

[illegible] stated in the MS. H. 3. 18, T.C.D., that the *Nos* [illegible] or Local Law, was made by a committee of nine per- [illegible], moreover, that no one could abolish it until they [illegible] to do so without a dissentient voice,—for if there [illegible] one of the nine disposed to retain it, it could not be [illegible].

Mode of making the *Nos Tuatha*, or Local Law.

[illegible] people made an illegal custom, however", says this [illegible] they may with safety abolish it";—that is, of course, [illegible] the sense of being contrary to the general law of the [illegible].

[illegible] persons who were required to make a lawful local [illegible]—a King, a Poet, a *Brughaidh* (a certain rank of [illegible]), a Bishop, a Teacher or Professor of literature, a Judge, [illegible], an *Airé Forgaill* (an official answering to a she- [illegible] *airchinnech* (or lay vicar).

[illegible] to which I have alluded, of the passing of one [illegible] laws (in that case, indeed, a code or body of [illegible] tribe or territory) is as follows: The committee of [illegible] to have been dispensed with, in veneration of a [illegible] singular reputation, whose skill and learning seem to [illegible] considered so great that the people consented to [illegible] as their lawgiver, though subject to the assent of a [illegible] convention or assembly of the tribe. The account in [illegible] preserved in the MS. H. 3. 18, in the Dublin Uni- [illegible]. It is that of the compilation of Twelve Books [illegible] West Munster, by *Amargin*, son of *Amalgaidh*, [illegible], a native of the Decies (a district which [illegible] modern county of Waterford, together with parts [illegible]), in the time of *Fingine*, King of Munster, who [illegible].

The Twelve Books of Laws for West Munster (by *Amargin*, son of *Amalgaidh*), circa A.D. 690.

[illegible] a distinguished scholar and poet, and the men [illegible] Munster pressed him to go and learn for them the [illegible] law. To this he consented, but on con- [illegible] he had finished his studies and compiled a [illegible] the men of Munster should assemble in one plain [illegible]. *Amargin* returned in due time with twelve [illegible] of his own compilation; and the men of Mun-

LECT. II.

ster, under their king, at once proceeded to select a plain sive enough for their multitudes to assemble in, and enough for fish, fowl, water, venison, etc., during blage. This plain they found between the Lake of and the Mangerton mountain. The land, however, inheritance of a local chief, named *Cormac*, he refused the use of it on any other condition than that of the body of laws ratified there named after himself land. To this the assembly were accordingly obliged to and the compilation has ever since been known not only *Fuithrimé*, that is, the Law of *Fuithrimé*, (that being of the plain), but by the name of the *Cain Chorm* Cormac's Law; and also by that of the *Da Leabhar* *Fuithrimé*, that is, the Twelve Books of *Fuithrimé*.

Edward O'Reilly, in his "Irish Writers", at the calls this a law tract on the privileges and punishments in different ranks in society. I am sorry to be obliged that I fear O'Reilly had no authority for this very loose tion, as, unfortunately, not a page remains that can be nized with certainty as any part of the Twelve Bo *Fuithrimé*.

The Rev. John Lynch (better known as "Gratianus L gives, in his "Cambrensis Eversus", a list—unauthorised defective indeed—of ancient law tracts, among which places the *Cain Fuithrimé;* but he ascribes its compila the time of *Cathal*, son of *Finginné*, King of Munster, died in 737.

Of the Laws or Ordinances not passed in Assembly.

Before I leave the immediate subject of Legislation, I observe that several rules or laws are to be found in our record which were *not* passed at any such assemblies as those to wh I have alluded. These laws or rules are generally quoted connection with the names of the persons by whom they introduced; and they could only have come into force, of by having been accepted, whether formally or not is question, by the princes or tribes amongst whom they are corded to have been put in force. Of this class of law I shall just give you one example, interesting chiefly bec it illustrates the strictness of thought which characterised early ages of Christianity in Erinn.

There is a law tract or rule extant, entitled *Cain Domh* or Law of Sunday, but the precise time at which it was mulgated is not exactly known; neither was it a law enac by the states of Erinn, nor by any section of them, but simp a rule brought over from Rome for the observance of Sunday

[illegible] totally free from labour, with certain unavoidable [illegible]". The prohibitions of this law, and the fines for its [illegible], would in our days be felt exceedingly severe. [illegible], "No out or in-door labour, not even sweeping [illegible] up the house; no combing; no shaving; no clipping [illegible] head; no washing the face or hands; no cutting; no [illegible] churning; no riding on horseback; no fishing; no [illegible]; no journeying of travellers,—but wherever a [illegible] to be on Saturday night, there was he to remain till [illegible] morning", etc. This Rule was brought over from Rome [illegible] *Conall*, the son of *Caelain*, founder of the ancient [illegible] *Inis Cail*; (now the island of Iniskeel, near the mouth [illegible] bay, in the barony of Boylagh, and county [illegible].

LECT. II.

The Cain Domhnaigh, or Law of Sunday.

[illegible] been able to ascertain the precise date of Saint [illegible], but it must be anterior to the year 594, as [illegible] the poet was killed on this island, in or about [illegible] buried at Saint Conall's church, according to the [illegible] to that poet's celebrated Elegy on Saint *Colum* [illegible] is, however, good reason to think that the rule [illegible] promulgated until more than a century after Saint [illegible].

[illegible] imperfect copies of this most curious tract pre[illegible] *Leabhar Mór Duna Doighré* (commonly called [illegible]) in the Royal Irish Academy, and in the [illegible] *of Lecain*", (classed H. 2. 16, in Trinity College [illegible] a perfect copy in MS., Egerton, 5280, in the [illegible].

[illegible] short account, or rather with these few observations, [illegible] of ancient Erinn, I pass now from this sub[illegible], which is, however, very nearly allied to it, that, [illegible] SYSTEM OF CLASSES into which society was [illegible] early ages. The contents of the *Seanchas Mór* [illegible], prove abundantly sufficient (as will I am [illegible] acknowledged) to substantiate all that I can say [illegible] very early civilization which distinguished this [illegible] among the nations of Western Europe. And [illegible] propriety make use of the materials in the study [illegible] been engaged for the Brehon Law Commis[illegible] able to occupy far more space than the whole [illegible] can extend to in profitable description of [illegible] which those materials abundantly disclose. [illegible] our inquiries must, however, be postponed for [illegible] even that division of the general subject

Division of Classes of Society in Ancient Erinn.

just alluded to is itself also closely bound up with the laws which the labours of the commission are to illustrate, I must take leave to content myself, just now, with a very short statement of the nature and division of the various classes of which ancient Irish society was constituted. Some short description of them is essential to our being able to take even the most general view of the state of society in the early ages of our history; but, tempting as the subject is, I must nevertheless dismiss it here with a very few words indeed.

Rank in society in ancient Erinn, as in almost every other part of the world, depended upon the quantity of a man's property (particularly in land), and the nature of his ownership of it.

It is not very easy to translate into modern language the technical terms of the ancient laws of Landlord and Tenant; but a very well-matured system existed, at a very early period indeed, under which, although there was no such thing as absolute property in land in any individual, independent of his tribe, still, within the tribe, individuals held exclusive property in land, and entered into relations with tenants for the use of the land, and these again with under-tenants, and so on, much as we see it in our own days. Now these relations constitute the first test of rank or condition. The *Flaith*,—a word which in some sense may be translated the Lord, or Nobleman,—was distinguished by being the absolute owner (within his tribe) of land for which he paid no rent; so that, if a man possessed but a single acre in this way, he was a *Flaith*. All other persons holding land held it either from a *Flaith* or from some tenant of his; and the rank and precedence of these persons depended upon the amount of their possessions. Tenancy (*Céilsine*) again, was of two kinds. One may call the two classes of *Céilé*, or tenant, Free *Céilés* and Bond *Céilés*, for want of better names in English. The Bond *Céilé* was, however, by no means a slave, though he was bound to assist or follow his landlord in war-time; he was merely a tenant, paying a higher rent (in kind) than the other. The true distinction was simply this:—the Free *Céilé* took the land which he stocked himself, and paid for it a rent in kind, the value of the occupation or use of the land;—the Bond *Céilé* took land without stock, and his landlord stocked it for him; so that he paid a greater rent in kind, as he paid for the use of the stock as well as the land; and at the end of his term of tenancy (which was generally for seven years), he had to give up not only the land, but also stock of the same number, kind, and value as had been originally supplied to him, if required. This distinction of tenancies applied to

The *Flaith*, or Land-owner.

The *Céilé*, or Tenant.

[illegible] however large the quantity of land taken, and [illegible] the tenant.(25)

I. THE TENANT CLASS.

[illegible] distinguishing the classes of society who enjoyed legal [illegible] privileges, we may, of course, pass over that large [illegible] the people who then as now occupied the honour[illegible] position of tenants of very small holdings; [illegible] with them the labouring class, servants and bond[illegible] general a view as that to which I must confine my[illegible] only speak of those classes already high enough to [illegible] social rank, and to be entitled to a certain fixed [illegible]

1. The Bo Aireach.

[illegible] of the *Crith Gabhlach*,—of which I have for [illegible] possessed a copy,—the scale of rank, beginning [illegible] commences with the degree of *Bo Aireach*, or [illegible] Cow-owner. Of these there were several classes; [illegible] *Aireachs* were tenants, paying rent in kind for all the [illegible] held. They were distinguished by the quantity of [illegible] they had; and were bound to have always at least a [illegible] quantity of property, houses, etc., in order to continue [illegible] the rank and privileges appointed them by law.

1. 1.—The Bo Aireach Febhsa.

[illegible] of the *Bo Aireach* was the *Bo Aireach Febhsa*. [illegible] of seven *Cumhal*; [a *Cumhal* was three cows: [illegible] seven *Cumhal* meant land sufficient for the grazing [illegible] seven, or twenty-one, cows.] He should have a [illegible] and an eating house of certain dimensions, being [illegible] visits from strangers and others privileged by [illegible] entertained for a certain time. He had a certain share [illegible] of the district; and he had of his own a kiln, a barn, [illegible] fees also were payable to him for the exercise of [illegible] privileges, such as that of being legal witness to a [illegible] on.

1. 2.—The Bruighfer.

[illegible] rank of *Bo Aireach* was the *Bruighfer*; who was [illegible] by the extent of his farm, which should consist [illegible] *Cumhal*; (that is, enough to graze sixty-three [illegible], as being what would now be called in Munster a [illegible]", he was to set an example to his neighbours; [illegible] of his duty to instruct the people by the arrange[illegible] house and establishment; and a list is given of all [illegible] household and farm utensils and conveniences [illegible] bound "to have always, without borrowing". He [illegible] by law to have always a stock of certain spe[illegible], "to sustain the visit of a king, or bishop, or [illegible] from the road". His property is fixed at much

[illegible] of remark that a very similar system of tenancy exists in [illegible] *Code Napoléon*.]

LECT. II. [I. THE TENANT CLASS.]

higher than the *Bo Aireach Febhsa*, and his fees are in proportion. All trespass upon his house or stock was punished by severe fines, prescribed for every case; and there is a curious list of irregularities, injuries, and offences which might be committed by such visitors as those just alluded to, or their attendants, while sojourning at his house, and which should be paid for according to a fixed scale of fines or compensation. The *Bruighfer* was already on the way to hereditary nobility; for the law required that he should have for wife "only the daughter of an equal, and one who had never been married before".

I. 3.—The *Fer Fothla*, or *An-Flaith*.

The next rank of *Bo Aireach* was the *Fer Fothla*, or leader of *Bo Aireach;* who was wealthier than the *Bruighfer*, for he had a greater quantity of cattle than he could support on his own land, and so let them to other persons, who became his tenants or vassals (if that be an appropriate word) in return for the stock they hired from him. One remarkable privilege appears to have been attached to this class of *Bo Aireach*, namely, that although an *Aithech* or tenant, he became a *Flaith* or noble, from being a tenant, in the progress of his grazing, whenever he should have amassed property to the amount of double that which marked the lowest order of nobility among the *Flaith*, namely, the *Airé Desa*, of whom I shall presently speak. This *Fer Fothla* was called an *An-Flaith*, and was in fact a sort of rich middleman. He was, however, only entitled to one-half the amount of compensation which a full *Flaith* might claim, for property injured, or insult or injury to his person.

I. 4.—The *Airé Coisring*, (the *Airé Finé*).

The highest rank of *Bo Aireach* was the *Airé Coisring;* one who bound (that is, entered into engagements with) the king and people on behalf of the particular tribe, name, or family to which he belonged, they having consented to grant him the leadership and power to speak for them. This Representative *Bo Aireach* was the *Airé Finé*, or family chief, who answered to the king or chief for the obedience of his tribe to the law. But any complete account of the nature of his rank would lead me too far into the details of his functions, and the peculiar system of law of which they formed a part.

The same law which defined the different degrees of *Bo Aireach*, and appointed to each its rank and privileges, prescribed, too, the punishment of degradation for any breach of the *Bo Aireach*'s official duties. The list of the misdeeds by which this officer became degraded, and the mode by which he was permitted to make amends before the people, and so to recover his honour, are very interesting, and throw a great light indeed

... of the times in which they were prescribed by ... law.

II. THE LANDLORD CLASS.

... to the same fragment, the order of *Flaith* comprised ... of Nobility. The *Airé Désa*; the *Airé Echtai*; ... the *Airé Tuisi*; the *Airé Forgaill*; the *Tanaisé* ... of the king); and the *Righ*, (or king). The ... Estate, and the right to protect his privileges; ... of the *Flaith* were those of the ancient Pro... people of his territory, the exercise of his Office ... within the territory, and that of Leader or Tanist ... war; and to have Serving Vassals and Free Vassals, ... (a class of tenants distinguished, and having ... responsibilities, as having been upon the land ... generations, either as tenants or as squatters, undis... the nobility of the *Flaith* was in these Estates ... Seven degrees of *Flaith*.

... *Désa* was so called, as distinguished from the *Bo* ... he was paid *Diré* (duty, rent, value), on account ... and not for his cows (*bo*), like the other. He had Ten ...; five free and five bond-*Céilés*;—and from each ... was entitled to fixed annual supplies of food and cattle, ... tribute. Certain houses and property were pre... law in the case of the *Airé Desa*, as necessary to ... just as in the different orders of *Bo Aireach*;—and ... he should have certain state equipments, (such ... with a silver bridle); and he wore a precious ... worth an *unga*, [about ten shillings]. His wife ... lawful wife in first marriage", of equal rank with ... equally richly dressed. But his rank and prece... the *Flaith* were according to his deeds: according ... done to deserve honour. The *Airé* guarded at ... of tenants among one another, and saw the law ... between them. II. 1.—The *Airé Désa*.

... *Echtai* was an *Airé*, or chief, of five men ... war; with whom he was in time of peace to ... punish all insults, and particularly violence by ... to his tribe. II. 2.—The *Airé Echtai*.

... *Ard* (or High *Airé*) preceded the *Airé Desa*. He ... *Céilés*;—ten bond, and ten free. His various pos... greater in proportion. II. 3.—The *Airé Ard*.

... *Tuisi* (or Leading *Airé*) took precedence over all ... by being of superior race or family. He had ... *Céilés*, of whom fifteen were bond-*Céilés*. His ... privileges were proportionately greater; but what... of an *Airé*, it was family alone that could give II. 4.—The *Airé Tuisi*.

LECT. II.

[II. THE LANDLORD CLASS.]

him this rank. He wore a golden bridle on his riding-steed, as well as a silver one.

II. 5.—The *Airé Forgaill*.

The *Airé Forgaill* was so called because "*fortgell*",—he testified,—to the character of the other *Flaiths* in court. The duties and legal privileges of this high functionary would also require, for proper description, a much more detailed examination of the laws than I can make here. The *Airé Forgaill* was richer than the preceding orders. He had forty *Céilés*, twenty bond and twenty free. His property in land and [illegible] was very extensive; his houses large and richly appointed, and his following powerful.

II. 6.—The *Tanaisé Righ* (Tanist of a King).

The *Tanaisé Righ*, (or Tanist of a King,) was next in [illegible] standing only second to the king himself. He was so called "because" (as the fragment already referred to explains [illegible]) "the whole territory" (or people) "adhere to him without opposition". He had five *Sen Cléithé* more than the *Airé Forgaill*, and was always attended by ten men. In all the other points as to wealth, etc., the *Tanaisé Righ* stood far higher than the other nobles.

II. 7.—The *Righ*, (King).

Next comes the *Righ* (or King); but it is not necessary for me to say anything of him here.

I have now concluded what I had to say upon the general system of Legislation and Law, and the division or distinction of Classes in ancient Erinn. It is to be remembered that I introduced the subject only as so inseparably and importantly connected with the history of our ancient civilization, that it could not be omitted altogether: and I think I have said enough to lead to an expectation from the forthcoming publication of the Laws of the most conclusive proofs of a civilization long denied by our enemies in modern literature, and doubted by our own writers.

Account of the Fair of *Carmán*; (A.D. 718–1023).

When speaking of the convocation of Tara,—the Fair or Feast of Tara, anciently held every three years,—I had at first intended to illustrate the account of it preserved by Keting, by reference to a very ancient poem upon a similar assembly, held as anciently for the province of Leinster, but which continued to be celebrated long after the abandonment of the ancient centre of government of all Erinn. I allude to the Fair of *Carmán* (now Wexford), which was revived, A.D. 718, by *Dunchadh*, King of Leinster, and last celebrated in A.D. 1023, by Donnchadh Mac Gillapatrick. There is preserved in the Book of Leinster (a MS. known to have been compiled about the year 1150) a great part of a celebrated old poem upon this fair; which I [illegible]

[illegible] been contemporary with the last celebration of [illegible] of even a more ancient date. And, on reflec- [illegible] seems to me to be of so much importance to [illegible] of the present course, that I have preferred to [illegible] the conclusion of this lecture, in order that I may [illegible] For though the allusion it contains to the legis- [illegible] of these assemblies is confined to a single verse, [illegible] quantity of important historical matter in the [illegible] to which I shall have frequent occasion to refer. [illegible] the Book of Leinster is unfortunately not all [illegible] about a third part of it is legible. It will there- [illegible] convenient if I precede my reading of the frag- [illegible] decipherable, by the account or version of the [illegible] which is preserved in the Book of Ballymote. [illegible] literally translated, as follows:

[illegible] who came from Athens, and one woman; these [illegible] sons of *Dibad*, son of *Dorcha*, son of *Ainches*; [illegible] and *Dother*, were their names; and *Carmén* was [illegible] their mother.

[illegible] wherever she went, blasted and blighted [illegible] spells, charms, and incantations; and it was by [illegible] and dishonesty that the men dealt out de- [illegible].

[illegible] into Erinn to bring evil upon the *Tuatha Dé* [illegible] blighting the fertility of the country against them. [illegible] *Dé Danann* were incensed at this; and they [illegible] *Ai*, the son of *Ollamh*, on the part of their [illegible] on the part of their Satirists; and *Lug* [illegible] of *Caicher*, on the part of their Druids; and [illegible] part of their Witches, to pronounce incantations [illegible] them; and they never parted from them [illegible] the three men over the sea, leaving behind [illegible] *Carmén* as a pledge that they should never [illegible] Erinn; and they also swore, by the divinities [illegible], that they would not return as long as the [illegible] Erinn.

[illegible], however, soon died of grief of her hostage- [illegible] requested of the *Tuatha Dé Danann* that they [illegible] a fair and games in her honour wherever she [illegible] and that the fair and the place should receive [illegible] name for ever; and hence *Carmán*, and the [illegible]. And the *Tuatha Dé Danann* observed this [illegible] they occupied Erinn".

[illegible] is, that old *Garmán* had followed the [illegible] *Eochaidh Belbuidhé*, King of *Ceanntiré* [Kintire

LECT. II. [Account of the Fair of Carmán; (A.D. 718-1033).]

or Cantire, in Scotland,] which cows had been carried off by *Lena*, the son of *Mesroeda*, whose mother was *Uca*, daughter of *Osca*, King of *Certa*, for she was the wife of *Misroeda*, son of *Datho*, King of Leinster; [about the time of the Incarnation].

"There were along with *Lena*, at driving these cows away, *Sen*, the son of *Durb*; and *Lochar* the Swift, son of *[illegible]*; and *Gunnat*, the son of *Succat*; and *Altach*, the son of *[illegible]*; and *Mothur*, the son of *Lorgach*.

"Old *Garmán* discovered them at the south side of *[illegible]* Dun; and he killed *Lena*, with his women and the men who assisted him to carry off the cows. And old *Garmán* then carried away his kine to *Magh Misca* [that is, *Mesca's* Plain, where Wexford now stands]; and she, *Mesca*, was the daughter of the great chieftain *Bodbh*, of the hill of *Finnchaidh*, in the mountain *Monach*, in Scotland; who had been carried off by him (old *Garmán*), in a trance; and *Mesca* died of shame in this place; and her grave was made there, namely, the grave of *Mesca*, daughter of *Bodhbh*.

"And the four sons of King *Datho* overtook old *Garmán* at this place, namely, *Mes Seda*, and *Misroeda*, and *Mesdeda*, and *Mesdelmon*; and old *Garmán* fell by them there; and they made his grave there; and so he begged of them to institute a Fair (or games of commemoration) for him there, and that the fair and the place should bear his name for ever: and hence the Fair of *Carmán*, and old *Carmán* have their names".

"And the people of Leinster observed this fair in tribes and families, down to the time of the monarch *Cathair Mór* [in the second century]. *Cathair* left the privileges of *Carmán* but to his own sons and their families, giving precedence to the race of his son *Rossa Failghé*, their dependent branches and their exiles, to keep the fair in perpetuity; namely, the Leinstermen proper, and the *Fotharts*"; [the present baronies of Forth].

"There were seven days for sport, or racing, there; and a week for considering and proclaiming the privileges and laws of the province for the three years to come.

"It was on the last day that the Leinstermen south of *Gabhar*, [the men of Ossory], held their fair or racing; and hence it was called the steed-contest of the Ossorians. The seat of their king was on the right hand of the King of *Carmán* or Leinster; and the seat of the King of *O'Failghé* [Offaly], on his left; and it was the same case with their wives.

"It was on the Kalends of August they assembled at it; and it was on the 6th of August they left it; and it was every third [illegible] and the preparations were going on for two [illegible]

[Account of the Fair of Carmán; (A.D. 718-1080).]

[illegible] five hundred and eighty years since the first fair [illegible] to the fortieth year of the reign of Octavius [illegible] in which Christ was born.

[illegible] Leinstermen were promised abundance of corn and [illegible] holding it, and that no other province should control [illegible] that they should enjoy righteous laws, and comfort [illegible] house, and fruit in great abundance, and their har-[illegible] and rivers teem with water (and fish). And if [illegible] not observe it, that failure and early grayness should [illegible] themselves and their kings".

[illegible] the same, but much expanded, in verse, as

[illegible] O Lagenians of the monuments,
[illegible] host who never opposed justice,
[illegible] you hear from me, in all directions,
The etymology of far-famed *Carmán*.
[illegible] the hill of a noble fair,
[illegible] a wide-spread unobstructed green
[illegible] the hosts who repaired there to occupy it,
[illegible] which they contested their noble races.
[illegible] cemetery of noble, valiant kings,
[illegible] dearly-loved of admiring hosts;
[illegible] are many, under the meeting mounds,
[illegible] their ever-loved departed ancestors.
[illegible] for queens and kings,
[illegible] forth great valour and great deeds;
[illegible] did the fair hosts of autumn assemble
[illegible] the smooth cheek of noble old *Carmán*.
[illegible] a man, or was it men, of great valour,—
[illegible] it a woman of violent jealousy,—
[illegible] gave name, not contemptible, pleasing,
[illegible] gave its true name to lovely *Carmán*?
[illegible] not men, and it was not angry man,
[illegible] a single woman, fierce and vengeful,
[illegible] her rustling and her tramp,
[illegible] whom *Carmán* received its first name.
[illegible] the wife of great *Dibad's* son.
[illegible] son of *Dorcha*, of armies and hospitality,
[illegible] of *Ainces*, of abounding prosperity,
[illegible] commanded armies in many battles.
[illegible] of profit could they pursue,
[illegible] ardent love of noble Erinn,

LECT. II.

[Account of the Fair of Carmán; (A.D. 718-1033).]

Righteous rules, and loyalty to kings,
With troops to coerce [i. e. to rule over] Erinn, (were its rewards).
"The hospitality of the *Hy-Drona*,
And the steed-contests of the men of Ossory,
And the clash of spear handles
From the entire host, was its termination.
"There comes of its not being holden,
Baldness, cowardice, early grayness,
With other numerous disasters,
To the noble Leinstermen. Listen!
"Though we had called it *Mesca's* Mound,
It should not be in mockery or in enmity,
Who, with old crooked *Garmán*, her husband,
Here was buried in far ancient time.
"Even though [we admit that] from these it were named,
Among the etymological writings,
It were due, without doubt, and were right,
O Leinstermen of the monuments. Listen!

This fine version is from the Book of Ballymote. The following is (so far as can be deciphered) a translation of what is preserved in the still earlier Book of Leinster:

"The Leinstermen held this, the fair,
Both as tribes and as householders,
From *Labraidh Loingsech* of the shining hosts,
To the powerful, red-speared *Cathair*.
"*Cathair* bequeathed not *Carmun*
But unto his great and mighty sons;
At the head of whom—with varied wealth,
Are the race of *Rossa Failghé*,—as you see.
"The throne of the King of noble *Argat-Ros*,
Stood at the right of the powerful King of *Carman*;
On his left hand, in his hereditary place,
The throne of the King of the plain-woody *Gabh*[illegible]
"Following these were the great race of *Lugaidh Laighsech*, the son of the powerful *Conall*;
And the *Fotharts* who knew no thirst,
In no paucity of splendour behind these.
"On the Kalends of August, without fail,
They repair thither every third year;
Here they proclaim boldly and loudly
The privileges of every law, and their restraints.
"To sue, to levy, to controvert debts.
To abuse steeds in their career

LECT. II.

[Account of the Fair of Carmán; (A.D. 718-1033).]

It is not allowed here by contending racers; [nor]
[illegible], oppression, or arrest.
No [illegible] goes into the women's assembly,
No women into the assembly of fair clean men;
No abduction here is heard of,
Nor repudiation of husbands nor of wives.
Whoever transgresses the Law of the Kings,
Which *Benen* so accurately and permanently wrote,[14]
Cannot be spared upon family composition,
But he must die for his transgression.
Here follow its great privileges [*i. e.* the splendid sights and enjoyments of the fair].
Trumpets, harps, wide-mouthed horns;
[illegible], timpanists, without fail;
[illegible], and groups of agile jugglers.
[illegible] Tales,—*Finn's* career, without limit;
[illegible] of courts,[15] Cattle-Spoils, Courtships;
Inscribed tablets, books of 'trees' [*oghams*];
[illegible], and sharp-edged philippics.
[illegible], Maxims, royal Precepts;
[illegible] the truthful Instructions of *Fithal;*
[illegible] poetry, topographical Etymologies;
[illegible] Precepts of *Carbré* and of *Cormac.*
[illegible], with the important Feast of *Teamar;*
[illegible], with the great Fair of Emania;
[illegible] there verified too;
[illegible] the divisions into which Erinn was divided.
[illegible] of the Hill of mighty *Teamar;*
[illegible] knowledge of every Territory in Erinn;
[illegible] history of bands of noblest Women;
[illegible]; Enchantments; Conquests.

[14] [illegible] of Benen is the *Leabhar na g-Ceart* before mentioned—(pub- [illegible] Society, Dublin, 1847.) [The *Leabar na g-Ceart* ("Book [illegible] a great portion of the law which in ancient Erinn settled [illegible] the several classes of society, and especially the relations [illegible] authorities and the Central and Provincial kings. "It [illegible] Introduction to the edition just referred to, p. vi.), "an ac- [illegible] of the monarchs of all Ireland, and the revenues payable to [illegible] kings of the several provinces, and of the stipends paid [illegible] the inferior kings for their services. It also treats of the [illegible] provincial kings, and the revenues payable to them from [illegible] the districts or tribes subsidiary to them, and of the sti- [illegible] superior to the provincial kings for their services",—(etc.). [illegible] of this work by the Celtic Society was prepared by the [illegible], with the assistance of Professor O'Curry; the valuable In- [illegible] work of the late W. E. Hudson, who superintended the [illegible] part of the Council of the Society.]

[15] [illegible] of these various classes of "Historic Tales", in the *Lectures* [illegible] *of Ancient Irish History;* pp. 241, *et seq.*

LECT. II.

[Account of the Fair of Carmán; (A.D. 718-1033?)]

" The noble Testament of *Cathair* the Great,
To his sons who excelled all wealthy kings;
Every one's inheritance, as he lawfully inherits,
That all of them should hear and know.

" Pipers, fiddlers, banded-men,
Bonemen, and fluteplayers;
The host of chattering bird-like flyers;
Shouters and loud bellowers.

" These all exert themselves to the utmost
For the impetuous King of the Barrow;
And the noble king by estimate bestows
Upon each profession its rightful honour.

" The history of Elopements, Conflagrations, musical Concerts;
The accurate Synchronisms of noble races;
The Succession of their gifted kings in *Bregia* [i.e. Tara];
Their battles and their hardy valour.([16])

" Such is the arrangement of the fair,
By the lively ever happy host;—
May they receive from the Lord,
A land teeming with choicest fruits.

" The saints of Leinster, on a certain day,
The saints of the alliance without guile,
Over the court of *Carmán's* bright lake,
Celebrate mass, genuflexions, and psalms.

" They fast in the autumn—it is true—
At *Carmán*, all of them together,
For the people of Leinster, against a season of scarcity;
Against tyranny; against oppression.

" The clergy and laity of Leinster, together,
Are a compact body of worthy men;
God, who knows how well they merit,
To their noble prayers will listen.

" The hospitality of the *Ui Drona* next;
And the steed-battle of the Ossorians;
And the clash of the shafts of spears
From the hosts, then, is the end.

" Though we should call it the mound of *Mesca*,
It would not be in idleness nor in enmity;
It was old *Garmán*—true is the knowledge,—
That there was buried a long time ago.

" Though [we should admit] it was from him it was named
Among the hosts who there were placed;
That name it deserved and was its due;—
O Leinstermen of the tombs, pray listen!

([16]) This verse is evidently misplaced.

"Twenty-one raths of lasting fame [there are],
In which hosts are laid [there] under ground;
A [illegible] cemetery of high renown [there is]
By the side of beloved noble *Carmán*.
Seven mounds without touching each other,
For the oft lamenting of the dead:
Seven plains, sacred, without a house,
For the sports of joyous *Carmán* were reserved.
Three markets were held within its borders;
A market for food; a market for live cattle; [and]
The great market of the foreign Greeks,
In which are gold and noble clothes.
[illegible] of the steeds; the slope of the cooking;
[illegible] of the assembly of embroidering women.
[illegible] of the happy host
[illegible] ululation, receives reproach.
[illegible] of not celebrating this feast
[illegible] cowardice, early grayness;
[illegible] without wisdom, without wealth,
Without hospitality, without truthfulness.
[illegible] they have been powerful and warlike,
[illegible] hosts of *Labhraidh's* house;
[illegible] host which is not aggressive is like a deer;
[illegible] but dares no one.
[illegible] by the saintly Host of Heaven,
[illegible] the beautiful, all-perfect God;
[illegible] of graceful Hosts may I reach,—
[illegible] prayers He will listen!—Listen!"

LECT. II.

[Account of the Fair of Carmán; (A.D. 718-1030).]

[illegible] be out of place to enter into any criticism on these [illegible] interesting accounts of the Fair of *Carmán*, or even [illegible] (as I should wish to do) the particular importance [illegible] number of allusions made in the poems. I [illegible] translated them here for the sake of the light they [illegible] was called the Fair of Tara; and because they [illegible] of these Assemblies, and how the grave busi- [illegible] was performed on appointed days, in the [illegible] set apart for pleasure or reserved for mercantile

LECTURE III.

[Delivered 2nd June, 1857.]

(III.) EDUCATION, AND LITERATURE. Of Education in Erinn in the ... ages. Schools of the *Fileadh*, or Poets. Account of some of the ... distinguished men of learning in the early ages in Erinn. Of the ... of the *Tuatha Dé Danann*. Of the Historians and Poets of the ... Of the ancient Genealogical Poem by *Finn*, father of *Concobar* ... *Ruadh*, (Monarch, B.C. 6.). Of *Adhna*, chief Poet of *Concobar* ... Of a very ancient Gaedhelic Grammar. Of literary offices connected ... the Courts of the early monarchs. State of learning in the time of ... *cobar MacNessa*. Of the "Pot of Avarice" of the *Fileadh*. List of ... men of learning (continued). Poems of King *Oilioll Oluim*. Poems ... *Art* "the Solitary". Foundation of a University by *Cormac Mac* ... the third century. Of the Book of O'Duvegan. Of the literary ... of *Finn Mac Cumhaill*. Of *Torna Eigeas*; and of learning temp. ... the presence of King *Corc* at Tara, at the time of the revision of the ... *chas Mór*. Of the Succession of the Kings of Munster.

AFTER having dwelt so long on the Laws and Institutions ... Ancient Erinn, and on the Classes who were qualified to ... part in enacting them, as well by right of social as of intell... rank, it is now time to give some short account of the Li... Institutions, or other sources of Literary Instruction, at w... those who drew their social position not from the possessi... land or wealth, but from intellectual acquirements alone, ... to become qualified to sit in the courts of kings and nobles, ... to take part in the national deliberations.

Of Literature and Education in Erinn in the earlier ages. It is much to be lamented that of distinct references to ... character and extent of literary Education in this country ... remote times, but few comparatively have come down ... As far, however, as we can collect from these few referenc... would appear that, down to the introduction of Christiani... the year of our Lord 432, the instruction of youth was ... in the hands of two classes of men: the *Fileadh*, or Poets ... the Druids; but it very often happened that these two ... racters were united in the same person.

Of the Druids I shall have to give some account on ... occasion, in a future Lecture.

Derivation of "Druid" and of "Fili" (Poet). Some of our old glossarists explain the name Dr... "doctus", learned; and *Fili*, a poet, by "*philo*", "ama... lover of learning.[17] But Cormac MacCullinan, in his Glos...

[17] See Note 2 (p. 2), and Appendix No. I. (p. 461), to *Lectures on the Materials of Ancient Irish History*.

LECT. III.

[illegible] reliable authorities we possess, and one of the [illegible] derives the word *Fili* from *Fi*, poison, or venom, and [illegible], or beauty; meaning that the poet's satire was [illegible], and his praise bright or beautiful.

Schools of the *Filedh* (Poets).

[illegible] Poet (and the Druid), according to *Seanchan*, when [illegible] the court of a king or chief, had his pupils about [illegible] and lectured them wherever he found it con- [illegible] within doors, but often in the open air; and [illegible] travelled through the territory, or from one territory [illegible] pupils accompanied him, still receiving his in- [illegible] however, they exceeded the number which [illegible] by law to have accommodated as his own com- [illegible] house, the excess were almost always [illegible] by the neighbours in the locality. The chief [illegible] have been always accompanied by a number of [illegible] degrees, who had not yet arrived at the [illegible] their profession. Of these, with their several [illegible] some account in a former Lecture.(18)

The Druids.

[illegible] his simple character, does not appear to have [illegible], but stationary. He is not recognized in any [illegible] ancient laws as entitled to any privileges or [illegible] the Poets, and Brehons or Judges, enjoyed; [illegible] place at court, and ranked with a particular de- [illegible] in the *Teach Midhchuarta*, or Banqueting [illegible] like the Poet, he appears to have been ac- [illegible] his pupils in the open air as well as wi- [illegible] general subject of what is known concer- [illegible], however, will be treated of in a subsequent [illegible] it over here, and confine myself for the [illegible] of the means and extent of general [illegible] country, in the earlier ages of our history, so [illegible] recorded in our various historical writings will [illegible] with the subject.

Account of some of the most distinguished men of learning in ancient Erinn.

[illegible], at this distance of time, and considering [illegible] dispersion that for ages have befallen our [illegible] attempt to find or to give any close and de- [illegible] the exact state of Education in this country [illegible] of the Christian era, or, indeed, I might [illegible] establishment of Christianity in it, in the fifth [illegible] all that can be done here is to recount a short [illegible] of those whose names have come down [illegible] in the several sciences of Law, of Poetry,

(18) [illegible] the *Lectures on the MS. Materials of Ancient Irish* [illegible]).

4

II. (if indeed the Gaedhelic *Filedheacht* is to be translated by insufficient name[19]), and History. And in giving such of these learned men as the materials we yet possess I shall in fact have furnished the most reliable sketch early civilization; because almost all of them are recorded distinguished in consequence of their having been the teachers of those who came after them, while they examples of the cultivation of the respective ages in which lived.

The earliest period at which I can begin to note of authorship and learning, so as to carry down the some connection, is not more remote than the reign great monarch *Ugainé Mór*, who flourished (according Annals of the Four Masters) some six hundred years Christian era. There are, however, some records the celebrity of many learned men, even before that

The following list of some of the persons who were to have preserved the ancient history of Erinn, is found Book of Ballymote, a manuscript volume compiled, has been already stated, so lately as in A.D. 1391, but rious very ancient Irish manuscripts now lost for ever. list is not chronologically arranged, but I have thrown chronological order, as far as I have been able to persons whose names are set down in it. The list is to the *Tuatha Dé Danann* and Milesian colonists, and no names of the Firbolgs, Nemedians, and Partholanians according to our old writings, preceded them. It is meagre yet an important catalogue, and looks like the of one of the early histories of Erinn, commenced by author, but never finished. Indeed, in a notice at the the list, but which was intended to be placed at the head list of Milesian writers, the author says: "These are torians of the Gaedhils, who formed the Historical Book Histories and in Annals".

The tract begins by stating that "ancient men history from the beginning of the world"; and then follows Irish Historians thus:

Daghda the great King of the *Tuatha Dé Danann*, about year of the world 3304. The *Mór Rigan*, or great Queen wife. *Etan* the Poetess, daughter to *Diancecht*, the *Tuatha Dé Danann* Physician, of the same period. *Coirpré*, the Poet of the Poetess *Etan*. *Senbec* the grandson of *Ebric*, of the

(19) See Note 2 (p. 2), and Appendix, No. I. (p. 461), to the former Lectures, already referred to.

LECT. III.

[illegible] (the inventor of the alphabet called Ogham), [illegible] son of *Delbaeth*, of the same period.

[illegible] the Historians of the *Tuatha Dé Danann*; and [illegible] (of the Milesians): *Amergin*, one of the Mile-[illegible] and their Poet, Judge, and Druid, A.M. 3500. [illegible] *Rosgadach*", or "the Glossarist", who invented the [illegible] the Wheel *Ogham*, and who was the son of [illegible] Monarch of Erinn, A.M. 4600.

Historians and Poets of the Milesians; (List in the Book of Ballymote).

[illegible] of *Lecain* and Ballymote contain a short piece, in [illegible] ascribed to this *Roighné Rosgadach*, son of King [illegible] to his brother *Mal*, on the peregrinations of [illegible] ancestors, from their departure from Egypt to their [illegible], with the names of their chiefs and leaders. The [illegible] construction of this piece bear, as far as I am able [illegible] of a very remote antiquity; and it was, I [illegible], preserved in the ancient chronicle of *Teamar*, [illegible] the Book of *Drom Sneachta*.

[illegible] in a former Lecture[(20)] that the Monarch *Labh-*[illegible] the great-grandson of *Ugaine Mór*, (and Mon-[illegible] about A.M. 4677,) was in his boyhood placed [illegible] tuition of the Poet *Ferceirtné* and the Harper [illegible] that these tutors so successfully conducted his [illegible] enable him while still a mere youth, unknown, [illegible] to win honour at a foreign court, and even to rise [illegible] distinguished military command.

[illegible] the List in the Book of Ballymote; it proceeds [illegible] to name *Morann* the son of *Maen*, the cele-[illegible] about the year of our Lord 14; *Nera*, the Druid [illegible] son of *Morann*; *Cathbadh*, the royal Druid and [illegible] Ulster, about the year of our Lord 40; *Concobar* [illegible] Nessa, King of Ulster, at the same period; *Fer-*[illegible] Conor's chief Poet; *Ferceirtné*, the chief Poet to [illegible], King of West Munster, at the same period; [illegible] Satirist of Ulster, and his school, of about the same [illegible] the Satirist, son of *Cairbré*, of Ulster, at the [illegible] *Amergin* the son of *Ecsolach*, "the smith", of [illegible] same period; *Critiné* the Poet, [whose precise [illegible] ascertained]; *Sencha*, the son of *Ailill*, chief [illegible] in Conor MacNessa's time; *Dubhdachonn* the [illegible] the learned; *Beathach* the grandson of [illegible] the Poet, and *Fuatach* the Poet "of the true [illegible] times and places I have not ascertained; *Cor-*[illegible] who was Monarch of Erinn in A.D. 266; *Fithal*

[illegible] the *MS. Materials of Ancient Irish History*; Lect. XII.,

LECT. III. [Historians and Poets of the Milesians.]

"the true and wise, of heroic words", King [illegible] Judge; *Finn-Ua-Baiscné*, or *Finn MacCumhaill*, [illegible] temporary; *Nera* the son of *Fincholl*, of *Sidh* [illegible] present county of Tipperary), whose time I have [illegible] tained; *Morann* the son of *Cairbré*, the stooped [illegible] farmer of hundreds of cows; and *Eithné* the daughter [illegible] *gaeth*, whose time I have not ascertained; *Cairbré* [illegible] Monarch of Erinn (son to King Cormac), A.D. 26[illegible] son of *Cairell*, who compiled the History of Erinn [illegible] Deluge, about the year of our Lord 430; *Dubhth*[illegible] of *Lugar*, of Leinster, the chief Poet and Historian [illegible] and the first who received the Christian faith from Saint [illegible] at Tara, about the year 432; the Committee of Nine [illegible] up the *Seanchas Mór*, or Great Body of the Laws of [illegible] whom the Monarch *Laoghairé* and Saint Patrick were [illegible] about the year 441; Saints *Colum Cillé* and *Finnian* [illegible] *Bilé*, after Patrick; *Dallan Ua Forgaill* the Royal [illegible] Great Scholar of Erinn, who wrote the celebrated [illegible] Saint *Colum Cillé*, in the year 592; *Finntan* the son of [illegible] after him; "and various Sages, Poets, and Druids, be[illegible] adds the writer of the tract. He then goes on to name [illegible] the son of *Comgellann*, one of the *Dalriada* of Scotland [illegible] arranged the misunderstanding between the Monarch [illegible] *Aedh* son of *Ainmiré*, and the King of Scotland, *Aedh*[illegible] *Gabran*, at the great meeting at *Drom Ceat*, in the year [illegible] *Cennfaeladh* the learned, about the year 640; *Seanchan* [illegible] *Cairbré*, the Royal Poet, about the year 670; *Cormac* [illegible] *linan*, who compiled Cormac's Glossary, about the year [illegible]

The extent of the List in the Book of Ballymote is [illegible] siderable; and notwithstanding all that may be said [illegible] remoteness and improbability of that part of it which [illegible] the *Tuatha Dé Danann*, it presents an important record [illegible] number of persons, stretching over a period of a thousand [illegible] whose names come down to comparatively late times as [illegible] who had by the means of prose or verse contributed [illegible] preservation or perpetuation of the history and antiquities of their country.

Beside this List, I may mention that there is another [illegible] men, (and some women), eminent as judges and expounders of the Law in Ireland, anterior to the coming of Saint Patrick; but as this List will appear in the publication of the Brehon [illegible] Commission, I shall omit it here.

Proceeding from that part of the List in the Book of Bally[illegible] mote, which brings us down to the commencement of [illegible] Christian era, we shall find a greater abundance of detail [illegible]

LECT. III.

[illegible] and among the earlier authors of this period, [illegible] most distinguished on the throne of Erinn. [illegible] the Annals of the Four Masters, *Concobar* [illegible] [Conor "of the red eye-brows"] was Monarch of [illegible] of the world 5193, that is, six years before [illegible] according to the chronology followed by the [illegible] was the son of *Finn* (also a poet and philo-[illegible] of Leinster, who at this very remote period wrote [illegible] poem on his own ancestors, the Kings of Leinster, [illegible] the Monarch *Nuadha Necht* up to Adam. [illegible] most curious and important piece of ancient [illegible] genealogy. The only copy of it that ever I have [illegible] is preserved in the Bodleian Library in Ox-[illegible], 502), a manuscript compiled about the year [illegible] in the most splendid angular Irish hand [illegible] seen. There are many other ancient poems in [illegible] that I have never seen elsewhere, and by writers [illegible] new to me, whose time I have not yet been [illegible]

Of Concobar Abradh-ruadh; (Monarch, A.M. 5193, or B.C. 6).

Ancient genealogical poem by Finn, the father of King Concobar Abradh-ruadh.

[illegible] the time of *Concobar Abradh-ruadh*, that [illegible] of, and immediately after, the Incarnation, [illegible] a native of Connacht, who was chief Poet [illegible] attached to the court of the celebrated King [illegible] at Emania. *Adhna* was succeeded by his [illegible] maintained and won the extraordinary literary [illegible] father's chair, against the learned *Ferceirtné*, [illegible] still extant, and known as the Dialogue of the [illegible] Professors), a Tract which has been often men-[illegible] former course of Lectures.[31]

Of Adhna, chief Poet of Ulster under Conor Mac Nessa.

[illegible] discussed the genuineness of the poem on the [illegible] *Fodhla*, ascribed in the Book of Leinster to [illegible] but this is not all that is known of his literary [illegible] presently seen.

[illegible] in the Books of Ballymote and *Lecain*, as [illegible] ancient tract on the Grammar of the Gaedhelic [illegible] comparing it, to some extent, with the Hebrew and [illegible] but more particularly and copiously with [illegible] Tract is divided into Four Books. The [illegible] First Book (first in point of composition, though [illegible] arrangement), is ascribed to *Fenius Farsaidh* [illegible] Antiquarian"], the ancestor of Milesius, and, ac-[illegible] very early Milesian traditions, the first person [illegible] Great School on the Plain of Shenar, where an

Ancient Gaedhelic Grammar; part attributed to *Fenius Farsaidh*, part to *Amergin*, part to *Ferceirtné*, part to *Cennfaeladh*.

[31] [illegible] the *MS. Materials of Ancient Irish History*, p. 383, (etc.).

[T. III. ient helic mar.]

attempt was made to collect and teach scientifically the various Languages, after the Confusion at the Tower of Babel. The second book, in point of composition, but the third in the [illegible] sent arrangement, is ascribed to *Amergin*, the son of Mil[illegible] Poet and Judge of the Milesian Colony; who, it is stated, [illegible] posed it at the *Tochar* of *Inbher Mór*, (which is the place [illegible] called Arklow). The third book, in point of composition, but second in the present arrangement, is ascribed to the [illegible] *Ferceirtné*, in the following words:

"The place of writing this Book was Emania; the time [illegible] the time of Conor MacNessa; the author was *Ferceirtné*, [illegible] Poet; and the cause of composing it was to bring the ignorant and barbarous to true knowledge".

The fourth book, in point of composition, but the first [illegible] the present arrangement, is the well-known book of *Cenn-faeladh* the Learned, (of whom more hereafter), who died in [illegible] year 678.

It is quite true that not one of these four parts of this cur[illegible] grammatical tract can now be found in its primitive simplicity of composition. This tract, as it now stands, was evidently compiled in the ninth century, when the writings of Isi[illegible] Priscian, and Donatus, became so familiar in the Irish Schools, and the object of the writer appears to have been to extend [illegible] comparison of the Grammar of the Gaedhelic Language w[illegible] that of the Latin, which it would seem had been already touched upon by *Cennfaeladh* about the year 650.

This grammatical tract bears, I think, internal evidence [illegible] its having been written in its present shape either by the cele[illegible] brated Cormac MacCullinan, King and Archbishop of Cashel, or by some one of the noble school to which he belonged, [illegible] wards the close of the ninth century.

This tract is too important to be treated of casually, wh[illegible] speaking on other subjects; and I cannot help remarking [illegible] a singular circumstance, that none of the numerous Irish Gram[illegible] mar writers of the last two centuries even refers to its existence, much less to having made any use of it. Indeed I believe [illegible] would not be in error if I should say that there are not [illegible] Irish Grammar writers, or rather compilers, now living, wh[illegible] ever read it, or even ever heard of it; nor is there now, perhaps, any one man living who could individually make it accessible to the student by reducing it to proper order, though there [illegible] scholars capable of accomplishing the task conjointly; and [illegible] until this is done, and Cormac's and other Glossaries published, it is, I think, premature to talk of a complete grammar of the Irish Language.

...doubt that from a very early period of our his-... the chief Monarch of Erinn not only ... own court, but also to encourage at those of ... Kings and other great local Lords, Poets, His-... as well as Druids and Musicians; and if ... proper place for doing so, I could show the exist-... of these officers, from an antiquity long ... of the Incarnation down to that period when ... was Monarch of Erinn, and Conor Mac-... Ulster. An early recorded instance of the ex-... officers is to be found in a very ancient tract, ... Battle of *Ros-na-Righ*, a battle fought between this ... Erinn and Conor King of Ulster; in which it is ... the Learned, *Diarmaid* the Poet, and ... or Romance writer, of the King, were ... battle, by *Conall Cearnach*.

LECT. III.

Of Literary officers in connection with the Monarch's court, in early times.

... that is, in Conor's reign, so far had the taste for ... kinds, but poetry, music, and druidism in parti-... the national mind, that it is recorded that more ... of the men of Erinn had then given themselves up ... and teaching of these seductive sciences; and ... into the ranks of the *Fileadh* and *Ollamhs*, ... organization was explained in a former Lec-... were enabled to gain legal privileges which secured ... of sustenance and rank, at the expense ... portion of the community. The producing ... began to feel the weight of supporting, in unpro-... so large a section of the population; and the ... them speedily became loud and threatening, ... East, South, and West of Erinn. The profes-... Poets, therefore, called a meeting of their body to ... for their own safety, and to consider whether ... take refuge in banishment, passing into ... the storm should have abated. When, however, ... well as powerful King Conor MacNessa heard of ... he, with the consent of his people, invited them ... and here, it is recorded, the legion of learned men ... were hospitably entertained for the space of seven

State of learning in the time of Conor Mac Nessa.

... subsequent occasions the poets received again the ... hospitality of the old Ultonians in their more ... of *Uladh* or Ulidia; namely, once in the time ... of *Baedan*, King of Ulidia, who was slain in the ... again in the time of his successor, *Maelcobha*, ... in the year 646; but the greatest danger that

LECT. III. ever threatened them arose in the reign of the
son of *Ainmiré*, son of *Sedna*, who reigned
A.D. 568 to 594. And though it is anticipating
chronological order, it may be as well to mention
stance, in connection with those just alluded to,
tion of the consequences of the ancient system of
ment to learning, even when education had already
generally diffused throughout the island.

Of the "Pot of Avarice" of the *Fileadh*.

At this time the *Fileadh*, or poets, it would
more troublesome and importunate than ever.
tom is recorded to have prevailed among their
a very early period. They were in the habit of
through the country, as I have already mentioned, in
companies, of thirty, composed of teachers and
single chief or master. In these progresses, when
to a house, the first man of them that entered began
the first verse of a poem; the last man of the party
to him; and so the whole poem was sung, each taking
that order. Now each company of Poets had a silver
was called *Coiré Sainnté*, literally the Pot of Avarice;
having nine chains of bronze attached to it by golden
and it was suspended from the points of the spears of
the company, which were thrust through the links at the
ends of the chains. The reason—(according to the account
custom preserved in the *Leabhar Mór Duna Doighré*, called
Leabhar Breac, [R.I.A.])—that the pot was called the "
Avarice", was, because it was into it that whatever of
silver they received was put; and whilst the poem was
chanted, the best nine musicians in the company played
around the pot. This custom was, no doubt, very picturesque
but the actors in it were capable of showing themselves
different characters, according to the result of their application
If their Pot of Avarice received the approbation of the
the house, in gold or silver, a laudatory poem was written
him; but if it did not he was satirized in the most virulent
that a copious and highly expressive language could supply

Now, so confident always were the Poets in the
which their satirical powers had over the actions of the
of all classes, that, in the year of our Lord 590, a company
them waited on the Monarch *Aedh* (or Hugh) son of *Ai*
and threatened to satirize him if he did not give them the
Croi itself,—the Royal Brooch,—which from the remotest
descended from Monarch to Monarch of Erinn, and which
recorded to have been worn as the chief distinctive emblem
the legitimate sovereign. *Aedh* (Hugh), however, had not only

[illegible] to refuse so audacious a demand, but in his [illegible] ordered the banishment of the whole pro-[illegible] country; and, in compliance with this order, [illegible] great numbers into Ulidia, once more, where [illegible] a temporary asylum.

[illegible] order of time, we shall have to return again to [illegible] in reference to the General Revision which [illegible] time, of the Laws concerning Education and [illegible] of Learning.

[illegible] adduced what I trust will be found satisfactory [illegible] cultivation of the native Language and Liter-[illegible] centuries before the introduction of Christianity, [illegible] a few of the prominent Scholars, lay and [illegible] from *Fercertné*, and those already mentioned, [illegible] second, third, and fourth centuries; in short, [illegible] Saint Patrick, in the fifth; and to continue the [illegible] eminent lay and ecclesiastical writers, in the [illegible] language, from that period down to the eleventh [illegible]

List of eminent men of learning continued.

[illegible] writers of Ancient Irish History, in the Book [illegible] find the Poet and Satirist *Athairné* and his [illegible] about the middle of the first century; suc-[illegible] *Fergus*, and his pupils, who must have con-[illegible] down to and into the second century.

[illegible] the ancient tract called *Bailé an Scáil*, de-[illegible] Lecture,[30] that *Conn* of the Hundred Bat-[illegible] his reign A.D. 123), had always in his company [illegible] mentioned in that tract were named *Ethan*, [illegible] and we have it from other authorities, that [illegible] *Righ Eigeas* or Royal Poet, was also attached to [illegible]

[illegible] King of Munster (who flourished from A.D. 186 [illegible] author of several poems, three of which are [illegible] the Book of Leinster. The first appears to have [illegible] to the chiefs of his own family or race, imme-[illegible] Battle of *Ceann Abrat*, (or *Feabhrat*,) which [illegible] *Cill Finan* (but in the county of Cork), and [illegible] defeated his stepson *MacCon*; the second, on the [illegible] sons, in the Battle of *Magh Mucroimhé* (in [illegible] Galway), fought in the year 195; and the third [illegible] his grandson *Fiacha Muillethan*, whose mother [illegible] him birth, and whose father, *Eoghan Mór*, [illegible] old king, was slain in the above battle. There

Poems of King Oilioll Olum.

[30] [illegible] MS. Materials of Ancient Irish History*, p. 385, (etc.).

LECT. III. can be no doubt of the great antiquity of these pieces, and scarcely any, in my opinion, of their authenticity. It is true that some Christian allusions enter into the third poem; but I am disposed to believe that these were introduced at a comparatively later but still remote time, though for what special purpose can not be now divined. But it would be impossible, consistently with the plan of these Lectures, to enter into any minute critical investigation upon such a subject; and I am forced to content myself for the present, with the expression of the opinion at which I have arrived as to the authenticity or antiquity of the various tracts of which I have to speak. To proceed.

Poems by King Art "the Solitary".

The Monarch *Art* "the Solitary", son and successor to Conn of the Hundred Battles, and who, with his nephews the seven sons of *Oilioll*, fell in the Battle of *Magh Muicroimhé*, just mentioned, was the author of a poem on the place of his own sepulture (*Treoit*, now Trevit, in Meath). A very ancient copy of this curious poem, with a gloss, is preserved in *Leabhar na h-Uidhré* (R.I.A.), a manuscript compiled before the year 1106.

Foundation of a University by Cormac Mac Airt; (third century).

The Monarch *Cormac*, the son of *Art* the Solitary, occupied the throne of Erinn from the year 227 to the year 268; and enough has been said in several former Lectures to prove that our national literature attained to the highest degree of cultivation during his illustrious reign, which covers so great a portion of the third century. It may be interesting, however, to introduce here a single extract respecting this king, because it contains an instance of the very early organization of Education, and its division into several departments; in fact, an early instance of a species of University, founded by Cormac at Tara, the seat of the monarchy. I quote from O'Flaherty's *Ogygia* (Hely's translation, vol. ii., page 239):

"*Cormac* exceeded all his predecessors in magnificence, munificence, wisdom, and learning, as also in military achievements. His palace was most superbly adorned and richly furnished, and his numerous family proclaim his majesty and munificence; the books he published, and the schools he endowed at Temor bear unquestionable testimony of his learning; there were three schools instituted, in the first the most eminent professors of the art of war were engaged, in the second history was taught, and in the third jurisprudence was professed. There is a poem consisting of 183 distichs of these three universities, of the grandeur of Temor in the reign of *Cormac*, and of his encomiums and exploits; this poem is compiled in O'Duvegan's book, fol. 175, which begins thus:

"Teamhair na riogh rath Chormaic".[1]

[1] ["Temor of the Kings is Cormac's royal seat".]

[illegible] is, I should observe, of great authority. The [illegible] was that compiled by the celebrated scho- [illegible] O'Dubhagan, *Ollamh* of *Ui Maini* (or O'Kelly's [illegible] Connacht), who died in the year 1372. This book [illegible] enlightened keeping of Lord Ashburnham, and is, [illegible] inaccessible to the historical student.

The Book of O'Duvegan.

[illegible] with Cormac was the celebrated *Finn Mac* [illegible] poet and warrior. *Finn*, according to an ancient [illegible] possession, was educated for the poetic profession, [illegible] under *Cathern* the son of *Fintan;* but having [illegible] with one of the daughters of the Monarch [illegible] than her father approved of, the young bard was [illegible] the court and to abandon his gentle profession for [illegible] and dangerous one of arms. *Finn* lived to the [illegible] he was slain, at a very advanced age. I gave [illegible] a very full list and description of the pieces [illegible] ascribed to him in our old books.(30)

Literary education of Finn Mac Cumhaill.

[illegible] succeeded, at least in his literary profession, by his [illegible] *Fergus*, and by his cousin *Cailtè;* from the com- [illegible] of whom quotations are made in the ancient [illegible] called the *Dinnseanchas.*

[illegible] century was not more deficient in native [illegible] undoubted authority. The celebrated *Niall* [illegible] Hostages" was born in the second half of this [illegible] succeeded his father in the monarchy in the year [illegible] slain on the bank of the river Loire, in France, [illegible] by his old enemy and competitor for the throne [illegible] the son of *Enna Ceinselach*, a prince of [illegible] was fostered and educated in the ancient dis- [illegible] (in which is situated the well-known "Abbey [illegible] the modern county of Kerry), by *Torna Eigeas* [illegible] learned poet"), from whom this district derives [illegible] it bears even to this day. *Torna Eigeas* fills [illegible] among the learned poets of ancient Erinn. [illegible] supposed compositions, I am acquainted with five [illegible] of which are of undoubted antiquity; but the [illegible] though still of an old date, must nevertheless have [illegible] modification in style, if ever they were written [illegible].

Of learning under Niall Naoi-Ghiallach. Of Torna Eigeas.

[illegible] two really ancient poems to which I refer, is [illegible] thirteen stanzas, or fifty-two lines, composed by [illegible] with his son, on the untimely death of the [illegible], as already described. The son opens the [illegible] following lines:

(30) [illegible] the MS. Materials of Ancient Irish History, pp. 301; 395;

LECT. III.

(Of Torna Eigeas.)

" When we used to go to the assembly
Along with the son of Eochaidh Muighmhead
As yellow as shining Sobairché[33] was the hair
Upon the head of the son of Cairen,[34]

Torna is pleased with the similitude; and answers:

" My worthy son, so well hast thou spoken,
A Cumal [three cows] to it is meet to be given
In honour of that hair which thou hast compared
With the [golden] top of the Sobairché".

Torna then describes the King's eyebrows, his eyelash eyes; comparing them in colour with certain berries, woods. The son replies by describing his cheeks, comp them to the opening blossoms of certain trees. Torna describes his pearly teeth and red lips, his countenance lik moon, like the sun, like a glowing fire. The son then com the lamentation of the people of Erinn, for Niall, wi moaning of the wind over a desert island; and says tha when he is gone, the Saxons, the Albans, and the Ga will roam uncontrolled in all directions. Torna says th screaming Saxons, and parties of the Lombards "from La will now seek to oppress the Gaedhils and the Picts. Th then bears witness to the bravery of Niall's sons; Eo Laeghairé, Enna, Fiacha, Conall, and Cairpré. And Torna winds up by bearing testimony to the happiness which hi self, and all men enjoyed, when they went to the Assem Tara with King Niall.

There is one point in this poem which would appear to something against its authenticity, namely, the introducti the Lombards into it, at a time in which it is supposed, th not clearly established, I believe, that they had not rec that name. And with this, which in my mind is not ho an exception, there is nothing in this curious poem to de from it a single year of the remote antiquity to which referred, namely, the year of our Lord 405, or twenty- years before the arrival of Saint Patrick.

This poem is to be found in the Library of T.C.D. (in " Yellow Book of Lecain", H. 2. 16.).

The next poem in point of antiquity, which I find ascri to Torna Eigeas, is one which I shall reserve until I com speak presently of the death of the Monarch Dathi, who, ceeded Niall, and who was slain in the year 428.

Of the other three poems ascribed to Torna, two of them,

(33) The "Sobairché" was the plant called "Herba Sancti Petri" [Hyperic quadrangulum—LIN.]

(34) The mother of Niall.

...should date farther back than *Niall's* death, and one ... of these poems consists of thirteen stanzas, or ... beginning: [LECT. III.] [Of Torna Eigeas.]

"... my precept, O noble Niall".(20)

... proclaims his love and affection for his two ... *Niall*, the future Monarch of Erinn, and *Corc*, ... of Munster; and says that each possesses half ... The learned tutor then addresses himself particu... and in good and forcible language lays down for ... instructions or rules for the govern... as well as for his own government.

... I know of this poem is that in a vellum ... (H. 4. 22); one not older than the fif... The poem, however, is much older than that ... certainly in its present style and diction, not ... hundreds of years of *Torna's* time. Indeed I am ... upon it rather as an imitation, on a very small ... an inferior style, of *Fotha-na-Canóiné's* ... of Instructions, written for his pupil *Aedh* ... elevation to the Monarchy of Erinn, in the

... of these three poems, in order of date, is one of ... in which *Torna* relates, that on one occasion ... of his pupil *Niall* that his other pupil *Corc*, ... had boasted of his intention to put forth his right ... and his determination to enforce that right ... He proceeds: As soon as King Niall had ... brother's designs, he raised an army at Tara, ... he would march into Munster, and reduce him ... obedience. When *Corc* received this account, ... marshalled four battalions of brave warriors, ... to meet his great opponent on the borders ... and to prevent his entering it, with all his ... relates that when he found matters come to this ... himself to the King of Cashel, and begged ... love and duty he bore and owed to him, *Torna*, ... and tutor, to stay his march, and allow him ... to heal the wounded pride of *Niall*, and dis... carrying his intended invasion of Munster into ... request was granted; and *Torna* repaired to Tara ... of peace, where he ascribed *Corc's* ambitious ... his more youthful inexperience, and to a boastful ... disposition in his race. To these unwarranted and

(20) ... mo teagasc, a Néill náir".

LECT. III. [Of Torna Eigeas.]

damaging excuses, *Niall* added very reproachful words against the King of Cashel; and having consulted the wishes of his people, it was unanimously decided to undertake the expedition. The army, consisting of nine battalions, marched forward until they arrived at *Lothra*, in Ormond (in the present county of Tipperary), where *Niall* pitched his camp, from which he pillaged and ravaged all the territory of Ormond and Ely, around him. Here *Torna*, who still continued with *Niall*, was sent by *Brian*, the Monarch's brother, and the actual leader of the expedition, to *Corc*, calling upon him to come in and deliver hostages, before the army marched further into the country. *Torna* went, and met *Corc*, nothing daunted, at the head of his troops, at *Bearnan Eilé*, (now called the Devil's Bit), where he delivered his message to him, and urged him to agree to it, which he found himself compelled to do. [illegible] then, at the head of five hundred horsemen, went for[illegible] *Niall's* camp, where he was joyfully received, and pea[illegible] amity were re-established between them; after which, [illegible] returned to Cashel, leaving hostages in the hands of [illegible] and receiving from him a present of "one thousand hor[illegible] hundred suits of armour, nine score rings of gold, [illegible] costly drinking horns".

This poem is well known in the south of Ireland; [illegible] more so, because about the year 1604, it gave rise to the [illegible]ous and valuable tract so well known by the title of the "[illegible]tention of the Bards", a series of historico-controversial [illegible] which sprang out of a poem written by Tady MacBruody[illegible] of the last, if not the last, of the hereditary poets and hi[illegible] of the O'Briens, and the other Dalcassian families of Tho[illegible] In this piece MacBruody severely criticises *Torna's* p[illegible] admitting its genuineness; but charging the author, w[illegible] of Ulster extraction, with partiality for *Niall*, and the n[illegible] or Eremonian, races. MacBruody was learnedly answ[illegible] *Lugaidh O'Clerigh*, of Donegal, and several other [illegible] scholars; but as I have given a pretty fair description [illegible] controversy in a former Lecture,[38] I shall not follow [illegible]ther on the present occasion. As the genuineness of T[illegible] poem, however, has for more than two hundred years [illegible] made the subject of criticism and doubt, I shall translate [illegible] the first stanza, for the purpose of identification; and the [illegible] concluding stanzas, for the purpose of offering a few rem[illegible] upon them.

The poem commences as follows:

(38) See *Lectures on the MS. Materials of Ancient Irish History*, p. 161.

LECT. III.

[Of Torna Eigeas.]

[illegible] of battle between *Corc* and *Niall*,
[illegible] at hand, or whether far distant;
[illegible] the tramp over every shore,
[illegible] *Niall*, the son of *Eocha Muighmheadhoin*.[35]

[illegible] concluding verses run as follows:

[illegible] my condition, now, at last,
[illegible] my relatives have passed away,
[illegible] grief for *Corc* and *Niall*;
[illegible] neither gifts nor spoils.
[illegible] Assembly of the world's men, at the end,
[illegible] the summit of Mount Sion,
[illegible] an account to all-just Christ,—
[illegible] I be brought to that great Assembly".[36]

[illegible] is nothing in the whole of this certainly very old [illegible] allowance for the present corrupt copies,— [illegible] be deemed inconsistent with its being the genuine [illegible] of *Torna Eigeas*, excepting these two concluding [illegible] first of which makes the poet alive after the year [illegible] year *Corc*, King of Cashel, is said to have attended [illegible] of Tara, to give his assent to the *Seanchas Mór*, [illegible] the arrival of Saint Patrick; and the last stanza [illegible] speaks the language of mature Christianity. [illegible] easy to believe that *Torna*, who was the foster- [illegible] of *Niall*, who was slain in the year 405, and of [illegible] down to the year 438, at least, could have sur- [illegible] pupils; but if we could believe that he survived [illegible] of his having been a Christian would be

Of the presence of *Corc* at Tara, on the revision of the *Seanchas Mór*; (A.D. 438).

[illegible] O'Flaherty, in his *Ogygia*, at the reign of *Niall* [illegible] Hostages, denies the possibility of *Torna* having [illegible] the coming of Saint Patrick, in 432, or of *Corc* of [illegible] alive in 438, to give his assent to the *Seanchas* [illegible] describing the present poem, he disposes, as he [illegible] authenticity, in the following words:
[illegible] return to the poem. I am of opinion that *Corc*,

[35] "Dál cata etir Corc is Niall,
A bfogus no a n-eidirchian;
Borb a treatan tar gach tráigh,
Niall mac Eachach Muighmeadhoin".

[36] "Truagh mo dhál-sa fa dheóidh,
Tanga mo chraobha coimneóil;
Dubhaidh Cuirc is Néill róm chráidh
Ni b-fágaim ág ná éadáil.
Dál fir n-domhain fó dheóidh
Ar mullach Sléibhe Sióin,
Ag tabhairt cirt do Christ chóir,
Beartar misi 'san mór dháil".

LECT. II. [Of the presence of Corc at Tara, A.D. 438.]

who, as he [*Torna*] declares, was very young in schools, and in his youth a contemporary with *Niall* in the kingdom, was much older, as he was cousin to the father-in-law of *Niall*; and I am convinced he died before the commencement of *Niall's* reign, because King *Crimthann*, the successor of *Niall*, [illegible] substituted *Conall Eachluaith* in the government of Munster, after the decease of *Corc*, as Dr. Keting assures us in his account of the reign of *Crimthann*, extracted from Cormac O'Culenan, Bishop and King of Munster, who was exceedingly well informed in the antiquities of his country.

"Wherefore their mistake appears the more manifest in Colgan, who insinuates that *Corc* was coeval with Saint Patrick, in the year of Christ 438; whereas *Aengus*, the grandson of *Corc*, was the first King of Munster, according to the accounts of all our antiquaries, who, by the means of Saint Patrick, embraced the Christian religion.

"Whether *Torna* was the author of that poem, or in what age he flourished, and whether he was a Christian, are matters with which I am not acquainted; this only I shall beg leave to intimate, that it has been a practice among the ancients to publish their works under the names of others, that their assertions might gain the greater weight and authority, as Cicero declares in *De Senectute*.—I shall also insinuate that *Torna* lived after *Dathi*, the successor of *Niall*, if that poem concerning the sepulchres of the Kings of *Cruachan* be ascribed to him, which I am very confident is of a later date".[31]

It will have been seen that O'Flaherty in these passages endeavours to show that this poem could not be genuine, because, in the first instance, *Corc*, the King of Munster who is mentioned in it as contemporary with the Monarch *Niall*, must have been much older than him, and died long before him; and he gives as the grounds of this opinion, a passage in Keting, in which it is stated that the Monarch *Crimthann*, the grand-nephew of *Corc*, and who died in the year 378, had given the government of Munster to *Conall Eachluaith* of the Dalcassian race, after the death of *Corc*, and consequently long before the death of King *Niall*, which took place in the year 405.

O'Flaherty is right in his calculations here, as far as Keting may be correct; for Keting states that the throne of Cashel, or Munster, having become vacant in the Monarch *Crimthann's* reign, the latter appointed to it his own foster-son *Conall Eachluaith*, of the Dalcassian race; that the nobles of the Eugenian or South Munster race felt displeased at this, alleging that they had of their own line a most eligible person to elect as their

(31) *Ogygia*, vol. ii. p. 340; Hely's (very inaccurate) translation.

King; and one who had a prior right to the succession, namely, [illegible], son of *Lugaidh;* that the monarch referred the question to the learned men of Munster; and that they decided that *Corc* should succeed to the government of the province, in the first instance, with reversion, on his death, to *Conall Eachluaith*, or if he should not be living then, to his next heir; and that this decision was acted upon, that *Corc* assumed the government (his years are not given), and that on his death *Conall Eachluaith* succeeded.

LECT. III.

[Of the presence of Corc at Tara, A.D. 438.]

This is the account given in all the copies of Keting that I am acquainted with, and some of these are as old as the author's time (though we have never seen his autograph, so as to be able to state positively that these are his words.)

This statement, however, is not correct; since it is well known that *Conall Eachluaith* never was King of Munster, and it is indeed more than probable that he died before *Corc*.

Of the oldest authorities for the succession of the Kings of Munster with which I am acquainted, the first is *Seaan Mór O'Dubhagain's* poem, who died in the year 1372; in which he gives both the names and the length of the reign of each of the Kings of *Caisel*, or Munster, from *Eoghan Mór*, who was slain in the battle of *Magh Lena*, in the year 153, down to *Domhnall Mór O'Briain*, the last of the Kings of Munster, who died in the year 1194. The poet does not give the years of *Eoghan's* reign, but begins his computation with his son, *Oilioll Oluim*, who reigned sixty years, and died in the year 234, of extreme old age. The reigns then counted are as follows:

The Succession of the Kings of Munster.

Cormac Cas, forty years; *Fiacha Muillethan*, forty years; *[illegible]*, twenty years; *Oilioll Flann Mór*, twenty years; *[illegible] Beg*, thirty years; *Eochaidh*, fifteen years; *Corc* (the subject of our discussion), thirty years.

If to the year 234, in which *Oilioll Oluim* died, we add these succeeding reigns, including that of *Corc*, they bring us down to the year 429, or three years before the coming of Saint Patrick, in the year 432, and nine years before the reputed compilation of the *Seanchas Mór*, at which he is said to have assisted.

After *Seaan O'Dubhagain*, the next authority is the Book of Leacan, compiled in the year 1391, at folio 38 of which is found the same list of reigns, in prose, and agreeing exactly with the poem, except in the matter of one year: for the poem gives the reign of *Eochaidh*, *Corc's* immediate predecessor, fifteen years, while the prose makes it sixteen, thus bringing *Corc's* death down to the year 430.

The third authority is *Dubhaltach Mac Firbisigh*, who com-

LECT. III. [Of the presence of Corc at Tara, A.D. 438.]

piled his great genealogical Book in the year 1650. At page 688 of that work this list is to be found, agreeing exactly with *O'Dubhagain's* Poem. The original list was also preserved in the ancient Book of Leinster; but the earlier part of it is now lost, as well as many other important articles from that valuable manuscript.

This list of reigns, extending from the year 174, in which *Oilioll Oluim* began to govern, down to the death of *Corc* in the year 429 or 430, disposes, I think, of O'Flaherty's assertion, founded on an erroneous passage in Keting:—that *Corc* died before the death of the Monarch *Crimthann*, which happened in the year 378; and that *Conall Eachluaith*, of the Dalcassian race, whose name is not found in any of the three copies, succeeded *Corc* before that year; and, therefore, that *Corc* could not have been present at, or have given his assent to, the *Seanchas Mór*.

O'Flaherty argues also that *Corc* could not have given his assent to the *Seanchas Mór*, because he could not have been a Christian; since his grandson, *Aengus* the son of *Natfraech*, who succeeded in 422, was the first Christian King of Munster, having been baptized by Saint Patrick in person. Now, this is not sound reasoning; for it is very clear that the six years which intervened between Saint Patrick's coming and the year assigned to the compilation of the *Seanchas Mór*, were quite insufficient for the conversion of the Irish people and their Kings and Chiefs. It is, therefore, quite possible, if not positive, that numbers of those who attended the Great Feast of Tara, on that occasion, were still unbelievers; and there is every reason to believe that the Monarch *Laeghairé* himself, who convened the meeting, and professed himself a Christian, did so more in obedience to the growing moral influence and popularity of Saint Patrick, than to the dictates of conscience, or any vivid appreciation of the Gospel.

It was stated in a former Lecture, that the compilation or revision of the laws of the land had been entrusted, by the Kings and Nobles who attended at this great assembly at Tara, to a Committee of Nine, to be composed of three Kings, three Bishops, and three Poets, or lay Philosophers; and that the nine persons so selected were, *Laeghairé* the Monarch, *Corc* King of Munster, and *Dairé* King of Ulster, to represent the Kings and Nobles; Saint Patrick, himself, Saint *Benin* (or Benignus), his pupil, and Saint *Cairnech*, to represent the Christian Church; and the Poets *Dubhthach*, *Ros*, and *Fergus*, to represent the lay literary professions. Now, it is very doubtful, as I have already said, that *Laeghairé* himself was a

LECT. III. [Of the presence of Corc at Tara, A.D. 438.]

[illegible] at this time, or indeed at any time. His son and [illegible] successor, *Lugaidh*, certainly was not. It is also [illegible], according to the Tripartite Life of Saint Patrick, [illegible] the King of Ulster, one of the Committee of Nine, [illegible] a Christian at the time, nor for nineteen years after, till the year in which Armagh was founded; though he had, indeed, [illegible] previously, given Saint Patrick the site of a church, [illegible] neighbourhood. It is certain that the Poet *Dubh-* [illegible] had been converted previously to the meeting; and there [illegible] reason to believe that the Poet *Ros* also had been con- [illegible] previously; but there is no reason whatever to believe [illegible] third Poet, *Fergus*, had become a believer at the time. [illegible] now shown that some members, at least, of the Com- [illegible] of Nine, were still pagans at the time of its constitution, [illegible] I trust, satisfactorily removed the second of O'Flaherty's [illegible] why *Corc* the King of Cashel could not have been one [illegible] namely, that he could not have been converted at the [illegible]. And this altogether passing over the possibility of *Corc* [illegible] become a Christian (which he is recorded to have done, [illegible] account of the *Seanchas Mór*), as many others [illegible] Erinn, before Saint Patrick's coming. If the *Sean-* [illegible] was compiled at all, at the time and under the cir- [illegible] laid down by all our ancient authorities without a [illegible] word, whoever was the King of Munster pre- [illegible] have been a pagan, since the baptism, but certainly [illegible] conversion, by Saint Patrick, of *Aengus* King of that [illegible] did not take place (supposing his grandfather *Corc* [illegible] in 430), until the year 442, or four years after the [illegible] acknowledged date of the compilation.

[illegible] argued that *Corc* could not have lived so late as the [illegible] because his nephew, the Monarch *Crimthann* (son to [illegible] his younger brother), was cut off in the prime of [illegible] year 366. This argument, however, falls to the [illegible], if we place any reliance on the Chronology of [illegible]'s poem, and the list in the Book of Ballymote; [illegible] which the death of *Oilioll Flann Beg*, the grandfather [illegible] brought down to the year 384; and surely there is [illegible] wonderful or incredible in the fact that a man should [illegible] years after his grandfather's death (that number [illegible] difference between the years 384 and 438, in which [illegible] *Mór* was compiled); neither is there anything [illegible] in the belief that the grandson's tutor might, by [illegible] survive his pupil say by a single year, and have [illegible] his death and that of his other and older pupil, [illegible] *Niall*, who was cut off prematurely in the year 405.

LECT. III.

[Of the presence of Corc at Tara, A.D. 438.]

It is a curious coincidence, too, that *Aengus*, the grandson of *Corc*, was, according to the Annals of the Four Masters, killed at the Battle of *Cell Osnadh*, near *Leithghlinn* (in the present county of Carlow), in the year 488, just fifty-eight years after his grandfather *Corc*, supposing him to have died in 430; and still, *Aengus*, as I have said, was killed in battle.

Having thus satisfactorily, I hope, though tediously, I fear, demonstrated the perfect possibility of *Corc* King of Cashel having been present at the compilation of the *Seanchas Mór*, it only remains for me, now, to dispose of the discrepancy of eight years, between the time of that compilation and *Corc's* death, as found in the authorities already quoted. On this part of the argument I need, I think, say but little, having already shown, in one of my early Lectures, how, in the lapse of centuries, chronology, which requires so much accuracy in its transmission, (and particularly with regard to mere numbers) was so very liable to irregularity and error; error arising both from the obscurity of old manuscripts, the carelessness or unavoidable mistakes of translators, and the probably inaccurate calculation of broken years, not to say anything of the use, from time to time, of different systems of computation.

It is, therefore, not a matter of suspicion, but a matter of admiration, that in a series of events, commencing in the year 234, and handed down, by manual transcription, to the year 1391, these accounts should, in one particular instance (or indeed in many), differ to the extent of some eight or nine years from the date of one or more other events transmitted through a medium equally liable to slight inaccuracy of this kind.

This, I find, has been a much longer and more unreasonable digression than I had at all intended; but as the subject has been discussed adversely by O'Flaherty, in his *Ogygia*, by the Rev. Dr. Lanigan, in his *Ecclesiastical History*, and by Dr. Petrie, in his valuable *Essay on the Antiquities of the Hill of Tara*, as well as by others; and as it will come under a more thorough examination in the forthcoming publication of the Brehon Law Commission; I have been tempted to throw together some of the more important of those facts which my own considerable reading and many years' attention to the subject have enabled me to collect; in order that such as have studied, or may hereafter devote attention to, this important event in our history, may see and know that there is a great deal more to be said on it than has been thought of in modern times.

LECTURE IV.

[Delivered 4th June, 1857.]

[illegible] AND LITERATURE; (continued). Of *Laidcenn* the Poet. [illegible] Belief in the power of a Poet's Satire. Of *Finnchaomh*, Poet of [illegible] *Torna Eigeas'* Poem on *Roilig na Righ*. Of the Poets of the [illegible] of King *Laeghairé*, (temp. St. Patrick). Druids of King *Laeghairé*. [illegible] cultivation of the Gaedhelic language in the early ages of the Church [illegible]. Of the early Gaedhelic writers after the introduction of Chris[illegible]—Bishop *Fiacc*, etc. The Ecclesiastical Schools of the early period [illegible] exclusively ecclesiastical. Of secular National Schools in the early [illegible] ages in Erinn. Of the *Feis* of *Drom Ceat* (A.D. 590);—revision [illegible] of the National system of Education. Of the Chief Poet *Dallan For-*[illegible] Of Laws concerning the Profession of Teaching. Of the nature of [illegible] Instruction in the early Christian Schools. Origin of "Sizars", or [illegible]". Story of St. *Adamnan* and King *Finnachta*. Early Edu-[illegible] of St. *Colum Cillé*. Students' Hut-Encampments. Of the foreign [illegible] of Armagh; (temp. Bede.) Of Secular Education in Ancient [illegible] Of *Flannan* the Poet, and *Cathal* the son of King *Ragallach*, (A.D. [illegible]). Of the qualification of a *Fer-Leighin*, or Head Master of a Public [illegible]. Of the Professors in a Public School or College. List of early [illegible] distinguished as Men of Letters. Of the Poet *Seanchan Torpeist* [illegible]. Story of *Seanchan* and King *Guairé*. Legendary account of [illegible] recovery of the heroic Tale of the *Tain Bo Chuailgné*.

[illegible] an account of the succession of learned men by [illegible] ancient Literature and History were preserved and [illegible], and in whom we have examples of the education [illegible] in ancient times, I had reached the reign of *Niall* [illegible] Nine Hostages", (at the end of the fourth century), [illegible] digression which I was obliged to make in order to [illegible] embarrassing difficulty as to the appearance of King [illegible] in Saint Patrick's time. I had just spoken of the [illegible] scholar of that age, *Torna Eigeas*.

[illegible] with *Torna* was *Laidcenn*, the son of *Bairced*, [illegible] poet and scholar who was also attached to the [illegible] Monarch *Niall* at Tara, but whose private resi-[illegible] at *Rath Beccé*, (a place now called Rathbeggan, near [illegible], in the county of Meath). Of Laidcenn the Poet.

[illegible] we have at least one anecdote. Among other [illegible] *Niall* had at his court *Eochaidh*, the son and [illegible] *Enna Ceinnselaigh*, King of Leinster. This young [illegible] some time became unhappy at his condition, and at [illegible] opportunity to escape from Tara, and fly to the south, [illegible] country. He had run as far as *Laidcenn's* residence

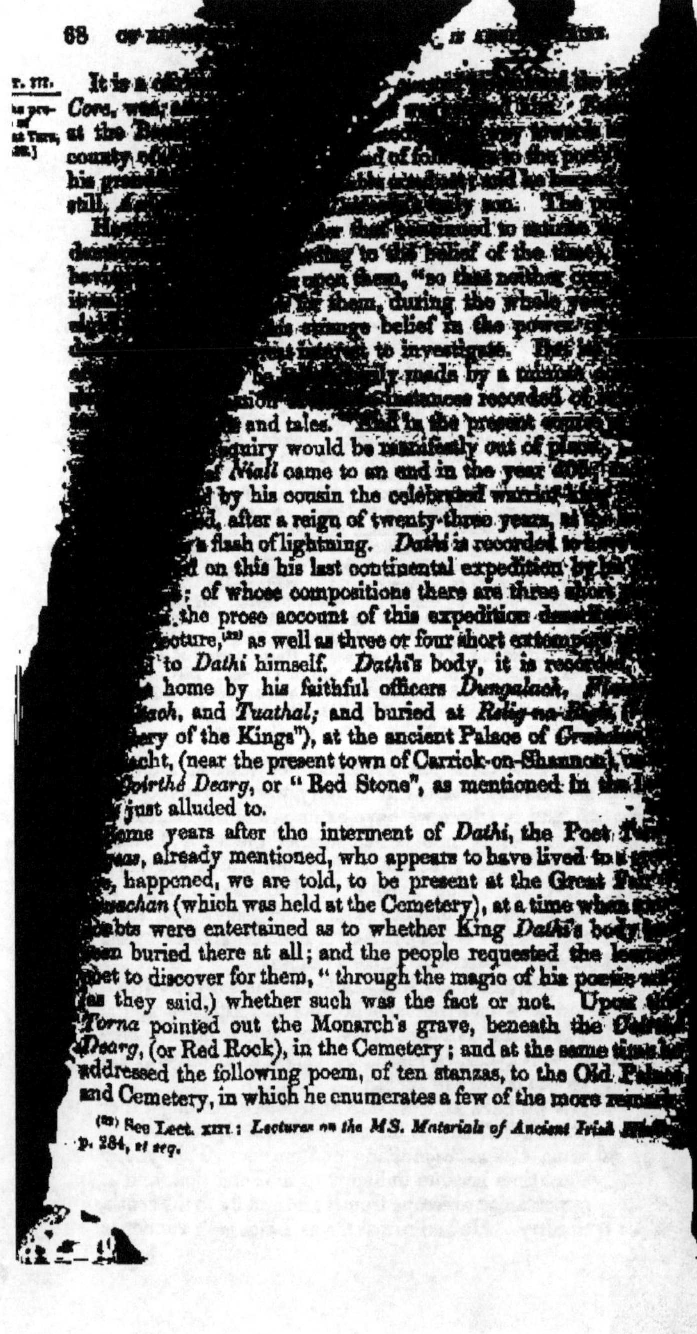

It is a [illegible]
Cora, was [illegible]
at the [illegible]
county of [illegible] of [illegible] to the poet
his [illegible]
still, [illegible] son. The [illegible]
[illegible] that continued to [illegible]
[illegible] to the belief of the time)
[illegible] upon them, "so that neither [illegible]
[illegible] by them, during the whole [illegible]
[illegible] strange belief in the power [illegible]
[illegible] to investigate. [illegible]
[illegible] made by a [illegible]
[illegible] instances recorded [illegible]
[illegible] and tales. [illegible] in the present [illegible]
[illegible] quiry would be manifestly out of place [illegible]
[illegible] *Niall* came to an end in the year [illegible]
[illegible] by his cousin the celebrated [illegible]
[illegible], after a reign of twenty-three years, [illegible]
[illegible] flash of lightning. *Dathi* is recorded [illegible]
[illegible] on this his last continental expedition [illegible]
[illegible]; of whose compositions there are three [illegible]
[illegible] the prose account of this expedition [illegible]
[illegible] ecture,[28] as well as three or four short [illegible]
[illegible] to *Dathi* himself. *Dathi*'s body, it is recorded [illegible]
[illegible] home by his faithful officers *Dungalach*, [illegible]
[illegible] *ach*, and *Tuathal*; and buried at *Relig-na-Righ* [illegible]
[illegible] ery of the Kings"), at the ancient Palace of [illegible]
[illegible] acht, (near the present town of Carrick-on-Shannon) [illegible]
Coirthe Dearg, or "Red Stone", as mentioned in [illegible]
just alluded to.

[illegible] ome years after the interment of *Dathi*, the Poet [illegible]
[illegible], already mentioned, who appears to have lived [illegible]
[illegible], happened, we are told, to be present at the Great [illegible]
[illegible] *achan* (which was held at the Cemetery), at a time when [illegible]
[illegible] bts were entertained as to whether King *Dathi*'s body [illegible]
[illegible] en buried there at all; and the people requested the [illegible]
[illegible] et to discover for them, "through the magic of his [illegible]
(as they said,) whether such was the fact or not. Upon [illegible]
Torna pointed out the Monarch's grave, beneath the [illegible]
Dearg, (or Red Rock), in the Cemetery; and at the same [illegible]
addressed the following poem, of ten stanzas, to the Old [illegible]
and Cemetery, in which he enumerates a few of the more [illegible]

(28) See Lect. XIII.: *Lectures on the MS. Materials of Ancient Irish* [illegible]
p. 284, *et seq.*

Torna Eigeas's Poem on Reilig na Righ.

the personages who had been previously buried there; from which poem it would appear that the Hill of *Cruachan* (which at first was called *Druim na n-druadh*, or the "Hill of the Druids"), must have been a pagan cemetery long before the building of the first Royal Palace there by the Monarch *Eochaidh Feidlech*.[30]

This poem never having been published (except a spurious and defective version by Dermod O'Conor in his inaccurate translation of Doctor Keting's *History of Ireland*, in the year 1723), I may venture to give here the following literal translation from the best copy of it now extant. It is found in the ancient *Leabhar na h-Uidhré*, in the Royal Irish Academy. It will be remembered that the verses are addressed to the Palace and Cemetery of *Cruachan:*

There lies under thee the King of the men of *Inis Fail*,
Dathi the son of *Fiachra* the triumphant,
O *Cruachan*, which doth this conceal
From foreigners and from the Gaedhils!
There lies under thee *Dungalach* the vehement,
Who brought the king home over the trackless sea;
There lie beneath thee, too, with similar renown,
Tuathal, *Flanngus*, and *Tomaltach*.
The three fair sons of *Eochaidh Feidleach*
Lie within thy mound, in thy pleasant mound;
And *Eocha Airemh*, lying low,
Who was killed by *Mael Mór*.
Eocho Feidhleach the kingly is
[illegible]; and *Deirbrin* the beautiful;
And *Clothra*, no reproachful fact;
And *Medbh*; and *Muiresg*.
Eri, and *Fodhla*, and *Banbha*,—
These young women, beautiful, admirable,—
Though it was not here they lived, [*lit.* spent their youth]
Yet it is *Cruachan* that [now] conceals them.
Mac Cuill; *Mac Greiné*, of bright career;
Mac Cecht, whose grave is not less famed;
In the Rath of *Cruachain* they are concealed.
Not a few does the single flag conceal!
Ailill Loingsech, no niggardly king;
Midir, of the *Tuatha Dé Danann* race;

(30) The Palace of *Cruachan* was erected by *Eochaidh* for his daughter, the [illegible] *Medbh*, or Meave, whom he had set up as Queen of *Olnegmacht*, as [illegible] now called Connacht was then named, about fifty years before

LECT. IV.

Cobhthach Cael Breagh, of dubious fame,
The ambitious, lies under thee.
" Side by side reclines that king
And *Eocho Feidlech* in his beauty;
And *Eocho Airemh* is there too,
In the north side, O *Cruacha!*
" The saint, upon his house being demolished,
Said unto him [*Dathi*], mysteriously,
That his grave [or his monument] here
Should not be illustrious, O *Cruacha!*
" There are fifty mounds around *Cruachan*'s hill,
Upon the grassy sloping plain;
There are, of men and women,
Fifty buried in each mound".

After what I have already said on the probability of [illegible] surviving his pupil *Corc*,—who must have been alive [illegible] at least,—there is no reason to think, as O'Flaherty does, [illegible] he did not survive King *Dathi*, who died in 428, [illegible] had embraced the faith before writing this poem.

There is another very ancient poem on other interments [illegible] *Cruachan* (among which are mentioned those of several [illegible] poets of Connacht), preserved in the same old book, [illegible] ascribed to the Poet *Dorban*, of whose time I am ignorant [illegible] is published, with a translation, among other curious [illegible] Dr. Petrie's *Essay on the Round Towers of Ireland*.

We now pass from the reign of *Niall*, which terminated [illegible] the year 405, and of *Dathi*, his successor, which ended in [illegible] year 428, to that of *Laeghairé*, who succeeded *Dathi*, [illegible] the fourth year of whose reign, that is, in 432, Saint P[illegible] arrived from Rome, upon his mission to convert our pagan [illegible] cestors to the Christian faith.

Poets, etc., of the Court of *Laeghairé*, at the coming of St. Patrick.

Saint Patrick found the country teeming with men di[illegible] guished for their acquirements in the native language and [illegible] rature, if not in other languages; philosophers, poets, dr[illegible] judges, etc. On his first appearance at Tara, he found the [illegible] *Dubhthach* installed there as the Monarch's chief Poet; and [illegible] have seen already that *Ros* and *Fergus* were also distinguished poets and scholars, learned in the laws and history of the country, as well as *Dubhthach*. We have also seen that *Laeghairé* had his Druids, who contended with Saint Patrick; and it [illegible] pears that he had entrusted the education of his two daughters to the druids *Mael* and *Coplait*, even at such a distance from [illegible] court at Tara as his Palace of *Cruachain*, (in the present county of Roscommon). From all our ancient records we have al[illegible]

The Druids in the time of *Laeghairé*, (A.D. 430.)

dant reason to believe that these as well as all the other druids, with whom the country abounded at this time, were men learned in the literature and poetry of the country as well as in druidism; and we have reason to believe that their druidic system was a more refined and a more philosophic one than that of their neighbours the Britons and Gauls. So, as these men as well as the poets were all active teachers to all comers, it is not to be wondered at that Saint Patrick found before him on his arrival many men among the people of Erinn of cultivated mind, sharpened by study, capable of appreciating new ideas, and thus quick to recognize the sublime truths of Divine revelation in preference to the unsatisfactory mysteries and secret ceremonies of their ancient mythology, however venerable it had become in their eyes.

[illegible] My object in dwelling so long on the learning and cultivation of the period of our history before the coming of Saint Patrick is, to show upon authority that we were, even at that [illegible] period, a nation not entirely without a native literature [illegible] a national cultivation, sufficient to sustain a system of so[illegible] and an internal political government so enlightened that, [illegible] history proves, Christianity did not seek to subvert but [illegible] endeavoured to unite with it; a system, moreover, which [illegible] sufficient vitality to remain in full force through all the vi[illegible] of the country, even till many ages after the intrusion [illegible] Anglo-Normans, in the twelfth century,—who themselves [illegible] found it so just and comprehensive that they adopted it [illegible] to the laws of the countries from which they came.

Cultivation of the Gaedhelic language in the early ages of the Church in Erinn.

[illegible] said so much on this important subject, let me now, [illegible] much brevity as possible, adduce some proofs that [illegible] Erinn adopted a new creed, whose preachers intro[illegible] literature new perhaps, as well as splendid, and one [illegible] cultivated with a fervour not often exceeded, still [illegible] ancient language was not abandoned or neglected but [illegible] cherished and cultivated with more ardour, if [illegible] ever. For it is certain that the ancient language [illegible] continued to be taught in all the schools and col[illegible] lay and ecclesiastical; and that there never was a [illegible] educated in Erinn, from Saint Patrick's time [illegible] year 1600, who had not deeply studied the [illegible] literature and history, as part of his college course. [illegible] that so many of the most learned and wise eccle[illegible] have adorned the Catholic Church of Erinn, and [illegible] seminaries, have left us more memorials of their [illegible] in their native language, than even in the [illegible] though the Latin tongue had in other countries

LECT. IV. so generally usurped the literature of the Christian world for many ages, and though our native clergy were educated in that language also, as many historical facts might be quoted to prove.

The introduction of Christianity, and with it of the classical languages, did not supersede the cultivation of the Gaedhelic then, but on the contrary it appears to have encouraged and promoted it. And this can be very clearly proved by the fact that several if not all our most eminent classical writers and divines were also the greatest Gaedhelic scholars of whom we have any reliable account. From the long array of [illegible] names among these venerable men I shall mention a few, of whose writings some pieces more or less numerous still remain.

Early Gaedhelic writers, after the introduction of Christianity.

The first distinguished writer in the native tongue,—after the three poets and scholars, *Dubhthach*, *Ros*, and *Fergus*, who were engaged on the *Seanchas Mór*,—was *Fiacc*, Bishop of *Sleibhté* (in the Queen's County), the first Bishop of Leinster. Saint Patrick, we are told, having made a journey from Tara into South Leinster, converted the people of that country, namely, the *Ui Ceinnselaigh*. Here he paid a visit to his distinguished convert *Dubhthach*, whom he requested to recommend to him, from among his pupils, a proper person to appoint as bishop over the newly-converted people; a man (he required him to be) without blemish of person, or stain of character, of easy circumstances, who had been the husband of but one wife, and to whom was born but one child. *Dubhthach* answered that he knew but one person who fully satisfied this description, namely, *Fiacc*, the son of *Erc*, who had shortly before gone into Connacht, with a poem to the kings of that province. "But", said Saint Patrick, as we are told, "even if he were here, would he consent?" And just then they perceived *Fiacc* coming towards them, on his return. Upon which *Dubhthach* said to the saint, "Pretend to cut off my hair". This the saint was preparing to do, just as *Fiacc* came up, and he said: "Why do you tonsure *Dubhthach*? thousands would feel his loss; why not take me?" Accordingly, Saint Patrick gave baptism and the tonsure to *Fiacc*; and so considerable was the young man's previous learning, that he is said (in the Tripartite Life of the saint) to have learned to read the Psalms (in Latin of course) in fifteen days, no inconsiderable feat of application.

Fiacc's Metrical Life of St. Patrick.

Of the writings of Bishop *Fiacc* nothing is known, to me at least, to be now extant, but his metrical Life of Saint Patrick. This poem, which consists of thirty-four stanzas, or one hundred and thirty-six lines, is written in the most ancient style and idiom of the Gaedhelic, and in the ancient rhythm and measure called *Cetal Noith*, or the "illustrious narrative measure"; a

LECT. IV. [Fiacc's Metrical Life of St. Patrick.]

[illegible] I may remark, with which the Irish grammarians of the [illegible] day seem to be totally unacquainted.

[illegible] narrative is, of course, short and simple. It recounts [illegible] saint's baptismal name,—the names and rank of his father [illegible] grandfather,—his captivity in Erinn,—his passing over the [illegible] into Italy, for his education,—his return again to Erinn, [illegible] of *Laeghaire MacNeill*, to convert the descendants [illegible] and Eremon,—how King *Laeghaire's* Druids foretold [illegible], and the destruction by him of the pagan system,— [illegible] of *Dun-da-leathghlas* (now Downpatrick) and of [illegible]—his last illness,—his receiving the communion from [illegible] of Bishop *Tassach*,—the wonders that happened at [illegible] his death,—and of his spirit passing "into the lov[illegible] of the Son of Mary".

[illegible] of learned discussion has been expended on a minor [illegible] important point connected with this poem,—namely, [illegible] France was not the country of Saint Patrick's birth,— [illegible] late Dr. Lanigan, in his Irish Ecclesiastical History. [illegible], too, has been expended upon it by those who [illegible] followed his authority, but pretend to make the [illegible] stronger, for the purpose of carrying themselves [illegible] to new discoveries and to an ultimate dogmatic decision [illegible] secondary point. Now it is somewhat remarkable, that [illegible] who have pedantically crowded together heaps of irre[illegible] and French authorities on this secondary point, [illegible] of asking themselves, or that other people might [illegible] a simple question as to what were the authorities to [illegible] the poem was authentic at all; and yet this is a very [illegible] question, and has moreover been put by Dr. Petrie, [illegible] on Tara; but it is one which our modern anti[illegible] far too patriotic or too confident to pretend to [illegible] however, a question that has occupied a great deal [illegible] of such mere Irishmen as myself for many years, [illegible] result quite favourable to the character of this vene[illegible] and its no less venerable ancient annotators, who [illegible] unjustly criticized by Dr. Lanigan and his fol[illegible] none of them could read or understand either [illegible] the annotations upon it.

[illegible] however, precluded from entering further here into the [illegible] of this curious poem, by the circumstance [illegible] Hymnorum,—a manuscript more than a thou[illegible], and which contains the oldest and most accurate [illegible] poem now known to be extant,—is at present in [illegible] publication by the Irish Archæological and Celtic [illegible] I cannot here anticipate the conclusions which will

LECT. IV.

there, I hope, be satisfactorily elucidated. The second part of the Book of Hymns is already at press; and when it appears every student will be able to satisfy himself at full length upon the interesting subjects to which I have alluded.

The Ecclesiastical Schools of the early Christian period not exclusively Ecclesiastical.

After the introduction of Christianity into Erinn, the enthusiasm which marked its reception by the people, and more particularly by the more learned and better educated among them, gave to almost all the great schools a certain ecclesiastical character. The schools of the early saints were, however, by no means exclusively of this kind; but as the most learned men were precisely those who most actively applied themselves to the work of the Gospel, and as it had always been the habit of students to surround the dwelling of the most learned, to dwell near the chosen master, and thus (somewhat as in ancient Greece) to make for themselves a true Academy wherever a great master was to be found, so did the laity also as well as those intended for the sacred ministry gather in great numbers round the early saints, who were also the great teachers of history and general learning. And so, while from such academies naturally sprung hundreds of priests, saints, and religious, there also were the great bulk of the more comfortable portion of the lay population constantly educated. Every part of educated Europe has heard of the great University of *Ardmacha*, where so much as a third of the city was appropriated even to the exclusive use of foreign, but particularly of Saxon and British, students, so great was the concourse to its schools from all the neighbouring nations. Who has not read of the great schools, with their hundreds and their thousands of scholars, of *Beannchoir* [Bangor, county Down], under Saint *Comgall* and his successors; of *Clonard*, under Saint *Finen;* of *Lothra*, under Saint *Ruadan;* of *Glas-Naoidhen* [Glasnevin, near Dublin], under Saint *Mobhi;* of *Clonmacnois*, under Saint *Ciaran;* of *Tallaght*, under Saint *Maelruain*, and the learned *Aengus Ceilé Dé;* of *Birra* [Birr] and *Cluainferta* [Clonfert], under Saint *Brendan;* of Roscrea, under Saint *Cronan;* of *Iniscelltra*, under Saint *Caimin;* of Killaloe, under Saint *Flannan;* of *Mungaret* [Mungret, near Limerick], under the holy Deacon *Nessan;* of *Emiligh* [Emly], under Saint *Ailbhi*, where the students were so numerous in the reign of *Cathal MacFinguiné* (about the year 740) that they were forced to live in huts in the neighbouring fields; of Saint *Finnbarr's*, in Cork; of the great lay school of *Colman O'Cluasaigh*, in the same place; of the great school of *Cluain Uamha* [Cloyne], under Saint *Colman MacLenin*, the converted poet; of *Ross Ailithri*, in the same county, under Saint *Fachtna;*—(I possess, myself, a copy of a most curious poem on universal

LECT. IV.

[illegible]graphy written and of course taught in this great school by [illegible], one of its professors, about the year 900);—of *Glenn-*[illegible] under Saint *Caoimhin* [or Kevin]; of *Tuam*, under [illegible] *Iarlaithe*; of Swords, under the successors of Saint *Colum* [illegible] of Monasterboice, under the successors of Saint *Buitè;* of [illegible] *Brecain*, under Saint *Brecin;* of Louth, under Saint [illegible] and of Kildare, under Saint *Brigid*, where Saint *Finnen* [illegible] preached before the foundation of Clonard by him.

Secular National Schools, in the early Christian era, in Erinn.

[illegible], however, these establishments, chiefly though not [illegible] ecclesiastical, were under the vigilant supervision of [illegible] of the Church, there were also at the same time a [illegible] of great secular schools, from the time of the great [illegible] of *Drom Ceata* down to the sixteenth century, and [illegible] continued under the inspection of the most distinguished [illegible] in the country. The office of teacher in these truly [illegible] Schools was ably discharged in the latter times by [illegible] members of the families of O'Mulchonry, O'Higgin, [illegible], etc.

The Feis of Drom Ceata, A.D. 590.

[illegible] meeting at *Drom Ceata* was the last great occasion on [illegible] the laws and general system of education were revised. [illegible] place in the year 590, in the reign of that *Aedh* the son [illegible], whose resistance to the impudent demands of the [illegible] of poets, I had occasion to refer to in the last Lecture. [illegible] after the refusal of the king to submit to the threats [illegible] on the part of the poets, and the consequences then [illegible] to follow from poetical incantations, he happened to [illegible] in two important political disputes. One of these [illegible] the case of *Scanlan Mór*, King of Ossory, who had [illegible] made a prisoner by the monarch some time before, [illegible] in long and cruel confinement; the other concerning [illegible] to the tributes and military service of the Dalriadian [illegible] colony of Scotland, to which King *Aedh* laid a [illegible] was resisted by *Aedan MacGabhrain*, the king of that [illegible]. For the more ample discussion of these weighty mat[illegible] convened a meeting of the states of the nation at [illegible] (a spot now called Daisy Hill, near Newtown[illegible] in the modern county of Derry); which meeting [illegible] according to O'Donovan's *Annals of the Four Mas*[illegible] year 574.

[illegible] meeting was attended by all the provincial kings, [illegible] chiefs and nobles of the island: and *Aedh* invited [illegible] the great patron of his race, Saint *Colum Cillé*, [illegible] benefit of his wise counsels in the discussion, not [illegible] the special subjects for which the meeting was [illegible], but many others of social and political import-

LECT. IV.

ance. And so it happened that at this meeting the [illegible] the poets and the profession of teaching were also [illegible]

Revision of the National System of Education at *Drom Ceata.*

It was solemnly resolved at this meeting that the [illegible] system of education should be revised, and placed upon [illegible] solid and orderly foundation; and to this end the [illegible] scheme (according to Keting) was proposed and [illegible] special *Ollamh*, or Doctor in Literature, was assigned [illegible] Monarch, as well as to each of the provincial kings, [illegible] lords of territories; and to each *Ollamh* were [illegible] lands, from his chief, and a grant of inviolability to [illegible] and sanctuary to his lands, from the monarch and men of [illegible] at large. They ordered also free common-lands, or endow[illegible] to the *Ollamhs*, for the purposes of free education, in the [illegible] of a University,—(such as *Masraighé* in *Breifné*, or [illegible] *Rath-Ceannaidh*, in Meath, etc.),—in which education [illegible] tuitously given to such of the men of Erinn as [illegible] become learned in history or in such of the sciences [illegible] then cultivated in the land.

Of the Chief Poet *Dallan Forgaill*, (sixth century).

The chief *Ollamh* of Erinn at this time was *[illegible]* [illegible] Poet Royal, who wrote the celebrated Elegy on the [illegible] Saint *Colum Cillé*, and who is better known under the [illegible] *Dallan Forgaill;* and to him the inauguration and [illegible] the new colleges were assigned. *Eochaidh* appointed [illegible] to the different provinces. To Meath he appointed *[illegible]* [illegible] Hugh), the poet; to Munster he appointed *Urmael*, the [illegible] poet and scholar; to Connacht he appointed *[illegible]* *[illegible] Cuairfertaigh;* to Ulster he appointed *Ferfirb MacM[illegible]* and so on.

It will have been observed that the endowed [illegible] establishments placed under these masters were in fact [illegible] Literary Colleges, quite distinct from the great literary [illegible] Ecclesiastical schools and colleges which about this time, [illegible] ing themselves round individual celebrity, began to cover the land, and whose hospitable halls were often (as we [illegible] crowded with the sons of princes and nobles, and with [illegible] and pupils from all parts of Europe, coming over to [illegible] ledge in a country then believed to be the most advanced in [illegible] civilization of the age.

Laws concerning the profession of Teaching.

That secular education was constantly recognized as a [illegible] the institutions of the country, and that it was sustained and pro[illegible] tected by the laws of the land for centuries after as well as [illegible] the meeting of *Drom Ceata*, could be easily shown from the [illegible] Laws,—revised, it is to be remembered, with the [illegible] Christianity, and constantly in force during the early ages of [illegible] Church; for instance, in the following short but important pas-

LECT. IV.

[illegible] (MS. H. 3. 18, T.C.D., 438 a.), which I quote here because [illegible] the legal existence of a profession of teaching, and the [illegible] provision for the remuneration and privileges of the teacher: [illegible] poet (or tutor) commands his pupils. The man from [illegible] education is received is free from the crimes of his pupils, [illegible] be the children of natives [*i.e.*, of the district], even [illegible] he feeds and clothes them, and that they pay him for [illegible] learning. He is free, even though it be a stranger he [illegible], feeds, and clothes, provided it is not for pay but for [illegible] he does it. If he feeds and instructs a stranger for [illegible] then he is accountable for his crimes".

Nature of Lay Instruction in the Schools of the early Christian period.

[illegible] appears, also, from the Brehon Laws, that the pupils were [illegible] the foster-children of the tutor. The sons of gentlemen [illegible] taught not only Literature, but Horsemanship, Chess, [illegible], and the use of Arms, chiefly casting the spear. [illegible] daughters were taught Sewing, Cutting or fashioning, and [illegible], or Embroidery. The sons of the tenant-class [illegible] taught horsemanship, nor did they wear the same [illegible] the classes above them.

"Sizarships", and "Poor Scholars".

[illegible] has, in the law, distinct reference to Public Schools, [illegible] the sons of the lower classes waited on the sons of the [illegible], and received certain benefits (in food, clothes, [illegible]) from them in return. In fact the "sizarships" [illegible] modern colleges appear to be a modified continuation of [illegible] system.

Saint *Adamnan* and King *Finnachta* "The Festive".

[illegible] is a very curious illustration of this custom in a short [illegible] the reign of *Finnachta* "the Festive", Monarch of [illegible] from A.D. 673 to 693. The story is preserved in an an-[illegible] Irish manuscript, lately in the possession of Mr. [illegible] Monck Mason, in England; of which a duplicate version [illegible] preserved in Duald MacFirbiss's Annals, in the Bur-[illegible] Library at Brussels.

[illegible] Finnachta had come to the throne, he received an invi-[illegible] his sister to visit her. He set out with a cavalcade; [illegible] were riding in the direction of Clonard (I should [illegible] Meath, they came up to a young student who was [illegible] the road, with a small cask or churn on his back. [illegible], on hearing the tramp of the horses, made a hurried [illegible] off the road, but having struck his foot against [illegible] fell, breaking the cask to pieces, and spilling the [illegible] which it was filled. The cavalcade passed on at [illegible], and the student recovering himself, set out along [illegible] and notwithstanding their speed and his own grief, [illegible] with them, with a fragment of the cask at his back; [illegible] he attracted the notice of the king, who smiled

LECT. IV. [Story of St. Adamnan and King Finnachta.]

when he saw the excitement under which he laboured ... the king accosted him (continues the story), and ... will make thee happy again, for we have sympathy ... unfortunate and the powerless; thou shalt receive, O ... said he, "satisfaction from me". And he continued to ... the student in this way. The youth (who was afterwards ... less a person than the great scholar and divine Saint Ad... the founder of the ancient church of *Rath-Botha*, or R... in Donegal, and afterwards Abbot of Iona), then spoke ... the king, whom he did not know at the time: "O good ... said he, "I have cause to be grieved, for there are three ... students in one house, and there are three lads of us that ... upon them, and what we do is, one of us three goes round ... neighbourhood to collect support for the other five, and ... my turn to do so this day; but what I had obtained for them ... been lost, and, what is more unfortunate, the borrowed ... has been broken, while I have not the means of paying ... *Finnachta* kept his word with *Adamnan*, and it appears ... over that he kept his eye upon him afterwards; for after ... conclusion of his studies and receiving holy orders, the king ... seeing his wisdom and sanctity, took him to his court ... appointed him to be his chief counsellor and director.

Here, then, we have a curious and a clear instance of ... remote antiquity of the "poor scholar" system in Ireland. H... were six youths who came for their education to this fam... school of Clonard [a school founded by Saint *Finnen*, who d... A.D. 548], from some distant country or province, and wh... whether they paid for their education or not were supported ... the bounty of the generous residents of the district. If they had not been, as well as many others, all strangers, like *Adamnan* (who came from Donegal), they would according to the system in force at this time have been either pensioners living ... at the college, or else they would be residing with their parents or friends in the town or surrounding district.

The house mentioned by *Adamnan*, in which they resided could scarcely be the dwelling of any of the resident famil... as it would be too much to suppose that any family could accommodate six or perhaps more such strangers at a time. However, whether such were the case or not, in the present instance we have abundant authority elsewhere to show that at and before and after the time of *Adamnan* (who died in the year 702), such in fact were the crowds of stranger students that flocked to some of our great schools of lay and ecclesiastical learning, that they were generally obliged to erect a village or villages of huts as near to the school as they conveniently [illegible] said, as in *Adamnan's* case, to find subsistence in the [illegible] of the surrounding residents.

Early education of St. Colum Cillé.

[illegible] custom we find an interesting example also in an early [illegible] of Saint *Colum Cillé*, in an ancient Irish Life of that [illegible] which it appears that after having finished his prepara[illegible] of education, under a local master in Donegal, he went [illegible] Saint *Finnen*, to Clonard, to enter upon his divinity [illegible] while that college was yet in its infancy. On his arrival, [illegible] that the young student asked Saint *Finnen* where [illegible] erect his hut. "At the door of the church", said Saint [illegible] whereupon *Colum Cillé* went to a considerable distance [illegible] the door, and fixed on a spot there. "You have not fol[illegible] directions", said Saint *Finnen*; "that spot is not at the [illegible] "True", said *Colum Cillé*, "it is not, but the door will [illegible] place hereafter". And so it came to pass, says this old [illegible] for the school which at first was kept in the small [illegible] in a short time after, from the literary fame and the sanc[illegible] founder, became so crowded as to include sometimes [illegible] thousand youths and adults, so as at last to require the [illegible] of the establishment to the very spot at which *Colum* [illegible] set up his hut, as he had thus prophetically foretold.

[illegible] we find in the same Irish life, that *Colum Cillé* after [illegible] left Clonard, and came to the select school of Saint [illegible] *Glas Naoidhen*, (now the little town of Glasnevin, on the [illegible] of the river *Tulchlaen*, or Tolka, near Dublin). The [illegible] of divinity students at this school, at the time, was fifty; [illegible] were *Cainnech* (or Canice), the founder of *Achadh* [illegible] Kilkenny; *Comgall*, the founder of *Bennchuir* (Ban[illegible]); *Ciaran*, the founder of Clonmacnois, etc.

[illegible] story is recorded in this ancient Life. The huts of [illegible] stated to have been situated on the west side of [illegible] On a certain night, we are told, the church bell was [illegible] There was a smart frost, and the river was [illegible] but *Colum Cillé* passed with his clothes through it; [illegible] continues our authority: "Bravely hast thou acted, O [illegible] *Niall*", said Saint *Mobi*. "God is competent", said [illegible] relieve us of this difficulty". And so, as we are told, [illegible] upon the return of the students from the church [illegible] the huts planted upon the east bank of the river, [illegible] the church.

Students' hut encampments.

[illegible] students' hut encampments were not confined to [illegible] province or locality, may be seen from the fol[illegible] found in a very ancient tract in the *Leabhar Mór* [illegible] (commonly known as the *Leabhar Breac*), in [illegible] Irish Academy. *Cathal* the son of *Finguiné*, was

LECT. IV.

King of Munster from the year 717 to the year 73 died. This prince was afflicted with the disease of unappeasable appetite, which he is stated to have got ing some apples into which certain "druidical charms" conveyed by an Ulster scholar. And we are told that the violence of his voracity, that the king, who sometim at *Imluich Iobhair*, [the ancient ecclesiastical city of Tipperary], was accustomed frequently to wrap himself mon gray cloak, and rush through "the huts of the stu the story calls them), with his drawn sword in his left to sweep away the cakes and fragments of bread from th

Foreign Students at Armagh. Bede's allusion to Saxon and British students in Erinn.

I have already alluded to the appropriation of one of the great seat of education at Armagh to foreign student cially those from the neighbouring Saxon nation. I haps, here quote what Bede (himself a British priest) cerning this period. (His death is recorded on the 26th A.D. 736):

"In the year of our Lord's incarnation, 664", he says, happened an eclipse of the sun, on the 3rd of May, a o'clock in the morning. In the same year a sudden (called the "Yellow Plague") also depopulated the south of Britain, and afterwards extending into the provinc Northumbrians, ravaged the country far and near, and a great multitude of men. To which plague the afore Tuda fell a victim, and was honourably buried in the of Pegnaleth. This pestilence did no less harm in the Ireland. Many of the nobility and of the lower rank English nation were there at that time, who in the Bishops *Finan* and *Colman* forsaking their native isla thither, either for the sake of divine studies, or of a tinent life; and some of them presently devoted them the monastical life; others chose rather to apply the study, going about from one master's cell to another. The [that is, the Irish, then so called] willingly received and took care to supply them with food, as also to them with books to read, and their teaching gratis. these were Ethelhun and Egbert, two youths of great of the English nobility; the former of whom was b Ethelwin, a man no less beloved by God, who also went into Ireland to study, and having been well returned into his own country, and being made bishop province of Lindsey, long governed that church worthily, creditably".(34)

(34) See Bede's *Ecclesiastical History*, chap. xxii.; (Bohn's edition, edited Mr. Giles; p. 162).

LECT. IV.

[illegible] enough that even this very matter of fact tribute [illegible] paid by the venerable Bede to our nation was deemed [illegible] English editor of Bede, (Mr. J. A. Giles, D.C.L.), [illegible]able an evidence of our early civilization, without some [illegible] comment. "The reader", says Mr. Giles, in a note, [illegible] heard much of the early civilization of Ireland will [illegible] that the description given in the text applies to a [illegible] earlier than the seventh century". As the vindication [illegible] ancient civilization of Ireland has not, however, much [illegible] the remarks of this gentleman, I only allude to his [illegible] here with a view to put students on their guard [illegible] expressions in English works, in which the [illegible] Irish history or antiquities may be alluded to. The [illegible] that modern writers, not only in England but in Ireland, [illegible] ignorant of our early history; and if ignorance or pre[illegible] prompts them to a sneer, let us Irishmen, on our [illegible] it by making ourselves better acquainted with that [illegible] which our critics are unwise enough to speak thus [illegible] the dark.

Secular education in ancient Erinn.

[illegible] may imagine from much that has been said of our great [illegible] establishments in early times, that their course of [illegible] was merely classical, ecclesiastical, and biblical or [illegible] and that no secular sources of education then [illegible] the country. That such, however, was not the case, [illegible] ample evidence in our old writings. The Annals of [illegible], at the year 645, record the death of *Ragh*[illegible] wicked", King of Connacht, who was ignominiously [illegible] man named *Maelbrighdé*, and a party of labourers, [illegible] about a stag which the king had pierced with a [illegible], having run in amongst them, they killed and [illegible] themselves, refusing to restore the prey at the [illegible]. I have in my possession a copy of a very [illegible] important elegiac poem written on this king by [illegible] king's poet, at the royal palace of *Cruachain*. [illegible] the more important events of the king's [illegible] among the many other valuable facts and allusions [illegible] we find that *Cathal*, who was the king's second [illegible] time pursuing his studies at the great school of [illegible] when he had heard of his father's death, he set [illegible] at the head of seven-and-twenty students of [illegible] and came directly to the house of the regicide [illegible] son of *Mothlachar;* and attacking him with [illegible] accomplices, he cut off his head and carried it, on [illegible] holly stake, to the palace of *Cruachan*, where he

Of *Flann-tain*, the poet of King *Ragallach*, (A.D. 645).

Education of *Cathal*, son of King *Ragallach*.

LECT. IV.

suddenly appeared with his trophy before his [illegible] midst of the astonished court. In this anecdote we [illegible] distinct instance of the use made even of the [illegible] by the young nobles of the laity.

Qualifications of a Fer-Leighinn, or Chief Master in a Public School.

It is to be remembered that the chief [illegible] every one of the divinity colleges was fully [illegible] native as well as in the classical and foreign [illegible] be a *Fer-Leighinn*, *Drumchli*, or Chief Master [illegible] great school, the candidate was obliged by law to [illegible] the whole course of Gaedhelic literature, in prose [illegible] (besides that of the Scriptures, "from the Ten Com[illegible] up to the whole Bible"), as well as the learned [illegible] already said. The legal arrangement of these [illegible] schools was as follows:

Of the Professors, or Teachers, in a public School, or lay College.

The College Professors, (according to law), includ[illegible]

1. The *Caogdach*, or "fifty-man"; who was the [illegible] ing only to chant the 150 Psalms.

2. The *Foghlantidh*, or scholar; who taught [illegible] twelve books of the college course of the *Fochoiré*, [illegible] education.

3. The *Staraidh*, or historian; who had also besides [illegible] thirty lessons of divinity in his course.

4. The *Foircetlaidh*, or lecturer; who professed [illegible] thography, criticism, enumeration, the courses of the [illegible] the courses of the sun and moon, (i. e. astronomy).

5. The *Saoi Canoiné*, or professor of divinity; who [illegible] "the Canons and the Gospel of Jesus, that is, the Word [illegible] in the sacred place in which it is; that is, who taug[illegible] Catholic Canonical Wisdom".

6. The *Drumchli*, or chief head; a master who kne[illegible] whole course of learning, "from the greatest book, which [illegible] *Cuilmen*, down to the smallest book, called the Ten Com[illegible] ments, in which is properly arranged the good Testament [illegible] God prepared for Moses".

As a further proof that the native language and [illegible] made no inconsiderable part of the divinity student's [illegible] course of education, there is scarcely one of our most [illegible] Irish ecclesiastics, from Saint Patrick in the fifth century do[illegible] to the eighteenth, that was not distinguished for his knowledge of the Gaedhelic language and history.

I shall content myself by enumerating a short list of the names of those among these early ecclesiastics whose verses are quoted in the notes and commentaries on a single work, the Festology of *Aengus Ceilé Dé*, (or "the Culdee"), in the *Leabhar Mór Duna Doighré*, (or *Leabhar Breac*).

Saint Patrick himself in the fifth century; Saint *Ciaran* of [illegible] of the same period;—Saint *Comgall* of *Bennchuir*; [illegible] *Colum Cillé*; Saint *Ité* the virgin, (of *Cill Ité*, in the [illegible] of Limerick); Saint *Caeimhghin* of *Glenn-da-locha*; [illegible] *Ciaran* of *Cluainmacnois*; Saint *Molaisé* of *Daimhinis*, in [illegible]; all of the sixth century:—Saint *Mochuda* of *Lis*-[illegible]; Saint *Moling* of Saint Mullins, in Carlow; Saint *Fechin* [illegible] (now Fore, in Westmeath); Saint *Aireran* "the [illegible] of Clonard; all of the seventh century:—Saint *Maelruan* [illegible] (or Tallaght); Saint *Adamnan* of *Rath Boith* [illegible] and *I Colum Cillé*, (Iona); and Saint *Aengus* "the [illegible] himself, of the eighth century.

List of early ecclesiastics distinguished as literary men, (from Aengus Ceilé Dé).

[illegible] to be recollected that these are but names found among [illegible] quoted in the notes and commentaries on Aengus's work, [illegible] was written in the year 798. But if I were to swell the list [illegible] other available sources, it would occupy the greater part if [illegible] whole of the space allotted for this Lecture. Now these [illegible] were all Irish scholars and literary teachers, as well as [illegible] divines; and we may be certain that that which they [illegible] taught themselves, and the language in which they con-[illegible] to write during their lives, they taught to their pupils [illegible] in like manner.

[illegible] the Poet *Fionntain*, we shall pass now to the celebrated [illegible] *Torpeist*, who flourished nearly at the same time, that [illegible] the year 600. *Seanchan* was by birth a native of Con-[illegible] by election chief poet of Erinn. He was the pupil of [illegible] *Righ Eigeas* (that is, *Eochaidh* "the king of the poets"), [illegible] known as *Dallan Forgaill*, author of the cele-[illegible] on the death of Saint *Colum Cillé*. On the death [illegible] the chief provincial poets of Erinn held a meeting [illegible] in *Breifné* (Breifney), for the purpose of elect-[illegible] to him; and their unanimous choice fell upon [illegible] who, after his inauguration, was requested by them [illegible] an elegy over the body of their late lamented chief. [illegible] *Seanchan* assented; and the following is a [illegible] of the short poem, as I have found it:

Of the Poet Seanchan Torpéist, (circa A.D. 600).

[illegible] the body that has fallen here!
[illegible] a weighty man, he was a light man,
[illegible] in body, weighty in followers:
[illegible] were the schools of which he was the master
[illegible] of us were his constant pupils,
[illegible] youths perfecting our knowledge.
[illegible] even though we had been more in number,
[illegible] learning he had to give us each day.

LECT. IV.

"The ocean's caverns, which armies dare not,—
The mighty cataract of the great *Eas Ruadh*,—
The rolling wave of a spring-tide's flow,—
Were the meet images of *Dallan*'s intellect.

"Until the shining sun is surmounted,
Which God has created above all creation,
No poet from north to south shall surpass
Eochaidh, the serene royal poet.

"He was sage, O God of Heaven!
He was a noble and a chief poet;
Until the wave of death swept placidly over him,
Uch! he was beautiful, he was beloved".

The only historical piece of *Seanchan*'s composition t[hat I] am acquainted with, is a poem of seven stanzas, or twenty-[eight] lines, which gives an account of the battles fought and wo[n by] the Monarch *Rudhraidhé*, who reigned over Erinn from [the] year of the world 4912 to the year of the world 4981, in w[hich] he died, according to the Annals of the Four Masters. [This] poem was evidently written for the descendants of *Fergus*, [the] grandson of *Rudhraidhé*, who is mentioned in the first lin[e of] it, and who, in *Seanchan*'s time, had become possessed of l[arge] territories in Connacht and Munster, where they are now re[pre]sented by the families of O'Ferrall and MacRannall (or R[ey]nolds), in Longford and Leitrim; by the O'Conors in Ke[rry]; and by the O'Conors, the O'Loughlins, and the *O'Grioh*[*tha*] (or Griffins), of Clare; the last-named clan rendered illust[rious] in our day by the name of the late distinguished writer Ge[rald] Griffin.

The copy of this poem to which I refer is that preserve[d in] the Book of Leinster, beginning:

"*Fergus* fought twenty battles;—
It is to be remembered".[85]

Edward O'Reilly, in his Irish Writers, at the year 647, [says] that this poem gives an account of the battles of *Fergus* [mac] *Rossa*, grandson of Roderick the monarch; but this is an e[rror], as the only mention of *Fergus*, in this poem, is what appear[s in] the above lines, whereas his grandfather's battles are given, [with] the names of the places in which they were fought.

The *Seanchan* to whose poems I refer here was the sam[e of] whom is related the recovery of the celebrated tale of the T[ain] *Bó Chuailgné*, of which I gave an account on a former occas[ion]. There is, however, another version of that account too inter[est]ing to be passed over in connection with him.

(85) original:—Ro ḟiċ Fergus fiċit caṫa,—
ba cuimnigi.

Story of *Seanchan* and King *Guairé* "the hospitable".

In the very curious tale to which I now allude we are told that after *Seanchan's* election to the rank of chief *Ollamh* of Erinn, and the formation on the usual scale of his household, his retinue, and his band of pupils, he consulted with them as to what king they should honour with their first or inaugural visit, according to ancient custom; and they agreed to pay their visit to *Guairé* surnamed "the hospitable", King of Connacht, who held his court alternately at *Gort Insi Guairé* (now Gort, in the county of Galway), and *Durlas Muaidhé* or *Durlas Guairé*, on the banks of the river *Muaidhé*, (now the Moy, in the county of Sligo). *Seanchan*, however, took with him but two-thirds of his establishment, consisting, indeed, of one hundred and fifty [illegible] poets, and one hundred and fifty pupils, with a corresponding number of women, servants, dogs, etc. He and his company were joyfully received by King *Guairé*, and hospitably entertained (according to the story) for a year, a quarter, and a month.[60]

[illegible] *Seanchan's* followers became so troublesome at the [illegible] of King *Guairé*, that the king's brother, the saintly *Mar*-

---

[illegible] in the introduction to this story of *Seanchan*, that the very odd anecdote [illegible] illustrative of the bardic legend of the poet's power to rhyme to death [illegible] and the lower animals, alluded to in a curious paper read by [illegible] Dr. Todd before the Royal Irish Academy in 1853 (Jan. 23rd). The [illegible] substantially as follows:

[illegible] that during the poet's sojourn at Gort (says the story), his wife, [illegible] one occasion sent him from her own table a portion of a certain [illegible] dish. *Seanchan* was not in his apartment when the servant arrived [illegible] the dish was left there, and the servant returned to her mistress. [illegible] he found a dish from his wife's table on his own; and, eagerly [illegible] it, he was sadly disappointed at finding that it contained nothing [illegible] fragments of gnawed bones. Shortly after the same servant returned [illegible] and *Seanchan* asked what the contents had been. The maid [illegible] it to him, and the poet eyed her with an angry look of suspicion. [illegible] protested her own innocence, and assured him that as no person [illegible] entered the apartment from the time that she left until he returned [illegible] must have been emptied by rats. The poet believed the girl's [illegible] vowed that he would make the rats pay for their depredations, [illegible] composed a metrical satire upon them. Of this we have but two [illegible] stanzas, of which the following is a literal translation:

"Rats, though sharp their snouts,
Are not powerful in battles;
I will bring death on the party [of them]
For having eaten *Brigid's* present.
"Small was the present she made us,
Its loss to her was not great;
Let her have payment from us in a poem,
Let her not refuse the poet's gratitude!
"You rats which are in the roof of the house
Arise, all of you, and fall down".

* * * * *

[illegible] (we are told) ten rats fell dead on the floor from the roof of [illegible] *Seanchan's* presence. And *Seanchan* said to them: It was not

LECT. IV. *bhan*, a holy hermit, laid an obligation on them to depart, and engaged them to devote themselves to the discovery of the ancient tale of the *Tain Bo Chuailgné*, which had been long previously carried "eastward over the sea", as has been stated in a former Lecture. *Seanchan* was much grieved that the unreasonable conduct of some of his party should force him to leave *Durlas* under such unsatisfactory circumstances; however, go they should; and upon his departure the arch-poet presented the following short farewell poem to King *Guairé*:

"We depart from thee, O stainless *Guairé*!
We leave with thee our blessing;
A year, a quarter, and a month,
Have we sojourned with thee, O high-king!
"Three times fifty poets,—good and smooth,—
Three times fifty students in the poetic art,
Each with his servant and dog;
They were all fed in the one great house.
"Each man had his separate meal;
Each man had his separate bed;
We never arose at early morning,
Without contentions without calming.
"I declare to thee, O God!
Who canst the promise verify,
That should we return to our own land,
We shall visit thee again, O *Guairé*, though now we
depart".

Account of the recovery by *Seanchan* of the Tale of the *Tain Bo Chuailgné*. *Seanchan* then set out with his company in search of the tale of the *Tain Bo Chuailgné*, which they thought might be preserved in Scotland; but after visiting that country, and afterwards the Isle of Man, without success, he returned again to Erinn, and repaired to Saint *Caillin* of Fenach, of *Magh Rein*, (in the county of Leitrim), who was the poet's brother on the mother's side, and to whom he complained of his difficulty. Saint *Caillin* and *Seanchan* then proceeded to *Guairé's* palace at *Durlas*, where they were well received; and the king having invited his brother, the holy hermit *Marbhan*, from his hermitage in *Glenn-an-Scail*, they held a consultation as to the most promising steps to be taken for the recovery of the lost tale of the *Tain Bó Chuailgné*.

you that should have been satirized, but the race of cats, and I will satirize them. And *Seanchan* then pronounced a satire, but not a deadly one, on the chief of the cats of Erinn, who kept his residence in the cave of Knowth, near Slane, in the county of Meath, etc.

This ancient tale appears to have been the origin of the well-known practice of "rhyming rats to death", in Ireland, to which reference is so often made in the works of Shakespeare and other eminent writers of his day.

The wise *Marbhan* gave it as his opinion that the tale in its entirety could at this time be received only from the lips of *Fergus MacRoigh*, who had been himself a chief actor in the great spoil of *Cuailgné*, and who, there was reason to believe, wrote the narrative of the expedition; and *Marbhan* proposed that they should call together the chief and most holy saints of Erinn, to fast, and pray to God that He would raise *Fergus* from the grave, to reveal to them this important ancient tale.

This counsel was adopted; and the saints who were called together were Saint *Colum Cillé*; Saint *Caillin*; Saint *Ciaran* of Clonmacnois; and Saint *Brendan* of Clonfert. These repaired to the tomb of *Fergus* on the brink of *Loch En* (in the county of Roscommon); and, after fasting and praying, their petition was answered, for Fergus (we are told) did appear to them, and related the tale, which was written down by Saint *Ciaran* and Saint *Caillin*, on the spot; after which Fergus disappeared.

I have already given you the substance of this account of the recovery of the tale of the *Tain Bo Chuailgné*, in one of my early Lectures, but the present version is taken from an ancient tract entitled *Imtheacht na Trom Daimhé*,—(literally "the Adventures of the great company of Learned Men"). My copy of this tract is, I am sorry to say, but a modern and inaccurately transcribed one, nor do I know where an older can be found. This circumstance, however, does not affect the antiquity of the original composition of the tract, as I find in the Book of Leinster a satirical poem on this "great company" of *Seanchan*, written by *Flann* of Monasterboice, who died in the year 1056; and in Cormac's Glossary, which was compiled in the ninth century, I also find (under the word *prull*) a quotation from it (the part which describes *Seanchan*'s visit to Scotland, with his company of fifty learned men and fifty pupils.

The whole tale forms a very curious specimen of an ancient legend, fantastically conceived, to account for the want of proof of the authorship of the celebrated Tale,—the history of the Irish Iliad,—a tale already so ancient even in ages before the time of *Flann* and of *Cormac*, that the prosaic truth of its history was already lost in antiquity.

LECTURE V.

[Delivered 9th June, 1857.]

(III.)—Education and Literature; (continued). Poems of *Colman O'Cluasaigh*, (vii. century). The "Liber Hymnorum". Of *Cennfaeladh* "the Learned". Of the School or College under St. *Bricin*, (vii. century). Of *Ruman*, "the Virgil of the Gaedhil". Of *Aengus Ceilé Dé*. Of *Eochaidh* "[illegible] *Cuncind*". Of *Flannagan*, son of *Ceallach*, (ix. century). Story of the [illegible] *Blanaid*, and *Ferceirtné* the bard of *Curoi Mac Dairé*. Of [illegible] *Fathan*. Of the poetess *Laitheog*. Of *Flann Mac Lonain*. Topographical poem by *Mac Liag*. Poems by *Mac Lonain*. Of *Cormac Mac Cuilennain*. Of learning in the x. and xi. centuries. Of *Dallan* Mac More. Of [illegible] "an *Eigeas*". Of *Cinnaedh* O'Hartagan. Of *Cormac* "*Fili*". Of *Eochaidh* O'Flinn. Of *Eochaidh Eolach* ("the learned") *O'Ceirin*.

Following the order which I have prescribed to myself, the next distinguished writer who is to claim our attention is *Colman O'Cluasaigh*, the *Fer-leighinn*, or head master, of the great seminary of Saint *Finnbarr*, in Cork, who died about the year [illegible].

Poems of *Colman O'Cluasaigh*, (vii. century).

Of the poetical compositions of *O'Cluasaigh* I know of but [illegible] specimens remaining. The first is a fragment of twelve lines of an Elegy written on his pupil Saint *Cumain Foda* (son of *Fiachna*, King of West Munster), who was Bishop of Clonfert, and died in the year 661. This fragment is given in the Annals of the Four Masters, who record the death of the author under the same year; but this date must be a mistake, as will appear presently.

The second piece by *O'Cluasaigh* is a Hymn, of twenty-[illegible] stanzas, or one hundred and eight lines, which is preserved in the ancient "Liber Hymnorum", in the Trinity College Library. This is an important piece with respect to ecclesiastical [illegible] general history, as it distinctly shows what the teaching of the ancient Catholic Church of Ireland was on the doctrine of the invocation of the saints; the same, from the very infancy of the faith, as it has unswervingly continued from that time to the present day.

The "Liber Hymnorum".

The Liber Hymnorum,—a MS. written in a magnificent Irish hand, and splendidly illuminated—is now eleven or twelve hundred years old, and with its arguments or prefaces to each of the hymns contained in it, and the scholia with which it is thickly enriched, is certainly one of the most valuable ecclesiastical documents in Europe. It is deeply to be regretted, however, that we have but a fragment of the ancient book [illegible]

[illegible] Ireland,—and that although there is another large fragment of it mouldering uselessly in the Irish College of Saint Isidore at Rome, we have as yet failed to procure even the loan of it here, where it might have been turned to the most important use.

[Poems of O'Cluasaigh, (VII. cent.).]

The argument of *O'Cluasaigh*'s Hymn, which is, of course, as old at least as the book, declares that it was written by *Colman Ua Cluasaigh*, Head Master of Cork, "as a shield of protection" to himself and his pupils against the mortality called [illegible] *[illegible]*, or Yellow Disease, which ravaged Erinn and [illegible] in the time of *Diarmaid* and *Blathmac*. *Diarmaid* [illegible] *Blathmac* were the two sons of the monarch *Aedh Slainé*; they reigned as joint sovereigns of Erinn from A.D. 657 to [illegible] in which year they both died of this "Yellow Plague". The [illegible] states, further, that it was in the year of their death that [illegible] wrote this poem. He wrote it, it is stated, on the eve [illegible] preparing to leave his college with his pupils, and repair to [illegible] island of the sea at no great distance from the land; the [illegible] belief being that no plague, mortality, or distemper [illegible] extend beyond the distance of nine "waves" from the [illegible]

[illegible] stated in the preface that some persons supposed that [illegible] wrote but the two first stanzas, and that his pupils wrote [illegible] twenty-five, by two lines, or half a stanza, each,—[illegible] would show that the number of the pupils was fifty. [illegible], as supplying a fact analogous to what we have [illegible] former Lecture,[w] as to Saint *Mobi*'s school at *Glas*-[illegible], near Dublin, where Saint *Colum Cillé* was one of [illegible] students who fled from an earlier visitation of the same mortality; and also as to the number of students attend-[illegible] individual master, with respect to which, passing over [illegible] instances, we may likewise refer to the case of the poet [illegible], who, on his visit to Scotland, was, according to Cor-[illegible], attended by "fifty" lay students.

[illegible]'s poem, consisting, as I have already stated, [illegible] stanzas, or one hundred and eight lines, begins [illegible]

[illegible] blessing of God come upon us;
[illegible] the Son of Mary screen us;
May He protect us this night,
Wherever we go,—though great our numbers"[x]

[illegible]

[illegible] Sén Dé donfé for donté;
Mac Maire rón félaðar;
Foessam dún innocht
Dia tiassa cain timaðar.

LECT. V.

The writer then invokes the intercession of the [illegible] the Apostles, the Blessed Virgin Mary, Saint J[illegible] Stephen, and many other saints of the New Testament [illegible]

Another important feature in this poem is, that [illegible] text is mainly Gaedhelic, it is interspersed with Latin [illegible] phrases, as for instance, the fifth stanza:[39]

I should feel tempted to enter much more at length [illegible] character and composition of this very ancient and [illegible] poem, were it not that it is now actually printed, with [illegible] ments and glosses, and elucidated by learned notes by [illegible] Doctor Todd, in the second fasciculus of the Liber H[illegible] shortly to be published by the Irish Archæological [illegible] Society.

Of Cennfaeladh "the Learned".

The next distinguished Gaedhelic and general [illegible] whom I have to call your attention is *Cennfaeladh* "the [illegible] of whom mention has been already made in this, as w[illegible] some of the former course of Lectures.[40]

Cennfaeladh was one of the most remarkable men of [illegible] His early life was devoted to military service; but, having [illegible] ceived a dangerous wound in the head at the celebrated [illegible] *Magh Rath*—(now Moira, in the county of Down),—in the [illegible] 634,[41] he was carried from the field of battle to Arm[illegible] the Primate *Senach*, the representative and successor of [illegible] Patrick. The Primate had him conveyed immediately to [illegible] *Bricin*, the learned Abbot of *Tuaim Drecain*—(now Toom[illegible] in the county of Cavan),—who appears to have combined [illegible] medical proficiency with his profound literary acquire[illegible] *Cennfaeladh* remained under Saint *Bricin*'s care for [illegible] months, until he was finally cured, but cured not without [illegible] loss of a part of his brain from the wound.

The School or College under S. Bricin, at Tuaim Drecain, (vii. century).

Saint *Bricin* at this time, we are told, conducted a College which consisted of three distinct Schools, in the town of T[illegible] *Drecain*; and these three schools were carried on in three distinct houses, situated at the converging points of three [illegible] and placed under the immediate superintendence of three distinct professors; namely, a professor of *Feinechas* or [illegible] Law; a professor of Poetry and general Gaedhelic learning; and a professor of the Classics.

(39) In the original as follows:—

Regem regum rogamus,	Anac noe a lucclad
In nostris sermonibus	Diluvii temporibus.

(40) See *Lectures on the MS. Materials of Ancient Irish History*, pp. [illegible], 418, etc.

(41) See *Battle of Magh Rath*, published by the Irish Archæological Society in 1842.

[Of Cennfaeladh.]

[illegible] *Cennfaeladh* became convalescent, he appears to have [illegible] the habit of listening to the lectures and lessons com[illegible] by Saint *Bricin* and his assistants to their pupils; [illegible] clear and retentive had his mind become, that it is said [illegible] retained everything which he had heard from all of [illegible] so that we learn that he became himself afterwards the [illegible] of three similar schools.

[illegible] passage in which this is recorded—(MS. H. 3. 18. T.C.D., [illegible])—is as follows:

[illegible] the place in which he was cured was *Tuaim Dregan*, [illegible] meeting of the three streets, between the houses of the [illegible] professors, *i.e.*, the professor of *Feinechas* [Law], the pro[illegible] of Poetry, [which included, in fact, Philosophy and ge[illegible] native Literature[40]], and the professor of Classics. And [illegible] was recited by the three schools, each day, he had [ac[illegible]] by the acuteness of his intellect, each night; and so [illegible] of it as he desired to show [or teach] he arranged in [illegible] order, and wrote into a white [or blank] book".[41]

[illegible] "Three Schools", spoken of in connection with Saint [illegible] and *Cennfaeladh*, always, and even to a comparatively [illegible], formed the necessary parts of a lay College among [illegible]. So, in the middle of the fifteenth century, *Diar*[illegible] *Clerigh*,—the ancestor of the celebrated Michael,—and, [illegible] his son *Tadhg Cam O'Clerigh*,—acting in his capa[illegible] hereditary chief *Ollamh* of the *Cinel Conaill*, (*i.e.*, the [illegible] O'Donnells), in Donegal,—kept also Three Schools: [illegible], for History, and for Poetry. In this division, [illegible]" would include the Latin and other literatures, [illegible] the Gaedhelic: while *Seanchas*, which is translated [illegible] certainly included the study of the *Feinechas* or [illegible] Law.

[illegible] summary of the history of the O'Clerys (and [illegible] this fact is stated) will be found in the *Irish Penny* [illegible] for January 16th, 1841 (p. 226). It is given in con[illegible] Kilbarron Castle, in the county of Donegal,—[illegible] residence of this great family of scholars.

[illegible] revised the ancient Gaedhelic grammars of [illegible] and *Ferceirtné*, and was perhaps the first person to [illegible]

[40] [illegible] p. 1; and Appendix, No. L, p. 461, to *Lectures on the MS.* [illegible] *Ancient Irish History*.

[41] [illegible]—Ocus is and do righned a leigis a Tuaim nDregain a [illegible] sraide toir tighib na tri suad .i. sai feinechais, ocus sai [illegible] sai leigind. Ocus in neoch do chanois na tri scola [illegible] aigirsium tre geire in intlechta gach naidche, ocus [illegible] tairsfenta leis de do beired glunsnaithe filidechta [illegible] aice he a caile libair.

LECT. V.

[Of Cennfaeladh.]

lay the foundation of comparative philology in Erinn, afterwards cultivated by Cormac Mac Cullinan. He, too (unless we may attribute it to Cormac himself), was probably the original writer of the Grammatical Tract preserved in the Books of *Lecain* and Ballymote, of which some account was given in the last Lecture.

Besides this grammar, *Cennfaeladh* compiled a Law Tract, which is still extant, and which will make part of the publication of the Brehon Law Commissioners.

Cennfaeladh was also author of a well-known poem, of fourteen stanzas, or fifty-six lines, on the migrations of *Golamh*, or Milesius, from "Scythia" into Spain, and the subsequent expedition of his sons, with their Milesian colony, into Erinn, and their conquest of and permanent settlement in the country. This celebrated poem begins as follows:

"*Golamh* departed out of Scythia".(44)

Edward O'Reilly, in his Irish Writers, at the year 678, states that in an old manuscript, in the possession of Mr. William Monk Mason, the authorship of the ancient poem describing the internal arrangements of the *Teach Midhchuarta*, or Great Dining Hall, at Tara, was ascribed to *Cennfaeladh*; but although there are two copies of this ancient and most curious poem still extant, one in the Book of Leinster and the other in the Yellow Book of *Lecain*, both in the Library of Trinity College, Dublin, (the latter of which, with an English translation, and with corrections from the former, is published in Dr. Petrie's Essay on the Hill of Tara), in neither of these books is the poem ascribed to *Cennfaeladh*.

There is, however, in the Book of Leinster, an extract of twenty-four lines, from a poem of *Cennfaeladh*. This poem is entitled *Aidedhaibh Uladh*, or the Deaths of the Ultonians; but I have never been able to discover any more of it than that extract; and from the character of that, the poem must have been a most valuable historical one, since it is evident that it contained a full description of the great achievements, the manner of death, and the places of sepulture of the series of the great Ultonian Champions of the "Royal Branch". The extract I allude to is introduced into a very ancient prose account of the death of *Cuchulainn*, the great Ulster champion of the *Tain Bo Chuailgné*. It gives the name of the spot in which he fell, and of the man who slew him, the number of the men he slew, and the monument of his head and hand at Tara, whither they had been carried from the field of battle. I feel perfect confidence

(44) original:—Do luid Golamh as in Scithia.

in expressing my conviction that this extract is preserved in its original purity, and that it has not undergone the alteration of, perhaps, one single word, since it passed from the hand of its author. LECT. V.

From *Cennfaeladh*, who died in the year 678, we pass now to *Ruman*, a native of Meath, who died in the year 742, and who is styled "the Virgil of the Gaedhil" by *Aengus Ceilé Dé*, in his pedigrees of the Irish saints. *Ruman*'s writings are now, unfortunately, lost, or not known; but there is a notice of two or three poems of his preserved in an ancient manuscript in the Bodleian Library at Oxford. Of *Ruman*, "the Virgil of the Gaedhil".

After *Ruman* comes *Aengus Ceilé Dé* himself, a celebrated saintly priest, and a great Gaedhelic scholar; the author of the celebrated *Feliré*, or Festology, and of the other important Irish compositions which I have so often spoken of in the course of my former Lectures. But I need not repeat what I have mentioned of his life, and of the position which he occupies in our literary history. *Aengus Ceilé Dé* died some time about the year 815. Of *Aengus Ceilé Dé*.

Confining ourselves still to those of our distinguished men of letters who may be considered the representatives of the education of their time, the next great name in the succession is that of *Fothadh na Canoiné*, of whom also I have given some account in one of my former Lectures, when treating of the reign of *Aedh Oirdnidhé*, Monarch of Erinn from 793 to 818. Of *Fothadh "na Canoine"*.

Contemporary with *Fothadh*, and after him, flourished *Flannagan*, the son of *Ceallach*, King of Bregia; who, as well as *Fothadh*, survived the Monarch *Aedh Finnliath*, who ruled from 861 to 877, in which year he died, at *Druiminesclainn*, on the 20th day of November. Of *Flannagan*, son of *Ceallach*; (ix. century.)

The Annals of the Four Masters, at the year 876, give two extracts from two poems written on this monarch's death, the one by *Fothadh*, and the other by *Flannagan*. The extract from *Fothadh*'s poem consists of twelve lines, beginning:

"Seven years over seven times ten,
Eight hundred and five thousand
[illegible], without falsehood,
To the death of *Aedh* are reckoned.
Seventy after eight hundred
And six years, are reckoned,
From the birth of Christ, without reproach,
To the death of *Aedh* of *Ailech*".

The extract from *Flannagan*'s poem consists of twenty-[illegible] lines, beginning:

LECT. V.

[Of Flannagan.]

" Long is the wintry night,
With fierce gusts of wind,
Under pressing grief we have to encounter it,
Since the red-speared king of the noble house lives not.
" It is awful to observe
The waves from the bottom heaving,
To these may be compared
All those who with us lament him".

The same Annals contain, at the year 890, a quotation from a poem by *Flannagan*, on the death of his son *Ceallach*, who was treacherously killed, in this year, by *Fogartach* the son of *Tolorg*. The quotation consists of the eight following lines:

" This is *Ceallach*'s servant coming from the west,
Leading *Ceallach*'s steed by hand;
The dreadful news is cause of tears,
It is no falsehood, the son of *Dearbhail* is dead!
" No son of a king reigned over chiefs
Nobler than *Ceallach* of the pure blushing face;
A household nobler than the household of that man
Exists not under Heaven of brilliant rays". [i. e. [illegible]
the bright shining heaven.]

This is immediately followed by a quotation from [illegible] *Mac Lonain*, on the death of the three sons of *Flann*[illegible] (whom he calls *Flann*), including the above *Ceallach*; [illegible] whom he surnames after the place of his residence.

This quotation consists of the eight following lines:

" Illustrious three, the three sons of *Flann*,
Who coursed over *Odhbha;*
Congalach of *Colt; Ceallach* of *Cearna;*
And *Cinaedh* of *Cnodhbha.*
" Though *Ceallach* for his faults may have been slain,
It is a pity he should have fallen but in battle;
Alas! that his fate was so premature
That he has not lived the life of an historian".

MacLonain must have written these lines in the year [illegible] as we find that in that year *Flannagan* himself was killed [illegible] the Danes, at *Olbha;* and his son *Cinaedh*, who is mentioned in these lines, died at *Dun Bric*. *Congalach*, *Flann*[illegible] third son, died in the year 889.

Besides these quotations from lost poems of *Flannagan*, [illegible] is a perfect poem of his preserved in the fine old manuscript called the *Leabhar Buidhé Lecain*, (H. 2. 16, in the Library [illegible] Trinity College.) In this poem the author enumerates a few [illegible] the great historical tales which an *Ollamh*, such as himself, should be able to recite; after which he gives a long list of the deaths [illegible] of persons eminent in Irish history, and the day of the week upon which each of them died, from the Monarch *Conairé Mór* down to *Flannabhra*, Lord of *Gabhra*, in Meath, who was killed in the year 876.

This poem is written in very ancient diction: it consists of twenty-eight stanzas, or one hundred and twelve lines, and begins:

"Let us relate the history of noble chiefs
Who bore over Erinn illustrious sway,
Of *Curoi* who in the conflict fell,
Which was the tragic death of three".(44)

Story of the lady *Blanait*, and *Ferceirtné*, the bard of *Curoi Mac Dairé*.

The three whose tragical deaths are spoken of here were: *Curoi MacDairé*, (King of West Munster, at the period of the [illegible]nation, who was treacherously killed at his Court of *[illegible] Conroi*, near Tralee, on account of his wife *Blanait*, by [illegible], the great Ulster Champion),—the lady *Blanait* her[illegible] *Ferceirtné* the poet.

[illegible] the death of *Curoi*, *Cuchulainn* carried the lady *Blanait* [illegible] into Ulster. *Curoi's* faithful poet and harper, *Fer*[illegible] who had fled to the mountains of Kerry on his mas[illegible]ath, soon bethought himself of taking vengeance of the [illegible] who betrayed him. He accordingly set out for the [illegible]nd in due time arrived at Emania, the royal palace of [illegible] where he was joyfully received by his former mistress, [illegible], and her new husband, *Cuchulainn*. In a short time [illegible]'s arrival at Emania, King Conor and the Ulto[illegible] a great assembly at a place called *Rinn Chinn Bear*[illegible] the brink of a high cliff. At this assembly, *Ferceirtné* [illegible]pportunity of engaging the lady *Blanait* in conversa[illegible] which he imperceptibly drew her to the brink of [illegible]ce, when he suddenly clasped his arms around her, [illegible] himself with her over the cliff, where they were both [illegible] this was the tragical death of "the three"; that is, of [illegible] *Dairé*, his faithless wife *Blanait*, and his faithful poet [illegible]*ceirtné*.

[illegible]luable poem, bearing undoubted evidence of the [illegible] of a great number of historic facts, as well as [illegible] historic tales such as those of which I formerly [illegible]

Of *Maelmura* of *Fahan*

[illegible]-na-*Canoiné* and *Flannagan*, we find in the [illegible]tral contemporary teachers, of whom the most

(44) [illegible]ium rcél rearcer nairic,
[illegible]rinic uar banba blocaic
[illegible]urgaet Cupaí ra gliaid
[illegible]enaig eóc cpoga cpiaip.

LECT. V. distinguished was *Maelmura*, the priest, poet, and hi *Fahan Mura*, in Ulster. He was the author of a poem in praise of *Flann Sionna*, Monarch of Erinn year 877 to 914; and of a more celebrated and important poem, on the origin and migrations of the The latter poem has been published, with the Irish Nennius, by the Irish Archæological Society (for 1847).

Of the poetess *Laitheog*. In this century also flourished the poetess *Laitheog*, of the poet *Flann Mac Lonain*, already spoken of; compositions one piece only has ever come under This is a short poem addressed by her to her son horting him to liberality and generosity, such as distinguished poet and scholar as he was: that he who whatever he asked from others ought himself to be keep a house of hospitality, and have a welcome for learned other guests. She advises him to write a poem, and to the north, to the four brave and generous chiefs of namely: *Maeldoraidh* [ancestor of the O'Muldorys]; *chan* [ancestor of the O'Donnells]; *Flaithbhertach* [ance the O'Lavertys]; and *Canannan* [ancestor of the O'C but she gives the preference to *Eignechan*.

This curious poem consists of twelve stanzas, or lines, beginning:

"Blessing upon thee, O *Flann* of *Aidhné*;
Receive from thy mother counsel;
Let not thy noble career be without hospitality,
Since to thee is granted whatever thou seekest".

This poem is quoted (and the poetess styled "the N the Learned") in a poem written by *Brian Ruadh Mac midhé*, in praise of *Neachtan* O'Donnell, chief of Tir who fell in battle in the year 1452.

Of Flann Mac Lonain. In this century also, as we have seen, flourished *Flann Lonain*, who was a native of *Aidhné*, or South Connacht, and poet of all Erinn. He was author of several poems still Two of the existing poems were written for *Lorcan*, K Munster, the grandfather of *Brian Boromha*; and a third scription of the Palace of *Ceann Coradh*, at *Cill-da-lua* (K in the days of *Ceinneidigh*, the son of *Lorcan* and *Brian*. These poems are described by Edward O'R his Irish Writers, at the year 891; but I have, in my

(48) original:—Bennact ort a Floinn Aiḋne,
Gaḃ ó'ḋ ṁaṫair coṁairle
Na bí gan gart ad' gníṁ glé
Uair is lat gaċ ní ċuinge.

[illegible] copies of four other poems, attributed, in ancient [illegible] to this author, which O'Reilly had not met. The [illegible] poems has a curious legend prefixed to it, by way [illegible] preface to the topographical narration of which the [illegible]: LECT. V.

[illegible] (we are here told) that on one occasion the poet [illegible], who was the successor of *Mac Lonain*, went from his [illegible] at *Loch Riach*, in the county of Galway, on a visit to [illegible] *Borumha*, at *Ceann Coradh*, accompanied by his usual [illegible] of learned men and pupils, and attended by *Ilbrechtach* [illegible], who had also been harper to his predecessor *Mac* [illegible]. Their path lay over the high and dreary range of [illegible] called *Sliabh Echtgé*, which separate the present [illegible] of Clare and Galway. In the course of their journey [illegible] rest and refresh themselves, on the side of one of [illegible] hills of the range, called *Ceann Crochan*, or [illegible] Head. Here, as they looked out over the prospect, [illegible] said: "Many a hill, and lake, and fastness, in this [illegible] it would be great topographical knowledge to know [illegible]". Upon which *Ilbrechtach* the harper said: "If it [illegible] *Lonain* that were here, he could name them all, and [illegible] origin of their names besides". "Let this fellow be [illegible] hanged", said *Mac Liag*. The harper begged a [illegible] next morning, and he was granted it. When the [illegible] came they saw the form of *Mac Lonain* coming to-[illegible]; and on his nearer approach he said: "Permit your [illegible] escape, and I will give you the name and origin of [illegible] locality in this range of *Echtgé*". His request [illegible] complied with; and thereupon he recited a poem [illegible] stanzas, or one hundred and thirty-two lines, be-[illegible] Topographical poem by Mac Liag.

[illegible], delightful, lofty *Echtgé*".[40]

[illegible] goes on then, in a vigorous and clear style, to give [illegible] of the history of the mountain, and the tribes and [illegible] in succession occupied it, made it their hunting [illegible] left their names on some parts of it;—among [illegible] *Finn Mac Cumhaill*, and his warriors. He [illegible] by name all the remarkable places; the hills, [illegible] rivers, fords, woods, etc.; and he concludes with [illegible] on the Dalcassians of Clare, their munifi-[illegible] of soul, of which the poet gives a very curious [illegible]. He relates that, on one occasion, he met a Dalcas-[illegible] *Find*, in the county of Galway, who had just con-

[40] [illegible]—[illegible]

LECT. V. [Of Mac Lonain.] cluded a service of twelve months to a man of that country, from whom he received a cow and a cloak for his wages; and as he met the poet, on his way home, he addressed him in these words, as he tells us:

"He said to me, in prudent words:
'Sing to me the history of my country;
'It is sweet to my soul to hear it';—
And the composition he instantly purchased.
"Thereupon I sang for him the poem,
Nor then did he show aught of loth;
All that he had earned,—not mean or meagre,—
To me he gave without deduction.
"The upright Dalcassians heard of this;
They received him with honour in their assembly;
They gave to him—the noble race—
Ten cows for every quarter of his own cow.
"No dearth of raiment or food has been heard of,
Upon the Dalcassians, or upon their king;
That friendly race, as I well know,
Are never without their sweet happiness".

The poem is thus carried on to the end, as if composed and recited by *Mac Lonain* after his death. His death had been a violent one; for he had been killed, in the county of [illegible] by a party of robbers from the county of Waterford; and [illegible] made to mention this circumstance, and the names of the [illegible] here.

This, as I have already said, is a very curious poem; [illegible] unless *Mac Liag* is taken to have recited but a known poem of *Mac Lonain*, and to have introduced it in the picturesque [illegible] described, it is clear that it was written by *Mac Liag* [illegible] and if so, then probably at the suggestion, and from the [illegible] niscences, of *Ilbrechtach* the harper, who must himself have been no ordinary personage to be selected as the constant companion of two such men as *Mac Lonain* and *Mac Liag*.

Poem by Mac Lonain. The second, hitherto unknown, poem of *Mac Lonain* [illegible] wild and romantic one too, as may be understood from the following prose legend, which is prefixed to it:

At a certain time that *Mac Lonain* and his company were passing through a desert place on these mountains, they were overtaken by a tempest, and detained so long that at last their stock of food was exhausted, and still the weather had not improved. While they were in the act of saying among themselves, that if they had food they would at least make an attempt to move notwithstanding the storm, they saw coming towards

LECT. V. [Of Mac Lonain.]

[illegible] rude, burly clown, holding a fat cow by the tail [illegible] hand, and a forester's axe in the other. The poet [illegible] if he were willing to sell the beef. He answered [illegible] would not, but that he would barter it for a cow such [illegible] himself should choose. *Mac Lonain* said that he would [illegible] such a cow if he would but give time. The clown [illegible] to do so; but requested to be allowed to slaughter and [illegible] the beef himself, a request that was gladly granted him. [illegible] cow was killed and cooked accordingly; and the poet and [illegible] ate heartily and were satisfied, and they heaped [illegible] presents on their benefactor.

[illegible] clown, after this, departed; but at the end of a year he [illegible] *Mac Lonain's* house, accompanied by four others like [illegible] each carrying a woodman's axe in his hand; and they [illegible], fierce, party of five men, (says the poet); and [illegible] was the space which they took up in the poet's house; [illegible] and voracious was their feeding; and they beat and [illegible] the women, and servants, and dogs, in and about the [illegible] they declared they should have nothing less than a [illegible] should never run dry, or to remain altogether in [illegible]

[illegible] then asked the chief of them his name: "I am [illegible] the son of Entangled Forest", said he.

[illegible] then addresses Forester, in a poem of twenty- [illegible] (or one hundred lines), on the unreasonableness of [illegible] the impossibility of complying with it, and the [illegible] himself and his companions on the establishment. In [illegible] of the poem the author pays a handsome compliment [illegible] a benison on, the Dalcassians, men, women, [illegible] and clergy, for their hospitality and liberality; from [illegible], perhaps, be inferred, that the poet's difficulty [illegible] *Forester*, was an innocent hint to afford the [illegible] another opportunity of indulging in their wonted [illegible]

[illegible] of the poem is well attested by the fact that [illegible] in it a particular compliment to *Sida-an-Eich-* [illegible] "*Sida* of the bay steed"), the chief of the *Clann* [illegible] tribe-name of the Mac Namaras of Clare), and to [illegible], who must have been very young at the time; [illegible] known personages in the pedigree of the MacNamaras, [illegible] have been both living, about the time of the [illegible] in the year 918.

[illegible] also bears evidence to the learning and literary [illegible] and critical, of his contemporary, Cormac Mac- [illegible] King of Munster and Archbishop of Cashel; while he

LECT. V.

celebrates the valour and munificence of the reigning monarch, *Flann Sinna*.[48]

MacLonain's poem on the sons of Eochaidh Muighmheadhóin.

The third of these hitherto unnoticed poems is one of twelve stanzas, or forty-eight lines, in praise of the five sons of the Monarch *Eochaidh Muighmheadhóin*; namely, *Brian*, *Fergus*, *Fiachra*, *Ailill*, and *Niall* ("of the Nine Hostages"). This rare poem begins:—

"The sons of *Eochaidh*,—high their renown".[49]

MacLonain's elegy on the death of Eignechan, son of Dalach.

The fourth of these very rare poems of *Mac Lonain*, and one of curious historical value, is his elegy on the death of *Eignechan*, the son of *Dalach*, hereditary Prince of Tirconnell (now Donegal), and ancestor of the great O'Donnell sept of that ancient territory. The chief of Tirconnell died in the year 902; and on hearing of the sad event, from his servant, *Mac Nagcuagh*, the poet, who, it appears, was no stranger to his mansion and his hospitality, wrote these verses, consisting of sixty-four stanzas, or two hundred and fifty-six lines, which he sent forthwith to the north; and in them he dwells, with considerable minuteness, on his own reception in former times by the deceased chief, and on the various gifts and presents which he had received from him. From the nature of the presents thus described, and the circumstances under which they were given, and sometimes procured by the donor, this poem presents to us a very interesting glimpse of the mode of life at the court of *Eignechan* at the time.

The most curious part of this poem, however, very valuable as it is in a historic point of view, is that in which we are told that the chief found himself compelled to purchase peace and exemption from plunder and devastation for his territory from the "Danish pirates", who were at this time committing fearful depredations along the sea-board of the island. This peace and exemption were purchased by the chief consenting to the marriage of his three beautiful daughters,—*Duibhlinn*, *[illegible]*, and *Bebhinn*,—to three of the pirate commanders, whose names were *Cathais*, *Turgeis*, and *Tor*. After the marriage the pirates sailed away with their wives and their booty to *Carraic Bracraighé*, in *Inis Eoghain* (now called Innishowen, in Donegal). Here, however, the Lady *Duibhlinn*, who had been married to

(48) This curious poem begins:

Fíoḋbaḋaċ mac feḋa fír-caiġ,	Forester, the son of the Entangled Wood,
Durcaib congeib gleóḋ,	Has taken upon him to make battle,
Iraiġ luaċ a bó do biuḋa,	He will eat the value of his cow in [illegible]
Béraiḋ a bó fa deóiġ.	And he must have his cow besides.

(49) original:—Maicne Echach, ard a n-glé.

the pirate chief *Cathais*, eloped from him while he lay asleep, taking with her a casket containing trinkets to the amount of one thousand *ungas* of gold; and she succeeded in safely making her escape to the house of *Cathelan*, son of *Maelfabhall*, the chief of that district, who had been formerly her lover, and under whose guardianship she was the more ready to place herself. When the pirate awoke and found his bride and his casket gone, he flew in a rage to her father, and threatened to have his territory ravaged if he did not restore to him his casket. This *Eignechan* undertook to do; and he invited the Dane to come on a certain day, with his brother commanders, and all their immediate followers, to his court at *Ceann Maghair*, (in Donegal;) where the gold should be restored, and the company royally entertained. The Danes arrived, and were well entertained accordingly; after which the company retired to the lawn of the court, where stood a tree upon which the Tirconnellian warriors were accustomed to try their comparative strength and dexterity, and the metal and sharpness of their swords, by striking their mightiest strokes into its trunk. The company, by *Eignechan*'s arrangement, sat in circles around the tree, for the usual purpose; the chiefs of both parties standing nearest to it. *Eignechan* then stood up to open the sports; and drawing his sword, he struck at the tree, but designedly missed it; and the weapon glancing off with immense force, struck his reputed son-in-law, the Dane *Cathais*, on the head, killing him on the spot. This was a preconcerted signal for the Tirconnellians, who instantly rushed on the rest of the band of their enemies, and quickly put them all to the sword.

The number of the Danes on this occasion may be inferred from the stated number of their ships, which was one hundred and twenty; and it is stated that not one of their crews escaped. *Eignechan* then demanded and received the casket of gold from his daughter; and he gave it all away on the spot, in proper [illegible], to the tribes and to the chief churches of his principality. Just, however, as he had concluded the distribution of the whole of the piratical spoil, *Mac Lonain* with his company of learned men and pupils happened to arrive on the lawn, on a professional visit to his patron. And here we have a characteristic trait of the manners of the times. When the chief saw the poet, and found himself with empty hands, he blushed, and was silent; but his generous people perceiving his con[illegible] immediately knew the cause, and came forward to a man, and placed each his part of the gold in the hands of his chief. *Eignechan*'s face brightened; he re-divided the gold, giving the poet a share of it proportionate with his rank and profession,

LECT. V. and disposing of the remainder among those who had so generously relieved him from his embarrassment.

This curious poem contains very many other points of interest,—and amongst them *Eignechan*'s pedigree. It begins as follows:—

"Fearful the news, O *Mac na-g-Cuach*,
Which thou hast brought us,—O sad fact!—
That *Eignechan*, the son of beloved *Dalach*,
Is buried beneath the heavy green earth".[80]

Of Cormac Mac Cullinan. I have now traced down the stream of learning, (more rapidly as I have approached the better known eras of our history,) to a period from which O'Reilly and other writers have so well illustrated the Literary History of Erinn that I shall only refer to a very few names more. Contemporary with *Flann Mac Lonain* was the celebrated Cormac MacCullinan, King of Munster and Archbishop of Cashel, who was killed in the year [illegible], at the battle of *Bealach Mughna*, fought by him against the Monarch *Flann Sionna*. Of Cormac's previous history some account has been given in a former Lecture;[81] and his connection with the eventful story of Queen *Gormliath*, *Flann Sionna*'s daughter, will be remembered. Cormac's fame is, however, so very generally familiar, that I need do no more than recall here that he has always been regarded as one of the most distinguished scholars in Europe of his time. He was educated in the Church of *Disert Diarmada*, (now Castle Dermot, in the county of Kildare); and besides the knowledge which he is recorded to have acquired of the Hebrew, Greek, and Latin, the British, the Saxon, the Danish, and other northern languages, he is regarded as having been one of the greatest Gaedhelic scholars that ever lived.

Of learning in the x. and xi. centuries. The tenth and eleventh centuries produced a very large number of men deeply versed in our native language and literature, as well as in the classical literature of the times. Of these, the space allotted to the present portion of our inquiry will permit me to give here but the names of a few, some portions of whose works, and whose dates, are given by Edward O'Reilly, in his Irish Writers, and a few more, whose precise time within this period I have not been able to ascertain, but whose names,

(80) original:—Ard do sgéal a Mhic na g-Cuaċ,
Do radair leat, is gníoṁ truaġ.
Eigneaċán mac Dálaiġ dil,
Do ḋul fó'n talṁain trom ġil.

(81) See *Lectures on the MS. Materials of Ancient Irish History*.—Lect. [illegible]; p. 182.

as well as those of the others, and some parts of their works, are preserved in the Book of Leinster. Of these, I may particularly mention: LECT. V.

Dallan Mac More (who is not mentioned by O'Reilly), a poet of Leinster, who was attached to the Court of *Cearbhall*, the king of that province, at Naas, and the recorder of his patron's achievements. He appears to have been present at the battle of *Magh Ailbhé*, in which Cormac MacCullinan was killed, in the year 903. Of Dallan Mac More.

And I should not pass over *Cormac "an Eigeas"*, a poet who was attached to the celebrated Palace of *Ailech*, near Derry, the royal residence of the Kings of Ulster, and who was the author of a long poem commemorative of the expedition made by *Muirchertach*, son of *Niall "Glun-Dubh"*, about the year 940, into Leinster, Munster, and Connacht,—from which that prince returned home with the hostages of these provinces, all of which he placed in the hands of his father-in-law, the monarch. This poem has been published by the Irish Archæological Society, in the first volume of their publications; and it is now popularly known as the "Circuit of Mortogh of the Leather Cloaks". Of Cormac "an Eigeas".

The next great name at this period is that of *Cinaedh* O'Hartagan, a distinguished poet and scholar, who died in the year [illegible]; he was author of several poems, copies of which have come down to our times, and of which Edward O'Reilly, in his Irish Writers, at this year, gives a description,—which is sometimes, however, incorrect. Of Cinaedh O'Hartagan.

A poem of twenty-eight stanzas, or one hundred and [illegible] lines, on the splendour of the *Tech Midhchuarta*, or [illegible] Banqueting Hall, of Tara, in the time of Cormac Mac [illegible] Monarch of Erinn, in the third century,—and of the [illegible]ance of that celebrated monarch's household appointments, beginning:

"[illegible] of perishable splendour".[(22)]

The [illegible] copy of this poem that I have seen, is preserved [in the Bo]ok of Leinster; but it is there ascribed to *Cormac Fili* ("the Poet"), a writer with whose time I am unacquainted. Cormac "Fili".

[illegible] poem of twenty-six stanzas, or ninety-six lines, on the [illegible] the name of *Rath Essa*, an ancient court in Meath. [illegible] *Airemh*, Monarch of Erinn about a century before the [illegible], had a favourite daughter named *Essa*, to whom he [gave] her choice of any situation in his kingdom, for her residence; and she selected a spot south of Tara, from which she [could see] not only Tara, but *Brugh-na-Boinné* (the Palace of the

[(22)] [Original]:—Doman duthain alainde.

LECT. V. [Of Cinaedh O'Hartagan.]

Boyne), and *Beinn Edair* (the Hill of Howth). Here, therefore, her father built a court for her, which ever after bore the name of *Rath Essa*, or *Essa's* Court. This poem begins:

"She stood here to observe".[33]

This poem is preserved in the *Dinnseanchas*, in the Book of Ballymote; but with no author's name.

3rd, A poem of eighteen stanzas, or seventy-two lines, on the origin of *Dumha Eire*, or *Ere's* Sepulchral Mound, and of the Hill of *Acaill* (now the Hill of Screen, near Tara, in Meath), beginning:

"*Acaill* near unto Tara".[34]

This poem is also found in the *Dinnseanchas*.

4th, A poem of thirteen stanzas, or fifty-two lines, on *Brugh Mic-an-Oig* (the ancient *Tuatha Dé Danann* Palace, on the Boyne, near Slane), and several of the mounds and wonders of that extraordinary locality. This poem begins:

"Noble thy appearance, O plain of *Mac-an-Og!*"[35]

The oldest copy of this very curious poem that I know is preserved in the ancient *Leabhar na h-Uidhré*, in the Royal Irish Academy.

5th, A poem of thirty-two stanzas, or one hundred and twenty-eight lines, on the origin of the name of Tara, beginning:

"It reflects credit on the women".[36]

The "credit reflected on the women", according to this poem, arose from the fact that the name *Teamuir*, (now, commonly Tara), comes of *Tea*, the name of King Eremon's wife, and *Mur*, a mound; and it means *Tea's* Sepulchral Mound, because she was buried on this hill, at her own special request.

6th, A poem of fourteen stanzas, or fifty-six lines, on the manner of the death and place of sepulture of each of the six sons of *Aedh Slainé*, Monarch of Erinn, who was slain in the year 600. This curious poem begins:

"*Oilioll* repaired into *Cailledh*".[37]

7th, A poem of thirty-six stanzas, or one hundred and forty-four lines, on the manner and places of death of a great number of the warriors whose names occur in Irish history, chiefly Ultonians, from Conor Mac Nessa, King of Ulster, at the time of the Crucifixion, down to the Monarch *Finnachta* "the Festive", who was slain at *Grellach Dollaigh*, in Meath, in the year 695. This poem begins:

[33] original:—Deṗcó oo muinimaṗ.
[34] original:—Acaill aṗ aice Ceṁṗaċ.
[35] original:—An ṗin, a ṁáġ ṁic an Og.
[36] original:—"Do beiṗ maiṗ oo na mnáib".
[37] original:—Do luiò Oilill iṗin Chailliò.

[Of Cinaedh O'Hartagan.]

"Champions who flourished at Emania;
In the palace of *Cruachain*; at Tara;
In *Luachair*, renowned for heroes;
In *Ailinn*, in West Munster".[38]

Of this most rare and valuable poem, which O'Reilly had not seen, I am well acquainted with two authentic copies. One of these copies was made by myself in the year 1849, from an [illegible] vellum manuscript, now in the possession of a private gentleman in England. This copy consists of thirty-eight stanzas, or one hundred and fifty-two lines, interlined with most valuable notes and commentaries to all excepting the last four stanzas.

The second copy is preserved in the Book of Leinster, but without the interlined notes. This copy, in its present condition, consists of forty-seven stanzas, two of which are mutilated; the stanzas, from thirty-six to forty-six, both included, are interpolated, and bring the history down from the death of [illegible] in 693, to the great battle of *Móin Mór* in Munster, which took place in the year 1151. This battle was fought by [illegible] O'Conor, King of Connacht, and Dermot Mac [illegible], the infamous King of Leinster, with all their forces, [illegible] Torlogh O'Brien, King of Munster, and his Dalcassians; [illegible] seven thousand of the latter were slain in it.

[illegible] noticed in the margin of the Book of Leinster, in the [illegible] hand, that these verses were added by *Finn* (Mac [illegible]), Bishop of Kildare, who, we know, was the transcriber [illegible] part of this old volume, and who died in the year 1160. [illegible] two concluding stanzas are O'Hartagan's, and conclude, [illegible] to ancient usage, with the first word of the piece, to [illegible] the poem is perfect.

[illegible] The next is a hitherto unknown poem of O'Hartagan's, [illegible] consists of eleven stanzas, or forty-four lines. Its subject [illegible] pillow of Saint *Buité*, in his ancient church of *Mainister* [illegible] the county of Louth, (now incorrectly called Monaster-[illegible]) The legend referred to in this poem is not sufficiently [illegible] in the text; but, as far as it is given, it contains a fair [illegible] of the cause and manner of the death of Conor Mac [illegible] King of Ulster, who had been struck in the head by the [illegible] warrior *Ceat*, son of *Magach*, with the fatal ball which [illegible] formed from the brain of *Mesgedhra*, King of Leinster, [illegible] he was killed by the great Ulster champion, *Conall Cear-*

[38] [illegible]—Fianna batar in Emain,
i Raith Cruachan, hi Temair,
i Luachair, Luaidter curaid,
hin Alind, in Iar-Mumain.

LECT. V.

nach, as has been related in a former Lecture.[29] But the part of the story which is not sufficiently explained in this poem is where the author calls this ball a stone,—saying that it lodged seven years in King Conor's skull,—that it fell out on the day of the Crucifixion,—and that this stone was afterwards the pillow upon which Saint *Buiti* was accustomed to lay his head when taking his scanty sleep; and as such, the poet addresses to it these most curious verses, which are preserved in the Book of Leinster, and begin as follows:

"Thou, yonder stone, on which often lay
Buiti the good, the son of *Bronach* the fair;
Thou wert often a diadem in battle-fray,
When lodged in the head of the brave MacNessa."[30]

9th, The last of O'Hartagan's poems which I feel called upon to mention, has also been unnoticed hitherto. It is one of seventeen stanzas, or sixty-eight lines, on the death of *Niall* "of the Nine Hostages", and his sepulture at *Ochun* in Meath. This poem is preserved in the Book of Leinster, beginning:

"Behold the warrior-grave of *Niall*".[31]

I think I need hardly call attention to the historical value of poems such as these, in which so many detailed references are to be found to some of the most interesting and important facts of our early history.

Of Eochaidh O'Flinn.

After this *Cinaedh* O'Hartagan, the next celebrated Gaedhlic scholar on our list is *Eochaidh* O'Flinn, an eminent writer of historical poetry, who died in the year 984. Edward O'Reilly, in his Irish Writers, at this year, gives a list of this author's poems, as found by him in various manuscripts, and describes them fairly enough; but he sometimes translates the opening line inaccurately.

The following are the poems ascribed to this author by O'Reilly:—

1st, A poem of fifty-six stanzas, or two hundred and twenty-four lines, interlined with a gloss, upon the invasion of Erinn by *Partholan*;—giving an account of the place from which he first set out for Erinn; the places he stopped at in his passage; the period at which he arrived in Erinn; the chief persons that

(29) See *Lectures on the MS. Materials of Ancient Irish History*, p. 596. *Appendix*, No. CLVI.

(30) original:—A ċloċ ṫall for é laiḋ uair,
Buite buain, mac Brónaiġ báin,
Ropsa mind ar tressa tóir,
Dia m-bá i cind mic Nessa náir.

(31) original:—Deċaiḋ ferta miċaiġ Neill.

LECT. V. [Of Eochaidh O'Flinn.]

[illegible]ed him in his expedition; the invasion of the Fomo-[illegible] the number of their ships and people; and the battle of [illegible], fought between them and *Partholan*'s people. This [illegible] begins:

[illegible]—from whence came he".[(62)]

[illegible] poem is preserved in the O'Clerys' Book of Invasions, [illegible] Royal Irish Academy; and copies are to be found (but [illegible] the gloss), in the Books of Ballymote and *Lecain;* [illegible] in none of these three books is it ascribed to O'Flinn.

[illegible] A poem, interlined with a gloss, containing twenty-six [illegible], or one hundred and four lines, on the Colonizations of [illegible], first by the lady *Ceasair*, and again by *Partholan;* giving [illegible] of the times in which both these colonies arrived in [illegible] the number and names of the lakes and rivers discovered [illegible] in the time of *Partholan;* and the extinction of the [illegible] colony. This poem begins:

[illegible] learned men of *Conn*'s beautiful even land".[(63)]

[illegible] copy is to be found in the O'Clerys' Book of Invasions; [illegible] (without the gloss), in the Books of Leinster, Bally-[illegible] *Lecain;* in all of which it is ascribed to O'Flinn.

[illegible] A poem of seven stanzas, or twenty-eight lines, upon [illegible] of Erinn between the four sons of *Partholan*, [illegible] the places where the boundaries of each met. This [illegible] begins:

[illegible] sons of Griffin-like voice".[(64)]

[illegible] poem is found in the O'Clerys' Book of Invasions, and [illegible] Books of Ballymote and *Lecain;* but in neither of the [illegible] the author's name given.

[illegible] poem of seventeen stanzas, or sixty-eight lines, giving [illegible] of the Druids, artizans, farmers, etc., who accom-[illegible] *Partholan* to Erinn. This poem begins:

[illegible] were the great family".[(65)]

[illegible] poem is found in the O'Clerys' Book of Invasions, [illegible] Flinn's name; and also in the Books of Ballymote [illegible], but with no author's name.

[illegible] poem of fourteen stanzas, upon the destruction of [illegible] Tower, (on Torry Island, on the coast of Donegal), [illegible] battles fought between the Fomorians and the Neme-[illegible] This poem begins:

[illegible] destruction of *Conaing*'s tower by valour".[(66)]

[illegible]—Partholan, can ar tainic.
[illegible]—A eamna chlair Chuinn coemfeing.
[illegible]—Ceathrar mac ba grinbda glor.
[illegible]—Ro bo maith an muinntir mor.
[illegible]—Togail tuir Conaing co n-gail.

LECT. V.

[Of Eochaidh O'Flinn.]

This poem is found in the O'Clerys' Book of Invasions, under O'Flinn's name; and in the Books of Leinster, Ballymote, and *Lecain*, but with no author's name given in those manuscripts.

6th, A poem of one hundred and ninety-six lines, interlined with a gloss. In this poem O'Flinn mentions the creation of Adam, and the time which elapsed from that era to the time at which the lady *Ceasair* is said to have landed in Erinn; the number of years that expired between the universal deluge and the colonization of Erinn by *Partholan;* and the interval between the destruction of *Partholan*'s colony, by the plague, and the arrival of *Nemedh*. He then gives an account of the Nemedian colony; of their coming from Scythia, and their passage to Erinn; and recounts the number of their ships, and the names of their leaders. The transactions of the Nemedians after their landing in Erinn are then related; such as the clearing of several plains by cutting down the timber, with which the country was overgrown; the discovery and bursting forth of lakes and rivers; the hardships the Nemedians suffered from the Fomorians; the battles they fought with them; and the destruction of *Conaing*'s Tower; the return of part of the colony to Greece; and the retirement of another portion of it into Britain, under their chief, *Britan Mael*, from whom that country is said to have derived its name. This poem begins:

"Great Erinn, made illustrious by the *Gaedhil*".(67)

This poem is preserved in the O'Clerys' Book of Invasions, under O'Flinn's name; and in the Books of Leinster, Ballymote, and *Lecain;* but in these with no author's name.

7th, A poem of eighteen stanzas, or seventy-two lines, giving an account of the Invasion of Erinn by the *Tuatha Dé Danann*, who were the descendants of another son of the above *Nemedh*, who passed out of Erinn after the destruction of *Conaing*'s Tower. This branch of the Nemedians, according to the poem, seated themselves in the northern islands of Greece, and now returned under the above name. The poem recounts their subsequent travels through the north of Europe; their battles; their proficiency in magic and other sciences; the names of their chief men, women, poets, poetesses, doctors, druids, artificers, etc.; the magical or talismanic articles that they brought with them into Erinn, namely,—the *Lia Fáil*, or Stone of Destiny, as it is generally called by Latin and English writers, on which the Monarchs of Erinn were anciently crowned at Tara; the wonderful spear of the champion *Lug;* and the gifted caldron of their King, the *Daghda Mór;* their manner

(67) original:—Eire oll oirdnit Gaedhil.

[Of Eochaidh O'Flinn.]

of coming into Erinn; their battle with, and overthrow of, the [illegible], at *Magh Tuiredh;* the institution of the public games [illegible] in Meath, on the first day of August in each year; and many other curious things. This valuable poem begins:

"[illegible] the proud and the warlike".(68)

This poem is preserved, with an interlined gloss, in the O'Clerys' Book of Invasions; but the copy there contains but [illegible] stanzas; and there are full copies in the Books of Leinster, Ballymote, and *Lecain;* in all of which O'Flinn is set down as the author.

[illegible] A poem of seventeen stanzas, or sixty-eight lines, giving the names of the principal leaders that came with the sons of Milesius into Erinn, and also the names of the places where several of them died. This poem is preserved in the Books of Leinster and *Lecain,* in both of which its authorship is ascribed to O'Flinn. It begins:

"The chiefs of the expedition from beyond the sea".(69)

[illegible] A poem of eighteen stanzas, or seventy-two lines, on the succession of the brothers *Sobhaircé* and *Cermna* (of the [illegible] race), to the government of Erinn, about fifteen hundred years before the Incarnation, according to the chronology of the Annals of the Four Masters; the partition of the island between them by a line drawn from *Inbher Colpa* (the mouth of the [illegible] *Boinn*), to Limerick; the Raths or Courts erected by them, particularly those of *Dun-Sobhaircé* (now Dunseverick, in the county of Antrim), and *Dun-Cearmna* (on what is now [illegible] the Old Head of Kinsale, in the county of Cork). This [illegible] begins:

"[illegible] *Sobhairce* of the numerous host".(70)

[illegible] preserved in the O'Clerys' Book of Invasions, with an [illegible] gloss, and under O'Flinn's name; and in the Book of [illegible] without either gloss or author's name.

[illegible] A poem of eighty-two stanzas, or three hundred and [illegible] lines, giving an account of the coming of the [illegible] or Milesians into Erinn, "at the time that the Greeks [illegible] sovereignty of the world"; and an account of all the [illegible] of Erinn, from beginning to end; but particularly [illegible] sons of Milesius of Spain. This poem begins:

"[illegible] sons of delightful wisdom listen".(71)

[illegible] of this important poem are preserved in the O'Clerys' [illegible] Invasions, with an interlined gloss; and in the Books

[illegible]—Eire co n-uaill co n-iodnaib.
[illegible]—Toisig na loingsi tar lear.
[illegible]—Dun Sobairce diar sluag linn.
[illegible]—Eistead aes egnai aibind.

LECT. V. [Of Eochaidh O'Flinn.]

of Ballymote and *Lecain*, without the gloss, and [illegible] but under the name of O'Flinn in all.

11th, A poem of twenty-seven stanzas, or one hu[illegible] eight lines, giving an account of the building of the [illegible] Emania in Ulster, by Queen *Macha* and her husband [illegible] (six hundred and forty-five years before the Incarnation [illegible] ing to the chronology of the Annals of the Four Ma[illegible] kings that ruled there from the time of *Cimbaeth* to the [illegible] of Conor Mac Nessa (contemporary with our Lord); [illegible] the death of Conor to the destruction of Emania by the [illegible] *Collas* (immediately after the battle of *Achadh-leith-derg* [illegible] which they defeated and slew *Fergus Fogha*, King of [illegible] A.D. 331). It also gives the names of the provincial K[illegible] Ulster who became Monarchs of Erinn. This poem begins:

"O delightful Emania of the spears".[72]

This poem is preserved in the O'Clerys' Book of In[illegible] with an interlined gloss, and in the Book of *Lecain* (but [illegible] without the gloss), in both of which it is ascribed to O'F[illegible] It is also preserved in the Book of Leinster, without g[illegible] author's name.

12th, A poem of eighteen stanzas, which gives the na[illegible] the fifteen kings that reigned over the province of Ulster, [illegible] the time of *Cimbaeth* to that of *Concobar Mac Nessa*, and [illegible] number of years that each king reigned there, from the t[illegible] *Concobar Mac Nessa* to the destruction of that palace by [illegible] three *Collas*. This poem, which appears to be a supplem[illegible] the last described, begins:

"*Cimbaeth*, the chief of the young warriors of Emania".[73]

Copies of this poem are preserved in the O'Clerys' Book [illegible] Invasions, the Book of *Lecain*, and the Book of Leinster, [illegible] without any author's name; there can, however, be little d[illegible] that it was written by O'Flinn.

13th, A poem of sixteen stanzas, on the reign of the Mo[illegible] *Ugainé Mór*, who is stated to have extended his rule over [illegible] whole of the West of Europe, as far as the Mediterranean [illegible] *Ugainé* had to wife *Ceasair*, the daughter of the King of Fr[illegible] by whom he had twenty-two sons and three daughters, a[illegible] whom he divided Erinn into twenty-five parts; and it is th[illegible] divisions and their names, and the names of *Ugainé's* childr[illegible] that form the principal subject of this poem, which begins:

"*Ugainé* the proud and illustrious".[74]

Copies of this poem are preserved in the O'Clerys' Book of

(72) original:—A ehain ronac arbino.
(73) original:—Cimbaeth cleithe n-óc n Emna.
(74) original:—Ugoine uallac ampa.

the Book of *Lecain*, and the Book of Leinster; all of O'Flinn as the author.

LECT. V.

[Of Eochaidh O'Flinn.]

A poem of fifty-eight stanzas, on the creation of the the names and ages of the patriarchs who lived before the the building and dimensions of Noah's Ark; the deaths his sons; the building of the Tower of Babel; the of languages; and the settlement in Egypt of *Niul*, *Farsaidh*, ancestor of the Milesians. This poem

Lord of Heaven is the Father of all men,
The gracious Son of Mary the Virgin,
Our chief, our safety, our head,
Without beginning, without limit, without end".[74]

is a fine copy of this poem preserved in the Book of but no author's name. Edward O'Reilly, however, in Writers, ascribes it to O'Flinn.

is", says Edward O'Reilly, "another poem that by is attributed to this author, beginning: 'The lakes is this southern lake'.[75] But it is by others, perproperly, ascribed to *Flann* of *Buiti*. It is to be the *Dinnseanchas*".

and those who with him attributed this poem either O'Flinn, or *Flann* of Monasterboice, are, however, wrong; as it now clearly appears that neither of them author. And not only were O'Reilly and those other whose opinions he refers, wrong, but even the geneand cautious Keating, who ascribes it to O'Flinn, mistaken. In the concluding stanza of several of the described, *Eochaidh* O'Flinn avows himself as the in the present poem, (which is one giving an account of the name of Loch *Carman*, now the Harbour the poet concludes by stating that *Eochaidh* "the Learned", wrote this poem. Now, this is a diswe never find given to O'Flinn, though I believe deserving of it; nor was there any *Eochaidh* or eleventh century, who bore this distinction, but the Learned" *O'Ceirin*, who was the contemporary Monasterboice, who died in the year 1056.

Eochaidh "*Eolach*", (or "the learned") *O'Ceirin*.

or transcriber of the ancient *Leabhar na* who died in the year 1106, states that the curious

athair chach coimṡiḋ nime,
Mac maith Muiṗe ingine,
Ar cumgiḋ, ar coimgi, ar cenn,
Cen tuṡ, cen ṡṙich, cen ṙoiṙcenn.
na Loch in Lochra tear.

LECT. V.

[Of Eochaidh O'Flinn.]

Tract on the ancient Pagan Cemeteries of Erinn, preserved in that valuable book, had been compiled and collected by *Eochaidh* "the Learned" *O'Ceirin*, and by *Flann*, from the Books of *Eochaidh O'Flannagan*, at Armagh, the Books of Monasterboice, and other choice books besides. There can, then, be no doubt that this *Eochaidh* "the Learned" *O'Ceirin* was the author of this poem on Loch *Carman*.

It was from this poem that Dr. Keating took the extract of three stanzas, on the triennial holding of the Great Feast of Tara, as given in a former Lecture;[97] and it is on this authority that he ascribes the poem to *Eochaidh O'Flinn*, in place of *Eochaidh O'Ceirin*, the true author, of whom I shall have occasion to speak more hereafter.

[97] See *ante*, p. 12; [and see same in Keating, (edition by John O'Mahony, New York, 1857;) p. 232.]

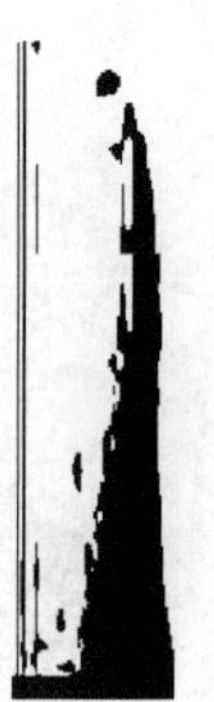

LECTURE VI.

(Delivered 16th June, 1857.)

[illegible] EDUCATION, AND LITERATURE; (continued). Of *Mac Liag*, and his works [circa A.D. 1000]. The History of the "Wars of the Danes". Life of *Brian Boromha*; by *Mac Liag*. Poems by *Mac Liag*. Of Poems of this writer not described by O'Reilly. Of the history of *Carn Conaill*. Of *Mac Coisé*, and his Poems. Of a prose piece by *Mac Coisé*. Of the Tale of the "Plunder of the Castle of *Maelmilscothach*".

We come now to *Mac Liag*, the chief historical Poet of Erinn, in his time, who died in the year 1015. This remarkable man was a native of South Connacht, and had in his early professional career been attached to the court of *Tadhg* O'Kelly, the hereditary prince of *Ui Mainé*, an extensive territory of south-eastern Connacht, bordering on the River Shannon; (a chieftain whose family is now represented in direct line of descent, by my esteemed friend, Denis Henry Kelly, Esq., of Castle Kelly, in the county of Roscommon).

On the death of Mahon, King of Munster, the elder brother of *Brian Boromha*, in the year 974, he was succeeded by the immortal *Brian* himself, who was then in the forty-eighth year of his age, having been born in the year 925.

Whether it was on his accession to the throne of Munster, in the year 974, or to the throne of all Erinn, in the year 1002, that *Mac Liag* became attached to Brian, I am not able to say; but I believe it was at the latter period, and that it was then that Brian raised him to the chair of the monarch's *Ollamh*, or chief Poet of Erinn, after which he lived in the monarch's residence of *Ceann Coradh* (at Killaloe, in the present county of Clare).

Edward O'Reilly, in his Irish Writers, at the year 1015, gives a list of seven pieces, prose and verse, which he ascribes to *Mac Liag*. Of *Mac Liag* (circa A.D. 1000) and his works.

[illegible] It is to be remembered that no monarch of Erinn held his residence at the ancient seat of the monarchy, ever since the death of *Diarmait*, the son of *Fergus Cerrbheoil*, in the year 558, in whose reign the hill and palace were cursed by Saint *Ruadan* of *Lothra* (in Ormond); so that, after the desertion of that ancient city, the monarch, of whichever of the different native families he happened to be a member, fixed his residence wherever he pleased, but generally if not invariably within his immediate provincial territory. And it was so with Brian, who fixed his residence on the plain of Killaloe, in the immediate neighbourhood of his own ancestral residence of *Grianan Lachtna*,—the ruins of which are still to be seen, on the south shoulder of the Hill of [illegible], about a mile north-west of Killaloe.

LECT. VI.

[Of Mac Liag.]

1st,—A book of the History and Annals of the wars [illegible] of Erinn; but which, notwithstanding its title, was [illegible] confined to an account of the battles of Munster [illegible] time of *Brian Boromha*. O'Reilly says that he had a cop[illegible] book in his own possession, made by John Mac Solly, [illegible] allen in the county of Meath, in the year 1710. Now [illegible] pens that this identical book is at present in the Royal [illegible] demy, (under the class-mark of 13. 5, in the original [illegible] of the Academy); but the book of the Wars of Munster [illegible] O'Reilly speaks, forms but a single tract, making but [illegible] pages of the volume; and there is not a word in it to [illegible] this tract was compiled by *Mac Liag*. Indeed, on the [illegible] there is internal evidence to show that it was written [illegible] *Mac Liag*'s death, and that it is no more than a [illegible] popular abstract of the Battle of Clontarf, taken chiefly [illegible] more important tract known as the "Wars of the D[illegible] Gaedhil", of which so much has been said in the cours[illegible] former Lectures.(79)

The History of the "Wars of the Danes".

Mac Liag, then, was certainly not the compiler of the [illegible] cular tract which O'Reilly without any authority [illegible] him. It is not, however, so certain that he was not the [illegible] of the more important tract of the "Wars of the Danes", [illegible] which the career of his great patron Brian is so faithful[illegible] so copiously recorded, and in which the terrible battle of [illegible] tarf, where the power of the Danish invaders was for ever [illegible] lated, is described in such graphic and minute detail that [illegible] some Danish words spoken on the battle-field are preserved [illegible] it. We know indeed from *Mac Liag* himself, that he was [illegible] present at the battle of Clontarf; but we know that his [illegible] mate friend, and fellow-poet and historian, *Errard Mac* [illegible] of whom we shall presently have to speak, was present in the train of the treacherous Malachy, King of Meath; and we also know that *Mac Liag* actually received from *Mac Coisi* a detailed account of the battle, a fact which is to be learned from a poem which I shall have presently to describe. We may suppose, then, that *Mac Liag* had this tract on the Wars of the Danes written, from the first coming in of the Danes, down to the battle of Clontarf; and that, not having been himself present at that battle, he sought from *Mac Coisi* the details of it, which the latter, as an eye-witness of the scene, must have been so capable of furnishing to him.

Mac Liag's Life of Brian Boromha.

2nd,—The second piece attributed to *Mac Liag*, described by O'Reilly, was a Life of *Brian Boromha*; an extract from which,

(79) See *Lectures on the MS. Materials of Ancient Irish History*, p. 232.

he states, had been given by General Vallancey, in the first edition of his Irish Grammar. Of this Life of *Brian Boromha*, I have never been able to see, or ascertain the existence of, any entire copy; but fortunately a very small fragment (the last leaf of it) remains in the well known hand of the last great Irish scholar, *Dubhaltach Mac Firbisigh;* and this copy must have been written by him before the year 1650, as he changed the character of his handwriting in or about that year. This single small leaf, which was discovered by me some years ago, was merely laid in between two folios of the *Leabhar Mór Lecain* (H. 2. 16, T.C.D.). But although this is an ancient piece of composition, it is quite certain, I think, that it could not have been written by *Mac Liag*. Indeed, from this little fragment, it would appear to have been a later semi-religious life of the great warrior,—something more in the nature of a sermon on his life and death than a historical biography. This is, however, but a mere inference from the little that remains of it. LECT. VI. [Of Mac Liag.]

The third piece described by O'Reilly, and attributed by him to *Mac Liag*, is a poem of forty stanzas, or one hundred and sixty lines, giving the names of the twelve sons of *Cas*, (from whom the Dalcassians of Thomond derive their tribe designation), and the different families which descended from each, down to the sons of *Brian Boromha*, in whose time the poem was evidently written. This poem begins: Poems by *Mac Liag.*

"Twelve sons that sprung from *Cas*".(90)

It is more than probable that *Mac Liag* was the author of this poem; but though there are copies of it preserved in the Books of Ballymote and *Lecain*, they are not accompanied by any author's name; nor does O'Reilly give any authority for his statement.

The fourth piece of *Mac Liag's*, described by O'Reilly, is a poem of eight stanzas, giving the names of the twelve sons of *Ceinneidigh* (Kennedy), the father of *Brian Boromha*, and the manner of the death of each. This poem begins:

"The twelve sons of brave *Ceinneidigh*".(91)

There are copies of this poem preserved in the Books of Ballymote and *Lecain*. It is in the latter only that it is ascribed to *Mac Liag*.

The fifth piece of *Mac Liag's*, described by O'Reilly, is a poem of eleven stanzas, written on the fall of *Brian Boromha*, and his eldest son *Murchadh*, and the flower of the warriors of Munster and Connacht, at the battle of Clontarf, in the year 1014, and on the consequent desolate state of the fallen monarch's palace at *Ceann Coradh*. This poem begins:

(90) original:—Da mhac déc do ċinn ó Ċhas.

(91) original:—Dá mhac déc Ceinneidiġ ċáiġ.

SECT. VI. [Mac Liag.]

"O *Ceann Coradh!* where is *Brian?*
Or where is the splendour that was upon thee?
Where are the nobles and the sons of kings,
With whom we drank wine in thy halls?"(82)

The concluding stanza of this plaintive poem shows [illegible] enough who the author was. It runs as follows:

"Woe that I live after *Brian!*
I am *Mac Liag* from the lake:
To invite me into his treasury,
He would come an hundred times, O *Ceann* [illegible]

An imperfect copy of this poem, with an English [illegible] was published by my late lamented friend, James [illegible] in his Irish Minstrelsy; and a full versification of it, by [illegible] James Clarence Mangan, from a literal prose translation [illegible] was published in the Irish Penny Journal, No. 28 ([illegible] January 9, 1841).

6th,—The sixth piece attributed to *Mac Liag* by O'R[illegible] which he does not describe, and of the first line of wh[illegible] gives an incorrect version in text and translation, is a poem [illegible] twenty-six stanzas, beginning:

"From the east has come the news of *Brian's* fall,
Alas! that I am in this world after him;
Thou messenger, who comest from the east,
Tell me, has *Murchadh* been slain too?"(84)

The messenger here addressed by *Mac Liag* was [illegible] *Errard*, or *Errad Mac Coisé*, poet and historian to *Maoilsech-lainn*, or Malachy the Second, King of Meath.

Malachy, with a thousand of the chosen warriors of [illegible] marched to Clontarf along with *Brian* to aid him; but wh[illegible] the battle commenced, he and his division fell out of the [illegible] and remained idle spectators of the bloody fight till its [illegible]tion. *Mac Coisé* the poet, who accompanied his patron on the occasion, had the best possible opportunity of witnessing the details of the battle; and as his person was held sacred and inviolable by both natives and foreigners, we may suppose that

(82) original:—A Chinn Choradh caidhi Brian;
nó caidhi in sciamh do bhi ort,
caidhi maithe no meic ríg,
ga n-ibmis fin ad port?

(83) original:—Is mairg atá beo gan Brian,
is misi Mac Liag o'n linn;
dom thogairm go tigh na séd,
do thigedh fá chéd, a Chinn.

(84) original:—An oir tainic tuitim Bhriain
mairg atá ar domhan na dhiaigh
a techtaire tic anoir
inois duine marbhadh Mhurchoidh.

he availed himself of that circumstance to mix with the combatants as much as was consistent with his safety from the accidents of a battle-field, so as to collect all the detailed information that could be useful to his task of recording a full account of the great scene at which he assisted.

At what place or time after the battle *Mac Coisé* visited his friend *Mac Liag*, and related to him the particulars of the great overthrow of the Danes, and the sad news of the fall of *Brian*, of *Murchadh*, and of the flower of the Dalcassian army, does not appear; but it is most probable that it was at *Ceann Coradh*; and it must have been immediately after the battle, since *Mac Liag* himself, as I shall soon show, visited the scene of the conflict [illegible] as before the interment of the slain had been concluded. [illegible] very probable that on the occasion of this visit *Mac Liag* [illegible] able to collect a great many additional details of the battle [illegible] the survivors of both parties, and that on his return home, [illegible] by himself or assisted by *Mac Coisé*, he compiled from the [illegible] this "History of the Wars of the Danes", or else added [illegible] part which he had already compiled the account of the [illegible] of Clontarf as collected by *Mac Coisé* and himself.

But to return to the dialogue between the two poets. *Mac Coisé*, in the fourth and fifth stanzas of this poem, bears testimony to the bravery and nobleness of *Brian*; and in the exag[illegible] of his feelings, goes so far as even to assert that so great [illegible] as his had not been offered on the altar of Justice, [illegible] and Religion, since the Great Sacrifice on Calvary [illegible] *Mac Liag*, then, in the sixth, seventh, eighth, ninth, and [illegible] stanzas, continues his inquiries as to whether *Murchadh* [illegible] other leaders whom he names, had really fallen. [illegible] answer to these questions, *Mac Coisé*, at the eleventh [illegible] gives the names of several of the chiefs who fell, and [illegible] the position in which they lay dead on the battle-field. [illegible] eighteenth stanza he launches out into exclamations of [illegible] grief; and he then continues to the end to review [illegible] important incidents in *Brian*'s life and reign. This [illegible] poem concludes with the following curious stanza:

"There were found at St. *Feichin*'s frigid bed,
Wells of overflowing blood,
The sign of kingly *Brian*'s death,
In the western border land of Erinn".[(88)]

The place mentioned here as Saint *Feichin*'s bed is the an-

[illegible] original:—Fríth in iomdoig Fheichín fuair
tobair 'na b-fuil robair bruaig;
comharta báis Bhriain na m-beann
i g-crích iartair na h-Eireann.

[Of *Mac Liag*.]

cient abbey of Cong, in the county of Mayo, which was founded by Saint *Feichin*, who died in the year 664; but of the legend of the bloody wells, and their connection with the death of *Brian Boromha*, I have never met any other account.

7th,—The seventh and last piece which O'Reilly attributes to *Mac Liag*, is a poem of five stanzas, or twenty lines, beginning:

"It is a long time to be without happiness,
Such as I never thought I should be;
When I was at the splendid *Ceann Coradh*,
Little did I fear that any one should rob me".[illegible]

O'Reilly states that: "This poem was written by the author, when he had retired to *Innsi Gall*, (the Hebrides), after the death of *Brian Boromha*, and in it bitterly laments his [illegible] from *Ceann Coradh*, and his want of the pleasures he was [illegible] accustomed to enjoy". He is mistaken as to the place at which *Mac Liag* is said to have written the poem, which was "*Inis an Ghaill Duibh*" (*i. e.* the Island of the Black Foreigner), in the Upper Shannon, and not *Innsi Gall*, the Hebrides—a [illegible] with which for the rest *Mac Liag* had no connection.

If *Mac Liag* was the author of this poem at all, it is the worst preserved, and the most corrupt and insipid, of all his poems with which I happen to be acquainted.

Poems of *Mac Liag* not described by O'Reilly.

So much for those of *Mac Liag*'s works mentioned in the list by O'Reilly; but I have also to mention a few more undoubtedly genuine pieces of that celebrated bard's composition, which are not described by that collector.

The first of these pieces of *Mac Liag*'s is one which O'Reilly had seen, though he has not described it,—a poem of thirty-three stanzas, or one hundred and thirty-two lines, which gives an account of why and when *Brian*'s town and palace of *Ceann Coradh* had received the alias name of *Boromha*. The poet describes in this piece how he happened to have been at *Ceann Coradh*, on one occasion when *Brian*'s tribute of cows from Leinster and Ulster was being driven home; that he went out from the court to look at them; and that he returned again, and said to *Brian*: "Here comes Erinn's tribute of cows to thee: many a fat cow and fat hog on the plain before thee". "Be they ever so many", said Brian, "they shall all be thine, O noble poet!" Whereupon it was that *Mac Liag* gave the name of *Boromha* to the town and plain; a name which literally means nothing more than a multitude of cows, either paid as tribute

([illegible]) original:—Fada beiṫ gan aiḃneas,
mar n'ar ṡaileas go bráṫ beiṫ,
mar do ḃíos a g-Ceann-Ċoraḋ ċaim
níor ṡaoil liom aon dam ċreiċ.

carried off as prey from, an enemy. It is probable that ... upon this occasion also that *Brian* himself received the ... to his name of *Boromha*, or "of the Tribute of Cows", ... the fact is not stated in this copy of *Mac Liag's* poem. ... poet proceeds to give an account of the amount and kind ... tribute sent to *Brian* to *Ceann Coradh* from the various ... paying provinces and territories of Erinn; among which ... find an item of one hundred and fifty butts of wine from the ... of Dublin, and one of a tun of wine per day from the ... of Limerick. He then describes the order in which the ... and noble guests of *Brian* sat around him in the great hall ... *Coradh*. *Brian* himself, we are told, sat at the head, ... King of Connacht on his right hand, and the King of ... (Ulidia or West Ulster) on his left, and the King of ... opposite to him. At the door-post, nearest to ... sat the King of Leinster, and at the other post of the ... sat *Donnchadh* (Donogh), son of *Brian*, and *Mael-*... (Malachy) the King of Meath. *Murchadh* (Mo-...), *Brian's* eldest son, sat in front of his father, with his back ... with *Aenghus*, the son of *Carrach*, a valiant prince of ..., on his right hand, and the King of *Tir Conaill* on his ... This position of *Murchadh* would seem to imply that *Brian* ... a seat elevated above the rest of the seats in the hall. ..., son of *Brian*, and *Tadhg* O'Kelly, King of *Ui Maini*, ... the end or side opposite to the door, on *Brian's* right ... and *Maelruanaigh*, chief of *Ui Fiachra* (in South Con-...), sat on *Tadhg's* right hand. Such, then, was the arrange-... as far as this poem goes;—a poem of which, I am sorry to ... know but of one copy, and that a bad one, made by ... O'Reilly, now in the library of the Royal Irish Aca-... It begins:

"...*omha*! home of the kings!
... of the renowned warriors of Munster!
Since *Brian* the illustrious has sprung up,
The noble chief of free-born clanns".[(97)]

The second piece by *Mac Liag*, not described by ..., is a poem of twenty-five stanzas, or one hundred lines, ... origin and history of an ancient sepulchral heap of stones, ... *Chenaill*, situated in the present county of Galway. ... poem begins:

"... ye the history from which", etc.[(98)]

(97) original:—boroma baile na ríg,
ópur na Muimnec, roéla an ríé,
ó do eirig Brian bregóa,
cenn ródaip gac raoir fonedu.

(98) original:—... in reancar ota ...

LECT. VI.

The history of Carn Chonaill. (Poem of Mac Liag.)

The history of *Carn Chonaill* is shortly this. After the defeat of the *Firbolgs* by the *Tuatha Dé Danann*, in the great battle of the southern *Magh Tuiredh* (as described in a former Lecture),[30] they fled the country, and a part of them took refuge in the Hebrides, where they remained until driven out by the Picts; upon which they returned to Erinn, in the reign of *Cairbré Nia-fear* (a short time before the Incarnation). At this time they were known as the Sons of *Umór* (*Clann Umoir*), and were led by their native chief *Aengus*, the son of *Umór*. On their arrival in Erinn, they went directly to Tara, and besought the King, *Cairbré*, to give them some rich lands in Meath, for which they were willing to pay him a fair rent. The King complied with their request; but obliged them to give him securities for their good conduct and integrity. They vouched to him, then, as pledges, the celebrated warriors *Cet Mac Magach*, of Connacht, *Ross Mac Deaghaidh*, of Munster, and *Cuchulainn* and *Conall Cearnach*, of Ulster. The Umorians, however, soon found that the burthens which the avaricious king laid on them were too heavy; and they therefore resolved secretly to fly from *Cairbré*'s rule, and to pass into Connacht, where they had contrived to conciliate the favour of *Ailill* and *Medhbh*, the King and Queen of that province. They set out, accordingly, by night, with all their property; crossed the Shannon in safety, and were allowed to settle themselves in the southern parts of Connacht, more particularly in the present counties of Galway and Clare, the latter forming at that time part of Connacht.

Aengus, the chief of the *Clann Umoir*, settled himself in the islands of Arann, and built the noble stone fortress which bears his name to this day, *Dun Aengus*, in the Great Island of Arran; *Cutra*, the son of *Umor*, settled at *Loch Cutra* (now called Lough-Cooter, in the present county of Galway); *Conall*, son of *Umor*, in *Aidhné* in the same district; *Adhar*, son of *Umor*, at *Magh Adhair*, the celebrated place of inauguration of the Dalcassian chiefs (in the present county of Clare); *Dael*, son of *Umor*, at *Daelach*, to the north of Ennistimon (in the same county); and so on as to the several other chiefs of the party.

In the meantime the King of Tara demanded of his securities their pledge, and the four warriors passed into Connacht, to take the sons of *Umor*; but the answer which they received was, an offer of combat to each. The combatants met; and *Cing*, the son of *Umor*, fell by the hand of *Rossa Mac Deadhaidh*, the Munster security; *Cimé*, the son of *Umor*, by *Conall Cear-*

[30] See *Lectures on the MS. Materials of Ancient Irish History*, p. 245.

LECT. VI. [Of Mac Liag.]

and; *Aengus* the son of *Umor*, by *Cet Mac Magach;* and *Conall Cael* ("the slender"), son of *Aengus*, the chief, by *Cuchulainn;* and it was over this young chief that his father and friends raised the heap of stones, which from him took the name of *Carn Chonaill.* Such is the history of that Carn, as related by *Mac Liag* in this poem.

There are copies of this curious poem preserved in the Books of *Leinster*, Ballymote, and *Lecain;* and in all these copies in the concluding stanza *Mac Liag* avows himself as the author.

3rd.—The third piece of *Mac Liag*'s which O'Reilly omits, being one which he had not seen; it is a poem of forty-four stanzas, or one hundred and seventy-six lines, in praise of *Tadhg* O'Kelly, chief of *Ui Mainé*, which begins:

"The blessing of *Abruin* be upon *Brighit*,
In my house is no small number of her gifts;
But *Abruin!* I say without anger,
That my friend excels your friend.
Tadhg the prosperous is my friend,
On whom poems by qualified bards are made;
He is the bravest man to guide a ship;
He is the distributor of small spoils".[56]

(The poet does not mean to assert in this last line, that the spoils which O'Kelly was accustomed to distribute were small, or of little value; but that his patron's soul was so great that the richest spoils and preys were but trifles in his eyes.)

It would appear from the opening of this poem, that *Mac Liag* addressed it to his own wife *Abruin;* who, it would also appear, had recently received some important marks of favour from O'Kelly's wife *Brighit*, to whom he makes acknowledgments; hinting at the same time that as O'Kelly was a better friend to the poet than O'Kelly's wife to the poet's wife, it was likely to be expected that O'Kelly's next exercise of his bounty in favour of his bard would be liberal in proportion.

It appears also that at some previous period the poet's homestead had been plundered of its cows, by a party from Westmeath; and that the plunderers were followed across the Shannon by Tadhg O'Kelly, with his household troops, and many of the chiefs of *Ui Mainé*, who recovered and restored them.

(56) [original:]—Bennacht Abruin ar Brighit,
fuil am thigh rim nach anait,
do chuaid, a Abruin, gan bara,
mo chara tar do charait.
Cara damsa Tadhg toirtheach,
da n-dentar dan bard n-dlethach,
is é is fearr iet im arthrach
is é marbthach na mincreach.

LECT. VI.

[Of Mac Liag.]

The names of the chiefs of *Ui Mainé* who took part in this enterprise are given in the poem, and the two concluding stanzas contain a handsome apostrophe to *Brian Boromha*, his son *Murchadh*, and his nephew *Conaing;* indicating that the poem was written before the fatal battle of Clontarf, in which these three warriors, as well as O'Kelly himself, lost their lives in the defence of their country.

4th,—The fourth piece of *Mac Liag*'s which O'Reilly had not seen, is a poem of sixty-eight stanzas, or two hundred and seventy-two lines, in praise of *Tadhg* O'Kelly and some of his allies on the east side of the Shannon; such as the chief of south *Eilé* (in Tipperary), and the chiefs of Delvin, and *Tebtha* (in Westmeath). This poem is something in the nature of a call to arms; in which all the chiefs of *Ui Mainé*, as well as their friends in South Connacht and on the east of the Shannon, are called upon by their respective names, to burnish their shields and prepare for battle. Many of the successful battles, preys, and plunders of *Tadhg* O'Kelly are given; and the poem ends with a call on *Brian Boromha* and his son *Murchadh* to burnish their shields and stand as usual to the defence of their country. This most curious and historical poem begins:

"Let the King of *Gaela*'s shield be burnished;
Bring dazzling flashes from its face;
Nine score and one shields that have been
Abandoned to the shield I now see".[91]

O'Kelly is here spoken of as King of *Gaela*, merely because the word *Gaela*, which was a minor chieftaincy in the territory of *Ui Mainé* (situate in the present barony of Leitrim, in the county of Galway), suited the measure of his verse.

5th,—The fifth piece of *Mac Liag*'s which O'Reilly had not seen, is a poem of unknown length, as, unfortunately, only the first fifty-four stanzas, or two hundred and sixteen lines, of it remain accessible to modern investigators. This fragment, as well as the two poems of *Mac Liag*'s, which have been last described, are preserved in a few folios of the ancient Book of *Ui Mainé*, now in the British Museum; a volume which was compiled by *Seaan Mór O'Duibhagain*, chief poet and historian to the princely house of O'Kelly, chiefs of *Ui Mainé*, who died in the year 1372. This ancient book, by some chance, passed into the hands of the late Sir William Betham, who sold it to the Duke of Buckingham for one hundred and fifty pounds; and at the

(91) original:—Sciath ríg Gaela, glantar hí
craeba caille for a clúi;
sciath ar nai fichit sciath
do fáged 'gon sciath adchíu.

sale of the magnificent library of Stowe, in London, in the year 1849, it passed by private sale, along with the other valuable collections of the Stowe Irish Manuscripts, into the possession of Lord Ashburnham. In his possession all Irish MSS. are concealed, as I had occasion to observe with sorrow before, with a churlish jealousy greatly at variance with what might have been supposed to be the intellectual cultivation of the owner, and in a spirit very hostile, indeed, to the general desire of the present age to facilitate the efforts now being made throughout the whole of Europe to investigate all such sources as can be deemed likely to throw new light on the migrations of men, and the march of civilization, in times long gone by. How or when the few folios now in the British Museum were parted from the original book, I cannot say; but they passed into that noble institution some twenty-four years ago, among the collection of Irish MSS. sold to it by the late James Hardiman. The fragment in the Museum contains these poems of *Mac Liag* and some other pieces, and breaks off from the original book just where the present poem stops, where the chasm appears to be a comparatively recent one; so that there is every reason to hope that the concluding part of this most curious poem, and several others of the same authors, remain still in the book itself, though it is to be feared it is doomed never to be made accessible in our time. This poem begins:

LECT. VI. [Of Mac Liag.]

"Heavily,—yet lightly,—have I come to Dublin,
To the Court of *Amlaibh* of the golden shields;
From Dublin of the swords and the graves,
Swiftly, yet slowly, shall be my departure.
O men of Dublin of the bells!
Including abbots and bishops,
Raise not the earth over *Tadhg* [O'Kelly],
Until I have bestowed upon him a last look.
Ye sons of Harold! ye reddeners of spears!
Ye remnant of Denmark's heroic bands!
Ui Maine's chief is of no foreign growth,
Or a remnant of an ignoble spurious race".[93]

(93) Original:—Leasg, amleasg, sind gu Ath Cliath
do dún Amhlaibh na n-ór sciath
o Ath cliath na lann 'sna lecht
is dian is mall mo imtecht.
A lucht Atha cliath na clog
etir abaidh is easbog
na cuiridh úir tar Tadhg toir
co tairsg duinn a dechsain.
A síl Arailt, ruadhar rand,
a iarsma laechraid Lochland,
ni gall da maig, ó Maine
ni rand dair na dergaine.

LECT. VI.

[Of Mac Liag.]

The poet then goes on to lament that O'Kelly had not taken the advice of his maternal uncle, *Maelseachlainn* (Malachy), the deposed monarch, (then King of Meath), who pressed him to abandon *Brian* and the Munstermen before entering the battle, offering him more substantial marks of his royal favour and consideration than he could expect to receive from Brian; all of which overtures the noble O'Kelly rejected with scorn; sealing with his life on the bloody field of Clontarf his fidelity to his honour, to his friend, and to his country. *Maelseachlainn*'s overtures to *Tadhg* O'Kelly (who was his sister's son) are fully described here; and they form the most complete evidence of the treachery of the King of Meath at Clontarf that has ever yet come to light.

After this the poet goes on to declare that he will not live after *Brian* and *Tadhg*. He then proceeds to bid adieu to various places in Connacht and Munster; after which he mentions several of the battles, plunders, and preys, won by Tadhg O'Kelly, and portions of the spoils of which were always bestowed upon himself. He then recounts a characteristic story concerning a meeting of the provincial kings and nobles of Erinn which, on a certain occasion, assembled at *Brian*'s court at *Ceann Coradh*; among whom were *Maelseachlainn*, King of Meath; *Aedh* O'Neill, King of Ulster; *Tadhg* O'Kelly, King of *Ui Mainé*, and several others. It happened, we are told, on this occasion, that while the henchmen of *Brian* and of Tadhg O'Kelly were burnishing the shields of their respective masters, a dispute arose between them, as to the claims of precedence respectively of the noble owners of the two shields. The dispute ran so high that at last *Tadhg*'s page raised his arm and struck *Brian*'s page a violent blow with his fist on the mouth, from which the blood flowed freely over the richly ornamented dress he wore.

Here, however, the poem breaks off abruptly: the remainder of it is, unfortunately, in the possession of Lord Ashburnham. Were it in that of any real lover of literature, he would surely send the fragment, and the old Book of *Ui Mainé* which contains it, over here, to be at least transcribed, so as to be made available for the important purposes of our antiquarian researches. But it is idle to expect so much of public spirit or scholarlike feeling at the hands of such a collector as the nobleman just referred to. It is probable that the Book of *Ui Mainé* contains many more of the poems of *Mac Liag* and his contemporaries; but we can only surmise about them for the present.

From *Mac Liag* we now pass to *Errard Mac Coisé*, who was

Of Mac Coisé, and his Poems.

chief poet to the court of *Maelseachlainn* (Malachy), the predecessor, and afterwards the successor of *Brian Boromha* in the monarchy of Erinn, who died in the year 1022.

Of *Mac Coisé's* compositions I know but five pieces to be now extant, four poems and one prose piece. Of the first two of these poems and of the prose tract I possess correct copies. Of the third poem there is a copy in the Royal Irish Academy, as well as an imperfect copy of the prose tract. Of the fourth poem there is, I believe, a copy in the possession of John O'Donovan, LL.D.[(93)]

[illegible] The first of these poems is one of twenty-seven stanzas, or one hundred and eight lines, in praise of the same king *Maelseachlainn*, and of the chief princes of Erinn his cotemporaries, among whom were *Brian Boromha* and *Tadhg* O'Kelly, who, it appears, however, were both dead at the time of writing this poem. This very scarce and valuable poem begins:

"*Maelseachlainn*, the senior line of the Gaedhils,—
It is fit that all men should celebrate him,—
The fierce destroyer of his foes,—
The brown-haired heir of *Domhnall*".[(94)]

2nd.—The second poem, which perhaps ought to have been the first described, consists of fifty-two stanzas, or two hundred and eight lines, and opens by way of a dialogue between *Mac Liag*, already mentioned, and *Mac Coisé*. This poem appears to have been written in Dublin, where both the bards must have been sojourning together at the time. *Mac Liag* opens the dialogue with a warm eulogy on *Brian Boromha* and the Dalcassians, and boasts loudly of the veneration he enjoyed, and of the [illegible] and gifts which he was at all times sure to receive from them. *Mac Coisé* interrupts him at the seventh stanza by asking [illegible] details of the Dalcassian munificence. *Mac Liag* answers in two more stanzas; and then at the tenth stanza *Mac Coisé* takes up the cause of the kings and nobles of Meath, Ulster, and Connacht, and in the remaining part supplies a number of [illegible] instances of the hospitality and munificence which he himself in his professional character received from those [illegible] personages. This poem begins:

"Long be thy life, O generous *Errard!*
Mac Coisé of the splendid intellect;

(93) [This great Irish scholar was still living when this lecture was delivered. [illegible] in November, 1861, at the comparatively early age of fifty-three—a few months before his distinguished brother-in-law, Professor O'Curry.]

(94) original:—Maelṡeaċlainn ṡinnsear Gaoiḋeal,
cóir do ċáċ a ċommaoiḋeam
foll foglaḋ na foirne, ua flainn
oigre donnaḋraċ Domnaill.

It is time that we return to our homes;
We have been here a whole year.
"Though short to you and to me may seem
This our sojourn in Dublin,
Brian of *Banba* deems it too long
That he listens not to my eloquence.
"Not to hear the history of the great sons of Milesius,
And of the brave and beautiful *Tuatha Dé Danann*,
And along with these that he hears not
The conquests of the noble monarchs of Erinn".[89]

This poem affords us what may be called a living illustration of the important office which the court poet filled of old, and the style of the social enjoyments of our ancient kings and princes. It affords also a clear verification of that part of the tract on the "Seven Degrees of the Poets", which relates to the office of *Ollamh*, or chief poet, to which reference has so often been made in the course of these Lectures.[90]

Edward O'Reilly, in his Irish Writers, at the year 1023, mentions this poem; but he appears not to have read it with sufficient care, since he says it was addressed to *Mac Coisé* himself, and that it is more likely it was written by some one of his contemporaries. O'Reilly also felt some difficulty about the identity of *Errard Mac Coisé;* because *Tighernach* the annalist mentions the death of one great scholar of the name at the year 990, while the Four Masters record the death of another great scholar of the same name and in the same words at the year 1023. But whether there were two poets named *Errard Mac Coisé*, and whether they died in those respective years, or not, does not affect the authorship of these two poems, as they bear internal evidence of their having been written by the same man, and that that man lived shortly after the death of King *Mael-seachlainn*, which took place in the year 1022.

3rd,—The third is a poem of twenty-six stanzas, or one hundred and four lines, in praise of *Maelruanaidh*, the second son

(89) original:—Marṫain duit a ṡraiṫ ḟéil,
a ṁic Coise go ccaiṁ ceill,
is miṫid duinn teaċt d'ar toiġ,
atamaid abus bliadain.
Giḋ gairid leatsa agus linn,
inḋenus sinn ag Duiblinn
is fada le Brian Banba
gan éisteaċt rem' urlabra.
Gan scéla mac Miliḋ ṁóir
is Tuaṫ De Danann dreaċ ṁóir,
gan a g-cloisteaċt ceann a cceann,
gabala ard-ríg Eireann.

(90) See *Lectures on the MS. Materials of Ancient Irish History*; p. 220, 240; *and Appendix, No. I.*, p. 461–3.

of *Tadhg* of the Tower, King of Connacht, and ancestor of the O'Conor family, who died in the year 954, and was succeeded by his eldest son Conor. *Maelruanaidh*, the second son, became lord of the territory of *Magh Luirg* in East Connacht, and was the ancestor of the families of Mac Dermot and Mac Donagh, of that country. The poet describes a visit which he paid to this chief at his princely residenbe, and the entertainment and gifts which he received on the occasion. Among these presents were, a chessboard; a valuable sword; fifty milch cows; and thirty steeds, "fit to appear at fairs and assemblies". This curious poem begins:

LECT. VI. [Prose piece by Mac Coisé.]

"Thou warrior of Queen *Meadhbh*'s plain,—
Thou king of popular *Cruachan*,—
Thou valiant guardian of thy people,—
Thou brave protector of Milesian Erinn".[97]

Edward O'Reilly had not seen this poem; and the only copy of it that I know to be extant is one in the Library of the Royal Irish Academy.

4th.—The fourth piece of *Mac Coisé*'s compositions, is a poem of twenty-two stanzas, or eighty-eight lines, written by him on the death of old *Fergal O'Ruairc*, King of Connacht, (the ancestor of the celebrated family of the O'Ruaircs of *Breifné*, or Brefney), who was killed in battle in East Meath, A.D. 964, according to the *Annals of the Four Masters*. This poem begins: "A poet is sorrowful after his king".[98]

I am not aware of any existing copy of this poem but one, which is in the possession of John O'Donovan, LL.D., and which I have not been able to examine. O'Reilly, in his *Irish Writers*, at the year 990, seemed to think that *Mac Coisé*, the author of this poem, (who, according to *Tighernach*'s annals, died in the year 990), was a different person from the *Mac Coisé* of whom we have been just speaking, who died in the year 1023. "The Four Masters", he says, "under the year 1023, record the death of an *Erard Mac Coisé*; but from the poem on the death of *Fergal O'Ruairc* above-mentioned, written immediately after the fall of that king in 964, when the writer must have been of full age, it would appear that the *Erard Mac Coisé* of the Four Masters, and the *Urard Mac Coisé* of *Tighernach*, were two distinct persons".

(97) Original:—a ḃeaṗṁaiḋ ṁuiġe Meaḋḃa,
a ríġ Cruaċan coṁḟéaḋma,
a ḃuaċaill taṗḃḋa na ttreaḃ,
a ḋíon Banba ṁac Míleaḋ.

(98) Original:—Brónaċ ollaṁ d'éis a ríġ.

LECT. VI.

[Prose piece by Mac Coisé.]

I have already stated my belief that O'Reilly was mistaken in his opinion; and that the *Mac Coisé* of *Tighernach* and the *Mac Coisé* of the Four Masters were one and the same person. For, supposing, as O'Reilly says, that *Mac Coisé* must have been a man of full age in the year 964, when he is believed to have written this poem, and supposing him to have been then twenty-four years of age, old enough to be a writer, and that he died in 1023, his age would be but eighty-two, or at most eighty-three years: but the *Chronicon Scotorum* gives the death of *Fergal O'Ruairc* at the year 966, which, on the same hypothesis, would reduce the poet's age to eighty, or at most eighty-one years, a span of life no way extraordinary in that age any more than in this. But whether or not a *Mac Coisé* died in the year 990, according to *Tighernach* and the *Chronicon Scotorum*, there is evidence enough remaining to prove that the *Mac Coisé* who died in the year 1023 was the author of the poem on *Fergal O'Ruairc*; for in the poem which *Mac Coisé* wrote on King *Maelseachlainn* (or Malachy) and his contemporaries, which I have already described, *Mac Coisé* mentions by name all the great Irishmen who had lived within Malachy's life-time; and among these he gives a distinguished place to old *Fergal O'Ruairc*, and winds up with a sorrowful expression of regret that he himself, who had been their contemporary, should have outlived them all.

5th.—The fifth and last piece of *Mac Coisé's* composition, is a prose tract of a very extraordinary character; and though it is in some sort a digression from the more direct subject of the present Lecture, I cannot refrain from giving some account of the details of a piece which contains so much, both in its matter and in its form, that is particularly interesting, in reference to the manners and habits of the time. The following short account of the cause of its composition is prefixed to the tract, in language as old as the original text, and, in my belief, in *Mac Coisé's* own words.

This account states that it was *Urard Mac Coisé* that framed this piece of composition for the O'Neils of Ulster, who had unlawfully plundered his castle at *Clartha* (now Clara, in the county of Westmeath), in revenge for his having wounded one of their people, named *Muiredhach*, son of *Eoghan*. They demolished the poet's castle, and carried off his household furniture, and his precious jewels, as well as his cows and his horses. The poet was absent at the time; and on his return to his family, he saw no prospect of redress against enemies so powerful, unless by the exercise of his art and the influence it gave him; and to this he had recourse. After some time, then, he set out to the palace of *Aileach* (near Derry), the ancient residence of the Kings of Ulster of the Clann Neill line, and at this time the abode of *Domhnall O'Neil*, Monarch of Erinn, (who died in the year 978).

[Prose piece by Mac Coisé.]

The poet arrived at *Aileach* rather early in the day, and before the king had risen; but when the monarch had heard of the arrival of such a guest, welcome as a great poet and historian was, everywhere, in those days, he at once ordered him to his presence; and having warmly received him, he proceeded to demand of him what tales he had to recite in the exercise of his art. *Mac Coisé* answered that he had a great many, and begged that the king would select from the ancient chief historic tales of Erinn, one or more that he should wish to hear. The king requested the poet to give him the names of those great tales, in order that he might be the better able to make a selection. *Mac Coisé* then repeats the list of those great tales, under the various heads, such as I have already presented them, when speaking of the particular qualifications of each of the seven degrees of the poets.[96] He began with the death of *Cuchulainn;* [illegible]'s decline after the assault of the two *Ben-Sidhes;* the [illegible] *Bo-Chuailgné;* and so on through the whole list;—into which, however, *Mac Coisé* introduces many tales not mentioned in the ordinary lists. With all these the king seemed to be familiar, except the last on the poet's list, to which he had given the title of: "The Plunder of the Castle of *Maelmilscothach*, the son of the Venerable Name, son of the Noble Teacher of the [illegible], son of the *Ollamh* in Poetry, son of Legitimate Poetry, [illegible] *Lugaidh*, Master of all the Arts, son of the Red Man [illegible] Knowledge, son of the Faith of the Holy Spirit with the [illegible] and the Son".[96]

[illegible] were the wild names, and such was the symbolical [illegible] which *Mac Coisé* made for himself; while the "Plunder [illegible] Castle of *Maelmilscothach*", of which he proposed to [illegible] history, was in fact but the plunder of his own castle [illegible].

Mac Coisé's Tale of the "Plunder of the Castle of Maelmilscothach".

[illegible] name *Maelmilscothach*, which *Mac Coisé* gave himself, [illegible] "of the honeyed words", from *mil*, honey, and *scoth*, [illegible] *Lugaidh*, "Master of all the Arts", whom he counts [illegible] ancestors, was the celebrated *Tuath Dé Danann* *Lug*, the son of *Cian*, more commonly called *Lug Mac*

[illegible] Lectures on the *MS. Materials of Ancient Irish History*, p. 220, 241, [illegible]:—Orgain cathrach Maoil Milscothaigh, mic anma airmice [illegible] Eolairde, mic Ollamhain aircetail, mic Dana Dligheadhaigh, mic [illegible] Denaigh, mic Ruaid Rofesa, mic Creitme in Spirita Naimh, acair

LECT. VI.

Mac Coisé's Tale of the "Plunder of the Castle of Maelmilscothach".

Ceithlenn, from his mother, of whom a full description was given in speaking of the Battle of the Northern *Magh Tuiredh*, in a former Lecture.[101] The *Ruadh Rofheasa*, or "Red Man of all Knowledge", was the celebrated *Tuath Dé Danann* king, the great *Daghda*. And *Mac Coisé* makes use of the names of these two personages to symbolize his intimate acquaintance with all the pagan literature of ancient Erinn, in the same way that he makes his descent from the Holy Spirit, the Father, and the Son, the symbol of his intimate knowledge of the Christian literature of the time.

When the king, *Domhnal O'Neil*, heard the title of this tale, and the name and pedigree of the lord of the plundered castle, he declared that he had never before heard of it, and eagerly desired to hear the full history of the plunder alluded to. *Mac Coisé* then commenced the tale, by relating the circumstances that led to his loss, and describing in a very imaginative style the character and prowess of the parties who took part in the violence of which he complained. It was somewhat as follows:

At the approach of the hostile party to the castle, the beautiful nymph Poetry, daughter of the Arts, who resided within, ascended to the top of the building, to beseech them to spare it on her account; for she believed that her inviolability would save it from any injury. With this view she accosted the spokesman of the party, asking who and what they were, what they wanted, and what were the names of their leaders. The spokesman answers by giving their names according to their etymological signification; such as "*Tené n-aen beimé*", which means literally "fire of one stroke", that is, the fire struck by one stroke on a flint. This fire is evidently but a spark; and the Irish for a spark of fire is *Aedh*, or *Udh*, as it is pronounced; and *Aedh* is the proper Christian name of a man, (now Anglicised Hugh). The name of the second chief man of the party, he said, was *Nuall Domain*, (from *nuall*, "noble", and *domain*, "the world",) that is, the noblest of the world; of which two words the Christian name *Domhnall*, (now Anglicised Donnell), is but a condensed transposition. The name of the third champion, he said, was *Nel Mac Laeich Lasamain*, that is, Light, the son of the Blazing Warrior, (from *nel*, "light", *laech*, "a champion", and *lasamain*, "blazing" or radiant). This *Nell* (or *Niall*, as the name is more commonly written), was son of the *Aedh* mentioned above, whose name was interpreted fire or flame; etc. And so the spokesman goes on to give the names of the chief men of his party under these obscure designations.

[101] See *Lectures on the MS. Materials of Ancient Irish History*, p. 249, 260.

Mac Coisé's Tale of the "Plunder of the Castle of Maelmilscothach".

The nymph Poetry then inquires whether the assailants would not prefer the precious jewels of poetic eloquence and eulogium, to the torturing lashes of poetic satire, of both of which she had, she said, an abundant stock to bestow, from the laudations of *Mac Lonain*, the satires of *Morán*, the eloquence of *Laidech*, the stories of *Laech Liathmhuim*, the obscure proverbs of *Fithal*, the philosophy of the *Ferceirtnés*, the intellect of the poetess *Edain*, the brilliancy of *Nera*, the clear truths of the Princess *Mór Mumhan*, etc.

The answer which the plunderers made to this inquiry was a furious assault on the mansion, which they soon entered and proceeded to strip of all its movable property. Having emptied the house above ground, they next approached the cellar under ground; and here they were met at its doors by *Dathghel*, the guardian of that important place. The assailants ask *Dathghel* who were the defenders of the cellar, and if they were brave. And *Dathghel* tells them that it was defended by the best and bravest of *Maelmilscothach*'s household, both men and women; and *Dathghel* gives them the names of a formidable band, by personifying the various articles of furniture, etc., in the house; such as *Criol mac Craeslinaidh*, that is, Chest, son of Fill-mouth; *Bolc mac Bith-thellaigh*, that is, Bellows, son of Constant Fireplace; *Breacan mac Ban-ghresa*, that is, Blanket, son of Woman's Work; *Fidhbha mac Fo-chraebhaigh*, that is, Hatchet, son of Tree Cutter; [illegible] *mac Dagh-shuaithé*, that is, Bag, son of Good Yarn; *Coiré mac Cruadh-ghobhann*, that is, Pot, son of Hardy Smith; *Cuagh mac Tornora*, that is, Wooden Mug, the son of Turner; *Loimdha mac Lomhthogha*, that is, Churn-staff, son of Choice Hands;—and so on. Such were the names of a few of the male defenders of *Maelmilscothach*'s cellar; and the following were the names of a few of its female inmates: *Lenn inghen Lamhthoraidh*, that is, Mantle, the daughter of Manufacturer; *Leiné inghen Lin-ghuirt*, that is, Shirt, daughter of Flax-field; *Ceirtlé inghen Suimhairé*, that is, Ball, or Bottom, daughter of Distaff; *Suathad inghen Inuamai*, that is, Needle, daughter of Stitcher; *Corthair inghen Druinighé*, that is, [illegible], daughter of Embroideress; *Scuap inghen Gaironta*, that is, Broom, daughter of Tidiness; *Cir inghen Scribairé*, that is, Comb, daughter of Scrubber; *Sust inghen Tren-truaircnigh*, that is, Flail, daughter of Powerful Thresher;—and so on

As I have dwelt at greater length than I intended on the names of these fanciful guardians of *Maelmilscothach*'s cellar, because, though I have given but a few of them, they will serve to show how the castle was furnished in articles of domestic conve-

LECT. VI.

Mac Coisé's tale of the Plunder of the Castle of Maelmilscothach".

nience, so as to afford some interesting examples (which, though somewhat out of place here, I should be loth to pass over) of the ordinary appliances of domestic industry in the home of an Irish housewife a thousand years ago. But on this subject I mean to speak at some length on a future occasion.

In the piece which I am now describing, *Mac Coisé* continues to relate, with much force, the progress of the plunder of the castle. The enormity of the act is considerably increased in his account, by his stating that it was while *Maelmilscothach* himself had been engaged in attending on the king in one of his expeditions, and in the king's presence, that an account of the plunder of his mansion reached him. Upon hearing this, continues *Mac Coisé*, the king exclaimed: "Reproach me not; for the sky shall fall on the earth, the sea shall overleap its boundaries, and the human race shall be swept away, or thou shalt have restitution of the plundered property, together with full compensation for the violation of thy castle, in such manner as the men of Erinn shall adjudge, in my presence". The king having thus promised material redress to *Maelmil-scothach*, the latter then recalls the "six bloodhounds" which the just administration of the king had induced him to banish from him twenty years before. The names of these hounds in the story are Satire, Disgrace, Shame, Abuse, Blush, and Bitter Words; and these he sent after the plunderers to bring them immediately before the king. They were foiled, however, by "six fanciful pigs", which the plunderers sent against them; so that the king had, at last, to send out his own herald to command them to his presence. In the meantime the king called a council of the chiefs of his country, to take their advice as to what should be done for *Maelmilscothach*; and they unanimously recommended that full restitution should be made to him.

When *Mac Coisé* had thus fully described the wrongs done to *Maelmilscothach*, and the justice rendered him, he ends by avowing to the monarch that he was himself the plundered *Maelmilscothach*, and that *Domhnall O'Neil* himself was the king whose people had plundered him. He then addressed the person whom he supposed to have been the leader of the plundering party, in a poem of eighteen stanzas; but, though addressed to this person, it was intended as a panegyric on the king himself, and his family and race (the Clann Neill of Ulster); and he takes care to remind the king that *Mac Coisé* had been the tutor of himself and his brother, and that he had been reared by their father, the celebrated *Muircheartach* "of the Leather Cloaks", son of *Niall Glundubh*. This curious poem begins:

Mac Coisé's Tale of the "Plunder of the Castle of Maelmilscothach".

"O thou, yonder man, by our words of knowledge,
If it be thou that hast caused this disturbance;
Verily it is not without punishment [or] without battle,
That *Maelmilscothach*'s cattle shall have been plundered".[180]

After this King *Domhnall O'Neil* really did call a council, to advise with them upon what should be done in *Mac Coisé's* case; and the chiefs left it in the king's own hands to inflict what punishment he should think proper on the guilty parties, but offered from themselves a cow for every commander and royal champion in all *Tir-Eoghain*, to *Mac Coisé*, as restitution. In the meantime the chief historians, poets, and judges of Erinn repaired to the king's presence, to demand, if necessary, a compensation proportionate with his rank for *Mac Coisé*, for the insult and violation offered to his sacred person and dignity; but the king having already conceded this, he had now only to call upon them to "assess the damages", according to the ancient law which provided for such cases. All parties, thereupon, agreed in requesting to have the case submitted to the decision of *Flann* "the eloquent", the head professor of the great school of Clonmacnois. This was done accordingly; and *Flann* awarded the poet full restitution of his property, full repairs of any injuries which his house might have sustained, and in addition fourteen *Cumals* (of three cows each), or forty-two cows, and "the breadth of his face of gold", as compensation for the violation of his personal and professional dignity. And the learned men present on the occasion confirmed this decision, and, with the consent of the king and his chiefs, fixed them as the damages to be ever after paid in all similar cases, but to such poets only as were capable of composing the "*Imbas Forosnai*", the "*Dichetul-do-Chennaibh*", and the "*Teinm Laeghdha*"; three species of composition, the nature of which I have described in a former Lecture.[181]

This tale is remarkable for the vigour and purity of the language in which it is told; but it is especially useful to the purpose of our present inquiry for the important corroboration which it contains of the authenticity of other ancient tracts and pieces, which go more or less into minute descriptions of the state of civilization and the social economy of the Gaedhil at the period spoken of; that is, so far back, at least, as a thousand years ago.

(180) Original:—A ḟir ṫall ðar ḟerba ḟis,
maṡa tu do gni an m-buaidris,
as derb ni gan cin gan cath
do airged Maelmilscothach.

(181) See *Lectures on the MS. Materials*, etc.; p. 240. See also, Lect. x.; *post*, p. 206, *et seq.*

LECTURE VII.

[Delivered 18th June, 1857.]

(III.) Education, and Literature; (continued). The Profession of Learning in ancient Erinn established by law. Professors sometimes employed as rulers, or ministers of state. Of *Cuan O'Lothchain*; (ob. A.D. 1024). Descent of the *O'Lothchains* from *Cormac Gaileng*. Of the Poems of *Cuan O'Lothchain*. Of the Legend of the origin of the name of the river *Sinann* (Shannon). The *Eo Feasa* ("Salmon of Knowledge",)—alluded to by *Mac Liag*; and by *Aengus Finn* O'Daly. Legend of the "Seven Streams of the Fountain of *Connla*". Of the History of *Druim Criaich*, (temp. *Eochaidh Feidhlech*, circa B. C. 100). Of the History of the *Cath Atha Comair*. Of the history of *Nial* "of the Nine Hostages". Of the origin of the Fair of *Tailtén*. Poems of *Flann Mainistrech*. Of the origin of the Palace of *Aileach*. Of the Poem on *Aileach* by *Cuaradh*, (x. century).

In tracing the evidences of literary cultivation among the Gaedhils, and the education which it implies, I could not but take the opportunity of recording more precisely than those who have gone before me, the principal specimens which have come down to us of the learning and literary ability of the more remarkable professors in each century. The examples I have referred to ought, I think, to satisfy every one that the Gaedhelic language was always carefully cultivated, not only as the ordinary medium of instruction, but also of the preservation of historic facts, even centuries after the introduction of the Latin language with Christianity among the learned. It is to be remembered that every one of the *Ollamhs* or *Fileas*,—(Poets they are called in English, because they wrote in verse, but they more properly correspond with the Philosophers of the classic nations)[164]—every one of these writers, whose lives and whose works I am here shortly recounting, was a learned man by profession; every one of them had successfully studied for a regular legal rank or degree; and every one of them was entitled not only to fees for his labour as a teacher, but to important privileges and to other advantages under the law, in order to enable him to devote himself the better to the investigation of legal science and history, and to the public exercise of his literary powers, for the benefit of the people. Accordingly, it is not unusual to find these "Poets", (Philosophers, or Professors of Literature,) associated with the governing powers as

The Profession of learning in ancient Erinn established by law.

[164] See *Lectures on the MS. Materials of Ancient Irish History*; p. 2, note; and App. No. I. p. 461.

political advisers to the king; and sometimes even themselves entrusted for a time with the cares of government, when particularly remarkable for their wisdom and ability. An instance of this honour is supplied in the case of the writer of whom I now proceed to speak, and whose name has been frequently mentioned before in the course of these lectures.

Professors sometimes employed as Rulers and Ministers of State.

Next after *Urard MacCoisé*, the most eminent historical poet, in the order of time, was *Cuan O'Lothchain*, whose death is recorded in the following words in the Annals of *Loch Cé* (in Roscommon,) at the year 1024: "*Cuan O'Lothchain*, Chief Poet of Erinn, was killed by the people of Teffia, [in Westmeath]. God manifestly wrought a poet's power upon the parties who killed him, for they were put to a cruel death, and their bodies putrefied until wolves and vultures had devoured them".

All the other annals record the poet's death in nearly the same words.

Of Cuan O'Lothchain; (ob. A.D. 1024.)

Edward O'Reilly, in his "Irish Writers", (at the year 1024) speaks thus of *O'Lothchain:*

"*Cuan O'Lochain*, the most learned and celebrated antiquarian and historian of Ireland in his time, was killed in *Teathbha* [Teffia], this year, according to the concurrent testimonies of the Annals of *Tighernach*, Inisfallen, and the Four Masters. His talents and his virtues were so highly appreciated by his countrymen, that he was made joint-regent of Ireland with *Corcran* '*Cleireach*', (or 'the Clergyman'), after the death of *Maoleachlainn*".

Dr. John O'Donovan, at page 42 of the Introduction to the "Book of Rights", (so ably edited by him for the Celtic Society, in the year 1847,) has the following remarks on *O'Lothchain*, whose poem on the Privileges and Restrictions of the Monarchs of Erinn, is prefixed to that most curious and important Book:

"*Cuan O'Leochain*, or *O'Lothchain*, as he is sometimes called, or, as the name is more generally spelled, *O'Lochain*, was chief poet to *Maelseachlainn* (Malachy) II., monarch of Ireland, who died in 1022. After the death of this monarch, there was an interregnum of twenty years, and we are informed that *Cuan O'Lochain* and *Corcran Cleireach* were appointed governors of Ireland; but *Cuan* did not long enjoy this dignity, for he was slain in *Teabhtha*, (Teffia) A. D. 1024. Mr. Moore states, in his History of Ireland, vol. ii. page 147, that—'for this provisional government of *Cuan* he can find no authority in any of our regular annals': and it is certain", continues Dr. O'Donovan, "that no authority for it is found in any of the original Irish annals, nor even in the Annals of the Four Masters; but the fact is

Of Cuan O'Lothchain; (ob., A.D. 1024.)

stated as follows in Macgeoghegan's translation of the Annals of Clonmacnoise:

"'A. D. 1022. After the death of King Moyleseaghlyn, this kingdom was without a king twenty years, during [a portion of] which time the realm was governed by two learned men, the one called Cwan O'Lochan, a well-learned temporall man, and chief poet of Ireland; the other Corcran Cleireogh, a devout and holy man that was [chief] anchorite of all Ireland, whose most abideing was at Lismore. The land was governed like a free state, and not like a monarchie by them.

"'A. D. 1024. Cwan O'Loghan, prime poet of Ireland, a great chronicler, and one to whom, for his sufficiencie, the causes of Ireland were submitted to be examined and ordered, was killed by one of the land of Teaffa; after committing of which evill fact, there grew an evill scent and odour of the party that killed him, that he was easily known among the rest of the land. His associate Corcran lived yett, and survived him for a long time after'".

It is a remarkable fact that the government of Ireland conjointly by the poet *Cuan O'Lothchain* and the priest *Corcran*, should be asserted or assented to by Charles O'Conor of Belnagare, in his pamphlet written against Sir Richard Cox, in 1749,—by Edward O'Reilly in his "Irish Writers", published in 1820,—by Thomas Moore in his History of Ireland, published in 1836,—and by John O'Donovan in the "Book of Rights", published in 1847,—without any more certain authority in support of it. It is probable, indeed, that Charles O'Conor was acquainted with the authority; but it is clear that none of those who followed him were so. It is undeniable that this fact is not to be found in any of our regular annals; it is, however, recorded in an older authority than any of the existing copies of our regular annals, namely, in the Book of Leinster itself, which was written about the year 1150. In a list of the succession of the Christian monarchs of Erinn, from *Laeghairé Mac Neil* down to Roderick O'Conor, preserved in this valuable book, the death of king Malachy the Second (*Maelseachlainn*), is recorded in its proper place (at the year 1022); and the following entry appears immediately after it:

"A joint government of Erinn during forty-two years, or fifty, *Cuan O'Lothchain* and *Corcran* the cleric".[103]

Along with the doubt of the scribe in the text of this article, as to whether the term was forty-two or fifty years, there is another correction or suggestion in the margin, in the original

(103) Original:—"Comflaitius for hErinn fri re da bliadain .xl. no l., Cuan O Lothchain, Corcran clerech".

hand and in the same Roman numerals, making the number of years sixty-four. LECT. VII.

Of Cuan O'Lothchain; (ob. A.D. 1024.)

Here, then, is a most respectable authority for this provisional government of Erinn; and one which Moore, with all his scepticism, would have gladly recognised. The doubt of the scribe as to the exact number of years could apply only to *Coveran*, in whom the term was prolonged, and must have arisen from some mistake or obscurity of the preceding scribe, which he endeavoured to correct.

From anything that I have been able to discover, *Cuan O'Lothchain* had never been chief poet to King Malachy; nor, indeed, could he have been so, since his contemporary *MacCoisé* had held that distinguished office down to the monarch's death.

The descent of the O'Lothchains from Cormac Gaileng.

The *O'Lothchains* were a family of distinction, and chiefs of the territory of *Gailenga Móra*, or Great Gailenga; (situated in Meath and Longford, and now known in the former county as the barony of Morgallion); but they were first settled in the district of *Eilé*, (in Tipperary and King's County). The history of their descent is worth alluding to for more than one reason.

The *O'Lothchains* were descended from *Cormac Gaileng*, the son of *Tadhg*, son of *Cian*, son of *Oilioll Oluim*, king of Munster. *Tadhg's* father *Cian* and his six brothers were killed in the battle of *Magh Macruimhé*, (near *Ath-an-Righ*, in the county of Galway), in the year 194, while maintaining the cause of their uncle *Art* (the father of the celebrated *Cormac Mac Airt*), the monarch of Erinn, who also fell there, against *Mac Con*, their step-brother and *Art's* nephew.

After the death of *Art* and the prolonged reign of *MacCon*, *Cormac* the son of *Art* at last came to the throne; but he was almost immediately attacked and expelled from power by *Fergus Dubh-deadach*, (i.e. "of the black tooth"), an Ultonian prince, who attempted to seize on the government of the nation by force. In this extremity *Cormac* went into Munster to seek assistance from *Oilioll Oluim*, the king of that province, who was married to his aunt *Sadhbh*, the daughter of *Conn* "of the Hundred Battles".

With the consent of the old king *Oilioll*, his grandson *Tadhg* the son of *Cian* already mentioned agreed to come to the assistance of his cousin *Cormac* with such forces as he could raise in Munster; but on the condition that if he were successful in driving out *Fergus* and his brothers from Tara, he should have a recompense out of the land which his valour had recovered; terms to which *Cormac* was but too glad to assent. *Tadhg* accordingly mustered as large a force as he could within his native province, and among the leading chiefs who joined his standard,

[LECT]. VII.

we are told, was his grandfather's brother, the aged warrior *Lugaidh Lagha*, who had been present at the battle of *Magh Macruimhé*, and who had himself actually cut off the head of the monarch *Art* on the battle-field, but who now resolved to make amends to his son *Cormac* by using his best endeavours to restore him to the throne of his ancestors. Thus prepared, *Tadhg* marched with his forces into Meath, and came up with the army of the usurper at *Crinna*, (near the place where now stand the noble ruins of the ancient abbey of Mellifont, on the bounds of Meath and Louth). Here a battle was fought in which the Ultonians were defeated by *Tadhg*, and Fergus the usurper and the other two Ferguses his brothers slain and beheaded.

Cormac having been thus restored to his throne gave *Tadhg* the promised territory, extending along the sea from the river *Glais Nera*, (at Dromiskin in Louth,) to the Liffey; a territory which was ever afterwards known by the name of *Cianachta*, in memory of *Tadhg*'s father *Cian;* and in which his descendants, (of whom the families of Mac Cormac are the representatives), continued to flourish as chiefs down to the tenth century, when they were at last reduced by the Danes.

Tadhg's second son, *Cormac*, had received the surname of *Gaileng*, (*Cormac Gaileng*, that is, *Cormac* "Shame-spear"), from having on a certain occasion made a treacherous use of the favourite spear of his father. And it is from this *Cormac* and his descendants that the territory of the Great and Little *Gailengas* (in Meath), as well as of *Luighné* (or Lune or Leney, in Meath and Sligo,) derive their names; and it is from him that the families of *O'Lothchain* in Meath, and O'Hara and O'Gara in Sligo, descend. From *Conla*, the elder son of *Tadhg*, sprang all the O'Carrolls, O'Reardons, and O'Meachars of Tipperary; and of his race too was the celebrated poet and scholar *Flann*, professor in the ancient abbey of Monasterboice, in Louth, of whom I shall have more to say hereafter.

[Poem]s by [Cuan O'Lot]hchain.

Of *Cuan O'Lothchain*'s works I have met with but six historical poems, but these are all of great value.

The first is a poem of forty-seven stanzas, or one hundred and eighty-eight lines, in praise of the monarch *Cormac Mac Airt*, who died A.D. 266; describing by name and situation every chief building and monument, every remarkable spot and object, within the precincts of Tara, in *Cormac*'s time or added afterwards; and not only those then remaining in ruins, but all those described in writings from the time of *Cormac* down to his own. This poem, with an English translation, (and a map of the ruins of Tara, deduced from it), is

LECT. VII.

Poems by Oisin O'Lothchain.

ated in Dr. Petrie's History and Antiquities of Tara, published in the year 1839, in the Transactions of the Royal Irish Academy, (vol. xviii. part ii.); a work to which I would direct the special attention of all who feel any interest in the genuine investigation of the antiquities of Ireland. As Dr. Petrie's published version of this most curious and important poem, and my own analysis of it in a former Lecture,[190] are already before the public, it is not necessary that I should dwell on it further here.

The second piece of *O'Lothchain* is a poem of thirty-seven stanzas, or one hundred and forty-eight lines, on the peculiar privileges and prerogatives, as well as restrictions and prohibitions, of the monarch and provincial kings of Erinn. According to this poem, the monarch was subject to seven "prohibitions", and had seven prerogatives, and each of the four provincial kings had five of each. The origin of those prohibitions (which are very analogous to those of our modern "lucky" and "unlucky" days), is lost in the obscurity of ages; but doubtless they had their rise in some untoward accidents or events which were at the time of sufficient importance to be handed down in existing traditions to generations long subsequent.

The "prohibitions" of the monarch of Erinn were such as the following: He should not let the sun rise upon him in his bed in the plain of Tara; he should not alight on a Wednesday in the plain of Bregia; he should not traverse the plain of *Cuillenn* after sunset; he should not urge his horse on the slope of *Comar*; he should not launch his ship on the Monday next after May-day; and he should not leave the track of his army upon the plain of *Maigin* on the Tuesday next after All Hallows. His seven "prerogatives" were: To be supplied with the fish of the river Boyne to eat; the deer of *Luibnech*; the fruit of Manann, (the present Isle of Man); the heath-fruit of *Brileith*; the cresses of the river *Brosnach*; the water of the well of *Tlachtga*; the hares of *Naas*. It was on the calends of August all these were brought to the king of *Temair* (Tara). And by way of a blessing on the king, it was said that the year in which he eat of these did not count in his age, and he defeated his foes on all sides.

The "prohibitions" and "prerogatives" of the provincial kings were of the same character as these; but, as they are published in the Book of Rights, already mentioned, I shall pass them over here.

From the opening lines of the poem it would appear to have

[190] See *Lectures on the MS. Materials of Ancient Irish History*; pp. 9, 10; and App., p. 496.

LECT. VII. Poems by O'Lothchain.

been addressed to the door-keeper of King Malachy the Second, who first assumed the monarchy in the year 979; and it is said that the object of the poet was to introduce himself to the notice of the monarch for the purpose of being chosen by him as his poet; but whether he was successful in this object or not we have now no means of knowing. The poem begins:(167)

"O noble man who closest the door!
I am *O'Lothchain* of the poems.
Allow me to pass by thee into the strong house
In which is the high monarch of Erinn.

"With me for him will be found
The knowledge—which is not a fiction—
Of his seven prerogatives of many virtues,
With the seven prohibitions of the high king".

In the last stanza but one we have a confirmation of what was stated in a former Lecture, that an accurate knowledge of these prerogatives and prohibitions was indispensable to the candidate who sought the distinction of *Ollamh* or chief poet and historian,—either to the monarch or to any of the provincial kings,—or to a free visitation of their provinces. The stanza is as follows:

"He is not entitled to the free visitation of a province,
Nor to the *Ollamh*-ship of Erinn,
Nor almost to anything he asks,—
The poet with whom these are not found".

The third piece of *O'Lothchain's* composition is a poem of sixteen stanzas, or fifty-six lines, on the origin of the name of the *Sinann*, now the river Shannon. This poem begins:

"The noble name of *Sinainn* seek ye from me;
Its bare recital would not be pleasant,
Not alike now are its action and noise
As when *Sinann* herself was free and alive".(168)

Legend of origin of name of river Sinann (Shannon).

The legend of the Shannon's origin affords an interesting example of the style of our very ancient literary compositions. It is shortly as follows:

Sinann was the daughter of the learned *Lodan*, who was the son of *Lear*, the great sea-king of the *Tuatha Dé Danann* colony of Erinn, from whose son and successor *Manannan* the

(167) See *Leabhar na g-Ceart* (Book of Rights), published by the Celtic Society, 1848; p. 9.

(168) original:—Saer ainm Sinna saighidh uaim
nabad loind a lom luaid
ni h-inand a gnim sa gléo
dia mbai Sinand co saer beo.

Isle of Man derives its name and ancient celebrity.[109] In those very early times there was a certain mystical fountain which was called *Connla*'s Well, (situated, so far as we can gather, in Lower Ormond). As to who this *Connla* was, from whom the well had its name, we are not told; but the well itself appears to have been regarded as another Helicon by the ancient Irish poets. Over this well there grew, according to the legend, nine beautiful mystical hazle-trees, which annually sent forth their blossoms and fruits simultaneously. The nuts were of the richest crimson colour, and teemed with the knowledge of all that was refined in literature, poetry, and art. No sooner, however, were the beautiful nuts produced on the trees, than they always dropped into the well, raising by their fall a succession of shining red bubbles. Now during this time the water was always full of salmon; and no sooner did the bubbles appear than these salmon darted to the surface and eat the nuts, after which they made their way to the river. The eating of the nuts produced brilliant crimson spots on the bellies of these salmon; and to catch and eat these salmon became an object of more than mere gastronomic interest among those who were anxious to become distinguished in the arts and in literature without being at the pains and delay of long study; for the fish was supposed to have become filled with the knowledge which was contained in the nuts, which, it was believed, would be transferred in full to those who had the good fortune to catch and eat them. Such a salmon was, on that account, called the *Eo Feasa*, or "Salmon of Knowledge"; and it is to such a salmon that we sometimes meet a reference among our old poets, where, when speaking of objects which they pretend to be above description, they say, "unless they had eaten of the salmon of knowledge they could not do it justice".

Mac Liag alludes to the "Salmon of Knowledge"; (the *Eo Feasa*).

Thus *Mac Liag* in the poem on *Tadhg* O'Kelly, who was killed in the battle of Clontarf, and whose body was laid on the shields of his clan, the warrior chiefs of *Ui Maine*:—

"I am not able to describe their shields,—
But the vultures are joyful through their means;
Unless I had eaten the Salmon of Knowledge,
I never could accomplish it".[110]

Allusion to the *Eo Feasa* by *Aengus Finn* O'Daly (A.D. 1400.)

And thus again *Aengus Finn* (or the Fair) O'Daly, popularly called *Aengus-na-Diadhachta*, ("of the Divinity"), and who flourished about the year 1400, applies this term to the

(109) See "Note on *Manannan Mac Lir*", ATLANTIS, vol. iv. p. 226.

(110) original:—Ní éiġ damh aireaṁ a sciaṫ
aċt ar failiḋ fiach dá fáṫ
muna eṫainn in t-éo fis,
ní féadainn beaṫ ris co bráṫ.

LECT. VII.

Blessed Virgin Mary, in one of his many hymns to her [illegible] which begins:

"Often is a kinswoman espoused", etc.[111]

The following is the fourth stanza of this graceful [illegible]

"Mary is not like unto ordinary women,
In regard to the love that I have contracted with [illegible]
I assert that no cloud ever obscures
The Salmon of Knowledge through whom God [illegible]
man".[112]

To proceed, however, with the legend of the Shannon [illegible]

It was forbidden to women to come within the [illegible] *Connla*'s wonderful well; but the beautiful lady *Sinann* [illegible] possessed above every maiden of her time all the accomplish[illegible]ments of her sex, longed to have also those more [illegible] masculine acquirements which were accessible at *Connla*'s [illegible] to the other sex only. To possess herself of these she [illegible] secretly to the mystical fountain; but as soon as she [illegible] its brink, the waters rose up violently, burst forth over [illegible] and rushed towards the great river now called the Shannon [illegible] overwhelming the lady *Sinann* in their course, whose [illegible] body was carried down by the torrent, and at last cast up [illegible] land at the confluence of the two streams. After this the [illegible] became dry for ever; and the stream which issued from it [illegible] that originally known by the name of the lady *Sinann* [illegible] Shannon; but having fallen into that great succession of [illegible] which runs nearly through the centre of Ireland, the [illegible] lakes subsequently appropriated the name to itself, which [illegible] still retains, whilst the original stream is now unknown. [illegible] original *Sinann* is, however, believed to have fallen into [illegible] present Shannon, near the head of *Loch Dearg*, not far [illegible] Portumna.

Legendary tradition of the Seven Streams of the Fountain of *Connla*.

According to legendary tradition, there were seven [illegible] streams of knowledge flowing from *Connla*'s sacred fountain [illegible] among which were the rivers now known as the Boyne, [illegible] Suir, the Nore, the Barrow, and the Slaney. And it is in allu[illegible]sion to this tradition that *Cormac Mac Chuillennain*, in a poem written by him a short time before his death, says, that he found his "nut of knowledge on the waters of the river Barrow"; for it was at *Disert Diarmada*, (now Castle Dermot, near that river, in the county of Kildare), that he studied in his youth.

(111) original:—Meinic berair bean gaoil.

(112) original:—Ni cosmail Muire is na mná
fán cumann do rinneas ria
bim ris nác ar cruinnig céo
an t-eo fis os duinig dia.

Poems by Cuan O'Lothchain, (continued).

This then is the ancient legend which *Cuan O'Lothchain* has handed down to us.

Edward O'Reilly, in his "Irish Writers", at the year 1024, gives a short mention of these three poems of *O'Lothchain*'s; but of the following poems he appears to have known nothing.

The fourth piece of *O'Lothchain*'s composition is a poem of fifty-three stanzas, or two hundred and twelve lines, on the origin of the name and the ancient history of the Hill of *Druim Criaich*, (now Drum Cree, in the parish of Kilcumney, barony of Delvin, and county of Westmeath). This poem begins:

"*Druim Criaich!* meeting-place of an hundred hosts!
Though now a desert, thy fame fades not,
Though thou art now *Druim Criaich*, thou wert once
also *Druim-Cro;*
As well as the cold *Druim Airthir* on the same day".[118]

Druim Criaich, the first of these three names, is composed of ... a hill, and *criaich;* which is composed of *cri*, the heart, ... a sigh or moan; because, ever after the monarch ... *Feidhlech* received the heads of his three rebellious ... this hill, sighs and moans never ceased to issue from his ... *Druim Cro*, the second name, means the Gory Hill; ... the blood that was shed there on the day of the great ... *Druim Airthir*, the third name, means simply the ... Hill; doubtless in reference to some other remarkable ... which must have stood to the west of it. The story told ... poem is shortly this:

History of Druim Criaich; (temp. Eochaidh Feidhlech, circa B.C. 100.)

... *Feidhlech* was monarch of Erinn about a century be... Incarnation. Besides the celebrated *Medhbh* (or Meave,) ... Connacht, and other daughters, he had three sons, ... one birth, who were named *Lothur*, *Nor*, and *Breas*, ... are better known in Irish history by the names of the ... *Eamhna*, or the Three Fair Twins, (or Triplets). ... these sons grew to man's estate, they became impatient ... father's rule, and proposed to dethrone him and seize ... sovereignty for themselves. For this purpose they mus... a large force of adherents at Emania, in Ulster, where ... had been educated, and marched through the northern ... westwards to *Eas-ruadh*, (Easroe,—Ballyshannon), and ... and from that to *Rath Cruachain* (in Roscommon), to ..., and so across the Shannon (into Westmeath). Their ... in the meantime having received information, at Tara, of ...

(118) Original.—Druim criaich céte cét cuan
cenoop [cerra—*Lecain*] dithrub ni dimbuan
cid druim criaid ba druim cró
is druim nuair nairthir in aen ló.

SECT. VII.

their movements and designs, hurriedly collected such forces as time would allow, and marching at their head to meet natural enemies, encamped on *Druim Airthir*, to watch gress and await their arrival. The young princes movement, advanced directly to the king's camp, battle immediately succeeded, in which they were feated, and forced to fly westwards across the Shannon; flight they were overtaken, made prisoners, and beheaded; their three heads were carried back to their father, however never after ceased to lament over their loss, and his own misfortunes.

story of
Cath
ha Comair.

By those who feel an interest in the authenticity of Irish history, and the class of native original documents which it is mainly founded, this poem will be regarded document of deep importance. The details to be many, and the topography of the march of the king's sons is scanty; yet still are they most valuable, afford strong evidence of the antiquity, and, as I am the authenticity, of a detailed prose version of this transaction which is still extant, though in a very form as to language, under the title of *Cath Atha* the battle of the Ford of *Comar*), the only copy of which am acquainted with is preserved in the Royal Irish A in the handwriting of John Mac Solly of the county of copied by him in the year 1715.

The poetic history of *Druim Criaich*, however, is to a period far later than that which forms the subject prose tract, coming down indeed to the time of the poet. The circumstances of the later transactions recorded in not sufficiently detailed in this poem, nor are they the Annals of the Four Masters. It appears that from cause, which is not explained, *Domhnall* the son of *D* (or *Donogh*), son of *Flann Sinna*, monarch of Erinn, (who the year 914), was driven out from Tara, the patrimony ancestors; that in his difficulty, accompanied by only lowers, he took a prey from *O'Duban* of *Druim Dairbreach*, neighbourhood of *Druim Criaich*; that he was pursued taken at the latter hill by *O'Duban*, accompanied by nine that a fight took place between them on the hill, in O'*Duban* was slain; that he was buried on the spot; his tomb was erected there by his vanquisher, to be for after ages as a memorial of the victory. This *Dom* was father of the celebrated monarch *Maelseachlainn*, Malachy), who died in the year 1022; and his pedigree, a valuable piece of history, is preserved here, being through thirty generations to the above-named monarch *Eochaidh Feidhlech*. LECT. VII.

There is a fine copy of this poem preserved in the Book of Munster; and it is also to be found in the Books of Ballymote and *Lecain*, but without the author's name, and wanting also the twenty-three last stanzas which record the second battle of [illegible] *Criaich*.

The fifth piece of *Cuan O'Lothchain's* composition is a poem of eighty-one stanzas, or three hundred and twenty-four lines, in praise of ancient Tara, and of the person, prowess, and life of *Niall* of the Nine Hostages, monarch of Erinn, who was slain in France A. D. 405. The poet gives a graphic account of the birth, education, and succession to the throne of his father, of the celebrated *Niall*. Poems by *Cuan O'Lothchain* (continued).

Niall's mother was a Scottish princess who had been taken captive by his father *Eochaidh*, whose "married queen" was *Mongfinn*, a South-Munster princess, by whom he had several sons older than *Niall*. When *Niall* was born, we are here told, the jealous queen had him conveyed out of the palace of Tara and exposed on the green side of the hill, where he was taken up by the celebrated Munster poet *Torna Eigeas*, the same of whom we had occasion to speak in a former Lecture. *Torna* took him home to his residence in Kerry, where he nurtured and educated him, and afterwards brought him to Tara and presented him to his father and his friends. The beauty and promise of the youth at once found favour with his father; and on comparing his appearance with that of his four elder brothers, the comparison was entirely in his favour. Now the king watching for some chance opportunity to try the comparative courage and bravery of his sons, it so happened that one day he found them all together in the forge of his chief smith; upon which he set fire to the building, and called upon his sons to save the smith's property. Immediately *Brian*, the eldest, rushed out with the smith's chariot, which happened to be in the forge; *Ailill*, the second son, carried out the smith's shield and sword; *Fiachra*, the third son, took out the forge trough; *Fergus*, the fourth son, took out a bundle of fire-wood; but *Niall* carried out the bellows, the sledges, the anvil, and the anvil-block. The story proceeds to recount, that when the old king saw that each of his elder sons had shunned the danger as much as possible, and ventured on saving but the lighter articles of the smith's property, while *Niall* seemed not to see danger at all, and chose the weightier and more important articles, he immediately made up his mind to adopt him as his successor. The four sons, either really feeling his superiority, or in obedience History of *Niall* "of the Nine Hostages".

LECT. VII.

to the general voice, quietly assented; and thus did [illegible], though the youngest of all, succeed his father in that monarchy on which he shed a lustre that has not faded from the page of Irish history even to this day.

The only copy of this fine old poem that I have seen, is preserved in the Book of Leinster, and begins:

"*Teamair* of Bregia, home of the brave;
Desert is thy state; it was God that brought thee low;
The inheritance of *Niall*, so well worthy of thee;
The noble great mansions of the Sons of *Milesius*".(114)

The sixth and last piece of *Cuan O'Lothchain's* composition that I have met, is a poem of fifty-eight stanzas, or two hundred and thirty-two lines, on the ancient history of the Hill of *Tailtén*, (now Teltown, in Meath,) and the institution of its ancient games and sports, from the destruction of the Firbolg power, in the battle of *Magh Tuiredh*, down to the last great fair held there by *Donnchadh*, or Donagh, the son of *Flann Sionna*, king of Meath, who died in the year 942.

Origin of the Fair of *Tailtén*.

The origin of the name of *Tailtén* (now Teltown), is shortly this. *Eochaidh Mac Erc* was king of the Firbolgs in Erinn, when the *Tuatha Dé Danann* colony arrived; and it was he that headed the former against the latter in the great battle of the southern *Magh Tuiredh*, in which he was slain and his people all cut off or routed. This king *Eochaidh* had to his queen *Taillté*, the daughter of *Magh Mór*, "king of Spain"; and she had been the fostermother and tutoress of *Lug*, son of *Cian*, the most valorous and talented of the *Tuatha Dé Danann*, who, in due time, after the triumph of his own people, became king of Erinn, and held his court chiefly at *Nás*, (now Naas) in the present county of Kildare). It was during his reign that his fostermother, *Taillté*, died; and he buried her in a plain (in the present barony of Kells, in the county of Meath), where he raised over her a large artificial hill or sepulchral mound, which remains to this day; and where he ordained a commemorative festival, with games and sports after the fashion of other countries, to be held in her honour for ever. These sports were appointed to commence each year in the middle of July, and end in the middle of August.

But as the matter of this important poem does not come within the scope of the present course of Lectures, and as its details will form part of, if not a whole Lecture, in another

(114) original.—Temair breg baile na fian,
forse dáil dia ra domian,
oiles neill mad cubaid cell,
minles mor mac mileo.

section of our National History, I shall pass it by for the present with this brief notice. For sake of identification, however, I may quote the first verse, which begins, LECT. VII.

"You learned men of the land of brave *Conn*,
Listen to me awhile, and take my blessing,
Until I relate to you the ancient history
Of the institution and arrangement of the fair of *Tailtin*".(118)

The beautiful copy of this poem preserved in the Book of Leinster contains fifty-eight stanzas; while the copies of it preserved in the Books of Ballymote and *Lecain* consist of but forty-three, and want the author's name.

I have now brought down my list of the chief professors of the ancient Irish Schools of Learning, almost as far as I need continue it for the purpose of the present Lectures, the illustration of the proofs of our ancient national civilization. I shall only add one other name, but it is one upon which I have still something to say, although in a former Lecture I had occasion to speak of this great teacher and historian in reference to his authority respecting the facts and chronology of our ancient history; I allude to the next great historical poet, in order of time, after *O'Lothchain*;—I mean *Flann Mainistrech*, or "of Monasterboice", as he is commonly called;—*Flann*, the chief professor or head-master of the great lay school at the monastery of Saint Buite, (now called Monasterboice, in the present county of Louth),—who died in the year 1056. Of Flann of Monasterboice.

I have in a former Lecture given a somewhat detailed account of the historical synchronisms compiled by this celebrated compiler;(119) but, besides these, he has left us a vast quantity of valuable contributions to the illustration of our history, as well as specimens of the cultivation of the native language of Erinn in his time.

Flann of the Monastery, as he is popularly called, was, like *O'Lothchain*, of Munster extraction, and descended from the same ancestor,—*Tadhg*, the son of *Cian*, son of *Oilioll Olum*,—but through a different line from the *O'Lothchains*; and he was not the only distinguished scholar of his immediate family.(120)

(118) original:—A chóemu críche Chuinn cáin,
éistid bic ar bennachtain,
co n-decius duib senchus sen,
suidigthe óenaig Tailten.

(119) See *Lectures on the MS. Materials of Ancient Irish History*; p. 53.

(120) See the Genealogical Table appended to the "Battle of *Magh Lena*";—published, with an English translation and notes, by the Celtic Society, in the year 1855.

. VII. of Main-

Of *Flann Mainistrech*'s historical poems, those comprised in the following list are preserved in the Book of Leinster, which was compiled in less than a century after his death.

The first is a poem of forty stanzas, or one hundred and sixty lines, on the manner of death and place of sepulture of the most distinguished persons, male and female, of the ancient *Tuatha Dé Danann* colony of Erinn. This poem, of which there is a copy also in the Book of *Lecain*, begins:

"Listen, O ye learned! without blemish".(118)

The second is a poem of thirty-seven stanzas, or one hundred and forty-eight lines, giving the length of the reigns and the manner of death of the Pagan monarchs of Erinn, from *Eochaidh Feidhlech*, in the century before the Incarnation, down to *Dathi*, the last of the Pagan rulers, who died "at the foot of the Alps", A. D. 428. This poem, of which there is also a copy preserved in the Book of *Lecain*, begins:

"The kings of *Teamar*, who were warmed by fire".(119)

The third is a poem of fifty-two stanzas, or two hundred and eight lines, giving the names and manner of deaths of the Christian monarchs of Erinn, from *Laeghairé*, who began his reign 428, to *Maelseachlainn* or Malachy the Second, who died 1022. This poem, of which the Book of *Lecain* also contains a copy, begins:

"The powerful kings of *Teamar* afterwards".(120)

These three poems are described by Edward O'Reilly in his "Irish Writers", at the year 1056; but with the following ten poems he appears to have been unacquainted, nor are they found in any other book that I am aware of, but the Book of Leinster alone, excepting two which shall presently be observed on.

The fourth is a poem of twenty-six stanzas, or one hundred and four lines, on the names of the persons who composed the *Tróm Dáimh*, or Great Company, of Poets, pupils, women, and attendants, which accompanied the chief poet *Seanchan Torpest* on his visit to the court of *Guairé*, king of Connacht, at *Durlas*, in that province, some time about the year 600, a visit which has been described in a former lecture.(121) It is difficult to discover what could have been the object of the author in writing this poem, unless we take it to have been a display of his rhythmical powers; for it contains no real name or useful fact, but consists chiefly of a harsh collection of fanciful descriptive names,

(118) original:—Eirtigh a eólcha cen ón.
(119) original:—Rig temra dia tearbann tnú.
(120) original:—Rig temra taebaige iartain.
(121) See *Ante*, LECT. iv.; p. 87.

Poems of Flann Mainistrech.

set down in good rhyme, but in tiresome alliteration. This poem, which appears to have been addressed to one of the author's pupils, begins:

"Thou youth of many high degrees,
Among the crowd of learned assemblies,
What were the names,—relate to us,—
Of the people of the Great Company.[129]

The fifth is a poem of fifteen stanzas, or sixty lines, on the names, length of reign, and manner of death, of the Christian kings of Munster, from *Ængus*, son of *Natfraech*, (who, with his wife, was killed in the battle of *Cell Osnadh*, [in Carlow,] in the year 489,) down to *Donnchadh*, (or Donagh,) son of *Brian Boromha*, who succeeded to the government of Munster about the year 1023. This important poem begins:

"Are ye acquainted with the ancient history."[130]

The sixth is a poem of fifty-one stanzas, or two hundred and four lines, chiefly on the monarchs of Erinn and kings of Meath who descended from *Niall* of the Nine Hostages;—from *Conall Cremthainne*, son of *Niall*, (the first king of Meath separately and as distinguished from the monarchy,) down to *Conchobhar*, king of Meath, who was slain by his kinsman Morogh the son of *Flann O'Maelseachlainn*, about the year 1030. This poem gives the name, length of reign, and manner of death, of each of these kings, forty-seven in number, and begins:

"Meath, the home of the race of *Conn*,—
The beautiful seat of brave *Niall*'s sons,—
The heart of far-renowned Erinn;
Meath, the plain of the great marshalled troops".[131]

The seventh is an interesting poem of thirty-five stanzas, or one hundred and forty lines, on the origin and history of the ancient Palace of *Aileach*, (near Derry; in the present county of Donegal). The origin of this celebrated palace, according to this account of it (containing a specimen of poetic etymology which I only quote for what it is worth), was shortly this:

Origin of the Palace of Aileach.

"When the Great *Daghda* was chief king of the *Tuatha Dé Danann* in Erinn, holding his court at Tara, he on one occasion entertained at his court *Corrgenn*, a powerful Connacht

---

(129) original:—A gilla gairm n-ilgráda,
etir drunga drong dála,
ca dé at anmand uncide,
muintire na trom dáma.

(130) original:—In eol dib in senchus sen.

(131) original:—Mide maigen clainne Cuind,
cáin forud clainne Neill neart-luind,
aird banba bricce,
Mide mag na mor cipe.

LECT. VII. Origin of the Palace of Aileach

chief, and his wife. During their stay at *Teamair*, *Corrgenn's* wife was suspected of being more familiar with the monarch's young son *Aedh*, (or Hugh) than was pleasing to her husband, who in a fit of sudden anger slew the young prince in the very presence of his father. *Corrgenn's* life would have paid for the murder on the spot, but that the old monarch's sense of justice was too strong to kill a man for avenging a crime so heinous as he believed his son to have been guilty of; but, although he would not consent to have his guest put directly to death, he passed on him such a sentence as, whether he intended it so or not, ended in the same manner. The singular sentence which the king passed on the unfortunate *Corrgenn* was, (according to the story,) to take the dead body of the prince on his back, and never to lay it down until he had found a stone exactly to fit him in length and breadth, and sufficient to form a tomb-stone for him; and then to bury him in the nearest hill. *Corrgenn* was obliged to submit, and accordingly set out with his burden. After a long search he found at last the stone he sought for, but found it only so far off as by the shore of *Loch Feabhail*, (now called Loch Foyle, at Derry.) Here, then, depositing the body on the nearest eminence to him, he went down, raised the stone, and carried it up to the hill, where he dug a grave, and buried the prince; and with many an *ach* (or groan) placed the stone over him; but, wearied by his labour, he had hardly done so before he dropped down dead by its side. And it was from these *achs* or groans of *Corrgenn*, that, (compounding the word *ach* with *ail*, an ancient Gaedhelic name for a stone,) the old monarch, when informed of what had happened, formed the name of *Ail-ach* for his son's grave; that is stone and groan; a name that the place has ever since retained. It was the custom in ancient times in Erinn, when a great personage had died, to institute assemblies and games of commemoration at his grave; and this was done at his son's grave at *Aileach* by the monarch *Daghda*.

The poem, however, contains two further explanations of the name of *Aileach*. In some time after the death of *Corrgenn*, it is said, *Neid*, son of *Indai*, (a semi-mythological personage, who may be called the Mercury of the *Tuatha Dé Danann*,) brother to the monarch the *Daghda*, built a palace and fortress here, after which it was called *Aileach Neid*. *Neid* was himself afterwards killed by the Fomorians or Pirates; and the place having gone to ruin, its history is not recorded from that time down to the reign of the monarch of Erinn *Fiacha Sraibtiné*, who was slain at the battle of *Dubh-Chomar*, A. D. 322. In this *Fiacha's* reign, however, it is stated that *Frigrinn*, a young Scottish chief, eloped with *Ailech*, "that is, 'the splendid'", daughter of *Fubtairé*, the king of Scotland; brought her over to Erinn; and put himself under the Irish king's protection. And it is said that King *Fiacha* gave the youthful lovers the ancient fortress of *Aileach* for their residence and security; and that here *Frigrinn* built the magnificent house which is described in this poem, whence the place got the name of *Aileach Frigrinn*, as well as the older name of *Aileach Neid*. LECT. VII. Origin of the Palace of Aileach.

Flann's curious poem begins:

"Should any one attempt to relate
The history of host-crowded *Aileach*,
After *Eochaidh* the illustrious,—
It would be wresting the sword out of Hector's
hand".[133]

I must observe here, however, that the ancient name of *Aileach* was certainly *Aileach Neid;* and the investigations of antiquaries, (including the cautious Dr. Petrie,) have led to the same conclusion to which we should come by following the ancient manuscript authorities,—that the *stone* ruins at *Aileach*, as well as several other similar stone erections in several parts of Erinn, must be referred to the *Tuatha Dé Danann*, if not to the *Firbolgs;* certainly to a race prior to the Milesians. A simpler etymology may easily be suggested for the name; for when we remember that the Milesians always used wooden buildings, in preference to the stone used by their predecessors, we can easily understand why they should emphasize such an erection under the name of *Aileach*. The word *aileach* itself may in fact signify simply "a stone building"; since *ail* is a stone, and *ach* the common adjective termination; so that *aileach* would literally signify "stony", i.e. of or belonging to, or made of, stone.

Who the *Eochaidh* was to whom *Flann* refers as having already written copiously of the history of *Aileach*, I cannot with certainty say; but I believe him to have been *Flann's* own contemporary, *Eochaidh* (called the "Learned") *O'Ceirin;* and that he was the author of the long poem on *Aileach*, preserved in the Book of *Lecain*, and published (with an English translation) by Dr. Petrie, in 1837, in the Ordnance Memoir of Derry. I believe that this very poem was the "copious history" to which *Flann* bears such honourable testimony; and this belief appears more likely to be well-founded, when we find that the

(133) Original—Dá ttriallaid neċ aisneis
senċais Ailiġ e altaiġ
d'éis Eachach áin,
is gait a cloidib a llaim Hectair.

author of this long poem states, in the sixty-seventh stanza, (the last but eight), that the monarch of Erinn then reigning was the sixteenth of the *Clanna Neil* line who had arrived at this high distinction; for we very well know that *Domhnall O'Neil*, grandson of *Niall* "*Glundubh*", was the sixteenth monarch of his line, and that he died and was buried at Armagh in the year 978. That the long poem on *Aileach* was written in the reign of *Domhnall O'Neil* is, therefore, pretty plain; but the author, whoever he may have been, does not set himself down as the chief author of the ancient history of that celebrated place, but quotes *Cuaradh*, some still more ancient writer of whom I have no other record, as the original compiler of its *Dinnseanchas*, or etymological history.

Of this short poem of *Flann*'s, on *Aileach*, there are copies preserved in the Books of Ballymote and *Lecain*, in the Royal Irish Academy.

The eighth poem of *Flann*'s is one of thirty-four stanzas, or one hundred and thirty-six lines, also on *Aileach*, and apparently a continuation of its history, from his former poem. It gives the names, and the lengths of the reigns of every king of the race of *Eoghan*, son of *Niall* of the Nine Hostages, who reigned in it as king of the northern O'Neills, from *Eoghan* himself down to the *Domhnall O'Neil* mentioned above, who died in the year 978. This poem begins:

"Four generations after *Frigrinn*,
By valiant battle,
The noble *Aileach* was taken by the warriors
Of the hosts of *Eoghan*".[184]

The *Eoghan* mentioned here, whose clann took possession of *Aileach* under compact with his other brothers, was *Eoghan* the son of *Niall* "of the Nine Hostages", who gave name to the territory which ever after bore his name, as *Tir Eoghain*, (or Tyrone; a name, however, now applied to a more limited district.) This *Eoghan* was visited at his palace of *Aileach* by Saint Patrick, when he embraced the Christian faith, and received baptism at the hands of the great apostle.

It would be difficult to discover the reason which induced *Flann* to write these two poems, so closely trenching on the poet *Eochaidh*'s history of *Aileach*, to the value of which he bears such honourable witness, were it not that we know that it was part of *Flann*'s system of teaching, as well as of all other teachers in

(184) original:—Cinn ceitri n-dini iar Frigrinn,
forraiġ gleóġal,
Aileċ agmar ro ġab anraċ,
anreċ Eoġain.

this country, to throw their lessons of history into poems of easy measure and rhyme, in order that their immediate pupils might with greater facility commit it to memory.

Poem on *Aileach*, supposed to be that by *Cuaradh*, (10th century).

There is another very ancient poem on the origin of *Aileach* preserved in the Book of Leinster, but without any author's name, and agreeing exactly with the history of the place given in the published poem, as well as in *Flann*'s. This poem comes down, however, but to the time of its passing into the possession of *Eoghan*, son of *Niall*; Saint Patrick's visit to him there; and the blessing which he left upon *Eoghan* and his descendants. It is probably *Cuaradh*'s poem, referred to in *Eochaidh*'s longer composition. The writer of this poem was evidently of the *Clann Neill*, as he calls Saint *Colum Cillé* his kinsman, alludes to his mission to Scotland, and invokes his intercession for his soul. This poem consists of twenty-eight stanzas, or a hundred and twelve lines, beginning:

"Behold *Aileach* from all sides around!
Home of the hosts of *Niall*'s brave race,
Mound of the assemblies of noble Erinn,
Grave of *Aedh*, son of vehement *Daghda*".[137]

Poems of *Flann Mainistrech* (continued).

The ninth poem of *Flann*'s is one of twenty-three stanzas, or ninety-two lines, on several of the battles and deeds of valour gained and performed by the descendants of *Eoghan*, son of *Niall*,—more familiarly known by the name of the *Cinel Eoghain*;—from the battle of *Sliabh Cua*, (in the County of Waterford), gained over the men of Munster in the year 593 by *Fiachna*, son of *Baetan*, king of Ulster, to the battle of *Cill-na-nDaighré*, (near Drogheda), gained by the Monarch *Aedh Finnliath* in the year 866, over *Flann* son of *Conaing*, lord of Bregia, and a great force of the men of Leinster and the Danes of Dublin, to the number of five thousand. This valuable poem begins:

"Let us follow,—it is no path of ease,—
Our history without faintness,
Until we relate, without omission,
The deeds of the race of *Eoghan*".[138]

The tenth poem of *Flann*'s is one of sixty-eight stanzas, or two

(137) original:—Decid Ailech n-imchill n-uaib,
Forad sluag sir-tenn sil Neill,
Fert fod aenaig Banba m-bain,
Aeda ain mic Dagda déin.

(138) original:—Aronam ni reól sadail
Iarrain slicht cen bréobail
co n-ecrem cen diuail
do gnimaib sil Eogain.

LECT. VII.

Poems of Flann Mainistrech (continued).

hundred and seventy-two lines, on several other of the batt[illegible] gained, and deeds of valour performed, by the Cinel [illegible] from the above battle of *Sliabh Cua*, gained in the year [illegible] down to the battle of *Magh Adhair* by *Mac Lochlainn* [illegible] battle of *Ceann Coradh* by *Domhnall*, and a battle over the [illegible]dians by *Mac Lochlainn* in the end of the tenth century [illegible] which that *Donnsleibhé*, king of Ulidia, was slain, whose [illegible] was carried to Armagh to be buried. The record by Flann [illegible] these three battles is the more important, as none of them [illegible] recorded in the Annals of the Four Masters. This valuable poem begins:

"What they have performed of valour,
These clanns of *Eoghan*,
Though it be attempted it cannot be
Recounted by the poets".(129)

The eleventh poem of *Flann's* is one of sixty-nine stanzas, or two hundred and seventy-six lines, also on the *Cinel Eoghain*. This poem gives an account of the life of the celebrated *Muirchertach*, son of *Muiredhach*, son of that *Eoghain* from whom descend the *Cinel Eoghain*. He was more popularly called *Muirchertach Mac Erca*, after his mother, who was *Erc*, daughter of *Loarn Mór*, King of *Albain*, (Scotland). *Muirchertach* reigned as monarch of Erinn twenty-four years, until he was burned to death in the palace of *Cleitech*, on the Boyne, in the year 527. The history of the elopement of his mother, *Erc*, with his father *Muiredhach*,—his birth, life, battles, and death,—are well described in this poem; as are also a great number of the victories of the *Cinel Eoghain*, down to the time of *Flaithbhertach O'Neil*, king of *Aileach*, who died in the year 1036. This most important historical poem begins:

"The deeds, the victories,
The devastations were so numerous
Of those men, so far renowned,
That even the poets cannot recount them".(130)

It would be difficult to over-estimate the historical value of these three poems. They are precisely the documents that supply life and the reality of details to the blank dryness of our

(129) original:—An do ronsat do cálma,
clanna Eógain,
Cia merraid ni etat,
a rim eolaig.

(130) original:—A n-gluind, a n-echta,
a n-orgni batar ili,
in fir is lia tuirim,
connach as cluinid o filid.

skeleton pedigrees. Many a name lying dead in our genealogical tracts, and which has found its way into our evidently condensed chronicles and annals, will be found in these poems, connected with the death or associated with the brilliant deeds of some hero whose story we would not willingly lose; while, on the other hand, many an obscure historical allusion will be illustrated, and many an historical spot as yet unknown to the topographer will be identified, when a proper investigation of these and other great historical poems preserved in the Book of Leinster shall be undertaken as part of the serious study of the history and antiquities of our country.

LECTURE VIII.

[Delivered 23rd June, 1857.]

(III.) EDUCATION, AND LITERATURE; (continued). Of the Poems of Flann Mainistrech (continued). Of the History of *Aedh Slainé*, (Monarch, vi. century). Of some Poems of *Giolla-Brighdé Mac Conmidhé* (xiii. century), attributed by O'Reilly to *Flann*. Of a Poem by *Eoghan Ruadh Mac an Bhaird* (or Ward), attributed by O'Reilly to *Flann*. Of *Flann's* Poem on the Pedigree of the Saints of Erinn. History anciently taught in verse. Of *Flann* and his descendants. Of general education in Erinn in early times. Continued cultivation of the Gaedhelic, after the introduction of Latin. Of the system of Academic Education in early times. The ancient Academic or University course. Of the legal relations between Teacher and Pupil. Teachers often employed as Ministers of State by their former pupils; *Fothaidh "na Canoiné"*. The Profession of Teaching not confined to the clergy in early Christian times. *Maelsuthain* O'Carroll, Teacher and afterwards Secretary of *Brian Boromha*.

THERE remain still some poems of *Flann* of Monasterboice to be mentioned before I close with him the sketch I proposed to trace of the succession of distinguished scholars and teachers in the Gaedhelic language during the earlier ages of our history. The cultivation of our ancient language, it need hardly be observed, by no means ceased with *Flann*. On the contrary it continued for centuries after his time to flourish vigorously; and it was during the succeeding ages to that of *Flann* that the greater portion of the extensive works still existing in the Gaedhelic were composed. But of the chief part of these an account has been given in a former course of lectures[131] in so much detail, that for my present purpose of illustrating the early civilization of Erinn, I need not repeat myself by continuing the chain below the eleventh century.

Poems of *Flann Mainistrech* (continued).

The twelfth poem of *Flann's*, not noticed by O'Reilly, is one of fifteen stanzas, or sixty lines, on the birth and history of *Aedh Slainé*, (a name commonly written Hugh Slaney), son of *Diarmait*, monarch of Erinn, who was slain in the year 558, after a reign of twenty years. This story of *Aedh Slainé* is as follows:

...ry of ...Slainé, ...arch, ...ntury).

Diarmait had to his second wife *Mughain*, the daughter of *Concraidh*, king of South Munster. Now, *Mughain*, as it happened, had no children for several years after her marriage; and as this was always considered as a reproach to our queens in ancient times, just as to those of the Hebrews, *Mughain's*

[131] *Lectures on the MS. Materials of Ancient Irish History.*

life soon became an unhappy one. To cure her grief, therefore, the queen, with the consent of her husband, piously besought the prayers of two holy saints, the bishops *Aedh*, of *Rath Aedh*, (in Meath), and *Finnen*, of *Magh-Bilé*, (now Movilla, in the county of Down). And it is recorded that soon afterwards she conceived, and in due time bore a son, the above-named *Aedh Slainé*, who subsequently succeeded to the monarchy in the year 595, and who was slain the year 600. *Flann*'s poem recounting this story begins:

"*Mughain*, the daughter of worthy *Concraidh*,
Son of *Duach*, king of South Munster,
Who followed munificence without guile,
The wife of *Diarmait Mac Cerbhaill*".[138]

Poems of *Flann Mainistrech* (continued).

The thirteenth poem of *Flann*'s is one of thirty-five stanzas, or one hundred and forty lines, composed for his pupils in history. In this poem he gives a list of the monarchs of Erinn and of the kings of Meath of the race of the above *Aedh Slainé*; together with the length of the reign and the manner and place of death of each, down to *Donnchadh*, who was slain by the *Clann Colman*, and *Muirchertach*, who was slain by *Maelseachlainn*; both of whom must have been kings of Meath, and both of whom must have flourished down to the close of the tenth century, though their names are not found in the Annals of the Four Masters. This valuable poem begins:

"The race of *Aedh Slainé* of the Spears,
Of whom grew many noble kings,
I will relate of their actions good,
Their deaths, and their lordly reigns".[139]

This is the last of the thirteen poems of *Flann Mainistrech* preserved in the Book of Leinster; but of the following list of poems, in addition to those already noticed, printed by O'Reilly and ascribed to him, some are genuine and some are not, as I shall now proceed to show.

The fourth poem of *Flann*'s in O'Reilly's list is one of thirty-three stanzas, or one hundred and thirty-two lines, on the family or household of Saint Patrick; in which the name and office of each person, male and female, are given; such as, his chaplains; his judges; his advisers; his workers in gold, silver,

(138) original:—Mugain ingen Chonchraid chain,
mic Duach do des-Mumain,
ro threm fialgarta cen faill,
bean Diarmata Mic Cerbaill.

(139) original:—Sil Aeda Slaine na sleg,
diar fasadar mor rig ra gal,
innisfet ara maithius,
a n-aided, a n-ardflaithius.

LECT. VIII. Poems of *Flann Mainistrech* (continued).

bronze, and iron; his embroideresses; his chariot-dr[illegible] etc.; and among the rest, singularly enough, appears [illegible] of *Aedh*, the keeper of his Tooth, a relic which [illegible] death preserved in the church of *Achadh Abhall*, (or th[illegible] tree field"), in *Connacht*, and the curious ancient shrine [illegible] is now in the museum of the Royal Irish Academy [illegible] only ancient copy of this curious poem of *Flann's*, th[illegible] ever seen, is preserved in the Book of *Lecain*, and beg[illegible]

"The household of Patrick of the Prayers".[133]

The fifth poem of *Flann's* in O'Reilly's list, is one [illegible] hundred and five stanzas, or one thousand two hundr[illegible] twenty lines, beginning:

"Make clear my way, O God of Heaven!"[134]

In this elaborate poem, (which is also a purely educa[illegible] one, and intended for his class), he gives the names and [illegible] of the emperors and kings of the Assyrians, Persians, G[illegible] and Romans, from Ninus to the Emperor Theodo[illegible] invasion of Britain by Constantine the Great; his adop[illegible] the sign of the cross on his banner; his conversion; and [illegible] Christian acts of his subsequent life. The only copy of [illegible] metrical abstract of ancient universal history with which I [illegible] acquainted, is preserved in the Book of *Lecain*.

The sixth poem of *Flann's* in O'Reilly's list, is one of eigh[illegible] stanzas, or seventy-two lines, on the taxes and tributes paid [illegible] king of *Tir-Chonaill*, (Tir-Connell) from the subordinate chi[illegible] his territory, and the stipends paid by him to them; the recei[illegible] of which stipends by them was, according to the legal custom [illegible] the time, the acknowledgment on their part of his superiority, [illegible] the earnest of their own fealty to him. This curious poem be[illegible]

"There is here a history not trifling".[135]

The seventh poem of *Flann's* in O'Reilly's list is one [illegible] eighteen stanzas, or seventy-two lines, on the Rights and [illegible] vileges of the kings of *Aileach*, or the O'Neil line, and of [illegible] kings of *Tir-Chonaill*, or the O'Donnell line. It begins:

"O book! there is in thy middle
A consistent, perfect history,
For the valiant king of great *Eoghan's* race,
And for the king of the brave *Cinel Chonaill*".[136]

From this valuable poem it appears that the sovereignty of

(133) original:—Muinnter Patraic na paiter.
(134) original:—Reidig dam a Dé do nim.
(135) original:—Ata sunn senchus nach suaill.
(136) original:—A Liubair atá ar do láir,
seanchus comcubaid comlán,
do rig cathach Eogain uill,
is do rig ceneoil Chonuill.

Ailech was common to the *Clann Eoghain* and the *Clann Chonaill*; and our author sets forth the tributes paid by either clann, when the king of the two races was chosen from the other, as well as when he was chosen from itself. This poem appears to have been addressed by *Flann* to his own Book; which Book, it would appear, or at least this part of it, he had copied from the ancient book of *Cill-Mic-Nenain*, the principal and patron church of Tir-Connell. In the last stanza of this poem, *Flann* avows himself as the author of it.

LECT. VIII. Poems of Flann Mainistreach (continued).

The eighth poem of *Flann's*, given in O'Reilly's list, is one of fifty-eight stanzas, or two hundred and thirty-two lines, chiefly in praise of *Conall Gulban*, the ancestor of the O'Donnells and all the *Cinel Chonaill*, who conquered from the *Clann Colla* and the tribes of North Connacht a territory for himself and his brothers, *Cairbré*, *Enna*, and *Eoghan*. *Conall*, it appears, was induced to go on this expedition during his father's lifetime and against the will of the king, because the northerns had slain his tutor, *Fiacha*, who was a Connacht-man. His father, *Niall* "of the Nine Hostages", prevailed on his three other sons, *Conall Cremhthainné*, *Fiachra*, and *Mainé*, not to join their brother *Conall* in what at first appeared to him to be a wild enterprise; and in order the more to encourage them in withholding their countenance from their brother, he gave them all lands in Meath. There, accordingly, *Conall Cremhthainné* became the founder of the great line of monarchs and kings of Meath of the *O'Maelseachlainn* line; there, also, from *Fiacha* descended the *Mac Eochagans*, O'Mulloys, and others; and from *Mainé* the *O'Cathernaighs* of Teffia, (who earned the name of Foxes), and various other families in Westmeath and Longford. These several clanns in aftertimes became distinguished in Irish History as the "Southern *Hy-Niall*", while the descendants of the northern brothers, (*Conall Gulban*, and *Eoghan*), are known as the "Northern *Hy-Niall*". The boundaries of the territories of the northern brothers are distinctly laid down in this valuable poem, which contains, besides, many other curious historical references. It begins:

"*Conall*, the chief of the sons of *Niall*,
Went forth from Tara's pleasant hill,
To wreak his vengeance on the northern land,
In the province of Ulster of the red weapons".[illegible]

It is stated in the concluding stanza of this poem that it was

([illegible]) original:—Conall cenngið ċlainne néill,
tainic a Temraiġ taoiḃ-réið,
d'aiṫe a ḟalaið 'ra tír ṫuaið,
a coigeaḋ Ulaḋ armruaið.

LECT. VIII.

written in Monasterboice, by *Ængus* and *Flann* [illegible] *Ængus* here mentioned we have no particulars.

Of some poems of *Giolla-Brighdé Mac Conmidhé*, (13th century), attributed by O'Reilly to *Flann*.

Edward O'Reilly says that there is another poem [illegible] ject, and beginning with the same words, written by [illegible] *Brighdé Mac Conmidhé*, of whom he gives some account [illegible] "Irish Writers", under the year 1350. O'Reilly is [illegible] ther correct in this assertion. The two poems agree [illegible] only in the first line. *Mac Conmidhé's* poem re[illegible] deal of what is recorded by *Flann* of the career of *C*[illegible] *ban*, and he places in a clearer light some unexplained [illegible] in it; but the main part of it is devoted to the history [illegible] of *Maelseachlain* O'Donnell, lord of Tir-Connell, who [illegible] by Maurice Fitzgerald at the battle of *Eas Ruadh*, (now [illegible] shannon), in the year 1247. As O'Donnell's reign [illegible] in the year 1241, and ended in the year 1247, it is evident [illegible] *Mac Conmidhé* wrote this poem between these two years [illegible] as he was also the author of several poems of an [illegible] (of one in particular, written in praise of *Donnchadh C*[illegible] O'Brien, who was lord of Thomond about the year 1[illegible] very clear that O'Reilly is inaccurate when he makes [illegible] rish in the year 1350. Having in my own possession [illegible] of all these poems, I have no difficulty in showing their [illegible] and where they differ.

The ninth poem ascribed to *Flann* in O'Reilly's list [illegible] of thirty-one stanzas, or one hundred and twenty-four lines [illegible] *Dalach*, son of *Muirchertach*, chief of Tir-Connell ([illegible] descended from *Conall Gulban*), who was slain in the year [illegible] It appears from this curious poem that *Muirchertach* ha[illegible] sons, among whom he divided his moveable property [illegible] time of his death. Of these five sons, *Dalach* was the f[illegible] and *Brodigan* (from whom descend the O'Brodigans [illegible] north), was the fifth. *Dalach* being more ambitious than [illegible] rest, employed the property bequeathed to him in the p[illegible] of the succession to his father's chieftaincy from his elder b[illegible] thers; and in this manner he became chief before his regular time. This *Dalach* was the immediate ancestor of the gre[illegible] O'Donnell family of Tir-Connell. This poem begins:

"Ye musical poets of Tir-Connell,
Inform us,—a matter of no small account,—
By what right did *Dalach* the beloved assume
Chiefship over all his brethren?"[189]

(189) original:—A eolċa Conaill ċeolaiġ,
ḟloinnig ḋúinn dáil naċ deolaiġ,
Gá ċéim ṗar ġab dalaċ dil,
Forlámas for a braiṫriḃ.

This poem, interesting as it is as an historical tract, bears [illegible] evidence, however, from its style and diction, that it [illegible] not written by *Flann* of Monasterboice. The author pro[illegible] in it to have obtained his historical materials from the [illegible] Book of *Cill-Mic-Nenain*, already mentioned; and he [illegible] to quote from it a prophecy of Saint *Colum Cillé*, con[illegible] the reign and fame of *Dalach* and some of his descen[illegible]—two of whom, *Eignechan* and *Cathbharr*, were destined [illegible] kings of Ulster, and the other two, *Conn*, and another [illegible], were to be monarchs of Erinn. Of the first two, [illegible], the son of *Dalach*, succeeded his father as king of [illegible], and died in the year 901. It was on his death [illegible] *Mac Liacc* wrote the remarkable elegy described in a [illegible] lecture. *Cathbharr*, the second of these destined kings [illegible] Connell, died in the year 1106; and it was under the [illegible] and at the expense of this *Cathbharr* that the beau[illegible] of Saint *Colum Cillé's* copy of the Psalms, now [illegible] as the *Cathach* or Book of Battles[139] (at present tem[illegible] deposited in the museum of the Royal Irish Academy), [illegible]. *Conn* and the second *Cathbharr*, who were, accord[illegible] to the supposed prophecy, promised to be monarchs of [illegible], do not appear in any list of the chief kings; but I be[illegible] the *Cathbharr* the son of *Domhnall Mór* O'Donnell, who [illegible] expected to succeed his father but was killed prematurely [illegible] in the year 1208, was one of them. And this surmise [illegible] exactly agree with the time to which I am disposed to [illegible] the writing of this poem, which I believe to have been [illegible] about the same time as the poem on *Donnchadh Cair-* [illegible] O'Brien, and by the same author, *Giolla-Brighdé Mac Con-* [illegible]. The *Conn* O'Donnell appears in our annals at or about [illegible].

LECT. VIII. Of some Poems of *Giolla-Brighdé Mac Conmidhé*, (13th century), attributed by O'Reilly to *Flann*.

[illegible] poem ascribed to *Flann* in O'Reilly's list, is one [illegible], or forty-eight lines, beginning:

[illegible], *Eoghan*, *Enda* the brave,
And great *Conall*, the sons of *Niall*,
Where, O you learned of noble Erinn!
Are the boundaries of their territories and lands?"[140]

[illegible] O'Reilly, in his account of this poem, falls into a [illegible] mistake when he says it was written on the territories of [illegible] of the sons of *Conall Gulban*, son of *Niall* "of the Nine

[139] [illegible] Lectures on the MS. Materials of Ancient Irish History, pp. 327, 331; [illegible] Ann., p. 596.

[140] [illegible] original:—Cairbré, Eogan, Enda éim,
ocus Conall Mor Mac Néill,
caide, a éolcha banba binn,
críocha a tíreacha sa fearainn.

LECT. VIII. [illegible] poems of Giolla-Brighdé Mac Conmidhé (13th century), attributed by O'Reilly to Flann.

Hostages"; it was in fact written on *Conall Gulban* [illegible] and his three brothers just mentioned, all the immediate [illegible] *Niall*. We have seen, in a former poem, that these [illegible] quered a territory for themselves in Ulster and North C[illegible] without the assent or assistance of the monarch [illegible] this poem professes to lay down the respective situations [illegible] and boundaries of each brother's separate division of the con[illegible] quered lands.

This is a curious and valuable poem; but with respect to [illegible] also it bears internal evidence that it was not from the [illegible] pen of *Flann*. Indeed there can be no reasonable doubt [illegible] having been written by *Giolla-Brighdé Mac Conmidhé*, [illegible] it was one of the series of historical poems which he [illegible] the northern *Hy-Niall* (the O'Donnells and O'Neills, [illegible] the early part of the thirteenth century. Of this I have, [illegible] some direct evidence; for, in a curious collection of [illegible] poems on the O'Donnell family and genealogy, now in my [illegible] session, *Mac Conmidhé* is actually set down as the author [illegible] poem.

The eleventh poem ascribed to *Flann* in O'Reilly's [illegible] one of forty-five stanzas, or one hundred and eighty lines, [illegible] ginning:

"*Enna*, the ward of hardy *Cairbré*,
Took to his share *Tir-Enna* of the red arms;
The chieftain left his noble sons
Under the protection of the sons of *Conall*".(161)

This poem, which was was also written by *Mac Con*[illegible] and not by *Flann*, gives a very curious and valuable his[illegible] the territory, and of the immediate descendants of *Enna*, [illegible] the three brothers of *Conall Gulban*, who sided him in his conquest in Ulster, and received for his share of the conquered lands a territory which after him was called *Tir-Enna*, or Enna's land, extending from the river *Suilidh* (or Swilly) [illegible] wards to the well-known mountain-pass of *Bearnas* [illegible] Donegal, and across from the present Lifford to Lett[illegible] This is one of the most curious pieces that I am acquainted with, in relation to the immediate branching off of the Northern Hy-Niall families from the above four brothers, *Conall*, *Eoghan*, *Cairbré*, and *Enna*.

The twelfth poem ascribed to *Flann* in O'Reilly's list was also written by *Mac Conmidhé*. It is one of twenty-two stanzas

(161) original:—Enna dalta Cairbre chruaidh,
ro gabh tir Enna armruaidh,
fagbhuidh an cuingidh a chlonn,
a fosgadh chlainne Chonuill.

[illegible] eighty-eight lines, and represents the discussion which is supposed to have taken place between *Conall Gulban* and his brother *Eoghan*, respecting the division of the territory which they had conquered in Ulster. This poem, which is one of no great value, begins: LECT. VIII.

"Listen ye to *Conall* the valiant,
And to *Eoghan* the noble and admirable,
How they held their council meeting
Upon the top of *Drom Cruachain* Hill".(140)

[illegible] thirteenth poem ascribed to *Flann* by O'Reilly is merely [illegible] by him as commencing as follows: Of other poems attributed to *Flann*.

"Here is a catalogue of the kings".(141)

Of this poem I know nothing more than what is said here, [illegible] having met a copy of it.

[illegible] fourteenth and last poem ascribed to *Flann* in O'Reilly's [illegible] one of fourteen stanzas, or fifty-six lines, upon the baptism of *Conall Gulban* by St. Patrick; on which occasion the Saint presented the chieftain with a shield and a crozier as symbols of the support which he was to give to the civil and ecclesiastical dignities. St. Patrick at the same time inscribed the sign of the cross on the shield with his sacred crozier, called the Staff of Jesus;(142) and he solemnly promised *Conall* that such of his descendants as should carry this sign in a just battle should be always victorious. And the Tir-Connellians did always inscribe this sign and the words that accompany it on their banner. The poet quotes the 137th chapter of Jocelyn's Life of St. Patrick as his authority for this story. This poem [illegible]

"Among all that has been written:
By the monk Jocelynus,
Of the works of Patrick, one with another,
Throughout the broad plains of Erinn".(143)

[illegible] will be seen at once, when the author of this poem [illegible] Jocelyn, a writer of the latter half of the twelfth century [illegible] his authority, that that author could not have been [illegible] since *Flann* died more than a century before that time.

[illegible] original:—Eirtig re Conall calma.
ocur re h-Eogan áro amra,
mar oo pinneaoar a n-oáil,
a mullač Opoma Cpuačain.

[illegible] original:—Aca ro(ro) pullaó na piog.

[illegible] See *Lectures on the MS. Materials of Ancient Irish History*; p. 338, *and* [illegible] 600.

[illegible] original:—Eroip gač obaip rgpiobčar,
an manach Ioreliner,
oo feapcaib Phacpaic ceann a ceann,
ileačc moig faobaig Eipeann.

LECT. VIII. Neither could *Mac Conmidhé* have been the writer of this poem, differing as it does most remarkably from his style.

Poem by *Eoghan Ruadh Mac an Bhaird*, (or Ward,) attributed by O'Reilly to *Flann*.

The real author of it was, in fact, *Eoghan Ruadh Mac an Bhaird*, or Ward, the chaplain and faithful companion of the great Red Hugh O'Donnell, who, after the battle of Kinsale in 1602, went to Spain, where he died. I have a copy of this poem in my own possession, made by James MacGuire in the year 1727, from the book of the family poems of the O'Donnells, and in this copy, its authorship is ascribed, and I have no doubt properly, to Father Ward. The legend on which the poem is founded, however, is much older than Jocelyn, as it is preserved in the oldest copy now known of the Tripartite Life of St. Patrick.

Flann's Poem on the Pedigrees of the Saints of Erinn.

There is another very remarkable poem, of which there is reason to believe that *Flann* was the author. This poem is noticed as follows in O'Reilly's "Irish Writers", at the year 908: "At the same time", he says, "with Cormac Mac Cullinan lived *Sealbhach*, the secretary of that prince. He wrote a poem reciting the names of the saints of Ireland, and distinguishing the tribe to which each saint belonged. It begins:

"'The sacred pedigree of the saints of Ireland'".(146)

This valuable poem is very properly described by O'Reilly, but he gives no authority to show that it was written by *Sealbhach*, while we have the distinct authority of the Annals of the Four Masters that it was written by *Flann*, for, at the year 432, the annals contain the following entry: "*Ath Truim* (now Trim, in Meath) was founded by St. Patrick, the place having been granted by *Feidhlim*, son of [the Monarch] *Laeghairé*, son of *Niall*, to God, to Patrick, to *Loman*, and to Saint *Forichern*. *Flann* of the Monastery cecinit". And they then give the following pedigree of St. Patrick, from this poem, beginning at the eighth stanza, leaving us no room to doubt their accuracy in ascribing it to *Flann*:

"Patrick, Abbot, or Christian chief of all Erinn,
Son of *Calphrann*, son of *Fotidé*,
Son of *Deissé*,—not liable to reproach,—
Son of great *Cormac*, son of *Lebriuth*,
Son of *Ota*, son of *Orric* the good,
Son of *Moric*, son of *Leo*, full of prosperity,
Son of *Maximus*, why not name him?
Son of *Encretta*, the tall and comely,
Son of *Philisti*, the best of men,
Son of *Fereni*, of no mean repute,

(146) original:—"Naeṁ ṡenċuṡ naeṁ inṡe Ḟáil".

Son of Britton, otter of the sea,
From whom the passionate Britons descend.
Cóchmas was his modest mother,
Nemthor was his native town;
Of Munster not small his share,
Which Patrick freed from all sorrow".[147]

I must observe here, that in a copy of this poem, in the handwriting of the Rev. Michael O'Clery, the chief of the Four Masters, described by me in a former lecture,[148] and now preserved in the Burgundian Library at Brussels, *Eochaidh O'Ceirin* is set down as the author, and under the peculiar distinction of "*Eochaidh* of the battle of *Craebh Tulcha*". The Four Masters record this battle of *Craebh Tulcha*, (which was, I believe, in the county Antrim), as having been fought between the people of Down and Antrim, in the year 1003; but there is no mention of this *Eochaidh* in their account of it.

History anciently taught in verse.

It is probable that the metrical compositions of *Flann* were much more numerous than we know of now. It was the universal practice of the teachers of history, and of the language in the early schools in Erinn, to compose their lessons in verse, according to the very artificial system of the Gaedhelic prosody; and in this manner it was that the student learned not only the facts which he was required to know, but also that dexterity in wielding the language which he was obliged to acquire before he could take even the lowest of those professional ranks of privileged men of learning, of whose distinction an account has been given in former lectures.[149] And the poems of *Flann*, as well as of the other historical writers already referred to, are all of this class.

In his Synchronisms, of which an account was also given on

(147) original:—Patraic, ab Erenn uile,
mac Calpraind, mic Fotaide,
mic Deisse, nar doig do lind,
mic Cormaic moir mic Leibriuth,
mic Ota, mic Orric mait,
mic Moric, mic Léo in lan raith,
mic Maximi, mairg na sloinn,
mic Encretta ard alaind,
mic Philistir ferr ar aig cach,
mic Fereni gan anfath,
mic Britain, do bra na mara,
o taic Bretain brucmara,
Cochmas a mathair malla,
Nemthor a baile baga,
don Mumain ni cael a chuid,
ro ḟaor ar ḟudar Patraic.

(148) *Lectures on the MS. Materials of Ancient Irish History*, p. 168.

(149) Idem. pp. 2, 204, 219, 220, 239, 241, 248, 255; and *ante* p. 84

LECT. VIII.

a former occasion,[180] *Flann* also followed the system of [illegible] pursued by his predecessors. He, however, greatly [illegible] the scope of their labours, corrected still more their chronology, and compiled at last a body of general comparative [illegible], which was found by scholars five centuries after him [illegible] full of valuable matter, but presenting that matter [illegible] ranged and in shape ready to their hands. These Synch[illegible] consist of parallel lines of the kings and chiefs of all the [illegible] nations, both of Asia and of Europe, from the very [illegible] cords of the human race, their proper dates being [illegible] each, and the parallel line of the monarchs of Erinn [illegible] down in regular order, corresponding to their dates, [illegible] year 918. For the better understanding of these Synch[illegible] or perhaps for their more convenient arrangement [illegible] sons or lectures, these chronological lines are divided [illegible] periods of a century each. And in addition to these Syn[illegible] nisms of general history, the master has also transmitted [illegible] similar parallel lines of the provincial kings of Erinn, [illegible] the kings and chiefs of those tribes of the Gaedhils who [illegible] migrated into, and settled in Scotland.

Of these important works of *Flann* I gave some [illegible] before; but I could not properly describe here his [illegible] a teacher, nor make clear the nature of the education [illegible] through the medium of the Gaedhelic language in our [illegible] schools, without recalling these labours also of one of [illegible] remarkable men of learning, of his day, in Europe.

Of the life of *Flann Mainistrech*; and of his sons after him.

So much for what remains to us of all the learning [illegible] one of the greatest of our mediæval scholars left behind [illegible] fortunately for his particular reputation, on the one [illegible] to serve as a witness of the nature and extent of the [illegible] taught in the secular schools of Erinn in his time on the [illegible] Of *Flann*'s private life or history nothing remains to [illegible] his public life we have on record the fact of his having [illegible] to the highest position in the profession of learning, [illegible] *Fer-Leighinn*, or head professor or master in the great [illegible] of Monasterboice: and we have evidence of his great [illegible] in after ages, in the high compliment paid to him by the [illegible] Masters (whose words of praise are always very [illegible] the following entry of his death, with the stanza from [illegible] cotemporary bard, recorded in the annals at the year 105[illegible]

"A.D. 1056. *Flann* of the Monastery, chief [illegible] Saint *Buite*'s Monastery, the wise master of the [illegible] literature, history, philosophy, and poetry, died on the [illegible] teenth of the kalends of December; as it is said:

(180) *Lectures on the MS. Materials of Ancient Irish History*; p. [illegible]

"*Flann* of the chief church of holy *Buité*,
Still is the brilliant eye of his noble head:
An enchanting poet was he whom we deplore,
The last great professor of Erinn, our *Flann*".

In a former lecture it was shown that *Flann* was not an ecclesiastic,[illegible] but only the principal teacher, head master, or rector of a great lay school or college, at Monasterboice. It is interesting to know that learning did not die in his family with *Flann* himself. He had three sons named *Eochaidh Erann*, *Echtighern*, and *Feidlimidh*. *Eochaidh Erann*, the eldest, appears to have left no issue, nor does his name occur at all in the Annals of the Four Masters; but the deaths of both the other sons, and of the sons of one of them, are honourably recorded, as follows:

"A.D. 1067. *Echtighern*, son of *Flann* of the Monastery, *Airchinnech*, [or land-steward] of Saint *Buité*'s monastery, died.

"A.D. 1104. *Feidlimidh*, son of *Flann* of the Monastery, a faithful soldier of Christ, who was an illustrious senior and an eminent historian, died.

"A.D. 1117. *Eoghan*, son of *Echtighern*, lay successor or representative of Saint *Buité*, died.

"A.D. 1122. *Feargna*, son of *Echtighern*, successor of Saint *Buité*, a wise priest, died".

The list of teachers and learned men could, of course, be very much extended, after *Flann*, and down to the time of the Four Masters and Duald Mac Firbis. The names of the principal of these are to be found in O'Reilly. I have, however, I think, sufficiently proved not only the existence of an early and general education in Erinn, but the continued exercise also of the practice of it in the Gaedhelic tongue, without interruption, to a comparatively recent period,—which was all I proposed to do at present.

General education in Erinn in the early ages.

The existence of a line of learned men in Erinn, through successive generations, beginning from the early colonization of the country by the Milesians, is evidence of the existence of means and opportunity for education, and of its encouragement from a very remote period. The constant succession, down to quite modern times, of men of learning formally honoured as well as protected by the laws, and equally so by the usages of society, no matter what the wars, invasions, or other troubles by which, on many occasions, the country was torn during the lapse of centuries, proves how constant and how general was the regard for education among the whole people. I have, however, not rested solely upon this fact alone, in endeavouring to con-

[illegible] Lectures on the MS. Materials of Ancient Irish History, p. 56.

LECT. VIII. vey something like a sketch of what social life must have been of old among our Milesian ancestors. I have shown from the ancient laws, as well as by examples of their operation, the nature of the Profession of Learning in Erinn before the Christian era; and I have shown that on the arrival of Saint Patrick, he found in the country many learned men, and a system of education flourishing on such a scale as to prove how well the wise encouragement of learning, instituted by our earliest lawgivers, had been carried out in practice for ages previous to his arrival. In those ages it will not fail to be observed, the knowledge of the Latin tongue not having penetrated so far west, the learning and literature of the Gaedhils was naturally preserved in their own rich and beautiful language alone. And I have shown that subsequently, when Saint Patrick and his clerical followers and successors introduced Latin with Christianity, it never superseded our native language in the works even of ecclesiastical writers, much less in the schools. All the early Gaedhelic saints and ecclesiastics had been, in their boyhood, educated in the Gaedhelic tongue; and all the more distinguished of them were poets and historians, who wrote ever in their own idiom in preference to that which the rest of Europe already appropriated to learning. And this general use of our native language by men of cultivation continued, it is to be observed, even down to the seventeenth century; so lasting was the influence of those early institutions which I have endeavoured to describe.

Continued cultivation of the Gaedhelic language after the introduction of Christianity.

In the course of the chronological account I have shortly given of the more remarkable of the learned men among the Gaedhils, I mentioned that each of them (with few exceptions) was a teacher, or lecturer, as well as a poet and historian. And in fact most of the metrical compositions which I have mentioned as the existing literary remains of so many of these professors, were nothing more than lessons of historical knowledge, composed in Gaedhelic verse for the use of the students over whose education they presided.

I have also called attention particularly to the fact that in Christian times the seminaries of education ever since so celebrated, in connection with the great ecclesiastics under whose fame they successively grew up, were by no means merely ecclesiastical colleges, but general schools for the laity at large. And it is this fact that explains the recorded accounts of the vast numbers of students who attended certain of these colleges at the same time, numbers only surpassed by the still more extensive establishments of Paris, and one or two other great seats of mediæval learning, some centuries afterwards.

Lastly, in describing the nature of the profession of teacher as such, and as distinguished from the *Filé*, *Ollamh*, or Philosopher, I have explained, from the ancient laws themselves, the nature of the rank and duties of the different professors and masters of a college, as established under the regulations prescribed by the national legislature of the period.

System of Academic Education in early times.

So far, the records of our ancient legislation which have escaped from the wreck of so many ages, supply us with sure and minute accounts. And it so happens, that upon the labours of the student, and even upon the course of his studies, the academic curriculum of the time, we are fortunate enough to possess equally clear and precise contemporary information. For, in the Book of Ballymote there is preserved a long and important tract upon this subject, under the name of the *Leabhar Ollamhan*, or Book of the *Ollamhs*, a tract which, singularly enough, appears to have escaped the notice of modern Gaedhelic scholars, so many of whom are, I regret to say, more inclined to invent general theories of our ancient modes of life, to the taste of the modern public, than to seek the real truth by examining the ancient books themselves, in which it is abundantly recorded. This curious record of the system of instruction of the schools, will best speak for itself. It begins as follows:

"The authority and order of the learning of the Gaedhil are, the twelve divisions (or books) of *Filedecht*", [that is, properly, as I have before explained, Philosophy, though ordinarily translated Poetry]; "and each book contains a year's learning (or lessons), as the ancient poet *Dithirné* says to his pupil *Amergin*: O praiseworthy *Amergin!* dost thou know the different divisions of poetry, the true knowledge of the *Dian* of the *Fochlachan*, the *Mac Mesnachan* of the *Fuirmid*, the *Dron-chetal* of the *Dos*, the *Ardreth* of the *Cana*, the *Cinntech* of the *Cli*, the *Adbreth* of the *Anradh*, the *Broenacha* of the *Sai*, the *Nath Cumarca* of the *Filidh*, the *Fochairech* of the *Eiges*, the *Sennath* of the *Saghdair*, and the *Anamain* of the *Ollamh?* Name for me each of the different degrees of these twelve kinds of exercise up to the *Ollamh*".—And so on.

The ancient Academic, or University, course.

The twelve divisions, books, or stages, of the native ancient collegiate study extended over twelve years; but as a full explanation of the nature of the study of each year would necessarily occupy the space of nearly a whole lecture, we must, for the present, pass them over lightly, and I can do little more than give here the original names of the different kinds of compositions which the student read, and by the gradual acquirement of which he ascended the ladder of intellectual cultivation,

LECT. VIII.

The ancient Academic, or University, course.

from the degree of *Fochlachan*, or mere learner of words, to that of the *Ollamh*, who was master of the entire course.

The first year's study, then, is stated to have embraced fifty "*Oghams*", or alphabets, and the *Araicecht*, or Grammar of the pupils; together with the learning of twenty Tales, and some Poems.

The second year's study consisted of fifty *Oghams* more; six minor lessons of Philosophy; thirty Tales; and some Poems.

The third year's study embraced Fifty more *Oghams* or alphabets; the learning of the correct diphthongal combinations; the six minor lessons of Philosophy; Forty Tales; and various Poems.

The study of the fourth year was Fifty Tales; then the *Bretha Nemidh*, or Laws of Privileges; and twenty poems of the species called *Enan*.

The study of the fifth year was Sixty Tales; and the critical learning of the adverbs, articles, and other niceties of grammar.

The study of the sixth year consisted of Twenty-four great *Naths*, and Twenty-four small *Naths* (certain kinds of poems); the style of composition called the Secret Language of the Poets; and Seventy Tales.

The study of the seventh year was the *Bromacha* of the Sai (or professor); and the Bardesy of the Bards; "for these" (says the writer of the tract from which I am abstracting) "the poet is obliged to know; and so they are the study of the seventh year".

The study of the eighth year was the knowledge of Prosody, or the Versification of the Poets; of Glosses, or the meaning of obsolete or obscure words; of the various kinds of Poetry; of the Druidical or Incantatory compositions, called *Teinm Laeghdha*, *Imbas Forosnai*, and *Dichetal-di-Chennaibh* (which I explained on a former occasion); also the knowledge of *Dinnseanchus* or Topography; and finally, of all the chief Historical Tales of Erinn, such as were to be recited in the presence of kings, chiefs, and good men; "for without this" (continues the tract) "the poet is not perfect, as the poetical proverb says:—

"'It is no palace without kings;
He is no poet without stories;
She is no virgin if not modest;
He has no good sense who does not read'".[188]

The studies of the ninth and tenth years consisted of Forty

(188) original:—Ni ba dúnad gan rígu,
ni ba fili cen scéla,
ni ba hingen minap fial,
ni maith ciall neich nad léga.

Sennadu; Fifteen *Luascas;* Seven *Nenas;* and an *Eochraid* of sixty words, with their appropriate verses; Seven *Sruths;* and six *Duili Fedha.*

LECT. VIII. The ancient Academic, or University, course.

The study of the eleventh year was Fifty great *Anamains,* and Fifty minor *Anamains.* The great *Anamain* was a species of poem which contained four different measures of composition; namely, the *Nath,* the *Anair,* the *Laidh,* and the *Eman;* and it was composed by an *Ollamh* only.

The study of the twelfth year was six score great *Cetals* (measured addresses or orations); and the four arts of Poetry; namely, *Laidcenn Mac Barceda's* art; *Ua Crotta's* art; *O'Brien's* art; and *Beg's* art.

The author of the tract does not favour us with any specimens of these "arts" of poetry, nor any further clue to their authorship than the mere names just quoted.

Of the first of them, *Laidcenn,* son of *Bairced,* some account was given in a former lecture,[130] when speaking of the monarch *Niall* of the Nine Hostages, to whom he was court poet about the year 400. *Ua Crotta,* and *Ua Brioné* I never heard of before; nor of the fourth, who is called *Beg,* unless he was *Beg Mac Dé,* a famous poet and "prophet" of Munster, who was attached to the court of the monarch *Diarmait,* at Tara, about the year 550. And I may observe here that the names given to all these different kinds of compositions are merely arbitrary, and quite incapable of any appreciable analysis; and this, even the great etymological glossarist, Cormac Mac Cullinan, acknowledges in his glossary, written about a thousand years ago, in which at the word *Anair,* a species of negative laudatory poem, he says: "It was the ingenuity of the poets that invented these names for their compositions, to distinguish their various species, and it was not their nature or character they took into account".

This curious tract, of the contents of which I have here only given a very meagre abstract, is of considerable extent, and is copiously illustrated with examples of all the different kinds of compositions known to, and taught by, the ancient Gaedhelic masters before the introduction of Christianity. The length of the academic course will, perhaps, be deemed subject of surprise, in comparison with those of modern colleges. But it is to be observed that it begins at the very beginning of literary education, and concludes only with an amount of special education carried far beyond the wants of any students but those who aspired to becoming themselves, in their turn, teachers or *Ollamhs* in learning.

(130) *Ante,* p. 69.

One thing only remains for observation [illegible] the subject of education, [illegible] course of lectures on the civilization and [illegible] ancient Erinn: I mean the social relation between [illegible] pupil, as established by the law. That relation [illegible] close one, and was the subject of enactments of [illegible] kind. The whole subject cannot be properly [illegible] publication of the general code of Laws enables the [illegible] Irish history to take a general view of all the [illegible] of society for which that code was framed. [illegible] properly enter it altogether, though I shall for [illegible] content myself with quoting but a short extract [illegible] the Law MSS. (H. 2. 15. in the Library of Trinity [illegible] The passage literally translated is as follows:

"The union (says the legal writer) which is [illegible] between the pupil and the tutor, or instructing father [illegible] was called, was this: the tutor bestowed instruction [illegible] reservation, and correction without violence, upon the [illegible] and he supplied him with food and clothing as long as [illegible] continued to pursue his legitimate studies, if he did not [illegible] them for anybody else".

This rule, it is stated, was derived from the great [illegible] *Fenius Farsaidh*, the remote ancestor of the Milesians, who [illegible] according to the ancient traditions, the first to collect and [illegible] the various languages after the confusion at Babel.

The pupil so supported during his pupilage by the tutor, [illegible] on his side, legally bound to assist or relieve the tutor in [illegible] of his being reduced in circumstances, and to take care of [illegible] in his old age; and whatever profession the pupil might [illegible] the tutor was entitled, at the hands of strangers, to a [illegible] fine, or "*logh enech*", appointed to him by law, for any [illegible] or bodily injury which should happen to be offered to the [illegible] in that profession. The tutor was also entitled to all the profits arising from any literary or other work of the pupil as long [illegible] he continued under his instructions, and also to the first fee [illegible] of his profession after quitting his school.

[illegible] relations as these between tutor and pupil, as laid down [illegible] our ancient laws, surely bespeak, like many others [illegible] institutions, a people deeply impressed with the value [illegible] and such laws afford curious proof of the equitable [illegible] ful, remembrance in which the pupil was bound [illegible] important care, solicitude, and benefits which the [illegible] bestowed upon him in his youth. And it is well [illegible] that such was the ancient Irish law, as well as [illegible] upon the important subject of Education, when we find our ancient laws so often ridiculed as "barbarous", by those whose ancestors took such pains to suppress every vestige of education among us, and who so lamentably succeeded in bringing down the civilization of the Gaedhil.

Of the kindly obedience of some of our greatest scholars to the law by which they were bound to cherish the old age of their teachers, an interesting instance may be pointed out in an allusion contained in one of the oldest of the existing Gaedhelic writings, an allusion explained distinctly by a very ancient scholiast. Every Irish student is familiar with the name *Aengus Ceilé Dé*, or the "Culdee", so often spoken of in the course of my former lectures. He was the pupil for a time of Saint *Maelruan of Tallaght*, near Dublin; and the following stanza (which is the fifty-seventh of the metrical preface to his Festology, where he gives a list of illustrious Irishmen who had then recently died,) alludes to his performance of the duties just mentioned, during the last years of the aged teacher's life:

"*Maelruan, after our nursing of him,*—
The shining sun of Meath's southern border,—
At his undefiled sepulchre
The wounds of all hearts are healed".(134)

And beside the direct assertion of *Aengus* in the text, the scholiast explains that it was Aengus's part, in particular, among all his pupils to take care of the beloved tutor in his old age.

Teachers employed as Ministers of State by their former Pupils.

In the case of kings and great chiefs, the pupil was not of course supported by the master. On the contrary, the master was supported at the court of the prince, where he generally occupied the highest rank. And on the termination of the education of a king, and his succession to power, it often happened, very naturally, that he availed himself directly of his former master's wisdom by making him at once his chief counsellor, or, as we should call it, his prime minister; and this he did entirely without regard to the family or original rank of the man of learning, or even his connection with the king's own name or clann. Instances of this kind occurred, for example, in the case of *Fothadh na Canóiné*, and king *Aedh Oirdnidh*, and in that of *Maelsuthain* O'Carroll, and king *Brian Boroimha*, of both of whom I gave some account on a former occasion.([illegible])

[illegible]

(134) Original:—Maelruan iar na gaire,
grian mar deᵹ muiᵹe Mide,
oca leacht co n-glaine,
icthar cneat cech cride.

([illegible]) See *Lectures on the MS. Materials of Ancient Irish History*, p. 76; and App., p. [illegible].

LECT. VIII.

Fothadh "na Canoine", the chief counsellor of the Monarch *Aedh Oird-nidhe* (circa A.D. 800).

Fothadh na Canoint was abbot of [illegible] in the county of Donegal), and he [illegible] (or Hugh) *Oirdnidhe*, who was [illegible] year 793 to the year 817. On the [illegible] monarchy, the learned tutor, as was [illegible] Precept, or Rule of Government for [illegible] of seventy-two stanzas, a fine copy of [illegible] Book of Leinster. And it appears that after [illegible] him altogether to himself, and introduced [illegible] as his chief adviser. Accordingly, we find the [illegible] year 799, submitting to him for decision, [illegible] respecting the compulsory presence of the [illegible] part of the army of the king, a controversy [illegible] *Aedh* and the body of the clergy of the north, [illegible] compelled to accompany him upon an hostile [illegible] Leinster. On this occasion, it will be remember[illegible] *adh* decided in the metrical sentence, or "Can[illegible] he has since been called by the name just referre[illegible] of the exemption of the clergy from such atten[illegible] monarch having acquiesced, this decision conti[illegible] to be the legal rule upon the subject throughout [illegible]

In the metrical precept, or poem on the duties of [illegible] posed by *Fothadh* for King *Aedh*, occurs a very [illegible] allusion to what has been mentioned as to the office [illegible] continuing to be a layman's function, even after [illegible] tion of Christianity; and as this fact seems to be little [illegible] I may quote here the explicit testimony of this very [illegible] rity. The passage occurs in the nineteenth stanza of [illegible] poem addressed to the king, which runs as follows:

"Your own tutor, [or adviser],
Let your alms be in his hand,
Whether he be a pure wise priest,
Or a layman, or a poet".[156]

The Profession of Teaching not confined to the clergy in early Christian times.

In this stanza the writer, though himself a priest, lays [illegible] the rule as he thought it ought to be, in accordance with [illegible] ancient practice. The object of the sentence is to recom[illegible] the king (and in these precepts addressed to young kings [illegible] poet always spoke generally, and traced as it were a [illegible] system of conduct for all kings to come), always to [illegible] the wisdom of the learned man to whom he had looked [illegible] his literary and philosophical instructor, the task of acting [illegible]

(156) original:—T-anmcara fadéin,
t-almsa 'na láimh,
gid cleireach glan gaeth,
gid laech, gid fear graid.

almoner: an office implying in those days far more than the dispensation of charities, for it included also the distribution of rewards, the payment and entertainment of vassals and followers, and perhaps most of the duties of a royal Treasurer and Minister of Finance of the present time. And this office the teacher advises should be conferred on the king's tutor, whether priest or layman; for the office was a secular political office, in effect; and on the other hand, the Profession of Teaching, the practice of Philosophy, and the acquirement of Literature and learning, were by no means confined to the priesthood. In the time of *Fothadh* and king *Aedh* it continued to be what it was long before the introduction of Christianity, the crowning glory of schools which were open to all alike, and in which all the knowledge of the age was publicly taught to the laity at large, whether intended or not for the sacred mission; and taught, not through the medium of the Latin tongue, as in many other countries, but through that of the ancient language of the Gaedhelic race itself.

Maelsuthain O'Carroll, the chief counsellor of Brian Boromha.

The other example to which I have referred of the teacher of a king being honoured as his minister, happens also to be an instance of a lay teacher, though one possessed of ecclesiastical property. *Brian Boromha*, who was monarch of Erinn from the year 1002 to the year 1014, was educated at the ancient monastery of *Inis Faithlenn*, [Inisfallen] in the Lakes of Killarney, by the learned *Maelsuthain* O'Carroll, who was chief of the *Eoghanacht* of *Loch Lein*, and hereditary lay abbot for the time (for he was not a priest) of that monastery.(137) *Brian's* education must, it is true, have been imperfect, as the constant disturbances arising from his wars with the Danes called him away from his studies to active life at the too early age of sixteen years, and from that moment to the end of his long life it is little likely that he could have ever found leisure to resume them. For the Dalcassian clanns, over whom his brother Mahon presided as king of Munster, were, during the whole of the next half century, engaged in almost incessant war; and Brian early became one of the most distinguished and formidable of their warriors. Mahon's career was closed by treachery and death about the year 974, upon which *Brian* succeeded to the government of Munster; and it was not without still more constant toil that he maintained that rule, as he did with skill and bravery, from that period down to the year 1002, when he assumed the government of the whole kingdom. At what time *Brian* called to his councils his old tutor, the same O'Carroll, I cannot say; but in or about the year 1002

(137) See *Lectures on the MS. Materials of Ancient Irish History*; p. 76; and p. 359 et seq., and 653.

LECT. VIII. we find him in the position of secretary to the king, in which capacity he accompanied *Brian* to Armagh, when Maelsuthain made that memorable record in the ancient Book of the Canon of St. Patrick, of which I gave some account in a former lecture,—in the presence, as he states, of *Brian*, "the Emperor of the Gaedhils", ["Imperator Scotorum"].(188)

I have referred to these familiar instances in our history, of the practical respect in which the profession of teacher was held of old, merely as instances. I need hardly repeat that the high social position of the teacher was the rule, not the exception; and such instances serve to show how those relations, which were determined by an enlightened system of law in the earliest ages, still continued to be cherished down to a comparatively modern period. In fact they flowed from the law and system of Gaedhelic society itself. And it is in this that we find so strong a proof of the real love of learning, the true civilization, of our remote ancestors.

I have now concluded what I had to say upon this branch of our general subject. When I stated, at the commencement of the present series of lectures, that I proposed to deal with the interesting theme of the social customs and manners of life in ancient Erinn, it was probably expected that I should at once take up those branches of it which relate to the internal family life of the people; their habitations and furniture; their dress and ornaments; their arms and mode of warfare; their music and musical instruments; and other similar matters. And these subjects will necessarily occupy an important portion of the present course. But to give anything like an adequate idea, however roughly sketched, of the nature and value of the kind of civilization enjoyed by our forefathers, it was indispensable to begin with the graver parts of their social system, upon which all else was founded. And therefore it was that I had first to deal with their system of Legislation and their Code of Laws; and, after this, with their system of Education, and the fruits it bore. This portion of my subject has, of necessity, occupied a somewhat longer space than I had originally expected; but is now at last concluded, and we approach the consideration of topics of, perhaps, more general interest.

(188) See *Lectures*, etc., ubi supra.

LECTURE IX.

[Delivered [illegible] June, 1857.]

(IV.) OF DRUIDS AND DRUIDISM in ancient Erinn. Vague statements as to Druids and Druidism in the Encyclopaedias. Account of the British Druids in Rees's Cyclopaedia. Rowland's account of the Druids of Anglesey. Nothing certain known of the Druids in Britain. Druidism originated in the East. Of the origin of Druids in Erinn, according to our ancient writings. Of the Druids of *Parthalon*; of the Nemidians, and the Fomorians; etc. Explanation of the name of *Mona*; (the Isle of Anglesey). Of Druidism among the *Tuatha Dé Danann*;—among the Firbolgs;—among the Milesians. Instance of Druidism on the occasion of the landing of the Milesians. The Invocation of *Amergin*. References to Druidism in ancient Irish writings;—the *Dinnseanchas* (on the names of *Midhe* and *Uisnech*). Druidical fire. Of the story of King *Eochaidh Airemh*, and Queen *Edain* (circa B.C. 100). The Irish Druid's wand of Divination made of the Yew, not Oak. Use of Ogam writing by the Druids. Of the story of *Cuchulainn* and the lady *Emer* (circa A.D. 1). Of the *Sidhe* or *Aes Sidhe*,—now called "Fairies". Of the story of *Lughaidh Reo-derg*. Of the school of *Cathbadh*, the celebrated Druid of king *Conchobar Mac Nessa*. The Druids Teachers in ancient Erinn.

Of all the systems of Religion or Worship, mixed with Philosophy and Science, of which the fertile mind of man was the parent, from the earliest period to the present day, there is not one, perhaps, which has obtained more early and lasting celebrity than that which has passed under the somewhat indefinite name of "Magic", as the description of the very imperfectly investigated Religion or Philosophy of the more ancient nations of the East. And there is, unfortunately, no system of which fewer satisfactory vestiges, or authentic historical details, have come down to our times.

Vague statements as to Druids and Druidism in the Encyclopaedias.

The compilers of modern Encyclopaedias have, I suppose, consulted all the ancient classical writers in an effort to present to the world some intelligible view of the Religion or Philosophy of "Magic" under one of its most interesting forms, and that which seemed the least unfavourable for historical investigation, that, namely, of Druidism; to which, as that form of the Western Philosophy or Religion which prevailed in early ages in our own as well as other western nations, I have now to direct attention. The best English article I have found on the subject, because free from the gross fabrications of Vallancey and Toland, touching Irish Druids, is to be found in Rees's Cyclopaedia. Yet, after all the labour of the learned writer, and although he has devoted many closely printed pages to the

[LECT.] IX.

[Vague] state-[ment]s as to [Drui]ds and [Druid]ism in [E]ncyclo-[pæd]ias.

subject, liberally quoting his authorities, still when we come to look for some specific description of Druids and Druidic Rites, we find nothing but the most vague and general assertions: that the Druids were Priests who sacrificed human and other victims; but how, or to whom, we are not satisfactorily told;— that they were Teachers of occult Sciences, and the domestic tutors of the children of the higher classes; but no instances are given;—that they were absolute Judges in cases of life and property; but by whom constituted, or under what laws, we are not told;—that they practised Magic and Augury; but we are not given any particulars;—not even furnished with so much as the name of any one great master of those arts among them, nor with any remarkable instance of their application.

As to the origin and history of Druidism, where and how it originally sprang, such books of reference as those I have alluded to, are equally unsatisfactory. Yet, perhaps the best general introduction by which I can preface what I have to say on the subject of Druidism in Erinn would be to quote the substance of the account given by the essayist in Rees's Cyclopaedia; for we shall then see to what extent our Gaedhelic authorities will enable us to define what this learned writer has been unable to make clear, and to supply what he has failed to discover from classical authorities.

"The Druids" (says this writer), "are said by some to have been a tribe of the ancient Celts or Celtae, who emigrated, as Herodotus assures us, from the Danube towards the more westerly parts of Europe, and to have settled in Gaul and in Britain at a very early period. Accordingly, they have traced their origin, as well as that of the Celts, to the Gomerians or the descendants of Gomer, the eldest son of Japhet. But little certain is known concerning them before the time of Caesar, who says that they were one of the two orders of persons that subsisted in Gaul, the other being the Nobles. The case was the same in Britain, where it is supposed the principles and rites of Druidism originated, and from which they were transferred to Gaul. This seems to have been the custom according to the account of the historian: Such of the Gauls as were desirous of being thoroughly instructed in the principles of their religion, which was the same with that of the Britons, usually took a journey into Britain for that purpose. It is universally acknowledged that the British Druids were at this time very famous, both at home and abroad, for their wisdom and learning as well as for their probity, and that they were held in high estimation as the teachers both of religion and philosophy. But it has been disputed whether they were the original in-

inventors of the opinions and system which they taught, or received them from others.

Vague statements as to Druids and Druidism in the Encyclopaedias.

"Some have imagined that the Gauls and other nations in the west of Europe derived the first principles of learning and philosophy from a Phoenician colony which left Greece and built Marseilles in Gaul, about B.C. 540. Others have suggested that the Druids derived their philosophy from Pythagoras, who flourished about five hundred years before Christ, and taught his doctrines at Crotona in Italy.

"It does not appear how widely the Druids were dispersed through Britain and the adjacent isles; but it is well known that their chief settlement was in the isle of Anglesey, the ancient Mona, which they probably selected for this purpose, as it was well stored with spacious groves of their favourite oak.

"As one principal part of their office was to direct the worship and religious rites of the people, the service of each temple required a considerable number of them, and all these lived together near the temple where they served. The Arch-Druid of Britain is thought to have his stated residence in the island of Anglesey above mentioned, where he lived in great splendour and magnificence, according to the custom of the times, surrounded by a great number of the most eminent persons of his order.

"The Druids were also divided into several classes or branches, viz., the *Vacerri*, *Bardi*, *Eubages*, *Semnothii* or *Semnothei*, and *Saronidas*. The *Vacerri* are held to have been the priests; the *Bardi*, the poets; the *Eubages*, the augurs; and the *Saronidas*, the civil judges and instructors of youth.

"Strabo only distinguishes three kinds: *bardi; eubages*, or *vates*, and Druids; though the last name was frequently given to the whole order.

"As several monuments were erected by the Druids for religious and other purposes, to say nothing of Stonehenge, we cannot question their having made great progress in the science of mechanics, and in the mode of applying mechanical power, so as to produce very astonishing effects.

"Medicine, or the art of healing, must also have been the object of attention and study among the Druids, for they were the physicians as well as the priests both of Gaul and Britain. To this purpose, being much addicted to superstition, those who were afflicted with a dangerous disease sacrificed a man, or promised that they would sacrifice one, for their recovery.

"The British Druids were great magicians, and much addicted to divination, by which they pretended to work a kind of miracle, and exhibited astonishing appearances in nature, to

SECT. IX. penetrate into the counsels of Heaven, to foretell [illegible] and to discover the success or miscarriage of [illegible] undertakings.

"'In Britain', says Pliny (N. H. l. 30, c. 1.) 'the [illegible] are cultivated with such astonishing success and so [illegible] monies at this day (A. D. 60), that the Britons seem [illegible] pable of instructing even the Persians themselves in [illegible]

"Of the British Academies the most consider[illegible] situated in the isle of Anglesey, near the mansion of [illegible] Druid. Here is a place that is called *Myfyrion*, [illegible] place of meditation or study; another called *Caer*-[illegible] is, the city of astronomers; and another *Cerrig-Brud*[illegible] astronomer's circle.

"Their great solemnity and festival was that of [illegible] the mistletoe from the oak. This festival is said to [illegible] kept as near as the age of the moon would permit to [illegible] of March, which was their New Year's Day. The [illegible] was also a great festival, in honour of Bellinus or the [illegible]

"Of the Druidical creed it was an article that it [illegible] lawful to build temples to the gods, or to worship them [illegible] walls, or under roofs. (Tacit. de Mor. Germ., c. 9.)

"The Druids, says Pliny, have so high an esteem [illegible] oak, that they do not perform the least religious [illegible] without being adorned with a garland of its leaves.

"The Druids had no image, but they worshipped a [illegible] tree as a symbol of Jupiter.

"They were selected from the best families. They [illegible] chief judges, and held their high court in Anglesey, [illegible] cirque. One of these is called *Brein Gwyn*, that [illegible] supreme tribunal, in the townland of Fér Dryid".

Rowland's account of the Druids of Anglesey.

So far the article in Rees's Encyclopaedia on the Dr[illegible] but let us see what Rowland, another and older Welsh[illegible] native, too, of Mona itself, or Anglesey, says of the [illegible] authority which existed for these glowing accounts of [illegible] Druids of that island.

"I think I may take it for granted", says this very [illegible] writer, "that it is the generally received account, among [illegible] sorts of people in Wales who pretend to anything of antiqu[illegible] that the Isle of Mona or Anglesey was anciently the seat of [illegible] British Druids: nay, there is not a book of late written of [illegible] tory or geography, which touches the isle of Anglesey, [illegible] gives the same account; though the opinion, for all I could [illegible] see, rather seems to have been taken upon trust, passing from hand to hand, among the authors who had lately mentioned it, than well settled upon its due foundation and evidence. 'T is [illegible] no purpose to recite instances which are too many, and which only serve to prove a consent, and that it has not been till of late years contradicted, which is all I propose in this part of the proof".(140) LECT. IX.

So far, then, Rees and Rowland upon the general character of the British Druids, their reputed learning and religion, and their establishment in the island of Anglesey; and I have here introduced so much on the subject, in order that we may be able to judge by comparison how far, and where the few notices of our Irish Druids which I have been able to collect, will agree with them.

We see from these English articles that nothing precise is known in England of the origin of Druids and Druidism in Britain; no native authorities of any kind quoted; in fact, nothing but a few opinions derived from foreign writers, and inaccurately stated on trust by modern English authors, as Rowland so honestly admits. Nothing precise known of the Druids in Britain.

It must occur to every one who has read of Zoroaster, of the Magi of Persia, and of the sorceries of Egypt mentioned in the seventh chapter of Exodus, that Druids and Druidism did not originate in Britain any more than in Gaul or Erinn. It is indeed probable that, notwithstanding Pliny's high opinion of the powers of the British Druids, the European Druidical system was but the offspring of the Eastern augury, somewhat less complete, perhaps, when transplanted to a new soil than in its ancient home. Druidism originated in the East.

I shall not, however, here attempt to trace the first origin of Druidism in Europe; nor shall I even endeavour, at present, to suggest any theory of what exactly constituted our own Druidism in ancient Erinn. Perhaps the time is not come for satisfactory inquiry, either into the nature of the Druidical Philosophy, (or "Religion", if it be proper so to call it), or into the details of the rites and ceremonies used by the Druids. For my own part I feel that I have at present more to do with the *materials* upon which hereafter to found a theory concerning this difficult subject of history, than with the imagination of one for myself. And so, merely calling attention to the rashness of such speculations upon Druidism as the writers I have just referred to, I shall confine myself here to a simple narration of what is to be found, upon Druids and Druidism, scattered over our own annals and earlier historic pieces; and that entirely apart from any comparison of the results of such an inquiry with what is to be found in the classic or other foreign authorities. Be it

(140) Rowland's *Mona Antiqua*, p. 89 (Dublin: 1723).

LECT. IX. for others to undertake the task of a final and exhaustive ex-amination of the subject of Druidism in Europe generally.

Let us begin with the earliest mention of Druids as [illegible] in our annals and historical traditions.

Origin of Druids in Erinn, according to our ancient writings.

The origin of Druids in Erinn is carried back by our [illegible] writings, (and I am convinced with great probability), [illegible] earliest colonizers of the country, who were all, it is [illegible] membered, referred to the race of Japhet; and whether [illegible] was or was not in the more ancient times anything [illegible] traditional authority for this belief, it is, I think, [illegible] show that the ancient Gaedhils never assumed the origin [illegible] Druidic system themselves, nor acknowledged to have [illegible] it, any more than any other part of their social system, from [illegible] neighbouring country.

Druids of *Parthalon*.

Parthalon is by our most ancient authorities recorded to [illegible] come into Erinn about three hundred years after the [illegible]. He is said to have come from "*Migdonia*", or Middle Greece, with a small company; but among these we are told that [illegible] were three Druids,—whose names are given: *Fios*, [illegible], and *Fochmarc*; that is, if we seek the etymological meaning of the words, Intelligence, Knowledge, and Inquiry. We have no record of any performance of these Druids of *Parthalon*.

Druids of the Nemidians and Fomorians.

The next colony, led by *Nemid* and his sons, is said to have come from "Scythia", about three hundred and thirty years after the coming of *Parthalon*. *Nemid*'s sons were: [illegible], *Iarbonel* "the Prophet", *Fergus* "the Half-Red", and [illegible]. And this colony soon, according to our oldest records, came in contact with the power of hostile Druidism, to which they opposed their own. *Nemid*, it appears, had not remained long in peace in the country, before he was disturbed by the [illegible]sions of the sea rovers, who are known in our old writings under the name of the Fomorians. These adventurers, under a valiant leader named *Conaing*, son of *Faebhar*, took pos-session of Tory Island (on the north-west of the coast of Donegal), which they fortified, and converted into a sort of citadel or depot, and by this means made themselves most formidable and oppressive to the Nemidians on the main land. The Nemidians, driven to despair at last, assembled all their forces, men and women, from all parts of the country, on the shore opposite Tory Island; which the Fomorians perceiving, sent their Druids and Druidesses, we are told, to confound them by their Druidic spells; but these were met by the Ne-midian Druids and Druidesses, under the leadership of [illegible], "daughter of the king of Greece", *Nemid*'s wife, and chief of the Druidesses. A fierce contest of spells as well as of blows ensued between them, in which the Fomorian party were defeated. A general battle ensued then, which resulted in the utter rout of the Fomorians, whose tower or fortress on Tory Island was demolished, and their chief leader, *Conaing*, and his sons, were killed.

The Nemidians did not long enjoy the peace and freedom which this victory brought them; for *More* the son of *Dela*, another famous rover or Fomorian chief, came, with sixty ships, took possession again of Tory Island, and renewed the oppressions practised by his predecessor upon the Nemidians. This led to another great battle, in which the destruction of the parties was mutual; *More* and a few of his followers, only, escaping to the island, and but one ship of the Nemidians, with only thirty warriors and three leaders on board, escaping to the land. These three leaders were: *Beothach*, the son of *Iarbonel* "the Prophet", son of *Nemid; Simeon Breac* (or "the speckled"), son of *Starn*, son of *Nemid;* and *Britan Mael* (or "the bald",) son of *Fergus* the Half-Red, son of *Nemid*. And it is to these three cousins that the races of the *Tuatha Dé Danann*, the *Firbolgs*, and the Britons, are traced by our early genealogists, from whom we learn that the three soon afterwards left Erinn, and proceeded to seek a better fortune elsewhere. *Beothach*, we are told, with his clann, went to the northern parts of Europe, where they made themselves perfect in all the arts of Divination, Druidism, and Philosophy, and returned, after some generations, to Erinn, under the name of the *Tuatha Dé Danann*. *Simeon Breac* with his clann wandered southward into Greece; and in many generations after, returned to Erinn under the name of the *Firbolgs*. And we learn that *Britan Mael*, with his father *Fergus*, and his clann, went to *Moinn* or *Mainn Chonaing*, the present Island of Mona (or Anglesey); "from which", says the Book of Ballymote (folio 15), "their children filled the great Island of Britain, which they inhabited until the coming in of the Saxons, who drove the descendants of Brutus to the one border of the country, and the descendants of *Britan Mael* back to *Moinn Chonaing* [or Anglesey], on the other border".

Explanation of the name of *Mona*; (the island of Anglesey).

And here, let me observe that it seems strange that Rowland and the other Welsh writers of modern times have not attempted to make any guess at the etymology of the name of Mona. This name is indifferently written in our ancient Irish manuscripts as *Moin*, *Main*, *Moein*, and *Maein*, and never but in connection with the name of *Conaing*, the great *Fomorian* chief already mentioned, who had occupied and fortified Tory Island on the coast of Donegal, from which he ravaged the

LECT. IX.

Of the Name of Mona; (Anglesey.)

mainland of Erinn, and perhaps other countries also. [...] was from the tower or fortress erected by him there, and [...] has been always called *Tor Chonaing*, or *Conaing's* Tower, [...] the island received the name of *Tor Inis*, or Tower [...] a name modified by the Danes, to Tor-eye, (eye being [...] Danish name for an island), and adopted in sound, and [...] in orthography, by English writers and speakers.

When we remember, then, that Tory was called [...] *Chonaing*, or *Conaing's* Tower Island (and also, for [...] *Tor Chonaing* or Conaing's Tower); and that in like [...] we find the Island of Anglesey invariably written [...] *Moen Chonaing;* we have established an analogy between [...] origins of both names, which to understand fully requires [...] to explain the word *Moin* or *Moen* through the [...] some recognised language. This we can well do; for, [...] ancient Gaedhelic glossary (preserved in MS. H. 3. 18, T.C.D.) [...] we find the following words and explanation:

"*Moen*": from [the Latin] Moenia, [signifying] a [...] of walls [or ramparts]".[188]

Now, if *Tor Chonaing* meant, as it is well known it [...] *aing's* Tower or Fortress, *Moen Chonaing*, or *Conaing's* [...] must have had simply a corresponding meaning; and that [...] it had, I have, I trust, sufficiently shown, from an [...] that cannot be questioned. *Moen Chonaing*, then, means [...] *Conaing's* Fortress, or fortified island; in the same way [...] *Tor Chonaing* meant *Conaing's* Tower, or Tower Island [...]

It is also but rational to suppose that the strait or [...] which divides this Island of Mona from the mainland of [...] and which is now called the "Menai Strait", did not [...] that name from any independent source, but that it borrowed [...] from *Maen*, the name of the island. And in fact it was anciently [...] called *Sruth Moena*, or *Muir Moena;* that is, the River [...] of *Moen;* the nominative *moen* taking a final *a* in the [...] case, and forming *Moena* or *Moenai*, the correct form [...] present name of Menai. That channels of this sort were [...] after the islands which they cut off from the main-land, [...] from the land itself, could be shown by many examples [...] were necessary; but it is too well known a fact to require [...] tration here.

It appears then that it was from Erinn that the Isle [...] (or Anglesey) received its earliest colony; and that that [...] was of a Druidical people.

Now going back to the ancient legendary history [...] Gaedhils, it is to be remembered that on the flight of [...]

(188) original:—Moen .i. a moenia, murorum aedificia.

grandsons from Erinn, one of them, *Simeon Breac*, the son of *Starn*, is said to have gone with his clann into Thrace, and into Greece. There, we are told, they remained and multiplied during more than two hundred years; when at last escaped from the oppression which, it seems, held them there in a state of slavery, and after many wanderings returned to Erinn again, and with little trouble made themselves masters of the country. These were the *Firbolgs*. These again, in their turn, were soon after invaded by the *Tuatha Dé Danann*, descendants of *Iobath*, the third grandson or great-grandson of *Nemid*; and their power and rule were overthrown in the first battle of *Magh Tuireadh*, of which some account has been given in a former lecture.[191]

Druidism among the Tuatha Dé Danann.

The *Tuatha Dé Danann*, or *Dadanann* tribes, as we have already seen, during the long period of their exile from Erinn, devoted themselves much to the cultivation of Divination, Druidism, and the Philosophy of the northern and eastern parts of Europe; so that they appear to have returned perfectly accomplished in all the secrets and mysteries of the occult sciences of those times. They had a druidical chief or demigod, the great *Dagda*, as he was called, who was also their military leader. They had, besides him, three chief Druids: *Brian*, *Iuchar*, and *Iucharba*; and two chief professional Druidesses: *Becuill* and *Danand*,—besides a great number of private Druids and Druidesses mentioned by name in the early accounts of the coming of the race.

On the first arrival of the *Tuatha Dé Danann*, they took up their position in the fastnesses of Middle Connacht, but soon discovered that the country was inhabited by the Firbolgs; they then moved farther south and west, to the plain called *Magh Tuireadh*, near Cong, in the present county of Galway, as described on a former occasion. The ancient tales record that while they were making this important movement three of their noble non-professional Druidesses, namely, *Bodhbh*, *Macha*, and *Mór Rigan*, went to Tara, where the Firbolg hosts were assembled in a council of war; and that there, by their Druidical arts, they caused clouds of impenetrable darkness and mist to envelope the assembled multitudes, and showers of fire and blood to pour down upon them from the heavens, so that for three days all business was suspended; that at last the spell was broken by the Firbolg Druids, *Cesarn*, *Gnathach*, and *Ingnathach*; but that during this time, the *Tuatha Dé Danann* had already established themselves without opposition in a new defensive position at a safer distance from their enemies. This

(191) *Lectures on the MS. Materials*, etc., p. 243 et seq.

LECT. IX. may serve as one instance of the [illegible] practical use of Druidical magic at a [illegible] Erinn.

Druidism among the Firbolgs.

Again we are told, in the oldest accounts [illegible] invasion of the *Tuatha Dé Danann*, the [illegible] *Eochaidh Mac Erc*, had an unusual dream, [illegible] for interpretation to his chief Druid, *Cesarn* [illegible] said to have had recourse to the secret agencies [illegible] have discovered from a vision the approach of a [illegible] and this he is said to have communicated to the [illegible] of short simple sentences, of which a few are [illegible] account of the great battle of *Magh Tuireadh*, [illegible] was extracted on a former occasion.[188] The [illegible] at last; and it is stated that the men of [illegible] ledge" of both parties took up their positions [illegible] stages on the battle-field, practising their druidic [illegible] of their friends and against their foes respectively [illegible] the *Tuatha Dé Danann* prevailed, and the *Firbolgs* [illegible] feated.

I need not describe here the curious druidic [illegible] tain or bath prepared by the *Tuatha Dé Danann* [illegible] this occasion, having gone fully into the whole [illegible] battle of *Magh Tuireadh* in a former lecture.[189]

So much for what is found in the few records [illegible] our very early colonists.

Ancient traditions of the Milesian Colony.

We now come to the Milesian Colony. According [illegible] cient traditions, these people, who were also Japhetian [illegible] in their migrations back from Scythia into Greece, [illegible] they had previously come; then into Egypt; then [illegible] and so, from Spain into Erinn, which they reached [illegible] hundred years after the conquest of the *Tuatha Dé* [illegible] that is, in the year of the world 3,500, or above 1,[illegible] fore Christ, according to the chronology of the *Annals* [illegible] Four Masters.

Druidism among the Milesians.

In the entire course of the migrations of this [illegible] Druids hold a conspicuous place. Among the most [illegible] was *Caicher*, who is said to have foretold to them, on [illegible] to Spain, that Erinn was their ultimate destination.

The chief Druids of the Milesians, on their arrival [illegible] were *Uar* and *Eithear* (who were both killed in the [illegible] *Sliabh Mis*, in Kerry), and *Amergin*, one of the Milesian [illegible] who was the Poet and Judge of the expedition, and a [illegible] Druid, though not by profession.

(188) See *Lectures on the MS. Materials*, etc., ubi supra.
(189) *Ibid.*

Instance of Druidism on the occasion of the landing of the Milesians

A remarkable instance of Druidism is stated to have happened even on the very occasion of the landing of the first Milesian colony. Having landed in Kerry, they marched direct to the seat of sovereignty, now called Tara, a place which at the time we are speaking of was called *Cathair Crofinn*, or *Crofinn's* City, from a *Tuatha Dé Danann* lady of that name, who had previously resided there.(160) On arriving at Tara, the Milesians demanded the sovereignty of the country from the three joint kings of the *Tuatha Dé Danann*, the brothers *Mac Cuill*, *Mac Cecht*, and *Mac Greiné*. These complained of their having been taken by surprise, alleging that if they had had notice of the intending invasion they would have prevented it, and offering to leave it with *Amergin* to give judgment between them. To this proposition the Milesians are said to have consented; and Amergin is recorded to have made the very singular decision that himself and his friends should reënter their ships, and should move to the distance of "nine waves", (as the authorities agree in stating), out from the land; and then that if they were able to land despite of the *Dé Danann*, the sovereignty of Erinn should be surrendered to them.

This decision, according to this most ancient tradition, was accepted by both parties; and the Milesians reëntered their ships, and went out the prescribed distance upon the sea. No sooner, however, had they done so, than the *Dé Danann* Druids raised such a tempest as drove the fleet out to sea, and dispersed them. One part of the fleet was driven to the south,—and round the island, to the north-east again,—under *Eremon*, the son of Milesius. The other part was suffering dreadfully from the tempest, when it occurred to them that the storm was raised by Druidical agency. *Donn*, the eldest of the Milesian brothers, then sent a man to the topmast of his ship to discover if the power of the wind extended as high as that point. The man descended, and announced that it was quite calm at that elevation; upon hearing which, *Donn* cried out: "It is treachery in our men of science not to allay this wind". [By this expression, "men of science", the Druids are referred to here as well as in many other places]. "It is not treachery", said his brother *Amergin;* and he arose and pronounced a Druidical oration,—of the ancient gloss on which the following

(160) The Hill of Tara had five names. The first was *Druim Decsain*, or the Conspicuous Hill; the second was *Liath Druim*, or *Liath's* Hill, from a *Firbolg* chief of that name who was the first to clear it of wood; the third was *Druim Cain*, or the beautiful Hill; the fourth was *Cathair Crofinn*, as shown above; and the fifth name was *Teamair* (now Anglicised Tara, from the genitive case *Teamhrach* of the word), a name which it got from being the burial place of *Tea*, the wife of *Eremon*, the son of Milesius.

LECT. IX.

The Incantation of Amergin.

is a literal translation, taken from the Book of [illegible] O'Clerys, in the Royal Irish Academy:—

"I pray that they reach the land of Erinn [illegible] riding upon the great, productive, vast sea. [illegible]

"That they be distributed upon her plains [illegible] and her valleys; upon her forests that shed [illegible] all other fruits; upon her rivers and her cataracts [illegible] lakes and her great waters; upon her abounding [illegible] upon her spring-abounding hills].

"That we may hold our fairs and equestrian [illegible] territories.

"That there may be a king from us in Tara [illegible] (Tara) be the territory of our many kings".[(184)] [illegible]

"That the sons of Milesius be manifestly seen [illegible] ritories.

"That noble Erinn be the home of the ship[illegible] sons of Milesius.

"Erinn which is now in darkness, it is for her [illegible] tion is pronounced.

"Let the learned wives of *Breas* and *Buaigne* [illegible] may reach the noble woman, great *Erinn*.

"Let *Eremon* pray, and let *Ir* and *Eber* implore [illegible] reach Erinn".

At the conclusion of this oration the tempest ceased [illegible] ing to our authority, and the survivors landed [illegible] then *Amergin*, upon putting his foot on dry land, [illegible] another propitiatory oration (couched in the same [illegible] general language), on the land, and on the waters, [illegible] them more prolific.

In this example we have a curious instance of the [illegible] of words in which it was anciently believed that, in [illegible] remote ages, the Druids framed their incantations. [illegible] however, perceive anything of druidic or magical [illegible] character, in this oration—nothing, in short, to dis[illegible] from the prayer of any Christian of the present day, [illegible] the expression of the speaker's wants and desire. [illegible] clearly appear to whom the prayer was addressed, or [illegible] ceremony or rite accompanied the delivery of it. [illegible] of course, quote it as the certainly genuine prayer of [illegible] but it is, without any doubt, a very ancient piece of com[illegible] tion, and it must, I am persuaded, have been written [illegible] some ancient Druid, or by some person conversant wi[illegible]

(184) The Hill had not at this time received the name of *Teamair* or *T*[illegible] but *Amergin* is made to speak of it by the name by which it was subseq[illegible] known.

style of Druidic practices, and probably at a time long before Druidism became extinct in this country. And as regards the intrinsic innocence of the words used, it is curious enough that the Irish people to this day have an old tradition, that in the most profane and forbidden performances of sorcery and witchcraft, harmless and blessed words have been always used. The common proverb still is: "Blessed words and cursed deeds".[188]

All that I have set down here is taken directly from our most ancient manuscripts, or those compiled from them; and they show clearly as the historical tradition of the country that each of the older colonies in Ireland was accompanied by its Druids; so that the suggestion of modern British writers that Druidism came first from Britain, or from Anglesey, into Erinn, is totally unfounded. I now proceed to select from the long list of Druidic references found in our old books, such as may serve to characterise the profession, so far, at least, as the limits of these lectures will allow. Very many other references there are, no doubt, which ought all to be gathered, all to be arranged and compared, if the subject of Irish Druidism, or indeed of Druidism at all, is to be completely investigated. But in these lectures I can hardly be expected to do more than give the general results, and to show where further information in detail may be obtained.

References to Druidism in ancient Irish writings.—The *Dinnseanchas*, (on the names of *Midhe* and *Uisnech*.)

The allusions and instances to which I shall refer are very widely scattered, and I cannot promise much arrangement in my treatment of the subject. I only propose to myself to give a few specimens of what was called Druidism by way of example: and I shall commence by citing from the earliest authority. The ancient tract called *Dinnseanchas*, (on the etymology of the names of several remarkable places in Erinn), gives the following singular legendary account of the origin of the names of *Midhe* (now Meath), and of *Uisnech*, in Meath.

Midhe, the son of *Brath*, son of *Detha* (says this legend), was the first that lighted a fire for the sons of the Milesians in Erinn, on the Hill of *Uisnech* in Westmeath; and it continued burning for seven years; and it was from this fire that every chief fire in Erinn used to be lighted. And his successor was entitled to a sack of corn and a pig from every house in Erinn, every year. The Druids of Erinn, however, said that it was an insult to them to have this fire ignited in the country; and all the Druids of Erinn came into one house to take counsel; but *Midhe* had all their tongues cut out, and he buried the tongues in the earth of *Uisnech*, and then sat over them; upon which his mother exclaimed: "It is *Uaisnech*

(188) original:—briatra beannaigte ɼ gníomarta mallaigte.

[i.e. proudly] you sit up there this night";—and hence the names of *Uisnech*, and of *Midhe* (or Meath).

Druidical Fire.

This, I believe, is the first reference to a Druidical fire to be found in our old books.

The story of king Eochaidh Aireamh and queen Edain, (circa B.C. 100.)

The next remarkable allusion to this subject that is to be found is the account of King *Eochaidh Aireamh*.

It was a century before the Incarnation that *Eochaidh Aireamh* was monarch of Erinn; and his queen was the [illegible] *Edain*, a lady remarkable not only for her beauty, but [illegible] learning and accomplishments. One day that *Eochaidh* [illegible] his palace at *Teamair*, according to this ancient story, a stranger of remarkable appearance presented himself before him. "Who is this man who is not known to us, and what is his business?" said the king. "He is not a man of any distinction, but he has come to play a game at chess with you", said the stranger. "Are you a good chess player?" said the king. "A trial will tell", said the stranger. "Our chess-board is in the queen's [illegible] and we cannot disturb her at present", said the king. "It matters not, for I have a chess-board of no inferior kind here with me", said the stranger. "What do we play for?" said the king. "Whatever the winner demands", said the stranger. [They played then a game which was won by the stranger.] "What is your demand now?" said the king. "*Edain*, your queen", said the stranger, "but I will not demand her till the [illegible] year". The king was astonished and confounded; [illegible] stranger, without more words, speedily disappeared.

On that night twelvemonths, the story goes on to tell [illegible] king held a great feast at *Teamair*, surrounding himself [illegible] queen with the great nobles and choicest warriors of his [illegible] and placing around his palace on the outside a line [illegible] rienced and vigilant guards, with strict orders to let no [illegible] pass them in. And thus secured, as he thought, he [illegible] with anxiety the coming night, while revelry reigned [illegible] As the middle of the night advanced, however, the [illegible] horrified to see the former stranger standing in the [illegible] the floor, apparently unperceived by any one else. [illegible] advanced to the queen, and addressed her by the [illegible] *Finn*, (Fair Woman), in a poem of seven stanzas, of [illegible] following is a literal translation:

"O *Béfinn*! will you come with me
To a wonderful country which is mine,
Where the people's hair is of golden hue,
And their bodies the colour of virgin snow?

"There no grief or care is known;
White are their teeth, black their eyelashes;

LECT. IX.

The Story of king *Eochaidh Airemh* and queen *Edain*, (circa B.C. 100.)

Delight of the eye is the rank of our hosts,
With the hue of the fox-glove on every cheek.
"Crimson are the flowers of every mead,
Gracefully speckled as the blackbird's egg;
Though beautiful to see be the plains of *Inisfail*,
They are but commons compared to our great plains.
"Though intoxicating to you be the aledrink of *Inisfail*,
More intoxicating the ales of the great country;
The only land to praise is the land of which I speak,
Where no one ever dies of decrepit age.
"Soft sweet streams traverse the land;
The choicest of mead and of wine;
Beautiful people without any blemish;
Love without sin, without wickedness.
"We can see the people upon all sides,
But by no one can we be seen;
The cloud of Adam's transgression it is,
That prevents them from seeing us.
"O woman! should you come to my brave land,
It is golden hair that will be on your head;
Fresh pork, beer, new milk, and ale,
You there with me shall have, O *Béfinn!*"

At the conclusion of this poem, the stranger put his arm around the queen's body, raised her from her royal chair, and walked out with her, unobserved by any one but the king, who felt so overcome by some supernatural influence, that he was unable to offer any opposition, or even to apprise the company of what was going on. When the monarch recovered himself, he knew at once that it was some one of the invisible beings who inhabited the hills and lakes of Erinn that played one of their accustomed tricks upon him. When daylight came, accordingly, he ordered his chief Druid, *Dallan*, to his presence, and he commanded him to go forth immediately, and never to return until he had discovered the fate of the queen.

The Druid set out, and traversed the country for a whole year, without any success, notwithstanding that he had drawn upon all the ordinary resources of his art. Vexed and disappointed at the close of the year he reached the mountain (on the borders of the present counties of Meath and Longford) subsequently named after him *Sliabh Dallain*. Here he cut four wands of yew, and wrote or cut an *Ogam* in them; and it was revealed to him, "through his keys of science and his *ogam*", that the queen *Edain* was concealed in the palace of the fairy chief, *Midir*, in the hill of *Bri Leith*, (a hill lying to the west of Ardagh, in the present county of Longford). The Druid joyfully

LECT. IX.

returned to Tara with the intelligence; and the monarch *Eochaidh* mustered a large force, marched to the fairy mansion of *Bri Leith*, and had the hill dug up until the diggers approached the sacred precincts of the subterranean dwelling; whereupon, the wily fairy sent out to the hill side fifty beautiful women, all of the same age, same size, same appearance in form, face, and dress, and all of them so closely resembling the abducted lady *Edain*, that the monarch *Eochaidh* himself, her husband, failed to identify her among them, until at length she made herself known to him by unmistakable tokens, [illegible] which he returned with her to Tara.

The Irish Druid's Wand of Divination made of the Yew, not the Oak.

This tale exhibits two curious and characteristic features of Irish Druidism; the first, that the Irish Druid's wand of divination was formed from the yew, and not from the oak, as in other countries; the second, that the Irish Druid called in the aid of actual characters, letters, or symbols,—those, namely, the forms of which have come down to our own times cut in the imperishable monuments of stone, so well known as *Ogam* stones (many of which may be seen in the National Museum of the Royal Irish Academy.)

Use of the *Ogam* writing by the Druids.

The antiquity of this story of *Eochaidh Airemh* is unquestionable. There is a fragment of it in *Leabhar na h-Uidhri* [illegible] the Royal Irish Academy, a manuscript which was actually written before the year 1106; and it is there quoted from the Book of *Dromsnechta*, which was undoubtedly written [illegible] or about the year 430. There is a better copy, but still [illegible] perfect nor so old, in the collection formerly in the possession of the late Mr. William Monk Mason, in England.

The Story of *Cuchulainn* and the Lady *Eithne*, (circa A.D. 1.)

From the reign of *Eochaidh Airemh* we now pass down [illegible] a century for our next remarkable instance in poetic [illegible] these early examples of druidical magic; namely, to the commencement of the Christian era, at which time *Cuchulainn* [illegible] great Ulster champion flourished. This *Cuchulainn*, [or *Cuchulaind*] of whom so much has been said in former lectures, [illegible] as much celebrated for the beauty and symmetry of his person [illegible] for his bravery and military accomplishments. It is [illegible] wondered at, therefore, that, in the ages of romance, so [illegible] a warrior should have had many personal admirers among the fair dames of his own and other countries, and that [illegible] should be made to attract his attention, and to secure his [illegible] tion, by those secret arts of sorcery, in the efficacy of [illegible] every one believed in those times. I gave, in a former lecture,[188] a free analysis of the ancient historic tale of *Cuchulainn* [illegible]

(187) See *Lectures on the MS. Materials of Ancient Irish History*, p. [illegible]
(188) *Ibid.*, p. 281 et seq.

successful courtship of the lady *Emer*, the daughter of *Forgall Monach* of Lusk,—(in the present county of Dublin). The following occurrence is reported in one of the same series of historic tales(149) to have taken place subsequently to his marriage with that lady.

LECT. IX.

The Story of Cuchulainn and the Lady Eithné, (circa A.D. 1.)

At one time, says this ancient story, that the men of Ulster were celebrating a fair in the plain of *Muirtheimné*,—(*Cuchulainn's* patrimonial territory, which was in the present county of Louth, and comprised the district in which the present town of Drogheda is situated),—a flock of beautiful birds appeared on the lock (or expansion of the Boyne) before them. *Cuchulainn* gave the birds a peculiar blow with the flat of his sword, called *taithbéim*, so that their feet and their wings adhered to the water, and they were all caught. *Cuchulainn* then distributed them among the noble ladies at the fair, two to each, until he came to *Eithné*, his own lady-love at this time, when he found that he had none left to give her. So *Eithné* complained bitterly of her lover's neglect, in thus preferring the other ladies to her. "Don't be cast down", said *Cuchulainn*; "should any more beautiful birds visit the plain of *Muirtheimné*, or the river *Boind*, [or *Boinn*] you shall have the two most beautiful among them". Shortly after they perceived two beautiful birds upon the lake, linked together by a chain of red gold. They sang low music, which cast all such of the assembly as heard them into a profound sleep. *Cuchulainn*, however, went towards them, and putting a stone into his *crann tabhaill*, or sling, cast it at them; but it passed them by. He threw again, and the stone went over and beyond them. "Alas!" said he, "since I first received the arms of a champion, I did not ever make a false throw before this day". He then threw his spear at the birds, and it passed through the wing of one of them; upon which they immediately dived under the water.

Cuchulainn, proceeds this singular tale, went away dispirited at his failure, and after some time, resting his back against a rock, he fell asleep. Immediately afterwards, two fairy women approached him, of whom one wore a green, and the other a crimson cloak, of five folds. The woman with the green cloak came up and smiled at him, and struck him a little blow with a horse-switch; then the other went up to him and smiled at him, and struck him in the same way; and they continued to do this for a long time, each striking him in turn, until he was nearly dead. All the Ultonians saw what happened, and they proposed to awaken him. "Not so", said Fergus, "let him not

(149) See the Tale of *Seirglige Conchulainn*, or "*The Sick-bed of Cuchulainn and only jealousy of Eimer*", in the ATLANTIS, vol. i. p. 362, et seq.; and vol. ii. p. 96.

LECT. IX. Story of Cuchulainn and the Lady Fand; (see [illegible].)

be touched till we see what shall happen". He soon after started up through his sleep. "What has happened you?" inquired the Ultonians. "Take me to the *Teti Breac*, [i.e. the speckled or painted court,] at Emania", was all that he was able to say to them. He was therefore taken thither; and he remained there a whole year without speaking to any one.

One day, at last, (the tale goes on), before the next November eve, the Ultonians were assembled about him in the house; *Fergus* between him and the wall; *Conall Cearnach* between him and the door; *Lugaidh Reo-derg* (or "the red-striped") at the head of his bed; and *Eithné In-gubai* (or "the sorrowful"), his mistress, at the foot. While they were thus placed, a strange man came into the chamber, and sat on the side of the bed or couch on which *Cuchulainn* lay. "What has brought you there?" said *Conall Cearnach*. "Now", said the stranger, "if this man were in health, he would be a protection to all Ulster, and even in the illness and debility in which he lies, he is still a greater consolation to them. I have come to converse with him", said the stranger. "You are welcome then", said the Ultonians. The stranger then stood up, and addressed *Cuchulainn* in the following stanzas:

"O *Cuchulainn!* in thy illness,
Thy stay should not be long;
If they were with thee,—and they would come,—
The daughters of *Aedh Abrat*.

"*Libán*, in the plain of Cruaich, has said—
She who sits at the right of *Labraid* the quick—
That it would give heartfelt joy to *Fand*,
To be united to *Cuchulainn*.

"Happy that day, of a truth,
On which *Cuchulainn* would reach my land;
He should have silver and gold,
He should have abundance of wine to drink.

"If my friend on this day should be
Cuchulainn, the son of *Soalté*,
All that he has seen in his sleep,
Shall he obtain without his army.

"In the plain of *Muirtheimné*, here in the south,
On the night of Samhuin [November eve], without luck,
From me shall be sent *Libán*,
O *Cuchulainn!* to cure thy illness".(179)

This, it will be perceived, was no other than a poetical invitation to *Cuchulainn* from *Aedh Abrat*, a great fairy chief,

(179) See original in ATLANTIS, vol. i. p. 378.

The Story of Cuchulainn and the Lady Eithné. (circa A.D. 1)

[inviting] him to visit his court, at the approaching November [eve], and to take his daughter *Fand* [or *Fann*] in marriage, [promising] that he would be then cured of his illness.

"Who are you?" asked the Ultonians. "I am *Aengus*, the son [of] *Aedh Abrat*", said he. The man then left them; and they [knew] not whence he came nor where he went to, says the tale. [Cuchulainn] then stood up and spoke. "It is time, indeed", said [the] Ultonians; "let us know what happened you". "I saw", [said] he, "a wonderful vision about November eve, last year"; [and] he then told them all that happened, as related already. The tale proceeds. "What shall I do now, my master, [Conchobar]?" said *Cuchulainn* to the king [*Conchobar Mac Nessa*]. "[You] will go", said *Conchobar*, "to the same rock again". [Cuchulainn], therefore, went till he reached the same rock again, [where] he saw the woman with the green cloak coming towards [him]. "That is well, O *Cuchulainn*!" said she. "It is not [well]", said he. "What was your business with me last year?" [said] *Cuchulainn*. "It was not to injure you we came", said [she], "but to seek your friendship. I have come now", said she, "[from] *Fand*, the daughter of *Aedh Abrat*, who has been [abandoned] by *Manannan Mac Lir*, and who has fallen in love with you; *Libán* is my own name, and I salute you from my husband, *Labraid* of the quick hand at sword, who will give you the woman in marriage for your assistance to him in one day's battle against *Senach* the distorted, *Eochaidh n-Iuil*, and *Eoghan I..bhir*". "I am not well able to fight this day", said *Cuchulainn*. "Short is the time until you are", said *Libán*. "You will be quite restored; and what you have lost of your strength will be increased to you. You ought to do this for my husband *Labraid*", said she, "because he is one of the best champions amongst the warriors of the world". "Where is he?" said *Cuchulainn*. "He is in *Magh Mell*, [i.e. 'the Plains of Happiness']", said she. "It is better that I depart now", said *Libán* "Be it so", said *Cuchulainn*; "and let my charioteer, *Laegh*, go along with you to see the country". *Laegh* was accordingly conducted to a certain island, where he was well received by *Labraid* "of the quick hand at sword". He then returned to *Cuchulainn*, and (in a very curious poem of twenty-eight stanzas) he describes to him his journey and *Labraid's* court. *Cuchulainn* himself then goes to visit the lady *Fand*, and to fight the battle for her brother *Labraid*; which they won.

Meanwhile, continues the story, the lady *Emer*, *Cuchulainn's* most cherished of women, was pining in grief and jealousy at her court at *Dun-delca* (now Dundalk); but, unable to brook her miseries in silence any longer, she at last repaired to

LECT. IX.

Emania, to King *Conchobar*, to crave his assistance for the recovery of her husband, who was now living with the lady *Fand* in Fairyland. Just at this time *Manannan Mac Lir*, the famous *Tuatha Dé Danann* (fairy)-chief, the former husband, as we have seen, of the lady *Fand*, repented his repudiation of her, and came and invited her to accompany him back to his court in the isle of *Manainn*, (now Man, which bears his name), to which she consented. *Cuchulainn*, upon her desertion, seems to have lost his senses, and fled in a delirious rage to the mountains, where he remained for a long time without eating or drinking. *Emer*, therefore, informed King *Conchobar* of his condition, and *Conchobar*, we are told, sent the poets, scholars, and Druids of Ulster to seek out the champion, and bring him to Emania. He thereupon attempted to kill them, but they pronounced "Druidic orations" against him, until he was caught by the hands and feet, when at length a glimpse of his senses returned to him. He was then taken to Emania, where, as he was begging for a drink, the Druids gave him a "drink of oblivion", and the moment he drank it he forgot *Fand* and all that had happened. The Druids then gave *Emer* also a drink "to cause oblivion of her jealousy"; for she was in a state of madness hardly less extravagant than that of her husband. And finally, when *Manannan* was going off with his wife *Fand*, it is stated that he "shook his cloak between her and *Cuchulainn*", so that they should never again meet. "And

The *Sidhe*, or *Aes-Sidhe*,—now called "Fairies."

this", continues the tract from which I quote, "was the vision of bewitching *Cuchulainn*, by the *Aes Sidhe*, or dwellers in the hills; for the demoniac power was great before the introduction of the Christian faith, and so great was it, that they (that is, the demons) used to tempt the people in human bodies, and that they used to show them secrets and places of happiness where they should be immortal, and it was in that way they were believed. And it is these phantoms that the unlearned people call *Sidhe* or fairies, and *Aes Sidhé* or fairy people".

This curious and very ancient medley of Druidism and fairyism I have abridged from the ancient *Leabhar na h-Uidhri*, so often referred to in these lectures. I have given it at greater length than the plan of the present lecture would, perhaps, strictly warrant; but as it affords a fair specimen of the ancient fairy doctrine, as well as an instance of Druidism described in a very ancient writing, I trust the digression will not be thought too long.

The Story of *Lughaidh Reo-derg*.

The next example of a druidical performance that presents itself has reference also to *Cuchulainn's* time; for the young prince *Lugaidh Reo-derg*, (*Lugaidh* "the red-striped"), [illegible] son of the monarch *Eochaidh Feidhlech*, was educated in literature and the science of arms by *Cuchulainn*. This druidical story (one of the most curious in detail which remains to us) runs as follows: LECT. IX. The Story of *Lughaidh Reo-derg.*

"A meeting of the four great provinces of Erinn was held at this time (at *Teamair*), to see if they could find a person whom they could select, to whom they would give the sovereignty of Erinn; for they thought it ill that the Hill of Sovereignty of Erinn, that is *Teamair*, should be without the rule of a king in it; and they thought it ill that the people should be without the government of a king, to administer justice to them in all their territories. For the men of Erinn had been without the government of a monarch upon them during the space of seven years, after the death of *Conairé Mór*, at *Bruighin Da Derga*, [*Brudin Da Derca*] until this great meeting of the four great provinces of Erinn, at *Teamair* of the kings, in the court of *Erc*, son of *Cairbré* [or *Coirpre*] *Niadh-fear*.

"These were the (provincial) kings who were present in this meeting, namely, *Medhbh* (or Meave), queen of Connacht, and *Ailill*, her consort; *Curoi* (*Mac Dairé*), king of South Munster; *Tighernach Tetbannach*, son of *Luchta*, king of North Munster; and *Find* or *Finn Mac Rossa*, king of Leinster. These men would not hold kingly counsel with the men of Ulster at all, because they were unitedly opposed to the Ultermen.

"There was a Bull-feast made by them there, in order that they might learn through it who the person was to whom they would give the sovereignty. This is the way in which that bull-feast was made, namely, a bull was killed, and one man eat enough of its flesh and of its broth; and he slept under that meal; and a true oration was pronounced by four Druids upon him; and he saw in his dream the appearance of the man who would be made king of them, his countenance and description, and how he was occupied. The man screamed out of his sleep, and told what he had seen to the kings, namely, a soft youth, noble, and powerfully made, with two red stripes on his skin around his body, and he standing at the pillow of a man who was lying in a decline at *Emain Macha*, (the royal palace of Ulster).

"The kings then sent messengers immediately to Emania, where the Ultonians were assembled round *Conchobar*, (their king), at this time; and *Cuchulainn* was lying in a decline there, (as stated in the story the substance of which was given in the last lecture). The messengers told their tale to *Conchobar* and to the nobles of Ulster. "There is indeed with us", said *Conchobar*, "a noble, well-descended youth of that de-

LECT. IX. scription, namely, *Lugaidh Reo-derg*, 'the son of the three twins', *Cuchulainn*'s pupil, who now sits over his pillow yonder, as you see, cheering his tutor".

The tale goes on to say that *Cuchulainn* then arose, and delivered a valedictory address to his pupil, (a very curious piece), chiefly on the conduct which should distinguish him in his new character of monarch; after which *Lugaidh* repaired to *Teamair*, where he was fully recognized as the person described in the vision, and proclaimed as monarch; after which the assembly broke up.

This *Lugaidh* was the father of the monarch *Crimhthann Niadhnair*, who had a famous court at *Beinn Edair*,—(now the Hill of Howth, the site of the court being that of the present "Baily" Light-House, according to Doctor Petrie),—where he died and was buried; and it was in the ninth year of his reign that our Saviour is supposed to have been born.

Of Cathbadh, the celebrated Druid of King Conchobar Mac Nessa, and his School.

At the time of which we are speaking, that is, about the time of the Incarnation of our Lord, *Cathbadh*, of the province of Ulster, and chief or royal Druid to king *Conchobar*, at Emania, was perhaps the most celebrated professor of the Druidic order in Erinn. There are a great many references to this *Cathbadh* in his Druidic character, but of these I shall content myself with one only, and translate from the ancient history of the *Táin Bo Chuailgné* (cattle spoil of *Cuailgné*) a short extract:

One day that *Cathbadh* was outside Emania, on the north-east, lecturing his pupils, who numbered one hundred, (that being the number which *Cathbadh* taught), he was questioned by one of them as to the signs and omens of the day, whether they were for good or for evil, and for what undertaking that day would be propitious. The Druid answered that the fame and renown of the youth who should take arms upon that day should last in Erinn "*go brath*"—that is, in Erinn "for ever". *Cuchulainn*, the great hero of the cow-spoil, of whom so much has been said, and who was one of the pupils, immediately begged of his master to recommend him to the king as a [illegible] date for championship, or knighthood, as we should now [illegible] to which *Cathbadh* assented. *Cuchulainn* then repaired [illegible] king, and in the proper manner solicited him for the [illegible] champion. "Who instructed you to seek them?" said [illegible] "*Cathbadh*", said the youth. "You shall have them", [illegible] king; and *Conchobar* then presented him with a sword, [illegible] and two spears,—a form which constituted him [illegible] knight or champion at arms.

From this extract we may see what the character [illegible] *badh*'s school was,—it was evidently one of those [illegible] often referred to in our ancient writings, an academy for instruction, not only in poetry and Druidism, but also in military accomplishments.

The Druids as Teachers in ancient Erinn.

That the Druids shared largely in the instruction of the youth of Erinn, of all classes, in ancient times, could be shown from innumerable passages in our old writings, (to which I shall make further allusion before I leave the subject); but one remarkable instance, from the ancient Tripartite Life of St. Patrick, will be sufficient for the present. According to this most ancient authority, St. Patrick, having overcome and confounded the monarch *Laeghairé*'s chief Druids at Tara, passed over the Shannon into Connacht, to prosecute his apostolic labours. Now, at this period, it happened that at *Magh Ai*, (a district of which the modern county of Roscommon forms part), in the royal palace of *Cruachain*, there resided two other of king *Laeghairé*'s Druids, the brothers *Mael* and *Coplait*; and that, to their joint tuition the monarch had committed his two beautiful daughters,—*Eithne*, "the fair", and *Fedelim*, "the rosy". When the Druids, in whose charge the king's daughters were brought up, heard of St. Patrick's coming into their country, and of his success against the Druids at Tara and elsewhere, they resorted to their magical arts to defeat him, and by an exertion of their demoniac power, brought a dense darkness over the whole of *Magh Ai* during the space of three days and three nights. Patrick, however, prayed to God, and blessed the plain; and it so befell that the Druids alone remained involved in the darkness, while all the rest of the people had the light restored to them.

Shortly after this, the saint, we are told, came to the palace of *Cruachain*; and the following incident, which is related to have occurred on the occasion, throws a curious light on the sort of theological education which the young princesses received from their Druidic preceptors. Thus says the Life:

"Patrick then repaired to the fountain called *Clibech*, at the side of *Cruachain*, at the rising of the sun. The clergy sat at the fountain; and while they were there the two princesses, the daughters of *Laeghairé Mac Neill*, came at an early hour to the fountain, to wash, as was their custom; and encountering the assembly of the clergy at the fountain in their white vestments, and with their books before them, they wondered much at their appearance. They thought that they might be men from the hills, i.e. fairy-men, or phantoms. They questioned Patrick, therefore, saying: 'Whence have ye come? whither do ye go? are ye men of the hills? or are ye gods?' To which Patrick answered: 'It would be better for you to believe in God than

SECT. X. The Druids as Teachers in ancient Erinn.

to ask of what race we are?" The elder [illegible] 'Who is your God, and where is he? Is he in the [illegible] or is he in the Earth, or under the Earth, or [illegible] or in the seas, or in the streams, or in the [illegible] valleys? has he sons and daughters? has he [illegible] there abundance of all sorts of wealth in his kingdom?' [illegible] these questions Patrick made, of course, suitable [illegible] the end of the conversation was, that not only the two [illegible] but even their tutors, the two Druids, were soon [illegible] verted to the true faith.

Here we have an example of the active [illegible] in St. Patrick's time. But it is to be observed, [illegible] by no means ceased, even with the introduction [illegible] ment of Christianity in Erinn, as we have [illegible] old books. For instance: in an ancient Life of [illegible] *Cillé*, preserved in the *Leabhar Mór Duna Doighré* [illegible] called the *Leabhar Breac*), in the Royal Irish [illegible] stated, that his mother even consulted a Druid as to [illegible] time to put him to the work of his education; and that [illegible] was in fact his first tutor.

LECTURE X.

[Delivered 2nd July, 1857.]

(IV.) Druids, and Druidism; (continued). Of Druidical Charms. Of the *Dlui Fulla*, or "Fluttering Wisp",—(A.D. 600). Story of Prince *Comgan*, (VII. century). Story of the Princess *Eithné Uathach*, and the *Deisi*; and of the Druid *Dill*. Of the *Imbas Forosnai*; or "Illumination" by the Palms of the Hands. Of the *Teinm Laeghda*; or "Illumination" of Rhymes, of the *Fileadh*; and of the *Dichetal do Chennaibh*. Story of *Finn Mac Cumhaill* and *Lomna* the jester. Story of *Mogh Eimhé*, (the lap-dog). Story of the Siege of *Drom Damhghairé*;—Druidic Fire. Of the use of the Roan- (or Rowan-) tree, in Druidical rites;—in the ordeal by Fire. Of ancient Poetical Satire, as a branch of Druidism. Of the *Glam Dichinn*; or "Satire from the Hill Tops". The *Glam Dichinn* (or Satire) of the Poet *Neidhé*,—(from Cormac's Glossary). Story of the Druid *Lughaidh Delbaeth* (or "the Fire-Producer"), son of *Cas*. No instance of Human Sacrifices at any time in Erinn. One instance, at least, among the Druids of Britain; (recorded by Nennius). Of Divination by interpretation of Dreams and Omens, in ancient Erinn. Of Auguries from Birds;—the Raven;—the Wren. Of Augury from the Stars and Clouds, by night. Recapitulation.

In the last Lecture,—after having shown from the most ancient historical MSS. the existence of Druids as a profession in the early ages, and among all the races which successively inhabited Erinn,—I collected a few instances of their professional interposition so as to show by example what was the nature of their knowledge or their power as far as we find it recorded. I proceed now to make a selection of some characteristic examples of Druidism as it is referred to in the old books. I have already observed that no definite account of the rites, any more than of the belief or of the magical or other powers of this mysterious order, has come down to us; it is only from a number of isolated examples and mere allusions in the historical tales and poems that we can form any conception, even the most general, of what Druidism really was.

Druidical Charms. The *Dlui Fulla*, or "fluttering wisp" (A.D. 600.)

One of the most remarkable of the druidical rites thus recorded was that, for instance, of the charmed handful of straw, or hay, to which allusion is made in more than one place as having been made use of with the most powerful effect by these magicians of the early ages. We learn from several authorities that the ancient Druids here had a curious practice of pronouncing an incantation or charm on a wisp of straw, hay, or grass, which, thus charmed, they used to throw into a person's face, and so, (as it was believed), cause him to become a lunatic

LECT. X.

and unsettled wanderer. This wisp or handful was called *Dlui Fulla*, or "fluttering wisp".

The first reference that I find to the exercise of this phase of Druidism, goes as far back as the time of *Nuadha Fullon*, one of the early kings of Leinster, who flourished so long since as about 600 years B.C. It is stated in an ancient tract on the etymology of ancient Gaedhelic surnames, that this *Nuadha Fullon* had received the addition of *Fullon* to his first name on account of his having been educated by a celebrated Druid named *Fullon*, who was the first person that practised the art of pronouncing druidical incantations on a wisp of straw or hay, of such a character as that, when thrown in any one's face, it caused him to run, jump, or flutter about, like a lunatic. And this was the origin of the *Dlui Fulla*, or *Fullon's* "fluttering wisp".

The Story of Prince *Comgan*; (VII. century).

The second reference is to the affecting case of the young prince *Comgan*, son of *Maelochtair*, king of the Decies,—the king who bestowed the site of the great ecclesiastical establishment of Lismore, in the county of Waterford, on St. *Mochuda*, who died in the year 636.

Comgan was the son of *Maelochtair* by his first wife, and was remarkable for beauty of person, grace, and manly accomplishments. His stepmother, (for *Maelochtair* remarried when advanced in life), who was much younger than his father, conceived a criminal passion for him, and made advances which he rejected with horror; upon which her love was converted into the most deadly hatred, and she sought anxiously for an opportunity to be revenged upon him. Now it so happened that, on one occasion, a fair and assembly having been held by the men of Munster, in South Tipperary, prince *Comgan* carried off the victory in all the sports and exercises of the day, and won the applause of all spectators. His father's Druid was especially delighted with his prowess, and celebrated his praises above all the rest. The malicious stepmother, seeing this, accosted the Druid, and said to him, "You are the last person who ought to praise *Comgan*, for he is in love with your wife, and has access to her at his pleasure. Observe him when he rides around to receive the congratulations of the fair ladies, and you will see that your wife regards him with peculiar favour". "If this be so", said the Druid, "his power of acquiring favour with her or any other woman, shall soon cease for ever".

Soon after, *Comgan* came up at the head of a troop of cavalry and rode around the assembly, according to custom, to receive the congratulations of the fair ladies who were witnesses of his success; and he addressed to each some courteous words, and to the Druid's wife among the rest. Although the unsuspicious *Comgan* in reality paid no more court to her than to others, yet to the Druid's eyes, already filled with jealousy, his passing compliment seemed an undoubted confirmation of all the suspicions with which his mind had been poisoned; and when *Comgan* retired to wash his horses and himself in a neighbouring stream, the Druid followed him, and suddenly, we are told, struck him with a druidic wand, or, according to one version, flung at him a tuft of grass over which he had pronounced a druidical incantation. The result, according to the story, was, that when *Comgan* arose from bathing his flesh burst forth in boils and ulcers, and his attendants were forced to carry him to his father's house. At the end of the year he had wasted away; his hair fell off; his intellect decayed; and he became a bald, senseless, and wandering idiot, keeping company only with the fools and mountebanks of his father's court.

Such was said to have been the fate of prince *Comgan*, brought about by apparently a very simple druidic process. This *Comgan* was brother, by his mother's side, to the holy bishop St. *Cummain Fada* ("*Cummain* the Tall"), of Clonferta, in the county of Galway, who died A.D. 661, and of whose history and life the full particulars will be found collected in Dr. Todd's Notes to the first part of the Liber Hymnorum, lately published by the Archæological Society.

There is yet another curious instance of the use of the magic wisp, recorded as having occurred shortly before the period just referred to; one which I cannot omit as an illustration of this form of Druidism, because the account is one given with so much detail.

The simple incident itself could be told in a few words, but it would scarcely be intelligible without some account, (which shall be as condensed as I can make it), of the circumstances which led to it. And first a few words as to the *Deisi* clanns,—for this tale also is connected with their eventful history.

The Story of the Princess *Eithné Uathach* and the *Deisi*; and of the Druid *Dill*.

The *Deisis* (Decies or Deasys) of Munster, just mentioned, were originally a tribe located in the present barony of Deisi, or Deece, in Meath, which derives its name from them. They were the descendants of *Fiacha Suidhé*, (brother to the monarch *Conn* of the Hundred Battles,) and his followers. One of the chiefs of this people was *Ængus Gae-buaifnech*, (*Æengus* "of the Poisoned Spear"), a valiant and high-minded man, and the champion of his tribe at the time their cousin *Cormac Mac Airt* was monarch of Erinn. *Cormac* had, besides *Cairbré Lifeachair*, his successor in the monarchy, another son named *Ceallach*, or "the Diviner". This *Ceallach* took away, by force or fraud,

LECT. X.

The Story of the Princess *Eithné Uathach* and the *Deisi*; and of the Druid *Dill*.

a young lady of *Æengus*'s people, who was also a near [illegible] his own. *Æengus*, enraged, followed the offender [illegible] entered the royal palace, and killed *Ceallach* in the [illegible] sence of his father the king, after which the champion [illegible] unhurt. King *Cormac*, however, immediately prepared [illegible] geance, and raised a force sufficient to drive the Decies [illegible] Meath southward into Leinster, in which province [illegible] journed for some time, and from which they afterwards [illegible] into Munster to king *Oilioll Olum*, who was married to [illegible] one of the three daughters of *Conn* of the Hundred Battles [illegible] consequently cousin to the Decian chief. *Oilioll Olum* [illegible] them the territory which still bears their name, in the [illegible] county of Waterford; and here and in other parts of [illegible] they remained for about two hundred years, until the [illegible] *Æengus*, son of *Nadfraech*, king of Munster, who was con[illegible] and baptized by St. Patrick. It is to about this latter [illegible] that the events recorded in the following story are referred.

About this time the Decies felt the need of a more ex[illegible] territory, to meet the wants of their growing numbers. [illegible] accordingly consulted, we are told, their Druid, who [illegible] that the wife of *Crimhthann*, king of Leinster, was then [illegible] nant; that she should bring forth a daughter; that they [illegible] contrive to procure that daughter in fosterage; and that [illegible] she should get married, her husband would extend their [illegible] tory. All was done according to the Druid's directions [illegible] Decies received the young princess, whose name was [illegible] fosterage; and under their assiduous care she grew [illegible] come eminent for ability as well as beauty. Some of [illegible] romances assert that her growth was promoted by her [illegible] on the flesh of infants, from which she got the nick[illegible] *Eithné Uathach*, or "the Hateful"; the only allusion [illegible] aware of to any instance of similar barbarity;—for as to [illegible] istence of cannibalism to any extent whatever among [illegible] dhils, even in the most remote ages, I am bound to declare [illegible] that there is no vestige of authority whatever. However, [illegible] shocking story of the princess *Eithné* as it may, having [illegible] grown to womanhood, she attracted the notice of *Æng*[illegible] of Munster, who sought her hand in marriage. His [illegible] promoted by the Decies, and gladly accepted by her [illegible] and they were forthwith married; after which *Æengus* [illegible] the Decies an addition of territory, lying north of the [illegible] in the present county of Tipperary, provided they [illegible] some tribes from the neighbouring district of Ossory, [illegible] some time previously settled themselves in it.

Now, these Ossorians had a famous blind Druid named [illegible]

The Story of the Princess *Eithné Uath-ach* and the *Deisi*; and of the Druid *Dill*.

the son of *Ui Creaga*. And *Dill* had a daughter who attached herself to the person of the newly-married *Eithné*, queen of Cashel, who in return provided her with a husband of the Decies, and a settlement at her court. "Good, now", said the queen to her one day, "your father is not kind to our people the Decies". "I have not the power to change him", said the Druid's daughter. "Go from me", said the queen, "with rich presents to him, to know if he will consent to turn away his enmity from us; and you shall also have an additional reward for yourself".

The daughter (the tale tells us) accordingly proceeded southwards from Cashel, and so reached her father's residence. "Whence have you come, my daughter?" said the Druid. "From Cashel", said she. "Is it true that you are attached to that hateful queen, *Eithné?*" said he. "It is true", said she. "Good, now, *Dill*", said she, "I am come to offer you wealth". "I will not accept it", said he. "I will light a fire for you", said she, "that you may eat, and that I may obtain your blessing". He raised his voice then, and said: "These (meaning the *Deisi*) are a bad swarm, who have planted themselves on the borders of the territory of Cashel; but", said he, "they shall depart at mid-day to-morrow. I am preparing incantations", said he: "the *Inneóin* (the name of a town at a certain hill near Clonmel) shall be burned on to-morrow; I shall be on the west side of the hill, and I shall see the smoke; a hornless red cow shall be sent past them, to the west; they shall raise a universal shout, after which they shall fly away; and they shall never occupy the land again". "Good", said the daughter; "sleep, now, when you please". He then slept; and the daughter stole the wisp of straw out of his shoes, and fled with it to Cashel; and gave it to queen *Eithné*, who immediately set out with it to the south, and stopped not until she reached the Decies, at their town of *Inneoin*. "Here", said she to the Decies, "burn this wisp, and procure for us a hornless red cow". Such a cow could not be procured. Upon which one of the Druids of the Decies said: "I will put myself into the form of the cow to be slain, on condition that my children be made free for ever". This was done; and the red cow passed westwards.

The Druid *Dill*, who at some distance was watching the effect, as he thought, of his own spells, now addressed his attendant: "What is doing now?" said he. "A fire is being lighted", said the attendant, "and a hornless red cow has been sent over the ford from the east side". "That is not desirable", said Dill; "is the wisp here?" said he. "It is not", said the

LECT. X.

attendant. "Bad", said the Druid; "do the men w[illegible] cow?" "They have let her pass, but the horseboys are [illegible] ing her"; said the attendant. "What shout is this I [illegible]" said the Druid. "The shout of the horseboys killing [illegible]" said the attendant. "Yoke my chariot for me", said the [illegible] "the town cannot be damaged, nor can we withstand it" [illegible] Decies rushed past him eastwards; the Ossorians were [illegible] and routed; they fled like wild deer, and they were [illegible] till they reached a place called *Luinina*, where the [illegible] day put an end to the pursuit; and this place became the [illegible] dary for ever after between Munster and Leinster. A[illegible] Ossorians, concludes the tale, who were previously [illegible] descendants of *Bresal Belach*, after a remote ancestor of [illegible] were from this time down called *Ossairghé*, from *Os*, [illegible] deer, and the wild-deer-like precipitance of their [illegible]

Of the *Imbas Forosnai*, or "Illumination" by the Palms of the Hands.

The next instance of Druidism in the selection I have [illegible] that of a peculiar rite of divination, which it seems might [illegible] formed by either a Druid or a Poet; it is described in the G[illegible] of the holy Cormac MacCullinan, King and Bishop of C[illegible] compiled about the year 890. The article is an expl[illegible] the words *Imbas Forosnai*, or (literally) "Illumination [illegible] Palms of the Hands". At this word (*Imbas For*[illegible]) [illegible] says: "This describes to the Poet what thing soever he [illegible] to discover; and this is the manner in which it is perfor[illegible] The Poet chews a bit of the raw red flesh of a pig, a dog, [illegible] cat, and then retires with it to his bed, behind the door, [illegible] he pronounces an oration upon it, and offers it to his idol [illegible] He then invokes his idols; and if he has not received the [illegible] mination' before the next day, he pronounces incantations [illegible] his two palms, and takes his idol gods unto him (into his [illegible] in order that he may not be interrupted in his sleep. He [illegible] places his two hands upon his two cheeks, and falls asleep [illegible] is then watched, so that he be not stirred or interrupted [illegible] one, until every thing that he seeks is revealed to him [illegible] end of a day, or two, or three, or as long as he continues [illegible] offering; and hence it is that this ceremony is called Pal[illegible] mination, that is, his two hands upon him, crosswise, [illegible] hand over and a hand hither upon his cheeks. And [illegible] Patrick prohibited this ceremony, because it is a [illegible] *Teinm Laeghdha;* that is, he declared any one who perform[illegible] should have no place in Heaven, nor on Earth". S[illegible] the *Imbas Forosnai*.

The *Fileadh*, ("poets", or rather "philosophers", as they [illegible] more properly to be called), had another very curious [illegible] and druidical rite for the identification of dead persons, [illegible] those who had been beheaded or dismembered. This art was called *Teinm Laeghdha*, that is, the "Illumination" of Rhymes. When the performance of this art was accompanied by a Sacrifice to, or an Invocation of, Idols, it was called *Teinm Laeghdha*, or the Illumination of Rhymes, and came under Saint Patrick's prohibition; but when not so accompanied, it was called *Dichetal do Chennaibh*, or the Great Extempore Recital, and was not prohibited.

Of the Teinm Laeghdha ("Illumination" of Rhymes) of the Fileadh; and of the Dichetal do Chennaibh.

Of the *Teinm Laeghdha* we have at least two instances on record, of nearly equal date, and referred back to the second and third centuries of the Christian era.

In one of those instances the celebrated *Finn Mac Cumhaill* was the performer; for *Finn*, as was shown in a former lecture, was a Poet and a Philosopher, as well as a Champion or knight-at-arms. *Finn*, from his infancy, was intended for the military profession, and in compliance with the Fenian rules must have studied philosophy, and letters also, to a certain extent; but after having made his profession of arms, and received a high appointment at the court of Tara, from the monarch *Conn* of the Hundred Battles, the young champion became involved in an affair of some delicacy with one of the king's daughters, which made it prudent for him to retire awhile from court. Abandoning, then, for a time, his military course, he placed himself under the tuition of *Cethern Mac Fintain*, a celebrated Poet, Philosopher, and Druid, under whose instructions he is said to have soon made himself perfect in occult studies. This curious statement is preserved in a very ancient poem, a copy of which is to be found in the Book of Leinster.

The account, however, in which *Finn*'s performance of the *Teinm Laeghdha* is recorded, is preserved in Cormac's Glossary, at the word *Orc Treith*, and may be shortly told as follows:

The Story of Finn Mac Cumhaill and Lomna.

Finn, at the time that we are speaking of, had to wife a lady of the tribe of *Laighné* (now Lune, in Meath); and he had in his household a favourite wit or buffoon, named *Lomna*. Now *Finn* chanced to go on one occasion on a hunting excursion into Teaffia (in Westmeath), accompanied by his wife, and attended by his domestics and his buffoon, whom he left in a temporary house or hut in that country, while he himself and the chief part of his warriors followed the chase One day, during *Finn*'s absence, *Lomna* the buffoon discovered *Cairbré*, one of *Finn*'s warriors, holding a rather suspicious conversation with *Finn*'s wife. The lady prayed him earnestly to conceal her indiscretion, and *Lomna* reluctantly promised her to do so. *Finn* returned after some time, and *Lomna* felt much troubled at being obliged to conceal a secret of such importance; and at

ECT. X.

last, unable any longer to do so, he shaped [illegible] drangular wand, and cut the following words [illegible] ters, in it: "An alder stake in a palisade [illegible] hellebore in a bunch of cresses; the willing husband [illegible] faithful wife among a select band of tried warriors [illegible] the bare hill of *Ualann* in *Luighné*". *Lomna* then [illegible] in a place where *Finn* was sure to find it. *Finn* [illegible] it, and immediately understood its metaphorical [illegible] gave him no small uneasiness. Nor did his wife [illegible] ignorant of the discovery, which she immediately [illegible] *Lomna;* so she forthwith sent privately for her [illegible] come and kill the buffoon; and *Cairbré* came, accord[illegible] cut off *Lomna*'s head, and carried it away with him [illegible] wards *Finn* came, in the evening, to *Lomna*'s hut, [illegible] found the headless body. "Here is a body without [illegible]" said *Finn*. "Discover for us", said the Fians, his [illegible] "whose it is". And then, says the legend, *Finn* put his [illegible] into his mouth, and spoke through the power of the [illegible] *Laeghdha*, and said:—

"He has not been killed by people;—
He has not been killed by the people of *Luighné*;—
He has not been killed by a wild boar;—
He has not been killed by a fall:—
He has not died on his bed,—*Lomna!*

"This is *Lomna*'s body", said *Finn;* "and enemies [illegible] carried away his head".

This piece of sorcery differs in one instance from any [illegible] that we know of; namely, that instead of a bit of any [illegible] kind of flesh, *Finn* chews his own thumb, which, of [illegible] thus makes his sacrifice to his idols.

he Story of
Mogh Eimhé.

Another instance of the *Teinm Laeghdha* occurs [illegible] Cormac's Glossary, at the word *Mogh Eimhé* ("the Slave of the Haft"); and though this story will seem in this place [illegible] longer than I should wish, still, as it contains other curious [illegible] important historical facts, I am tempted to give a translation [illegible] it at length.

"*Mogh Eimhé*", says *Cormac*, "was the name of the [illegible] *Oircné*, or lap-dog, that was known in Erinn. *Cairbré* [illegible] the man who first brought it into Erinn, out of the country [illegible] Britain. For at this time the power of the Gaedhils was [illegible] over the Britons; and they divided Albion among them [illegible] farms, and each of them had his neighbour and friend [illegible] the people; and they dwelt no less on the east side of the [illegible] than in Scotia",—[that is, the land of the Scots or Gaedhil [illegible] term then only applied to Erinn]. "And they built their [illegible]

The Story of Mogh Eimhé.

dances and their royal Duns (or courts) there; as, for instance, *Dun Tradin*, or *Dun Tredin*, [the three-walled court] of *Crimhthann Mór Mac Fiodhaidh*, monarch of Erinn and *Alban* [Scotland], as far as the Ictian sea; and also *Glastimberi* [Glastonbury], now a church on the brink of the Ictian sea, in the forest of which dwelt *Glas Mac Cais*, swine-herd to the King of *Irfuaté*, to feed his pigs on the mast,—the same who was resuscitated by St. Patrick six score years after he had been slain by *Mac Con's* huntsmen. And one of these divisions [of land] is *Dun Mac Lethan*, at this day, [A.D. 890], in the country of the Britons of Cornwall; that is *Dun Mac Liathain*. And so, every tribe of them [i.e. of the Scots, or Gaedhils of Erinn] divided the lands into portions on the east side of the channel; and so it continued for a long time after the coming of St. Patrick into Erinn.

"It was on this account, therefore, that *Cairbré Musc* was in the habit of going over frequently to visit his family and his friends. Down to this time no lap-dog had come into the country of Erinn, and the Britons commanded that none should ever be given, either for satire, or for friendship, or for price, to the Gaedhils.

"The law which was then in force in Britain was, that every transgressor became forfeited for his transgression, if discovered.

"At this time a friend of *Cairbré Musc* was possessed of a celebrated lap-dog in the country of Britain; and *Cairbré* procured it from him in the following manner. *Cairbré* went on a visit to this man's house, and was received with a welcome to every thing but the lap-dog. Now *Cairbré* had a costly knife, the handle of which was ornamented with gold and silver; a most precious jewel. In the course of the night he rubbed the knife and its haft thickly over with fat bacon and fat beef, and laid it at the lap-dog's mouth, and then went to sleep. The dog continued to gnaw the knife until morning; and when *Cairbré* arose in the morning, and found the knife disfigured, he made loud complaints, appeared very sorrowful, and demanded justice for it from his friend; namely, 'the transgressor in forfeit for his transgression'. The dog was accordingly given up to him, then, in satisfaction for its crime; and thus it received the name of *Mogh Eimhé*, or 'the Slave of the Haft', from *mogh*, a slave, and *eimh*, a haft.

"It so happened that dog was a female, and was with young at the time of its being brought over. *Ailill Flann Beg* was the king of Munster at the time, and *Cormac Mac Airt* monarch of Tara. Each of these claimed the dog, but it was agreed that she should remain for a certain time, alternately,

LECT. X. in the houses of *Cairbré* himself, and of each of the [illegible]
In the meantime the dog brought forth her whelps [illegible]
of the royal personages took one of them; and it was [illegible]
little dog that sprang all the breed of lap-dogs in E[illegible]
lap-dog died in a long time after; and in many years [illegible]
again, *Connla* the son of *Tadg*, son of *Cian*, son of *O*[illegible]
king of Munster, found the bare skull of the lap-[illegible]
brought it for identification to *Maen Mac Ethna*[illegible]
guished poet, who had come with a laudatory [illegible]
father.

"The poet had recourse to his *Teinm Laeghd*[illegible]
said:

"Sweet was your drink in the house of *Eogan's* gran[illegible]
Sweet was your flesh in the house of *Conn's* [illegible]
each day;
Fair was your bread in the house of *Cairbré M*[illegible]
O *Mogh Eimhé!*"

"This", said the Poet, "is the skull of *Mogh Eimhé*, [illegible]
lap-dog that was ever brought into Erinn".

Cairbré Musc, by whom, by no very fair means, [illegible]
Oircné or lap-dog was brought into Erinn, was son of [illegible]
monarch of Erinn. He fought at the battle of *Cenn*[illegible]
A.D. 186; and he was ancestor to the O'Connells, the O'[illegible]
the O'Sheas, and other families of ancient distinction [illegible]
Munster, as well as of others in East Munster.

So much for the *Teinm Laeghda*, which seems to [illegible]
a charm of rhyme, by which it was supposed that [illegible]
would be led to name the name of that which he [illegible]
sort of magic inspiration, the nature of which is not [illegible]
to us save by such examples as that contained in [illegible]
legend.

The Story of the Siege of *Drom Damhghairé*; Druidic Fire. To this period may be also referred another occu[illegible]
ancient historic interest, namely, the Siege or Encamp[illegible]
Drom Damhghairé, of which some account was given [illegible]
mer lecture[171], and in the Historic Tale concerning wh[illegible]
wild druidical performances are described in some det[illegible]
this Tale, therefore, as containing another series of exam[illegible]
what was called Druidical Art, I have next to refer.

The Encampment of *Drom Damhghairé* took pla[illegible]
the following circumstances. The celebrated *Cormac* [illegible]
commenced his reign as monarch of Erinn at Tara, A.[illegible]
It would appear that his hospitality and munificence [illegible]
hausted the royal revenues, so that in a short time he [illegible]
necessary not only to curtail his expenditure, but to [illegible]

(171) *Lectures on the MS. Materials of Ancient Irish History*, p. 27[illegible]

The Story of the Siege of Drom Damhghaire; Druidic Fire.

mediate means of replenishing his coffers. In this difficulty he was advised to make a claim on the province of Munster for a double tribute, on the plea that although there were properly two provinces of Munster, yet they had never paid more than the tribute of one. *Cormac*, therefore, on these very questionable grounds, sent his messengers into Munster to demand a second tribute for the same year. *Fiacha Muilleathan* (the son of *Eoghan Mór*, son of *Oilioll Oluim*) was king of Munster at the time, and he received the messengers of the monarch (at *Cnoc Raffann*, in Tipperary) with all the usual honours and attention. He denied the justness of *Cormac's* demands, but offered to send a sufficient supply of provisions to him as a present, for that occasion. The messengers returned to Tara with this answer, but *Cormac* would not listen to it, and he consulted his Druids on the probable success of an expedition into Munster. They, however, after having recourse (as we are told) to their divinations, gave him an unfavourable answer. Still, he would not be persuaded by them, but insisted on undertaking the expedition. He therefore mustered a large force, and marched directly to the hill of *Damhghairé* (now *Cnoc Luingé*, or Knocklong, in the south-east part of the county of Limerick, bordering on Tipperary). Here *Cormac* fixed his camp; and from this, with the aid of his Druids, by drying up the springs and streams of the province, he is said to have brought that great distress on the people of Munster which was described in a former lecture.[172] Ultimately, the monarch and his Druids were overmastered by the superior power of the great Munster Druid, *Mogh Ruith*. This celebrated sage, one of the most renowned of those ages, is recorded to have completed his Druidical studies in the east, in the school of no less a master than Simon Magus; and it is even stated in this tract, that Simon Magus himself was of the race of the Gaedhils of Erinn.

After *Magh Ruith* had relieved the men of Munster from the drought and famine which *Cormac's* Druids had brought upon them, *Cormac* again took into council his chief and oldest Druid, *Ciothruadh*, and inquired of him what was best to be done. *Ciothruadh* answered, that their last and only resource was to make a druidic fire against the enemy. "How is that to be made?" said Cormac. "In this way", said *Ciothruadh*: "let our men go into the forest, and let them cut down and carry out loads of the quickbeam, (i.e. the Mountain-Ash, or Roan-tree), of which large fires must be made; and when the fires are lighted, if the smoke goes southwards, then it will be well for you to press after it on the men of Munster; and if it is

(172) *Lectures on the MS. Materials of Ancient Irish History*, p. 272.

x. x. bither or northward the smoke comes, then, indeed, it will
tory of time for us to retreat with all our speed". So, Cormac
ge of forthwith entered the forest, cut down the wood
Dam- brought it out, and set it on fire.
the Fire.

Whilst this was going on, *Mogh Ruith*, perceiving what the northern Druids were preparing for, immediately ordered the men of Munster to go into the wood of *Lethard*, and each to bring out a faggot of the roan-tree in his hand; and the king only should bring out a shoulder-bundle from the side of the mountain, where it had grown under three shelters, shelter from the (north-east) March wind, shelter from the wind, and shelter from the conflagration winds. The men returned with the wood to their camp; and the Druid *Ceann-mhair*, *Mogh Ruith*'s favourite pupil, built the wood up in the shape of a small triangular kitchen, with seven doors; while the northern fire, (that prepared by *Ciothruadh*), on the other side, was but rudely heaped up, and had but three doors. "The fire is ready now", said *Ceannmhair*, "all but to light it". *Mogh Ruith* then ordered each man of the host to give him a shaving from the handle of his spear, which, when he had got, he mixed with butter and rolled up into a large ball, at the same time pronouncing those words in rhythmical lines:

"I mix a roaring powerful fire;
It will clear the woods; it will blight the grass;
An angry flame of powerful speed;
It will rush up to the skies above,
It will subdue the wrath of all burning wood,
It will break a battle on the clanns of *Conn*";—

and with that he threw the ball into the fire, where it exploded with a tremendous noise.

"I shall bring the rout on them now", said *Mogh Ruith*, "let my chariot be ready, and let each man of you have his horse by the bridle; for, if our fires incline but ever so little northwards, follow and charge the enemy". He then blew a druidical breath (says this strange tale) up into the sky, which immediately became a threatening black cloud, which came down in a shower of blood upon the plain of *Cláiré* before him, and moved onwards from that to Tara, the Druid all the while pronouncing his rhythmical incantations. When the noise of the bloody shower was heard in the northern camp, Cormac asked his Druid, *Ciothruadh*, what noise it was. "A shower of blood", said the Druid, "which has been produced by a violent effort of Druidism. It is upon us its entire evil will

After this, (the tale proceeds), *Mogh Ruith* said to his pupil, "What is the condition of the flames from the two fires now

LECT. X.

The Story of the Siege of *Drom Damhghaire*; Druidic Fire.

[for *Mogh Ruith* was blind]. "They are", said they, "chasing each other over the brow of the mountain, west and north, down to *Druim Asail*,—[now Tory Hill, near Croom, in the county of Limerick,]—and to the Shannon, and back again to the same place". He asked again the state of the flames. "They are in the same condition", said they; "but they have not left a tree in the plain of middle Munster that they have not burned". *Mogh* asked again how the flames were. His people answered that "they had risen up to the clouds of Heaven, and were like two fierce angry warriors chasing each other". Then *Mogh Ruith* called for his "dark-gray hornless bull-hide", and "his white-speckled bird-headpiece, with its fluttering wings", and also "his druidic instruments", and he flew up into the air to the verge of the fires, and commenced to beat and turn them northwards. When *Cormac*'s Druid, *Ciothruadh*, saw this, he also ascended to oppose *Mogh Ruith*; but the power of the latter prevailed, and he turned the fires northwards, and into *Cormac*'s camp, where they fell, as well as [*i.e.* where also fell] the Druid *Ciothruadh*. *Cormac*, on this, ordered a quick retreat out of the province.

They were hotly pursued, (we are then told), by the Munster men, led by *Mogh Ruith* in his chariot drawn by wild oxen, and with his druidic bull-hide beside him. The pursuit continued beyond the border of the province, and into *Magh Raighné*, in Ossory. And here *Mogh Ruith* asked, though he well knew, who were the nearest parties to them of the retreating foe. "They are three tall gray-headed men", said they. "They are *Cormac's* three Druids, *Cecht*, *Ciotha*, and *Ciothruadh*", said he, "and my gods have promised me to transform them into stones, when I should overtake them, if I could but blow my breath upon them". And then he "blew a druidic breath" upon them, so that they were turned into stones; "and these are the stones that are called the Flags of *Raighné* at this day"—and so on.

This extraordinary tale contains more of the wilder feats of Druidism than any other Irish piece known to me. But not only is the main fact recorded in it true, but some of the principal personages, at least, are historical; for it is a curious fact, that the great Druid, so celebrated in this piece, *Mogh Ruith*, for this or some other singular piece of druidic service rendered to the men of Munster, is recorded, in truly historic documents, to have received from them the extensive territory anciently known as *Magh Meiné*, or the "Mineral Plain", (now the district of Fermoy, in the county of Cork); a territory which the race of *Mogh Ruith*, moreover, continue to inhabit even to this

LECT. X.

day, in the families of O'Dugan, O'Cianin, etc., [illegible] neighbouring districts.

Use of the Rowan, or Rowan-tree, in Druidical rites.

The use of the quicken or roan-tree in druidical [illegible] cumstance by no means incidental to this tale alone [illegible] of its uses for superstitious purposes may be found [illegible] writings, and some of them have come down [illegible] sent day, in connection, for example, with the [illegible] peculiar to the dairy. I have myself known [illegible] in Munster who would not have a churn for their [illegible] out at least one roan-tree hoop on it,—or without [illegible] of that sacred tree twisted into a gad, and formed [illegible] placed upon the churn-staff while churning,—for the [illegible] putting it out of the power (as they conceived) of [illegible] neighbour, to deprive them of the proper quantity of [illegible] any trick of witchery.

In the ordeal by fire.

The following short article from an ancient [illegible] 3. 17, T.C.D.) is conclusive, on the use of the [illegible] druidical rites. It is the case of a woman clearing her [illegible] from charges affecting it, by an ordeal, when she had [illegible] find living compurgators. The ordeal she was to go [illegible] was, to rub her tongue to a red-hot adze of bronze, [illegible] melted lead (but not, it appears, to iron), and the adze [illegible] be heated in a fire of blackthorn, "or of roan-tree"; and [illegible] says the book, was a druidical ordeal.

Of ancient Poetical Satire, as a branch of Druidism.

When St. Patrick had purified the laws and the [illegible] education in Erinn, in the ninth year of his mission (about [illegible] year 443), he, of course, prohibited all druidical rites and [illegible] formances, but particularly those which required sacrifices to idols. He left, however, to the lawfully elected [illegible] poet, liberty to write satires, according to ancient custom, [illegible] the kings or chiefs in whose service he was retained, whenever the poet wrote an historical, a genealogical, or a laudatory poem for his patron, and was not paid for it the reward which custom or the law of the land had provided in such cases. How far the spirit of Druidism may have pervaded these compositions it is now out of our power to ascertain; but, considering the prevailing belief in the effects ascribed to them, it is very probable, to say the least, that in such incantations the [illegible] poet must have dealt largely in Druidism as known or practised in times not yet far removed from his own.

The *Glam Dichinn*, or "Satire from the Hill-tops".

Some curious, though apparently simple examples of this species of poetry have come down to us; and the following account of the ceremony of its composition, (from the Book of Ballymote), stands, perhaps, unique in the annals of satire. The composition was called *Glam Dichinn*, or Satire from the

Hill-tops; and was made in this way. The poet was to fast upon the lands of the king for whom the poem was to be made; and the consent of thirty laymen, thirty ecclesiastics, (bishops, the tract says), and thirty poets, should be had to compose the satire; and it was a crime for them to prevent it when the reward for the poem was withheld. The poet, then, in a company of seven, (that is, six along with himself), upon whom had been conferred literary or poetic degrees,—namely, a "*Fochlac*", a "*MacFiurmedh*", a "*Doss*", a "*Cana*", a "*Cli*", and an "*Anrad*", with an "*Ollamh*" as the seventh, went at the rising of the sun to a hill, which should be situated on the boundary of seven farms, (or lands), and each of them was to turn his face to a different land; and the *Ollamh's* face was to be turned towards the land of the king who was to be satirized; and their backs were to be turned to a hawthorn which should be growing upon the top of the hill; and the wind should be blowing from the north; and each man was to hold a perforated stone and a thorn of the hawthorn in his hand; and each man was to sing a verse of this composition for the king,—the *Ollamh* or chief poet to take the lead with his own verse, and the others in concert after him with theirs; and each, then, should place his stone and his thorn under the stem of the hawthorn; and if it was they that were in the wrong in the case, the ground of the hill would swallow them; and if it was the king that was in the wrong, the ground would swallow "him, and his wife, and his son, and his steed, and his robes, and his hound". The satire of the *Mac Fiurmedh* fell on the hound; the satire of the *Fochlac*, on the robes; the satire of the *Doss*, on the arms; the satire of the *Cana*, on the wife; the satire of the *Cli*, on the son; the satire of the *Anrad*, on the steed; and the satire of the *Ollamh*, on the king.

This is a very singular instance of Druidism, as it was believed to have prevailed in Erinn even after the introduction of Christianity.

It is now too late in the world's age to canvass the power and nature of Satire; all that I can say on the subject is this: that from the remotest times down to our own, its power was dreaded in Erinn; and that we have numerous instances on record of its having driven men out of their senses, and even to death itself.

The *Glam Dichinn*, or Satire, of the Poet *Neidhe* (from Cormac's Glossary.)

Of the antiquity of satire in Erinn, and of the belief in its venomous power, we have the very important authority of *Cormac's* glossary, in which the word *Gairé* is explained and illustrated in the following manner:

"*Gairé;* that is, *Gair-seclé* (short life]; that is, *Gair-ré;* that

LECT. X.

The *Glam Dichinn*, or Satire, of the Poet *Neidhé*; (from Cormac's Glossary)

is, *re-ghair;* ut est, in the satire which the poet *Neidhé* [illegible] *Adhna*, son of *Guthar*, composed for the king of [illegible] was his own father's brother, namely *Caier*, the son [illegible] for *Caier* had adopted *Neidhé* as his son, because [illegible] sons of his own.

"*Caier*'s wife", (continues Cormac) "conceived [illegible] passion for *Neidhé*, and offered him a ball of silver [illegible] his love. *Neidhé* did not accept this, nor agree [illegible] posals, until she offered to make him king of [illegible] his uncle *Caier*. 'How can you accomplish [illegible] *Neidhé*. 'It is not difficult', said she; 'make you a [illegible] him, until it produces a blemish upon him, and you [illegible] a man with a blemish cannot retain the kingly rule[illegible] not easy for me to do what you advise', said *Neidhé*, [illegible] the man would not refuse me anything; for there is [illegible] possession anything that he would not give me'". [Th[illegible] only fulminated their satires in case their privileges [illegible] lated, or their requests refused.] "'I know', said the [illegible] 'one thing that he would not give you, namely, [illegible] which was presented to him in the country of *Alba*[illegible] land]; and that he would not give you because it is pro[illegible] to him [*i.e.* because he is under a vow or pledge not] [illegible] it away from himself'. *Neidhé* went then and asked [illegible] for the knife. 'Woe and alas', said *Caier*, 'it is prohi[illegible] me to give it away from me'. *Neidhé* then", continues Cor[illegible] authority, "composed a '*Glam Dichinn*', or extempore [illegible] him; and immediately three blisters appeared upon his [illegible] This is the satire:

"Evil, death, and short life to *Caier;*
May spears of battle slay *Caier;*
The rejected of the land and the earth is *Caier;*
Beneath the mounds and the rocks be *Caier*".[173]

Caier, we are then told, went early the next morning [illegible] fountain to wash; and in passing his hands over his [illegible] found three blisters on it, which the satire had raised; na[illegible] (says the story), "disgrace", "blemish", and "defect",—in [illegible] of crimson, green, and white. On discovering his mis[illegible] he immediately fled, in order that no one who knew him [illegible] see his disgrace; and he did not stop until he reached [illegible] *Cearmna*, (now the Old Head of Kinsale, in the coun[illegible] Cork), the residence of *Caichear*, son of *Eidirsgel*, chief [illegible]

(173) original:—Maili, baire, gaire Caier;
cot m-beodur cealtru catae Caier;
diba cach dire, cach furo Caier;
fumara, focara Caier.

district, where he was well received, as a stranger, though his quality was not known. *Neidhé*, the satirist, then assumed the sovereignty of Connacht, and continued to rule it for a year. LECT. X.

The conclusion of this strange story, (the historical meaning or foundation of which is now lost to us), is worth telling. After a year's enjoyment of his ill-gotten rank, *Neidhé*, it is said, began to repent of having unjustly caused so much misery to *Caier*, and having after some time discovered his retreat, he resolved to visit him. He set out accordingly in the favourite chariot of *Caier*, and accompanied by the king's treacherous wife; and he arrived in due time at *Dun Cearmna*. When the beautiful chariot arrived on the lawn of the *Dun*, its appearance was curiously examined by *Caichear* and his people. "I wonder who they are", said every one. Upon which *Caier* rose up and answered: "It is we that used to be driven in its champion's seat, in front of the driver's seat". "Those are the words of a king", said *Caichear*, the son of *Eideregul*, who had not recognised *Caier* until then. "Not so, alas!" said *Caier*;—and he rushed through the house, and presently disappeared in a large rock which stood behind it, in a cleft of which he hid himself. *Neidhé* followed him through the house; and *Caier*'s grayhound, which accompanied him, soon discovered its master in the cleft of the rock behind the house. *Neidhé* approached him, but when *Caier* saw him he dropped dead of shame. The rock then "boiled", we are told, "blazed", and "burst", at the death of *Caier*; and a splinter of it entered one of *Neidhé*'s eyes and broke it in his head; whereupon *Neidhé* composed an expiatory poem,—which is, however, omitted by *Cormac*, and by all the authorities that I am acquainted with.

This extravagant legend is valuable as exhibiting one of the earliest illustrations of that peculiar belief, in Erinn, concerning the satire of a Poet, of which I have before given more than one less singular and more modern instance. This belief also may be taken to have preserved to us one of the traditions of that Druidism into whose mysteries we are unable to prosecute inquiries exact in detail.

The Story of the Druid *Lughaidh Delbaeth*, or "the Fire-Producer", the son of *Cas*.

I have now given instances of almost all the kinds of Druidism to which we find allusion in any of our Tales or any of our Historical pieces. And I shall add but one other example, which, as usual, I shall give in the form of an abridgment of the account itself, as it has been handed down to us. It is an instance of the mention of a Druid and some druidical operations of his, preserved in the history of the Dalcassian race of Thomond. The story is shortly as follows:—

CT. X. Story of Druid aidh aeth, or Fire- ucer", on of

Cas, (from whom the Dalcassians derive the race-name), was the son of *Conall* "of the swift was contemporary with the monarch *Crimhthann*, 379. *Cas* had twelve sons, from whom descend cassian tribes; and of these twelve *Lugaidh Del* *gaidh* "the Fire-producer"), was the twelfth. This six sons; and one daughter, whose name was *Aeifé* were named: *Gno Beg*, *Gno Mór*, *Baedan*, *badh*, and *Sighi*. *Lugaidh* the Fire-producer had large territory from his father; and in time gave *Aeifé* in marriage to *Trad*, son of *Tassach*, who chief and Druid, but without much land.

After some time *Trad* found himself the father ous family, with but little provision for their vancement in life. Accordingly he said to his wife, thou and ask a favour from thy father; it would be well for our children to get more land". *Aeifé*, therefore, asked her father to grant her a favour. "Then *Lugaidh* his oracles", says the writer of this account, "and daughter: 'If thou shouldst order any one to leave now, he must depart without delay'. 'Depart said she, 'and leave us the land which thou inherit may be ours in perpetuity'". Whereupon, we are told, her father immediately complied, and with his six sons inheritance assigned to him by his father to his daughter and her husband *Trad*. And I may add that this territory to the present day, retains the name of *Trad*, forming the deanery of *Tradraidhé*, in the present barony of county of Clare (a tract which comprises the parishes *finnlocha*, *Cill-ogh-na-Suloch*, *Cill Mailuighré*, *Cill*- *Cluain Lochain*, *Drom Lighin*, *Fiodhnach*, Bunratty, *Eoin*, and the island of *Inis-da-dhrom*, in the river

The story proceeds to inform us that the Druid having been thus deprived of his inheritance by daughter, crossed the Shannon with his sons and and passed into the south-western district of West *Carn Fiachach;* where *Fiacha* was buried, the son of arch *Niall* of the Nine Hostages, (ancestor of the *Mac Eochagan*, O'Mulloy, etc.). On arriving at this built up a large fire; and this, we are told, he ignited druidic power,—from which circumstance he acquired *Delbhaeth*, or "the Fire-producer"; a name that to preserved both in that of the territory and in the of his principal descendants, the family of *Mac* *Dealbhna*, (now called Delvin), in Westmeath. The

The Story of the Druid *Lughaidh Delbaeth*, or the "Fire-producer", the son of Cas.

however, does not stop here. From this fire we are told there came forth five streams of flame, in five different directions; and the Druid commanded his five elder sons to follow one each of the fiery streams, assuring them that they would lead them to their future inheritances. The two elder sons, *Gno Beg* and *Gno Mor*, accordingly followed their streams across the Shannon into Connacht, where they stopped in two territories, which retained these names down to the sixteenth century, when they were united under that of the Barony of Moycullen, in the county of Galway; a district of which *Mac Conrai* (a name now Anglicised King) was the chief in ancient times. The three other sons were led by their streams of fire to various parts of Westmeath, where they settled, and after whom those territories took the name of *Dealbhna*, (Anglicised the Delvins), from their father *Delbaeth* the Druid. Of these "Delvins", *Dealbhna Ethra* was the most important, of which *Mac Cochlan* was the chief, whose residence was at the town now called Castletown-Delvin, in Westmeath; a house that preserved a considerable degree of rank and importance down even to our own times. *Sighi*, the sixth son of *Lughaidh Delbaeth*, remained in his father's neighbourhood; and it was to his son *Nós* that belonged the place in which the celebrated church of St. *Ciaran* of *Cluain-muc-Nois* was built. The field in which the church was built had been appropriated to the use of the hogs of *Nós*, son of *Sighi*, and was therefore called *Cluain Muc Nóis*, or the field of the hogs of *Nós;* and the present name of Clonmacnoise is but a slightly Anglicised corruption of the old name. In fine, the old Druid *Lughaidh Delbaeth* himself settled on the brink of a lake near *Carn Fiacha*,—which lake was thenceforward from him called *Loch Lugh-phorta*, or the lake of *Lughaidh's* Mansion;—and after his death his people buried him on the brink of this lake, and raised over him a great heap of stones which was called *Sidh-an-Caradh*, or the Friendly Hill.

In this story of *Lughaidh* we have allusion to two separate arts of professional Druidism; the one, that of ascertaining Fate by consultation of "oracles", that is, Soothsaying, I suppose; and the other, the production of the magical Fire, of which we have already had so many other examples in these ancient legends.

From these various instances recorded or alluded to, either in the ancient annals, on the one hand, or in ancient tales which at least preserve what men believed of the Druids, on the other, we can gather much information as to the rank and authority, and something, at least, as to the ceremonies of the Druids of ancient Erinn. We have, indeed, no precise record of their specific rights, powers, or privileges; nor of the forms in which

LECT. X.

they exercised their magical arts; nor of the [illegible] perstitions or religious belief which they taught. [illegible] amples I have collected, (mere examples out of a [illegible] of similar cases to be found in ancient MSS.), will [illegible] that the historical student has a vast quantity of [illegible] investigate before he can pronounce with any [illegible] any of the details connected with this subject, [illegible] rize upon it with any safety as a whole.

No instance known, or even alluded to, of the existence of human sacrifices at any time in Erinn.

It is a matter worthy of remark, that in no tale [illegible] the Irish Druids which has come down to our [illegible] any mention, as far as I know, of their ever having [illegible] recommended to be offered, human sacrifices, either [illegible] or to propitiate the divine powers which they [illegible] Not so, however, as to the British Druids, of whose [illegible] few also have come down to us, voluminous as are the [illegible] modern "antiquaries" on their history. One reference [illegible] for its antiquity at least, and well worthy of notice, [illegible] the *Historia Britonum* of Nennius, a work believed [illegible] been written about the year 800. Of this ancient [illegible] tory the oldest version now known, I believe, is the [illegible] lation of it made by the learned Poet and Historian [illegible] *Caeimhghin*, who died in the year 1072. This [illegible] been published, with an English translation and [illegible] Irish Archaeological Society, in the year 1848, under [illegible] editorship of the Rev. Doctor Todd, assisted by the [illegible] the late learned, but sometimes very fanciful, Rev. [illegible] Herbert. At page 91 of this volume, where the [illegible] British king, Gortigern, pressed by the treachery of [illegible] invaders, is related, the old author speaks as follows:

One instance, at least, recorded of human sacrifices among the Druids of Britain, (from Nennius.)

"Gortigern, with his hosts and with his Druids, [illegible] all the south of the island of Britain, until they [illegible] Guined; and they searched all the mountain of [illegible] there found a hill over the sea, and a very strong [illegible] to build on, and his Druids said to him: 'Build [illegible] tress', said they, 'for nothing shall ever prevail [illegible] Builders were then brought thither, and they [illegible] rials for the fortress, both stone and wood; but all [illegible] rials were carried away in one night, and materials [illegible] gathered thrice, and were thrice carried away. And [illegible] of the Druids, 'Whence is this evil?' said he. And [illegible] said, '*Seek a youth whose father is unknown, kill him,* [illegible] *blood be sprinkled on the fort, for by this means only* [illegible] *built*".—The youth thus indicated proved [illegible] know, the celebrated philosopher Merlin, of whom [illegible] poetical legends are current among the traditions of [illegible] gain. The Druids' recommendation was not carried into effect; and this is, I think, the only instance of ancient allusion to human sacrifice even in Britain. In Erinn, as I have already said, there appears never to have been an instance even of a suggestion made to take such means of propitiating the Fates, or the Deity.

Of Divination, by interpretation of Dreams and Omens, in ancient Erinn.

I have now, I think, given specimens of all the magical arts ascribed distinctly to the Druids, as such, in our old books. Whether the interpretation of dreams and of auguries drawn from the croaking of ravens, the chirping of wrens, and such like omens, (of which we find, of course, a great many instances alluded to), formed any part of the professional office of the Druid of ancient Erinn, I have not been able to ascertain. But whoever it was, or whatever class of persons, that could read such auguries, there is no doubt that they were observed, and apparently much in the manner of other ancient nations. There is indeed a small tract devoted specially to this subject, among the valuable MSS. preserved in the library of Trinity College, Dublin, to which I may direct attention in connection with the general subject. This tract is divided into three sections, which contain the three classes of Omens I have just alluded to; that concerning Dreams and Visions, being, however, much more copious than either of the others. As it would not be possible, perhaps, to investigate the subject of the Druids and their rites without reference to whatever can be gleaned of the superstitious beliefs and observances of the people of their time, I cannot wholly pass by this matter in concluding what I had to say, though I shall not do more than to mention generally what it contains.

As to Dreams and Visions.

And first, as to Visions or Dreams: the list of them is in extent very copious, though the subjects are very meagrely treated; and though the connection between the several articles mentioned and the vision of the dreamer to whom they may occur does not seem very clear, it may however, perhaps, become so when all the various examples of such visions preserved in the Tales, etc., are critically considered. For the present purpose I need do no more than give a literal translation of some few of the entries or memoranda in the tract, as specimens of this interesting record. Those on dreams run as follows:

"A dead King denotes shortness of life. A King dying denotes loss. A King captured alive denotes evil. A brilliant Sun denotes blood. A dark Sun denotes danger. Two Suns in one night, disgrace. The Sun and Moon in the same course, battles. To hear Thunder denotes protection. Darkness

CT. X. notes disease. To cut the Nails denotes tribulation; Girdle around you denotes envy. To sow Tares bats. To catch Birds by night denotes spoils by flying from you by night denote the banishment mies. To carry or to see Arms denotes honour

aries Birds. The divisions of the tract concerning Auguries Croaking of Ravens and the Chirping of Wrens, same style, but more specific, because the subject of the distinctions taken respecting the sounds are very curious, almost suggesting the recognition species of language among them. I should the Ravens and the Wrens, whose croaking and the subject of the augury, seem to have been domesticated (probably domesticated for the very purpose of as will be perceived at once, even in the few about to select. These, as before, shall be literally

Raven. Of the Raven the writer says: "If the Raven closed bed within the house, this denotes that a guest, whether lay or clerical, is coming to you. difference between them. If he be a layman that it is '*bacach! bacach!*' the Raven says. But if it holy orders, it is '*gradh! gradh!*' it says; and is day that it croaks If it be a soldier or a satirist it is '*grog! grog!*' or '*grob! grob!*' that it croaks behind you that it speaks, and it is from that guests are to come". And again: "If it be in a that the Raven speaks", says this tract, "namely, '*ur! ur!*', there is sickness to come on some person or on some of its cattle. If it is wolves that are to sheep, it is from the sheep-pens, or else from beside of the house, that he croaks, and what he says is '*grob! grob!*' '*coin! coin!*'; (that is, wolves, wolves) again: "If the Raven should accompany or precede expedition, and that he is joyous, your journey will ous. If it is to the left he goes, and croaks at you is at a coward he croaks in that manner, or his croaking disgrace to some one of the party";—and so on.

Wren. Of the chirping of the Wren a similar list of recorded, and in the same manner; but I need not of further specimens of this class.

gury from Stars and ads by ht. As may be imagined, the practice of Augury, or was not confined to these observations, and one instance remembered of another class of Auguries as already a former lecture [174] I mean that of the auguries

(174) See *Lectures on the MS. Materials*, etc. pp. 284–5.

[illegible] of the stars and clouds by night, by the Druids of Dathi, the last of our pagan monarchs. In that instance the divination is stated to have been conducted by the Druids by night. And I suppose it is but probable that all such Auguries as those of which I have just been speaking were generally practised by the same influential order. I have, however, (as already remarked), no positive proof that these divinations were confined to the class of Druids. Indeed, this class of learned men is not anywhere sufficiently defined to us in the old MSS., either as to their privileges, their doctrines, or their system of education; and we have, as may be observed, many instances of kings and chiefs who happened to have been also Druids, though no instance of a Druid, as such, arriving at or exercising any civil or military authority. LECT. X.

In this too short account of what is really known from authentic histories of this mysterious class or order of men, I have, as I already observed, by no means exhausted the subject; on the contrary, there are vast numbers of allusions to the Druids, and of specific instances of the exercise of their vocation,—be it magical, religious, philosophical, or educational,—to be found in our older MSS., which in a course of lectures like the present it would be quite impossible to unfold at full length. For these examples generally occur in the midst of the recital of long stories, or passages of history; and they could not be made properly intelligible without giving the context at so much length as often to lead us entirely away from the more immediate subject. And yet, considering the meagreness of facts and of any specific statements in all that has been yet published concerning the Druids of Britain and of Gaul, (who, I may observe, appear to have differed materially from those of our island in many of their most important characteristics), I believe I have already described so many instances of Druidism as recorded in Gaedhelic MSS. as will be found to throw a great deal of light upon the path of the investigator of this difficult and curious subject.

Recapitulation.

From the records of the earlier stages of our history instances have been adduced of the contests in druidical Spells between the Nemidians and Fomorians; of druidical Clouds raised by the Incantations of the Druidesses before the celebrated battle of *Magh Tuireadh;* of Showers or Fire and of Blood said to have been produced by the same agency on that occasion; of the Spells, broken, after three days, by the counter arts in magic of the Firbolg Druids; of the Healing Fountain gifted by druidical spells, at the same battle; and of the Explanation

LECT. X. Recapitulation.

the Dream of the Firbolg King *Eochaidh Mac Erc*, [illegible] the means of a Vision raised by the "prophetic [illegible] Druid *Cesarn*.

After this period we have, on the coming of the [illegible] colony, the Tempest raised by the Druids of the [illegible] *Danann*, when they had persuaded their invaders to take [illegible] ships again; and the discovery of the magical [illegible] tempest by that observation from the topmast of [illegible] vessels, which proved that it only extended a few [illegible] the level of the water. And I quoted from an ancient [illegible] the very words attributed to *Amergin* the Druid, [illegible] sons of Milesius, in the druidical oration by which [illegible] this magical tempest.

Passing on in the course of time we had an instance [illegible] druidical Fire, in the story of *Midhé*, the son of *Brath* [illegible] *Detha;* and in the singular tale of *Edain* (*Bé-finn*), the [illegible] of *Eochaidh Airemh*, (in the first century before Christ [illegible] example of Druidical Incantation; of the early science of [illegible] letters; and of the use of the Yew-wand, which, and [illegible] oak, nor the mistletoe, seems to have been the sacred [illegible] Tree in Erinn.

In the stories of *Cuchulainn*, again, we had an instance [illegible] Trance produced by magical arts; of the mad rage of the [illegible] and of how, in the midst of that rage, he was caught as it [illegible] by the hands and feet, through druidical Incantation [illegible] another kind of druidical charm instanced by the Drink [illegible] Oblivion, finally given to the hero and to *Emer*, his wife [illegible]

In the account of the means taken to discover the [illegible] tined successor of king *Conairé Mór*, we had then in [illegible] detail the description of a Vision produced by Druidical [illegible] cantations; and of the Omens of a day, an instance in [illegible] observed by *Cathbadh*, the Druid, on the day of the [illegible] of *Cuchulainn* to the arms of knighthood; while of the [illegible] observation of the Stars and Clouds, those made by the [illegible] of king *Dathi*, before his foreign expedition, and [illegible] a former lecture, afford a very distinct example. Of [illegible] Oracles, that which I have just referred to in the [illegible] *Lughaidh Delbaeth*, and *Aiefé*, his daughter, is a fair [illegible] The singular sorcery of the "Wisp of Straw", [illegible] the curious stories of *Nuadha Fullon* and of the prince [illegible] son of *Maelochtar*, is another remarkable case of [illegible] ceremony, very minutely described. And in addition [illegible] example, we had that, in full detail, of the use of the [illegible] connexion with the Druidical Fire, in the story of the [illegible] Druid *Dill* and queen *Eithné* of Cashel, so lately as the [illegible] century. Lastly, the very extraordinary account of the siege of *Drom Damhghairé*, or Knocklong, with the druidical contests of *Mogh Ruith* and *Ciothruadh*, proved even still more specific in the details of the same kind which it preserves to us. And the stories of Saint Patrick's contests with the Druids again afforded instances of Druidical Darkness magically produced, even in his time.

Closely connected with the druidical rites and belief were the systems of poetical divination, such as the *Imbas Forosnaí*, and the *Teinm Laeghdha*, prohibited by Saint Patrick, as connected with idol worship; and this species of Druidism we found practised by the famous *Finn MacCumhaill* in the third century. Another curious instance of it was preserved in that story of the recognition of the skull of *Mogh Eimhé*, the lap-dog, two centuries after its death, by the poet *Maen Mac Etnae*. Lastly, of the effects of the poetical satires I gave some further instances, as they were evidently the remains of the more ancient magical usages.

As to the Religion, and the Organization of the Druids.

It is unfortunate that we have no certain account of the Religion of the time of the Druids. We only know that they worshipped idols, from such examples as that of the Idol Gods taken into the Druid's bed, so as to influence his visions, as described in Cormac's Glossary, and that of the invocation of idols in the case of the *Teinm Laeghdha;* and we know that in certain ceremonies they made use of the Yew tree, of the Quicken or Roan tree, and of the Black-Thorn, as in the instance of the ordeal or test of a woman's character by means of fire made of these sacred woods. That the people of ancient Erinn were idolaters is certain, for they certainly adored the great idol called *Crom Cruach*, in the plain called *Magh Slecht*, as I showed on a former occasion.[175] But it is remarkable that we find no mention of any connexion between this Idol and the Druids, or any other Class of Priests, or special Idol-servers. We have only record of the people, generally, assembling at times, to do honour to the Idol creation.

As little, unfortunately, do we know of the organization of the Order of the Druids, if they were indeed an Order. They certainly were not connected as such with the orders of learned men or Profession of Teachers, such as before explained. The Druids were often, however, engaged in teaching, as has been seen; and it would appear that kings and chiefs, as well as learned men, were also frequently Druids, though how or why I am not in a position to explain with certainty at present.

(175) See *Lectures on the MS. Materials*, &c. p. 103; and App. pp. 538, 631-2.

LECT. X.

I have, therefore, simply endeavoured to bring together such a number of examples as may give some general idea of the position and powers of the Druids, so far as special instances are preserved in our early writings, of their mode of action and position in society And I have refrained from suggesting any theory of my own upon the subject. This negative conclusion, nevertheless, I will venture to draw from the whole: that notwithstanding the singularly positive assertions of many of our own as well as of English writers upon the subject, there is no ground whatever for believing the Druids to have been the priests of any special positive worship,—none whatever for imputing to them human sacrifices,—none whatever for believing that the early people of Erinn adored the sun, moon, or stars,—nor that they worshipped fire;—and still less foundation for the ridiculous inventions of modern times, (inventions of pure ignorance), concerning honours paid to Brown Bulls, Red Cows, or any other cows, or any of the lower animals.

There are in our MSS., as I have already observed, a great number of instances of Druidism mentioned besides those I have selected. I have merely taken a specimen of each class of druidical rites recorded. I only hope I have so dealt with the subject as to assist the student, at all events, in attaining some general idea of our ancient life in respect of the superstitious observances of the people, though I cannot satisfactorily specify the forms and doctrines of our ancient system of paganism.

There are some curious allusions to an educational connexion with Asiatic Magi, in some of the stories of the very early Gaedhelic Champions, many of whom seem to have travelled by the north of Europe to the Black Sea, and across into Asia. But these will, perhaps, more properly come under our consideration in connexion with the subject of Military Education, and especially that of the professed Champions.

LECTURE XI.

[Delivered 1st June, 1858.]

(V.) Weapons of Warfare. Scope of the present lectures. The earliest positive descriptions of Weapons, in Irish History. The first settlers. The colony of *Parthalon*. The colony of *Nemidh*. The *Tuatha Dé Danann* and Firbolg colonies. The first battle of *Magh Tuireadh*; (B.C. 1272). Of the arms of *Sreng*, the champion of the Firbolgs. The *Craisech*; or "thick-handled spear". Hurling-match between the armies of the *Tuatha Dé Danann* and the Firbolgs. Of the construction of the arms used at the Battle of *Magh Tuireadh*. The *Manais*; or "trowel"-shaped spear. The *Fiarlann*; or "curved blade". Difference between the arms of the early *Tuatha Dé Danann* and Firbolgs. Of the arms of the Firbolgs;—the *Craisech*;—the *Fiarlann*. Different shapes of ancient Sword-blades. The Iron-mounted Club, or Mace, of the Firbolgs, (the *Long-Iarainn*.) Of the arms of the *Tuatha Dé Danann*; (Tale of the Battle of *Magh Tuireadh na b-Fomhorach*.) The Spear of the *Tuatha Dé Danann*. Of *Nuadha* of the Silver Arm. Of the Three great Artificers of the *Tuatha Dé Danann*. Of the Forge of *Goibniu*.

In the preceding lectures we have disposed of the more important general subjects connected with the present inquiry, in their legitimate order, in relation to the Civilization of the people,—the system of Legislation in ancient Erinn,—the division of society into Classes,—the system of Education,—and the system of religion, if Druidism is to be so considered. I have not allowed myself to theorize upon any of them. I have strictly confined myself to an inquiry as to what is to be gathered on each of these subjects from the histories and literature which have come down to us in the ancient language, and the authorities recognized by the earliest writers and teachers of the country. I only regret that it was impossible for me, within the necessary limits of such a course as the present, to do more than merely present the results of my examination of those authorities, together with some examples of each of them selected from a great store which has yet to be searched out completely before a full history of the Civilization of ancient Erinn can be properly undertaken. We come now to another class of subjects in the consideration of details equally important in connexion with the yet undeveloped study of our early history, and in themselves, perhaps, likely to prove even more generally interesting than the contents of the preceding lectures.

LECT. XI.

Of Weapons of Warfare.

The first class of these details forms the necessary [illegible] to the subject of the Military Institutions of the [illegible] namely, which embraces the Description and Class[illegible] the various WEAPONS OF WARFARE, offensive and [illegible] known in ancient Erinn. And the interest which I [illegible] student will find in forming some acquaintance with [illegible] pons cannot fail to be increased by the opport[illegible] every one in this city possesses of visiting the museum [illegible] Royal Irish Academy in which is preserved so grea[illegible] dance of specimens of almost all the various [illegible] have occasion to mention, including even those of [illegible] liest ages of our history.

Scope of the present lectures.

To trace the history of a people's progress in the [illegible] lized life, through a long series of generations, from [illegible] settling down in some temporary hut on the brink of [illegible] on the skirts of a forest of one or more poor families, [illegible] the proper implements for the cultivation of the soil, the [illegible] of the rivers, the clearing of the forest, the housing and [illegible] of themselves,—the history of the gradual progress of [illegible] from so helpless a beginning, to its eventual development [illegible] populous and prosperous nation not only possessing an [illegible] system of agriculture, but skilled in all domestic and [illegible] manufactures (including that of the finest weapons of [illegible] warfare), enterprising in commerce, and happy in free [illegible] tions, good laws, and a vigorous national government,—[illegible] history, (if the history of Ireland could be so described), [illegible] be, indeed, a subject highly worthy of the study of the [illegible] pher, and of the indefatigable labours of the antiqua[illegible] historical student. It is well that I have not to deal with [illegible] a history, or the task would be but poorly performed. [illegible] it is not without great diffidence that I venture to approa[illegible] examination of even a section of our primitive history, [illegible] scious as I am of my inadequacy to do anything like [illegible] to a subject now so difficult and obscure, and one which [illegible] already engaged the attention of so many scholars and inv[illegible] gators, both at home and abroad. And this diffidence [illegible] creased by the consciousness that the conclusions I hav[illegible] rived at, after the most mature consideration, are often [illegible] at variance with the opinions of many of the writers I allud[illegible]

It does not come within the scope of my lectures to [illegible] the various ethnological hypotheses which from time to [illegible] have been proposed regarding the origin, or condition of [illegible] earliest inhabitants of Europe or of Erinn. The cou[illegible] have strictly prescribed to myself is simply to set down [illegible] results of such positive information as I have been abl[illegible] collect from our own early authorities, taken in connexion with the positive remains of genuine ancient workmanship preserved in our museums and elsewhere. I shall thus distinctly state all the foundations for my own conclusions, and I shall leave it to others to examine the value of these for themselves; fully trusting that when the authorities and remains to which I shall refer shall be investigated as they deserve, the truth will at last come out in its proper colours. Nor is the subject interesting to us alone; for it has a direct bearing upon similar investigations in the history and antiquities of other nations also, and in particular of France, of Northern Germany, of Denmark, and of Norway, as well as of Great Britain; so that I would earnestly claim the assistance also of all sincere students of early history in these different countries, for their own sake as well as ours. When each produces the evidence which his own language can afford of the state of civilization in arts and manufactures during the first ages, then and not until then historians will really be able to sift and compare the scraps of knowledge so preserved, and really to undertake the true solution of these interesting questions of archæology.

Whether our remote colonists brought with them military teachers, or at what time, if ever, Military Schools were first established in Erinn, it would be vain to pretend to lay down, with any degree of certainty, or upon any reliable authority; but upon this part of my subject I shall have something to say on a future occasion. All that I propose to do at present is to give, from ancient Irish writings, as many references as may seem necessary to explain what was known or believed many centuries ago, relative to the use, material, and manufacture of the Military Weapons of ancient Erinn, and the times and the people to which such references belong, according to our native books of history, chronology, and genealogies. And in order to do this in something of a regular order, I believe it will be convenient in as brief a manner as possible to refer chronologically to the unanimous ancient accounts of our early colonists, and of the countries from which they are stated to have come, introducing what is said of the various weapons and their uses just as they occur in the accounts of the successive contests here recorded.

Earliest positive description of Weapons in Irish History.

The earliest positive description of the forms and nature of the weapons used by the primitive races in Erinn, is found in the tracts concerning the two battles of *Magh Tuireadh*, of which I had occasion to speak at some length on a former occasion; the first of these battles having been fought between the Firbolgs and the *Tuatha Dé Danann*, (two races long anterior to the Milesian Gaedhils in the occupation of the country); and

LECT. XL.

the second between the latter people and the [illegible] rovers, known in our history as the Fomorians. [illegible] annalists and ancient historians make very posi[illegible] the existence in the island of more than one tribe [illegible] even these, in the successive march of the waves of [illegible] towards the west from the cradle of the human race [illegible] Asia. And these early tribes also had arms and [illegible] of which they appear to have made active use. [illegible]

Traces of a colonization before that of *Parthalon*.

Even before the coming of *Parthalon*,—call him [illegible] legendary character if you will,—mention is [illegible] ancient story of a previous colonisation, under the [illegible] a chief sprung from the ruler of "*Sliabh Ughmoir*" [illegible] the ancient Gaedhelic name for the Caucasus. Th[illegible] said to have lived here for some generations, until [illegible] defeated and almost extirpated by the followers of [illegible] at a battle fought by him, on his landing, in the plain [illegible] *Ita*, in Ulster. Perhaps the statement of the exi[illegible] first colony may be more satisfactory to the advo[illegible] theory of primitive barbarism, when I add that they [illegible] have lived only by fishing and fowling. The leg[illegible] count of them is extravagant enough; but so much, [illegible] certainly be gathered from it with some degree of c[illegible]

Parthalon's Colony.

After this most ancient colony, the next historical [illegible] dary tribe that appears on the scene is that of *Parth*[illegible] genealogy is minutely given by the old historians, [illegible] said to have landed in Erinn so long ago as in the [illegible] generation after the general deluge. He is explicitly [illegible] to have come from "Migdonia", or Middle Greece [illegible] have landed, with about a thousand families, at [illegible] small island in the River Erne, near Ballyshannon, [illegible] present county of Donegal. No detailed account [illegible] *thalon*'s exploits is to be found; but he is stated to have [illegible] not only the battle in which he subdued the tribe [illegible] settled in Erinn before him, but two great battles [illegible] parties of the Fomorians or northern Sea-Rovers, [illegible] was victorious. The arms used on these occasions [illegible] however, mentioned. But that his people were provi[illegible] implements of peace, as well as warlike arms, and [illegible] civilized as to be acquainted with the practice of agri[illegible] proved by the record which states that it was by the[illegible] that the plains called *Magh Eithrighé* in Connacht, [illegible] in Ulster, *Magh Lir* in Meath, and *Magh Latharna* [illegible] *Araidhé* in Ulster, were cleared from forest and brought [illegible] cultivation. And he is distinctly stated to have possessed [illegible] and ploughmen, (which, I presume, implies also plough[illegible]

The colony of *Parthalon* is recorded to have been almost entirely cut off by a plague or mortality which destroyed about nine thousand of this people, in the plain of the *Lift*, or Liffey, about three hundred years after the first landing of the tribe in Erinn. And the early histories note that the remains of this people are marked by those very mounds which still exist on the hill of *Tamhlacht*, or Tallacht, in this county; a place, indeed, whose very name is derived from this account, being called in the Gaedhelic *Taimh-Leachta Muinntiré Phartalain;* or, literally, The Mortality-Tombs of the People of *Parthalon;* a name by which it has been known from the earliest ages.

The Nemidian Colony.

After *Parthalon* yet another wave of population reached our shores, before the coming of the Firbolgs and the *Tuatha Dé Danann;* a people, indeed, who were said to have been not only the predecessors but the actual progenitors of both these tribes. These were the "Nemidians", or followers of *Nemidh*, a chieftain of the same Japhetic race, who is said to have come out of "Scythia" into Erinn, with about a thousand followers, some thirty years after the Partholanian mortality. This nation seems also to have been comparatively civilized; for it is recorded in all the ancient books that these Nemidians built two royal Raths or Courts in Erinn;—one called *Raith Cinneich*, in the territory of *Uibh Niallain*, (now the barony of Hy-Nelland, in the county of Armagh); and the other called *Raith Cimbaeth*, in *Leimné*, (on the east coast of the present county of Antrim). And under them, too, the improvements begun by *Parthalon* were immediately resumed; for *Nemidh's* people are said to have cleared twelve great plains, from the forest, in different parts of the Island. The Nemidians also fought several fierce battles against the Fomorians or Sea Rovers of the time; but no account has come down to us supplying any details regarding their military weapons, any more than the agricultural and other domestic implements used by them. This colony is recorded to have held the country for more than two hundred years, until they had at last become so enfeebled by the frequent descents of the Fomorians, (particularly after the great battle of Torry Island, on the north-west coast of the present county of Donegal, in which they suffered most severely), that their leading men fled out of the Island, leaving behind them but a few defenceless families. Of the fugitives one party is said to have taken refuge in Britain; and another to have made its way into Thrace; while a third passed into the north of Europe, and is reported by some writers to have settled in Bœotia. The party which passed into Thrace are recorded to have been the ancestors of the Firbolgs; and that which passed into the north of Europe the ancestors of the

LECT. XI. *Tuatha Dé Danann*. The Firbolgs are said to [illegible] about two hundred years after the flight of the [illegible] the *Tuatha Dé Danann* thirty-seven years later [illegible] date is placed by the Four Masters about eighteen [illegible] years before Christ.

The *Tuatha Dé Danann* and *Firbolg* Colonies. There seems to have been no intercourse between [illegible] great branches of the early colonists of Erinn during [illegible] centuries and a half which elapsed since their common [illegible] had abandoned the island. During that period it would [illegible] that the branch since known as the *Tuatha Dé Danann* [illegible] their residence in the north of Europe attained a [illegible] degree of civilization to that of the Firbolgs, who [illegible] Greece, according to the national traditions, in a state [illegible] slavery for the greater part of this time. Certain it is that [illegible] very early traditions respecting the *Tuatha Dé Danann* [illegible] cate that they were a people possessed of an amount [illegible] chanical skill and philosophical knowledge, as well [illegible] degree of general refinement, so much greater than that [illegible] of the Firbolgs whom they subjugated, but even of the [illegible] quent Milesian immigration by which in their turn they [illegible] themselves subdued, that for ages afterwards they were [illegible] believed by their less-educated successors, and enslaved [illegible] scure descendants, to have been gifted with supernatural [illegible]

The *Tuatha Dé Danann*. It is much to be deplored that so few historic vestiges [illegible] to testify the very remote civilization of this ancient [illegible] Unfortunately the Annalists and Historians whose works [illegible] in the whole or in part, come down to us are of the [illegible] ing Milesian race alone; and the notices they give of [illegible] conquered predecessors are very slender. Perhaps [illegible] investigation of those very arms, of which I am now [illegible] report the very little that is known, will be found to [illegible] almost all that can with certainty be gleaned from our [illegible] concerning them. For it is in the account of the two great [illegible] in which, immediately after their arrival, they established [illegible] selves in sovereignty, against the Firbolgs on the one side [illegible] the northern sea rovers on the other, that we find almost [illegible] particulars known to Irish history of the *Tuatha Dé Danann* [illegible] and it is in the details of this account also that the only [illegible] description of the various ancient arms is preserved.

On a former occasion I described at length the recorded [illegible] count of the two battles of *Magh Tuireadh*;[178] and I need [illegible] more now than shortly refer to them before I extract from [illegible] ancient histories what specially relates to the arms used [illegible] occasion.

(178) See *Lectures on the MS. Materials*, etc., pp. 244, 247, etc.

The first Battle of *Magh Tuireadh* was fought between the Firbolgs and the *Tuatha Dé Danann*, shortly after the former discovered that like themselves the latter people had also returned into Erinn to take possession of the ancient inheritance of their common ancestors. Its date is fixed, according to O'Flaherty's chronology, A.M. 2737, or B.C. 1272; and according to the chronology followed by the Four Masters, A.M. 3303, or B.C. 1890.

The First Battle of *Magh Tuireadh*.

The Firbolgs had settled their seat of sovereignty at Tara, where they lived under the government of a distinguished warrior, king *Eochaidh Mac Erc*, when they heard of the appearance of their rivals, who had entered the island on the north-west and had established themselves in the strongholds of the present county of Leitrim. The Firbolgs, on consultation, determined to send a picked champion of their force to enter into communication with the strangers, and to ascertain what their intentions were; and their choice fell upon *Sreng*, the son of *Sengann*; and it is in the description of the meeting of this warrior with *Breas*, the equally redoubted champion messenger of the *Tuatha Dé Danann*, that the first description of the weapons on both sides, both offensive and defensive, is found Without occupying any unnecessary space, then, in detailing the description of the battle itself, I shall proceed to refer to those passages only which contain any description of the shape, size, construction, and use of the various arms employed; and I shall afterwards endeavour to classify these, as well as I can, with reference to the collection of specimens open for examination in the Museum of the Royal Irish Academy.

Arms of *Sreng*, Champion of the *Firbolgs*, (B.C. 1272.)

Upon the selection of *Sreng* by the council of the Firbolgs: "he arose then", says the ancient writer, "and took his hooked, firm, brown-red shield; and his two thick-handled spears, called *Craiseachs;* and his keen-gliding sword; and his elegant quadrangular [square?] helmet; and his thick iron club; and he set out from Tara",—etc. And when *Sreng* arrived in sight of the camp of the *Tuatha Dé Danann*, *Breas*, the champion of the latter, came out to meet and speak with him,—"with his shield upon him", proceeds the history, "and his sword in his hand, and having two huge spears with him".

The two champions, we are told, wondered each at the peculiar arms of the other, their form and character being different; and when they came within speaking distance, each of them, it is said, "stuck his shield firmly into the ground", to cover his body, while he looked over the top of it to examine his opponent. On conversation they agree to raise and put away their shields; and *Sreng* observes that he had raised his in dread

LECT. XII. of the "thin sharp spear" of his adversary, ... presume similar respect for the "thick-handled ... Firbolgs, and asks if all their arms are like the ... give Breas an opportunity of examining them; ... the fixings off his two thick-handled Craisech ... spears), and asks Breas what he thinks of them; ... surprise and admiration of the "great, pointless ... sharp-edged arms", and refers to the sharpness of ... their power when cast at an enemy, the wounds ... cause of rubbing to their edge, and the deadliness ... thrust; thus describing both the form and mode ... peculiar kind of spear. Sreng then explains that ... the weapon is Craisech; that they are "gorers of ... "crushers of bones", and "breakers of shields", and ... thrust or stroke is death, or perpetual mutilation. ... ing they exchange weapons, we are told, that the host ... side might thus form an opinion of the other, by ... of a specimen of the arms. Breas gives Sreng his ... or spears, and sends word by him that the Tuatha Dé ... will insist on half of the island; that they would take ... in peace, but if so much were not conceded by the ... they must try the issue of a battle between them. ... returns to the Firbolg camp, and it is in his account ... champion of the *Tuatha Dé Danann* that we have a ... of their weapons. "Their shields", he says, "are ... firm; their spears are sharp, thin, and hard; their ... hard and deep-edged". And *Sreng* recommended ... accordingly to agree to the proposed terms, and to ... country equally with the strangers. This, however, ... not consent to do, for they said if they gave the *Tuatha Dé Danann* half, they would soon take the whole.

The Craisech.

On the other side, the *Tuatha Dé Danann* were ... impressed with the report of *Breas*, and with the ... the terrible *Craisechs*, that they resolved to secure ... by taking up a better military position before the ... battle, and they retired, accordingly, farther west ... nacht, where they fixed their camp in the plain of ... (close to the present church and village of Cong, in the ... county of Mayo); and at the west-end of this plain ... trenched themselves, we are told, so as to have the ... the great mountain, *Belgatan*, in their rear, through which ... retreat could be safely made, if necessary.

The Firbolgs, (continues the story,) subsequently ... their levies and encamped "in eleven battalions", at the ... end of the same plain. Then *Nuadha*, the king of the *Tuatha* ...

Dé Danann, (the celebrated *Nuadha* "of the silver hand"), sent envoys to make the same proposition formerly made through *Breas*. King *Eochaidh Mac Erc* referred them for an answer to his nobles present, and these at once declared that they would not consent. The Poets, (that is, the envoys), asked in reply when then did they propose to give battle; and the Firbolgs made the very remarkable answer, that "delay is necessary, for", said they, "we require time to put in order our spears, to repair our armour, to burnish our helmets, and to sharpen our swords, and to make proper preparation for battle; and we require too", said they, "to have spears like yours made for us, and ye require to have *Craisechs* like ours made for you". So they agreed on a delay of 105 days for preparation.

Pointed Spears known also to the Firbolgs.

From this passage it would appear that the Firbolgs had no other spears but the *Craisechs*, which were "pointless". However, the writer of this history observes that the Firbolgs must have had pointed spears too, (or at least must have been acquainted with them); because, he says, the weapon had been introduced among them by their former king, *Rinnal*, the grandfather of king *Eochaidh*. And that this was the common belief of other ancient writers, is evidenced by an ancient tract on the etymology of proper names (called *Coir Anmann*), of which copies are preserved in the books of Leinster, *Lecain*, and Ballymote, from which the following stanzas are quoted from a poem on the reign of the Firbolg kings, written by *Tanaidhé O'Maelchonairé* [O'Mulconry], (who died A. D. 1136):

"Until *Rinnal* arose, there were no points
To arms, at first, in Erinn;
Rude spears without smooth handles,
And they only like forest-axes". * * *

"The brave *Tuatha Dé Danann* brought
Pointed spears in their hands with them.
Of these was killed king *Eochaidh*,
By the victorious race of *Nemid*.(177)

Hurling Match between the *Tuatha Dé Danann* and the *Firbolgs*, (B.C. 1272.)

The day of battle came at last; the first day of the sixth week of summer. The battle proceedings were opened by a sort of hurling match or game of hurl, in which the three times nine hurlers on each side of the *Tuatha Dé Danann* were not only defeated but

(177) Original:—Gur ḟas Rinnal ní ḃoí rinn
for arm ar túr in Eirinn
forgaib garga gan cleiṫ ċaim
sa mbeiṫ mar ḟiḋċrannaiḃ.
Tucrat Tuath De Danann dil
laigne leó ina lámaib,
dibrein ro marbad Eoċaid
la síl Nemid nertbreċtaig.

LECT. XI. themselves slain by the Firbolg party. A mess[...] sent by king *Eochaidh* to the camp of the *Tuatha* [...] (such was the chivalrous custom, it seems, of those [...] range how the contest should be carried on, [...] should be every day or only every second day. [...] agreed, on the demand of the *Tuatha Dé Danann*, [...] be fought always with equal numbers; an arrangement [...] disagreeable, says the writer, to the Firbolg king, [...] largely the advantage in the numbers of his army. [...] then commenced, and the description of it is that [...] of successive feats of gallantry, now on one side, [...] other, conceived much in the manner in which [...] would have appeared to the author of the Iliad. [...] also, on both sides, are said to have had healing [...] with medicinal herbs and plants, into which the [...] each day were put, so as to be healed and strength[...] next morning's engagement.

Allusions to the construction of Arms in the Tale of the Battle of *Magh Tuireadh*. The description of the various single combats by wh[...] a struggle was naturally distinguished offers occasional [...] only of the use but of the construction of the weapons [...] in the passage which relates the combat between the [...] *Aidleo* and the Firbolg warrior *Nertchu*, it is stated that [...] firmly-clutched shields were torn from their fists, their [...] broken at their hilts, and their spears wrenched fr[...] rivets",—an expression which at once distinguishes th[...] spear in which the blade was received into the handle [...] shall afterwards see.

The *Manais*. Again, when the advance of the two kings, and the [...] the select bands led by each, is described, the line of Fir[...] riors is said to have appeared: "sparkling, brilliant, and [...] with their swords, spears, blades, and trowel-spears", ([...] different weapon from any yet mentioned) flashing in [...] while that of the *Tuatha Dé Danann* is also called a [...] line, "under their red-bordered, speckled, and firm [...] And in the shock of battle both are said to have fou[...] sharp spears, till the thick spear-handles were twist[...] their hands, and the swords broken upon what are de[...] "the polished surfaces of the curved shields". So, [...] tion is made of the havoc caused by their "curved blad[...] the reverberating "strokes" of the *craisech* are spoke[...] tearing and splitting the shields of the warriors. So, [...] weary combatants stopping to take breath are descri[...] springing up again to the upper edges of their shields, [...] tempt "blows of decapitation" upon the exposed necks [...] other; and they are described as "raising their powerful [...]

on high to shower down crushing blows of the sword upon each other's helmets, so as to break or cleave them". And the blow by which king *Nuadha* lost that right arm which is said to have been afterwards replaced by an artificial one of silver, was the blow of the sword of the champion *Sreng*, which is stated to have not only severed the arm at the shoulder, but to have carried with it to the ground a third part of the monarch's shield. And when *Sreng* is then pressed on by *Aengabha* of *Iruaidh*, and a crowd of the *Tuatha Dé Danann*, in assistance of their king, the exact nature of the *Craisech* is well indicated in the description of his thrusts, which are said to have been more powerful because of the "sharp breadth of his spear, and the thickness of its handle". *Craisech.*

The subsequent combat, again, between king *Eochaidh Mac Erc* and *Breas*, the great champion of the *Tuatha Dé Danann*, (in which *Breas* is eventually killed), is commenced by the clashing together of the shields of the two warriors. And the use of the "curved blade" is indicated in the passage immediately following, where the four brothers of *Breas*, springing forward to his rescue, are met by the four sons of *Slaingé*. Both parties begin by striking fiercely at each other's shields, but it is observed (and it is this I wish to lay some stress on) that not only did their bodies suffer from the blows of the swords, but in the ardour of their fight "the hair of the champions was cut off behind" by their "curved blades". The "curved blade"; *Fiarlann.*

The event of the battle at last (according to the tale) was unfavourable to the Firbolgs, who, before resolving to abandon the island altogether, made one final attempt to recover their ground, by challenging their opponents to risk the issue of the war on a fight between three hundred men on each side. But the *Tuatha Dé Danann*, themselves exhausted, proposed in return that there should be no more fighting, but that the Firbolgs should be accorded one province of Erinn at their own option, the remainder being reserved to their hardly victorious rivals, and that both parties should in future live in peace with one another. And this offer the Firbolgs gladly accepted, choosing for themselves the province of Connacht, in which both parties then were; (and so Duald Mac Firbis mentions, in his great Book of Genealogies, finished in 1650, that some of their descendants were still known in Connacht, even down to that day).

If there be any credence due to our ancient histories and Historic Tales,[176] I think it will be admitted that the account

(176) See as to the authority of the "Historic Tales", *Lectures on the MS. Materials*, etc., pp 239-241.

LECT. XI. of the famous battle of *Magh Tuireadh*, to wh[illegible] copiously referred, is fully sufficient to prove [illegible] earliest population possessed no small knowledg[illegible]

Differences between the arms of the early Tuatha Dé Danann and Firbolgs.

It is to be observed that in this ancient account [illegible] of *Magh Tuireadh* the arms of the Firbolgs are [illegible] scribed as "broad", "heavy", "sharp", and "po[illegible] that they are said to have consisted of a *Craisech*, [illegible] a *Claidheamh* and a *Long-Iarainn*; while the [illegible] *Tuatha Dé Danann* are distinguished as "pointe[illegible] said to have consisted of a *Sleigh*, a *Goth-Mhanais*, [illegible] *eamh*. It would be impossible satisfactorily to d[illegible] different weapons in mere words, so as to distingui[illegible] their various shapes and features; and it has occurred [illegible] it would be very desirable to make my hearers acqu[illegible] their appearance by a more direct representation. [illegible] happy to be able to do, through the kindness of the [illegible] the museum of the Royal Irish Academy, who has [illegible] me to make use of some most accurate drawings, of the [illegible] of such of the weapons to which I have alluded as I [illegible] able, so far as my judgment goes, to identify among [illegible] preserved in the museum of the Academy.[179]

The arms of the Firbolgs. The Craisech.

The first is the Firbolg *Craisech*. It was, accordin[illegible] description in the ancient account of the battle, a [illegible] thick weapon, sharp-edged, and rounded at the [illegible] (judging by the specimen) it was made of fine bro[illegible] finished with much skill. It must have been receive[illegible] end of the pole or handle, and fastened by those [illegible] (preserved in the specimen),[180] which passed through [illegible] socket and blade, and were flattened down at both [illegible] handle. The handle must have been thick and hea[illegible] point of receiving the blade, for such it is describe[illegible] account of the battle, where these weapons are [illegible]

[(179) As to the Catalogue by Sir W. R. Wilde, published by the [illegible] Academy, see INTRODUCTION, *ante*. Professor O'Curry [illegible] of the guesses of Sir W. Wilde as to the uses and as to the date [illegible] ments and ornaments of early ages referred to in that pu[illegible] engravings in it are, however, accurate.]

[(180) The specimen referred to by Professor O'Curry is not [illegible] Academy Catalogue. Figures 1, 2, 3, (see INTRODUCTION), however, [illegible] erroneously supposed by Sir W. Wilde to represent the blades of [illegible] *Catalogue*, p. 489), though smaller in size, will furnish almost [illegible] examples of this weapon. The blade of fig. 1 (fig. 356, No. 25[illegible] is 3¾ inches long (the whole bronze is 5¾ inches), and 3½ inches [illegible] (fig. 357, No. 269), which is drawn one-fourth of the original, [illegible] inches long, and 3¾ broad. Another *Craisech* is that figured in Sir [illegible] catalogue as a sword (No. 232, Fig. 327), which is 12¾ inches lon[illegible] broad at the bottom, and 1½ inches within an inch of the end.—[illegible] called a *Craiseha crannremra Catha*", that is, "thick-handled battle *Craisechs*".

The shaft was probably flattened thin, and mounted with a thick plate or ferule of bronze, on which the rivets were fastened at both sides; else the wood would have been in danger of splitting. Indeed an instance of this actually occurs in the combat between *Aidleo*, the son of *Allai*, of the *Tuatha Dé Danann*, and *Nertchu*, the grandson of *Semeon*, of the Firbolgs, of which the writer says: "Their shields were wrested from their firm grasp, their swords were broken at the hilts, and their spears were wrenched from their rivets"[(141)] And although such plates or ferules as I have been speaking of are not mentioned in this tract, there is frequent mention made of them in other ancient tracts, into which they are introduced under the names of *fethána*, or flat rings, both for ornament and use, as shall be shown at another place.

Ferules or Rings for Spear-Rivets. (*Fethána*).

It does not appear distinctly from the authority from which I have been quoting that the spears of the *Tuatha Dé Danann* were mounted in a way different from those of the Firbolgs; on the contrary, the only difference spoken of between them, in any way, is that the former were "sharp-pointed", whilst the latter were "rounded at the top". Still, however, the shape might have been, and, in fact, was different; because all the spears with sockets ever discovered, (and there are great numbers of both kinds in our various collections,) are pointed; whilst the *Craisechs* and the *Fiarlanna* which were received into the handle are rounded at the top. There is, indeed, another class, (of which very early specimens are to be found in the Museum of the Academy), which embraces the supposed characteristics of both; being sharply pointed after the *Tuatha Dé Danann* fashion, and having been received into the handle, like that of the Firbolgs.[(142)] It could not, however, have belonged to them, according to the distinction laid down in this tract, unless, indeed, it be an exceptional weapon, for which we have, as already mentioned, some authority in old writings;—and perhaps others, in what is stated in *O'Maelchonaire*'s poem, that [illegible], the grandfather of the Firbolg king *Eochaidh Mac Erc*, had in his own time introduced sharp-pointed spears among his people. It is certain from the tract, however, that such a form was, at least, not generally adopted or preserved among them. Be this as it may, there is a weapon among the oldest in the

Mounting of the Spear-points among the *Tuatha Dé Danann* and the *Firbolgs*.

(141) [illegible]—Ro mergait a sceith as a n-glacaib comolúta, ro claic[illegible] in inormadaib a n-urdorn, ro snit a slega da semannaib.

(142) The specimen Fig. 4. (fig. 340, No. 156, Acad. Catal.) is a bronze spear-[illegible] inches long, and half an inch wide at the middle of the blade.

LECT. XI. Academy, certainly as old as any that we are acq bearing the recorded characteristics of both nati positively referable to either in particular, as the but the blade and mounting are more of the Fi

The *Fiar-lann*, of the *Firbolgs*. In the Academy collection we have next a spe Firbolg *Fiarlann*, or "curved blade", which, like was received into the end of the pole or handle, by rivets.[188] It is clear from the curvature in beautiful double-edged blade, that it was not cast from the hand like the *craisech*, (which as used in striking), or like the ordinary spear, that it was used only for striking and thrusting at c

We are told in the Tale of the battle of *Magh* king *Nuadha* had his arm cut off from the should of the sword of *Sreng*, the Firbolg champion; there is no weapon among those assigned to either would appear so capable of performing such a *fiarlann*, or "curved blade".

The *Fiarlanna*, or "curved blades", are twice men battle of *Magh Tuireadh*, in the fight of the fourth it is first said that they were cooled or tempered in blood of the noble warriors;—and again, in the comb the four brothers of the *Daghda*, the great chief of *Dé Danann*, and the four sons of *Slaingé* of the F where it is stated that the combat was firmly them with their swords, and that their hair was cut by the sharp edges of the *Fiarlanna*. In this com no allusion to *craisechs* or spears, but only to swords *lanna*; which may perhaps be considered to show latter weapon was used in close fight only, or chief

The *Fiarlann*, or "curved blade", from its great shank, would require, one should think, a very handle, and so it surely would if the handle were wood; but very fortunately we are in a position to existing example of the highest interest as well as that the superior skill and taste of the manufacture curious blade to a handle the most perfect for use, graceful of form. My talented friend, Mr. George V having visited Rouen in the summer of last year, covered in the museum of antiquities of that city sev weapons, of which he made the beautiful colour

(188) Fig. 5, (fig 329, No. 240 Acad. Catal.) is 16 inches broad at the bottom, and 2¼ inches at the middle of the blade. 330, No. 271, which is drawn on a larger scale) was, when inches long, and is 3⅜ inches broad at bottom, and 1⅝ across the

presented by him to the museum of the Royal Irish Academy. It requires not, I think, a word from me to show that our own *fiarlann*, or "curved blade", with its three and sometimes five short rivets, was mounted in a metal handle exactly like the beautiful specimens[(184)] there figured of the *colg*, or straight blade; and it is not unimportant to remember that the country in which these *colgs* have been found closely adjoins that of the *Belgæ*, who are said to be the same race as our own Firbolgs.

Different shapes of ancient Sword-blades.

In examining the collection of Sword-Blades in the Academy, if we strictly apply to this weapon the test which applies to the *craiseach* and *fiarlann*,—that is, that the rounded top is the mark of all *Firbolg* weapons, as distinguished from the pointed weapons of the *Tuatha Dé Danann*,—we can scarcely think that any precise specimen of the *Firbolg* sword has come to our time. Among them will be found some two or three types of ancient swords of the flagger-leaf shape; that is, widening gradually from near the hilt to about two-thirds of their length, and then narrowing gradually but more suddenly, until they terminate in a decidedly sharp point. Among them, however, will be found some which, although not decidedly rounded at the top, yet can scarcely be believed to have ever terminated in a fine sharp point. And although there are doubtless some with sharp points among them, still they are not of the flagger-leaf shape, nor have they, on close examination, much in common with that shape at all. Their solidity is great, and they are marked from hilt to top by two well defined raised lines, running along the shoulders of the blade, breaking the bevel of the edge, and marking themselves with precision the line from which the edge is to start.[(185)] In a second form of sharp-pointed sword it will be perceived[(186)] that solidity is given by a single sharp bevelled line, or ridge, running through the centre from hilt to top, and agreeing with the general character of what we shall have occasion hereafter to designate as the spear of the *Tuatha Dé Danann*. Now if this slightly round-topped sword to which I have alluded cannot be brought within the range of the Firbolg family of round-topped weapons, one of two things must necessarily be supposed: either on the one hand that this pecu-

(184) [See Fig. 7.]

(185) The construction alluded to is represented in all but the rounded top in Figs. 8, 9, 10. These figures are drawn one-sixth the size of the originals. Fig. 8, (fig. 316, No. 45, Cat. R.I.A.), is 18½ inches long by 1 inch broad at the broadest part. Fig. 9, (fig. 318, No. 5, Cat. R.I.A.), is 23½ inches (including the hilt, 4⅛ inches), and 1⅜ broad at the centre. Fig. 10, (fig. 318, No. 40, Cat. R.I.A.), is 29⅝ inches long (including hilt, 2¼ inches); and 1⅞ broad.

(186) See Fig. 11, (fig. 317, Cat. R.I.A.).

LECT. XI. liarity did not extend to the sword; or, if it did, of that type has come down to our time, as found in the collection of the Royal Irish Academy, known (to me at least) to exist anywhere else.

The iron-mounted Club (or Mace) of the Firbolgs; (Long Iarainn.) The next of the Firbolg weapons would be the Club or Mace, which it is stated was carried by *Sreng* along with his two *craisechs* and his Sword, interview with *Breas*, the champion of the *Tuatha Dé* but which is not further spoken of in the battle. cise character of this club, however, we are at present give any account, as no such weapon is now known; but it was probably similar to that recorded to have by the Assyrian contingent in the great army of are described as having been armed with brass helmets, daggers, and "large clubs pointed with iron". What pointed with iron may have been I cannot clearly unless it is meant that the head of the club was mounted spiked ring or head, like the mediæval Mace; and if the case, and that bronze be substituted for iron, existing a few specimens, three only, at the Academy, that description of club-mounting, which will give a of what a formidable weapon this club or mace was, its power must have been in breaking shields and arms and skulls at the same time.

The form of this bronze weapon, however, is opposed I believe to be the Firbolg construction; because not received into the handle, but it receives the handle its cylindrical socket. It is therefore difficult to discover rule derived from the peculiarities recorded in the what party or colony it belonged; but there can be from the specimens known to us that it was invented for the purpose of shattering helmets and shields, belonged to a period of great antiquity, and to a versed in the manufacture of bronze.

No Arrows, Slings, Stones, or Axes, mentioned in connection with the First Battle of Magh Tuireadh. It is remarkable that in this account of the battle or southern *Magh Tuireadh*, there is no mention Bows, Arrows, Slings, Stones, or Battle-Axes, Academy's collection contains many specimens of construction of which agrees with the recorded of both parties; one kind having been received into the handle,[(188)] the other receiving the handle

[(187)] [Fig. 12, (fig. 861, No. 297, Cat. R.I.A.), is of bronze half the real size.]

[(188)] [Fig. 13, (fig. 247, No. 27, Cat. R.I.A.), is 12½ inches long; broad, at the broadest; ⅛ of an inch thick. Fig. 14, (fig. 248,

socket,[188] and both apparently of equal antiquity. It is to be noted, however, as a very remarkable distinction, that while we have axes of very large size and great weight, and of various diminishing sizes, of the Firbolg or wedge-back form, we have not one large or heavy axe of the *Tuatha Dé Danann* or socket-kind, nor has any such been found anywhere else that I am aware of.

The Arms of the *Tuatha Dé Danann.*

Having so far disposed of the arms of the Firbolgs, as described in this first battle of *Magh Tuireadh*, we shall now turn our attention to the arms of the *Tuatha De Danann.*

Descriptions of Arms in the Tale of the Second or Northern Battle, (*Magh Tuireadh na b Fomhorach*).

About thirty years after the battle of the southern *Magh Tuireadh*, the Second called the Northern battle of *Magh Tuireadh*, or more commonly the Battle of *Magh Tuireadh na b-Fomhorach*, was fought between the victorious *Tuatha Dé Danann* and the Fomorians or Sea Rovers. And as their arms are better described in the ancient account of this second battle than in the first, and as they do not appear to have undergone any modification in the intervening time, I shall refer to that account for a description of some curious particulars relating to them.

It is stated, as I have already observed, in all our ancient authorities, that the *Tuatha Dé Danann* were the first to introduce pointed weapons into Erinn; and as these pointed weapons must have consisted, as they are stated to have done, of spears and swords, of various sizes and forms, we have no difficulty in distinguishing them generally from the round-topped weapons of the Firbolgs. In the description in the first battle of the interview between *Breas*, the champion of the *Tuatha Dé Danann*, and *Sreng*, the Firbolg, *Breas* is said to have gone armed with two great spears and a sword; but there is nothing in this allusion to the spears to convey any idea of their particular form or characteristics. The general ancient statement, however, of these spears being pointed, and the fact that no pointed great spear has been found without a socket into which the handle was received, may of itself, I think, be received as some proof that the spears with sockets preserved in the museum of the Academy were really those ascribed to the *Tuatha Dé Danann*.

The Spear of the *Tuatha Dé Danann.*

We are not, however, dependent on mere inference or deduction, as we have in the Tale of the Battle of the second *Magh*

[illegible] natural size), is 7½ inches long, 8¾ thick. Fig. 15, (fig. 249, No. 608), [illegible] inches long, ½ an inch thick. Fig. 16, (fig. 250, No. 135), 7 inches long; [illegible] inches broad. Fig. 17, (fig. 251, No. 145), 7 inches long; 3½ inches broad. Fig. 18, (fig. 256, No. 175), is 4½ inches long. Fig 19, (fig. 262, No. 632), is [illegible] inches long, and 4½ wide in the blade. Fig. 20, (fig. 273, No. 858), is [illegible] times the size represented in the figure.]

[189] [Fig. 21, (fig. 276, No. 444), is 4 inches long. Fig. 22, (fig. 277, No. [illegible]), is [illegible] inches long. Fig. 23, (fig. 282, No. 468), is 4½ inches long.]

LECT. XI. *Tuireadh* such an allusion to the Spear of the [illegible] *Danann*, as leaves no doubt whatever that our [illegible] the first battle are correct.

Of *Breas* and *Nuada* "*airgid-lamh*". After the victory of the *Tuatha Dé Danann* over [illegible] in the first battle, in which *Nuadha* their king lost [illegible] was, consequently, according to our ancient law, [illegible] hold the reins of government), they set up in his [illegible] champion *Breas*, who was, as it happened, of the [illegible] *Danann* by his mother, though a Fomorian on [illegible] his father's side. When *Breas* found himself invested [illegible] supreme power, he began to encourage the visits and [illegible] of the rovers, until by degrees they succeeded in [illegible] ascendancy over the *Tuatha Dé Danann*, laying heavy [illegible] on them. The *Tuatha Dé Danann*, however, though [illegible] to bend their necks to these wrongs and ignominies [illegible] time, did not bend their minds to them, but continued [illegible] years to hold secret councils among their most influential [illegible] wise men; until at last their plans being matured and [illegible] put in execution, they succeeded in banishing their [illegible] king *Breas* from the throne, and recalled thereto their [illegible] monarch *Nuadha*, who had by this time recovered [illegible] wound, and had even, we are told, had a silver arm [illegible] him by the master artists and surgeons of his people.

The three great artificers of the *Tuatha Dé Danann*. The *Tuatha Dé Danann*, according to their history, [illegible] among them three remarkable artizans, namely, *Goibniu* [illegible] smith; *Creidné* the *Cerd*, or worker in gold, silver, and [illegible] and *Luchtiné* the carpenter; and during the three years [illegible] they held their secret councils, they secretly employed [illegible] smith in making spears and swords for the insurrection which they intended to make against their oppressors, and the [illegible] fare which was sure to follow, should they succeed in driving them out.

The forge of *Goibniu*. According to a copy of an ancient tract, prose and verse, [illegible] my possession, the forge of *Goibniu* the Smith was, during these years, situated in the depths of the forest of *Glenn Treithim*, some where near the well-known and since so celebrated hill of *Mullach Maisten* (Mullagh Mast), in the present county of Kildare [illegible] Leinster. The name and situation of this primitive Irish [illegible] were well known at the time of compiling the tract. It was [illegible] called *Cerdcha Ghaibhinn* (or the forge of *Goibniu*) in [illegible] *Treithim*, where the place of the furnace and the *debris* of [illegible] and coals then still remained. As this glenn lay eastwards [illegible] *Mullach Maisten*, and in the direction of the river *Liff* [illegible] there scarcely can be a doubt but that it was situated in the [illegible] ern part of the present county of Wicklow. And the [illegible] this place having been selected for the situation of the forge is quite obvious, when we recollect that Wicklow was at all times known to abound in copper ore, of which metal all those ancient spears and swords are made; and also that the northern parts of the present county of Wicklow, joining and running into the county of Dublin, must of old have contained superior facilities for smelting, since we find that several generations after this period the same district, namely, that of the forests on the east side of the Liffey, is recorded to have been selected by the Milesian monarch *Tighernmas* for the smelting of gold and the manufacturing of vessels and trinkets therefrom.

Unimportant, in some respects, as this tradition of the Forge of *Goibniu* and its peculiar situation may appear to some, the fact of its existence there being handed down and believed from very remote times throws more light on the history of the manufacture of these military weapons in ancient Erinn than anything that has been hitherto advanced on the subject. It is true that although the late lamented John Mitchel Kemble, accomplished scholar and antiquarian as he was, acknowledged that the early manufacture of spears and axes could not be denied to this country, because the ancient moulds for both were found in it, still he appeared to entertain doubts whether swords were also made here; but I trust that an extract which I shall subsequently have to refer to will be sufficient to show that Mr. Kemble's doubts on this subject were not well-founded.

LECTURE XII.

[Delivered 4th June, 1858.]

(V.) Weapons of Warfare; (continued). Of the manufacture [illegible] of arms by the *Tuatha Dé Danann*. No mention made of [illegible] except Swords and Spears, with a single exception only, in [illegible] *Cath Muighe Tuireadh*. Of the Sling-Stone of *Lugh*, and [illegible] "*Balór* of the Evil Eye". Sling-Stones of composition [illegible] the *Tathlum*. Of the *Caer-Clis*; (a missive ball). Of [illegible] *raic*; (a composition ball of several colours). Use of Armour [illegible] of *Magh Tuireadh*. Of the inscribed Sword of *Tethra*. [illegible] charmed weapons. The weapons of the Firbolgs and Tuatha [illegible] Weapons of the Milesians. Of the "broad green" Spear [illegible] troduced by *Labhraidh Loingsech*, (B.C. 307.) The "[illegible] *Táin Bo Chuailgné*. Of the arms used in the time of *Eochaid* [illegible] (B.C. 123.) The Battle of *Ath Comair*;—description of the arms [illegible] and among others of the "Champion's Hand-Stone". ([illegible] *Laich*.) The stone weapon unmeaningly called a "Celt", [illegible] classification of M. Worsaae and other Northern Antiquaries; [illegible] of the "Stone, the Bronze, and the Iron Periods". Sir R. [illegible] J. M. Kemble, as to the arms found at Keelogue Ford. [illegible] "Arrow-Heads" (so called), found in Ireland. Bows and Arrows [illegible] luded to in any of our ancient Historic Tracts.

In considering the arms of the *Tuatha Dé Danann*, [illegible] with the ancient account of the Second Battle of [illegible] *Tuireadh*.

The anticipations of the *Tuatha Dé Danann* were [illegible] the Fomorians collected all their forces, and landed on the [illegible] eastern coast, from which they marched into the [illegible] *Magh Tuireadh*, (in the present county of Sligo,) [illegible] battle was, after some time, fought. The *Tuatha Dé* [illegible] had just at this juncture, we are told, received a great [illegible] to their strength in the person of a young warrior [illegible] people, named *Lug*, or *Lugaidh*; a distinguished hero, [illegible] long been travelling in remote countries, and had [illegible] highly accomplished in the arts and sciences of the [illegible] military and civil; and to this young chief they un[illegible] gave the command and preparation for the battle.

Manufacture and Repair of Arms by the Tuatha Dé Danann.

Lug, accordingly, among many other professional [illegible] called to his presence, the Tale tells us, the three [illegible] whose names I have already mentioned, namely, *Goibniu* [illegible] the Smith; *Creidné*, the *Cerd*, or Gold- and Silver-Smith [illegible]

(190) [This is the form of the name in Cormac's Glossary; gen. [illegible] the St. Gall incantations, according to Zeuss (926). The more mod[illegible] the genitive, according to Prof. O'Curry's MS., is *Gaibhnim* or [illegible]

Luchtiné, the Carpenter; and addressing the smith first, he asked him (according to the curious old tract from which I extract) what aid he could give them in the battle. Then the smith answered:

LECT. XII. Manufacture and Repair of Arms by the *Tuatha Dé Danann*.

"Though the men of Erinn should continue the battle for seven years, for every spear that falls off its handle and for every sword that breaks I will give a new weapon in place of it; and no erring or missing cast shall be thrown with any spear that is made by my hands, and no flesh into which it will enter shall ever taste the sweets of life after; and this", said he, "is more than *Dubh* the Fomorian smith can do".

"And you, *Creidné*", said *Lug* to the Gold- and Silver-Smith, "what aid will you give us in the battle?" "This", said *Creidné*, "Rivets for Spears, and Hilts for Swords, and Bosses and Rims for Shields, shall be supplied by me to all our men".

"And you, *Luchtiné*", said *Lug* to the carpenter, "what aid will you give us in the battle?" "This", said *Luchtiné*, "a full sufficiency of Shields and of Spear-handles shall be supplied by me to them"—(etc.)

When the time of battle came, the Fomorians wondered at what they saw of the arms of the *Tuatha Dé Danann* in the course of the conflict, as the tale relates:

"They saw their own arms, that is, their spears and their swords, injured and useless after the fight; but it was not so with the *Tuatha Dé Danann*, for if their arms were rendered useless to-day, they were in perfect order for battle the next day, because *Goibniu* the Smith was in the forge, making swords, and javelins, and spears; and he made these arms by three turns, or spells, and they were perfectly finished by the third turn. And *Luchtiné* the carpenter made the spear-handles by three chippings, and the third chipping was a finish".

"When the smith had finished a spear-head", says the tract, (describing as usual in exaggerated poetical language the mode of operation, which in substance was that in all probability really pursued by the artificers), "he threw it from his tongs towards the door-post, in which it stuck by the point; and then *Luchtiné* the carpenter had the handle ready, and threw it so exactly that it entered the socket of the spear, and became firmly fixed, that it required no further setting".

Creidné the *Cerd*, again, according to the same authority, (in the same extravagant style of language), made the rivets by "three turns";—"and the third turn was a finish; and then he pitched them from his tongs into the holes in the socket of the spear, so as, without further boring, to pass

LECT. XII.

Manufacture and Repair of Arms by the Tuatha Dé Danann.

through it and the handle, fastening them so quire no further attention".—(etc.)

Then the Fomorians, continues this history, effects of the unfailing weapons of their oppone their people to discover the order and arrange of the *Tuatha Dé Danann*. This man's name he was the son of *Breas* of the Fomorians, but *Brigh*, daughter of *Daghda*, the great chief the *Tuatha Dé Danann;* and on the strength ship he gained free access to their camp. its arrangements, accordingly, *Ruadan* rians, and informed them of the performances the Carpenter, and the *Cerd;* and they sent him instructions to kill the Smith if possible. the camp, therefore, *Ruadan*, we are told, head from the Smith, and its rivets from the handle from the Carpenter, and they were given a fourth artificer is here also mentioned; for we that there was in the camp a woman whose grind the arms on a grinding or whet-stone, and was *Cron*, and that she was the mother of she, says our authority, that ground this new spear who no sooner received it finished, than he smith, and threw the spear at him and wounded him smith drew forth the spear from his own person, *Ruadan* with such force, that it passed through killed him on the spot.

Such is the account given of the arms used by *Dé Danann*, at the battle of the second *Magh* the mode and manner of making, fitting, mounting, ing them. It is extravagant in the details, (as in ing the manufacture and putting together of the there can be no difficulty in extracting the plain from this poetic account of them. And that it supposed that this Tale is merely a romantic one, comparatively modern times, I have the satisfaction the part of it which describes the three artisans, Carpenter, and the *Cerd*, is preserved, word for authority no less respectable than the celebrated piled at the close of the ninth century (nearly years ago), by the learned Cormac MacCullinan, king ster and archbishop of Cashel, who extracts it the old story, and this story must even at that early been very ancient, else Cormac would not have authority as he does. I may add, that it is with

too, apparently, of its historic truth, that he alludes to the Tale, for he refers to a circumstance which he says occurred in the smith's family, whilst he was engaged during the battle in the making of the spears as described.

No mention but of Swords, Spears, and (in one instance) a Sling-Stone in the *Cath Muighé Tuireadh*.

It is remarkable that there is no reference whatever in this tale, any more than in the preceding account of the battle of the Southern *Magh Tuireadh*, to the *Tuatha Dé Danann* having any other arms but swords and spears; nor any reference to arrows, darts, axes, clubs, stones, or slings,—excepting, indeed, that the Sling and a Sling-Stone are once mentioned in it. This sling and stone, however, belonged to, and were used by, the champion *Lugh*, who ordered and conducted the battle on the side of the *Tuatha Dé Danann*, but who may, perhaps, be supposed to have learned the use of the weapon during his long travels abroad.

The Sling-Stone of *Lugh*, and death of *Balór* "of the Evil Eye".

This allusion to the use of the Sling is as follows. In the heat of the battle, a Fomorian warrior and chief named *Balór*, was dealing fearful destruction among the *Tuatha Dé Danann*, not more by the sword and spear, than by a certain natural (or rather very unnatural) gift which he possessed. This was no other, says the tract, than an Evil Eye, which he generally kept covered, but to the effect of which he gave free range in this battle. (And here may be observed an example of the manner in which supernatural powers were, in these historic tracts, just as in Homer, frequently attributed to the more aggressive heroes whose feats are described, as if to account for their intolerable superiority.) Among those who were struck down by the power of this evil eye, according to the story, were *Nuada* "of the silver-hand" himself, the king of the *Tuatha Dé Danann*, and the lady *Macha*, daughter of *Ernmas*; after these deaths it appears *Balór* closed the magical eye again. Thereupon the champion of the *Tuatha Dé Danann*, *Lugh*, [illegible] what had happened, dauntlessly went up, we are [illegible] the tale, to the fierce warrior, whose fatal eye was at [illegible] closed, and denouncing his cruelty threatened him [illegible] death. Then *Balór*, hearing such taunts and [illegible] proceeded to raise the lid of the evil eye; but no sooner [illegible] see the movement of the lid, than he darted a Sling-[illegible] says the ancient writer of the tale, at the eye, which [illegible] attaining its mark, drove it through his skull; and [illegible] *Balór* fell dead among his people.

[illegible] passage it is not said, however, that it was from a [illegible] stone was cast, but only that it was a "sling-stone", a [illegible]"; and whether or not *Lugh* alone of all the warriors [illegible] in this battle was acquainted with the use of the sling, [illegible] no satisfactory means of determining, unless we admit

LECT. XIII. the value of the negative evidence in the first allusion to it is to be found in this ancient to observe, however, that in the Book of Le that it was with a stone from his sling, " killed *Balór*, (who was, we are also told in this story, *Lugh*'s own grandfather).

Sling-Stones of composition manufacture. There is a short but very curious ancient istence, which gives an extravagant origin and composition of this very sling-stone by "evil eye" was destroyed; from which it an artificial composition, a "*tathlum*", or following is a literal translation of the passage:

"A *Tathlum*, heavy, fiery, firm,
Which the *Tuatha Dé Danann* had with
It was that broke the fierce *Balór*'s eye,
Of old, in the battle of the great armies.
"The blood of toads and furious bears,
And the blood of the noble lion,
The blood of vipers, and of *Osmuin*'s
It was of these the *Tathlum* was compos
"The sand of the swift Armorian Sea;
And the sand of the teeming Red Sea;—
All these, being first purified, were used
In the composition of the *Tathlum*.
"*Briun* the son of *Bethar*, no mean warrior,
Who on the ocean's eastern border reigned,
It was he that fused, and smoothly formed,
It was he that fashioned the *Tathlum*.
"To the hero *Lugaidh* was given
This concrete ball,—no soft missile;—
In *Magh Tuireadh* of shrieking wails,
From his hand he threw the *Tathlum*".

Of this very curious poem I have a transcript from the only copy I have ever seen, one cient vellum manuscript formerly in the possession Monck Mason, but lately sold at a public auction

The Tathlum. But this is not the only instance of a *Tathlum* in our ancient writings; for it occurs, though name, in an article on the origin of the name of (now Dublin), in the ancient topographical tract *Dinnseanchas*, preserved in several of our oldest This article gives an account of the death of the from whom the river Liffey derived the name of *D* (the word literally means the Black Pool, if we late the name of the lady *Dubh*);—and the followi verse from it in which such a ball as that of which I have been speaking is mentioned:—

> "*Mairgen* the pure and happy, perceived her,
> He was the high-favoured servant of *Ochinn;*
> He cast a *Caer-Clis* at her path,
> By which he killed the daughter of king *Rodubh*.(191)

This *caer-clis* was a missive ball, though every ball or ordinary missive was not called a *caer*. A *caer* was always a ball formed of many ingredients, and sometimes of many colours; and when it happened to be of a mosaic character, as having many distinct lines or ribs, or ingredients or colours, it was then called a *caer-comraic*, or ball of convergent ribs or lines. The *Caer-Clis*. (a missive Ball).

The stanza quoted above is taken from the Book of Leinster, and the line which runs there, "He cast a *caer-clis* on her path", is written in the same article in the Book of *Lecain* thus: "He cast a stone from his sling on her path"; thus establishing without any doubt that the *tathlum* and *caer-clis* were artificial Sling missives.

From this digression let us return again to the battle-field of the second *Magh Tuireadh*, in the account of which there are still some particulars respecting arms and armour, which we cannot afford to pass over.

It is stated distinctly in the Tale that there was not a chief or a man of valour in the whole army of the Fomorians, who was not furnished with a "*lorica*" on his body, a helmet on his head, a *manais* (or broad-spear) in his right hand, a "heavy sharp sword" at his girdle, and a "firm shield" at his shoulder. And in describing the battle at its greatest heat, the writer again enumerates the weapons which were used by both parties, in the following words: Use of Armour at the Battle of *Magh Tuireadh*.

"Fearful, indeed, was the thunder which rolled over the battle-field; the shouts of the warriors, the breaking of the shields, the [illegible] and clashing of the swords, of the straight tooth-hilted [illegible];—[that is, hilted with hilts formed of the tooth of the [illegible]],—the music and harmony of the 'belly-darts', and [illegible] and winging of the spears and the lances".(192)

[illegible] again, a curious circumstance regarding the construction [illegible] hilted swords is referred to, where the tract records that

(191) Original:—Ros rathaig Mairggin glan grind,
gilla, co n-ard réir Ochind,
focheird chaer clis ar conair,
diar bris ingen rig Rodub.

(192) Original:—Ammas din, an cairneach ruboi and rechnon an catha .i. [illegible] Laechraid, ocus brosnib na sciath; loindrech ocus feadgairi [illegible] ocus na calc n-déd; cairchiu ocus grindegar na saigid-bolc; [illegible] ocus eitigud na sogaid, ocus na ngabluch.

LECT. XVI. in the flight of the Fomorians from the battle... their king, lost his sword. This passage is as fo...

The inscribed Sword of Tethra.

"It was in this battle that *Ogma* the champion... *Ornai*, the sword of *Tethra*, king of the Fomorians... opened the sword and cleaned it. Then the sword... the deeds that had been performed by it; for it was... of swords at this time, when opened, to recount ... had been performed with them. And it is therefore... are entitled to the tribute of cleaning them wh... opened. It is on this account, too, that charms are ... in swords, from that time down. Now, the reason ... were accustomed to speak from weapons at that ... cause arms were worshipped by people in those ... were among the protections (or sanctuaries) of those...

References to charmed Weapons.

There are many references to charmed swords ... be met with in our ancient writings, as will appear in ... of these lectures; but I have never met any accoun... that "spoke", except this; and the legend is, perhaps... unless we take it in the sense that the names of the... deeds in which the sword had been employed had ... scribed on it, perhaps in *Ogham*, or some sort of ... or symbols. I have, indeed, met with a curious in... hilt of a sword being opened in much later though ... times, when an inscription was found on the shank ... cided the ownership. The particulars of this curious ... have to relate on another occasion.

I have been thus tedious in recounting the names ... ber of the weapons which are stated to have been ... ancient battle, in order that no one should have ... that anything has been left out which would in any ... with the opinions which have been for the first time ... in the course of this lecture, on the variety and dis... acters of the offensive weapons mentioned in these ... tracts on the two battles of *Magh Tuireadh*. And ... markable circumstance, and one that ought to stamp ... authority the traditional history of these battles ... that the fewness of the weapons mentioned in the... rangements of the fight described, and the simpli...

(188) original:—Is an cathsin din, fuair Ogmai trenfer ... Techra ri Fomoire. Do sorlaic Ogma in claidem ocus ... and imois in claidem nach(a) ndernad de, ar (ba) bés do ... tan sin do sorsilcitis, do adbadis na gnima do gnethea ... de sin dlegaid claidme cis a nglantai iar na sorlaicad ... forcométar brechta hi claidme ó sin amach. Is aire ... demna d'armaib is an aimsirsin, ar no adradis airm ó ... sin; ocus bado comairchib na haimsire na hairm.

description of it, should bear a character so widely differing from the more glowing, and sometimes I may add much less probable, descriptions of the warfare of subsequent ages.

Distinction between the Weapons of the Tuatha Dé Danann and the Firbolgs.

It will be remembered that the weapons used in the battle of the first, or southern *Magh Tuireadh*, fought between the Firbolgs and the *Tuatha Dé Danann*, were, on the part of the former, first, the *craisech*, or broad-blade spear, with an oval, not a pointed end, not unlike that of a duck's bill; second, the *fiarlann*, or curved blade; third, the sword; fourth, the iron or bronze mounted club; and (probably) a fifth in what may be called the hybrid spear or lance, which embraced the peculiar characteristics of the spears of both parties,—namely, in having a flat blade received by a shank into the handle like the Firbolg weapons, and sharp sides, but no deep socket and swollen centre to receive the handle and receive the blade, like the *Tuatha Dé Danann* spear. These were the well-defined arms of the Firbolgs; while those of the *Tuatha Dé Danann* were, first, the sharp-pointed narrow spear or *sleigh*, for casting,—which had sockets hollowed in the blades, running gradually almost to the very point, and forming on the upper surface either a gracefully diminishing rounded ridge, or more generally a low spine, broad at the bottom, and rising to a sharp external edge;[194] second, the *manais* or broad trowel-shaped spearhead for thrusting, having a socket similar to the *Sleigh*;[195] and third, the *slaidheamh* or sword, generally flagger-shaped and pointed, and invariably double-edged. And in the battle of the second or northern *Magh Tuireadh* we find a distinct account of the manufacture on the spot of the Sword and the Spear, as the only weapons of the *Tuatha Dé Danann*. Whether the spear varied in size we cannot say, nor does the description of the arms of the Fomorians add a single weapon to those, except that the writer makes use of some synonymes. It is remark-

[illegible] [See Fig. 24, (No. 6, fig. 362, R.I.A. Catal.,) is 18¼ inches long. Fig. 25, (No. 26, fig. 364, R.I.A. Catal.,) is 15 inches long. Fig. 26, (No. [illegible], fig. 374) is no less than 26¾ inches long. Fig. 27, (No. 252, fig. 373), [illegible] inches. Fig. 28, (No. 34, fig. 374), is 11½ inches long. Fig. 29, (No. 215, fig. [illegible]), is 5¾ inches long. The illustrations Figs. 30, 31, 32, 33, 34, (figs. 369, [illegible], 385, 386, R.I.A. Cat.), by their shape seem to belong to the class of *manais*, or broad thrusting spear, next described; but their eylet holes, employed to fasten the spur chord used in drawing back the spear when thrown, would show that they were casting spears like the *Sleigh*. Fig. 35, (No. [illegible]), is 4½ inches by 1¾. Fig. 36, (No. 239, fig 370), is 6½ inches. Fig. 37, (No. 191, fig. 384), 7¼ inches. Fig. 38, (No. 192, fig. 385), [illegible] inches long, by 1½. Fig. 39, (No. 234, fig. 386), is 7½ inches long.

[illegible] [Fig. 40, (No. 125, fig. 368, R.I.A. Cat.), is 5¾ inches long, by 2 inches across the widest part of the blade. It is a rude specimen, but presents a characteristic type of the shape above described. The broad spears referred to in the last note may also, perhaps, be classed under this category.]

LECT. XII.

able, too, that neither the *cruisech*, the *fiarlann*, nor the *ferad* (club) of the Firbolgs is at all spoken of in this second battle, from which it might perhaps be inferred that the arms of the Firbolgs had disappeared with their power in the country, and that from that time down the *Tuatha Dé Danann* type, (which appears to be identical with that of the Fomorians), with some variety in the spear as to size and style of manufacture, continued as the universal model in use in all the country.

Weapons of the Milesians.

There is no account preserved of the arms which the subsequent Milesians brought with them at their coming; and no distinction can, therefore, be drawn between them and those of their immediate predecessors, if any such existed. And as we have no detailed description of the various battles which their descendants fought among themselves for many centuries after, we are shut out from all means of comparison. There is, however, in our ancient writings some slight reference to what, perhaps, may be considered the introduction of a new, or at least a modified type, into Erinn, many years after the Milesian conquest, so late as three hundred years before the birth of Christ. This was the "Broad Spear" brought from Gaul by *Labhraidh Loingsech*, whose adventures, it may be remembered, formed the subject of one of the historic tales of which I gave a detailed account on a former occasion,[196] and in which this reference is found.

Of the Gaulish "broad green" Spear introduced by *Labhraidh Loingsech*, (B.C. 307, according to O'Flaherty.)

I shall not here recapitulate the story of Prince *Labhraidh's* flight into France on the murder of his father and grandfather by his grand-uncle *Cobthach Cael*, nor of his subsequent return to Erinn when he grew up to manhood at the head of an army of Gauls given him by the friendly king of that country. The battle of *Dinn Righ*, in which *Labhraidh* and his Gauls slew king *Cobthach* and recovered his kingdom, is placed by O'Flaherty at A.M. 3682, or, according to his chronology, B.C. 307; and the death of *Labhraidh* (who reigned under the title of *Labraidh Loingsech*), A.M. 3696, or B.C. 293. O'Flaherty's account of this king introduces the new weapon brought by him from France, but does not describe it correctly. An investigation of the authorities will, however, I think, make this curious subject clear enough.

O'Flaherty, accounting for the name of the province of Leinster, (*Laighean*), says that "it has obtained that appellation from the word *lancea*, a javelin; and the broad-pointed weapons which these foreigners imported hither, were till then unknown to our countrymen".[197] Now, if O'Flaherty were

(196) See *Lectures on the MS. Materials*, etc., p. 251.
(197) *Ogygia*; vol. ii.; p. 138; (Hely's Translation.)

LECT. XII.

Of the Gaulish "broad green" Spear, introduced by *Labhraidh Loingsech*, (B.C. 307, according to O'Flaherty.)

...in describing the spears or javelins of those Gallic war... who came into Ireland with *Labraidh Loingsech* as "broad-... weapons, the opinion which I have put forward in ... lecture, that this was the peculiar character of the ... of the Firbolgs, would be incorrect. And the authority ...laherty is in general a high one upon such subjects. I ... however, be allowed to say (and I think I can very satis-...ly prove it), that O'Flaherty, in his translation of Irish ..., and in his rendering of passages from ancient Irish ..., is very often inaccurate. And I think a little examina-... will prove the present to be one instance among those of ... of this kind.

...may be remembered that in a former lecture,[198] I quoted ... the Book of Leinster a poem which I endeavoured to ... had been written by *Fercsirtné*, an Ulster poet, who ...ished at the beginning of the Christian Era, and which ... contains the presumed origin of the provincial names of ..., Munster, and Leinster. The following is the stanza of ...portant poem which gives the origin of Leinster:—

"It was *Labhraidh Loingsech* of ample force,
That slew *Cobthach* at *Dinnrigh*;
With a spear-armed host from beyond the broad sea,—
It is from these [spears] that *Laighen* (Leinster) was
named".[199]

...d another stanza, quoted in the ancient tract on the etymo-... of proper names, and which is also quoted by the Rev. ...ting, runs thus:—

"Two hundred and twenty hundreds of Gauls
With broad-spears hither came;
From these spears, without reproach,
It was that Leinster received its name".[200]

... Keating quotes these stanzas; and very strangely precedes ... stanza by the following observations:

"It was by him (*Labhraidh*) that broad-green *laighins* were ...de in Erinn. *Laighins* are the same as *sleaghs* [spears], ... had broad-green heads [or blades] of iron; and it was ... these *laighins* the Gailian province, which is now called

[198] ... ante, Lect. I., p. 3.

[199] ...iginal:—Labparo Loingreċ, lóp a lín,
Ro opt Cobtac i nOinn pig,
Co rlúag laigneċ ᵭap lino lip,
Oib po h-ainmnigṫe Laigin,

[200] ...iginal:—Oá ċét ap ficic ċét n-gall
Co laignib leṫna léo anall;
Oe na laignib rin, cen ail,
Oib po h-ainmnigṫea Laigin.

[... See ante, where the translation of this stanza is somewhat different; that ... given appears to accord better with the original text.]

LECT. XVI. the *Laighin* province, was named[(331)]—[that is the province of Leinster.]

Of the Gaelish "broad green" Spear, introduced by *Labhraidh Loingsech*, (B.C. 307, according to O'Flaherty.) Dr. Keting appears to have departed a little from his accustomed accuracy here, in stating that *Labhraidh* himself was the first to invent or make the "green [spear]", when he had the above two stanzas before him, which state, as do all the ancient prose authorities, that [his] troops brought those particular spears into Erinn [with them from] over. Keting, moreover, adds a very important [statement, if it] were but true; namely, that those broad-green sp[ears were made] of "iron". For this assertion, however, there is [no] foundation, as in no authority in which the [...] these spears is mentioned, is there the remotest [allusion to the] metal of which they were made; but from their [being] called *Laigné Leathan-glasa*, literally "Broad-gre[en spears]", there can be no doubt whatever that the first [...] story had green Bronze spears in their view, and [not] Iron, which never could have been called *glas*, or [green]. [I] need scarcely add that O'Flaherty's assertion, that [these] were "broad-pointed" weapons, had no better foun[dation than] his own mere idea of applying the term "broad" [...] and not to the general shape of the whole weapon, [which is] that is described in the old stanzas from which [...] Keting derived their information.

I have already quoted a verse from an ancient p[oem] that the *Sleagh*, or Spear, of the *Tuatha Dé Danann* [was] also a *laighin*, so that the term *laighin* does not [...] distinction between their spears and those of the G[aedhil; the] distinction is that the latter are, as I have said, [re]presented as being "broad" and "green". I may a[dd that] in all my readings I find that both the *sleigh* and [...] whatever their particular form, were weapons to b[e cast from] the hand, as well as to be used in thrusting into th[e ...] whilst the *manais* and the *craisech* of the later [...] however, are very seldom mentioned as of later [...] mainly used for thrusting or stabbing only.

It would be carrying scepticism to an unreasonab[le length to] deny that those foreigners who came into Erinn in the [reign-] ing of *Labhraidh Loingsech* did, in fact, bring with [them a de]scription of spear which in some particulars differed [from the] weapon of the same kind with which the natives had [...]

(331) original:—"ar leir do ronad laigne leathan-glasa [...] eirinn. Inann, umorro laigne agur rleaga ar a m-bloig [...] glara iarainn; agur ar ó na laignib rin gairmtear laig[...] Gailian rir a raidtear cuigead laigean anir".

remote times acquainted. Nothing else could have induced our ancient writers to notice and put on record such an apparently insignificant incident, if it had not, even during the course of ages, continued to be believed as a fact, and as one, moreover, connected with the distinctive name of the people, and the territory into which they were first introduced.

There is, in my opinion, even still stronger evidence of the authenticity of this ancient story, in the existence, even to this day, of a few specimens of these "broad green" Gaulish spears. I need only refer to the splendid specimen of a broad bronze spear-head, of the most ancient workmanship, in the Academy Museum, one of the most remarkable specimens in the whole collection,[illegible] and then appeal to the eye as to whether this broad spear, with very rounded hips and rapidly tapering point, does not agree fully with the description of the Gaulish spear, the true *laighin lethan-glas*.

Probable variety in the Gaulish Spears.

It is probable that there were much larger specimens of these spears in use in ancient times, though not known to us now; but it is also probable that there was some variety in the shape, and that the *manais*, or trowel-hip, may have characterized some of them at the root with a straighter outline from that to the point. And this also is explainable.

The foreigners who attended *Labhraidh Loingsech* back to his own country were not all of the same nation, but were, we are told, composed of three different sections or parties, under three different names: *Domnans*, *Gailleans*, and *Laighins*. Of these three parties the *Gailleans* appear to have been the bravest and most warlike; and, in fact, they continued to flourish and distinguish themselves in the military affairs of Ireland from the time of *Labhraidh Loingsech* down to the period of the *Táin Bo Cuailgné*, when *Ailill*, the husband of *Medbh*, queen of Connacht, (himself a Leinsterman), invited a body of three thousand of them to take part in that famous cattle spoil.

The *Gailleans* at the *Táin Bo Chuailgné*.

It will be remembered, (for I have given an account of the *Táin Bo Cuailgné* on a former occasion), that preparatory to setting out on this great expedition, the men of Connacht, Munster, and Leinster, assembled at *Rath Cruachain*,—(the royal palace of Connacht, which was situated near the present town of Carrick-on-Shannon in the county of Roscommon). From *Cruachan* they proceeded in the direction of Athlone, in order to cross the Shannon into Meath; and at the end of the first day's march, according to the history, they halted at a place called *Cuil Silinni* (now the name of a parish and church in the

[illegible] This splendid spear-head—Fig 41, (No. 249, fig. 365, R.I.A.)—is 13½ inches long, and 2½ inches broad at the broadest part.

LECT. XIII.

The Gailleans at the Táin Bo Chuailgné.

barony and county of Roscommon). Here [illegible] the night; and it is in reference to this [illegible] tains the following curious allusion to the [illegible] the description of whose activity, dexterity, [illegible] remind us of that of the French troops, [illegible] similar circumstances, on a late remarkable [illegible]

When Queen *Medbh* saw the superior [illegible] leans in providing for the comforts of the night [illegible] she felt jealous of it for her Connacht people, [illegible] leans were her husband's countrymen; and she [illegible] them and even send them back again, lest they [illegible] more of the credit of the expedition, should it prove [illegible] than her own people. The story runs thus:

"Queen *Medbh* did not permit that her chariot [illegible] up or her horses unyoked, until she had gone [illegible] whole camp. Then *Medbh*'s chariot was put up [illegible] unyoked; and she went and sat by the side of [illegible] *Ailill* the son of *Magach*: and *Ailill* asked her [illegible] covered among the troops those who were pleased [illegible] or unwilling to go on the expedition.

"'It is idle for any one to go upon it', said *Medbh* [illegible] one party only, that is the three thousand Gaillean[illegible] good have they done that they are thus praised [illegible] 'They are deserving of praise', said *Medbh*. 'At the [illegible] all others had commenced to make good their [illegible] these had finished their huts and their tents: at the [illegible] all others had finished their huts and their tents [illegible] finished the preparation of their food and drink [illegible] that all others had finished the preparation of food [illegible] these had finished the eating of their meal; at the [illegible] others had finished the eating of their meal, these [illegible] asleep; and in the same way that their slaves and [illegible] have excelled the slaves and the servants of the men [illegible] so also will their brave champions and their brave [illegible] excel the other brave champions and the brave [illegible] the other men of Erinn on this expedition"'.[illegible]

[illegible] original:—Ni aplacair Meob ara cupnta a carpan, no ara [illegible] eiċ co ra lao cop oi ipin ounao. Anopaim ra oiḃairc eoċ [illegible] ra turnac a carpac, ocur oeirio ar láim Ailella mic [illegible] Conporoa Ailill rcéla oi Meob ar co rerrec Meob cia lar [illegible] no nemlainn, no lar mao lorc in rluagao.

Neppać oo neoć a ċriall acc oono aen ṗuallać, ar Meob [illegible] ċrićac céc na nGailleon. Cia maić ro ġniac in ċan molcar [illegible] Ailill. Fail olug molca ṗeirṗo, ar Meob. Oráċ ro ġab [illegible] ocur longpopc oo oenam, ro rcaich ooibrium boċa, ocur [illegible] oenam; orać rorcaich ra caċ boċa acar bélrcalam, [illegible] uprgnam biḋ ocur lenna; oráċ carnaic oo caċ uprgnam biḋ [illegible]

Notwithstanding Queen *Medbh's* jealousy of the brave Gailleans, she eventually consented, though with reluctance, to allow them to share in the expedition; and all our accounts of them testify to the efficiency with which they filled every post of valour and danger which fell to their lot during that tedious war. Such, however, was the envy and jealousy, if not the fears, which their valour and fame had raised against them in the country, that the Druids of Erinn, whether at the instigation of Queen *Medbh* or not I cannot say, pronounced withering satires and incantations against them, (according to the story); so that their whole race became extinct in the land, excepting a few, and these few of the "Gallians", as well as the whole of their fellow foreign tribes, the *Laighinns* and the *Domnanns*, were afterwards totally extirpated by the monarch *Tuathal Teachtmar*, on his accession to the throne of Erinn, A.D. 79.

This is, however, a digression for which I must ask indulgence, while I resume the thread of my account of the various arms known to our early history.

Arms used in the time of Eochaidh Feidhlech, (B.C. 123).

After the reign of *Labhraidh Loingsech* (which terminated, as I have already said, about three hundred years before the Incarnation), we have no account of any particular addition to the national weapons of warfare, down to the time of the monarch *Eochaidh Feidhlech*, whose reign ended 5069, according to the annals of the Four Masters, or B.C. 123, according to their chronology. This monarch was the father of the celebrated *Medbh*, queen of Connacht, of whom we have been just speaking; and besides ... other daughters he had three sons, who were born at ... birth, and were in consequence called *Na Tri Finn Emhna*, ... three Fair Twins" (or Triplets). These young princes ... nursed and educated at the royal palace of Emania in Ul... and as the great House of the Royal Branch was then in ... glory, it is to be presumed that it was there that they re... their military education among the many valiant cham... who then graced it.

Battle of Ath Comair.

The ambition of these brothers grew with their manhood; ... they resolved to request their father, who was then old, to ... the sovereignty of Erinn and the palace of Tara in ... favour. The old king on hearing this request indignantly ... to grant it; whereupon the princes sent him a challenge

... ódibrium praind acas tomailt; tráth roscaich do chách praind acas ..., bacassom na cotlad andsaide. Feib ra deligetar a ndaer... dé doeraib acas mogadaib fer n-Erenn, deligsit a ... acus a ndegóic do deg laichaib acas de degócaib fer n-Erenn ... sor in tslúagad.

LECT. XII.

Battle of *Ath Comair.*

of battle; and collecting a large body of
they marched at their head round by the
Ballyshannon, into Connacht, and did not
the palace of *Cruachan*, in that country.
while was not idle; he collected about him
and all his forces, and marching at their head
wards, he encamped at the hill of *Drum*
cree, in the parish of Kilcumny, barony of
of Westmeath). His rebellious sons
Shannon, and marched directly to *Drum*
took up a position in the immediate neighbourhood
at *Ath Comair*, [the "Ford of the Confluence"]
passes by the hill into *Loch Dairbreck*. The
quotation from the old tract makes mention of
were used on both sides, when the two parties

Descriptions of the Arms used.

"Then the brave battalions on both sides
swelling faces of their bright shields, and with
their broad green *laighins*; and they threw thick
of their battle missiles at each other, until they
easy distance of flying their wide-socketed
spear-like sharp *manaisés*, and they rushed
with their long, narrow, flame-flashing swords

The *Craisech* at this time, I should observe,
having a socket.

And again:

"And it was in such manner that the battalions
each other their red, most venomous, weapons
whirring swift-flying darts, and their sharp-pointed
dripping javelins, and their smooth well-riveted
sleaghs [or spears"].[305]

So far it will be observed that the missive weapons
ral, at both sides, consisted of darts, javelins,
full spears, or *craisechs*.

Of the Arms and mode of fighting of *Lothar* in the Battle of *Ath Comair*; and of the "Champion's Stone".

The particular achievements of each of the three
sons of the king—*Breas*, *Nar*, and *Lothar*—are
in this tract; but as none of them merits particular
here but those of the youngest son, I shall only

(304) original (fol. 18): Is annsin do comraicsead na cath
tarda, do chulaib na sciath sciathda, sgeallbalgacha, ocus do
laigen letan-glas; ocus tucsat frasa trena trena trig,
igtib catha for a cheile, no go rangatar fo fo-chur a craisech
ocus ar a manaisib móra muirnecha, miroir-gera; ocus ro
ceile dib le cloidmib caelfaebracha, coinnill-faebracha.

(305) original (fol. 19): Is amlaid sin tra, ro dicuirsedar na cath
a n-airm gaile ruada, ro neimnecha .i. a saighde sianghaile,
a foghada biorracha braoin neimnecha, ocus a slegha, reimnecha,

much of the text as relates to his share and that of his party in the battle:

Battle of Ath Comair.

"And there came not a man of *Lothar*'s party without a broad-green *laighin* [spear], or without a burnished shield, or without a Champion's Hand-Stone in the hollow cavities of their bent shields. * * * *

"As to *Lothar* himself, he went forward to the brink of the ford, to where he perceived his father; and he saw his father in the middle of the ford, with *Conall Cearnach* on his right, and *Cet*, son of *Magach*, on his left, guarding him. And as each of these men brought a champion's stone, *Lothar* himself came with it likewise; and *Lothar* then raised his arm quickly, and he put the strength of his body to his wrist, and the strength of his wrist to his hand, and the strength of his hand to the champion's stone, and he hurled a straight unavoidable throw of it towards his father, where he stood in the rear of the battle; and he sent the thick stone with a rotatory motion to the middle of the ford, and it sailed directly towards the high king. And when *Cet*, son of *Magach*, and *Conall Cearnach*, son of *Amergin*, saw it, they simultaneously raised their two great shields against it. Notwithstanding this, however, the powerful champion-stone passed between the two, onwards, until it struck the high king fully on the breast, so that it struck him down prostrate across the middle of the ford, with his broad kingly shield and his panoply of valour and bravery laid low in the dark waters of *Ath Comair*, throwing up black frothy blood into the stream.

"The King of Erinn soon started up, however, and he put his foot on the stone where he saw that it fell, and buried it, so that there remains but a third part of it over ground; and he kept his foot on it as long as the battle continued; and it lives still in the ford, and the print of his foot is in it, and will live in it for ever".[306]

(306) original (fol. 28): Ocus ní ṫainic fear do ṁuinntir Loṫair gan laiġin [illegible]glas, ocus gan sgeit ċoinnleaċ, ocus gan lig laṁa laoiċ a ccuas[illegible] na ccrumm-sciaṫ. * * * *
[illegible] Loṫair, immorro, do ċuaiḋ-sen go bruaċ an aṫa, áit a ḃ-facaiḋ a [illegible]; ocus do ċonnairc-sen a aṫair a ccertan áṫa, ocus Conall Cearn[illegible] a deis, acas Cet mac Magach for a ċli agá imċoiméd. Ocas [illegible] tuc gaċ fear a ċloċ leis tuc Loṫar mar an cedna. Ocas ro [illegible] Loṫar iarsin an láṁ go deas, deġtapaid, ocus tuc neart a colna [illegible], acas neart a riġe ar a dorn, ocus neart a ḋuirnn forsan lia [illegible], ocus do rad urċar díreaċ do ḋingbala, d'innsaiġe a aṫar di, áit [illegible] ar ċúl an ċaṫa: ocus do rinne roṫa reimdiubraicṫe don reamar [illegible] lár an áṫa, ocus do ro gaḃ go seolta d'innsaiġe an aird[illegible] do ċonnairc Cet mac Magach ocas Conall Cearnaċ mac Aimir[illegible] sin, ro ṫógbadar an dá sgéiṫ lánmóra an aon-uair ina haġaid. [illegible] acht do ċuaid an lia foirtille feḋma idir in dá sgéiṫ sian, go [illegible] leaṫan ucṫa ocus urbruinne do, n airdriġ, innus gur leag saen, [illegible] for lár-meaḋón an áṫa hé; go na sciaṫ ríoġa, ro leaṫan, ocus

LECT. XVI. I may add to this extract that the three [illegible] defeated, and fled with the remnant of their [illegible] back again over the Shannon, into Connacht [illegible] their father's forces, who overtook and killed [illegible] turned in triumph to the old king.

Of the '*Lia Lamha Laich*', or "Champion's Hand-Stone" Having spoken of this battle more at length [illegible] lectures, I should not have referred to it again [illegible] pose of introducing the important archaeolog[illegible] weapon of offence which appears for the first [illegible] tle of *Ath Comair*, save that it is mentioned [illegible] torical tract which has reference to a period [illegible] fore this, and of which you shall immediately [illegible] weapon of offence is the "*Lia Lamha Laich*", [illegible] Hand-Stone".

It will be observed that this formidable weapon [illegible] of as having been carried by every man in the [illegible] by the men in general of either side, but only [illegible] who belonged to the party of which *Lothar*, the [illegible] three brothers, was commander, and by *Lothar* [illegible] as the army of the rebellious brothers probably [illegible] regulars, taken up chiefly from the people of [illegible] haps, not too much to suppose that those men [illegible] armed with "Champions' Hand-Stones" were [illegible] ticular tribe, or else the natives of some particula[illegible] which the use and manufacture of these stone weap[illegible] generally if not peculiarly practised at the time.

It cannot be supposed for a moment that the "[illegible] *Laich*", or Champion's Hand-Stone, was any [illegible] a stone which offered itself for the occasion. We [illegible] this ancient tale that *Lothar* and his men came with [illegible] "stowed" away in the hollows of their shields; and [illegible] fact of itself implies distinctly enough that the stone [illegible] been of a shape and size the most convenient for [illegible] probably that which was found to be the best [illegible] throwing from the hand, and the best calculated [illegible] for cutting, or for penetrating the object at which [illegible]

The Stone Weapon unmeaningly called a "Celt". Now, it is satisfactory to find all these requisite[illegible] developed in what is unmeaningly called the stone [illegible] Ireland, the simple stone weapon which is so often [illegible]

gona treallaim goile ocus gaisgid, a brotar-linnib [illegible] cuirestar dan-cubar dub-fola tar a bél is in linn.

Ocas ro eirig rig Eirenn suas annsin, ocas an d-[illegible] cloch do tairisin do thuc a chos fuirre, acas ro adnaad is [illegible] fuil acht aen trian ós talmain di; ocas ro chuir a chos [illegible] cur in chatha, ocus mairid fós is an n-ath, ocus slicht a [illegible] mairfid co tig an brath".

from the bottoms of our rivers, and from the depths of our soil, a weapon of which the Museum of the Royal Irish Academy contains a large collection.[207]

The Stone weapon unmeaningly called a "Celt".

This stone weapon being of an oblong form, more or less flattened on two of its four sides, narrowed at one end, and sharpened at both ends, it required no more provision for conveniently carrying it than to nail a strap of leather by both its ends to the concavity of the shield, under which to thrust the stone by its narrow end; and there it safely and without inconvenience remained, on the march and even in the heat of battle, until the time for using it had arrived, when a single instant released it from its mooring, and sent it in its "rotary" course on its deadly mission.

The second effective requirement of the Champion's Handstone was a proper balance, and this our stone "celt" possesses in the highest degree; for, as every one knows, in hurling anything of a conical form from the hand, its power and velocity are greater by holding it by its smaller end than by the larger; and the blow of such a stone, so thrown, is much greater than that of one of which both ends are of the same thickness.

The third requirement was the edge at both ends; so that when either of them struck, the weapon was sure to leave its mark, and should it strike the face or head, was sure to enter, and with such force as easily to pass, as we are sometimes told it did, clearly through the skull from front to back.

That this particular half-flat half-round stone weapon may have been used in cases of necessity as an axe or chisel, in the absence of a better tool, is indeed more than probable; but I cannot at all agree with those who assert, (and I must add without the least authority), that for this purpose it was received into a slit handle, fastened with cement and cord, and that the more it was used the firmer it became fixed in its handle; whereas, the shortest trial would prove that the more such an axe was used the looser it would become, by the wood receding with the pressure of the blows. No, this "Champions' Handstone", if used at all as an axe, must have been held naked in the hand.

There is, however, another description of stone "celt" (as modern theorists call them), much more flat and disproportioned at the ends, and this may have been used, or intended, chiefly as an axe, either to be set in a stick or held in the hand; but even if this be so, let me observe that nothing has been yet

(207) See Fig. 42; (No. 481, fig. 37, Catal. R.I.A.); this is of felstone, 5¾ inches long, and about 2 broad. Fig. 43; (No. 13, fig. 54, R.I.A.); felstone, 13¾ inches long, by 3¾ broad.

LECT. XII. written to prove, or even to show any probability ... these kinds of stone implement was the ... civilized man, in this or the neighbouring countries ... or Scotland, or in Denmark.

Unfounded classification of M. Worsaae, and other Northern Antiquaries; their theory of "the Stone, the Bronze, and the Iron periods".

I am led into these observations from circumstances ... occurred within a comparatively recent period, ... have been put forward, on assumed authority, to ... man in his uncivilized state had first recourse to ... tools of stone for offensive and domestic purposes ... yet learned the art of the fusion and manufacture of ... which, however, he subsequently became gradually ... On this assumption, the Society of Northern A... Copenhagen were, I believe, the first who undert... tematic classification of their great museum of ... quities into three periods or classes, namely, "the S... "Bronze", and the "Iron periods", assuming that ... classes marked a distinct period and people in the ... their country.

M. Worsaae.

The first work in which I saw this theory propo... book written by an able northern antiquarian, M... Worsaae, in the year 1844, on the Primeval An... Denmark; and the following short extract from Tho... translation, (published in London in 1849), will be ... show the whole drift of the original author, and of ... society of which he is, I believe, a distinguished mem...

"As soon as it was first pointed out", says Mr. ... "that the whole of these antiquities could by no m... ferred to one and the same period, people began ... clearly the difference between them. We are now ... pronounce with certainty that our antiquities belong... times of paganism" [which in Denmark, observe, came ... the tenth century], "may be referred to three ... referable to three distinct periods. The first class ... antiquarian objects formed of stone, respecting which ... assume that they appertain to the stone period, as ... that is, to a period when the use of metals was in a great ... unknown. The second class comprises the oldest ... objects; these, however, were not as yet composed of ... of a peculiar mixture of metals,—copper and a small ... tin melted together,—to which the name of 'bronze' ... given; from which circumstance the period in which ... stance was commonly used has been named the bronze ... Finally, all objects appertaining to the period when ... generally known and employed, are included in the third ... and belong to the iron period".

Such are the fundamental dogmas laid down by the northern antiquaries; dogmas laid down, I must say, without any reference whatever to historic or traditionary authority. LECT. XII. M. Worsaae.

Mr. Worsaae, however, is of opinion that the transition from the stone to the bronze period in Denmark, developed itself gradually, or step by step; but that the transition was so marked, that the bronze period must have commenced with the irruption of a new race of people, possessing a higher degree of cultivation than the early inhabitants. Mr. Worsaae then goes on to say (p. 24):

"As bronze tools and weapons spread over the land, the ancient inferior implements of stone and bone were, as a natural consequence, superseded. This change, however, was by no means so rapid as to enable us to maintain with certainty that from the beginning of the bronze period no stone implements were used in Denmark. The universal diffusion of metals could only take place by degrees, since in Denmark itself neither copper nor tin occurs, so that these metals being introduced from other countries, were of necessity expensive, the poorer classes continued for a long series of years to make use of stone as material; but it appears also that the richer, at all events in the earlier periods, in addition to their bronze implements, still used others of stone, particularly such as would have required a large quantity of metal for their formation. In tombs, therefore, which decidedly belong to the bronze period, we occasionally meet with wedges and axes, but most frequently hammers, all of stone, which must have been used at a much later period. A great number of these are very carefully bored through with round metal cylinders. But although implements of stone and bronze were at a certain period used together, yet it is an established fact [!] that a period first prevailed during which stone alone was used for implements and weapons; and that subsequently a time arrived when the axe of bronze appears to have been the all-prevailing custom".

These very plausible archæological dogmas of the Northern Antiquaries were received with seeming satisfaction and perfect faith by, I believe, the far greater part of the antiquarians of Europe, but perhaps less generally in Dublin than anywhere else. The Northern Antiquaries were, however, greatly sustained in their opinions, if not primarily set in motion, by a communication made to the Royal Irish Academy on the 9th of January, 1843, by Mr. (now Sir Richard) Griffiths, chairman of the commissioners for improving the navigation of the Shannon, on the occasion of presenting to the Academy a large and important collection of weapons and other implements in

LECT. XII. stone, bronze, and iron, turned up when ... the river, at the ancient ford of Keelogue, ...

Sir R. Griffiths.

After some observations on the ... ford, as the chief pass from the counties of ... into the county of Tipperary and the King's ... employment by the commissioners of ... their plans, Sir Richard Griffiths proceeds: ...

"Towards deepening this ford the contract... portion of the river one hundred feet in width, ... dred feet in length, and have commenced ... nearly six feet in depth; the material to be ... at the top of two feet of gravel, loose stone, ... the bottom, of four feet of a mass composed of ... limestone, which, in some parts was found to ... compact, that it became necessary to blast it ... in preference to excavating, according to the ... through detrital matter. * * * * * *

"I have already mentioned that the ... the excavation consisted of two feet of loose stones, ... sand, and the lower part of four feet of a very ... composed of indurated clay and rolled limestone. ... in the loose material of which the upper two ... posed, the labourers found in the shallowest part of ... considerable number of ancient arms, consisting ... swords, spears, etc., in excellent preservation, which ... lar to those which have been frequently discovered ... parts of Ireland; and towards the lower part of the ... feet they discovered a great number of stone hat... similar in many respects to those which have so ... been met with in different parts of this country. ... to the stone hatchets, I would merely observe, that ... number, which are black, are composed of the ... called Lydean stone, which occurs in thin beds, ... with the dark gray impure limestone called Calp, which ... dant in the neighbourhood of Keelogue and Banagher; ... others, some of which present a blueish gray, and ... lowish colour, are composed of a sub-crystalline and ... igneous porphyritic rock, none of which occurs in ... bourhood, or possibly in the south of Ireland. ... probable that the latter, which are much more perfe... cuted than the black, or those composed of Lydean st... brought from a distance, and probably from a foreig...

"The important and interesting subject for conside... the antiquities before us is, that they are evidently ... very different and probably distant periods. Owing ...

rapidity of the current at Keelogue ford, it is extraordinary that any comparatively recent deposit should have been formed, and at all events the annual increase must have been inconsiderable; hence, though not more than one foot of silty matter may be found between the stone weapons of a very remote age, and the swords and spears of another period still remote from us, yet under the circumstances described, centuries may have intervened between the periods of mortal strife which must have taken place in the river probably between the Leinstermen and Connaught men of old, disputing the passage of the river at two distinct, and, no doubt, very distant, periods".[308]

LECT. XII.

Sir R. Griffiths.

This description of the discovery of the Keelogue antiquities would be much more interesting and valuable if Sir Richard Griffiths had given us his ideas as to the probable length of time which the condition of the ford would allow to expire for the formation of the one foot of loose stone and gravel which appears to have intervened between the metal and the stone weapons found in it. It would also be satisfactory if Sir Richard Griffiths, as well as other writers, could have set some probable limits to what they call "a very remote age", and "a period still remote from us". This, however, neither he nor any one else that I am aware of has attempted to do, so that we are left by them without any resting point in the history of man's existence from the beginning of the world down to almost our own times. There is a general belief (in Ireland at least) that with the introduction of Christianity into Ireland in the fifth century, the use of bronze as the material of military weapons and mechanical implements gave way to the more enduring and efficient materials of iron and steel. And assuming this probability as a guide, and supposing that the bronze weapons discovered in the Keelogue ford had been dropped there in the third century, and the stone weapons six hundred years before that, I should then be glad to know whether these two periods—both of them remote enough in our views—would in any way approximate to Sir Richard Griffiths' notion of "a very remote age", and of "a period still remote from us".

Vaguely, however, as Sir Richard Griffiths, Mr. Worsaae, and some other writers of a somewhat earlier period, have touched upon the times to which the stone and the bronze weapons might be referred, a gentleman not inferior at least to any of them, as a scholar, a philosopher, and an antiquarian, has within a recent period offered so strong and decided an opinion

(308) *Proceedings of the Royal Irish Academy*, vol. ii., p. 313.

LECT. XII. on the length of time which must have intervened [illegible] deposits of the stone and the metal weapons in [illegible] ford,—though still proposing no positive [illegible] either,—that it is impossible to consider the [illegible] vations without some degree of impatience, [illegible] This opinion was expressed by the late lamented [illegible] learned John Mitchell Kemble, in an address on "[illegible] antiquarian collections, as throwing light on the [illegible] annals of the European nations", delivered by him [illegible] Royal Irish Academy, February 9th, 1857. The [illegible] the passage in Mr. Kemble's Address in which he [illegible] opinion to which I have alluded:

Mr. J. M. Kemble.

"There is no doubt, gentlemen, that in the earli[illegible] culture, weapons and implements are formed of the [illegible] terials accessible to man; that he is acquainted with [illegible] horn, and stone, before he obtains a sufficient master[illegible] metals to convert them to the purposes he desires; [illegible] ingly, we do find implements or weapons both [illegible] stone, to the exclusion of the metals, at periods [illegible] lessons of geology compel us to place at an almost [illegible] tance from our own. I would remind you of the [illegible] the commissioners for the improvement of the navi[illegible] Shannon. The men of science connected with [illegible] dertaking will assure you that the lowest stratum [illegible] of human life contained implements of stone and [illegible] below the first appearance of implements of metal, [illegible] an almost *incalculable* lapse of *centuries* between [illegible] posits".

These are certainly high-sounding words and [illegible] tions, and assertions which, if true, it would be very [illegible] bring within the range of man's received creation; [illegible] nately, they cannot be correct, since, according to [illegible] of the Shannon commissioners themselves, the stone [illegible] found in the Keelogue ford were but *a foot* of "[illegible] gravel, and sand", below the bronze weapons; and [illegible] one will believe that "an incalculable lapse of cent[illegible] required to produce this foot in depth of a deposit [illegible] stones, gravel, and sand" in the mighty waters of the [illegible]

It appears, however, that Mr. Kemble acted on inaccurate [illegible] aggerated information on this occasion; and as it was [illegible] that was never believed by myself, I took occasion at the [illegible] of the Royal Irish Academy held on the 8th of Febru[illegible] to put the question to the president, the Reverend D[illegible] to the authority on which Mr. Kemble's statement [illegible] To this question Dr. Todd answered that Mr. Kemb[illegible] vations were incorrect, and had in fact arisen from a mere mistake; and Dr. Wilde in addition said that he had lately waited on Sir Richard Griffiths and others of the Shannon commissioners, to ascertain if there had been any error in their communication to the Academy as to the facts of the case; that is, whether there was really but one foot of loose stuff between the bronze and the stone implements; and they all stated positively that there was not; and more, that there was no evidence whatever to show that they were not found mixed up together. I may remark, however, that this was the first time that Sir Richard Griffiths' and Mr. Kemble's error was publicly announced in the Academy.

The arms found at Keelogue Ford.

And now I, for my part, question much whether even any appreciable period of time must, of necessity, have elapsed between the deposits of the stone and the metal implements found at Keelogue. If we consider the shape and weight of a cylindrical stone from four to six or seven inches long, and weighing from two to four pounds; and the shape as well as the weight of a spear from twelve to sixteen inches long, and weighing, independently of its long handle, two pounds; and the shape and weight of a sword twenty or twenty-six inches long, and weighing three pounds; and if we consider the extent of superficial surface which each of those implements covers, and the resistance to their sinking which that extent of surface presents,—particularly in a bed of "loose stones, gravel, and sand", constantly undergoing disturbance from the current of water which flows over it;—if, I say, we consider all these circumstances, our wonder will not be that the shorter thicker more compact and heavier stones have gone down to a far greater depth than the lighter less compact and more lengthy implements of metal and timber, but that they have not gone to a much greater depth, which they certainly would if the same layer of "loose stones, gravel, and sand" had been deeper.[209] Whatever inferences or evidences, therefore, might reasonably be drawn from the fact of finding implements of stone and horn at lower depths than bronze or iron ones, in situations not liable to the disturbing influences of unequal resistance or natural or accidental pressure, no such deductions can, I think, be fairly drawn from the two deposits found in the Keelogue ford. And here I may add, that no implements of horn, such as Mr. Kemble speaks of, have been ever found in Ireland, as far as I am aware of.

Of the flint "arrow-heads" found in Ireland.

To the same remote and indefinite antiquity as that given to the stone "Celts", as these antiquarians insist on calling them,

[209] See, as to this question, INTRODUCTION.

LECT. XII. are also referred the barbed flint "Arrow-Heads
with above and below the surface of the land
plements which have, however, I may observe
greater quantities in the north than in any of the
the country.

Why or how these generally beautifully
formed implements could be charged to man's
cultivation, I confess myself at a loss to
appear to have been formed on the model of
described as the Trowel-shaped Spear of the *Tuatha*
nann; the barb of the "arrow" commencing where
the spear commences, sometimes forming a deep
the broad end of the "arrow", and leaving no
to be received into the shaft;[210] in other instances
between the barbs;[211] and in a third class neither
shank, such as I have mentioned, but a continuous
part behind the hips,[212] more or less extended and
which, if ever mounted, it was held in the slit end

It is to be noticed that the barbs are seldom, if ever
to a sharp point, and that in most cases, instead
outwards, like the generality of arrows of the
times of the use of the bow and arrow, they are
wards, so that if the tapering outlines were con
would meet in an obtuse point at a short distance
hips.

Bows and Arrows not alluded to in any of our ancient Historic Tracts.

It is remarkable that in none of our more ancient
or romantic tracts, is there any allusion whatever to Bows
Arrows; and what is more remarkable, indeed I might
what is more important, there is no model found for
the other stone and metal weapons which have come
from the ancient times, either in Erinn or any of the
bouring countries. No barbed implement in ordinary
bronze has been yet discovered; nor has there been ever
in Erinn, as far as we know, a flint arrow-head in con
with any one or more bronze spears, darts, or swords.

It is quite clear that if the barbed arrow had been known
the *Firbolgs* and the *Tuatha Dé Danann* at the battle of
Tuireadh, they would have used it; and we would undoubt

(210) [See Figs. 44, 45, and 46; (Figs. 10, 12, 13, Nos. 514,
R.I.A.), same size as originals.]

(211) [See Figs. 47, 48, 49, 50, and 51; (Figs. 15, 17, 18, 19,
658, 657, 716, 724, Cat. R.I.A.), same size as originals.]

(212) [See Figs. 52 and 53; (Figs. 22, 27, Nos. 771, 954, Cat. R.I.A.)
size as originals. The last is of large size, but all the smaller heads
likely to have belonged to the small casting-spears which we
used (as in the combat between *Cuchulainn* and *Ferdiadh* in
Chuailgne), as to "arrows", of which we have no record.]

have specimens of it among the immense number of their other bronze weapons which have certainly come down to our times; and not only that, but its efficiency and convenience, I should say, would be so obvious to their successors in all after ages, that (from its peculiar liability to be lost when once shot) in place of its total non-existence in metal, thousands of bronze arrow-heads would long ere this have been picked up in all parts of Ireland. LECT. XII.

Resting on these reasons, then,—reasons drawn from a history not yet overthrown, nor likely to be,—I have come to the conclusion that the barbed "arrow"-head is not, in Ireland at least, a weapon to be referred to man's uncultivated state, but a new weapon either devised or brought into Ireland within her undoubted historic period, and manufactured, whether here, or wherever else, by a people who had been well acquainted with the best types of the metallic spears.

Finding flint and bronze spears and "arrows" in the same spot, or in the same grave, in Denmark or in Britain, cannot shake the opinions that I have put forward; since it is, I believe, well known that the general use of brass or bronze came down to a much later period in those countries, especially the first, than in Ireland. I have yet, however, something more to say here, both as to the Champion's Hand-Stone, and the first probable introduction of the barbed "arrow"-head into this country.

LECTURE XIII.

[Delivered [illegible]]

(V.) Weapons of Warfare; (continued). Of the [illegible] of *Aenach Tuaighé*, B.C. 160; temp. *Congal* [illegible] 161). Of the use of "Round Stones" in battle. [illegible] *nech*. Use of the "Champion's Hand-Stone" by [illegible] use of stone missiles in general. Use of the "[illegible] Siege of *Drom Damhghairé*, (A.D. 270.) Use of [illegible] Description of the form of his Hand-Stone. Story [illegible] of *Enna Cennselach* (circa A.D. 400); and of the death [illegible] Hostages" by an Arrow, A.D. 405. Of the Sling, and [illegible] Eriun. The *Caer Chlis*, or Sling-Stone, at the [illegible] *sadh*. Of the story of *Dubh-lina*. Death of queen [illegible] Shape of the Sling-Stone. Use of Sling-balls of [illegible] the Sling by *Cuchulaim*. Of the *Taball*. Of the [illegible] *Deil-Chlis*. Of the *Tailm*.

The next reference to stone weapons belong[illegible] shortly anterior to the battle of *Ath Comair*, [illegible] the last lecture, and should have taken prece[illegible] battle, but that the coincidence of the broad [illegible] which we had been previously speaking, and the [illegible] *Láich* or Champion's Hand-Stone happening to [illegible] together in that tract, induced me, at the expense [illegible] anachronism, to let that transaction take precedence [illegible]

Of Congal Cláiring- nech; (Monarch B.C. 161.)

The monarch *Eochaidh Feidlech*, the principal [illegible] mentioned in the battle of *Ath Comair*, assumed the [illegible] B.C. 111, according to the Annals of the Four Masters [illegible] *Congal Cláiringnech*, of whom I am now to speak, [illegible] monarch B.C. 161, or forty-one years before *Eochaidh* [illegible]

This *Congal Cláiringnech* was the son of *Rudhraighe* [illegible] monarch; but three kings in succession had intervened [illegible] the reigns of the father and the son. Of these [illegible] was *Lughaidh Luaighné*, who, when he came to the [illegible] gave the provincial kingship of Ulster to the prince [illegible] *Leité*, to the prejudice of *Congal Cláiringnech*, the [illegible] former monarch, and hereditary king of Ulster. *Congal* [illegible] venge for this affront and wrong headed a large body of [illegible] followers consisting of displeased or disaffected men [illegible] rent parts of the country, and on his way home from [illegible] an adverse decision had been given against his claim, [illegible] the son of the monarch, *Lughaidh Luaighné*, he slew [illegible] gether with the chief part of his attendants; and then, after ravaging and devastating his native province, looking for a secure defensive position, he marched with his followers to a place called *Aenach Tuaighé*, at the mouth of the river *Bann*. Here he took up as strong a post as circumstances would allow him, and awaited the issue. He had not long to wait; he was speedily overtaken, and challenged to battle by *Fergus Mac Léidé*. A battle accordingly took place; and though *Congal* was victorious, he deemed it prudent to leave the country, and to wait for a more favourable time to assert his right to the sovereignty of his native province.

Arms used in the Battle of *Aenach Tuaighé*; (B.C. 160.)

The following short passage from the ancient historical account of the Battle of *Aenach Tuaighé* gives us the names of the weapons which the combatants used on the occasion:

"And then both parties of them advanced upon each other with long blue darts, and with sharp, bloody spears, and with round [or globular] stones; after which they had recourse to their thrusting and striking weapons, until slaughtered hosts had fallen there".[313]

In this passage we have nothing new as regards weapons except the reference to "globular stones"; save that the long "blue" darts may argue an iron and not a bronze material in that weapon. On this last matter I have but one remark to offer; namely, that the word *gorm*, which I translate "blue", means a colour certain shades of which so nearly approach the green called *glas*, that the word might possibly be applied to a weapon of that tint. It is possible, however, that the use of iron had either been discovered or introduced into Erinn at this time, for we certainly find frequent reference to it shortly after the same period, in the Tale of the *Táin Bo Chuailgné*; though not to the exclusion of bronze, as we shall see bye-and-bye.

Of the use of "round stones" in battle.

The reference to the general use of round stones in this battle is curious indeed; but the round stone must not be taken to be the same as the *Lia Lamha Laich* or "Champion's Handstone"; for the latter weapon was apparently always reserved for some particular occasion, or opportunity of a more important character, in some difficult contest of skill; while the round stones are here represented as having been cast promiscuously with the darts and spears, on the advance of both parties to the close combat in which their "long heavy spears", and their "broad green spears" for thrusting, and their swords for cleaving, were called into requisition.

(313) Original:—Iṡ annṡin ro innṡaiġ cáċ a ċéile díb do ḟoiġdiḃ ṡíoċ-ḟada, ocuṡ do ġaiḃ faebraċa, fuileaċa, ocuṡ do ċlaċaiḃ cruinne; ocuṡ ro [illegible] iar ṡin ar na h-armaiḃ iomgona, ocuṡ iombuailte, co ndorċ[illegible] [illegible] tuiġ-ár na ṡloaġ.

LECT. XIII.

It is remarkable that in no details of any [illegible] after this Battle of *Aenach Tuaighé* is there any [illegible] "showers" of stones such as we have here, down [illegible] fought near Limerick by the celebrated *C*[illegible] against the Danes, so late as about the year [illegible] is stated (Book of Lismore) that "their youths, [illegible] and their proud, haughty veterans, came to the [illegible] battle to cast their stones and their small arrows [illegible] and their smooth spears, on each side, at one another [illegible]

Story of *Congal Cláiringnech.*

To return to *Congal Cláiringnech*: After the Battle of [illegible] *Tuaighé*, he passed, with a band of followers, into [illegible] and took military service from the king of that [illegible] here, as always in the adventures of the brave, a [illegible] romance is introduced into the narrative. The king [illegible] navia, or *Lochlainn*, had a beautiful daughter, who [illegible] fell in love with the exiled Ultonian prince; but as he [illegible] gifts or dowry to bestow on her, according to the [illegible] her own country, he declined her hand until he should [illegible] by his valour some precious object, such as she should [illegible] out to him. So she requested of him to obtain for her [illegible] beautiful birds which perched on the shoulders and [illegible] amazon *Saighead*, the daughter of *Carrtann Cas*, the [illegible] dian of the castle of the amazon *Muirn Mollbhach* [illegible] and his party accordingly set out by sea to reach this [illegible] castle, which was situated on the eastern shore of a [illegible] in the story "the cold country", (probably Iceland,) [illegible] time they reached.

When they approached the fortress and landed upon [illegible] *Saighead* came out to meet them; but as she came [illegible] her three beautiful birds began to sing so enchanting [illegible] such plaintive and soothing tones, that *Congal* and all [illegible] ple, who heard it, fell insensibly into a deep sleep, [illegible] *Fergus Mac Róigh* alone. And the following passage from [illegible] old tale tells how *Fergus* escaped the potent spell:—

Use of the "Champion's Hand-Stone" by *Fergus Mac Róigh.*

"In short, sleep fell on them all except *Fergus* alone [illegible] what saved him from sleep was this: he plucked the [illegible] brooch which was in his cloak out of it, and he began to [illegible] his feet, his fingers, and his palms with it; and looking [illegible] and seeing all the people asleep, it became certain to him [illegible] what their Druid foretold of their expedition was about [illegible] fulfilled; whereupon, he put his hand into the hollow [illegible]

(214) original: do riaccader a n-óig, acas a n-errid, acas a n-[illegible] foruallach a núrcorać na hirgaile, do caiteṁ a cloć acas a [illegible] acas a coirr-sleg da gać leit.—(B. of Lismore, fol. 149 a.)

LECT. XIII.

shield, and drew forth from it a *Leacán Laoich Milidh*, [that is, a 'Champion-Warrior's semi-flat Stone'], which he threw with brave and manly force; and it struck the hag on the front of her skull, through which it entered, and carried with it its own measure of her black face and brain out through the back of her head, so that the hag fell dead in the middle of the strand".[218]

Here then is a description of the "Champion's Hand-Stone", so particular that no one can mistake its form. It was *leacán*, that is a "half" or modified "flat stone"; for *leac* means a perfectly flat stone, so that *leacán* must mean a stone partaking somewhat of the flat form, but not entirely flat; and, than this, no more accurate description need be desired of those stone implements in our museums which it has been the unmeaning fashion to call "celts".

It will have been observed too, that like the prince *Lothar* and his men at the Battle of *Ath Comair*, described in the last lecture, *Fergus* had his *leacán* hid away in the hollow of his shield, in reserve for some important feat of valour and victory; and that, therefore, it could not have been an ordinary stone picked up for the occasion; nor, on the other hand, one of those "round" stones which were used generally by both parties, at the battle of *Aenach Tuaighé*.

Of the use of missiles of stone in ancient Erinn.

So far I have been speaking of military and offensive weapons in the chronological order in which they happen to be mentioned, in such ancient Irish documents as have come under my notice; but as the subject of scientific stone missiles has been introduced, it is one that would suffer by dispersion; and I shall, therefore, add here the few other references to them which I have been able to collect, in chronological succession as regards themselves, though I shall have to return again in order to take up the remaining metal weapons in their proper chronological order.

My reason for dwelling so much and so particularly on these stone weapons is, to show by all the evidences within my reach, that the *Lia Lámha Láich*, or Champion's Hand-Stone, or by whatever other name it was designated by different writers, was not an ordinary chance stone which a man may pick up any-

[218] Original:—Cid ṫra, aċt do ṫuit a ccodlaḋ uile orra, aċt Fearġus [illegible] aonar; acus aread tuc dorum gan codlaḋ eḋon, tug an dealg óir do [illegible] ina ḃratar, acus do ġaḃ ag guin a ċroiġed acus a ṁér, acus a ḋean-[illegible]. Ocus do féc tairis ocus do connairc an sluaiġ uile ina codlaḋ, [illegible] lais go tiucfaḋ fairoine an Druaḋ dóiḃ, ocus tuc a láṁ a cob-[illegible] a roiċh, ocus tuc leacán laoiċ miliḋ as, ocus tuc urċar ferḋa [illegible]ṁail de go tarla a ttul a cruaiḋ ċinn don ċailliġ, go ruc a coiṁeis [illegible] a duiḃéḋain tré na ceann siar seaċtair, gur ṫuit an ċailleaċ [illegible] lár na tráġa.

[illegible] where, but a stone of a particular shape, and [illegible] chance or random shots but for a proper [illegible] portant object.

The next reference to this Champion's Hand [illegible] find is one that contains some legendary [illegible] ment, and teaching which the story through [illegible] much of the marvellous to be available as history [illegible] legitimate and in point as regards the weapons [illegible] present object to draw from it.

Of the "Champion's Hand-stone" at the Siege of Drom Damhghairé. (A.D. [illegible])

It will be remembered that in two former lectures [illegible] myself to the subject of Druids and Druidism in [illegible] One of these lectures[118] was chiefly devoted to [illegible] feats of the Druid *Mogh Ruith*, at the siege of [illegible] ghairé, in Munster; and the reference to the *Lia* [illegible] I am now about to call your attention occurs in the [illegible] count of this siege.

The battle was fought between *Cormac Mac* [illegible] reigned as monarch of Erinn from A.D. 227 to 266 [illegible] *Muilleathan*, king of Munster, who had refused [illegible] demands of the chief king for a double tribute on [illegible] that Munster included two kingdoms in one. [illegible] *Drom Damhghairé* is that now called Knocklong, [illegible] the south-east corner of the county of Limerick; and [illegible] this hill that *Cormac* pitched his camp, from which [illegible] indeed its present name is derived.

Powerful as *Cormac*'s army was, he had, it would [illegible] more confidence in the magical power of his druids [illegible] good many of the most celebrated attended him; and [illegible] to the singular tract from which I quote, the [illegible] power soon made the Munstermen feel that they [illegible] must have recourse to superhuman agency to [illegible] fluences so baleful, since all their natural efforts had [illegible] do so. It was on this account that, according to the [illegible] sent an urgent message with offers of large and [illegible] to the old Druid *Mogh Ruith*, (who then resided [illegible] *Dairbré*, now the well-known island of Valencia, on [illegible] of Kerry), begging of him to come to their assistance [illegible] druid complied; and he had no sooner arrived at the [illegible] action than he made the monarch's druids feel themselves [illegible] presence of a superior power.

King *Cormac* himself, we are told, soon perceived [illegible] ness of his druids, and reproached them sharply for [illegible] which *Colptha*, one of the chiefest among them, [illegible]

(118) Lect. x.; *ante*, p. 212.

Of the "Champion's Hand-Stone" at the Siege of Drom Damhghaire. (A.D. 270.)

and goes forth to the ford which lay between the two armies, for the purpose of giving single combat. *Mogh Ruith*, who was blind, is told this, whereupon he calls up his pupil and companion, *Ceannmhor*, and orders him to go to meet the druid *Colptha*, at the ford, and give him combat.

Then *Mogh Ruith* says to *Ceannmhor*:

"Let me have my poison-stone and my *Lia Láimhé*, and my 'victory over an hundred', and my 'destruction upon my foes'. And the stone was given to him; and he began to praise it; and putting poisonous charms into it, he pronounced the following address to it:

"I beseech my *Leo Láimhé*, [Hand-Stone]—
That it be not a flying shadow;
Be it a brand to rout the foes,
Before the brave host of *Clairé*, [Munster].

"My fiery hard stone,—
Be it a red water-snake;—
Woe to him around whom it coils,
Betwixt the swelling waves.

"Be it a sea eel, like a seal,—
As long as seven ox-horns;
Be it a vulture among vultures,
Which shall separate body from soul.

"Be it an adder of nine coils,
Around the body of gigantic *Colptha*,—
From the ground into his head,
The smooth spear-headed reptile.

"The spear-armed, royal, stout wheel
Shall be as a galling, strong, thorny briar;
Woe is he around whom it shall come,
My fiery, stout, powerful dragon.

"Nobles and authors shall relate
The woe of those whom it shall reach;
The high valour of *Colptha* and of *Lurga*
It shall dash against the rocks.

"The prostrate one which it prostrates,
In bonds shall it bind;
The bonds which it binds on,
Are like the honey-suckle round the tree.

"Their ravages shall be checked;
Their deeds shall be made to fail;
Their bodies shall be food for wolves;
At the great ford of slaughter.

"So that children might bear away,
Without combat and without conflict,

SOC. XIII. Of the Champion's "Hand-Stone" at the Stage of Drom Damhghaire.

Their trophies and their heads,
If such were what they sought. [I. [illegible]

It will, I think, be pretty clear to everyone [illegible] of this extraordinary poetic address was no [illegible] one that had not on previous occasions given [illegible] deeds which it was invoked to perform on this [illegible] not to be sought from it in vain. And so it [illegible] when the druid *Ceannmhor*, *Mogh Ruith's* favourite [illegible] companion, comes to the ford of combat to meet [illegible] *mac's* chief druid, hand to hand,—and when the [illegible] height between them, and *Ceannmhor* is getting [illegible] it,—he suddenly pulls out the stone, and casts it [illegible] where they fought; and, according to this strange [illegible] sooner did the enchanted stone touch the water [illegible] changed into a monstrous snaky eel, which, coiling [illegible] legs and body of the Druid *Colptha*, brought him [illegible] the ground, and there detained him fast until *C*[illegible] off his head, and returned himself in triumph to [illegible] and friends.

On the following day, according to this tale, *Ceannmhor* [illegible] again challenged to the combat by *Lurga*, another [illegible] *mac's* chief druids; and they repaired to the same [illegible] the previous day, as the story says:

"*Ceannmhair* went towards the ford with his [illegible] in his hand; and he began to praise it, and to implore [illegible] foretell the slaughter which it would perform; and he [illegible] his gods, and the chief druid of the world, namely, *Mogh* [illegible] and he said:

(317) original:—Dom roiched mo ċloċ neime, ocus mo lia [illegible] mo ċomlann cét, ocus mo dichugad ar mo naimdib. [illegible] ocus ro bói ica molad, ocus ag cur breaċta neime inni, [illegible] in retoiric so:

ailim mo lic láime,
narab taidbri taidi,
bid breo brissfeas báiri
re cat cróda Cláiri.
Mo ċloċ teinntiġeaċ teann
bid naċair dearg dobair
mairg gus a bhfillfid a fortuim
iter ċonnaib treall.
Bid muireascaing, mulaċ,
fod fect congna rodaim,
bid badb ider badbaib
sceaṁas corp re hanmain.
Bid naċair noi snadma
um ċorp Cholpa allmair,
o ċalam co a ċeann
an boic sleaṁain birceann.
In roċ ruibneaċ rigteann
bid uir agarb imċeann,
mairg a tiosa [illegible]
mo draic ċairpċeaċ [illegible]
Cantait dair is [illegible]
mairg co a [illegible]
ardgail do colpa [illegible]
Laisid ear re all[illegible]
In trasrad nos [illegible]
is fasdad nos [illegible]
is nascad nos [illegible]
mar bis rénd [illegible]
Coisceidear a [illegible]
meaċsaidear a [illegible]
beit a cuirp ra co[illegible]
ar aċ olam [illegible]
Comberdais leo [illegible]
cin troit is [illegible]
a cosnam re a [illegible]
cemad eaċ bud [illegible]

LECT. XIII.

Of the "Champion's Hand-Stone" at the Siege of *Drom Damhghaird*.

"A flat stone, a flat stone;
 A stone that will kill as before;
 A narrow stone, a thick thin stone;
 A choice weapon for success.
"A stone that will cut, a stone that will cut,
 Over well secured shields;
 A stone that will spring over waves,
 Without stooping or curving.
"As thou hast overpowered in the contest,
 By hardy valour, *Colptha;*
 Go forth strongly in fierce action,
 Until by thee shall *Lurga* fall.
"A valuable stone, a precious stone,
 A guardian stone, a thunderbolt stone,
 A powerful stone, an accurate stone,
 An expedition stone, a victorious stone.
"*Ethor's* stone, Daniel's stone,
 A hard stone, a battle stone;
 Mogh [*Ruith*]'s stone, Simon's stone,
 An immense stone, a swift stone.
"A stone to relieve the fears of Munstermen,
 A stone ready to fly without command,
 A stone of power, a stone of death,
 A noisy stone, a silent stone.
"A stone that will fill the ford
 Into sweeping-torrent dimensions,
 A stone that will distribute the full flood
 Over fields and over banks.
"A stone that will quickly overpower,
 This horse-boy that seeks me;
 A stone that will defeat the foes,
 A stone that will scatter them is my stone". [319]

(319) original:—Gabas Ceannmhair for amus an áċa, acus a lia cloiċe 'na laim, acus gabas ica molaḋ acus ica h-eadarguide, acus ic faiṫsine in air do ḋénaḋ, acus teit i muingin a ḋée ocus prim ḋruaḋ in doṁain, edon, Mog Ruiṫ, ocus do raiḋ:

Lia cloiċe, lia cloiċe,
 cloċ ċeana gun béba,
 lia ċael, lia tiuġ, tana,
 arm toġa for méla.
Lia fillfear, lia fillfear,
 tar fosalla gu nallaḋ;
 lia lingfear tar tonna
 gan croma gan camaḋ.
Mar do ċraeċais in argain
 tria forrġail ċruaiḋ, Colpṫa,
 eirig go talċair tria ḃorrfaiḋ gnim
 co noroċair dit Lurga.

Lia lóġa, lia lóġmar,
 lia coma, lia luaġa,
 lia bruġa, lia beaċta,
 lia feaċta, lia buaḋa.
Lia Eċóir, lia Dhaneol,
 lia ċalaḋ, lia caṫa;
 lia Mhoga, lia Shimoin,
 lia dimór, lia daṫa.
Lia foirfeas báiġ Muimneaċ,
 lia lioṁṫa gan aslaċ,
 lia ċuingin, lia tuirmim,
 lia ċnúċaċ, lia ċastaċ.

LECT. XIII. Of the "Champion's Hand-Stone" at the battle of Drom Damhghaire.

This singular poem, as well as that which [illegible] withstanding its exaggerated style, must [illegible] describing the *Lia Lamha Láich*, or Champion's [illegible]

Even though there were no closer description [illegible] it was, by the Arch-Druid's incantations, to [illegible] poisonous eel or water-snake, on touching the [illegible] implies plainly enough that its shape must have [illegible] but the first verse of the druid *Ceannmhair's* [illegible] doubt whatever on the matter.

"A flat stone, a flat stone;
A stone that will kill as before;
A narrow stone, a thick thin stone,
A choice weapon for success".

Surely no attempt with plain words could [illegible] describe the stone of which the drawing is an [illegible] these words of this ancient and most wonder-loving [illegible] ever he may have been.

It is needless to say that the stone so highly [illegible] fervently invoked performed in the story all that [illegible] from it; it not only crushed the northern druid [illegible] but in its shape of a monstrous eel, with a long [illegible] mane, it flung itself upon the dry land, and pursued [illegible] *Liffeachair*, king *Cormac's* son, who had been [illegible] combat, in the direction of his camp, and would have [illegible] him also, if *Ceannmhair* had not again addressed it [illegible] words, by which its fury was calmed; and then he [illegible] to its old blind owner, who immediately restored it to [illegible] form of a Champion's Hand-Stone!

The fifth stanza of this last poem requires some [illegible] if we could give it,—which we unfortunately cannot, [illegible] a single instance: It runs thus:—

"*Ethor's* stone, Daniel's stone,
A hard stone, a battle stone,
Mogh [*Ruith*]'s stone, Simon's stone,
An immense stone, a swift stone.

We know very well, of course, who *Mogh Ruith* [illegible] great druid was; and we also know that the "Simon" [illegible] was Simon Magus, under whom *Mogh* had, it was [illegible] his druidic education; but we do not know who [illegible] Daniel were, save that they too must have been [illegible] known ancient Eastern professors of the magic art, [illegible]

Lia linfas na h-áṫa,
in árd deilb fuaṫaiġ;
Lia ṡaiṫfeas in lán tṡruiṫ
far bánta tar bruaċa.

Lia traeṫfas go [illegible]
in eaċlaċ [illegible]
Lia fraeċfas ar [illegible]
Lia maiḋfeas, [illegible]

our Irish druid appears to have taken lessons. And one reason for my referring to their names a second time is, in the hope that some of the learned better acquainted than myself with classical mythology, with mediæval history, and with eastern lore, may happen to know something about these personages, and kindly communicate it to me. LECT. XIII.

The next "Champion's Hand-Stone" that I have any note of, is one with which the name of our long celebrated fellow-countryman, *Find Mac Cumhaill* is connected. The history of this stone is preserved in the ancient topographical tract called *Dinnseanchas*, in an article on the origin of the name *Ath Liag Find*, or the Ford of Finn's *Liag*, or "flat stone"; (now the ford of Ballyleague, at Lanesborough, on the Shannon above Athlone). The story is given in prose and verse, as follows: Of the "Champion's Hand-Stone" of Find Mac Cumhaill.

"*Ath-liag Find*, why is it so called? Answer: A battle which was fought there between *Find Mac Cumhaill* and *Fland* the son of *Eochaidh Abrad-Ruaidh*; and it was at this precise time that *Sideng*, the daughter of *Mongan* of the fairy hills, came with a flat stone (*lic*) and a chain of gold to *Find*, who gave them into the hand of *Guairé Gull*, [a familiar name for *Oisin*, the celebrated son of *Find*]. *Find* having used up all his weapons in the battle, snatched the stone [from *Oisin*], and with it killed three other sons of *Eochaidh Abrad-Ruaidh*, namely, *Bran*, *Seanach*, and *Senan*. And the stone fell into the ford; and no one shall find it until it is found by *Be-thuindé*, [the nymph of the waves], the daughter of *Calad* son of *Concinn*, who will bring it to land on a Sunday morning; and there will be but seven years from that to the morning of the day of judgment; and hence the ford is called *Ath Liag Find*".

[This is the prose account; and the verse scarcely differs from it, except in one important fact—the form of the stone:]

"*Ath-liag Find*, what stone is it named from?
Ascertain for us, O ye historians;
What was it that darkened his [*Find's*] memory,
At the time that he forgot his stone there?

"A victorious battle of high renown
Here was won by *Mac Cumhaill*,
Over a hero of the northern country,
The son of *Eochaidh Abrad-Ruaidh*.

"At this very time came *Seigeng* [*Sideng*] the fair,
Daughter of noble *Mongan* of the fairy hills,
And gave a stone, with a chain of gold,
To the son of *Cumhall* son of *Tlirenmór* [*Trenmhor*.]

"*Find* now placed his missive stone,
In the battle, on the back of *Guairé Guill*,

SECT. XXII.

f the Cham- on's Hand- tone" of ind Mac umhaill.

Until all his weapons at length had failed, [illegible]
Between the rising day and the close of [illegible]
"A shout then reached them from the north, [illegible]
It was *Fland*, the son of *Eochaidh Abrad*[illegible]
His face distorted with mighty rage,
The valiant chief of the furious combat.
"*Find* forthwith put forth his hand
For the stone of three angles and of three [illegible]
And that which was placed upon the back
Of *Guairé Gall* he bravely threw.
"By this he felled into the ford
Four *Conalls*, and four *Colmans*,
Four *Suibhnés*, two *Mac Brics*,
Four *Dubhthachs*, two *Diarmaids*.
"*Find* his stone cast into the ford,
Now that his heroic rage had risen;
And *Bran*, and *Senach*, and *Seanan*,
By that cast together were slain.
"The stone was lost, amid the waters,—
That stone by which *Find*'s honour was saved, [illegible]
And from thence thither no one has found it, [illegible]
Though truly it was a precious jewel.
"But it will be found by a gifted maiden,
Whose name will be *Bethuindé*,
Who shall thrust her fair right foot,
Through its connecting link of red gold.
"Up to land will she then bring
This stone by its attached hook;
And she will leave it on the strand,
On a Sunday in the latter days.
"Seven years from that auspicious day,
Until the day of judgment comes;—
And such is the deed from which arose
The ancient name of this famous ford".[819]

(819) original:—Achliag Find canas ro hainmniged. Ni [illegible] Cath do radad itir Fhind mac Cumaill ocus Fland mac [illegible] ruaid, conid annsin do reacht Sideng ingen Mongain [illegible] slabrad oir do Find mac Cumaill co tard sin a laim [illegible] tairmic airm Fhind do chaithim, conid iarsin, tairlig [illegible] co torcradar de tri mic Echach Abradruaid .i. Bran ocus [illegible] Senan, ocus torchair in liag is an ath, acus ni fuaib [illegible] conas Bechuille [Betuinde] ingen Chalaid mic Conchind, [illegible] beir ar aird madain domnaig, ocus secht iaram co brach; [illegible]

Achliag Find ca lia dia tá
Finnaid duind a [na] sencada
Ciasa cumne ro dus dall [cia
dia cumne ro don dall],
Can forfacaib a lig and.

Imairec chatha [illegible]
do mac Cumaill [illegible]
For milg don [illegible]
Sri mac Echach [illegible]

In more than one point of view this is a most curious and valuable legend. It clearly and distinctly shows us, not only that stones such as our stone "celts", (as modern "antiquarians" call them), were used in battle within historical times; but also that such stones, formed perhaps after a particular fashion, were deemed worthy presents from fair ladies to brave champions.

Description of the form of the Stone in the Story of *Finn.*

The stone in this legend appears not only to have had three angles or edges, and three sides, but to have been perforated at the smaller end, and suspended by a chain and hook of gold; but whether this implies that the stone was not to be thrown from the hand, but swung round and struck with by the chain, we have nothing now to show, as far as I am aware of.

Story of Prince *Eochaidh* son of *Enna Cinnselach.* (circa A.D. 400.)

One instance more of the use of the Champion's Hand-Stone is all that I shall cite at present; and it is the latest to which I have found any particular historical reference.

The celebrated *Niall* "of the Nine Hostages" was monarch of Erinn from A.D. 379 to 405. Among the hostages whom he carried with him to *Teamair*, from the provincial kings, and kept prisoners as security for their fealty, was *Eochaidh*, the son of *Enna Cinnselach*, King of Leinster. Discontented with his captivity *Eochaidh* after some time succeeded in making his escape, and took his way southwards, in the direction of his own

Do leig Seigeng sel iarsin
ingen Mongáin sáir sroaig,
co tuc lic co slabrad nóir
do mac Cumaill meic Tren-
móir.
Ar do rad Find a lic laind
sin chath for muin Guairi
glaind [gaill],
co tairnic airmid in tloig
[airmidéo a sloig],
o thrath eirgi co hiarnoin.
Gairit is in [ann dun], leath
atuaid [as in lech atuaid],
Fland mac Echach abradruaid
ro marb a cruth comall ngle
tren [tre in] coimchind na hirgaile [hurlaige].
Sind Find a laim iar sin
dou lig treill tre eochair
do tuc in cenn bai for bail
[muin]
Gaeth Guill for eblongair
[forcoeblongair.]
Adrochratar sin san ath
deichiu Conaill, da Cholmain,
ceithri Suibni, da Mac Bric,
ceithri Dubthaigi da Diarmaid.
Gaibleog Find a lia san ath
ón uair thainic anniech cách
[alonn lat],
Bran ocus Sendc na [is] Seanan
as de sin do rochradar.
Do rochair in lia sin linn
dia ndearmad enech fial Find
iaram nocho nadaib [nagaib
.i. nfagaib] nech
conache [conad] in sed som-
aineach.
Fogeb ingen comall ngle
dianad comainm Bechuinde,
focheard acas [acois] liasaid
choir
tre na hurdoman ndeargoir.
Cond tairring [tairrgend] suas
iar sin
in lia sin cona drolaim [dro-
laib]
cond farcaib is in [sor a]
craid
dia domnaid isin tiugnair.
Secht mbliadna uad sasad
ngle,
co tic Laichi in messaite
cond he sin gnim dia tá
dindsenchus in nachasa [deg
ata]. [&c.

—[MS. H. 3. 3. T.C.D. 53, and *Lecain*, 261, a, b.]

LECT. XIII.

Story of Prince Eochaidh, son of Enna Cennselach, (circa A.D. 400.)

country. Hungry and exhausted during his [illegible] he could think of no better step than that of [illegible] house of *Laidcend*, son of *Barced*, who was one of [illegible] *Niall's* chief poets, in order to obtain some food [illegible] fused him, and he was obliged to pursue his way [illegible] forget the inhospitality; and returning from [illegible] afterwards with a party of followers, he burned the [illegible] and in the attack upon it killed his only son. [illegible]

The poet after this continued for a whole year [illegible] against the men of Leinster, and to urge the [illegible] his personal wrongs as those of the whole order [illegible] belonged, which was by law privileged against [illegible] tion". *Niall* at last complied with his entreaties, [illegible] with a large force into Leinster encamped at [illegible] (now Tullow, in the county of Carlow), laying [illegible] try all round, until the men of Leinster were [illegible] liver their young prince *Eochaidh* once more [illegible] The poet now prepared for vengeance; and at [illegible] the young prince, we are told, had a chain put [illegible] the end of which was passed through a perforated [illegible] flag-stone", and made fast by an iron bar at the [illegible] prince had not been long in this condition when a [illegible] men went out from the camp to kill him; but when [illegible] ceived their design, he gave, says the historian, a [illegible] and tug at the chain, which broke it; and seizing [illegible] with which it had been fastened to the stone, he [illegible] bravely that his nine assailants fled before him to [illegible] Lagenians, who were encamped near, seeing him [illegible] liberty, pressed on along with him into King [illegible] which they suddenly entered, spreading confusion [illegible] on all sides; and the Chief King himself was forced to [illegible] wards and to quit the province with all his speed.

Niall, however, soon afterwards went to the south [illegible] overrunning the whole province did not stop until he [illegible] on the shore of the bay of Wexford, on the brink [illegible] Slaney. The poet *Laidcend*, who accompanied him [illegible] pedition, then begged of him to spare the country [illegible] ple; but he besought him to order the young prince, [illegible] to come into the poet's presence, at the opposite [illegible] river Slaney. The prince consented, and immediately [illegible] had him deprived of his arms, and then began to [illegible] abuse him bitterly. Whilst thus engaged, however, [illegible] youth, we are told, suddenly drew from his girdle a " [illegible] or Champion's flat Stone, which he threw at him; [illegible] struck him in the forehead, and killed him on the spot. [illegible]

It was on this occasion that the Poet *Ua Torta*, who had been *Laidcend's* pupil, commemorated the sad fate of his tutor in the following stanza:—

"A champion's hand-stone by a fool was cast,
Over the saltwater eastwards;
It was *Eochaidh* son of *Enda* that threw it,
At *Laidcend* the son of *Barced*.[(330)]

After this unfortunate deed, (for a Poet was always privileged against all violence, whatever the provocation), *Eochaidh* fled into Scotland, and sought and received protection, concealment, and hospitality from *Loarn*, the king of that country.

Of the Death of *Niall* "of the Nine Hostages", by an arrow, A.D. 405.

King *Niall* returned home; and some time after this it was that collecting a large force of the men of Erinn and of Scotland he proceeded at their head on his last expedition, into France, with the intention of taking "the hostages of Italy"; and he stopped, says the history, only when he reached the banks of the Loire, "near the foot of the Alps", where he encamped.

Now the young prince *Eochaidh* marched with this expedition in the train of the king of Scotland, but in disguise; and while *Niall* one day sat conspicuously on an eminence, on the bank of the river, taking counsel with his officers, he passed to the opposite side unobserved, and shot the king dead with an arrow (*saigst*), from his *fidbac*, (or bow); after which he fled, and succeeded in reaching his own country of Leinster in safety.

This short article is valuable for two reasons; the first that it shows that even down to shortly before the year 405, in which year *Niall* was killed, the *Lia Lámha*, or Champion's Hand-Stone, remained in use in Erinn; and secondly, because it contains the earliest reference to the Bow and Arrow that I have ever met with in Irish writings. It is quite possible, however, that later reference to the use of the Champion's Hand-Stone, and earlier to the Bow and Arrow, than those that I have noticed here, may be to be found in old Irish books still extant; I can only say that they have not come under my observation.

Of the Sling and Sling-Stone in ancient Erinn.

To these few notices of the offensive use of the Champion's Hand-Stone, I shall now add a few brief notices of the Sling and Sling-Stone in ancient times. I have to remark, however, that in no instance have I ever met with any account of the general use of the Sling, in battle; it seems that, like the champion's hand-stone, they were always used on certain special occasions,

(330) original, (MS. T.C.D.; H. 2. 16, fol. 784;—B. of Ballymote, fol. 77. b.):
Lia Lamhe, orrut fochres, Eochaid mac Enda forla
tar fan fál faerchá, for Laidcend mac Baircedа.

LECT. XIII.

where no other weapon would reach the object
sailed.

At the second Battle of *Magh Tuireadh*.

The first reference to the Sling-Stone, but
out the Sling itself, is in the second battle of
where, as has been shown in a former lecture,
Danann champion, *Lug*, struck the Fomorian
"of the stout blows", in his "evil eye", and
skull. It is not, as I have already said, stated
the battle of *Magh Tuireadh* that the stone
Sling; it is only said that he threw a "*lic*
Stone", at him; and it could hardly be otherwise,
talking face to face at the time.

This, it will be recollected, was not an ordinary
the famous *tathlum*, or Composition-Ball, of which
is given in the ancient poem quoted in a former
however, stated in the version preserved in the
ster, that in this case it was with a stone "out of
struck him.

Story of *Duibhlinn*; (instance of the use of the Sling-Stone).

The next reference to a Sling and Sling-Stone,
already mentioned, is found in the *Dinnseanchas*,
on the origin of the name *Duibh-linn*, or Black-pool
the name of Dublin is but a corruption); a spot which
bably that part of the River Liffey which in later
known by the name of *poll*, or "the hole", or pool
name of which is now preserved to some extent in
Poolbeg Street, that is, Little Hole, or Little Pool
lower quays of the city of Dublin; and in the
lighthouse on the south side of the river. The legend
is a wild one, refers to circumstances and persons of
other accounts are now lost, probably for ever, and
lows, in prose and verse:—

"*Duibh-linn*, why so named? It is not unpleasant
Dubh, the daughter of *Rodubh*, son of *Cas*, son of
was the wife of *Enna*, son of *Nos*, of the hill of
[near Dublin]. *Enna* had another wife unknown to
name was *Aelé*, daughter of *Ochand*, son of
the lady *Dubh*, who was a druidess and poetess,
infidelity of her husband, she became jealous; and she
took a walk along the sea-side, till she came opposite
house. Here she pronounced a druidical charm on
which swelled up so as to overwhelm the house and
rival lady *Aelé*, the water having risen above her.
had a servant whose name was *Margen*, who
baneful effects of the incantation, turned on the
shot a *Caer Clis* [or "Composition-ball",] equal to

lenn, from his *taball* [or sling], towards her (from the opposite side of the river), which struck her, and she fell into the pool; and hence the name of *Duibhlinn*, and also of *Ath Liag Mairgené* [or the Ford of *Margen*'s Sling-Stone], because it was there *Margen* threw his cast, of which the poet sang :— LECT. XIII. Story of *Duibhlinn*; (instance of the use of the Sling-Stone.)

"The daughter of *Rodubh*, son of brave *Cas*,
Son of gentle *Cas*, son of *Glas-gamhna*;
The wife of *Enna*, son of comely *Nos*,
Who ruled in the Hill of *Forcharthan*.

"She was a druidess and a generous poetess,—
The daughter of *Rodubh* of noble mien,—
She was a prophetess to foretell all occurrences,
Till she was drowned through one fatal shot.

"*Enna* had also to his fair blooming wife
Até the daughter of *Ochand*,
Who was the son of friendly *Cnucha*,
A fact that brought misery to *Rodubh*'s daughter.

"Jealousy seized on the daughter of *Rodubh*,—
It was not a very cheerful visitor,—
Whereupon she spoke a sea incantation
Because she loved not her favoured rival.

"She was perceived by honest cheerful *Margen*,
The highly trusted servant of *Ochand*,
Who threw a missive ball in her path,
Which struck the kingly daughter of *Rodubh*.

"Then died, though by no enemy slain,
Her noble and illustrious father;
The fair towering tree died before night,
After the death of his (*Rodubh*'s) daughter".

We have here, too, another *Athliag*, or "stone-ford", deriving its name from a circumstance, such as *Athliag Finn*; but the obliteration of ancient local names by the spread of Dublin as a city has given some new name to that part of the Liffey which must have been known as *Ath Liag Mairgené*. It seems probable that it was somewhere about Wood Quay.

In this very ancient legend we have another important instance of the use of a peculiarly shaped stone to be cast from the Sling, as well as from the hand, in ancient times; and though it is said here to have been a *caer clis*, or Conglobate missive, "equal to" or like the *tathlum* of the Battle of *Magh Tuireadh*, still we may safely take it to have been a stone specially fashioned for the sling and reserved for some extraordinary occasion, while the first stone that came to hand may have been used on ordinary occasions.

We have another curious instance of the use of the Sling and

LECT. XIII. Ball in the ancient account of the death of ... or Meave, queen of Connacht, so often ... lectures.

Death of Meave (Medbh) Queen of Connacht, by a Sling-Stone.

This *Medbh* had been first married to the ... *Mac Nessa*, king of Ulster; but she ... govern many men than to be governed by ... abandoned *Concobar* and returned to her ... *Eochaidh Feidhlech*, to Tara, who shortly ... independent queen of the province of Connacht ... implacable jealousy and hatred, carried out ... border warfare, continued to rage for many ... *Medbh* and her former husband; until at length ... the course of one of his expeditions against the ... quondam wife, received his death-wound (as will be remem-bered) from the "ball made out of the hardened ... *gedhra*", the King of Leinster, which was ... the Connacht Champion *Ceat Mac Magach*; ... which I gave a full account in a former lecture.[121]

Now, at the time that king *Concobar* found himself ... by *Medbh*, he repaired to her father, to Tara, and ... obtained the hand of another daughter of his, ... *Eithné*,—(a name which means, literally, the ... nut). By this princess *Concobar* had a son who ... world after his mother's death; for, having fallen ... anciently called *Glaisé Bearramain*, (in Westmeath) ... died of the effects of the accident, though ... life was extinct; and having been near her confinement ... time, her side was cut open, and the infant, which ... a son brought forth alive, who received the name of ... —*Furbadh* being the ancient Gaedhelic name of ... science now calls the Cæsarian operation. (I may ... that the river which before was called *Glaisé Bearramain* ... been called *Eithné* ever since that princess lost ... and that it is now the well-known river Inny,[122] in ... of Westmeath.)

Young *Furbaidhé* grew up in time to be a ... warrior; and when long afterwards his father ... consequence of the wound inflicted on him through ... nant contrivance of Queen *Medbh*, he was resolved ... venged of her, though the undertaking was ... performed, seeing that she was always well ... cumstances, however, favored his design, for *Medbh* ...

(121) See *Lectures on the MS. Materials*, etc., p. 275.

(122) [A slight corruption of the correct pronunciation of ... *Eithné*.]

Ailill, was slain near his own palace of *Cruachan* by the celebrated Ulster hero *Conall Cearnach;* and *Medbh* being then old, withdrew from public life to *Inis Clothrann*, (an island of Lough Ree, in the Shannon above Athlone, between the present counties of Roscommon and Westmeath, but nearer to the latter). Here the aged queen was accustomed to wash every morning in a certain spring on the east side of the island; and *Furbaidhé* having discovered this circumstance, came stealthily, unperceived; and measured with a thread the exact distance from the spring to the opposite bank of the river, on the Westmeath side. With the measure of this distance *Furbaidhé* returned home to Ulster, where he set up two poles at the distance of the length of the thread asunder, and with the thread or line extended between them. On the top of one of the small poles he placed a ball, and taking his stand at the other, with his *crann-tabhaill*, or Sling, in his hand, he commenced shooting at the ball, his aim following the direction of the thread. He continued this practice until he became so expert and accurate that he never would miss striking the ball on the [illegible] pole; and now being thoroughly certain of the unerring accuracy of his aim, he set out from Ulster, and arriving on the bank of the Shannon opposite to his enemy's favourite washing-place, he took his stand there by night, and waited for her coming at early morn. The aged and unsuspecting queen, true to her custom, repaired early to the spring, and commenced her ablutions. *Furbaidhé's* time had now come: he placed a well-balanced stone in his *crann-tabhaill*, and took deliberate aim; the stone flew unerringly, struck queen *Medbh* in the forehead, and killed her on the spot.

Death of Meave, (Medbh) Queen of Connacht, by a Sling-Stone.

It does not appear from this tale of what particular form the stone or ball was which *Furbaidhé* used on this important occasion. It will be collected, however, from the accounts of the *Tathlum* and the *Caer Clis* already described, and from a few other references to the Sling, which shall follow below, that the most approved shape was the globular, though in time of necessity any shaped stone may have been used.

Of the shape of the Sling-stone.

It will be seen also that iron or bronze balls were sometimes used in the sling; and such balls must have been too precious to be wasted on any but objects worthy the attainment of a champion.

Of the use of Sling-balls of Iron and Bronze.

In all our ancient writings there is found no man whose name is so much connected with the use of the sling as the celebrated Ultonian champion* *Cuchulainn;* there scarcely occurs a reference to him anywhere that his practice and accuracy of aim at the sling are not spoken of, but more particularly in the nar-

Use of the Sling by Cuchulainn.

LECT. XIII.

Use of the Sling by Cuchulainn.

rative of the celebrated *Táin Bó Chuailgné*, of which so much has been said in the course of these lectures.

On the very day on which *Cuchulainn*, who was still in his teens, received the arms of championship at Emania, from *Concobar Mac Nessa*, king of Ulster, he, in accordance with ancient custom, directed his chariot to a border of the province, to consecrate his arms by bathing them in the blood of an enemy. The border to which he directed his course, we are told, was that of East Meath, or Bregia; and at a point at which it meets the province of Ulster, on the right bank of the little river Mattock, where it falls into the Boyne, (a little below the chief entrance to Neterville house, on the road between Drogheda and Slane, in the county of Meath). Here stood an ancient fort, (the ruins of which are still I may observe, in ample preservation). This fort was the residence of *Nechtan Sceiné*, his three sons, and his wife. *Cuchulainn* came up to the gate, where he was met by *Foill*, the eldest of *Nechtan Sceiné*'s three sons. But when the boy-champion's charioteer saw this mature warrior coming towards his young master, he apprised him of the disparity between them, and the hopeless issue of a successful combat with him. To this discourse *Cuchulainn* answered:

"'It is not to me it is proper to speak thus, O *Ibar*', said the boy. 'I shall put my hand to the *deil clis* [sling-rod,] that is, to the iron ball, and it shall strike him on the front of his shield and on the front of his forehead; and it will carry the measure of the ball of his brain out through the back of his head, so that it shall become a flaming red mass outside, and that the light of the sky shall be visible through his head'.

"*Foill*, the son of *Nechtan*, then came forward; and he (*Cuchulainn*) put his hand to his *deil clis*, [or sling-rod], and threw a choice throw of the ball at him; and it struck him on the front of his shield, and on the front of his face; and it carried the measure of the ball of his brain out through the back of his head".(323)

Again it is stated that, on *Cuchulainn*'s return to Emania after slaying the three sons of *Nechtan Sceiné*, his horses flew so fast that the missive which he threw from his *tailm*, or Sling,

(323) original:—Ni fuimsa is cóir duitsi sain do rád, a Ibair, ar in mac bec. Do bersa mo lam for deil cliss .i. forn-uball n-iarnaide, ocus tecma illaind a sceith ocus illaind a etain ocus beraid comthrom in uballi dia inchinn tria chuladaig co ndingne rechen derg de sin a chend a nechtair combat leiss lesbaire aedir tria na cend.

Tainic immach Foill mac Nechtain. Tucsam a lam fon deil clis do. Ocus focherd focurt n-urchair dond uball uad cu tarla illaind a sceith, ocus illaind a étain ocus beirid comthrom in n-uballi da inchind tria chuladaig co ndearna rechendoer de sin a cend in echtair comba leir lesbaire aedir tria na cend.

before him, was caught by him before it fell to the ground. All these incidents, however, are stated to have taken place previous to the *Táin Bo Chuailgné;* but the following references to his sling achievements are taken from that curious old tale.

LECT. XIII. Use of the Sling by Cuchulainn.

"*Cuchulainn* declared then at *Methin Port* [the name of a ford on the border of Meath and Louth], that when he would first see *Ailill* or *Medbh*, [the king and queen of Connacht], he would hurl stones at them from his *taball*, [sling]. And this he did too; for he cast a stone from his *tailm* and killed the *Togmhall* [squirrel] that sat on *Medbh*'s shoulder on the south side of the ford; whence that place is called *Meithé Togh;* and he killed the bird which perched on *Ailill*'s shoulder, on the north side of the ford; whence that place is called *Meithé an Eoin*".[314]

And again: "*Cuchulainn* killed thirty warriors of them with his *tailm*, [sling]".[315]

And again: "In this place *Cuchulainn* killed an hundred men of them each night of the three nights that they encamped there, by plying his *taball* against them".[316]

In another place, queen *Medbh* sends her beautiful daughter *Finnabhair*, accompanied by one of her simpletons (a class of people whose infirmity rendered them inviolable), to *Cuchulainn*, with terms of peace; but the simpleton was dressed like king *Ailill*, the maiden's father, and intended to pass himself as such on *Cuchulainn;* the latter, however, detected him, and threw a *lüc tailmé*, or sling-stone, which he had in his hand, at him, and which struck him in the head, and knocked his brains out".[317]

And again, in the combat between *Cuchulainn* and the Connacht warrior *Caur*, it is said:

"*Caur* had been throwing missives at the face of his (*Cuchulainn's*) shield, until a third part of the day had passed; and he was not able to send a single blow or thrust home to him, such was his (*Cuchulainn*'s) scientific dexterity. * * * *Cuchulainn* then glanced at him, and shot the missive ball which he had in his hands at him, over the boss and border of his shield, and it passed through the skull of the giant clear out.[318]

(314) original:—Bagais Cuculaind hi Methin Port iarsin, in accigeo Ailill no Medb, ro cíbred cloich as a thabaill forru. Do gnisom on [illegible]adon do leici cloich as a thailm, conort in togmall boi for gualainn Medbe fris in áth andess, is de atá Meith Tóg. ocus ro ort in n-én [illegible] for gualainn Ailella fri áth antuaid; is de atá Meithe in n-Eoin.

(315) original:—Brisid Cuculaind tricha laech dib cus in tailm.

(316) original:—Dorsnechat Cuchulainn isuidiu orgain ced fer cacha aidche na tri aidche m-batar ann, gabais taball doib.

(317) original:—Srethis liic telma boi ina láim fair, con sescaind ina cend co tuc a inchind as.

(318) original:—Robói dna Caur oc airmimbeirt gaiscid hi tuamaim a

LECT. XIII.

This certainly was not a cast from a sling, that it was a sling-ball, or *Caer Clis*, cast from the distance between the combatants being too short the convenient use of the *Deil Clis*, or Sling Rod,

It would be tedious and unprofitable to follow end these short quotations from the *Táin Bo* other tracts, relative to the use of the Sling, under names of *Taball*, *Crann-Tabhaill*, *Deil-Clis*, and

Of the *Taball*.

The word *Taball*, a sling, would appear to be the Greek word "Ballo", from which "Ballista" warlike engine to throw or shoot stones, is derived.

Of the *Crann-Tabhaill*.

Tabhaill, or Staff-Sling, on the other hand, suggests "Fustabulum", an engine which was formed a thong or strap of skin or leather through somewhat flattened end of a staff of from three feet in length; in using which by placing the staff and the strap, at the point of intersection, tapering end of this strap of leather tightly up staff, and swinging and letting it go, like the you have a kind of sling or casting engine of and certainty of aim than the string sling. This called *Crann-Tabhaill*, because of the *Crann* or annexed word being *Tabaill* (ending in the with the slender vowel *i*, the sign of a plural not the singular *Taball*, without the final *i*,) the instrument contained a plurality of parts.

Of the *Deil-Clis*.

The *Deil Clis* is also a compound word, formed a Rod, wand, or slender staff, and *Cleas*, any weapon, but in this instance a round ball of bronze, etc. Wherever the use of this instrument *Clis* is spoken of, it is always found that the it was a ball, and not a common stone, as ways, in the *Taball* or *Crann-Tabhaill*.

Of the *Tailm*

The third kind of sling is called *Tailm*; and this rived by Cormac's glossary from *tell* and explains as "the clashing of the thongs and their and however far-fetched this derivation may leaves no doubt as to the nature of the slinging often mentioned in our old writings under the name

sceit corrice trian ind lai frisseom, ocus in concerrtaid fair la decra na cles. * * * Danecat Cuchulainn n-ubull-chles tarraid ina láim; colluid isin cobrad, sceit, colluid tria na chenn ind aig siar.

(338) original:—Tobeim na n-iall ocus an-uaim.

LECTURE XIV.

[Delivered 11th June, 1858.]

(V.) WEAPONS OF WARFARE; (continued). Recapitulation of names of Weapons anciently in use in Erinn. Descriptions of Arms and of Costume in the Tale of the *Táin Bo Chuailgné*. Story of the *Táin*. Description of the Herald, *Mac Roth*. Description of the Champion, *Fergus Mac Roigh*. Of the *Cletine*, or Little Spear, of *Cuchulainn*. Description of the "Armed Chariot" of *Cuchulainn*; and of the Charioteer, *Laegh*. Description of the several combats, with various different weapons, between *Cuchulainn* and *Ferdiadh*. Of the "*Gae-Bulga*", of *Cuchulainn*.

During the last three lectures we were occupied with the names, fashions, and materials in general, of the different weapons of offence and warfare of which our most ancient writings make any mention. The number and variety of such weapons is comparatively limited; and it may be better to recapitulate them here before we enter upon another period of our history, in which the same weapons, indeed, with one exception, are still found in use, but with some addition to their number and variety.

The weapons mentioned as having been in use in the battle of the first or southern *Magh Tuireadh*, were; the *Craisech*, or pointless Spear; the *Fiarlanna*, or curved pointless Blade; the Swords, and the Clubs, of the *Firbolgs*; and the *Manais*, or Broad thrusting Spear; the *Slegh*, or Pointed Spear (for casting); and the Sword, of the *Tuatha Dé Danann*. Recapitulation, (of Weapons anciently in use).

In the battle of the second or northern *Magh Tuireadh*, we find, in common, among the *Tuatha Dé Danann* and their invaders, the Fomorians: the *Slegh*, or Pointed long Spear; the *Gotha*, or Short Spear; the *Saighead-Bolg* [*Saiget Bolc*], or Belly-Dart; the *Claidheamh*, or Sword; and the *Lic Tailmé*, or Sling-Stone, or, according to the second version, the *Tathlum*, or Composition Sling-Ball.

To these primitive weapons we find added, in the time of *Labhraidh Loingsech*, the *Laighen Leathan-ghlais*, or "Broad-green thrusting-Spear", of the Gauls; and to these, again, in the time of the monarch *Eochaidh Feidhlech*, and the battle of *Ath Comair*, were added the *Lia Lamha Laich*, or Champion's Hand-Stone, which we have traced down to *Mogh Ruith* the druid, and *Find Mac Cumhaill*, in the third century, and to *Eochaidh*, the son of *Enna Ceinnselach*, king of Leinster, in the fifth.

It is remarkable that there is no mention made of the Champion's Hand-Stone in the battles of the *Táin Bo Chuailgné*, nor

LECT. XIV. in the battle of *Ros-na-Righ*, which were fought in the intermediate period, or about the time of the Incarnation.

Descriptions of Arms and Costume in the "*Táin Bo Chuailgné*".

These battles, however, particularly the battles of the *Táin Bo Chuailgné*, supply us with much more minute details of the dress, weapons, and other particulars of the warriors who took part in them, than anything which has gone before them; the ancient account of the battle of the first *Magh Tuireadh* which has come down to us being written in a much more matter of fact and less exuberant age than that of the *Táin Bo Chuailgné*, which, in its present form, is ascribed to the close of the sixth century.

Story of the *Táin Bo Chuailgné*.

As this *Táin Bo*, or Cow-spoil, of *Cuailgné*, has been so often mentioned already, and partially described in former lectures, it will be sufficient here to recall to mind that it is the history of an hostile expedition made by *Ailill* and *Medbh*, (or Meave), the king and queen of Connacht, at the head of the forces of Connacht, Munster, and Leinster, into the southern part of the province of Ulster, (namely, into *Cuailgné*, the district lying between Drogheda and Dundalk), for the purpose of carrying away by force a famous bull called the *Donn Chuailgné*, or the Brown-Bull of *Cuailgné*; that at the time this expedition was undertaken all the men of Ulster above a certain age were, according to the story, lying in a state of torpor or debility, under a spell which a certain woman whom they had wronged had worked on them, and which attacked them periodically, and for a certain time; and that thus, at the time of the hostile incursion into their country, there was no one to check the course of the invaders but the young hero *Cuchulainn*, who was not affected by the spell, in consequence of his youth at the time. *Cuchulainn* was the son of the chief of that territory of *Cuailgné*, into which the invaders first passed.

Immediately on the appearance of the invading host, *Cuchulainn* confronted them, and claiming the observance of the strict laws of ancient Gaedhilic Chivalry, demanded single combat, insisting that the invaders should not intrude farther into his territory until the victory of their champion and his own defeat should justify their progress. And we learn from the story that in fact according to this arrangement, the advance of the invaders was regulated by a succession of single combats, in which several of the most celebrated warriors of the king and queen of Connacht met their death at the hands of *Cuchulainn*.

But although the invaders undertook to regulate their advance into the province of Ulster by the results of those combats, still they continued to advance farther north after every one of them, until at last they took up a very threatening position on the brink of the little river on which stands the present town of Ardee (*Ath-Firdiaidh*), in the county of Louth. LECT. XIV.

Before arriving so far, however, queen *Medbh* proposed favourable terms to *Cuchulainn*, not indeed in good faith, but with the view of gaining the object of her expedition by means more expeditious and less expensive of the lives of her best warriors.

These terms were conveyed to the young hero by *Mac Roth*, the queen's chief herald; and I may here quote the whole passage of the story in which this officer is introduced, so interesting is it not only in reference to the military customs of the time, but also for the sake of the description it contains of the arms, dress, and accoutrements of an ancient herald.

When *Mac Roth* approaches *Cuchulainn*'s quarters, he is perceived by the vigilant charioteer of the latter, so celebrated in our legendary history, *Laegh Mac Riangabhra*:

"'Here comes a single champion towards us, O *Cuchulainn*', said *Laegh*. 'What sort of a champion is he?' said *Cuchulainn*. 'A brown-haired, broad-faced, beautiful youth; a splendid brown cloak on him; a bright bronze spear-like brooch fastening his cloak. A full and well-fitting shirt to his skin. Two firm shoes between his two feet and the ground. A hand-staff of white hazel in one hand of his; a single-edged sword with a sea-horse-tooth hilt, in his other hand'. 'Good, my lad', said *Cuchulainn*, 'these are the tokens of an herald'."[a] Description of the Herald, Mac Roth.

Mac Roth's mission to *Cuchulainn* proved fruitless, as the latter would not accept the conditions offered him; and queen *Medbh* then called up *Fergus Mac Roigh*, an Ulster prince, and one of the greatest champions of the time, who had been for some years in exile at her court, to go from her with conditions of peace to *Cuchulainn*, who had been formerly the pupil of this very *Fergus* in the great military school of Emania. *Fergus* consented to undertake this mission; and in the following short account of his personal appearance, as he appeared to *Cuchulainn*'s charioteer, *Laegh Mac Riangabhra*, we have a vivid picture of a prince and warrior of the highest class in these remote ages. The language is that of poetical exaggeration; but it is only the exaggeration of expression.

At the time that *Fergus* approached them, *Cuchulainn* and

[a] original:—Oen laeċ ċucainn, Cuċulainn, for Laeg. Cinnas laeċ? ar Cuċulainn. Gilla donn, dreċlethan, alainn; bratt donn derrgaisidi imm; brut-gáe umaide ina brut. Tarbléni trebraid fria ċness. Da bróicc etir a dá ċoiss is talam. Matad-lorg finnċuill is in dara láim; claideb letfaebraċ, co n-eltaib déċ, isind laim araill. Maith, a gillai, ar Cuċulainn, comarta eċlaige sin.

his charioteer were amusing themselves at [illegible] spear; when the charioteer suddenly exclaimed [illegible]

"'A single champion approaches us, O [illegible] *Laegh*. 'What description of champion [illegible] 'As large as a mountain on the plain appears [illegible] in which the warrior is seated [said *Laegh*] [illegible] top of a noble tree which stands on the lawn of [illegible] appears to me the branching, flowing, fair yellow [illegible] manly fleece of hair on his head. [He wears] [illegible] with a deep fringe of golden thread on him [illegible] golden brooch in that cloak. [He bears] a [illegible] [or heavy spear], blazing red, in his hand. [illegible] tering, well-studded shield, with a boss of red [illegible] A sword as long as the oar of a canoe, in a [illegible] lies across the two thighs of the huge haughty [illegible] within that chariot'".(331)

The mission of *Fergus* was unsuccessful; [illegible] combats went on day after day, always to the [illegible] *Cuchulainn*. Queen *Medbh* and her people were [illegible] at loss of so many of their bravest warriors; and [illegible] them that there was something supernatural in [illegible] Spear, the weapon with which he generally slew [illegible] (and which was called *cletiné*), they held a [illegible] some stratagem besides the uncertain one of combat [illegible] he could be deprived of it. The determination [illegible] came to was, to send *Redg* the court satirist and [illegible] *Ailill* and queen *Medbh*, to ask *Cuchulainn* to [illegible] present of the spear, for it was not usual in those [illegible] any request which a man of that profession made: [illegible]

"And after this *Redg*, *Ailill*'s satirist, went by [illegible] for the *cletiné*, that is, *Cuchulainn*'s spear. 'Give [illegible] spear', said the satirist: 'Not so, indeed', said *Cuchulainn* [illegible] I shall give thee other gifts'. 'I shall not accept [illegible] the satirist. [*Cuchulainn*] then rebuked the [illegible] would not receive from him what he had offered [illegible] the satirist said that he would disparage his [illegible] would not give him the *cletiné*. *Cuchulainn* then [illegible] *cletiné* at him, and transfixed him through the [illegible]

(331) Oen laech ducuind, a Chucu laind, ar Laeg. Cinnas [illegible] laind. Meticir lim den na prim-sliab is mó bis for [illegible] carpat sil fond oclaig. Meticir lim den na prim-bile bis [illegible] prim-duin, in folt craibach, dualach, findbuid, forordha, [illegible] imme ceno. Fuan corcra corrcharach ór fnaithi imm [illegible] n-ecorta, sin brut. Manais lethan-glas ar derg-lassar [illegible] Sciath chobradach, condualach, co cobraid óir deirg, fare [illegible] fithlai, co n-ecrasaib sennda, for dib sliastaib sairighti [illegible] móir, borrfaid fail isin carpat ar medón.

'That is an overpowering gift', said the satirist; [and he dropped dead.] It is from this circumstance that the ford of *Ath-Tolam-Sed* has its name. There is also a little ford to the east of it, into which the bronze of the *cletiné* fell; the name of this ford is [thence known as] the *Uman-Sruth*, or the Bronze Stream". [illegible]

Of the "Cletiné", or Little Spear of Cuchulainn.

This short quotation is valuable as showing that the *Cletiné*, *Cuchulainn's* favourite light spear, was made of bronze; indicating clearly that though perhaps iron may have been introduced in the manufacture of military weapons in Erinn at this time, still bronze continued also to be used. Positive evidences of this fact, such as this, are scarce in our ancient writings; doubtless because things that were common at the time, just as in our own times, were not deemed worthy of special record.

After several successful combats, *Cuchulainn* at length, (so the tale goes on to tell us), began to fail in strength and vigour, from constant exertion; and it appears that at last he fell suddenly into a deep sleep, which lasted for three days. During this time a party of one hundred and fifty of the noble youths of Ulster who had heard of his distress came to his relief, and kept the enemy in play during his sleep; but they were all slain at last, one after another.

Description of the "Armed Chariot" of Cuchulainn; and of the Charioteer.

When *Cuchulainn* awoke and saw the slaughter of his friends, his rage knew no bounds. So he ordered his charioteer, *Laegh* the son of *Riangabhra*, to yoke for him his "armed Chariot", that he might rush through and around the host of his enemies, and deal death and destruction on all sides. The descriptions of this charioteer, the chariot, the horses, and the champion himself, in this passage, are rather long; but the passage contains so much of importance to the subject of this lecture that I cannot omit any part of it. Here also, as generally throughout this ancient tale, the picture is highly painted, and the details full of poetic exaggeration; but there can be little doubt but that the groundwork is correct in all its essential features.

"Then", says the tale, "arose the charioteer, and put on his wild charioteering dress. Of this wild charioteering dress which he put on was his graceful frock of skins;—which was light and airy, spotted and striped; made of deer skins; close-fitting, so as not to interfere with the free action of his arms outside,

[illegible] original:—Is iarom luid Reog cainte Aililla a comairli Cuchai do [illegible] in cletine .i. gai Conculaind. Tuc damsa do gai, or in cáinte. [illegible] dim, or Cuculainn, act do ber seota dait. Nad gebsa ón, ar in [illegible]. Gegna som dna in cainte, uair na gaet uad a targid do. Ocus [illegible] in cainte no berad a enech mani berad in cletine. Focheird [illegible] iarum in cletine do colluid tria na cend sor tarsna. Is [illegible] [.i. set talman] in set so, ol in cainte. Is de ata Ath Tolam Sét. [illegible] dna at fuirt anair airm in arrasar an uma don Cletiniu; humansrut [illegible] ata sain.—(Leabar na h-uidhre, fol. 34, b,b.)

LECT. XIV.

Description of the "Armed Chariot" of Cuchulainn; and the Charioteer.

"He put on, outside this frock, his raven-black [illegible] Simon Magus had made for the king of the Romans [illegible] to *Concobar Mac Nessa*, [king of Ulster,] who [illegible] *lainn*; and *Cuchulainn* gave it to his charioteer. [illegible] then put on his crested, dazzling, quadrangular [illegible] in various colours; inscribed with various devices [illegible] tain falling over his shoulders behind. Much did [illegible] add to his grace, and not at all to his incumbrance [illegible]

"With his hand he set [then] upon his forehead [illegible] yellow band, like a blade of red gold which had [illegible] over the edge of an anvil. This he put on in [illegible] Charioteership, to distinguish him from his master [illegible]

"He took [then] the spurring-goads of his horses [illegible] long whip, in his right hand; he took the restraining [illegible] ments of his horses, that is, the reins, in his left hand [illegible] late his charioteering.

"Then did he throw their 'loricas of beautiful [illegible] his steeds, which covered them from their faces to [illegible] studded with little blades, little spikes, little lances [illegible] pointed spears; and every motion of that chariot [illegible] sharp point next anyone whom it approached; so [illegible] angle and every face, and every point, and every [illegible] same chariot, was a sure path of cutting and lacerating [illegible]

"Then did he cast a spell of invisibility over the [illegible] over his companion, [or master], so that no one [illegible] could see them, whilst they could distinctly see every [illegible]

"It was no wonder that he should cast such a [illegible] them, since he possessed the three perfections of a [illegible] on that day; namely, to leap over the rails of the [illegible] drive unerringly, and to poise his whip correctly.

"It was then the champion and warrior, and [illegible] martial heroes above all the men of earth, namely [illegible] the son of *Soaltann*, equipped himself in his array of [illegible] fighting and combat. Of that battle array which [illegible] may be counted seven and twenty shirts,[330] cered and [illegible] and closely braced on with strings and lines, and rollers [illegible] bodkins or pins?], so that his fury may not exceed [illegible] whenever his manly rage should boil up. He put [illegible] these his battle-girdle of hard-tanned leather, cut from [illegible] of seven full-grown ox-hides, which encircled him from [illegible] to his arm-pits, and which he wore for the purpose of [illegible]

(330) [This passage of the Tale requires investigation. Unfortunately [illegible] translator's notes, in explanation of the existing form of the Tale [illegible] completed up to the time of his death; and this among other [illegible] therefore appear without comment.]

javelins [gai], points [rend], and [sharp-pointed] irons [iaernn], spears [sleg], and darts [saiget]; so that they always rebounded from him in the same way as if it had been from a stone, or a rock, or a bone, they had rebounded.

LECT. XIV. Description of the "Armed Chariot" of Cuchulainn.

"He then put on his apron of striped satin [srebnaide sróil], with its border of mottled white gold, over the softer part of his lower body: he then put on his apron of brown leather, cut from the backs of four full-grown well-tanned ox-hides, over his battle-girdle of ox-hides, and his apron of striped satin.

"Then did the royal champion take his arms of battle, and fight, and combat.

"Of these battle-arms which he took, were his eight little Swords, [claidbini], along with his bright-shining, tooth-hilted Sword [solgdet]. He took his eight little Spears, [sléigini], along with his flesh-piercing Spear, and his Belly Spear, [saiget bolc.] He took his eight little Darts, [gothnada], along with his Ivory Dart, [goth-ndét]. He took his eight short Spears, [cleitini], along with his Sling-rod.

"He took his eight Missive Shields, [sciatha clis], along with his great, curved, black-red shield; in the hollow of which a full-grown hog would fit; [and which was] bound all round with a scalloped keen-edged rim, so sharp as to cut a hair against a stream, so that whenever the champion used it as a weapon, it was equally that he cut with his shield, and with his spear, and with his sword.

"And he then put on his helmet of battle, and of combat, and of fighting, on his head, from every recess and from every angle of which issued the shout, as it were, of an hundred warriors; because it was alike that women of the valley [de bananaig], and hobgoblins [bacanaig], and wild people of the glen [geinti glinde], and demons of the air [demna aeóir], shouted in front of it, and in rear of it, and over it, and around it, wherever he went, at the spurting of the blood of warriors and heroes upon it.

"He then threw his mantle of invisibility over him, manufactured from the precious fleeces of the land of the immortals, which had been brought to him by *Manannan Mac Lir*, [the great navigator of the *Tuatha Dé Danann*], from the King of Sorcha",—[now Portugal].

Cuchulainn being thus equipped, (we are told), mounted his chariot, and drove around the hosts of his enemies in a furious succession of narrowing circles; driving them closer and closer together; assailing them with his deadly weapons at all points; and brushing close to them and through them, with his armed chariot, tearing, maiming, and killing them in all directions,

[LECT. XIV. Descriptions in the Tain Bo Chuailgne (continued).]

and escaping himself in the sudden confusion
which he threw them.

When the invading host had recovered
after the sudden panic into which
had thrown them, queen *Medbh* lost no time
her entreaties and gifts several of her bravest
succession, to fight with *Cuchulainn*; each
turn received his death, at the hands of the
tonian youth At last, and after considerable
and the promise of large gifts and immunities,
her fair daughter *Finn-abhair*, in marriage,
Ferdiaidh Mac Damain, to engage in single
Cuchulainn.

This *Ferdiaidh* was one of the Damnonian
Firbolg race of the sea-board of Connacht; (from
the well-known Bay of Erris, in the present
was anciently called *Irrus Domnain*, or Erris
nonians). He and *Cuchulainn* were old acquaint
both been pupils at the same time in the celebrated
college of the lady *Scathach*, (a famous school
those ages on the north-east coast of Scotland).
friendship contracted by the champions at this foreign
continued warm and unbroken after their return
country; and nothing could surprise *Cuchulainn*
when he discovered that his attached friend and
had been induced by the blandishments of the wily
Connacht to undertake to engage in battle with
such unequal circumstances. He knew, too, that,
ception of the "*gae bulga*", or "belly-dart", alone,
was as accomplished as himself in the use of all military
and feats of championship, as well as in all the
manly vigour, strength, and courage.

Ferdiaidh at length came to the ford at which
was to be fought, where *Cuchulainn* came to talk to
remonstrate with him on the unfairness of the combat
he had undertaken; and after a good deal of conversation
old reminiscences, (conversation which in the story
on chiefly in rhyme), *Cuchulainn* ends the conference
following words, which are given in prose and verse:

"'Well, *Ferdiaidh*', said *Cuchulainn*, 'it is for
thou oughtst not to come to fight and combat with
when we were with *Scathach*, and with *Aifé*, it was
always went into every battle and battle-field, to every
bat and every fight, through every forest, and every
through every dark, and through every lonely place'

And having so said, he repeated the following words in verse: LECT. XIV.

"We were hearty friends;
We were companions in the woods;
We were fellows of the same bed,
Where we slept the balmy sleep,
"After mortal battles abroad,
After many foreign expeditions,
Together we went, and accomplished
Every forest lesson along with *Scathach*".

Cuchulainn having concluded this short address, *Ferdiaidh* asks him with what weapons they should commence the battle on that day. *Cuchulainn* answers, that as it was *Ferdiaidh* that first sought the ford, it was for him to choose the weapons for that day. *Ferdiaidh* then asks him if he remembered the missive weapons of valour [*airigtib gaisced*] which they practised when with *Scathach*? and *Cuchulainn* answers, that he did. "If thou dost", said *Ferdiaidh*, "let us try them". So they then had recourse to their "missive weapons of valour". Description of the Combats between Cuchulainn and Ferdiaidh.

The description of this protracted combat preserves for us an account as minute of the weapons and mode of warfare of the time, as Homer's of those of the Greeks before Ilium.

"They took up", (proceeds the tale), "two equally-balanced shields for defence against missiles, and their eight *ochar-chlis* or Missive-Shields, and their eight *cletiné*, or Little Spears; and their eight *colg-dets*, or Ivory-hilted Small Swords; and their eight *gotha-ndéts*, or Ivory-shafted Spears; and they cast them at and from each other, so that they resembled a swarm of bees on a summer's day; and they threw no cast that did not strike. Each of them continued to cast those missiles at the other from the dawn of early morning to the full middle of the day, until all their various missiles were destroyed against the faces [*tilib*] and bosses of the missive shields; and although the throwing was of the best description, the defence was so superior that neither drew the other's blood during that time.

"'Let us desist from these weapons now, *Cuchulainn*', said *Ferdiaidh*, 'because it is clear that it is not by them that our combat shall be decided'. 'Let us stop if thou thinkest the time has come', said *Cuchulainn*. They then threw their missiles away from them into the hands of their Charioteers".

The tale proceeds:

"'What weapons shall we turn to now, O *Cuchulainn*?' said *Ferdiaidh*. 'Thou hast thy choice of weapons until night', said *Cuchulainn*, 'since it was thou that first came to the ford'. 'Let us now', said *Ferdiaidh*, 'turn to our straight,

LECT. XIV.

Description of the Combats between Cuchulainn and Ferdiaidh.

elegant, smooth, hard *sleighs* (Light Spears)
fectly-hard strings of flax in them'. 'Let
Cuchulainn. They then took two hard,
and they then turned to their straight,
spears, with perfectly-hard lines or strings
Each of them began to cast the spears at the
full middle of the day till the close of the
the warding off was of the best, still the
superior, that each of them bled, reddened,
other, in that time. 'Let us desist from this, now
said *Ferdiaidh*. 'Let us desist', said *Cuchulainn*
then, and threw their arms away from them
their charioteers.

"Each of them then went towards the other,
arm around the other's neck, and embraced
Their horses were in the same enclosure that
charioteers sat at the same fire; and their
beds of green rushes for them, and supplied
pillows of wounded men. Then there came
ing and curing, to heal and cure them;
healing and salving herbs and plants to their
cuts and their many wounds. Every herb and
was applied to the sores, cuts, and many wounds
he sent share of the same over the ford westward
in order that the men of Erinn should not have
diaidh fell by him, that it was the consequence
of healing.

"They rested so for that night, and early on the
ing they repaired again to the ford of combat.

"'What arms shall we turn to on this day, O
Cuchulainn: 'To thee belongs the choice till
diaidh, 'because I had my choice of weapons in
have passed'. 'Let us then', said *Cuchulainn*,
aisibh muirnecha, [or great heavy spears, (dat.
this day; because the thrusting on this day is more
us than the casting (or shooting) of yesterday:
caught and our chariots yoked, until we fight from
on this day'. 'Let us indeed then', said *Ferdiaidh*
took upon them two broad, exceedingly firm shields
to their great heavy spears, on that day. Each of
pierce, to perforate, and to lacerate the other, from
early morning to the close of the evening. If it
tomary for flying birds to pass through human
might have passed through their bodies on that day
off lumps of gore and flesh from their cuts and

LECT. XIV.

Description of the Combats between Cuchulainn and Ferdiaidh.

[illegible]rounding clouds and air.[394] And when the closing hour of [illegible] came, their horses were tired, and their charioteers were [illegible]ed, and the champions themselves were exhausted.

"'Let us cease now O *Ferdiaidh*', said *Cuchulainn*, 'be[illegible] our steeds are tired, our charioteers are fatigued, and if [illegible] are wearied, why should not we be wearied too?' And [illegible] spoke this verse:

"'We are not bound to persevere
With Fomorian obduracy;
Let the cause be put in abeyance,
Now that the din of combat is over'.

"'Let us cease indeed, now', said *Ferdiaidh*, 'if the time [illegible] come'.

"They ceased then: they cast their weapons away from them [illegible] the hands of their charioteers: each of them came towards [illegible] other, put his arms around his neck, and embraced him [illegible] times. Their steeds were put into the same enclosure [illegible] night, and their charioteers sat at the same fire. Their [illegible]oteers prepared a litter-bed of green rushes for them, and [illegible] the pillows of wounded men for them. Professors of [illegible] and curing came to examine, and attend, and watch [illegible] them for that night; however, they found nothing to be of [illegible] to allay the pain and danger of their sores, their cuts, [illegible] their many wounds, but the application of charms, and [illegible], and incantations, to check their blood, and their pain, [illegible] the agonies of their wounds. Every charm, and every [illegible], and every incantation that was applied to the sores and [illegible] of *Cuchulainn*, he sent an equal share of them across [illegible] ford, to the west, to *Ferdiaidh*.

"They arose early the next morning, and repaired to the ford [illegible] combat. *Cuchulainn* perceived a great change of counte[illegible] and great gloominess upon *Ferdiaidh*, this day. 'Thou [illegible] in a bad state, to-day, O *Ferdiaidh*', said *Cuchulainn*. [illegible] hair has become dark, thine eye has become dull, and [illegible] own form, and thy countenance, and shape, have de[illegible] from thee'. 'It is not dread or terror of thee that makes [illegible] this day indeed', said *Ferdiaidh*, 'because there is not [illegible] this day a champion whom I am not able to subdue'.

"*Cuchulainn* then began to groan and to lament; and he [illegible] these words (in verse); and *Ferdiaidh* answered:

"'O *Ferdiaidh*, if it be thou indeed,

[394] [This is another extreme instance of style—one of those upon which the [illegible] had intended to offer some remarks in a special note, which was un[illegible] not prepared before his death. The reader may be referred to the [illegible] Tale of the Battle of *Magh Rath*, published by the Irish Archaeol. [illegible] 1842.]

LECT. XIV.

Description of the Combats between *Cuchulainn* and *Ferdiaidh*.

Certain I am that thou art a poor-souled being,
To have come at a woman's will
To fight with thy fellow-pupil'.

F "'O *Cuchulainn*, 't is a wise decree,—
Thou true warrior, thou true champion,—
That a man is forced to come
To the sod whereon his death shall be'.

C. "'*Finn-abhair*, the daughter of queen *Medbh*,
Whose superior beauty all must allow,
To thee was given, not for thy love,
But in order to prove thy mighty strength'.

F. "'My strength a while ago was proved,
O *Cuchulainn*, by a fair gauge;
One so brave I have not heard of,
Nor until this day have I ever found'.

C "'Thou hast caused all that has happened,
O son of *Daman*, son of *Dáiré*,
To have come by the counsel of a woman
To measure swords with thy fellow-pupil'.

F. "'Should I have returned without combat with thee,
Though we were fellow-pupils, O comely Cu,
Bad should be my fame and my renown,
With *Ailill* and with *Medbh* of *Cruachan*'.

C. "'No person has conveyed food to his mouth, [who
ever lived]
And no more [i.e. nor] has there been born
Of king or queen, without exception,
[Any] one for whom I would [be induced to
thee'.

F. "'O *Cuchulainn* of many deeds,
It is not thou but *Medbh* that has betrayed
I shall obtain victory and renown,
But it is not on thee the fault shall lie'.

C. "'My heart within me is a mass of gore,
My life has nearly from me fled;
I deem it no addition to my other deeds
To fight with thee, O *Ferdiaidh*'.

"After this dialogue *Ferdiaidh* spoke and said [illegible] thou hast been complaining of me', said *Ferdiaidh*, [illegible] pons shall we turn to this day?' 'Thou hast thy choice [illegible] pons till night', said *Cuchulainn*, 'because it was I [illegible] choice on yesterday'. 'Let us then', said *Ferdiaidh*, [illegible] heavy, mighty, blow-dealing swords, this day, as [illegible] that the cleaving to-day will bring us nearer to the [illegible] of the battle than the thrusting on yesterday'. Let us', [illegible]

lainn. They took upon them two great long shields this day. They turned to their great, mighty, blow-dealing swords. They began to cleave and cut down, to strike and to slash, until every piece of flesh which each of them cut from the shoulders and hips, and thighs of the other, was as large as the head of a month-old infant. They continued, each, to cleave the other in this manner, from the dawn of morning till the close of evening.[illegible]

Description of the Combats between Cuchulainn and Ferdiaidh.

"'Let us cease now, O *Cuchulainn*', said *Ferdiaidh:* 'Let us cease, indeed, if the time has come', said *Cuchulainn*. They stopped: they threw their arms away from them into the hands of their charioteers. Though their meeting (in the morning) was that of two pleasant, happy, joyous, high-spirited persons, their separation at that night was the separation of two displeased, sorrowful, dispirited persons. Their steeds were not in the same field that night: their charioteers were not at the same fire.

"They spent that night as before; and in the morning *Ferdiaidh* was up early and came alone to the ford of combat, because he knew that this was the day which should decide the combat and the fight; and he knew that either of them should fall on that day, there, or that both of them should fall. It was then he put on his suit of battle, and combat, and fighting, before *Cuchulainn* came to meet him; and, as part of that array of battle and fighting, he put on his apron of striped satin, with its border of fretted gold, next to his white skin. He put on his apron of brown leather, well sewn, over that outside. He then took a great, huge flag-stone, as large as a millstone, and secured it over this outside. He put his firm, deep apron of refined iron [literally, double-melted], over the great flat stone as large as a mill-stone, outside, in fear and in terror of the *gae bulga*, (or belly-dart) on that day. He put his crested helmet of battle, and combat, and fight, upon his head; in which were set four carbuncle gems, in its four sides; and it was garnished with bronze and crystal, and brilliant stones of the oriental world. He grasped his fretted, firm-pointed spear in his right hand. He slung his battle-sword by its bent hooks to his left side, with its hilt of pale gold and jointings of red gold. He threw his great shield with its beautiful pinnacles, over the declivity of his back; on which were fifty pointed bosses on each boss of which a full-grown hog might be spitted, besides its great centre-boss of red gold. *Ferdiaidh* on this

[illegible] [The reader may be referred to an interesting example of the exaggerated [illegible] style in descriptions of combats such as this, in that of the combat of [illegible] and Olivier, in "Le Mariage de Roland",—in *La Legende des Siècles*, [illegible] Victor Hugo.]

day exhibited various noble and wonderful feats of gladiatorial dexterity, which he never learned from from tutoress or from tutor, neither from [the lady *Scathach*, nor from *Uathach*, nor from *Aifi*, but [invented] by himself on that day, in preparation for

" *Cuchulainn* in due time reached him at the the weapons and feats which *Ferdiaidh* put forth. all this, my man *Laegh*', said *Cuchulainn*, 'and once with such other weapons as these; and besides be I that shall be yielding this day, you are to proach me, and speak evil of me, so that thereby and my anger may be increased; and should I be quisher, you are to cheer me and praise me, and me, so that my courage may be the greater'. 'It O *Cuchulainn*', said *Laegh*.

(*Cuchulainn*'s battle-array having been described is omitted in the text as well as here).

" Then *Cuchulainn* put on his array of battle, and fight; and he performed many noble, wonderful torial feats, on that day, which he had never learned one, not from *Scathach*, nor from *Uathach*, nor *Ferdiaidh* saw these feats; and he knew that they brought to bear against himself in their turn.

" 'What feat shall we decide upon, O *Ferdiaidh*', said *lainn*. 'To thee belongs the choice of weapons till *Ferdiaidh*. 'Let us come to the game of the Ford, *Cuchulainn*. 'Let us, indeed', said *Ferdiaidh*'. Al *diaidh* said this, he was sorely grieved to go there, knew it was at that game *Cuchulainn* had destroyed champion and every warrior who fought him, that Game of the Ford.

" Each of them then began to shoot at the other weapons, from the dawn of early morning to the full and when mid-day came, the anger of the champions more furious; and each of them approached the other. then *Cuchulainn* sprang from the brink of the ford, and on the boss of *Ferdiaidh*'s shield, seeking to strike him head over the border of the shield; upon which *Ferdiaidh* the shield a blow of his left elbow, and cast *Cuchulainn* from him as if he were a bird, back to the brink of *Cuchulainn* again sprang from the brink of the ford, and on the boss of *Ferdiaidh*'s shield, for the purpose of him on the head. *Ferdiaidh* gave the shield a stroke knee, and cast *Cuchulainn* from him, like a little to the brink of the ford. *Laegh*, (*Cuchulainn*'s

Description of the Combats between Cuchulainn and Ferdiaidh.

perceived all this. 'Alas!' said *Laegh*, 'the man who opposes you chastises you as a loving woman would her son; he spins you as a bubble spins on the water; he grinds you as a mill grinds dried malt; he pierces you as a lance pierces an oak; he entwines you as the woodbine entwines a tree; he pounces on you as a hawk pounces on a titmouse; so that you have no relation, or claim, or right, to bravery or to valour, henceforth, to the end of the world, you little deformed wretch', said *Laegh*.

"*Cuchulainn*, then, the third time, with the swiftness of the wind, with the fleetness of the swallow, with the spring of the dragon, leaped upon the buoyancy of the air, and alighted on the boss of *Ferdiaidh*'s shield, to endeavour to strike his head over the edge of the shield; upon which the champion shook the shield, and threw *Cuchulainn* off into the middle of the ford. It was then, indeed, that *Cuchulainn*'s fury first arose; he became inflated and swollen like a blown bladder, so that he became a terrible, awful, many-coloured, wonderful rainbow; so that the great, brave champion stood the height of a Fomorian (i.e. a man of the sea,) over the head of *Ferdiaidh*, in proper height. Such was the closeness of the fight between them, that their heads met above, and their legs below, and their arms in the middle, over the borders and bosses of their shields. Such was the closeness of the fight between them that their shields were split and cloven, from their borders to their centres. Such was the intensity of the fight between them that their spears were turned, and bent, and strained from their points to their heels: such was the intensity of the fight between them, that they forced the river out of its bed and out of its power, so that the middle of the ford might afford a bed which a king or a queen might sleep in.

"It was at the feat of sharp swords they fought all this time; and at last *Ferdiaidh* found an unguarded moment upon *Cuchulainn*, and he made a blow of his tooth-hilted sword, and buried it in his body, so that his blood flowed into his girdle, so that the ford was brown from the hero's blood. *Cuchulainn* did not return this feat, because *Ferdiaidh* continued a succession of wonderful, heavy, quick blows on him; until at last *Cuchulainn* called to his charioteer, *Laegh Mac Riangabhra*, for the *gas bulga* or 'belly-dart'.

The "Gas Bulga" of Cuchulainn.

"This was the character of that dart: it was upon a stream it should be set, and it was from between his toes he should cast it. It made but the wound of one dart in entering the body; but it presented thirty inverted points against coming back; so that it could not be drawn from a person's body without opening it. And so when *Ferdiaidh* heard the 'belly-dart'

[. XIV.] [Gae] [of] [ulainn.] called for, he suddenly dashed his shield down [illegible] lower part of his body; upon which *Cuchulainn* [illegible] from the palm of his hand, with a spiky, short, [illegible] border of the shield and through the breast of [illegible] it was visible out at his back after piercing his [illegible] body! *Ferdiaidh* threw the shield suddenly up [illegible] the upper part of his body, though it was a relief [illegible] the meantime the Charioteer had set the "belly-[illegible] stream; and *Cuchulainn* caught it between his [illegible] darted it at *Ferdiaidh* with such unerring aim and [illegible] it passed through the deep, firm, iron apron, broke [illegible] hard flag, which was as large as a mill-stone, in [illegible] and passed through the lower part of his body into [illegible] so that every part of him was filled with its inverted [illegible] 'Enough!' said *Ferdiaidh*, and he fell dead in the ford [illegible] *Cuchulainn* sprang to him, and took him up in his arms [illegible] carried him to the north side of the river, so that it [illegible] himself, and not queen *Medbh* and her people that [illegible] obtain his trophies".—

And so, *Cuchulainn*, after lamenting in many pathetic [illegible] the untimely fall of his early friend and fellow-pupil, [illegible] charioteer to strip him of his armour to obtain the [illegible] gold brooch which queen *Medbh* presented to him; and [illegible] cut open his body and recover the fatal Belly-Dart [illegible] of which the dexterous charioteer soon performed. And [illegible] ended the celebrated combat of *Cuchulainn* and *Ferdiaidh* [illegible] extravagantly told in this ancient tale of the *Táin Bo Chuailgné* [illegible] but the fact of which is preserved in the name of the [illegible] which it was fought, which from that day to the present [illegible] been called *Ath Firdiaidh* or *Ferdiaidh*'s Ford, now A[illegible] the present county of Louth.

The combat with *Ferdiaidh* was not the only occasion [illegible] which *Cuchulainn* had availed himself of the fatal [illegible] the *Gae Bulga*, or Belly-Dart, of which he alone is [illegible] in our old writings as being master. Concerning this [illegible] if we only knew of it from the exaggerated description [illegible] manner in which it tore its way through *Ferdiaidh*'s [illegible] tionable armour, its existence at all might be very well [illegible] as simply an exaggeration introduced for effect in this [illegible] lar Tale of the *Táin Bo Chuailgné;* but in another [illegible] we have, in my belief, very fair authority to show that *Cuchu*-*lainn* had unwittingly killed his own son *Conlaech* with [illegible] weapon, in an ordinary combat on the shore near [illegible] and in precisely the same way that *Ferdiaidh* is [illegible] have been killed with it.

LECT. XIV. The "Gae Bulga" of Cuchulainn.

Like the *Tathlum*, or wonderful Sling-Ball, with which the champion *Balor* was killed in the battle of the northern *Magh Tuireadh*, the *Gae Bulga*, or Belly-Dart, has been assigned an eastern and fabulous origin, by some ancient Irish poet whose name and precise time are not known to me. This poem consists of ten stanzas, and the only copy of it that I have ever met is one made about the year 1714 by John Mac Solly, of the county of Meath, a tolerably fair scribe.

The poem, the language of which is certainly older than the tenth century, and which has suffered but little by transcriptions, appears to have been written in answer to a question, and runs as follows:—

"How was the *Gae-Bulga* discovered?
Tell us without being ignorant,—
Or by whom was it brought hither,
From the eastern parts of the world?

"Inform those who are ignorant
That this weapon originally came hither
From *Bolg Mac Buain*, in the east,
To *Cuchulainn*, in *Muirtheimhné*.

"Two monsters that were upon the sea,
Which fought a fierce, angry battle;
Their names, I well remember, were
The *Curruid* and the *Coinchenn*.

"*Curruid* fell in the furious fight
By the noble, fierce *Coinchenn;*
Upon the boisterous, proud, Red Sea,
On the ridge of the cool and deep abyss.

"*Bolg Mac Buain*, a champion famed,
Discovered the skull of *Curruid* upon the strand,
Whither it fled from the sea abroad,
Closely pursued by the *Coinchenn*.

"*Bolg Mac Buain*, the renowned,
Many were the hosts whom he defeated;
By him was made the wild spear,
From the bones of the kingly monster.

"*Mac Buain* gave the *Gae Bolg*
To *Mac Iubar*, the brave subduer;
Mac Iubar next consigned the gift
To *Lena* his own fellow-pupil:

"*Lena* gave to *Dermeil*
The spear of hard sharp-pointed head;
And *Dermeil* gave it, without grudge,
Unto his tutoress, unto *Scathach:*

"*Scathach* gave it to [her daughter] *Aifé*,

LECT. XIV.

The "Gae Bulga" of Cuchulainn.

She never did a more foolish act;
And by her was made the fatal spear
By which her only son was slain.
"*Cuchulainn* brought the *Gai Bolg*
Into Erinn, with all its barbs;
By it he slew *Conlaech* of the battle-shields,
And *Ferdiaidh* afterwards, without mistake".

Such, then, is the account of the origin and subs[illegible] tory of the famous *gai* or *gae bulga*, as preserved in th[illegible] poem; but from the third line of the last stanza but one [illegible] appear that the *gae bulga* brought by *Cuchulainn* [illegible] was not the original spear, but one made on its model [illegible] the daughter of his tutoress *Scathach*, and the mo[illegible] son *Conlaech;* and given to him by her on his re[illegible] own country, after finishing his military education [illegible] mother.

The extracts given above have been somewhat [illegible] it would have been impossible perhaps to have given [illegible] intelligible account than they embrace of the use of th[illegible] weapons alluded to; and these were some of the princ[illegible] pons in use in ancient Erinn.

LECTURE XV.

[Delivered, 15th June, 1858.]

(V.) Weapons of Warfare; (continued). Examples of Weapons used in the *Táin Bo Chuailgné*;—the Iron Spear of *Cethern*;—"Double-bladed" Spears;—the antiquated arms of *Ilbach*;—etc. Shields with sharp rims; "Missive Shields". Story of the death of *Soaltainn*, father of *Cuchulainn*. Example of a Two-Handed Sword. Of the incribed Sword of *Cuchulainn*, of the *Gai Buaifneach*, (or "Venomed Spear"), of *Cormac*. Of the Shields used in ancient Erinn. The Shield of *Corb Mac Ciarain*. Early references to Shields. Of the use of the Compasses in engraving devices on Shields. Of the Shield of *Aedh Oirghialla*. The *Sciath*. The Shield-strap (*Nasc*), and Shield, of *Mac Con*. List of celebrated Shields, in the Book of Leinster.

If it were the special purpose of these lectures to make a complete investigation into the subject of the arms and modes of warfare among the early Gaedhils, it would be necessary to translate in the first place, the whole of the historic tale of the *Táin Bo Chuailgné*. For that remarkable piece is all through full of descriptions, names, and allusions, throwing light upon the details of this subject. But my design at present is only to offer some general account of our ancient weapons and of the use of them, in connection with the general subject of the manners and customs of early civilization in Erinn. I do not, therefore, propose to do more than select from ancient authorities a few examples of each kind of weapon, and mode of combat, used by the different races, down to a comparatively late period of our history; taking them in chronological order, but only taking so many of each as may be necessary to mark such changes of form, or such additions to the number of a champion's arms, as from time to time took place. I shall, accordingly, proceed in the first place to instance a few others of the more remarkable among the descriptions and allusions in the *Táin Bo Chuailgné*; but I shall not further refer to the incidents described in the tale, confining myself merely to noting the passages in which arms and warlike accoutrements are directly referred to.

Examples of weapons used in the *Táin Bo Chuailgné*.—The Iron Spear of *Cethern*.

The first of these to which I have got to refer is that in which an Iron spear is described, as having been borne by a warrior named *Cethern*. This *Cethern* was a chieftain of the Rudrician race, of Ulster; and he is stated to have been one of the first of the Ulster champions who came to the assistance of *Cuchulainn*, when he lay disabled by his many wounds after his desperate combat with *Ferdiaidh*. In his haste to reach the scene of

LECT. XV conflict, *Cathern* seems to have left home without [illegible] self with all his weapons. For he is described as ha[illegible] the north armed only with a single weapon [illegible] i.e. literally, a Spit of Iron: and this is the first [illegible] weapon so called. This word is often applied [illegible] ancient forms of the Gaedhalic language. The *b*[illegible] ever, as may be supposed, the only weapon [illegible] warrior; and accordingly the tale proceeds to [illegible] *Cathern* was slightly recovered from his first [illegible] against the men of Connacht, his wife arrived from [illegible] his sword, which had been forgotten by himself [illegible]

"Double-bladed" Spears.

Another species of spear, not hitherto mentioned, [illegible] on the scene; for, we are told in continuation of [illegible] of *Cathern*, that scarcely had he retired from [illegible] the enemy, when his father, *Finntann*, arrived [illegible] action, from *Dun-da-Bheann*, (on the river *Bann*), [illegible] one hundred and fifty men, each armed with a "[illegible] spear", that is, a spear with a blade at each end of [illegible] so that it wounded alike with either end. They [illegible] ever, excepting *Finntann* himself and his second son [illegible] who were saved by king *Ailill* and queen *Medbh*. [illegible]

After the defeat of *Finntann* again came *Menn*, [illegible] *cholga*, from the points of the Boyne, with a [illegible] men only, each armed like those who went before [illegible] a spear having a blade at each end. These twelve [illegible] killed, but *Menn* himself escaped.

Description of the antiquated arms of *Iliach*.

A curious description next occurs of the worn-out [illegible] champion so old as to have been superannuated at [illegible] queen *Medbh*'s invasion; but who seems to have been [illegible] to new vigour by the danger of the province. It is [illegible] for the details it contains respecting the materials and [illegible]tion of the war-chariot, as well as of a chieftain's [illegible] early date.

This aged warrior was *Iliach* the son of *Cas*, the son [illegible] *Ruadh*, a champion of the clann *Rudhraidhé*, the royal [illegible] Ulster, whose territory lay on the very northern coast. [illegible]

When this old warrior heard of the hostile descent [illegible] his native province by the queen of Connacht, he resolved [illegible] set out at once to the scene of action, and devote even [illegible] remnant of his life to the honour and security of his [illegible] His two old steeds, says the story, which had been let loose [illegible] life, were once more caught and yoked to his old [illegible] chariot, "which had neither cushions nor skins in it". [illegible] slung over his shoulder "his rough, dark shield of iron, [illegible] its hard rim of silver"; he girded "his rough, gray-[illegible] heavy-striking sword" to his left side. He placed his two "shaky-headed, many-gapped *sleghs*" (or spears), beside him in his old chariot. His people supplied the chariot around him with stones, and rocks, and great flags, and so he went to the scene of action.

In the battle, the old warrior seems to have recovered the power of youth. For it was not till after he had broken his old spear, and exhausted his heap of stones against his enemies, killing numbers of them, that he retired, barely alive, to the spot where *Dochs Mac Magach* stood, an old Connacht friend of his; and him the wounded old chief requested to cut off his head, since he could now do no more for his country, and begged of him to convey his old broken sword to his friend *Laeghairé*, another celebrated Ulster warrior, as the last token of his friendship; all of which was accordingly done.

According to the story of the *Tain Bo Chuailgné*, after *Cuchulainn* was disabled queen *Medbh* passed the bounds of the province and ravaged all Ulster, burning down even the extreme northern fortress and royal residence of *Dun Sobhaircé;* [the place now called Dunseverick, near the Giant's Causeway, in Antrim]. She succeeded then in possessing herself of the famous Bull of *Cuailgné*, the original object of all the war; and with this trophy of victory, she returned with the army of Connacht, in the direction of Athlone.

Descriptions in the *Táin Bo Chuailgné*.

The Ultonians had, however, by this time quite shaken off their lethargy, and assembling all their forces they pursued the queen, whom they succeeded in overtaking at *Clartha* (now Clara, near the present town of Mullingar).

It is at this stage of the history that occurs one of the most curious passages in the whole tract, as to the arms, dresses, and personal appearance of the princes and warriors of this age.

When *Ailill*, the husband of queen *Medbh*, perceives that they are overtaken by the Ultonians, he sends forth *Mac Roth*, his courier or herald, to observe more closely who are coming; and at the end of each of *Mac Roth*'s observations, he describes the appearance of each party and each chief exactly, in order that *Fergus Mac Róigh* (the exiled Ulster champion, who was, as will be remembered, with the Connacht army), might identify each to the king and queen.

All these descriptions of the different chieftains are highly picturesque, as well as full of antiquarian and historical interest. Much of them, however, relates rather to the dress and ornaments and the personal bearing of the various individuals described, than to their arms; and the consideration of this part belongs more properly to a future lecture, when I come to treat of the

LECT. XV.

Descriptions in the Táin Bo Chuailgné.

costume and domestic life of those ages. This part is moreover somewhat lengthy, and could not be abridged. I shall, therefore, here, simply extract specific descriptions of the various arms and armour it contains allusions, giving them in literal translation without any attempt to connect them together. They will be found to contain clear accounts of shields, swords, and spears; and of the latter, some and some of iron. And all these descriptions will show how very various were the forms materials and employed at the time, while yet the nature of the weapons is exactly similar to that of those with which already familiar.

One of the Ulster chiefs is described by *Mac Roth* as

—"A white Shield, with devices of red gold, long, gold-hilted Sword in one hand, and a Broad-(*manais lethan-ghlas*), in the other".

Of another he says, that he bears:

—"A Spear like the candle of a king's house in with rings of silver and bands of gold; wonderful which the spear the champion carries in his hand rings of silver [seem to] run upon it over the bands once from its heel to its socket; and the next time bands of gold that [seem to] run over the rings of the socket to the heel. [He carries a] sharp-rimmed over him; and a Sword with an ivory hilt, overlaid thread, at his left side".

Another bears:

—"A bright Shield, with silver devices, over him hilted Sword, in a flaming Scabbard, at his side; a column of a king's palace, beside him".

Another has:

—"A curved Shield, with a sharp rim, and rivets, a flesh-seeking Spear in his hand; and an ivory-hilted his side".

Another again carries:

—"A well-mounted, broad-edged, blood-dripping Spear) in his hand".

The next:

—"A wounding, Shadowy Spear at his shoulder black Shield at his shoulder, with a hard rim of white on it; a Sword with an ivory hilt, overlaid with thread hanging over his clothes outside".

Another bears above him:

—"A round Shield with a hard silver rim all around

deep-edged heavy-Spear (*gae*); and a long light-Spear, (*slegh*) in his hand; and an ivory-hilted Sword at his left side".

LECT. XV. Descriptions in the *Táin Bo Chuailgné*.

The next bears:

—"A bright Shield, with devices in red gold, above him; a gold-hilted, long, Sword, at his left side; a long, green-edged heavy-Spear, (*gae*), together with a sharp, threatening short-Spear (*fagha*), with hard strings (*suaineamain loga*), and rivets of white bronze, in his hand".

(This is the second instance of "strings" being attached to Spears; allusion was also made to them, it will be recollected, in the combat of *Cuchulainn* and *Ferdiaidh*.)

Another warrior bears:

—"A Shield with devices in gold over him; a hard, firm straight-edged Sword, girt to his side; and a straight-ridged light-Spear (*slegh*), flaming red in his hand".

Another wears:

—"A long, gold-hilted Sword at his left side; a flesh-seeking light-Spear (*slegh*), which dazzled the multitude, in his hand".

The two chieftains next described carry:

—"Two bright-hilted Swords, at their girdles; two flesh-seeking or light-Spears, (*slegha*), with bright rings of silver, in their hands".

Another warrior bears arms of iron: [for the "gray" spear was, doubtless, of that metal]: he is described as having:

—"A Sword of seven layers of re-melted iron, at one side of his back; a brown Shield over him; a great, gray Spear, with thirty rivets through its socket, in his hand".

The next has:

—"A long Sword at his side; a great trowel Spear (*manais*), in his right hand; a gray Shield at his shoulder".

The next:

—"A green Shield above him; and a thin, blue heavy spear (*gae*), at his shoulder".

Then comes a champion with:

—"A blood-red Shield, with rim and bosses, over him; a Sword with a silver hilt, at his left side; an elbowed or light Spear (*slegh*), with a golden socket over him".

And another:

—"A Shield with a rim of gold, over him; a Sword with a hilt of gold, at his left side; and a flesh-seeking, gold-shaded [that is, bronze] light-Spear, (*slegh*) in his hand".

Another again bears:

—"A bright Shield with fastening-hooks of red gold, and a rim and boss of red gold; a small, gold-hilted Sword at his side; and a sharp, light, shadowy Spear above him".

LECT. XV.

Descriptions in the *Táin Bo Chuailgné.*

Lastly come a group:

—"Armed with blue, shining Spears; yellow [illegible] ing Shields; gold-hilted, long Swords, at their [illegible]

There are a great many other similar descriptive [illegible] the tract; but as already observed I have selected [illegible] which offered some variety worthy of notice, either [illegible] the material, or the ornamental work of the different [illegible] In these passages the descriptions are not always [illegible] to enable us, to determine with perfect certainty, [illegible] which the various arms were composed; but sufficient [illegible] appears to warrant us in believing that they were [illegible] of iron both. The exact time at which the latter [illegible] known here, or extensively worked, is a subject [illegible] investigation. I have no doubt however that it was [illegible] and much used at a period very much earlier than [illegible] imagined.

No Axes or slings in the *Táin.*

It is remarkable that among the various groups of [illegible] either side, no one is described as armed with [illegible] with battle-axes, or with slings. In fact the sling [illegible] appear to have ever been a general weapon of warfare [illegible]

Shields with sharp rims, or edges.—"missive shields".

Before taking leave for the present of the *Táin Bo* [illegible] I wish to direct attention, a little more closely, to the [illegible] made there of shields with sharp rims or edges, which [illegible] in several of the passages just quoted.

In the first place, it will be recollected that, in the [illegible] combat between *Cuchulainn* and *Ferdiaidh*, there [illegible] little "missive shields" enumerated among the missive [illegible] with which that day's combat was fought. Now these [illegible] must have been metallic ones and with sharp [illegible] whether they were thrown horizontally or vertically [illegible] stated. It is probable, however, that they were thrown [illegible] ways. That shields were thrown vertically is clearly [illegible] the passage, in which it is mentioned that when *Cuch*[illegible] *Finntain*, after his cure by the physician *Fingin*, [illegible] his assaults on the men of Connacht, and meets *Ma*[illegible] one of the sons of king *Ailill* and queen *Medbh*, he [illegible] shield at him, the rim of which as it fell cut [illegible] Connacht warrior, wounding his charioteer, and his [illegible] cleaving the chariot itself at the same time.

There is another extraordinary passage relating to [illegible] edged shield, to which no previous reference has been [illegible] that in which the singular death of *Cuchulainn's* [illegible] recorded. The description is indeed very extravagant, [illegible] passage is important, as indicative of the exact nature of this curious species of shield. LECT. XV.

Story of the death of Soaltainn, the father of Cuchulainn.

When *Cuchulainn* had partially recovered from the effects of his combat with *Ferdiaidh*, his father, *Soaltainn*, came to visit and console him. The hero, however, would receive no consolation, but vengeance on the enemies of his province; and knowing that the time had nearly come for king *Concobar* and the men of Ulster to recover from the enchanted sleep, (*esamnaidhean*,) he determined to send his father to Emania to apprise them of the insulting intrusion of an enemy into their country, and to rouse them to exertion and vengeance. *Soaltainn*, accordingly, took *Cuchulainn*'s celebrated gray steed, *Liath Mhacha*, and rode directly to Emania; and when he came to the palace he shouted these words: "Men are wounded; women are captives; cows are driven away; O Ultonians";—but he received no answer, because it was the custom of the Ultonians that they were bound not to speak before their king, and their king was bound not to speak before his druids.

Soaltainn went then to *Leac na n-giall*, (i.e. the Flagstone of the Hostages), at Emania, and shouted the same words: "Men are wounded; women are captives; cows are driven away".

"Who has wounded; who has captured; who has driven off cows?" said *Cathbadh* the druid. "Ye have been plundered by *Ailill* and *Medbh*", said *Soailtainn*; "your wives, your children, and your youths, your steeds, your studs, and your flocks have been carried off. *Cuchulainn* has been fighting and obstructing the great four provinces of Erinn, in the gaps, defiles, and passages of the cantred of *Muirtheimhné*. * * * But he is no longer able to contend with them; and if you do not now avenge your own wrongs, they shall never be avenged".

"It is better to allow the man who offers such combats to a king to come on to death and destruction": said *Cathbadh* the druid. "All that you say is true", said king *Conchobar*. "It is true": said all the Ultonians at the same time.

Soailtainn then rushed out in a fury, because he had not received the answer he had expected from the Ultonians.

The *Liath Mhacha* (*Cuchulainn*'s steed), however, returned with him again to the side of the palace; but in *Soailtainn*'s confusion, his own shield, (says the tale), turned against him, and cut off his head, which fell into the hollow of the shield.

From all the various allusions quoted, and particularly from this last strange story, it is clear that some if not all the shields of the ancient champions had sharp borders, and might have

SECT. XV.

been often as we have seen they sometimes were [illegible] for offence as defence.

Example of a two-handed sword.

There is another remarkable weapon also [illegible] same tract to which special attention may be called [illegible] in a passage in a subsequent part of the tale, after [illegible] tions of men and arms of which I have been speak[illegible] passage in question mentions a Two-Handed Sword [illegible] a sword wielded occasionally with both hands. The [illegible] sword spoken of belonged to *Fergus Mac Roigh* [illegible] prince who had been exiled into Connacht by king [illegible] who now took part in the final battle of *Clartha*, [illegible] lingar), against his own countrymen.

The immediate cause of the banishment of *Fergus* [illegible] death of the sons of *Uisneach*, at the instigation of [illegible] in violation of *Fergus*'s honour, which had been pl[illegible] their safety; but besides this there was an older [illegible] between *Fergus* and *Concobar*, because *Fergus* had [illegible] rightful heir to the kingdom of Ulster and had actu[illegible] it for some time until *Concobar* supplanted him [illegible] ingenuity of his mother, whom *Fergus* had taken to [illegible]

Some short time before the battle of *Clartha*, [illegible] discovered *Fergus* asleep in a place and under circu[illegible] of pain and insult to him; but not deeming it pruden[illegible] time to have an open quarrel with him, he ordered his [illegible] to remove *Fergus*'s great sword from its scabbard, [illegible] replace it by a wooden one, in order that he might have [illegible] putable proof of the wrong which he had done him. [illegible] wards when the day of battle came, and king *Ailill* [illegible] *Fergus* to exert himself to the utmost of his power ag[illegible] countrymen, *Fergus* answered that he had unaccount[illegible] his sword, that with it he would hurl destruction on the [illegible] but that without it he was quite powerless. *Ailill* [illegible] the sword brought to him, and he placed it in the h[illegible] *Fergus*; who on receiving it exclaimed, "Thou art w[illegible] O *Calad-Bolg*, sword of *Leite!*"—[*calad bolg* literally [illegible] "the hard-bulging".]

Leité, whose sword it appears to have been, was [illegible] famous warrior of Ulster; and his son, *Fergus Mac L*[illegible] was slain about this time, was equally celebrated with hi[illegible] It is stated here that *Leité* obtained this celebrated swo[illegible] some one of the "fairy mansions" of Erinn, and that [illegible] was raised for a stroke it expanded to the dimensions of [illegible] bow in the firmament.

In the heat of the battle, *Fergus* came up to *Conco*[illegible] planted three mighty blows on his shield; which shield [illegible] called the *Ochain*, that is, the Groaner, because it emitted a loud groan whenever *Concobar* was in danger; and all the shields of Ulster groaned in answer to it. But although *Fergus* planted the three mighty blows on *Concobar's* shield, yet so bravely did *Concobar* carry that shield, that the ear of the shield was not even driven so near to his ear as to touch it. "Who is this", said *Fergus*, "that dares to hold a shield against me this day, when the four provinces of Erinn meet in the great battle of the *Táin Bo Chuailgné?*"

Example of a Two-handed Sword.

To this question *Concobar* answered: "A man younger and more accomplished than thou art, and of better father and mother; a man who banished thee from thy country and from thy lands and thy inheritance; a man who sent thee to the haunts of the deer, the hare, and the fox; a man who has not left thee the extent of one step of thy territory or thy lands; a man who has driven thee to accept unmanly subsidy from a woman, (that is, from the queen of Connacht); a man who insulted thee by killing the three sons of *Uisneach* while under thy protection at one time; a man who will defeat thee this day, in presence of the men of Erinn: *Concobar*, the son of *Fachtna Fathach*, son of *Ross Ruadh*, son of *Ruadhraidhé*, high king of Ulster, son of the high king of Erinn. And whoever insults thee, now", added *Concobar*, "thou art not entitled to any fine [*eric*], for the injury to thy person, or violation of thy honour, because it is in a woman's service that thou art".

"Now, when *Fergus* heard these insulting words", (says the tale), "he put his 'two hands' to the *Calad Bolg*, and in sweeping round, the edge came in contact with three small hillocks which were immediately at his back; and such was the force of the action, that he cut the three tops off them, and hurled them to a distance into the adjoining swamp, where they remain to this day, as well as the three decapitated trunks, which have ever since been called *na tri maela Midé*, or 'the three bald hills of Meath'".

Before passing away from *Cuchulainn*, the hero of the *Táin Bo Chuailgné*, it may be worth while to give a short extract relating to his sword, from a legend preserved in the Book of Ballymote, into which it was transcribed at the time of its compilation, in the year 1391, from the more ancient *Leabhar na h-UaChongbhala*, or book of Navan. It is the same which I referred to in a former lecture when alluding to the inscriptions placed within the hilts of ancient swords, by which they were said to tell of their performances, and the names of the champions to whom they belonged. The legend is referred to the time and court of king *Cormac Mac Airt*, who died A. D. 266;

Of the inscribed Sword of Cuchulainn.

LECT. XV. (that is, about as many years after the death of [illegible] and it is not more interesting from the account of [illegible] sword which it contains, than it is in connection [illegible] curious customs of *Cormac's* time, which are [illegible] The story runs thus:

"*Cormac*" [as chief king] "had the hostages of [illegible] his custody. One of these was *Socht* the son of *F*[illegible] genealogy is thus minutely given in the text: "[illegible] of *Fithal*, son of *Aengus*, son of *Glangein*, son of [illegible] *Socht*, son of *Fachtna*, son of *Seanchadh*, son of *A*[illegible] son of *Rudhraighé*, as the book of *UaChonghbhail* [illegible]

"*Socht* had a beautiful sword, with a hilt of [illegible] with silver, with a golden suspension (or belt), and [illegible] mented scabbard; it had a sharp point which [illegible] night like a candle. If its point were bent back to [illegible] would become straight again like a dart. It would [illegible] on the water; it would chop off a hair on one's [illegible] approaching the skin; it would cleave a man in two [illegible] one half of him would not miss the other for some ti[illegible]

(In this poetically exaggerated description, it [illegible] served that a vivid account is given of the temper and [illegible] of the sword-blade; and this is important.)

"He (*Socht*) said that this was 'the *Cruaidin Cai*[illegible] (or "hard, hard-headed"), *Cuchulainn's* sword; and [illegible] looked upon that sword as an heir-loom of their race [illegible] down from their fathers before them. Now there wa[illegible] brated court-steward at Tara at this time, whose name wa[illegible] *reann*, the son of *Uirgreann*. This steward requested [illegible] to sell the sword to him; and he told him that he sh[illegible] the same meals as himself every night, and that eve[illegible] his attendants should have four men's food [every day] [illegible] pliment to the sword, and its full value, at his own [illegible] besides that. 'Not so'; said *Socht*; 'I am not competen[illegible] my father's property as long as he is alive'.

"Things remained so for some time, *Duibhreann* [illegible] talking of the sword: at last he invited *Socht*, on [illegible] sion, to partake of some pleasant drink with him; and [illegible] *reann* instructed the cup-bearer to ply him well with [illegible] mead until he became drunk. This was done, acco[illegible] so that *Socht* did not know where he was, and so fe[illegible] The steward then took the sword from him, and wen[illegible] king's *Cerd* [or worker in precious metals], *Coua*[illegible] name]. 'Could you', said he, 'open the hilt of this [illegible] 'I could', said the *Cerd*. So the *Cerd* then took th[illegible] asunder, and inscribed the name *Duibhreann* in the [illegible] it, and fixed the sword again in the same way that it had been before.

Of the inscribed Sword of Cuchulainn.

"Things continued so for some time longer; and the steward was still asking the sword, but he could not get it from *Socht*. The steward then claimed the sword, and went through the legal form of enforcing his claim; and he asserted that it was his own, and that it was from him that it had been taken. *Socht* declared that the original sword was his by right, as well as its trappings and ornamentation; and he had a *Cerd* [or artificer] to prove this. He then repaired to his father *Fithal*, [who was the wisest and most celebrated of king *Cormac*'s judges], to ask his opinion on the case, and to beg of him to come along with him to defend his right to the sword.

"'I shall not', said *Fithal;* 'you must yourself sustain your causes, and it is not I that shall ever arbitrate for you, because you prosecute and are prosecutor in too many causes. Speak the truth without falsehood; falsehood shall not be answered by falsehood; but I will go if you fail to prove the ownership of the sword, and it will be the easier for me to cross the proceedings'".

The cause was opened before the monarch in due course, and *Socht* was allowed to prove that the sword was his; and he made oath that the sword was an heir-loom in his family, and that it was his own. Then the steward said:

"'Good, O King *Cormac;* the oath which *Socht* has sworn is a falsehood'. 'Who is to prove for you?' said *Cormac*, 'that it is a falsehood?' 'This', said he; 'if the sword is mine my name is written in it, and it is concealed in the hilt of the sword'. *Socht* was then called up by *Cormac*, who told him what had been said. 'The case is suspended', said *Cormac*, 'until this is ascertained; and let the *Cerd* be called before us'. The *Cerd* came, and ripped open the hilt; and the steward's name was found written in it.

"*Socht* (then spoke, and) said: 'Ye have heard, O men of Erinn, and [king] *Cormac* along with you, that this man acknowledges that the sword is his. I give up [said he to the steward] its possession along with its liabilities from me to you'. 'I acknowledge, indeed', said the steward, 'its ownership with its liabilities'.

"*Socht* then said: 'This is the sword that was found in the (headless) trunk of my grandfather; and I know not who it was that committed that deed, even to this day: and do thou, O *Cormac*, deliver judgment in that case'. 'That is a liability greater [than the value of the sword]', said *Cormac*. There were then seven *cumals* adjudged by *Cormac* for that crime,

LECT. XV. Of the inscribed Sword of Cuchulainn.

[on the steward], and to return the sword back [illegible] acknowledge', said the steward, 'the history of [illegible] and he then related the whole story of his find [illegible] the *Cerd* [or artificer] also told the same story [illegible] sword. Upon this *Cormac* ordered seven cumals [illegible] one cows] from the steward, and seven more [illegible] [or artificer]; and he said: 'It is a profitable injunction [illegible] *Neré* bound (on all; namely), to deliver a just [illegible] judgment'".

(The *Neré* alluded to was himself a judge, and [illegible] son of the celebrated judge, *Morann*, "of the Golden [illegible]

"'True', said *Cormac*, then; 'this is *Cuchulainn's* [illegible] and it was with this sword that my grandfather, *Conn* [illegible] hundred battles, was killed by the hand of *Tibraidé* [illegible] of which it was said:

"With an army of valiant companies,
If the men of Connacht have come,
Alas! to have seen *Conn*'s blood
Upon the sides of *Cuchulainn's* sword".

"*Cormac*, then, and *Fithal* [his judge] gave judgment [illegible] the sword; and it was *Cormac* that prepared it; and [illegible] himself was adjudged the sword, as *eric* [or fine] for [illegible] by it of his grandfather *Conn*".

Of this sword it was said, that it could not be [illegible] battle, nor the man in whose hand it was carried [illegible] was one of "the three precious jewels in Erinn", which [illegible] possessed, namely, his Cup, and his Branch, and this [illegible]

This history of *Cuchulainn's* sword offers a remarkable [illegible] ample of the care with which certain celebrated weapons [illegible] preserved, and the respect with which they were [illegible] among the Gaedhils; and that down to a period but little [illegible] Saint Patrick's time. But this is by no means a solitary [illegible] stance of the kind, as will be seen from the following [illegible] of another possession of the same king.

The Gae Buaifneach, or "Venomed Spear" of Cormac.

Besides *Cuchulainn*'s famous sword, the *Cruaidin* [illegible] *cheann*, or *Cataid-cheann*, king *Cormac* possessed another [illegible] ancient and not less celebrated weapon, known in [illegible] writings by various names, but more particularly by the [illegible] of the *Gae Buaifneach*, or "the Venomed Spear". The [illegible] of this spear is very remote, being indeed involved in the [illegible] tory of the *Tuatha Dé Danann*.

In the course of these lectures we have had occasion [illegible] than once, to mention the name of *Lug*, or *Lugaidh* [illegible] *Eithlenn*, the famous chief and king of the *Tuatha Dé Danann*, who killed his grandfather, *Balor* "of the evil eye", with a [illegible]

LECT. XV. The Gae Buaifneach, or "Venomed Spear" of Cormac.

from his sling of a ball of the kind called *tathlum*, at the battle of the second or northern *Magh Tuireadh*. The name of *Lugaidh*'s father was *Cian*; and this *Cian* was murdered by the three sons of *Bicrenn*, who were of the same race as himself.(336)

For this murder *Lugaidh* imposed an *eric* or fine of compromise on the three young warriors: and the fine which he imposed on them was, to procure for him certain things from foreign countries, which he was satisfied would cost them their lives to get; and amongst these was the famous Spear of *Assal*, or "*Pisris*", as others call him, the king of Persia. The youths, however, returned to *Erinn* with *Lugaidh*'s demands, after many years' travel and dreadful suffering, but so enfeebled that they died after landing on this east coast of Leinster, before they could reach Tara. The sufferings and tragical fate of these young warriors, I may remark, form one of the ancient tales known as the "Three Sorrows of Story-telling"; the other two being, the story of the tragical fate of the children of *Uisneach*, and that of the Children of *Lir*.(337)

The objects of *Lugaidh*'s demands, however, were safe; and among them was the famous spear, which at the time was called *Ibar Alainn Fidh-bhaidhea*, (or, "the Yew, the finest of timber"),—perhaps from the shaft being formed out of the yew tree,—though I believe that the ancient spear-handles were generally made of ash.

No farther account of the spear is found from *Lugaidh* down to *Celtchair Mac Uithir*, a famous chief and champion of Ulster in the time of *Concobar Mac Nessa*, whose residence was at *Dun Celtchair*, (now Downpatrick, in the county of Down). In *Celtchair*'s time the spear was called *Luin Cheltchair*, that is, *Celtchair*'s Spear; and it is described (in terms of unusual extravagance) both in the Tale of the *Táin Bo Chuailgné*, and in that of the *Bruighean Da Derga*.

From a poem on the manner of the deaths of the chief heroes of the Royal Branch, written by *Cinnaeth O'Hartigain*, who died in the year 975, it is stated that *Cumscraigh Menn*, the son of king *Concobar Mac Nessa*, was killed with the *Luin Cheltchair*, by *Ceat Mac Magach*, a famous Connacht champion; from which circumstance we may infer that the spear had at this time passed, probably in the vicissitudes of warfare, from Ulster into Connacht.

After this we hear nothing more of the *Luin Cheltchair*, until we find it in the possession of King *Cormac*, about the year

(336) Book of *Lecain*, fol. 28. a.

(337) [The Three Tales have been published in full in the ATLANTIS, vols. iii. iv. (Dublin, 1862-3), in the original, with Translation and notes by Professor O'Curry.]

LECT. XV. The Gae Buaifneach, or "Venomed Spear," of Cormac.

260, but then under the name of the *Crimall*, [illegible] "Blood-spotted". But in connexion with the [illegible] *Cormac*, it is reported to have borne a very [illegible] deed; no less than causing the abdication of one of [illegible] and wisest monarchs recorded to have filled the [illegible] The following are the circumstances, as preserved [illegible] history.

In the time of King *Cormac Mac Airt*[229] there [illegible] remarkable champion, of the people called the Desies [illegible] (or Bregia), whose name was *Aengus*, the son of [illegible] This champion took upon himself the office of *Aire* [illegible] the holder of which, under the Brehon laws, was [illegible] one who righted the wrongs of his own tribe against [illegible] doers from without, and maintained the cause of the [illegible] the poor against all wrongs and oppressions within. [illegible] happened that on a certain occasion in the performance [illegible] office *Aengus* had to proceed into Connacht to inflict [illegible] ment for some wrong done by the people of that [illegible] his own; and on his return he discovered that his [illegible] daughter had in his absence been forcibly carried off and [illegible] by *Cellach*, one of King *Cormac*'s younger sons. On [illegible] this outrage he made directly for Tara; but the door[illegible] refused him admission until he had put off his arms, [illegible] ancient regulation, no armed champion was allowed [illegible] the palace. *Aengus* complied with the rule, and entered [illegible] in passing through the hall he perceived the king's [illegible] spear, the *Crimall*, resting on its rack. He immediately [illegible] down the spear, and passed on into the council chamber [illegible] he saw the king in his chair of state, and his guilty son [illegible] sitting behind him.

The moment the enraged champion saw the offender [illegible] the spear by a single thrust through his heart. "Now [illegible] were three chains attached to the spear", (continues the [illegible]) "and three hooks to each chain; and on *Aengus* pulling [illegible] the spear, one of these hooks caught *Cormac*'s eye, and [illegible] asunder, while at the same time the heel-blade of the [illegible] struck *Cormac*'s high steward on the forehead, and [illegible] through his skull behind". The champion fled at [illegible] the palace towards his own house, closely pursued by the [illegible] attendants, no less than nine of whom he is said to have [illegible] with the spear himself, escaping finally from the [illegible]

From this circumstance, we are told, the *Crimall* received the name of *Gai Buaifneach*, or "Venomed Spear"; and [illegible]

[229] See *ante*, pp. 18, 58, 212, etc.

[230] See *ante*, p. [illegible]

has been ever since known in Irish history as *Aengus Gai Buaifneach*, or "*Aengus* of the Venomed Spear". But after this record the celebrated weapon disappears, so far as I know, from history.

The last mentioned anecdote of the *Crimall* is especially preserved by our historical writers, because it is connected with the retirement from the throne of so celebrated a king. The loss of his eye by the accident just described occasioned one of those "personal blemishes" which, according to the national law, were held to be inconsistent with the possession of the chief sovereignty; and *Cormac* accordingly resigned the throne, to devote the remainder of his life to the cultivation of the philosophy of the period, in the honourable retirement of a comparatively humble residence at *Acaill*, close to the royal seat of Tara.[340]

Of the Shields used in ancient Erinn.

I have now referred, I believe, to the greater part of the specific information preserved in the early manuscripts relative to the Sword and the Spear. It remains to speak of the structure of the Shield, which almost equalled in variety that of the weapons of offence of which we have been speaking. And I cannot better introduce the subject than by a curious extract from the "Yellow Book of *Lecain*" (a manuscript of about the year 1390, preserved in Trinity College, Dublin, H. 2. 16), which defines the meaning of the ancient name of this portion of a warrior's arms.

"*Lumman* was a name for every shield; that is, *Leoman* (a lion); because there is no shield without the picture of a lion inscribed on it, in order that its hatefulness and its terror might be the greater; because the lion is a furious, combative, fighting animal;—and it was through charms and incantations that this was done".

Of the Shield of Corb Mac Ciarain.

The tract from which I quote then proceeds to give an account of a particular Shield,—that, namely, of *Corb Mac Ciarain*, who flourished in the reign of king *Art*, the father of that *Cormac*, the cause of whose abdication has just been described.[341] This shield had belonged in succession to seven monarchs of Erinn; and it was believed to be a shield against which no force could prevail.

There was, says my authority, at this time, a certain

(340) [*Cormac's* wound is mentioned in the Ann. IV. Masters, at A.D. 265. His abdication in consequence of it is not stated by these Annalists, who record his death, at *Cleitach*, the following year, 266.]

(341) [*Art* reigned (according to the Annals of the IV. Masters), from A.D. 166 to 195. His father *Conn*, "of the Hundred Battles", reigned from 123 to 157.]

LECT. XV.

(Leinster) warrior, who was both a poet and a [illegible] *berna*, the son of *Regaman*, was his name. And [illegible] composed a poem for *Corb*, the owner of the [illegible] sented it to him; begging of him at the same time [illegible] the shield. *Corb* accordingly, unable to refuse the [illegible] a poet, gave him the shield; and his joy and [illegible] boundless. Now, it was just at this time that a [illegible] the eve of being fought between the monarch *Art*, [illegible] and some marauders from the Hebrides; and the [illegible] availed himself of so favourable an opportunity to try [illegible] acquired shield. He accordingly repaired to the [illegible] action, (which was at the Hill of *Cuarna*, near the [illegible] called Garristown, in Meath), and took an active [illegible] fight; but despite the protection of his gifted shield [illegible] unfortunate enough to have received no less than one [illegible] and fifty wounds in the battle. He then returned [illegible] but he was so exhausted by the time he reached T[illegible] (the place now called Straffan, in the county of [illegible] he died there of his wounds;—"his sharp spear in his [illegible] shield slung at his neck, and his sword with its [illegible] brass at his side; and so it was that he died",—says the [illegible] authority. He had ordered his servant to dig his grave [illegible] to bury him with his spear stretched at the one side, [illegible] at the other, and his shield over him";—and the place of [illegible] was ever after called *Lumman*, from the shield. Unfortunately I cannot identify the spot under any existing name.

Early references to Shields.

The first reference to the making and repairing of shields in ancient Erinn, is found in the account of the first Battle of [illegible] *Tuireadh*, where the Firbolgs required from the *Tuatha De Danann* time "to make and repair their arms and Shields", before coming to the fight. In this instance, however, there is no reference to the material of the shield; but we may, I think, presume that it was framed of wood, and that it was [illegible] with leather, or hides, and plates of metal.

We find it stated in the Annals of the Four Masters (A.M. 3817) that the monarch *Enna Airgtheach*, of the Milesian race, fell in battle this year; and that it was by him that silver Shields were made, at *Airget-Ros*, (in the present county of Kilkenny), which he bestowed on the men of Erinn, together with horses and chariots. Whether we insist on the truth of this statement, or not, it may be fairly inferred from it that the Gaedhils had among them very ancient traditions that metal shields, or shields covered or adorned with discs, at least, or plates of the precious as well as of other metals, had been known and used in the country from a remote period. And this tradition is well-sustained by a curious account of a shield made for *Cuchulainn*. LECT. XV.

The story of this shield is so short that I may give it verbatim. It is wild enough, as usual; but it will be found to contain some curious and valuable details as to the process of manufacture followed by the metal workers of the earliest times.

"There was a law made by the Ultonian knights that they should have Silver Shields made for them, and that the carved device of each should be different from those of all the others.

"*Cuchulainn* was at this time pursuing his military education at the school of *Buanann* and *Scathach*; and on his return home he found the shields in process of being made. *Cuchulainn* repaired to the manufacturer, whose name was *Mac Engé*. 'Make a shield for me', said he, 'and let me not find upon any other shield of the shields of the Ultonians the same carved devices that shall be on it'. 'I cannot undertake that', said *Mac Engé*, 'because I have exhausted my art on the shields of the Ultonians'.

"'I swear by my arms (of valour)', said *Cuchulainn*, 'that I shall kill you if you do not make my shield according to my order'. 'I am under (king) *Concobar*'s protection before you', said *Mac Engé*. 'I shall violate *Concobar*'s protection, then', said he, 'and shall kill you besides'; and *Cuchulainn* then repaired to his home.

"*Mac Engé* was greatly distressed at what happened; and as he was musing over it he saw a man advancing towards him. 'You are distressed', said he to *Mac Engé*. 'I have cause to be so', said the shieldmaker; 'namely, that I am to be killed unless I make *Cuchulainn*'s shield'.

"The man said to him: 'Clear out the floor of your workshop, and spread ashes upon its floor, until the ashes are a man's foot in depth'. It was done according to his directions.

"As *Mac Engé* was standing, after this, he saw the same man coming over the outer wall to him, with a fork in his hand, and two prongs projecting from it; and he planted one of the prongs in the ashes, and with the other described the devices that were to be engraven on *Cuchulainn*'s shield. *Luaithrindi*, [or 'ashes-engraver',] was the name of this prong; as *Dubditha* said: 'Were I *Mac Engé*, it is so I would engrave'. And *Dubhan* [the Black] was the name of the Shield".

Use of the Compasses in engraving devices on a shield.

This is a fanciful legend enough; but still it could hardly have been altogether an idle invention; and it seems likely enough that the object of the writer was simply to connect with the name of the great champion *Cuchulainn* the origin of some

LECT. XV.

remarkable new design in the engraving of shields, and at the same time to mark the (supposed) first application in ancient Erinn of the compasses, or two-pronged fork, to [illegible] in the engraving or casting of ornaments in metal of [illegible]

This legend is found in an old vellum manuscript [illegible] brary of Trinity College, Dublin (H. 3.17); but the [illegible] left us in the dark as to whether the shield was actually [illegible] the mould formed by the patterned ashes, or whether the [illegible] traced in the ashes was transferred to or copied on a [illegible] metal or wooden shield. The former, however, is [illegible] sistent with the circumstances, and if so, it would afford [illegible] instance of the antiquity of the founder's art in this country.

Of the Shield of *Aedh*, son of *Duach Dubh*, king of *Oirghiall*.

The next reference to the Shield to which I have to [illegible] attention, is important as regards the material employed [illegible] making it. That shields were not always wholly of [illegible] have perfectly authentic authority, from *Dallan Forgaill's* celebrated poem on the shield of *Aedh*, son of *Duach Dubh*, [illegible] of *Oirghiall* (or Oriell). This poem was written about [illegible] and it states that the shield had been made from the [illegible] a particular tree, namely, of the *Eo Rossa*, or Yew-tree of [illegible] [near *Leithghlinn*, in the present county of Carlow].

This "Yew of *Ross*" was one of the great ancient trees [illegible] tioned in our history, blown down by storms about this [illegible] after having stood, as it was believed, from the time of [illegible] monarch *Conaing Beg-eaglach*, a period of about fourteen hun[illegible] dred years.

It can be gathered from *Dallan Forgaill's* poem that [illegible] Shield of the king of *Oirghiall* had been made in a house under ground, by a druid named *Eochaidh*, who is said to have [illegible] dowed it with druidical protective properties, which gave [illegible] value and importance that did not attach to ordinary shields.

The *Sciath*.

The Shield, like the Spear, had various names among the ancient Gaedhils; but *Sciath* was the most common; and it is a fact not without some interest, that this very name, probably because the particular kind of shield represented by it had [illegible] come the most general form of the ancient Gaedhelic shield, is still preserved universally in almost every farmer's or peasant's house in Ireland, in connexion with a common household im[illegible] plement, which is framed like the kind of shield no doubt [illegible] merly used by the common soldiers at least. I allude to a no [illegible] peaceful an article than the *sciath*, or "scuttle", as it is some[illegible] times Anglicised, in Munster, in which I dare say many of [illegible] have often seen potatoes carried to the stream to be washed; an article probably very little if at all different from the ancient *sciath* used for defensive purposes. The common potato-*sciath* is a simple construction of stout wicker-work, of an oblong form, about three feet long and nearly two feet wide; having a depth in the centre of about six inches; the oblong not squared or of equal width at both ends, but tapering gradually to its termination, to a rounded and somewhat broad end at the top, and more gradually to a much sharper angle at the lower end

LECT. XV.

The Sciath.

This *Sciath* is made by first bending a good strong osier hoop to the form just described. To this hoop, at both ends, are lashed, with osier withes, in longitudinal lines, a sufficient number of strong rods to form ribs, bulging out to the required depth, and interwoven across from the sides with strong twigs, so as to form a light, compact, firm piece of wicker-work; which if covered, as the ancient shield was, with one or more layers of raw ox-hide, would offer no inconsiderable resistance to the assaults of the heaviest sword or spear.

It will now be readily understood that when a shield is described as being capacious enough to stow away "a young pig", we need not wonder at it, nor consider it as any very extravagant exaggeration; for I can testify that I myself, as I am sure thousands besides me, have seen children from one to two years old rocked to sleep in one of those modern potato-*sciaths*, which are probably indeed coarser in make, but are certainly not larger nor probably at all different in shape from the ancient shields.

It appears from various ancient Gaedhelic readings, that the *Sciath* or shield was in some way strapped to the arm; as we find, for instance, in the account of the combat between the young warrior *Conlaech*, the son of *Cuchulainn*, and the great champion *Conall Cearnach*, that when the former subdued the latter, instead of killing him he led him captive, "with his hands tied", says the story, "with the *sciathrach*, [i.e. straps], of his Shield".

The Shield Strap, and Shield, of Mac Con.

There is a very extraordinary but very short reference in the Brehon Laws to the *Nasc* or "strap" of a Shield, and to the Shield itself, of *Mac Con*, a prince of Munster, who fought the battle of *Magh Macruimhé*, [near Athenree, in the county of Galway], against *Art*, the monarch of Erinn, in which the latter was slain, in the year of our Lord 191; [or 195,—Ann. IV. Mag.]

This curious note runs as follows:

"*Mac Con* was a famous champion; he was a champion, a king, and the son of a king, and he was also a poet. His shield was always fastened to *Mac Con's* leg; and the *nasc* [band] of it was gold; and there were seven chains of red bronze attached to it, [that is, to the band]; and there was a champion at the end of each chain, whose support and obedience were com-

LECT. XV. manded by him when going to battle. When [illegible] entered on his combat, this band and the seven [illegible] were used to prevent any one of them taking [illegible] other, though the one should be more powerful [illegible] because [in such a case] they were immediately [illegible]. And this *nasc* [band] could not be taken in pledge [illegible].

The last observation refers to a general law, [illegible] *nasc*, as an exception, was, it seems, not subject, [illegible] seizure of arms for debt. The law of seizure [illegible] peculiar as regarded weapons of warfare, as well as [illegible] used on festive occasions. When Knives were [illegible] were left two days in the hands of the owners to give [illegible] opportunity of paying or settling the debt;—when [illegible] seized, they were left three days;—Swords were left [illegible] and "Emblazoned Shields" ten days.

List of celebrated Shields, in the Book of Leinster.

I cannot better conclude this part of my subject [illegible] referring to a very curious extract from the Book of [illegible] which records the names of the more celebrated Shields [illegible] at the royal palace of Emania, in the time of king [illegible] *Mac Nessa*. It is remarkable also as containing an [illegible] of one phase at least in the social life of the fierce [illegible] the Royal Branch, of which I shall have again to [illegible] future occasion. And it is historically important, [illegible] cause this entry forms the chief authority respecting [illegible] arrangements of the Courts or Halls of the Champions [illegible] gave name to the most celebrated order of warriors [illegible] in our ancient history.

"King *Concobar* had three houses, namely, the [illegible] *Ruaidh;* and the *Teité Brec;* and the *Craebh Derg* [illegible] the "Royal Branch", or court; and the "Speckled [illegible] and the "Red Branch"]. In the Red Court were kept the [illegible] [of the enemies], and their spoils and trophies. In the Royal Court sat the kings; that is, it was *Ruadh*, [or Royal,] because of the kings. In the Speckled Court were kept the Spears, and the Shields, and the Swords; that is, it was speckled from the hilts of golden-hilted swords, and from the glistening of the green spears, with their rings or collars, and their bands of gold and silver; and the scales and borders of the shields, composed of gold and of silver; and from the lustre of the vessels and [drinking] horns, and the flagons.

"The reason why they always put their arms away from them into one house, was: at everything harsh they heard [in their dining-hall] if not avenged on the spot, each man of them arose against the other, so that each of them would be assaulting the other with his shield and his head, throughout the house; and hence their arms were taken from them all, into the *Teitë Brec*. [These were the shields which were hung up] there: king *Concobar's Ochain*, i.e. *Concobar's* shield, with its four rims of gold around it; and *Cuchulainn's Fabán*, [the famous *Dubhan* already described]; and *Conall Cearnach's Lamh-tapaid*; and [the lady] *Flidas's Ochnech*; and *Furbaidh's* 'Red Bordered'; and *Causcrad's Coscrach*; and *Amargin's Echtach*; and *Condere's Ir*; and *Nuadat's* "Candle"; and *Fergus's Leochain*; and *Dubhthach's Uathach*; and *Errgé's Lettach*; and *Mend's Brattach*; and *Noisé's Luithech*; and *Laeghairé's Nithach*; and *Cormac's Croda*; and [the poet] *Seancad's Sciath-Arglan*; and *Celtcar's Comla Catha* ['gate of Battle'].

LECT. XV. List of celebrated Shields, in the Book of Leinster.

"Great indeed would be the enumeration of the shields that were there besides these".[348]

(348) original:—Tri tigi la Conchobar, edon in Chroeb Ruaid, ocus in Teite Brecc, ocus in Chroib Derg. Issin Chroeb-deirg no bitis in Chennail, ocus na cuind. Issin Chroeb-ruaid, imorro, no bitis na rig, edon ba ruad do no rigaib. Isin Teite-bricc, dna, no bitis na gae ocus na sceith ocus na claidib; edon ba brecc do imdornchoraib na claideb nor-duirn, ocus do chaindlib na nglas-gae, cona moncib ocus cona fethib ór ocus argait, ocus do lannaib ocus imthimchellaib na sciath di ór ocus argat; ocus do intinorum dna na hescra ocus na cuirn ocus na m-bailgend.

Is airi no bertis a n-arma n-adib in oen tech: Cech ní garg ro chluintis mam-poscis digail fair fechetóir, atraiged cech fer dia laslin combid cach dib oc tuarcain a chind ocus a sceith for a cheiliu rethnón in taige, comberthis a n-arma uadib uile isin Teite mbrecc. Ind Ochoin Chonchobair and, edon sciath Conchobair; ceitre imle óir impe; ocus Fabán Conculainn; ocus Lamtapaid Conaill Cernaig; ocus ind Ochnech Flidais; ocus ind Orderg Furbaide; ocus ind Choscrach Causcraid; ocus ind Echtach Amargin; ocus ind Ir Chondere; ocus in Caindel Nuadat; ocus ind Leochain Fergusa; ocus ind Uathach Dubthaig; ocus ind Lettach Errgi; ocus in Brattach Mind; ocus ind Luithech Noisen; ocus ind Nithach Loegaire; ocus in Chroda Chormaic; ocus in Sciath-arglan Senchada; ocus in Chomla-chatha Celtchair.

Mod tairrn, dna, arrobói do sciathaib and olchena.—[B. of Leinster; (H. 2. 18; T.C.D.); fol. 69. b. b.]

LECTURE XVI.

[illegible]

(V.) Weapons of Warfare; continued. Continued use of [illegible] down to the ix. century. Of the Burial of *Eoghan Bel*, [illegible] Spear". Story of St. *Ciaran* and Prince *Diarmaid*. A Spear [illegible] of the emblems of royalty;—account of the crowning of [illegible] Story relating to the Sword of *Crimthann*, and the Shield [illegible] headed weapons. Allusions to Iron and Bronze weapons, [illegible] Chief Poet of King *Laeghaire*, (temp. S. Patrick.) Of [illegible] *Leamhdhy*; (A.D. 594);—instance of a combat on horseback [illegible] Weapons used at the Battle of *Magh Rath*; (A.D. 637). The "[illegible] (*Gaerr*) of *Congal*, and of *Conall*. Account of the Military [illegible] *Kegh[illegible]*, (circa A.D. 640); from an ancient poem. [illegible] to the time of the Danish invasions, (A.D. 820). Weapons [illegible] Battle of Clontarf; (A.D. 1014). Account of the Battle, in [illegible] *Gall re Gaedhealu*";—"lurica" of the Danes;—description [illegible] from this History. Use of the *Lochlann*, or foreign Battle-Axe [illegible] backed Swords", of the Dalcassians. Use of Two Swords, [illegible] by *Murchadh*, at the Battle of Clontarf. Account of the [illegible] and of the stand of *Donnchadh* against the Ossorians, at [illegible]

We have been occupied so far with such references [illegible] gathered from history as to the military weapons [illegible] Erinn, from the earliest days of Firbolgs down to a [illegible] proaching that of the introduction of Christianity into [illegible] try, with which some more intimate acquaintance [illegible] manners and customs of continental nations may [illegible] to have been introduced. Little, if any, alteration [illegible] appears to have taken place in consequence of the [illegible] communication with other parts of Europe, either in the [illegible] of warfare or in the military weapons of the ancient [illegible] such as we have found them in the various descriptions [illegible] allusions I have collected. The Sword, the Spear, the [illegible] and the Shield appear to have continued still to be the [illegible] if not the only, weapons of offence, from the time of the [illegible] of Saint Patrick, in the year 432, to the Danish invasion [illegible] the year 820, when we first note the use of Battle-Axes [illegible] Bows and Arrows. It would therefore be but mere [illegible] of what has already been said, to follow the history of [illegible] weapons by quoting any further instances in detail from [illegible] of *Cormac Mac Airt*, in the third century, to that of the [illegible] Invasion in the ninth. I shall only take a few instances [illegible] the history of our own domestic warfare between the intro[illegible] Christianity and the invasion of the Danes, to show [illegible] change appears to have taken place between these periods [illegible]

Instances showing continued use of the same Weapons down to IX. century.

In the Annals of the Four Masters, at A.D. 537, we find it recorded that *Eoghan Bel*, king of Connacht, was mortally wounded in a battle near the present town of Sligo, by *Fergus* and *Domnall*, the kings of Ulster, who had made a plundering expedition into his country. King *Eoghan* survived the battle a few days; but when he found that his end was drawing near, he ordered a grave to be dug for him in the side of the mount on which his own palace stood, and that he should be buried in it "with his Red Spear in his hand and his face to the north" against his Ulster enemies. The mount on which the grave was opened, in which *Eoghan* was buried according to his own direction, overlooked the road by which the Ulstermen were accustomed to pass into his territory; and it would seem that the grave must have been left open, as the Ulstermen became so terrified at it that they are stated to have made an incursion into the district afterwards, when, raising the body, they took it away past Sligo to the north, and buried it there with its face down, on the banks of *Loch Gilé*.

Of the Burial of *Eoghan Bel*, with his "Red Spear".

This example proves that the Spear was still, in 537, a century after the time of Saint Patrick, the favourite among the Christian Gaedhils.

Story of St. *Ciaran* and Prince *Diarmait*.

In the Annals of the Four Masters, at the year 528, it is stated that *Tuathal Maelgarbh* assumed the monarchy of Erinn in this year, to the prejudice of the young prince *Diarmait*, the son of *Fergus Cerrbheóil*, whom he drove out of Meath, over the Shannon, into Connacht. It happened that it was just at this time that Saint *Ciaran* came out, from the island in the Shannon in which he had founded his first church, to the mainland of Westmeath, for the purpose of establishing himself on a broader foundation; and just as he was about to set up the first pole on the site on which the famous ruins of Clonmacnoise yet stand, he was joined by the young prince *Diarmait* and his few attendants, who had landed from their boats, curious to see where Saint *Ciaran* and his followers would stop. Saint *Ciaran*, recognizing the prince, invited him to lend his assistance to the setting up of the pole. This prince *Diarmait* did; and thereupon Saint *Ciaran* gave him his blessing; and said in addition, that the time for mounting the throne of his ancestors was at hand.

Hardly was the prophecy pronounced, when *Diarmait*'s step-brother, *Maelmordha Mac Argatan*, having heard the saint's words, and placing implicit confidence in his promise, set off with all speed to where he knew the monarch *Tuathal* was at the time holding an assembly,—at a place called *Grellach Eilti*, in the same district. When *Tuathal*'s people saw an

LECT. XVI. armed horseman coming at full speed towards them, lieved him to be a courier coming with news of to the king, and they accordingly opened a way for reaching the place where the king was, however, threw himself from his horse, rushed up straight to, and plunged his Spear into his breast, killing him This daring deed cost *Maelmordha* his life, as he we are told with "hundreds of spears" at once, by dants of the murdered monarch. *Diarmait*, however, diately assumed the monarchy of Erinn without and thus the saint's blessing was fulfilled.

A Spear of Honour one of the emblems of royalty.

In the history of the reign of this king a very curious stance indeed is recorded, concerning a Spear of Honour seems to have been taken as the ensign of royalty. lusion occurs in connection with the quarrel which important historical fact of the desertion of the royal Tara in consequence of Saint *Ruadan's* curse, I state the substance of the account in full.

Of the cursing of Tara by St. *Ruadan*.

Strictly administering the laws, as they then stood king *Diarmait* kept up a constant visitation by his great and *Fianns*, or standing army, throughout the country force them. Now, it happened that on one occasion officers passed into the province of Connacht, preceded of the king's heralds,—whose business it was to announce approach at any noble residence at which they claim the free quarterage due to their official dignity engaged in the examination of the state of the the administration of the laws, by the king's command the mode of proceeding of the royal agents was this they came to the house of a provincial king or chief, they intended to take up their temporary abode, who carried (we are told) as his insignia of office and the monarch's favourite Spear, always approached the residence, holding that famous weapon "horizontally" across his hands; and wherever the door was not wide to admit the spear in that position, the herald used to walls at either side to be taken down until the requisite was obtained; a curious relic of the peculiar sumptuary usages of more ancient times.

The king's stewards and his heralds having gone nacht on their tour of inspection, they came to the *Guairé*, king of *Ui Mainé*; (a large district situated present counties of Galway and Roscommon, and of ancient sept of the O'Kellys were chiefs). Here they the Royal Spear would not enter "horizontally", and were obliged to be broken down in consequence. But *Aedh*, the lord of the place, becoming enraged at this, in his anger attacked and slew the king's herald, who carried the spear.

When his anger had cooled so far as to see what he had done, knowing the stern disposition of the monarch, *Aedh Guairé* fled precipitately from his house across the Shannon, taking refuge in Lower Ormond with his cousin, the bishop *Senach*. The bishop however did not deem himself sufficient protection in such a case; and he accordingly conveyed the fugitive without delay to the more powerful and sacred sanctuary of the celebrated Saint *Ruadan* of *Lothra*, [now Lorra], in that district. Saint *Ruadan* himself felt some uneasiness as to his power of appeasing the king in so serious an affair; and he again conveyed the prince secretly to some friends in Wales, but the king's influence followed him even into that country; and his friends there were forced to send him back to Saint *Ruadan*.

Diarmait having received information of the return of *Aedh*, went directly from Tara, with a party of his people, to *Lothra*, and demanded of Saint *Ruadan* to deliver him into his hands. This the saint refused to do; whereupon the king took him by force, in violation of the well-established privilege of his saintly sanctuary. Saint *Ruadan* therefore, accompanied by Saint *Brendan* of Birr, followed the king to Tara; but *Diarmait* would not listen to them. And then the two saints went round the hill of Tara, ringing their bells, and cursing it, and prophesying that no king of Erinn should ever again reside there. And this was fulfilled; for *Diarmait* having been soon after murdered in *Dal Araidhé*, in Ulster, (in consequence, it was believed, of his insult to Saint *Ruadan*), the succeeding kings of Erinn chose to reside in other places; and Tara in fact was abandoned, and was never afterwards occupied as a place of residence.

The immediate value of this historic story to the object of these lectures is of course only to show how important a place the spear continued to hold down to the close of the sixth century, among the military weapons of the country; so important as even to represent symbolically, as in this case, the authority of the monarch.

Story referring to the Sword of Crimhthann, and the Shield of Eana, as celebrate weapons.

The next citation I have to make is one chiefly connected, indeed, with the history of the manufacture and use of ordinary household articles; but it contains a curious reference to a celebrated Shield and Sword of more ancient times, apparently preserved and regarded with the highest honour at the comparatively late period to which the history refers.

In the year 568, *Aedh Mac Ainmiré* assumed the monarchy of Erinn. Now, it happened that shortly after his accession to the

LECT. XVI. Story referring to the Sword of Crimhthann, and the Shield of Bran, as celebrated weapons.

throne, *Cumascach*, the youngest of his four son[illegible] consent to make a princely circuit of visitations to [illegible] and chief courts of the kingdom, in accordance [illegible] custom. The pleasure of prince *Cumascach*, howev[illegible] no means that his visits should carry any [illegible] residences at which he proposed to make them; [illegible] trary, he was resolved that his presence should be [illegible] and as insulting to his entertainers as he could mak[illegible]

The first court that he visited was that of *Bran* [illegible] of Leinster, at *Bealach Conglais*, [the place now [illegible] tinglass, in the county of Wicklow]. His characte[illegible] ever, preceded him. When therefore king *Bran* [illegible] so unwelcome a guest was on his way to him, with [illegible] and oppressive retinue, he dressed himself in the [illegible] his own domestics, and desired that the prince [illegible] seemingly well received; at the same time that [illegible] tell him that he, *Bran*, was away in Britain, raisin[illegible] from that people. The prince and his company [illegible] due time at *Bran Dubh*'s court, and where they [illegible] parate spacious hall, fitted up for their reception, [illegible] propriate repast prepared for them.

While this was going on, there came to *Bran Dubh* [illegible] bearing some useful presents, anticipatory, as it [illegible] of the events which were to ensue. This friend [illegible] than Saint *Maedhog* of *Cluain-Mór*, [in the county [illegible] and the homely presents which he brought to *Bran* [illegible] flesh fork and a boiler; but besides these he brough[illegible] a Shield and a Sword; all which the saint showed to [illegible] whilst he recited the following short poem:

"Here are presents meet for a king,
O Son of *Eochaidh*, never-cheerless,—
A fork with carving prongs;
A shield; a sword; and a boiler.

"The fork, for the purposes of the cooked flesh,
Is a gift becoming a high king;
The boiler, for the boiling of the raw,—
For such our Lord Himself ordained.

"The Shield, for the front of battle
Against wicked tyrants;
The Sword, to rout the battalions,
Thou mayest have, O son of *Eochaidh*.

"*Connlaid*, Saint *Brigid*'s artificer,—it is not forgott[illegible]
It was he that made this flesh-fork;
Gressach (the smith) made this boiler,
For the son of *Niall*, for king *Laeghaire*.

Story referring to the Sword of *Crimhthann*, and the Shield of *Enna*, as celebrated weapons.

"The Sword of *Crimhthann*, the Shield of *Enna*,
From me thou shalt receive;
The Flesh-fork of Fair *Mac-in-Egis*;
And the Boiler of *Dubhthach* of Dublin.
"*Laeghairé* of the mantles gave it [this boiler]
To *Dubhthach* the chief poet of Erinn;
Dubhthach of overspreading fame gave it
To *Fiach*, the son of his sister.
"*Fiach* gave it to *Dunlaing* of his own race;
Dunlaing gave it to *Ailill;*
Ailill gave it to me afterwards;
I give it to thee, O *Bran Dubh!*
"Good are the gifts which thou receivest,—
A Flesh-fork; and a strong boiler;
The Sword of *Crimhthann* who was never vanquished;
The Shield of *Enna*, which is all red with blood".

* * * * * * * * * *

"My flesh-fork of three uplifting prongs,
I have brought hither to *Bran* of the fierce battles;
My straight, red, carved boiler,
I have given to the noble victorious *Bran*", [etc.].

This curious little poem is to be found in the Book of Leinster, (a manuscript, it will be remembered, compiled before the year 1150); much of the interesting matter it contains is not pertinent to our present purpose, though I shall have to make use of it hereafter; it records however this curious fact of the transmission from generation to generation of the instruments of warfare of distinguished men. It is still more curious that in this instance it should be so saintly a man as Saint *Maedhog*—[pron. Mogue; not of Ferns, but of Clonmore]—that figures as the preserver of such arms. This Saint *Maedhog*, however, was himself of the royal race of Leinster.

The shield of *Enna* was that of *Enna Cinnselach*, the celebrated king of Leinster, whose son *Eochaidh* slew the great monarch *Niall* "of the Nine Hostages", in France, A.D. 405.

Crimhthann, whose shield is alluded to, was the other son and successor of *Enna*. *Crimhthann* was king of Leinster at the coming of Saint Patrick, at whose hands he received baptism at *Rath Bhiligh*, [in the present county of Carlow]. He continued to be the enemy of the monarch *Laeghairé*, (who was son of *Niall* "of the Nine Hostages",) and of his successor *Ailill Molt*, against whom he fought at the battle of *Ocha*, near Tara, A.D. 478, where that monarch was killed.

The poet *Dubhthach*, mentioned in Saint *Maedhog*'s poem, had been chief poet to the monarch *Laeghairé*, and was the first person who received the Christian faith from Saint Patrick, on his first visit to Tara. I possess a copy of an ancient [illegible] praise of *Crimhthann* son of *Enna Cinnselach*, [illegible] battles, the authorship of which is ascribed to this [illegible] which I believe to be genuine, and in which the [illegible] curious verse occurs, in reference to this battle *Ochó* [illegible]

"It was my mantle that was on *Crimhthann*,
In the Battle of *Ochá*;
My iron lorica, my shield of bronze,—
My children and my friends".[343]

It will be perceived that the allusions to an "iron [illegible] a "bronze shield" are as important in reference to [illegible] of arms at the beginning of our Christian era, as they [illegible] timony of the co-existence of iron and bronze at that, [illegible] have no doubt an earlier period.

But to return to *Bran Dubh*, the king of Leinster, [illegible] *mascach*, the son of *Aedh Mac Ainmiré*, monarch [illegible] When Saint *Maedhog* departed from king *Bran*, leaving [illegible] the presents enumerated above, the latter took an opp[illegible] in disguise, of closing fast the door of the house in [illegible] monarch's insolent son and his friends were making [illegible] comfortable; and placing a guard around it, he ignited [illegible] wood against it on the outside, so that it was soon [illegible] fire. The young prince, however, availed himself of the [illegible] rosity of his poet, who exchanged clothes with him, [illegible] the universal privilege of inviolability accorded to [illegible] was allowed to escape from the flames, but only to be [illegible] the steward of the neighbouring church of *Cill Ran*[illegible] which he sought sanctuary.

News of the untimely death of his son soon reached the [illegible] arch *Aedh*, at his palace of *Ailech*, [near Derry]; who witho[illegible] lay raised a powerful force, marched into Leinster, and [illegible] in the immediate vicinity of *Bran Dubh*'s residence. T[illegible] neral incidents of this encampment and of the battle that [illegible] in which the monarch was slain, are outside our present [illegible] and it is sufficient to state that the account makes [illegible] mention of swords, spears, and shields, as well as of "b[illegible] flying from the tops of spears placed at the doors of all the [illegible] of the camp,—this last a very curious entry.

There is, however, one incident of a kind unlike [illegible] which we find mention in our ancient writings, I mean [illegible] stance of combat on horseback.

When *Bran Dubh* in the first instance saw the dispo[illegible] the monarch and his forces, "he mounted his single hors[illegible]

(343) orig. :—ıſſé mo chımchach pobo ım Chpımchann,—ı cath [illegible] mo luıpech ıapainn, mo ſcıath uma,—mo chınaı, [illegible]

are told, rode up to their line alone, and challenged the best of them to single combat. The challenge was taken up by *Blathach*, the chief marshal of the monarch of Erinn, "who came out mounted on the monarch's favourite steed". This *Blathach* was one of the most expert champions of his day, and is praised for that he never threw an erring cast of his spear; but, notwithstanding, he was no match for the famous *Bran Dubh*, who soon overthrew him and cut off his head, with which, as well as the monarch's favourite steed, he returned in triumph to his own people.

The year in which this occurred, and in which the monarch *Aedh* was slain in the battle of *Dunbolg* [near Baltinglass], was the year 594.

We now come down a generation or two later, to the battle of *Magh Rath*; and we find the same weapons still in use.

Weapons used at the battle of *Magh Rath*; (A.D. 634.)

The battle of *Magh Rath*, [a place believed to be that now called Moira, in the county of Down], was fought A.D. 634, by *Domhnall* the monarch of Erinn, against *Congal Claen*, a rebellious prince of Ulster, who passed into Scotland and Britain, and returned with a large number of auxiliaries and mercenaries, to make war on the monarch. An ancient Gaedhelic tract exists containing a minute and florid account of this battle and its causes. This piece was published in full with an English translation, by the Irish Archaeological Society in the year 1842. To that publication I may once for all refer, without going into an unnecessary account of what will be found in it.

In the controversy between the monarch *Domhnall* and the prince *Congal*, the latter reminds the former of the time in which they were both in banishment in Scotland, for disloyalty to the Irish monarch *Suibhné Menn*; and how *Congal* was the means of restoring him, not only to his country but to its sovereignty also:

"Thou didst afterwards return to Erinn, (said *Congal*), and I returned along with thee, for I was in exile along with thee. We put into port at *Traigh Rudhraidhe*, [now the bay of Dundrum, county Down], and there we held a short consultation. And what thou didst say, was, that whoever thou wouldst get to go and betray the king of Erinn, thou wouldst be bound to restore his territory to him, whenever thou shouldst become king over Erinn. I went on that enterprise, O king, for a promise that my patrimony should be wholly restored to me whenever thou shouldst become monarch of Erinn; and I delayed not until I reached *Ailech Neid*, [*Aileach*, near Derry] where the king held his residence at the time. The king came out upon the green, surrounded by a great concourse of the men of

LECT. XVI.

Erinn; and he was playing chess amidst the host, [illegible] came into the assembly, passing, without the permission [illegible] one, through the crowds; and I made a thrust of my [illegible] Spear, (the *Gearr Chonaill*) which I held in my hand, [illegible] breast of the king, and the stone which was at his back [illegible] ded to the thrust, and his heart's blood was on the [illegible] spear, so that he fell dead of it".[344]

The "Short Spear" (*Gearr*) of *Congal*.

This is a very clear reference to a short Spear, [illegible] "*Gearr*" *Chonaill*, that is, "the short spear" of Conall [illegible] but though we learn from this that the weapon was [illegible] that the king was struck with it directly from the hand, [illegible] have no means of determining its precise form.

The "Short Spear" of *Conall*, the son of *Baedan*.

There is, in another passage of the same tale,[345] another [illegible] ence; but it makes no nearer approach to an exact description [illegible] the "short spear". When the monarch *Domhnall* had [illegible] his forces to *Magh Rath*, he exhorted his northern [illegible] relatives to prove their valour in his behalf, in words [illegible] to express his doubts of their fidelity and bravery; and the [illegible] says that:

"To whomsoever this speech of the monarch [illegible] superfluous, a haughty, fierce-faced northman from the [illegible] part of the protecting battalion of (*Tir*) *Chonaill*, [illegible] raged at the verbal exhortation and lordly instruction [illegible] monarch, the grandson of *Ainmiré*; his name was *Con*[illegible] son of *Baedan*, who was the son of *Ninné*, from *Tul*[illegible] and the high-cliffed shore of Tory, in the north; [illegible] not like to be exhorted at all, and he did not like to [illegible] cited; so he poised his 'black-darting spear', and sent [illegible] of it spitefully and suddenly at the grandson of *Ain*[illegible] king). But three select, lordly chieftains from the [illegible] the defensive battalion of (*Tir*) *Chonaill*, namely *Maine*, [illegible] and *Airnelach*, (observing his design) sprang before the king, and between him and the east, and raised their three [illegible] hard shields before the king and between him and the [illegible] but, however, the short spear of *Conall* passed through the [illegible] shields, one after another, and through the red-backed [illegible] the king himself, until it passed into the ground between the feet of the monarch of Erinn".

Account of the military array of King *Raghallach*; (circa A.D. 640); from an ancient poem.

It is drily recorded in the Annals of the Four Masters, [illegible] year 645, that *Raghallach* the son of *Uathach*, king of [illegible] was killed on a Sunday, by *Maelbrighdé* the son of *M*[illegible] The circumstances of the murder are not there recorded; [illegible]

(344) *The Banquet of Dun na n-gedh, and the Battle of Magh Rath*, [illegible] by John O'Donovan, for the Irish Archaeological Society. Dublin, 184[illegible]

(345) Ib., p. 153.

elsewhere preserved. The king being out hunting, pierced a large buck with his spear, and then followed him into a bog where some men were engaged in cutting turf. These men had finished the buck before the king came up; and on his demanding what he deemed to be his lawful game, they set upon himself and killed him also with their ignoble spades. King *Raghallach's* family poet, *Fintan*, wrote a poem on his royal master's ignominious death, in which he recounts the chief exploits of his life and reign; and as this singular poem gives an undoubtedly correct illustration of military array, in the middle of the seventh century, I venture to give here a few verses of it, from a fine copy in my own possession.

LECT. XVI. Account of the military array of king *Raghallach*; (circa A.D. 640); from an ancient poem.

According to this poem *Muirenn* was the name of *Raghallach's* wife; and he had three sons, *Fergus*, *Cellach*, and *Cathal;* the latter of whom, at the time of his father's death, was a divinity student at Clonard; a situation which, however, did not deter him from taking signal vengeance on the murderers of his father. After enumerating several battles gained by king *Raghallach*, *Fintan* proceeds to describe an event which took place during his reign, on an occasion when *Nindé*, prince and lord of *Tir-Chonaill*, made a predatory incursion into Connacht, at the time that the king and queen and their sons, with the assembled nobles of the province, were holding the ancient games of *Lughnasad* or Lammas, (on the 1st of August), on the sporting green of the palace of *Cruachan*.

"*Raghallach*, on Lammas-Day,
Cellach, and *Fergus* the choleric,
And *Muirenn Mael*, with her necklaces,
Were preparing for the Games of *Cruachan*.

"When came *Nindé* the vindictive,
The son of the plundering *Duach* son of *Conall*,
With *Fraechan*, son of *Sanasan;*
And they burned all before them to *Ceis Corann*.

"We perceived the conflagrations;
They moved not in quiet progress;—
The land was filled with burnings
From *Sliabh Gamh* to *Sith Seaghsa*, ["the Curlews"].

"*Raghallach* said unto us,
It is the *Clanna Neill* that perpetrate this treachery;
If we do not haste to the rescue,
They will slip away from us over *Ath Seannaigh;* [Bally-Shannon].

"We mustered from the horses of the Fair
Ten hundred bridle-steeds in rank;
The sons of warriors and of noble farmers

LECT. XVI.

Account of the military array of king *Raghallach*; (circa A.D. 640); from an ancient poem.

Of the race of *Brian Mac Echach*.
"Ten hundred well trained sons of chiefs,
With *Cellach*; many were their achievements;
This was the number of his household,
Who accompanied him on his expedition.
"There were of the household troops with *Rag*[hallach]
Ten hundred champions, with their shields;
The front of battle they always held;
Theirs was the first Spear in the conflict.
"Smoothly did they prepare their light-Spears [...]
Because their captains were severe;
High was the anger of their men;
Their heavy-Spears [*craiseach*] were not shak[en].
"The order of our march was,
With a shield (*sdarga*) on the shoulder of each [...]
Our Spears in our own hands,
And no servant [*gilla*] to carry any man's arms.
"*Raghallach*'s kingly shield
In his white hand inciting us;
His two heavy-spears [*Craiseachs*] of equal leng[th]
In his hand, to rescue the prey.
"Into the *Corrsliabh* ["Curlews"] we went,
Passing by *Ceis*, the first day of autumn,—
Into *Corann* straight after them,
In three bands, not very great.
"To us their numbers seemed immense,
The clanns of *Conall* and of *Eoghan*;
But *Raghallach* said unto us,
'Give them the battle bravely!'
"To the call of their trumpets they mustered
Seven battalions,—who does not know it?
With captives, pledges, and plunders,
The van of their host reached *Sligech*, [Sligo].
"*Cellach* advanced to check them
Until the full tide had filled in;
Ten hundred heads of the Conallians,
Was their loss ere they reached *Eas-darra*, [Bal...]
"The defeat of the flood we gave
To *Ninné* and his shouting hosts;
We changed the name of the cold cataract;
From thenceforth it is called *Martra*.
"The preys were turned back,
From the *Clanna Neill* by the strength of hosts;
There was scarcely of them, on that night,
A cow that was not in its own *buailedh*.

"Numerous were we on that night:
Joyful was our assembly;
Were it not for the numbers of the biers,
Beautiful would have been our return.
"Though our losses were numerous,
We did not miss them in our pride;
On the steeds of the men of *Tir Eoghain*
We performed the games of *Cruachan*".

It is remarkable that this poet speaks only of shields, *Sleghs*, (or light Spears), and *Craisechs* (or heavy Spears), without any mention whatever of swords, axes, or of smaller weapons. Enough, however, appears to show that in *Raghallach*'s time the very arms were still in use which his ancestors had used two thousand years before him, and so they continued down to the Danish wars.

No change in weapons to the time of the Danish invasion (A.D. 820.)

It would be easy to continue a list of examples of the military weapons of this middle age, from the time of *Raghallach*, in the middle of the seventh century, (that is, A.D. 645,) down to the invasion of the country by the northern robbers commonly called the Danes, which happened about A.D. 820; but, as absolutely no change appears to have taken place in either the mode of warfare or the implements of war in the country in this interval, it is unnecessary to cite passages in mere repetition of what has been already quoted.

No account of the weapons of the Danes before Clontarf.

Nor can we say with certainty what were the arms of the Danes themselves at this time, as their own antiquarians are doubtful whether that rude people were acquainted with the use of iron even at that late period. But however this may be true of their country in general, still there can be little doubt but that professional warriors who came here after many hostile visits to the more southern countries of Europe could not have failed to make themselves acquainted with the fashion and materials of the weapons of those countries, and that at their coming here, they came armed, if not wholly, at least to a great extent with arms and armour of steel or iron. Be this, however, as it may, we have no account, as far as I know, of what the precise character of their weapons was, down to the battle of Clontarf, which was fought in the year 1014.

Of the weapons used at the Battle of Clontarf, (A.D. 1014.)

Of the arms, and of the use of armour described in the accounts of the various contests between the Gaedhils and the Danish invaders, perhaps the examples supplied by the history of the battle of Clontarf will serve to give a complete account, without risking too frequent repetition by following the various descriptions of these contests in chronological order, through so many centuries. And even at Clontarf the mode of fighting is but little changed from that of the primitive [illegible] bolgs and *Tuatha Dé Danann*.

Account of the Battle in the History called *Cogadh Gall re Gaoidhealaibh*.

Of the weapons used at this battle, there is indeed [illegible] all, to be said. Both parties, Gaedhil and foreign[illegible] presented as having been armed alike. The be[illegible] their respective weapons, as well as of the details [illegible] cisive battle itself, is preserved in the tract now so [illegible] as *Cogadh Gall re Gaoidhealib*,—that is "the W[illegible] Foreigners with the Gaedhil"; a history popularly kn[illegible] name of "the Danish Wars";—and perhaps the bes[illegible] make of it here is, to abstract the whole description [illegible] especially as this is the last battle to which I shall [illegible] claim attention here.

In the year 1002, *Brian Boromha*, who had some [illegible] fore succeeded his father as hereditary king of Munster [illegible] or pretending to find, that the monarch of all Erinn [illegible] *seachlainn* [or Malachy] the Second, though personally a [illegible] brave man, had from supineness or some other cause [illegible] inspire with the necessary respect for the central supre[illegible] the foreigners of the Danish settlement at Dublin, a[illegible] turbulent native chiefs who were but too ready to [illegible] with them, compelled him to resign the supreme auth[illegible] himself. *Maelseachlainn* accordingly submitted to the [illegible] of the abler and more powerful *Brian*, and retired to [illegible] his own hereditary kingdom of Meath, without further [illegible] with the sovereignty of the whole island.

In the early part of the year 1014, the dethroned [illegible] acting as king of Meath alone, complained to *Brian* [illegible] foreigners of Dublin and some of their Leinster allies [illegible] tered and ravaged his kingdom; and he acknowledged [illegible] ability, with the limited powers at his command, to [illegible] against them and protect his property and his people [illegible] the assistance of the chief monarch. *Brian* did not [illegible] moment, upon receiving tidings of the distress of the [illegible] Meath, but raising a large force, marched at once to [illegible] where he encamped [at Kilmainham], about the 17th [illegible] (Saint Patrick's Festival), in the year 1014.

When the foreigners heard of his preparations, [illegible] heralds in all directions to invite and collect au[illegible] them, to give him battle; and amongst others they [illegible] hither the earls Brodar and Amlaff, the sons of the [illegible] Lochland, and the leaders and retainers of all the [illegible] bands of the west of Europe, whom they endeavoured [illegible] semble in overpowering numbers, to strike, if possible [illegible] blow, and to reduce all Erinn beneath their yoke.

"In the following of these two princes" (says the curious tract from which I quote) "came also two thousand cruel, hard-hearted, branded Danes, the mercenary instruments of piracy, plunder, and murder in the hands of any one who chose to purchase their infamous service. Now, there was not a single branded Dane of these two thousand without a polished, strong, highly-carved, shining "lorica" of re-melted iron, or cold rustless brass, to cover their sides and their bodies from their heads to the soles of their feet.

Steel loricas of the Danes.

"They invited to them also *Sigraid Mac Lotar*, earl of Orkney and the neighbouring islands, with the whole muster of the fierce, barbarous, maniac, unrestrainable hordes of the islands of Orkney, Skye, Lewis, Cat, and Man; and two barons from Cornwall. They invited to them, too, *Carlus* and *Ebric*, the two sons of the king of France; and *Plait*, the brave champion of Lochland. All these foreigners crowded from their respective places to Dublin, where there was an immense host of men collected before them, amounting to three great and powerful battalions, to which were added the entire muster of the men of Leinster, under the traitor king *Maelmordha*, the son of *Murchadh*, and father-in-law of *Brian*".

On the other side, *Brian* found himself at the head of the men of north and south Munster, a large body of the men of Connacht, and the men of Meath; but these latter were not, as he believed, faithful; and their subsequent desertion of his cause in the hour of danger justified his belief.

The following passages will sound strange to the modern ear. The extravagant use of descriptive adjectives will seem contrary to good sense as well as good taste. The style is, however, that of the fashion of the period; and faulty as it may now seem, it is for the present purpose not to be carelessly condemned, since the very adjectives used will be found to supply the place of long and detailed description:—

"The battle having become inevitable, there stood on the one side the active, vigorous, valorous, fierce, restless, unrestrainable, [etc.] host of the audacious, hard-hearted, inhospitable Danes, and of the blue-green infidel *Galls* (foreigners), without mercy or reverence, without recognition or sanctuary to God or man.

Descriptions of arms, etc., from the ancient History of the Battle.

"They had with them, to maintain battle and combat, long, keen, bloody, reddened, barbed, sharp, bitter, wounding, fearful, galling, dangerous, heroic, poisonous, Darts; which had been tempered and browned in the blood of dragons and toads, and water-adders and others, and various venomous serpents besides; to be thrown and cast at champions of battle and

LECT. XVI. combat. They had besides bulging, [illegible] Arrows, and smooth, neatly-finished, yellow Bows, [illegible] broad-green *laighins* [heavy Spears], sharp, [illegible] in the valiant, bold, cruel hands of these [illegible] They had also beautifully-ornamented, smooth, [illegible] mets; and polished, strong, supple, firm, engraved, [illegible] secure 'Loricas' of re-melted iron, or of coal, [illegible] protect their bodies, and sides, and heads from the [illegible] gerous arms and weapons of battle. They had [illegible] heroic, heavy, force-striking, stout, powerful, [illegible] beautiful Shields; and dazzling, bright, strong Axes [illegible]

The Dalcassians (that is, the followers of *Brian*) [illegible] auxiliaries, were armed with "beautiful, well-[illegible] ous (*i.e.* piercing) Spears (*slegh*), mounted on [illegible] of white hazel; and great, sharp-pointed Lances [illegible] beautiful silken strings, so that they were like [illegible] bright whistling nails, when cast at chiefs of valour [illegible] They wore their long, shining, elegant, graceful, [illegible] fitting shirts, with splendid, many-coloured frocks. [illegible] heroic, bright, many-coloured Shields, with [illegible] bronze', and beautiful Chains of 'white bronze'. [illegible] on their heads crested, gold-emblazoned Helmets, [illegible] pure crystal gems and precious stones. They [illegible] shining, powerful, stunning, sharp, dazzling, [illegible] *Lochlann* Axes, in the hands of chiefs and [illegible] and brave champions, with which to strike down [illegible] armour and helmets. And they had hard, straight, [illegible] ornamented, smooth, polished, bright-bladed, sharp, [illegible] flaming Swords; in the white right hands of chiefs, [illegible] and champions, to cut and hack, to wound and [illegible] sides, bodies, and heads of their enemies".

Use of the *Lochlann*, or foreign Battle-Axe.

At first sight it would seem, from this description [illegible] of both the parties in this celebrated battle, that the [illegible] were armed with *Lochlann* or foreign battle-axes like [illegible] the foreigners themselves. This, however, appears not [illegible] for this reason, that in the details of the battle, though [illegible] references to battle-axes in the hands of the foreigners, [illegible] no reference whatever to their use by the Gaedhils. [illegible] be clearly seen in some passages taken from the [illegible] the separate battle which took place between the two [illegible] mail-clad Danish veterans and the Dalcassians alone.

The description of the day proceeds to tell how the [illegible] battle was now arranged; and how the Danish commanders [illegible] their traitorous Leinster auxiliaries gave the front of the [illegible] to those foreign captains already mentioned. [The [illegible]

Use of the *Lochlann*, or foreign Battle-Axe.

of the Danish array follows.] The tract then goes on to state that *Brian* now drew up his men face to face with his terrible foes; and the front of the battle, (in accordance with a well-known ancient right), was assigned to "the lively, fierce, brave, irresistible Dalcassian clanns", *Brian*'s own friends and relatives. The leadership of these celebrated clanns was assigned to "the Hector of Erinn"; namely *Murchadh*, *Brian*'s eldest son and heir, then in his sixty-third year, the most distinguished champion among all the Gaedhil of his time, if we may believe the annals of the country, for, according to these, there was no man of his time capable of holding a Shield against him in battle.

Murchadh was attended by his own son *Torlogh*, the best youth of fifteen years then in Erinn; and *Conaing*, the son of *Donnacuan;* and *Niall O'Cuinn*, Lord of Inchiquin, [an ancestor of the present earl of Dunraven]; and *Eochaidh*, the son of *Dunadach;* and *Cudiuligh* the son of *Cennedigh* [Kennedy]; and these last three champions were *Brian*'s own rear-guard in all his battles; and along with these stood *Domhnall* the son of *Diarmait*, king of *Corca Baiscen*, supported by the noblest and best men of the Dalcassian race. [The description of the remainder of the Irish array follows.]

When the arrangements of the battle had been finished at both sides, a rather singular circumstance occurred. On the previous evening a dispute happened between *Plait* the son of the king of *Lochland*, the chief hero of the foreigners, and *Domhnall Mac Eimhin*, the *Mór Maer* or Great Steward of Scotland, who had come over specially to give his aid to *Brian*. The dispute ended in an engagement of combat in the morning. And as both sides were ready for the attack, *Plait* sprang out from the ranks of his own people, and shouted "Where is *Domhnall?* where is *Domhnall?*" "Here", said *Domhnall*. So they advanced towards each other, and each attacked the other with equal fury until both fell and expired together, and when taken up next day, they were found each "holding the other by the hair of the head, and the sword of either plunged through the heart of the other".

On seeing the two warriors lying dead between them, the front ranks of the foreigners and of the men of Munster rushed over their dead bodies at each other; and the historian, after attempting to compare the shock of meeting of the two forces with the wars of the elements or the terrors of the last Judgment, says:

"To all these might I compare the fulminating, fierce, barbarous, distinct blows on the beautiful, deep-bordered, brown-radiating, starry Shields of the *Clann Luigdech*, [that is, the

LECT. XVI. Dalcassians] under the stout, shining Axes (or hatchets) [illegible] Danes and pirates, in shattering and crushing them [illegible] the other hand, the gleaming, bright descent of [illegible] straight-backed Swords of the Dalcassians, reverberating [illegible] and powerfully on the supple, bright, carved, stout, [illegible] cure 'Loricas' of the Danish foreigners, shattering [illegible] and their skulls along with them".

"Straight-backed" Swords of the Dalcassians.

If the Dalcassians had been armed with the Axe [illegible] would have been the very place where we might expect [illegible] so stated; but here they seem to be actually disting[illegible] the Danes by the use of the "straight-backed sword" [illegible]

Use of Two Swords, (one in each hand), by *Murchadh*.

The weapon used by the hero *Murchadh*, the eld[illegible] *Brian*, was the Sword; or rather indeed he used two [illegible] the same time, one in each hand,—for we are told [illegible] grasped two Swords, one in each hand, and rushing th[illegible] hostile ranks like a wild and infuriated 'Ox', or [illegible] enraged Lion which had been robbed of his whelps, [illegible] a breach as if by an hundred men, through the [illegible] compact line";—and even "his enemies after him" [illegible] Leinster and Danish writers), the historian tells us, [illegible] dence, that "fifty men fell at his right and fifty on his [illegible] that fearful rush; and that he did not deal a second blow [illegible] one; and that neither shield, nor coat of mail, nor [illegible] afforded protection against any one of his blows, [illegible] through them he wounded the bodies and clove the [illegible] his enemies".

And an extraordinary instance of performance w[illegible] Swords is mentioned in a subsequent passage, in [illegible] described with some extravagance of language a [illegible] feat of strength in *Murchadh*'s combat with *Sitric*, the [illegible] earl of Orkney, a champion clothed in complete armour [illegible] the Dalcassian prince is related to have rushed upon [illegible] dable enemy "with a sword in each hand"; and he is [illegible] have cut off the head and the legs of the Dane at [illegible] moment, with the two swords.

In the account of *Murchadh*'s final combat, with [illegible] the son of the king of *Lochland*", he is also described [illegible] ing with the sword alone; but he wore a dagger, [illegible] sword, in addition, for in the last struggle it was [illegible] weapon that his antagonist, who succeeded in snatching [illegible] his belt, despatched the hero.

Account of the death of King *Brian*.

The account of the death of king *Brian* himself [illegible] mentions the Sword as his only weapon. It runs as [illegible]

About the time of the final defeat and dispersion [illegible] Danes, an attendant reported to *Brian*, who wa[illegible] battle from a little distance, his great age having induced him to leave it to his son to command in the field), "that he saw three naked men running towards them". But *Brian* said, "they are not naked men, but they are a part of the mail-coated battalion";—and this was, indeed, true, for the party consisted of the great Danish champion earl *Brodar* and two other warriors. *Brian* immediately started to his feet, and "drew his sword". But *Brodar* passed without noticing him. However, one of his two companions, who had been formerly in *Brian*'s pay, called out in the Danish language, "king, king!" "No, no", said *Brodar*, "priest, priest". "Not at all", said the same man, "it is the chief king himself that we have here". And then *Brodar* turned about, "with a bright double-edged (or double-headed) battle-axe in his hand"; and "when *Brian* saw this, he dealt him a blow of his sword, by which he cut off the warrior's left leg at the knee, and the right at the ankle". The Dane at falling, however, inflicted on *Brian* a tremendous blow with his axe which clove his skull in two. This was the last event of the great Battle.

I shall conclude this part of my subject with one more example taken from the history of this period, and as it offers more than one trait of military manners in the heroic age of *Brian*, I may be excused for relating the whole passage.

Of the stand of *Donnchadh* against the Ossorians, at *Baile-atha-Aoi*.

After the melancholy death of *Brian*, and of *Murchadh* his eldest son, with the flower of their forces, at Clontarf, *Donnchadh*, *Brian*'s second surviving son, collected the shattered remains of the Dalcassian clanns, "not leaving behind him a single man who had any signs of life in him": and with these he proceeded on his way home, without any molestation from Dane or Leinsterman, until he reached the place now called Athy, [*Bailé-atha-Aoi*, i.e., the town of the *Ford of Ae*], on the river *Bearba*, [now called Barrow, in the co. Kildare]. Here, however, he received a message from *Donnchadh Mac Gilla Padraicc*, king of Ossory, who, with all his people was posted on a hill in the neighbourhood, calling on him to give up hostages of submission to him as a condition of permitting him to pass by that way towards his own country, or else prepare to give him battle.

To this insolent demand *Donnchadh* the son of *Brian* answered, that, if he were trusting to only one servant in the world to support his cause, he would not refuse a challenge of battle from *Mac Gilla Padraicc* and the men of Ossory. Then he ordered a third of his sound or partially sound men to take charge and guard of the disabled victims of Clontarf, and the other two-thirds to give battle to *Mac Gilla Padraicc*. But "when

Of the stand of *Donnchadh* against the Ossorians, at *Belld-atha-Aoi.*

the wounded men heard this, they started up so [illegible] their wounds and cuts which had been closed [illegible] burst open". However "they stuffed them with [illegible] the field", grasped their spears and their swords, [illegible] ghastly array took their place with their friends. They [illegible] of Brian's son to send men into the neighbouring wood, [illegible] down and bring out strong stakes to be fixed in [illegible] and said they: "Let us be tied to them, with our [illegible] hands; and let our sons and our friends be placed [illegible] is, two sound men, one at each side of each wounded [illegible] so that our action may be the more cordial and ardent [illegible] for surely, said they, the sound man will not [illegible] until the wounded tied man of us leaves his post".

This was done, accordingly; and when the men [illegible] saw the order into which the Dalcassians had put [illegible] disgust and terror seized on them: "and what they [illegible] It is not an attempt to retreat; it is not fear or terror [illegible] cassians seem disposed to exhibit, they said, but [illegible] formed themselves into a close, compact battalion; [illegible] reason, said they, we will not give them battle, [illegible] are prepared alike for life or for death".—And so [illegible] ing all the remonstrances of *Mac Gilla Padraice*, [illegible] persuade the men of Ossory to attack the desperate [illegible] and the remnant of the Dalcassian clanns were allowed [illegible] the best of their weary way back to their native [illegible] recorded of these, however, that no less than one [illegible] fifty of the wounded heroes died of the effects of [illegible] burst of anger and ardour on this occasion.

LECTURE XVII.

[Delivered 26th June, 1858.]

(VI.) Military Education. Keting's account of the *Fianna Eireann*. O'Flaherty's allusion to a Military School under *Cormac Mac Airt*. Ancient System of Fosterage explained. Education of boys and girls in ancient Erinn. First Historical allusion to a Military Teacher, in the account of the Battle of *Móin Trogaidhé*, (B.C. 1000). Of *Trogaidhé*. Of *Cimbaeth*, (A.M. 4480); the head of the champions of the "Royal Branch". Instances of the system of Fosterage, under *Eochaidh Bég*. The Champions of the "Royal Branch". Of the "Gamannrians"; and the *Clanna Deaghaidh*. Accounts of *Cuchulainn*, in the Tale of the *Táin Bo Chuailgné*. Of the Early Education of *Cuchulainn*; (his boyish feats). Early training of young warriors at this time. Of the later Education in arms of *Cuchulainn*, (in *Alba*,—Scotland). List of the "Feats of Championship", learned by *Cuchulainn*, in the School of *Scathach*.

In the last six Lectures I have endeavoured to state the substance of what is recorded as to the fashion, the material, and the manner of use, of the various offensive and defensive Weapons of Warfare in ancient Erinn, from the period of our earliest historical references down to the battle of Clontarf, fought in the year 1014. Such an inquiry should properly be considered, however, only as preliminary to the discussion of the system of Military Education of the ancient Gaedhils, as far as it can be gathered from the same sources. And here I have to express my regret that there is less of direct information on this subject to be found amongst the wreck of ancient national records which have come down to us, than could be wished; and that much of what has been confidently taken for granted by a certain class of "historians", who prefer the pleasure of eloquent expatiation on our ancient military glory to the trouble of investigating what history really assures to us, belongs to the domain not of fact, but of mere assumption. So far as I can testify to the contents of the very large body of Irish MSS. which I have closely examined, including all the old MSS. in the Royal Irish Academy, in Trinity College, Dublin, and in the British Museum, as well as most of those in the Burgundian Library at Brussels, and to some extent those at Oxford, and so far as I know of the contents of those at Rome and Edinburgh, I am sorry to say that they do not contain, I believe, any reference to the existence at any time of any regular general school or college of Military Education in ancient Erinn. Some authorities there are, however, on the subject.

LECT. XVII.

Keting's account of the Fianna Eireann.

The Rev. Dr. Geoffrey Keting, in his valuable abstract of ancient Gaedhelic History,—a work [illegible] the year 1630, from various ancient books [illegible] now lost,—gives us, and doubtless on ancient authority [illegible] precise sketch (and one in itself in all probability [illegible] the military education, mental and physical, of [illegible] Militia of the Third Century, commonly called [illegible] *Eireann*, who obtained such lasting fame under [illegible] of the celebrated *Finn Mac Cumhaill*, a warrior [illegible] it will be remembered, a mere soldier either, but [illegible] may be called the accomplishments of the education [illegible] his time,—a Druid, a Poet, and a Scholar.[346]

O'Flaherty's allusion to a Military School under Cormac Mac Airt.

Again, the learned Roderick O'Flaherty, in [illegible] his *Ogygia*, (Part iii.) already quoted,[347] in which [illegible] of *Cormac Mac Airt*, (who flourished in the middle [illegible] Century,) alludes to a school of the Art of War [illegible] Three great Schools instituted by that enlightened [illegible]

It is very unfortunate, and among other things [illegible] pose of our present inquiry, that the important [illegible] to by O'Flaherty in this passage is not to be found [illegible] the MS. collections available to us; it is only known [illegible] among those locked up in England in the custody [illegible] Ashburnham, by whom Irish scholars are not permitted [illegible] amine treasures which properly belong to our own [illegible] the legal ownership of which is at present unhappily [illegible] a stranger unsympathising alike with our pursuits [illegible] and with those of the literary world at large. [illegible] there is probably much calculated to throw light on [illegible] of education in ancient Erinn, though O'Flaherty [illegible] casion to refer more closely to it in reference to [illegible] his work.

In the absence, therefore, of this poem of O'D[illegible] of the original authorities used by Keting, we are [illegible] upon the only sources of information on the subject [illegible] our reach, namely, the references met with from [illegible] so many MSS. to private or individual military [illegible] references which frequently occur in the old books, [illegible] after all probably represent accurately enough the [illegible] tem of education in which the peculiarly favoured [illegible] alluded to by O'Flaherty and Keting formed but [illegible] exceptions in the history of ancient Erinn.

(346) See *Lectures on the MS. Materials*, etc.; p. 300, etc. *And* [illegible] *History of Ireland*, (translated by John O'Mahony); New York, [illegible] 347, et seq.

(347) See ante, p. 56.

Ancient system of Fosterage explained.

We may premise at the outset, that a system of fosterage, governed by accurately defined laws, prevailed universally in Erinn from the remotest period of her history; a system, indeed, which in many of its features continued to prevail even down so late as to the sixteenth and seventeenth centuries. And we have ample proofs that this fosterage was not a mere indiscriminate custom among all classes of the people, nor in any case one merely confined to the bare physical nurture and rearing of the child which in early infancy was committed to the care of a nurse and her husband; but that the fosterhood was generally that of a whole family or tribe; and that in very many cases it became a bond of friendship and alliance between two or more tribes and even provinces. In those cases the fosterers were not of the common class, poor people glad to perform their nursing for mere pay, and whose care extended to the physical rearing only. On the contrary, it is even a question, and one not easily settled, whether the term nursing in the modern acceptation of the word, should be applied at all to the old Gaedhelic fosterage, and whether the term pupilage would not be more appropriate. As the present, however, is not the time to go into this very curious subject, I must content myself with stating as a matter of fact that the old Gaedhelic fosterage extended to the training and education not only of children up to the age of fourteen, but sometimes of youths up to that of seventeen years.

Education of boys and girls in ancient Erinn.

The daughters of peasants were taught by their fosterers to grind, to sift, and to knead, as well as the needle-work suited to their way of life; whilst the sons were taught the rearing of all sorts of young cattle, besides the kiln-drying of corn, and the preparation of malt, etc.

The daughters of the better and higher classes were instructed in sewing, cutting, and embroidering cloth; whilst the sons were taught the game of chess, the art of swimming and riding, and the use of the Sword and Spear.

In fact, the Gaedhelic foster-parents in some sense filled the place among the ancients of what would now be called masters of boarding schools, and they did often actually keep large establishments for the accommodation of many pupils;—though sometimes also they were simply private tutors residing in the family or within the domain of the parents of their pupils. All this will be found in the Brehon Laws in full detail, when that great collection sees the light.

To return to our immediate subject.

The earliest, indeed I might say the only, reference to a regular Professor of the Military Art that I have met with, occurs as

LECT. XVII. First historical allusion to a Military Teacher, in the account of the Battle of *Móin Trogaidhé*.

far back as the reign of the monarch *Siorna* [illegible] who was killed at the battle of *Aillinn* [now [illegible] county of Kildare,] A.M. 4169; that is, according to [illegible] of the Annals of the Four Masters, about B.C. 1,000 [illegible] great battles recorded to have been fought [illegible] *Siorna*, was the battle of *Móin Trogaidhé* in the [illegible] wards called *Ciannacht* in East Meath, which took [illegible] these circumstances. *Siorna* was a great warrior [illegible] other distinguished feats of arms, it was he that drove [illegible] cient Rudricians from the sovereignty of Tara; and [illegible] reduced Munster to obedience to the king of Tara. [illegible] of Munster, however, (*Lugair*, the son of *Lugaidh* [illegible] of the Eberean line), did not remain long obedient [illegible] secretly invited the Fomorians to come in and join [illegible] effort to recover his independence. These [illegible] great force, headed by *Ceadarn* [or *Ceasarn*] their [illegible] having been joined by *Lugair* and his Munstermen, [illegible] of *Móin Trogaidhé* was fought between them and the [illegible] in which the latter was victorious, but in which the [illegible] were killed, as well as great numbers on both sides. [illegible] cient authorities state, however, that it was by a sudden [illegible] which descended on them when the battle was at its [illegible] the two adverse leaders and the greater part of the [illegible]

Of *Trogaidhé*, a Military teacher before B.C. 1000

Who *Trogaidhé* was, from whom the bog, (*móin*), [illegible] this battle was fought received its name, we do not [illegible] but from the following two stanzas from a short [illegible] commemorative of the battle, which is preserved in [illegible] of Leinster, we gather that he was the great Teacher [illegible] Military Art in Erinn, in his time:

"The battle of *Móin Trogaidhé* in the east,
In which the Fomorians were cut down;
He who fought it, at the swelling hill,
Was *Lugair* the son of *Lugaidh Lamh-fhind*.

"He from whom *Móin Trogaidhé* is named,
Was *Trogaidhé*, the Tutor of the young W[illegible]
And even of the Fomorians too,
Before the fight of this great battle".[(340)]

Of *Cimbaeth*, (A.M. 4480); the head of the Champions of the "Royal Branch".

From *Trogaidhé* we come down to *Cimbaeth*, [illegible] monarch of Erinn A.M. 4484, and who appears to have [illegible] accomplished warrior. He reigned as the husband of [illegible] sovereign queen that ever owned legitimate sway [illegible]

(340) orig.:—Cath Móna Trogaidhe toir,
i corcratar Fomoraig;
hé do rat con tulaig find,
Lugoir mac Lugdach Lam-find.

Do ach Móin Trog[illegible]
Trogaidhe, ait[illegible]
ocus Fomorach [illegible]
ren imbualad [illegible]

Erinn, the famous *Macha Mong-ruadh*, who succeeded to the monarchy in right of her father, and maintained her exclusive right by force of arms against the three sons of *Dithorba*, and others, who claimed an alternate septennial right, and of whom *Cimbaeth* was one. *Macha*, however, when she succeeded to the throne, married *Cimbaeth*, and gave him the chief command of her army; and *Cimbaeth* appears to have been previously the head, if not the founder, of the champions of the Royal Branch of Emania.

This may be inferred from an ancient poem preserved in the Book of Leinster, of which the following is the first stanza:

" *Cimbaeth*, the Chief of the Young Warriors of Emania,
Possession took of the lordly lands of Tara,—
The husband of *Macha* full of pride,
The director of the battalions of the Royal Branch".[349]

It is stated, on the authority, also, of the Book of Leinster, that this *Cimbaeth* was the tutor of the celebrated monarch and warrior, *Ugainé Mór*, who afterwards carried the fame of his arms so far as into Italy itself. *Ugainé Mór* was the direct ancestor of all the great Eremonian families of Ulster, Leinster, and Connacht.

From *Cimbaeth* and *Ugainé Mór*, we pass now to the century immediately preceding the Incarnation, at which time the Royal Branch and its champions appear to have attained their highest degree of celebrity.

Instance of the system of Fosterage under *Eochaidh Beg.*

A fair instance of the fosterage system of the Gaedhils at this time, is preserved in the *Leabhar na h-Uidhré* in the case of *Eochaidh Beg* the son of *Cairbré*, king of the ancient territory of *Cliach*, (a district situate about *Cnoc Ainé*, in the present county of Limerick). This *Eochaidh* had at one time forty foster-sons, or pupils, under his care, the sons of the chiefs and nobles of Munster; and when he had received an invitation from *Ailill* and *Medbh*, the king and Queen of Connacht, to visit them at *Cruachan*, he is said to have gone there attended by his forty pupils each mounted on a richly-caparisoned steed.

The Champions of the "Royal Branch".

It was at this time, as I have said, that the champions of the Royal Branch had attained their highest degree of celebrity. Among these champions the most celebrated were: *Conchobar Mac Nessa*, king of Ulster; *Cuchulainn Mac Soaltainn*; *Fergus Mac Roigh*; *Fergus Mac Leité*; *Celtchair Mac Uithir*; *Eogan Mac Durthacht*; *Dubhthach "Dael Uladh"*; *Conall Cear-*

(349) original:—Cimbaeth, cleite nóc nemna,
ꝛoᵹab tiꝛ toꝛad Temꝛa,
ceile Maċa meit ualle,
conn caṫa na Cꝛaeb Ruaiḋe.

LECT. XVII. nach (*Mac Amergin*); three sons of *Uisnach*, namely, [illegible]
Annlé, and *Ardán*; and *Laeghairé Buadhach Mac* [illegible]

The "Gamanrians"; and the Clanna Deaghaidh.

There were besides these champions of the Royal [illegible]
Emania, two other great bands of champions in [illegible]
time, namely, the "Gamanrians" of Connacht, a tribe [illegible]
Firbolg race, of whom *Ferdiaidh Mac Damain* was the [illegible]
this time; and the *Clanna Deaghaidh* of Middle Munster [illegible]
were of Ulster origin, and the chief of whom was the [illegible]
champion *Curoi Mac Dairé*. Little, however, has come [illegible]
to us of the particular history of the Gamanrians and [illegible]
Deaghaidh; whilst the champions of the Royal Branch [illegible]
filled a large space in our bardic and romantic history. [illegible]

Accounts of Cuchulainn in the tale of the Táin Bo Chuailgnè.

It does not appear, as far as we know, that there [illegible]
special college for Military Education at Emania; but [illegible]
evidence to show that the use of arms and military [illegible]
formed no unimportant part of the general course of [illegible]
which the noble youths of the province certainly [illegible]
there. The chief references to this education are found [illegible]
somewhat romantic life of *Cuchulainn*, as preserved in [illegible]
of the *Táin Bo Chuailgnè* and other ancient tracts; [illegible]
therefore through him that we must attempt to arrive [illegible]
thing like distinct notions on the subject. In order to [illegible]
therefore, we must have recourse again to the tale of the [illegible]
Bo Chuailgnè.

When the forces of Connacht in their first [illegible]
advanced as far as the neighbourhood of Slane in [illegible]
their way into Ulster, we are told that they were [illegible]
prised to find their advanced guards and guides [illegible]
cut off, their headless trunks being sometimes fastened [illegible]
horses, and these turned back to the main army, [illegible]
caused no little consternation. The king and queen of [illegible]
being at a great loss to know who they were that [illegible]
destruction of their men, sent for *Fergus Mac Roigh*, the [illegible]
Ulster chieftain who had been for years in exile at [illegible]
under the displeasure of *Conchobar* the king of Ulster. [illegible]
having been questioned as to who he thought might [illegible]
killed the advanced guards and scouts of the army, [illegible]
that he could not guess unless it was his own pupil, "the
boy *Cuchulainn*"; but the king and queen of Connacht [illegible]
at the notion that a youth of *Cuchulainn*'s age, (for he was
but in his seventeenth year), could have performed [illegible]
or could be dreaded as capable of offering any serious [illegible]
tion to the march of so formidable an army as [illegible]
they commanded. To this *Fergus* had no answer [illegible]
but that from what he had known of the mere boy [illegible]

Cuchulainn, they might expect extraordinary deeds from him in his now more mature years; and he then gives the following sketch of the feats of the boy among his fellow-pupils and playmates at their sports and exercises at Emania. The passage is somewhat long, but it contains so much that is pertinent to the subject of our inquiry here, that I shall not hesitate to quote it in full.

Early education of *Cuchulainn*. (His boyish feats.)

"This boy, said *Fergus*, was nursed in the house of his father and mother in the plain of *Muirtheimné*, where he soon heard the history of the youths of Emania. This was the way in which the king *Conchobar* spent his time, ever since he has taken upon him the government of the province. He divides the day into three parts. The first third part he spends in superintending the noble youths of the province at the games of military exercise and ball hurling. The second third he spends in playing *Brandabh*, (that is Draughts, or some similar game), and *Fidchell*, (that is, Chess;) and the last third in eating, and drinking, until sleep seizes on the company, professors of music and amusements entertaining them at the same time. And though we are a long time in exile through him", said *Fergus*, "I pledge my word that there is not in all Erinn nor in Alba a man like unto *Conchobar*".

"And, as we have said, the boy *Cuchulainn* had heard the story of the youths and princes of Emania; for there were at all times an hundred and fifty youths at exercise there; and he said to his mother, who was sister to king *Conchobar*, that he wished also to go and practise his exercises in the play-ground of Emania. 'It is too early for you to do this, my little son', said his mother; 'not until some one of the champions of Ulster conducts you thither, or some one of *Conchobar*'s companions shall be security for your protection and safety from the youths'. 'I think that too long, mother,' said the little boy; 'and I shall not wait; but tell me where Emania lies'. 'The place in which it lies is far from you,' said his mother;' and the mountain *Sliabh Fuaid* is between you and Emania". 'I will guess at where it is', said he".

"The boy set out then, taking with him his 'instruments of pleasure'. He took his 'Shield of Laths'; and his 'Red-Bronze Hurl'; and his 'Silver Ball'; and his 'throwing Dart'; and his (mock) 'Wooden Spear', with the burned top; and he shortened the way by means of them. He would give his ball a stroke of his hurl, and drive it to a great distance before him; he would throw his hurl at it, and give it a second stroke that would drive it no shorter distance than the first. He would cast his dart and hurl his wooden spear, and run himself after

LECT. XVII. Early education of Cuchulainn. (His boyish feats.)

them. He would take up his hurl, and his ball
and the end of his wooden spear would not have
ground before he had caught it by the top while
In this manner he went on until he reached the
is, the lawn ranged with seats,] of Emania, where
princes were at their sports.—

"The boy ran at once into the play-ground
and he snatched up the ball between his legs
he did not let it pass his knees up nor his ankles
he kept it and closed it between his two legs
them could reach it with a prod, a blow, a stroke
and in that manner he carried it over the brink
from them. They all looked at him together
surprise and a wonder to them. 'Good, O youths
main the son of king *Conchobar*, 'attack yonder boy
and let him get his death at our hands; for it is
you that any youth should presume to come
without having first claimed your protection; and
him all of you together, though we know that he is
one of the champions of Ulster, for he has omitted
into our play-ground, to put himself under our
They all attacked him then. They threw their
fifty hurlies at his head; but he raised his single
and warded off the three times fifty hurlies. They
their three times fifty balls at the boy; but he
his wrists, and his palms, and he warded off the
fifty balls. They then threw at him their three
mock spears of wood burned at the end; but the boy
little lath-shield, and he warded off the three
wooden spears. Then did he rush furiously upon
dashed fifty of them against the ground; five of
tinued *Fergus*, "rushed between me and *Conchobar*
chess-board at which we were playing on the ground
towards the palace; and the little boy followed
but in springing over our table the king caught
wrists and addressed him thus.—

"'Holla, my little boy', (said the king), 'I
are dealing harshly with the youths'. 'I have great
said the little boy; 'I have not received from the
honour due to a stranger, though I have come from
is this, and who are you?' said *Conchobar*. 'I am
the son of *Soaltann* and of *Dectere*, your own sister
not at your hands I should expect to be thus
the little boy. 'What, my little son', said *Conchobar*
not aware of the privilege of the youths, that it is

them that a stranger youth should enter among them until he had first put himself under their protection.' 'I was not aware of that', said the little boy; 'had I known it, I should have been more cautious'. 'Good, now, O youths', said *Conchobar*, 'take upon yourselves the protection of this little boy, forthwith'. 'We are content to do so indeed', said they. So the boy put himself under the protection of the youths, and *Conchobar* released his hands.—

LECT. XVII. Early education of Cuchulainn. (His boyish feats.)

"No sooner was this done however, than the little boy rushed on them again, and dashed fifty young princes of them in succession to the ground under him, with such force that their fathers thought that they were dead; it was not so, however, but they were stunned with surprise and terror. 'Holla', said *Conchobar*, 'what do you mean towards them further?' 'I have sworn by my gods whom I adore', said the little boy, 'that until they have all come under my protection and under my defence, in the same way that I have gone under theirs, I shall not take my hands off them until I have laid them all prostrate on the ground'. 'Good, my little boy', said *Conchobar*, 'take thou on thee the protection of the princes'. 'I do so', said the little boy. The young princes then put themselves under his protection and defence".

"A little boy who performed these deeds at the age of five years", said *Fergus*, "who prostrated the sons of the warriors and champions of Ulster, at the door of their own palace, it is no wonder that he should perform the deeds which appear so surprising to you, now, when he is in the seventeenth year of his age".

After *Fergus* had finished this relation of the first display of the strength and dexterity of *Cuchulainn*, (who was, it is to be remembered, at the next stage of his career, the pupil in arms of *Fergus* himself), another of the Ulster exiles takes up the second part of the wonderful "little boy's" history, and relates it also to the king and queen of Connacht. This portion also of the tale I must give at the same length, because it embraces a great variety of allusions to the gymnastic practices which formed an essential part of the training of a young champion, in the days of king *Conchobar* and the "Royal Branch". It is also interesting as describing the feat which gained for the young *Setanta* the since so famous name of "*Cuchulainn*". The narrator in the present instance was *Cormac Conloingeas*, one of king *Conchobar*'s own sons:

"'The same little boy', said he, 'performed another great deed in the year that followed'. 'What deed was that?' said *Ailill* [king of Connacht]. 'It was this', said *Cormac*. 'There was in

Ulster a certain artificer in metals [a card, i.e. an
name was *Culand*. This *Culand* on one occasion
for king *Conchobar*, and went to Emania to invite
he asked the king to come to his house with a
because it was not a territory or land that he had
but "the profits of hammers, his anvil, his
tongs": and *Conchobar* said that he would go with
company. So *Culand* returned to his house to
and drink for the king's party".

"*Conchobar* remained at Emania until his
up at the approach of the close of the day. The king
on his light travelling suit, and went out to the
take his leave of the young princes, where he
prised him very much; namely, three times fifty
one end of the green, and only one boy at the other
the one boy gaining every game and goal at the
the three times fifty boys. When it was the game of
they played, and when it was their turn to throw
defend, he would catch their three times fifty balls
hole, and would not let one of them pass him into it
it was their turn to defend, and his to throw, he
the three times fifty balls into the hole without
in spite of them. When it was the feat of pulling
other's clothes, he would snatch away their three
cloaks off them; and they would not be able to
much as his brooch from his cloak. When the time
ling came, he would bring down the three times fifty
ground; but from among them all there could not be
sufficient number to lay hold of him. Then king
said on seeing the boys: Ah youths, said he, happy
land from which has come the boy whom you see,
only been as well instructed in the feats of championhood
is in those of boyhood". "It is not proper to speak
Fergus, "for, according to the manner in which the
has performed his actions, [it is clear] he must [already]
the feats of championhood".

Cormac Conloingeas goes on to tell how, after this
king *Conchobar* asked the boy to accompany him to
to which he was then going; but the boy refused to
he and his comrades had finished their sports and
but promising that when these were over for the day,
then follow the royal party. When evening came,
youths retired to the house of his father and mother,
of his nurse and tutor; and their meeting broke up.
Setanta, then set out in the track of the royal cortege,

little difficulty in making his way to the smith's house. When arrived there, however, he found his approach to the door prevented by a huge, ferocious watch-dog, whose inhospitable growl at seeing him rang through the Armourer's establishment, as well as throughout all the neighbourhood. On hearing this, the Armourer asked king *Conchobar* if he had appointed with any one to follow him. The king said he had not; but immediately recollecting the boy's promise to do so, he shouted to his friends to go out and save him, as he was certain that the dog had torn him to pieces. When they went out, however, they found the great dog lying dead on the platform, and the boy standing over him in triumph. *Fergus* at once snatched him up on his shoulder and carried him into *Conchobar*'s presence, who received him with joy. The Armourer too bade him welcome, but said that the honour of his company was too dearly purchased by the loss of his noble dog, which not only guarded his own house and flocks, but those also of the whole district around him. Make yourself easy on that head, my friend, said the boy, for if there be a pup of the breed of your dog in all Erinn, I will procure him for you; and I shall myself take on me the duties of your former dog, until the young one comes to the age of efficiency. Upon which *Cathbad*, the celebrated Druid, who always attended the king on his excursions, proposed to the "little boy" to relinquish his name of *Setanta*, and called upon him to adopt in future that of *Cu-Chulaind*, "the Hound of *Culand*", the Armourer; and he declared that under that name his fame would live for ever in the mouths of the men of Erinn and Alba. And so it was that he obtained that name which, in verification of the Druid's prophecy, has been preserved with honour and distinction in the records of the men of Erinn and Alba even to this day.

LECT. XVII. Early education of Cuchulainn. (His boyish feats.)

Cormac Conloingeas having finished his part of the relation before the king and queen of Connacht, the theme of *Cuchulainn*'s exploits was taken up in continuation by *Fiach Mac Fir-Aba*, another of the Ultonian exiles at the Connacht court, as follows:

"'The boy performed a third series of exploits in the year which followed', said *Fiacha Mac Fir-Aba*. 'What deed did he perform?' said king *Ailill*. '*Cathbad* the Druid was lecturing his pupils on the north-east side of Emania, where he had a hundred youths industriously learning Druidism from him; that was the number that *Cathbad* always instructed. One of his students asked him what that day would be propitious for? *Cathbad* answered: The young warrior who shall receive the arms of championhood on this day, the fame of his name and

[ECT. XVII. rly educa- on of ... his boyish ats.]

deeds shall live in Erinn "*go brath*", [i.e. for ever]. ... *lainn* (who was on the south side of the palace) ... and he immediately repaired to king *Conchobar* ... was taking repose in his sleeping house. 'All ... thee, O king of Champions', said the boy. ' ... tation of a person who is about to ask something ... *chobar*. 'And what is it you want, my little ... 'To take arms', said the boy. 'Who instructed ... my boy ?' said *Conchobar*. '*Cathbad* the druid', ... 'I shall not disappoint you then', said *Conchobar*. ...

"*Conchobar* then presented him with two Spears, ... and a Shield. The boy poised and balanced the ... he shivered them to atoms. *Conchobar* gave him ... Spears, and a Shield and Sword; and he poised and ... and shook them also, until they were shivered to ... the others. In fine, the fifteen suits of arms which ... *chobar* had always in reserve for the youths,—for ... of them embraced knighthood, it was *Conchobar* that ... him with the accoutrements of battle, in virtue of ... candidate received 'the gift of superior valour',— ... suits of arms, I say, in succession, the boy shivered ... 'These are not good arms my master, *Conchobar*', said ... 'they are not worthy of my acceptance'. Then *Con*... sented him with his own two Spears, his Sword, and ... He poised and balanced and shook them, and he bent ... their points touched their heads, and none of them ... but they withstood his test. 'These are good arms ... the boy, 'they suit me exactly'; and he thanked the ... arms, and said: 'Happy the people and the race of ... whose arms these are is king'. 'Good, my boy', said ... 'go into your chariot now, for that is the first thing you ...

"He went then into a chariot; and the first chariot ... into he jolted and shook until he shivered it to pieces ... of the fifteen chariots which *Conchobar* always had ... the acceptance of the youths at Emania, was shattered ... by him in the same way. 'These are not good ... master, *Conchobar*', said the boy; 'there is not ... sufficient for my purpose'. 'Where is *Ibar* the ... *gabhra*?' said *Conchobar*. 'Here, indeed', said *Ibar* ... my own two steeds for this boy, and yoke them to ... said *Conchobar*. So the Charioteer brought the ... yoked them to the Chariot; and the boy went ... jolted and shook it with all his strength, but it ... his efforts to break it. 'This', said he, 'is a good ... exactly suits me'. 'Very well then, boy', said the ...

'let the horses go to their grazing now'. 'It is too soon, yet, *Ibar*', said the boy; 'drive around Emania this day, as this is my first day of taking arms, that it may be the "gift of valour" to me'. So they drove three times round Emania.—

LECT. XVII. Early education of Cuchulainn. (His boyish feats.)

"'Let the horses go to their grazing, now', said *Ibar*. 'It is too soon yet', said the boy: 'go forward until the young princes salute me on this my first day of taking arms'. They went forward accordingly to where the young princes were. 'Is it arms he has taken?' said each to the other. 'It is, indeed', said he himself. 'May you have victory, and trophy, and "first wounding" with them', said they; 'but we think it is too soon you have taken them, because it will separate you from us at our exercises', said they. 'I shall not separate from you at all', said he; 'but it was for luck I took arms on this day'.—

"*Cuchulainn* then asked his Charioteer where the great road which passed by Emania led to; and he answered that it led to *Ath na Forairé*, (i.e. the Ford of Watching), at *Sliabh Fuaid*; (a well-known mountain lying at the south of ancient Emania, in the present county of Armagh). 'Why is this ford called the Ford of Watching?' said *Cuchulainn*. 'Because', said *Ibar*, 'there is an Ultonian champion constantly watching and guarding there, in order that no warriors nor foreigners should come unperceived into Ulster, without being challenged by him to battle; and that champion must answer any such challenge on the part of the whole province; and if any "professional parties" (i.e. poets, etc.), were to leave the province in displeasure at the manner in which they had been rewarded there, it would be his duty to conciliate them, by the bestowal on them of such gifts and presents as may be sufficient to preserve the honour of the province; and also if any professional parties passed into the province, it is this champion that acts as their safeguard until they reach the presence of king *Conchobar*; so that their poems and their songs should be the first sung at Emania, after their arrival there'. "Do you know who is at that ford to-day?' said *Cuchulainn*. 'I do, indeed; it is the valiant and victorious *Conall Cearnach*, the Royal Champion of Erinn', said *Ibar*. 'Well, then', said *Cuchulainn*, 'you drive on until we reach that ford'.—

"They drove on accordingly till they came to the brink of the ford, where *Conall* was. 'Is it arms he has taken?' said *Conall*. 'It is, indeed', said *Ibar*. 'May they be arms of victory, and triumph, and first-wounding to you', said *Conall*; 'but we think it is too soon that you have taken them, because you are not arrived at the age of valour yet'. 'What do you do here, my master, *Conall*?' said *Cuchulainn*. 'I keep watch

LECT. XVII. Early education of Cuchulainn. (His boyish feats.)

and guard for the province here, my little son'; [illegible] 'Go you then to Emania for the present, my [illegible]' said the boy, 'and leave me here to keep watch [illegible] the province'. 'Not so, my little son', said *Conall*, [illegible] yet strong enough to fight with a brave champion [illegible] go on to the south then, to the Ford of *Loch* [illegible] if I can dip my hands in the blood of a foe to-day', [illegible] *lainn*. 'Then I will go to protect you, that you [illegible] to the border of the province', said *Conall*. 'You [illegible]' *Cuchulainn*. 'But I shall', said *Conall*; 'else the [illegible] would censure me for allowing you to go alone to [illegible] of the province'.—

"Then *Conall's* horses were yoked to his chariot [illegible] went forth to protect the boy. But when *Conall* [illegible] abreast with him, knowing well that if any opportunity [illegible] forming a creditable action should occur, *Conall* would [illegible] him no share, *Cuchulainn* stooped, and picked from the [illegible] a stone the full of his hand, and threw it with all his [illegible] the yoke (*cuing*) of *Conall's* chariot, so that he broke [illegible] two; and the chariot fell down, and *Conall* was hurled [illegible] it with such force as to dislocate his shoulder. 'Who [illegible] this, my son?' said *Conall*. 'It was I that threw it, [illegible] if my throw was straight, or how I could shoot, or whether [illegible] am "the makings" of a brave champion at all', said *Cu*[illegible] 'There is venom on your throw, and venom on yourself [illegible]' *Conall*, enraged; 'and if I were sure that you would [illegible] head with your enemies on this occasion, I would not [illegible] step to save you!' 'That is what I have sought from [illegible]' the boy, 'because I know that you Ultonians are bound [illegible] obligations not to proceed in a chariot with insecure [illegible]

After this adventure *Conall Cearnach* makes the [illegible] his way northwards [back to Emania] to repair his chariot [illegible] to obtain aid for himself; while *Cuchulainn* presses [illegible] south, and does not halt until he has crossed the border [illegible] province of Ulster, into Meath, at the place in which [illegible] river Mattock falls into the Boyne, about three [illegible] Drogheda. Here the boy champion draws up at the [illegible] the formidable *Dun*, or court, of the lady of *Nechtan* [illegible] where he sounded a challenge, and was soon answered [illegible] three sons in succession. Each of them, however, [illegible] death in fair combat at the hands of the hero; and after [illegible] returns in triumph to Emania, where he exhibits the [illegible] three of the most formidable enemies of his native province [illegible] the fruits of the first day of his championhood.

Such, then, was *Cuchulainn's* early military training [illegible] other passages in the *Táin Bo Chuailgné*, as well as from equally ancient and independent tracts, we know that *Fergus Mac Róigh* himself had been the special military tutor of the hero. This is clearly asserted in an ancient tale called the *Seirgligi Coinchulainn*, the "Sick Bed of *Cuchulainn*"), preserved in the *Leabhar-na-h-Uidhré*.[366] In this tract *Cuchulainn* speaks distinctly of *Fergus* as his tutor, and of *Conall Cearnach* as therefore his "fellow-pupil"; though the latter must have been so much older than himself, his education having been probably completed before *Cuchulainn* was born.

Early training of young warriors at this time.

From these references to what is recorded of *Cuchulainn's* early life, we may fairly collect what constituted the military education of a champion of the "Royal Branch", or, I suppose, of any other order, in the storied days of Erinn's military glory, that period which is spoken of in ancient Irish manuscripts as the *Aimsir na cCuradh*, that is, "The Time of the Champions". It appears clearly enough that the sons of the chiefs and nobles received from their infancy an elaborate training in athletic exercises, as well as in the use of the spear and shield; but it does not appear from any original authority that I know of, that there was any such institution as a special military School, with regular Professors and a regular system, as in the Schools of Literature and Law. The allusion in the *Táin Bo Chuailgné* to the retirement of the youths at Emania from their play ground at the close of day, each to the house of his parents, or to that of his nurse, and his tutor, indicates pretty clearly indeed that the tuition of the future candidates for admission to the order of Champions was individual; and there can be indeed but little doubt that each distinguished Champion in his time was the effective teacher of his profession to one or more pupils, either as a matter of friendship or emolument. In this way *Cuchulainn* himself, in his time, was military tutor of *Lugaidh Riabh-Derg*, ("the Son of the Three Fair Twins", as he was called), who was subsequently Monarch of Erinn, and probably of others of less note of whom no particular record has come down to us.

Later education in arms of *Cuchulainn*, (in *Alba*—Scotland.)

Passing on then from this point for the present, we have still to draw from the history of *Cuchulainn*, as it is preserved in the various ancient tracts devoted to the life of that hero, something more interesting still in the account of that part of his education for which he is said to have travelled into *Alba*, or Scotland, a course which seems to have been frequently

(366) [This very ancient Tale has been published in full, with Translation and Notes, by Professor O'Curry, in the ATLANTIS, (Dublin, 1858, 1859),—vol. i. p. 362, and vol. ii. p. 98.]

LECT. XVII. Later education in arms of Cuchulainn, (in Alba,—Scotland.)

taken by young warriors of peculiar promise. The [illegible] on which he was induced to take this means of [illegible] accomplishments as a champion, is stated as follows [illegible]

It seems that at length when he arrived at man's [illegible] ing that his exploits and fame as a knight had fully [illegible] with his years, *Cuchulainn* bethought him of taking a [illegible] able to his rank; and after no inconsiderable search [illegible] to his taste, he at last found her in *Emer*, the second [illegible] of *Forgall Monach*, a "chief *Brughaidh*", or "noble [illegible] who held extensive lands along the north-eastern [illegible] present county of Dublin, and who kept one of the [illegible] Courts of Hospitality in Erinn", at *Lusca* [the place no[illegible] Lusk]. His visit to *Lusca* was for the moment fruitl[illegible] *Emer* could not be persuaded to accept his hand with[illegible] consent of her father; and that personage, it would appear [illegible] no high regard for the position of a professional Cha[illegible] *Cuchulainn* accordingly returned to Emania, without for[illegible] demanding the alliance, but without abandoning his [illegible] to take another opportunity of prevailing with the lady [illegible] was not long before *Forgall Monach*, the father of *Emer* [illegible] ceived information of the suspicious visit of the great Ch[illegible] of Ulster to his daughter; and not doubting but that [illegible] understanding had been established between them, he [illegible] to take immediate measures to put a stop to any chance [illegible] renewal of their intercourse. With this view, then, he "[illegible] his countenance and his dress to the countenance and d[illegible] a foreigner", (so we are informed); and having done the [illegible] for two of his most trusted adherents, the three rep[illegible] Emania, where they represented themselves as am[illegible] "from the king of the *Galls*" [i.e. foreigners], who h[illegible] with presents from their royal master to king *Conchob*[illegible] story tells us that they were hospitably received; [illegible] there was a review of the knights of the Royal Bra[illegible] before them, at which all the feats and evolutions of [illegible] approved military education of the country were p[illegible] This was the opportunity sought by *Forgall Monach* [illegible] ing in the guise of a foreign ambassador, he was lavi[illegible] praises of the noble performance of the knights, and pa[illegible] of *Cuchulainn*, whom he pronounced to excel in all [illegible] of the art which could be acquired at home; but he [illegible] recommended him to pass into Scotland and place him [illegible] some time under the tuition of the Champion *Dom*[illegible] which he should, he said, cross that country as far as [illegible] Military College of the celebrated lady *Scathach*, up[illegible] he enlarged; and he concluded by saying that, after [illegible]

Later education in arms of Cuchulainn, (in Alba,—Scotland.)

his studies with these famous teachers, he would certainly be the most accomplished champion in Europe. *Cuchulainn* listened, we are told, with natural satisfaction to these disinterested recommendations, and he immediately began his preparations for a journey into Scotland; though it appears that before his departure he contrived to secure a private interview with the beautiful *Emer*, in which they are said to have exchanged the vows of constancy usual on such occasions.

Cuchulainn, however, did pass into Scotland; and we learn that in due time he proceeded at once to the residence of the champion *Domhnall*, (though where exactly that was, I am unable to say); and he seems to have spent some time in taking lessons from him; but he soon set out again to the more distinguished establishment of the lady *Scathach*. The description of the young hero's journey thither partakes largely of the wild and wonderful; but all dangers and difficulties having been at last escaped and every obstruction overcome he succeeded in arriving safely at the court in which the pupils of *Scathach* resided. The ancient tale then goes on.

"He asked them then where *Scathach* was. 'In yonder island', said they. 'By what path do people reach it?' said he. 'Over the Bridge of the Pupils', said they; 'but no one can pass that until he is perfect in his championship', said they. (For this, "continues this very wild tale," was the way in which that bridge was fashioned: it had two low heads, or ends, and it was high in the middle; and when a person stood on one end of it, the other end would rise up and he would be cast off to the bottom".) It is stated in other copies, that there was a party of Champions from Erinn at this court when *Cuchulainn* came there, learning additional feats of arms from *Scathach*; among whom were *Ferdiaidh Mac Damain* from Connacht, [he who was slain by *Cuchulainn* afterwards in the *Táin Bo Chuailgné*]; also *Naoisé Mac Uisnech* from Ulster, [the unfortunate husband of the beautiful *Deirdré* and the hero of the celebrated tale;][351] *Loch Mor Mac Morfebis* from Munster; *Fiamain Mac Forai* from Ulster; and a great number beside. *Cuchulainn* made three efforts to pass the bridge, but he did not succeed; and the pupils began to reproach him. "Then", continues the story, "he became vexed, and he leaped on the end of the bridge, and springing a champion's salmon-sault, he alighted on its centre, not giving the bridge time to raise its other head before he

[351] [The first of the "Three Most Sorrowful Tales" of Erinn is that of the "Exile of the Children of *Uisnech*" and the death of *Deirdré*. The oldest version of this celebrated Tale was published (with Translation and Notes) by Professor O'Curry, in the ATLANTIS (Dublin, 1862), vol. iii. p. 377;—the two other tales in ATLANTIS, vol. iv. p. 118.]

[illegible]CT. XVII.

[illegible]er educa-[illegible]n in arms Cuchu-[illegible] (in [illegible]o-[illegible]tland.)

reached it, and with another spring from that he alighted [illegible] the ground in the island. There he saw the court [illegible] and made directly for it; and in his anger he broke the [illegible] that stood in the way, and passed through it. This was [illegible] the lady *Scathach*. 'True', said she, 'this is a man [illegible] finished his Championship in some other place',—and [illegible] her daughter *Uathach* to know who the youth was. So [illegible] went out to meet him; but when she came to see him [illegible]tinctly, (says the old tale, with great simplicity) she [illegible] utter a word, so much did the beauty and symmetry [illegible] man astonish her. And she returned to her mother; and [illegible] recovered her speech on the way, she described in [illegible] highest praise the appearance of the man she had seen. [illegible] have fallen in love with this man', said her mother;—'[illegible] indeed'; said *Uathach*".

We are then told how *Cuchulainn* was kindly received by [illegible] mother, and joyfully by the daughter; whose attentions [illegible] were however for some time thrown away, as he had [illegible] thought of breaking his pledge to *Emer*. But after [illegible] rested three days, the ancient narrator records that he had a [illegible]versation with the young amazon, *Uathach;* when she [illegible] if it was to perfect his Championship he had come, he [illegible] well to go to her mother *Scathach* where she was giving [illegible] lessons to her two sons, *Cuar* and *Cett;* that having [illegible] the spot "he should spring a 'Champion's salmon-[illegible]' into the great thick yew-tree, in which she was lying; [illegible] he should then place the point of his sword between her [illegible] until she had promised him his three requests, which [illegible] to teach him all, without reservation; to marry herself (*Uathach*) to him; and to tell him his future destiny, for she was [illegible]phetess". And *Cuchulainn*, who appears to have readily [illegible] every portion of these suggestions, accordingly at once [illegible] to where *Scathach* was, "placed his two feet on the edge [illegible] exercise basket, [whatever that was], sprang into the [illegible] bared his sword and placed its point to her heart: 'A [illegible] death', said he. 'You shall have any three requests [illegible] they come with your breath without consideration', [illegible] So he accepts her terms and binds her to performance [illegible] *Scathach* fairly performs her promises; for, she gives [illegible] daughter to wife; teaches him all her secrets in the [illegible] art; and when at last *Cuchulainn* leaves her to return [illegible] tells him all the events of his future life.[348]

(348) The Tale above quoted proceeds to narrate another passage [illegible] *lainn's* life in *Alba*, or Scotland, which, though too diffuse to be [illegible] into the text, may be abridged here by way of note. It offers some [illegible]

The tract then proceeds to enumerate an interesting list of the names of the various feats (*cleasa*) of championship which it is recorded that *Cuchulainn* learned perfectly from *Scathach*:

LECT. XVII. List of the various "Feats of Championship" learned by Cuchulainn in the School of Scathach.

sions to other military exercises, mixed with the wildest fancies of extravagant story telling:—

During *Cuchulainn*'s sojourn with *Scathach*, a quarrel sprang up between her and a neighbouring nation which was governed by another famous amazon like herself whose name was *Aifé*. Both the ladies assembled their forces respectively to decide their differences by battle. *Cuchulainn* accompanied the two sons of *Scathach*,—*Cuar* and *Ceat*,—to the battle, to meet the three bravest champions of the lady *Aifé*, whose names were also *Cuar* and *Ceat*, and *Craifné*, the three sons of *Ilsuanach*. But when *Cuchulainn* came face to face with these three champions, he fought and slew them single-handed, without waiting for the general battle which was to take place on the next day.

The next day came, and the forces of both sides stood face to face; and the lady *Aifé* put forward three other brave knights, *Ciré*, and *Biré*, and *Bailené*, the three sons of *Eisse Enchinn*. These three knights challenged *Scathach*'s two sons to combat;—and here occurs one of the strangest scenes of combat which imaginative romance has ever suggested. The challenge was accepted; and the three challengers "sprang on the *Téd Chlis*", (which, it seems, was something like a tight-rope for dancers), on which these strange knights performed their feats of arms and their combats. *Cuchulainn*, however, who was to have gone with *Scathach*'s sons, sprang alone upon the rope and attacked the three knights, whom he slew in succession. Then the lady *Aifé*, on seeing the death of her best champions, challenged the lady *Scathach* herself to single combat; but *Cuchulainn* took up the challenge. Before proceeding to engage the sorceress, however, *Cuchulainn* asked *Scathach* what she thought was most prized by her great opponent *Aifé*; and *Scathach* answered, that it was her chariot and her two steeds. Then they sprang upon the rope, *Cuchulainn* and *Aifé*, and they fought a fierce combat upon it, in which the sorceress shivered her spear and her sword. "Holla!" said *Cuchulainn*, "*Aifé*'s charioteer and her two chariot horses have fallen into the glen and are killed!" So *Aifé* looked about her; whereupon *Cuchulainn* snatched her up suddenly on his shoulder, and descending to the ground with her, laid her prostrate at his feet, and placed the point of his sword at her breast. And *Aifé* shouted out: "Life for life, O *Cuchulainn*!" said she. "Let me have my three requests", said he. "You shall have them, such as you ask in one breath", said she. "My three requests, then, are", said he, "that you submit to *Scathach*; that you revolt not against her; and that you take myself into your cherished friendship". "All is granted", said she;—and so the strange combat ended.

Cuchulainn having thus established peace between the warlike ladies, proceeded to return in triumph to his new conquest; but having to pass over the same rope again, he now found it occupied by "a fierce half-blind hag". She requested of him to make room for her and allow her to pass. He answered that he had not any other path on which to move except down the great cliff which was under him. She begged of him, however, to clear the way for her; and he accordingly dropped himself down from the rope, "holding by it with his forefinger and thumb only". The hag passed over him then, and endeavoured with her foot to remove his thumb from the rope, that he might drop down the cliff. But he perceived her motion and intention; and he "gave a champion's salmon-sault" up again, and with his sword cut off the hag's head. Now this hag was, it appears, the mother of the three sons of *Eissé Enchinn* whom he had already slain on the rope; and she had met him designedly on the rope, "knowing that under his vows of Championship he would make way for her on it"; and in the hope that by such means she would cause his death in revenge for that of her sons.

Cuchulainn then returned with *Scathach* and her forces to her own country, where in accordance with her promise she instructed him in the full perfection of the science of arms, as far as it was known to her.

LECT. XVII.

List of the various "Feats of championship" learned by Cuchulainn in the school of Scathach.

"*Ubhall-chleas*, (the ball feat); *Faebhar-chleas*, (the sword or sharp-edged shield feat); *Torand-chleas*, (the "thunder feat", which was performed with the chariot around the enemy); *Faen-chleas*, (the "prostrate feat", one which I cannot explain from the name, unless it means that from lying flat on the ground, perhaps in ambush, the champion sprang suddenly to his feet:) *Cleas-cletenech*, (dart-feat); and the *Ted-chleas*, (rope feat; which probably was that feat of the rope in which *Cuchulainn* overthrew the lady *Aifé*, and killed her three champions and the old hag their mother, [see note below,(382)]; it was another feat which is mentioned in the Brehon Laws as one of three perfections of the education of a knight, and which will be presently described;) the *Cleas-Cait*, ("cat feat"; of which I know nothing); the *Coriech n-Errid*, (champion's salmon-sault, or -leap); the *Imarchor n-delend*, (the proper carrying of the charioteer's switch); the *Leim-dar-n-aimh*, (the leap over a fence (?); the *Filliud erred nair*, (the "whirl of a valiant champion"); the *Gae-bolga*, (the feat of casting the belly-dart, already described); the *Bai-braissé*, (literally, "sudden death" (?); the *Roth-chleas*, ("wheel feat"; a gymnastic performance resembling the casting of the sledge(383) at the present day;) the *Other-chleas* ("invalidating feat",—as well as I can understand the term); the *Cleas for analaibh*, (literally, the "feat of his breathings"); the *Bruid-giné*, ("gnashing of the mouth", as well as I can understand it); the *Sian-Cauradh*, (the champion's war-whoop); the *Béim co famus*, (cutting of his opponent's hair off with his sword); the *Taith-béim*, ("vertical stroke", which fixed his antagonist to the ground); the *Fodh-béim*, ("sod-blow", by which he cut the sod from under the feet of his antagonist, by a stroke of his sword; this was done in contempt); the *Dreim fri fogh-uist*, (climbing against a rock, so as to stand straight at its top); the *Fonaidhm niadh for rinnibh Slegh*, "coiling of a champion around the blades of upright Spears"); and the *Carbad-Searrdha*, (the feat of the armed, or scythed, chariot, in battle).

The tale from which these latter notes of *Cuchulainn's* achievements are taken, is the ancient tale known as that of the "Courtship of *Emer*, and the Education of *Cuchulainn*", (*Tochmarc nEimiré, ocas Foglaim Coinchulaind*).(384) At the beginning of this Tale it is stated, that the feats (*cleasa*) of Championship which distinguished the knights of Emania at home, were limited to three, namely, the *Cleas-Cletineach*, or feat

(382) [So described, apparently, in the ancient Tale of the *Fledh Bricrind*, ("*Bricrind's* Feast"); concerning which see *Lectures on the MS. Materials of Ancient Irish History*, p. 346, etc.]

(384) See *Lectures on the MS. Materials*, (etc); p. 278.

LECT. XVII.

List of the various "Feats of Championship" learned by Cuchulainn in the School of Scathach.

with darts; the *Ubhall-Chleas*, or feat with balls; and the *Faebhar-Chleas*, or feat with edged weapons, (such as knives, swords, or sharp-edged Shields). And we have it on the same authority, that all these feats were practised by the champions *Conall Cearnach*, *Fergus Mac Róigh*, *Laeghairé Buadhach*, *Celtchair Mac Uithir*, *Dubhthach Dael-tenga*, and *Cuchulainn Mac Soaltainn*, as well as the rest of the knights. Yet although these special feats are set down as part of the necessary education of a finished knight or champion, it can, I think, be clearly shewn that some of them at least were merely ornamental accomplishments by way of evidence of skill and dexterity, and not at all regarded as feats of arms intended for use in actual combat.

LECTURE XVIII.

(Delivered [illegible].)

(VI.) Military Education; continued. Instances of [illegible] pions acting as the military tutors of young champions. [illegible] fosterage, which continued, more or less, down to A.D. 1[illegible] the ancient custom of military education. No reliable [illegible] tral military organization until the time of *Conn* "of the Hundred [illegible] probability however of the existence of such an organization [illegible] the name *Fianna*. Mention made in the "Book of Navan" of the [illegible] tion of a military force by *Cormac Mac Airt*. Mention made [illegible] barrack at Tara in poems of *Cinaedh O'Hartagan* and *Cuan* [illegible] Dr. Keting's account of the *Fianna Eireann*. List of Fe[illegible] in the Yellow Book of *Lecain*. Account of the battle of *C*[illegible] the *Fianna* under *Finn Mac Cumhaill* were engaged. Destruction of [illegible] *Fianna* at the battle of *Gabhra*, A.D., 284. Instances of the [illegible] a regular army in Erinn after the time of the battle of *Gabhra*.

It has been already observed that from all that can be [illegible] in the existing relics of our old historical literature, we must [illegible] to the conclusion that the Gaedhil had not among them [illegible] stitutions which could strictly be called Military Colleges, [illegible] term is understood in modern times. That there were [illegible] schools for literary and military instruction together, [illegible] by individual professors, there can, I think, be no doubt, [illegible] ever; but we have no satisfactory information as regards the [illegible] ber of pupils or how these schools were efficiently worked [illegible] one time.

Military tutors of celebrated Champions.

We find it recorded that the celebrated monarch of [illegible] *Ugaine Mór*, who flourished about three hundred years [illegible] the Christian era, was educated by the famous champion *C*[illegible] *baeth*, king of Emania. So *Cuchulainn*, and *Conall C*[illegible] famous knights of Emania, were educated by *Fergus Mac* [illegible] of the same place; *Lugaidh Riabhderg* (afterwards [illegible] of Erinn) by *Cuchulainn; Conall Claringnech*, a famous [illegible] and Champion of Ulster, by *Finntann Mac Rudhraidhe*, [illegible] the same period, that is, about the commencement of [illegible] *Conn* "of the Hundred Battles", monarch of Erinn, by [illegible] *Cruachua*, king of Connacht, (who was of the Firbolg [illegible] about the middle of the second century; *Laigsech C*[illegible] son of the champion *Conall Cearnach*, (the ancestor of the *O'*[illegible] *radh's* or O'Mores of *Laighis*, or Leix, in Leinster,) by [illegible] *Finn*, brother to the monarch *Conn*, also in the second century;

Eoghan Mór, king of Munster, the great opponent of the monarch *Conn*, by *Nuadha Dearg*, a celebrated Munster chieftain; *Cormac*, the son of *Art*, son of *Conn*,—who was monarch of Erinn in the third century,—by *Lughna Firtri*, a chieftain of Connacht; *Fiacha Muilléthan*, the son of *Eoghan Mór*, son of *Oilioll Oluim*, by his maternal grandfather, *Dill* the Druid, and under the superior direction of the celebrated Druid *Mogh Ruith*; *Connla*, the son of *Fadg*, son of *Cran*, son of *Oilioll Oluim*, king of Munster, by the monarch *Cormac*, the son of *Art*; *Conall Echluaith*, (the ancestor of the great Dalcassian families of Thomond,) by *Crimhthann Mór*, monarch of Erinn in the fourth century. So *Niall* "of the Nine Hostages", monarch of Erinn, and *Corc Mac Luighech*, king of Munster, were educated together by the poet *Torna Eigeas*, (of the district of O'Torna in Kerry), also in the fourth century. And lastly *Conall Gulban*, the son of *Niall* "of the Nine Hostages", was educated at *Beinn Gulban*, in Connacht, by a sub-tutor named *Muiredhach Meann*, under a superior tutor named *Fiachra*.

Military Education in Erinn, a system of Fosterage.

These few instances are sufficient to show what the general system of the country was in regard to the education in arms; the principal champions, whether kings or inferior chieftains, presiding over the military education of the more promising youths and young champions of each period. However, there can be but little doubt that at Tara, as well as at each of the provincial courts, there were (as by law it was certainly prescribed there should be) more regular establishments of a public kind, and upon a more extended system; though it is true that no particular detailed account of these schools has escaped the wreck of ages, as far as I am informed on the subject, excepting what has been quoted from the Brehon Laws, namely, that the sons of the kings and chiefs, under the Law of Fosterage and Tutorage, were taught riding, swimming, chess, draughts, or backgammon, with the use of the sword, spear, and all other weapons offensive and defensive. And as these fosterage laws, preserved—though irregularly—by the natives, and adopted by the Anglo-Normans continued in full force in one form or another down even to about the year 1600, the custom may be very fairly accepted as a living representation of an ancient universal system. It is in consequence of this ancient and universal custom of military education by way of Fosterage, that we find in genealogies and histories such names as *Domhnall Connachtach* O'Brien, so called because he was fostered and educated in Connacht with the O'Conors; *Donnchadh Cairbrech* O'Brien, so called, because he had been fostered with the MacCarthy of Carbery in the county of Cork *Brian Luighnech* O'Conor, so called because he had

XVIII. been fostered with (I believe) the *O'Haras of Leyney* [illegible] *chadh Muimhnech*, and *Donnchadh Cairbreach O'Kelly* [illegible] *Maine*, because they were respectively fostered [illegible] Munster and in Hy-Kinsella in Leinster; and so [illegible] others.

Notwithstanding the numerous references in our [illegible] to the chivalry and military fame of individual champions, [illegible] no reliable authority for the existence of any central [illegible] ganization under the monarch of Tara, for the general [illegible] of the nation and the defence of the country at large, [illegible] time of *Conn* "of the Hundred Battles", who reigned [illegible] monarch from the year of Our Lord 123, to the [illegible] which he was slain. Still there is good reason to [illegible] national military organization did actually exist [illegible] time; since we find it stated in the ancient historical [illegible] as the battle of *Cimcha*, that before *Conn* had come to [illegible] narchy (after the intervention between his reign [illegible] his father, the monarch *Feidlimidh*, of the reign of [illegible] who ruled for three years), he appears to have been [illegible] mander of the celebrated national militia, or standing [illegible] popularly known as the *Fianna Eireann*, of whom [illegible] the father of the celebrated *Finn MacCumhaill*, and [illegible] self, were afterwards in succession the most distinguished [illegible] manders.

Origin of the word "*Fianna*". The name *Fianna* is explained in an ancient glossary [illegible] in a volume of Brehon Laws.[365]

"*Fianna*, a Venatione, id est, It was from the Hunting [illegible] they practised they were so named. Or, *Fianna*, that is, [illegible] *dha*, [families,] because it was in tribes they were formed [illegible] *Fianna*, that is, *Feinneadha* [champions], because they [illegible] Champions of the monarch of Erinn".[366]

This is a very curious and indeed important explanation [illegible] rather, attempt at the derivation of the name. It [illegible] doubt or difficulty as to the existence of the force; [illegible] commentator is at a loss only to know which of three [illegible] was that gave occasion to the name. And the value [illegible] difficulty is, to induce him inadvertently to preserve to [illegible] smallest possible space, allusions to the clear and distinct [illegible] tertained in his time of the peculiar formation, habits, [illegible] of the Feinnean force.

(365) In the library of Trin. Coll. Dublin: MS. classed H. 3. 18.

(366) original:—Fianna, a venatione, .i. o'n tseilg do gnidis [illegible] fianna friu. No fianna .i. fineada, ar is ina fine [illegible] bitis siat. No fianna .i. feinneada rig Eirenn iat.

First, he thinks the name *Fianna* may have been derived from *Fiadach*, that is, *Venatio*, or Hunting; clearly implying that these warriors were habitually addicted to the chase; and that this would be a reasonable derivation will appear as we go on. Secondly, the commentator thinks that the name *Fianna* might be derived from *Fineadha*, that is, Families, or Clanns; because it was of such they were composed,—as for instance, the *Clanna Baiscné*, who were *Finn MacCumhaill*'s own clann, and made up the chief part of the Leinster contingent; the *Clanna Morna*, who were *Goll Mac Morna*'s clann, and supplied the chief part of the Connacht contingent; the *Clanna Deaghaidh* and others, under the command of *Glas-donn*, of *Beara* (Berehaven), who were the Munster contingent; and so on. Thirdly, the commentator thinks that the name may have been derived from the word *Feinnid*, a Champion; because they were "the champions of the monarch of Erinn"; and this last derivation is indeed the most probable and rational. XVIII.

The Rev. Dr. Keting, in his well-known abstract of the history of Erinn, quotes from some ancient book, (most probably the *Leabhar-na-h-Ua Chongbhala*, or Book of Navan), a curious tract on the formation, education, discipline, and laws of the *Fianna Eireann*, of which I have never had the good fortune to meet with another copy; and that it was from the Book of Navan that Keting did take it, is to some extent borne out by the fact of finding the following note, on this very subject, quoted in the Book of Ballymote, from the Book of Navan, in a sketch of the high personal qualities and the magnificence of the monarch *Cormac Mac Airt* and his reign. Mention of the *Fianna* in the "Book of Navan".

"The monarch of Erinn, (*i.e. Cormac*) appointed an army over the men of Erinn; and over it he appointed three times fifty royal Feinian officers, for the purpose of enforcing his laws, and maintaining his sovereign rule, and preserving his game; and he gave the command of the whole, and the High-stewardship of Erinn to *Finn Ua Baiscné*, [that is, *Finn Mac Cumhaill*]".[357]

It appears from a poem written by *Cinaedh* O'Hartagan (who died 975) on the glories and magnificence of Tara in *Cormac Mac Airt*'s time, that there existed at Tara at this time a spacious barracks in which were lodged no less than seven thousand five hundred men.[358] The following are the stanzas of this most curious poem, which refer to the great barrack at Tara. Great Barrack of Tara described by *Cinaedh* O Hartagan.

[357] original:—Ro ordaig din, rig Erenn (.i. Cormac), a amsaig for feraib Erenn; ro ordaig tri caecait Rig feinnig, forraside fri comus a chána, ocus a smachta, ocus a fiadaig; do rat a cennacht uile, ocus ardmaeraidecht Erenn d'Find ua Baiscne.—[B. of Ballymote, fol. 145, a.]

[358] This poem is published in Dr. Petrie's *Antiquities of Tara*, page 164, and printed in the eighteenth volume of the Transactions of the Royal Irish Academy.

XVIII.

"Its great house of thousands of soldiers,—
To generations it was not obscure;
A beautiful, brilliant fortress of brave men;—
Seven hundred feet was its length.
"It was not filled with the foolish and ignorant,
Nor over-crowded with the wisely and arrogant;
It was no small thing to be cut up:
Six times five cubits was its height.
"The king had his place there, the king of Erinn,
Around whom the fairest wine was distributed;
It was a fortress, a castle, a wonder;—
There were three times fifty compartments in it.
"Three times fifty Champions with swords,
(No silly defence for a fortress,)
That was the number, among the wonders,
Which occupied each compartment".[359]

This poem, it is to be remembered, was written by the great bardic historian *Cinaedh* O'Hartagan (who died in 975), while the remains of Tara were still distinct and intact, and whilst the written history of that famous hill was still clear and abundant, and its traditions vividly cherished.

Mentioned also in *Cuan O'Lothchain's* poem on Tara

In *Cuan O'Lothchain*'s poem, written also on the wonderful remains of ancient Tara, we find the following stanza relating to this great barrack or army house:

"I speak farther of the fortress of the champions;
(Which was also called the fortress of foolish women);
The House of the Champions was not a weak one,
With its fourteen opening doors".[360]

Cuan O'Lothchain, the author of this poem, and of whom mention has been often made in the course of these Lectures, died in the year 1024.[361]

[359] orig. :—a tech mór milibh amuss,—
con ndáinib, nír bo dolúss;
cathair glan glerib glain-
ser;—
trí cét [secht cét] traiged
a tomus.
Nír tairmchell bairr burbae,
na cumga gaissi gargai;
nír bo beg fri therba:
se coic cubat a hardae.

Auba ríg, ri uas [illegible];
[illegible] [illegible] [illegible];
ba [illegible], ba [illegible],
[illegible];—
trí caecad [illegible]
[illegible] caeca laeċ co [illegible],
nír bo [illegible] [illegible]
[illegible],
ba ne [illegible], [illegible] [illegible]
ceċa [illegible] [illegible].

[360] orig. :—Imráidim fós long na laech;
fris anaber barc ban mbaeċ;
teċ na laeċ nír [illegible];
co ceitre doirrib [illegible].

The whole of this poem also is published in Dr. Petrie's *Antiquities of Tara*, page 121.

[361] See ante, Lecture V., p. 105.

XVIII.

Dr. Keting's account of the Fianna Eireann.

The Rev. Dr. Keting, after a glance at various exaggerated tales and fables concerning *Finn Mac Cumhaill* and the *Fianna*, which were in popular favour in his own time, goes on to speak on the subject, as follows

"Notwithstanding these fables, it is certain that truthful, reliable histories have been written of them; and it is certain that they were not taller or larger in their persons than the men in general who lived in their time; and that they were nothing more than the *Buanadhs*, or permanent soldiers of the kings of Erinn, to defend and preserve the country for them, in the same way that all kings at this day have officers and soldiers to defend their own countries.—

"The way in which the *Fianna* were disposed was this.—

"They were freely quartered on the men of Erinn, from November to May; and they were employed in enforcing right and preventing wrong, under the kings and lords of Erinn; and further to guard and defend the harbours of the country against the oppressive intrusion of foreigners.—

"From May to November they employed themselves in fowling and hunting, and in discharging such duties as the monarch of Erinn assigned them; such as to check thieves, to enforce the payment of taxes, to check outlaws, and all other evils which may affect the country. For all this they had a fixed stipend, such as all the kings of Europe at the present give to those who are captains and officers under them.—

"The *Fianna*, however, were obliged to subsist from May to November on the fruits of the chase, both in regard to their food and their pay, in accordance with the rule of the monarchs of Erinn, who assigned them the flesh of the animals for their food, and their skins for their pay.—

"They were accustomed to make but one meal in the day and night, and this at evening time; and this was their custom. The chase which they ran down in the morning they sent by their attendants at midday to an appointed hill, contiguous to a wood and moorland: there they lighted great fires, into which they put a great quantity of sandstones. They next dug two trenches in the yellow clay of the moor; and, having set part of the venison upon spits to be roasted before the fire, they bound up the remainder in *sugans* or sedge-ropes, or bundles of sedge, which they placed to be cooked in the larger of the two trenches previously cut. There they set round them the stones which had been heated in the fire, and kept heaping them on the bundles of meat until they had made them broil freely, and the meat had become thoroughly cooked. And these fires were so great that their black, burned sites remain to be seen in various parts of Erinn to this day; and it is these that are called by [illegible] *Fulachta Fiann*, (the cooking-places of the *Fianna*).—

"As to the *Fianna*, when they were assembled at the hillock [illegible] was the fire, every man of them stripped himself to the [illegible] tied his shirt around his waist; and they then gathered [illegible] the second pit which we have mentioned above, bathing [illegible] heads and washing their limbs, to remove the sweat from [illegible]. They then began to supple their thews and sinews (by [illegible] exercise), until they had in this manner put off from [illegible] fatigue, after which they ate their meal. That being over, [illegible] commenced constructing their *Fianbhotha*, (i.e. Hunting-[illegible]), and preparing their beds, and putting themselves in [illegible] sleep. Of the following three materials then did each man [illegible]struct his bed, namely, of the brushwood of the forest, of [illegible] and of fresh rushes. The brushwood was laid next the [illegible]; over it was laid the moss; and lastly the fresh rushes were [illegible] over all. It is these three materials that are designated in [illegible] ancient books as the *Tri Cuilceda na Feinne* (i.e. the Three Beddings of the *Fianna*)".

I may observe here, in corroboration of the learned and [illegible]worthy authority of Keting, that the *Fiann-bhotha*, or [illegible] booths of the *Fianna*, and even of *Finn MacCumhaill* [illegible], are spoken of in Cormac's Glossary, a compilation of the close of the ninth century, as well as in several other ancient books, of equal authenticity.

Keting enters into farther proofs of the authenticity of the rational history of the *Fianna Eireann*, or Militia of Erinn, [illegible] defends them and their celebrated commander from the [illegible] account published of them by the Scottish historian [illegible] Boetius.

"It is improperly", says Keting, "that Hector Boetius, [illegible] his History of Scotland, calls *Finn MacCumhaill* a '[illegible]', and he speaks falsely when he says that he was fifteen [illegible] height; because it is quite manifest from our ancient [illegible] books, that he was not larger than the men in general of his [illegible]; and it is also manifest that there were several men of the [illegible] yet taller, stouter, and stronger than he was. The reason [illegible] was made chief of the Champions of Erinn was, because his [illegible] and grandfather had been such before him, and also [illegible] excelled in knowledge, learning, wisdom, acuteness, and [illegible] all the warriors of his time; and it was on this account [illegible] was appointed Royal Commander of the *Fianna*, and [illegible] the size and stature of his person above other men.—

"The ordinary strength of the force which *Finn* [illegible] and which was generally quartered freely throughout the [illegible] was Three *Caths* or Battalions, each consisting of three thousand men. This was when peace reigned between all the men of Erinn and the *Ard Righ* or monarch. But when dissensions arose between any large section of the men of Erinn and the monarch, or when it was necessary to send an army into Scotland to sustain the Dalriadian colony of the Gaedhil against foreign foes, then *Finn* commanded Seven *Caths* or Battalions; so that he had troops sufficient to relieve the Dalriads in Scotland, and to protect Erinn from foreign tyranny, at the same time.—

XVIII. Dr. Keting's account of the Fianna Eireann.

"Many were the chief captains or leaders that were in command under *Finn*, such as a *Cath-Mhiledh*, over a *Cath* or Battalion, the same as the colonel of a regiment now; a *Ceann-feadhna-Cead*, the same as a Captain of an hundred now; a *Taoiseach-Caogaid*, or Leader of Fifty, the same as a lieutenant now; and a *Taoiseach-Tri-nonbair*, or Leader of Twenty-seven, the same as a corporal now; and a *Taoiseach Nonbair*, or leader of nine, the same as the Decurion with the Romans. For, when an hundred men were thrown into ten platoons or ranks, there was an officer to each rank of them; and it was he that was called the Leader of Nine.—

"There were four conditions which every man who was received into the *Fianns* was obliged to fulfil—

"The first condition was, that he should not accept any fortune with a wife, but to select her for her moral conduct and her accomplishments.—

"The second was, that he should not insult any woman.—

"The third was, that he should not refuse any person for trinkets or food.—

"The fourth was, that he should not turn his back on (that is, fly from) nine champions".

Here follow the additional conditions which *Finn Mac Cumhaill* attached to the military degrees, and which every man was obliged to accept before he was received into the *Fianna*.

"The first condition was, that no person was admitted into them at the great meetings of *Uisneach*, nor at the fair of *Tailltin*, or at the feast of Tara, until his father and his mother, his tribe and his relatives, gave security that they would never avenge his death on another person; in order that he should not expect any one to avenge him but himself; and no matter what evils he might commit, that his friends were not to be sued for them.—

"The second condition was, that no man should be taken into the *Fianna*, until he was an accomplished poet, and had read the Twelve Books of Poetry.[388]—

[388] [*Fileadeacht*,—Philosophy.

XVIII. Dr. Keting's account of the Fianna Eireann.

"The third condition was, that no man was received into the *Fianna*, until a wide pit had been dug for him, in which [illegible] to stand up to his knees, with his shield in one hand, [illegible] hazel stake the length of a champion's arm, in the other. [illegible] warriors armed with nine *sleghs* (or spears) came to within the distance of nine ridges (of ground) of him; and then [illegible] throw their nine spears all at once at him; and should [illegible] wounded, despite the shield and the hazel staff, he was [illegible] ceived into the order of the *Fianna*.—

"The fourth condition: No man was received into the [illegible] until his hair was first plaited, and till he was then [illegible] through several forests, with the whole of the Feinnian [illegible] pursuit of him, with full intent to wound him, the distance between them being but one tree; and if they came up with him they wounded him, [and then he could not be taken into the *Fianna*].—

"The fifth condition: No man was received into the *Fianna* if the arms trembled in his hands.—

"The sixth condition: No man was received into the *Fianna* if a single braid of his hair had been loosened out of its plait by a branch in the wood (as he ran through it).—

"The seventh condition: No man was received into the *Fianna* whose foot had broken a single withered branch in his course.—

"The eighth condition: No man was received into the *Fianna* unless he could jump over (the branch of) a tree as high as his forehead, and stoop under one as low as his knee (without [illegible] to his speed), through the great agility of his body.—

"The ninth condition: No man was received into the *Fianna* unless he could pluck a thorn out of his heel with his [illegible] without hindrance to his speed.—

"The tenth condition: No man was received into the *Fianna* until he had first sworn fidelity and obedience to the king (or Commander) of the *Fianna*" —

So far Dr. Keting on the organization and use of this celebrated ancient militia, in the time of their last and most distinguished leader *Finn MacCumhaill*. I say last, because [illegible] having broken his allegiance to the monarch *Cairbré Liffeachair*, the son and successor of the wise monarch *Cormac Mac Airt*, [illegible] *Fianna* were annihilated soon after at the battle of *Gabhra* [illegible] *Cairbré* and his forces.

Although, as I have already stated, I have not been able to meet with any copy of the tract which Keting quotes, older than his own version of it, I have met with several ancient authorities on the actual existence of the Feinnian Militia under *Finn Mac Cumhaill* and his predecessors. One of these authorities [illegible] curious list of the names, and sometimes the pedigree and entry of the native district, of one hundred and fifty of the subordinate officers or Captains of Nine men, who held command under *Finn* himself. This list is preserved in the ancient manuscript known as the "Yellow Book of *Lecan*," in the library of Trinity College, Dublin, (class H. 2, 16), a manuscript which was compiled in the year 1391, from more ancient records, by *Gilla Isa Mór Mac Firbis*, of *Lecan Mac Firbisigh*, (in the county of Sligo). The original compiler adds that it was *Finn Mac Cumhaill* and his *Fianna* that gained the following battles: the battle, of *Cuil Cuilleann*, (the situation of which I am not acquainted with); the battle of *Cliach*, (on the border of Tipperary and Limerick); the battle of *Cumar-Tri-Nuisci*, (near Waterford); the battle of *Magh Mis*, (in Kerry); the battle of *Sliabh Mis*, (in the same county); the battle of *Sidh Femen*, now *Sliabh-na-m-ban*, (in Tipperary); the battle of *Feaa*, (in the county of Wexford, I believe); and the battle of *Inis Derglocha*, (the situation of which I do not know).

List of names of Feinnian officers in the "Yellow Book of Lecan".

Battles won by the Fianna of Finn Mac Cumhaill.

It is not stated, however, for whom or in what cause these battles were fought, nor is there mention of any of them in the Annals of the Four Masters; but these annals are very meagre about the occurrences of this period. But although these annals are silent on any of the achievements of the *Fianna*, (except in the one instance of the battle of *Gabhra*, near Tara, fought A.D. 284, but of which I shall speak bye and bye), still there is a remarkable and doubtless true account of another battle in which *Finn Mac Cumhaill* and his warriors took a decided part, but one most unfortunate for the stability of his forces.

The first place in which I find *Finn* and his men engaged was at the battle of *Cnamhros*, fought somewhere in the present Queen's County, I think towards its south end, and on the brink of the river *Bearbha* [Barrow]. This battle of *Cnamhros* arose out of the fatal imposition of the tax called the Boromean Tribute, of the origin of which I detailed to you the history on a former occasion.[383] This tribute continued to be paid with reluctance, and often levied by force of arms, from the time of king *Tuathal*, who reigned from A.D. 76 to 106, down to that of *Cairbré Liffeachair*, who was monarch from A.D. 268 to 284.

Battle of Cnamhros fought by Finn Mac Cumhaill and his Fianna.

When Cairbre assumed the reins of government, he immediately, according to ancient custom, demanded the Boromean Tribute from *Breasal Belach*, the king of Leinster; but *Breasal* refused to pay it without a battle. *Cairbré*, accordingly, pro-

(383) See *Lectures on the MS. Materials*, etc., p. 230, etc.

[illegible]

ceeded to muster the men of the northern half of Erinn, (that part known as *Leath Chuinn*, or Conn's Half); and at their head he marched into Leinster, penetrating as far as the *Cnamhros* above mentioned, on the bank of the *Bearbha*.

The king of Leinster, who knew that he was to expect nothing less than such an invasion, was not idle in the meantime. He held at once a meeting of the chiefs of the province, to deliberate on the best course to be pursued in case of the advance of an army so much superior to his own as that of the monarch of all Erinn, to make an attack on him at his own door. The determination at which they arrived was, to invite *Finn Mac Cumhaill* and his *Fianna* to abandon the cause of the monarch to whose service he was bound, and to join his forces to those of his immediate countrymen, (*Finn* being himself a Leinsterman), against the alleged unjust demands of the chief king. *Breasal* accordingly set out immediately to wait upon *Finn*, whom he found at his residence, at a place called *Rinn Dubhain*, on the east side of the river *Bearbha*, some distance below *Tech Moling*, (now Saint Mullin's, in the county of Carlow). There he received a hearty welcome, and at once proceeded to communicate to *Finn* his distress and the object of his visit, telling him that no person was more imperatively called on to endeavour to cast off the hated impost than *Finn* himself; and he then addressed him in the following verses:

"O *Find!* wilt thou come in friendship?
Wilt thou and the Leinstermen be of one accord?
If thou wilt come, arise! give battle
To the powerful hosts of Tara.

"Hast thou heard of the oppressive tribute
Which is carried from us to *Conn's* Half?
Thirty cows and nine thousand,—
Of beautiful Cows of one age.

"Hast thou heard how the men of Leinster
In crowds have fallen on the battle-plain?
Or hast thou heard that twenty kings
Have fallen for the first evil deed?(384)

"Oh! my inmost heart will burst
If I do not avenge my father;
If I retort not his lofty pride
Upon the fierce, haughty *Cairbré Liffeachair*.

"Woe is he who attempts the sea without a ship!
Woe is he who descends from a high to a low position!
Woe the house that is divided in two parts!
Woe that a noble race should be contemned!

(384) The first battle of Rath Inil.

XVIII.

Battle of *Cnamhros* fought by *Finn Mac Cumhaill* and his *Fianna*.

"O son of *Cumhall* of renowned deeds!
Array thyself, and let us begone;
Grasp ye your arms with pleasure;
And arise, ye *Fianna* of *Find!*—O *Find!*"[386]

Finn arose at once after this address, the eloquence of which seems to have been irresistible, and accompanied by such of his *Fianna* as happened to be then about him, he marched northwards, keeping the river *Bearbha* on his left hand, until they reached *Ros Broc*, (the ancient name of the place now called Saint Mullin's, in Carlow). Here resided three fellow pupils of *Finn*, the three sons of *Conga*, whose names were *Molling* the Swift, *Ceallach*, and *Braen*; and from them he received a hearty welcome. Having explained to those friends the cause of his march, and his intention to join the king of Leinster against the monarch, he was pressed by *Molling* the Swift, the eldest of the three brothers, not to hazard an attempt with his then small party to face the monarch with the muster of all the northern half of Erinn at his back. Now the number that *Finn* had with him at this time was fifteen hundred men, with an officer to every thirty of them. Therefore, when *Molling* the Swift saw that *Finn*'s high spirit had got the better of his judgment, he begged of him to remain where he was at least until he had summoned the remaining part of his *Fianna* to his presence, who were dispersed over their native districts through the island,—apparently in a way not unlike that in which a modern militia, disbanded during the pleasant times of peace, are scattered amongst the population of the country until the time comes for being called out again on the approach of war. *Molling* at the same time addressed *Finn* in a very curious poem (of thirty-one stanzas), offering the hospitalities of his house until his troops had gathered around him from their different localities. And this account is particularly interesting, because in the

(386) orig.:— A Find in n-ergi ri báig?
in bia ocus Laigin doen-láim?
ma tici, erig! fer chach,
ra prim thuathaib Temrach.
In cualadais in cain truim
berar uain illech Cuind?
tricha bó noe mile,
do buaib caema conidine.
In cualadais in Lagin
do thuitim in oen magin?
n'ón cualadais fichit rig
do thuitim tririn mignim?
Or memais mo chride cain
acht mani diglorsa m'a-thair;
mani timris a uabar ard
ar Coirpre Lifechair lan-garg.
Mairg triallas cen luing dar ler!
mairg triallas a hard in isel!
mairg bale bis ar da raind!
mairg do beir sás ar saerclaind!
A mic Cumaill aidble glond!
geib immocus imthigeom;
gebid bar narma co grind;
ocus eirgid a fian Find.
A Find.

XVIII.

Battle of *Cnamhros* fought by *Finn Mac Cumhaill* and his *Fianna*.

poem the writer names many of these localities, as well as the chiefs and captains of the troops dispersed among them; such as *Agruan* of *Magh Ené*, (in the west of Donegal); *...choll* of *Druim-da-Chonor*; *Donn Mac Daghar* of *Magh Adhair* in the present county of Clare); *Caeman* at *Sliabh Grot*, (on the borders of Limerick and Cork); *Aedh*, from the banks of the Boyne; *Duban* from *Druim Dacili*; *Lugard* and *Gilld*, ... who are not named in connection with any particular place; *Idland*, from *Leith* (in Kerry); *Garad*, from ... county of Limerick; *Breasal*, the grandson of ... own brother, from Leinster; *Crimhthann* and *Dithrabh*... the same country; *Maelorund*, from *Creamhchaill*; ... *Flaithchins* the Valiant; and *Cuan* the Victorious, from ... places, etc. And so *Molling* goes on to name the various ... nian chiefs.

Finn followed the advice of *Molling*, and delayed at the residence of his friend, until all the captains whom he had summoned came up to him with their troops. As soon as all were assembled, he reviewed his little army, and then set forward to the place where he had heard the monarch was encamped; ... this was at *Rath Inil*, which was also called the *Gardhtha*... that is, the "Cruel Grave" of the two daughters of the monarch *Tuathal*, who were here buried, at their death, two hundred years before, but whose bodies (we are told) were soon afterwards exhumed by their valiant father and interred by him at *Fionn*... or the "White Heap", (among the Pagan sepulchral mounds in the vicinity of New Grange on the left bank of the river Boyne). *Finn* and his troops rested for the night at the *Gardhtha*..., and early on the following morning they marched to the encampment of the king of Leinster, which was in the immediate neighbourhood. Both leaders then went forward at the head of their respective forces to *Cnamhros*, where those of the monarch *Cairbré Liffeachair* were drawn up in order of battle.

A hard and equally-well-contested battle was fought then between both parties. The monarch's forces, however, found themselves unable to withstand the vehement valour of the Leinstermen and their allies, and they were forced to give way and retreat in all directions, leaving, it is said, nine thousand men dead on the field of battle, as well as the monarch's ... sons themselves, namely, *Eochaidh*, and *Eochaidh Dom*... *Fiacha Sraibtiné*.

The time of this battle of *Cnamhros* is not given by the annalists, and we have little to say farther of *Finn Mac Cumhaill* and his warriors till the battle of *Gabhra*, which was fought in the year 284.

After this revolt of *Finn Mac Cumhaill* against the monarch *Cairbré Liffeachair*, he lost all trust for ever in the fidelity and loyalty of the *Fianna*, and his confidence was transferred to *Aedh Caemh*, (Hugh "the beautiful"), of the *Clanna Morna*, captain of the Connacht *Fianna*, a brave hero, to whom the monarch then gave the chief command, not only of his own contingent, but also of such new levies or recruits as he might deem proper to add to their ranks.

Fianna of the Clanna Morna.

It is recorded in the Annals of the Four Masters, at the year 283, that *Finn MacCumhaill* was killed by *Aichleach*, son of *Duibhdreann*, at *Ath Brea*, on the Boyne.

There was at this time a violent feud existing between the Monarch *Cairbré* and *Mogh Corb*, son of *Cormac Cas*, king of Munster (the ancestor of the Dalcassians of Thomond). This *Cormac Cas* had been married to *Samair*, the daughter of *Finn Mac Cumhaill*, by whom he had three sons, namely, *Finné*, *Connla*, and *Mogh Corb;* and when the estrangement took place between the monarch and *Finn*, and after the death of the latter, this *Mogh Corb* took his uncle *Oisin* the poet, who succeeded his father as commander of the *Fianna*, into his confidence and pay, together with his men. The *Clanna Morna*, who were now the monarch's favourite standing army, had long been jealous of the important hold which the *Clanna Baoiscné*, that is *Finn Mac Cumhaill*'s clann, had so long held in the country, and being now in the monarch's favour, they induced him to improve his enmity against *Mogh Corb* into a war on him and his province of Munster. The Munster king, however, was beforehand with *Cairbré;* for, collecting rapidly all the forces he could muster, and uniting them with the battalion of the *Fianna* under the command of his uncle *Oisin*, he marched straight towards the seat of monarchy itself, and threatening the very household of the chief king, he encamped at *Gabhra Aiclé* (now the hill of Skreen, near Tara.) To this place the monarch came out against them, and a fierce battle ensued, in which the Munstermen, inferior in number, suffered sorely.

Destruction of the Fianna at the Battle of Gabhra.

Among the slain in this battle was *Oscar*, the famous son of *Oisin*, who was killed by the cast of a spear (cast from on horseback, it is curious to observe), by the monarch *Cairbré*. *Cairbré* himself at the same time received a wound from *Oscar;* and he was soon after slain on the field of battle by *Simeon* the son of *Cerb*, a warrior of the people of Forth in Leinster. Of the brave band of the veteran *Fianna*, who so often fought and won under the command of *Finn Mac Cumhaill*, and his father and grandfather, scarcely one survived the fatal battle of *Gabhra*.[366]

[366] Some of the incidents of this battle are related in an ancient poem as-

XVIII.

It does not appear, as far as I can discover, that the *Fianna Eireann*, or Irish Militia, were ever afterwards embodied [illegible] maintained under the same conditions as formerly, after the death of *Finn* and *Oscar* and the fatal issue *of the battle of Gabhra*.

It would serve the purpose of these lectures but little to [illegible] into any minute accounts or enumeration of all the other references to the existence of a permanent central military force in Erinn, supported under the direct control of the monarch, and for national purposes. Many such allusions are to be found, and all bear upon the existence of a regular military system, the nature of which can best be realized in the example already given of the institution in its best time, that of the *Fianna* of *Finn* and of *Mac Morna*. Nor was this system confined to the support of a central army or national militia; for there are abundant references to be found to the existence of a similar organization under the provincial and even minor kings, for the defence of each province and smaller division of the country.

Instances of a regular army in Ireland after the battle of *Gabhra*;

A few instances of the employment of a regular army by the kings of Erinn, an army commanded by professional officers, and organized in a permanent manner, may here however be given, in proof that the institution by no means disappeared after the disaffection and destruction of the *Fianna*.

We have it on record in the Book of Ballymote, in a [illegible] ancient tract, that *Niall* "of the Nine Hostages", who reigned as monarch of Erinn from A.D. 379 to 405, sent an organized army into Munster; that this army fought a battle at *Caen-raighé*, (now Kenry, in the county of Limerick), where they defeated the Munstermen, and returned with fifty hostages from among the nobles of that province; and that this army was commanded by *Fiacha*, who was the monarch's own brother, as well as his "*Tuairgnidhe Catha*", (Leader of his army in battle), an office, apparently, such as that which we should now call "Commander in Chief", or "Commander of the Forces".

Battle of *Caenraighé*;

Fianna under king *Diarmait*;

Again we find, in an ancient tract, quoted in a former lecture,[287] that the monarch *Diarmait*, son of *Fergus Cerrbheoil*, who died A.D. 558, had sent his stewards and his *Fianna* [illegible] standing army all through the country to collect his [illegible]

cribed to *Oisin*, and preserved in the old Book of Leinster which has been published, with an English translation, by the "Ossianic Society", [illegible] with part only of another poem, much more modern indeed, but still [illegible] the same subject: and I may add that my learned friend the [late] Rev. [illegible] Hamilton Drummond, (the librarian of the Royal Irish Academy), [illegible] lately published a spirited but very free translation in verse of the whole in his *Ancient Irish Minstrelsy*.

(287) See *ante*, p. 356.

to enforce the laws, and to maintain ancient important social customs; and this, it will be remembered, was the indirect cause that led to the abandonment of Tara as the royal residence of the monarchs of Erinn ever since his reign.

Amhuis, or mercenaries of *Raghallach*; A.D. 645;

And again, from the poem already quoted,(368) on the death, in the year 645, of *Raghallach*, son of *Uathach*, king of Connacht, we find him marching with the whole concourse of people who attended at the ancient public games and sports of his palace of *Cruachan*, in pursuit of the Ulstermen who selected that great day to enter his province for the purpose of plunder. And among this great concourse, the king's Royal Guard of a thousand regular soldiers was not the least important body, as may be seen from the following stanza of the poem:

" His royal Mercenaries around *Raghallach*;
Ten hundred champions with their shields;
The front of battle was theirs to maintain;
Theirs was the first spear in the conflict".(369)

One thousand regular professional soldiers, who constantly attended on the king's command, and had their chief residence at his court, formed no trifling force at this remote time.

Amhuis, or mercenaries at the battle of *Almhain* [Hill of Allen], A.D. 718;

And lastly, we find in the detailed account of the battle of *Almhain*, (now the Hill of Allen in the county of Kildare), fought in the year 718, between the monarch *Fergal Mac Maoile-duin*, and the men of Leinster, that the monarch was killed there, with six thousand(370) of his *Amhuis* or " Mercenaries", and a great number of the northern chiefs and warriors.

This was one of the last great battles which arose out of that long and fatal cause of domestic warfare, the Boromean Tribute. The monarch *Fergal*, who then resided at the provincial palace of *Aileach*, (near Derry), spent a long time in collecting a sufficiently strong force with which to march into Leinster to demand the Boromean Tribute, which if not paid him voluntarily, he was determined to raise by force from the king of Leinster, *Murchadh*, son of *Bran Muité*. He set out on his march at length; but having employed bad guides, they led him through the most rough and difficult roads and passes of the country, until after much toil and fatigue they found themselves at last in the neighbourhood of *Cluain Dolcain*, (now Clondalkin in the county of Dublin), and here they pitched their camp in the immediate vicinity of the church.

(368) See *ante*, p. 343.

(369) original:—Riġ aṁuis im Raġallaċ;
deċ céd seál cona sciaṫaiḃ;
cosaċ caṫa ċosnaidis;
ba leó an céd ga go cliaṫaiḃ.

(370) 160, according to other accounts.

XVIII. *Amhais*, or mercenaries at the battle of *Almhain* [Hill of Allen], A.D. 718;

The northern soldiers behaved, it appears, with [illegible] ness towards the church, and particularly to a poor [illegible] cluse who had a separate hut in its precincts, and to [illegible] authorities of the church had assigned a milch cow for his [illegible] use. This hut the northerns tore down over his head, [illegible] his person with a spear; and they killed his only cow. [illegible] sacrilegious conduct on the part of his countrymen, so [illegible] the pious feelings of *Cubretan*, son of *Aengus*, king of the [illegible] of *Ross* (the district around Carrickmacross, in the present [illegible] of Monaghan), that he wrote the following three stanzas on the spot, deprecating the impious act, and anticipating its [illegible] consequences:—

"Our men are already red with gore,
O valiant *Fergal*, it is true!
Sorrowful are the People of Mary's Son,
For having torn down his house over the leper's head.

"The leper's cow, the leper's cow,
Was killed after all the oxen:
Woe to the hand that pierced his cloak,
At going into battle against the son of *Bran*.

"Should it be that we give battle,
Though brave our opponent, the son of *Bran*,
Much more do we dread than the battle-field,
The loud lamentation which the leper sends forth."

The monarch *Fergal* then led his men, who are said to [illegible] numbered twenty-one thousand, to the hill of *Almhain* [illegible] county of Kildare), where they were met by *Murchadh*, [illegible] *Bran*, with a force of only nine thousand, raised [illegible] and marched precipitately. A battle immediately [illegible] the fiercest, says the historian, that was ever fought in [illegible] in which the northerns were defeated, not by [illegible] strength, the historian says, but by the powerful aid of [illegible] *Brigid* of Kildare, who was actually seen hovering over [illegible] ranks of the Leinstermen.

Fergal, son of *Maelduin*, himself fell in this battle by the [illegible]

(311) original:—Atát ar cat forderg glano,
a ríg Fherġaile aṡglind!
aobrónaig muintir Mic Muire,
ar mbreith a taigi dia chinn.
Bó in ċlaim, bó in ċlaim,
do gaed andegaid in daim:
mairg láim ler tollad a brat,
ma tect i cat co mac mBrain.
Da mbeith neach do berad cat,
ma trén dreman fria, mac mBrain,
andsa leam olvar indras,
in cae ro ċanad in ċlam.

Amhuis, or mercenaries at the battle of *Almhain* (Hill of Allen), A.D., 718;

of *Aedh*, son of *Bran*, king of South Leinster, and brother to the chief king of Leinster. With him fell twenty of the chiefs and petty kings in attendance on him, besides seven thousand of their men. This account states, that among these seven thousand, were only one hundred and sixty-three of his *Amhuis* or Body Guard; but that this number bore no proportion to the entire number of his Royal Guard, or permanent army, we have clear evidence in the following three stanzas, written on this disastrous battle, at the the time, by the poet, *Nuadha O'Lomthuilé*, who says:

"At mid-day, at *Almhain*,
In defence of the cows of *Breaghmhainé*,
A red-mouthed beaked vulture raised
A shout of exultation over the head of *Fergal*.

"*Murchadh* put off his former debility,
Many a brave man did he cut to the ground;
He turned his arms against *Fergal*,
With his immense body of *Fianna* at *Almhain*.

"There fell there one hundred brave, gifted chiefs,
With one hundred valiant officers;
Besides nine who ran to madness;
And seven thousand armed men".

In a fine old detailed account of this famous battle, in my possession, the number of the monarch's *Amhuis*, or Guard of *Fianna*, killed there is set down as *sesca ced*, which I would certainly read as sixty hundred, or six thousand. The Four Masters, however, and the compiler of the *Chronicon Scotorum*, make it but a hundred and sixty; and to their reading of these words I bow.

From these and many other similar instances, some relating to the forces of the chief king, some to those of the provincial kings, we may form a clear opinion that the monarch of Erinn, as well as the provincial and smaller kings, had always a regular standing army, of numbers more or less, whether under the name of *Fianna* or of *Amhuis*, on whom he could call on all sudden emergencies, either to enforce his laws, or to repel his domestic or foreign foes.

The Danish wars having set in soon after the battle of *Almhain*, there was after this period, indeed, little time given to the monarch or to the minor kings to organize and maintain special bodies of regular troops, because, in fact, the whole country had to take up arms; and the men of every province and chieftaincy were liable to be called out at a moment's notice to oppose the ever active and cruel foreigner. There are, however, in our old writings, references to bodies of men who are

XVIII. Lucht Tighé, or household troops.

called the "*Lucht Tighé*", or Household Troops, of kings and chiefs; and particularly in the account of the battle of Clontarf, (fought in the year 1014), where the *Lucht Tighé* of *Tadhg* O'Kelly, king of *Ui Mainé* in Connacht, and of *Ferghal O'Ruairc*, king of *Breifney*, did great execution on the foreigners, independently of the general Connacht contingent. And even so late as the year 1593, we find Hugh McGuire, Lord of Feranagh, marching to battle with the people of his own territory and a body of *Amhuis*, or Mercenary Household Troops drawn from other territories or countries.

The regular organization of these household troops or body guards of the chieftain is instanced besides in the names of certain places, as, for example, we know that there was anciently a district in Monaghan, which was called *Lucht Tighé mhic Mathgamhna*, that is Mac Mahon's Household, because it was exclusively devoted to the maintenance of that chief's household troops or standing army.

And in the Brehon Laws this institution is made the subject of positive rule; for, it is stated there that every king of a *Tricha Céd*, or Thirty Hundreds of Land, should support seven hundred warriors: a law, the necessity of which is intelligible enough, when we remember that the duty of these regular forces included all those which are in modern times performed by the police as well as by the military authorities of a civilised nation.

END OF VOL. I.

CPSIA information can be obtained
at www.ICGtesting.com
Printed in the USA
LVHW081446030321
680478LV00031B/866